Houghton Mifflin Company   Boston

Dallas
Geneva, Illinois
Hopewell, New Jersey
Palo Alto
London

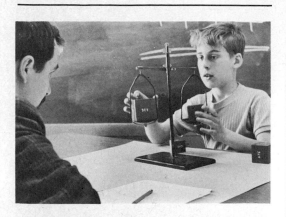

Psychology applied to teaching

THIRD EDITION

Robert F. Biehler

Library of Congress Catalog Card Number: 77-077665

ISBN 0-395-25489-2

Material in Chapters 3 and 4 appeared in Child Development by Robert F. Biehler (Boston: Houghton Mifflin, 1976).

Credit for photographs on title page:
Left page (top left) Cary Wolinsky/Stock Boston, (top right) Francis Laping/DPI, (bottom) Courtesy of IBM; right page (top left) The New York Times, (top right) Peter Travers, (bottom) Paul Conklin.

The author is grateful for permission to quote from the following copyrighted works:

Teaching: A Course in Applied Psychology by Wesley C. Becker, Siegfried Englemann, and Don R. Thomas. Copyright © 1971 by Science Research Associates, Inc. Reprinted by permission of the publisher.

Taxonomy of Educational Objectives, Handbook I, Cognitive Domain by Benjamin S. Bloom, editor. Copyright 1956 by David McKay company, Inc. Reprinted by permission of the publisher.

The Process of Education by Jerome S. Bruner. Copyright © 1960 by Harvard University Press. Reprinted by permission of Harvard University Press.

Toward a Theory of Instruction by Jerome S. Bruner, Harvard University Press, 1966.

Essentials of Educational Management by Robert L. Ebel, pp. 126, 130, 131, 136. Copyright © 1972. Reprinted by permission of Prentice-Hall, Inc., Englewood Cliffs, N.J.

Childhood and Society, 2nd edition, revised, by Erik H. Erikson. Copyright 1950, © 1963 by W. W. Norton & Company, Inc., New York, N.Y. Reprinted by permission of W. W. Norton & Company, Inc., and The Hogarth Press, Ltd.

Identity: Youth and Crisis by Erik H. Erikson. Copyright © 1968 by W. W. Norton & Company, Inc., New York, N.Y. Reprinted by permission of W. W. Norton & Company, Inc., and Faber and Faber, Ltd.

Wad-Ja-Get? The Grading Game in American Education by Howard Kirschenbaum, Rodney W. Napier, and Sidney B. Simon. Copyright © 1971 by Hart Publishing Company, Inc.

Taxonomy of Educational Objectives, Handbook II, Affective Domain by David R. Krathwohl, Benjamin S. Bloom, and Bertram B. Masia. Copyright © 1964 by David McKay Company, Inc. Reprinted by permission of the publisher.

"An Experimental Study of Leadership and Group Life" by Ronald Lippitt and Ralph K. White in Readings in Social Psychology, 3rd edition, edited by Eleanor E. Maccoby, Theodore M. Newcomb, and Eugene L. Hartley. Copyright © 1947, 1952, 1958, by Holt, Rinehart and Winston. Reprinted by permission of Holt, Rinehart and Winston.

Toward a Psychology of Being by Abraham H. Maslow, 2nd edition, D. Van Nostrand Company, New York, 1968. Reprinted by permission.

Summerhill: A Radical Approach to Child Rearing by A. S. Neill. Copyright © 1960. Reprinted by permission of Hart Publishing Company, Inc.

Beyond Freedom and Dignity by B. F. Skinner. Copyright © 1971 by B. F. Skinner. Reprinted by permission of Alfred A. Knopf, Inc.

The Technology of Teaching by B. F. Skinner, pp. 21, 24, 49, 109–111. Copyright © 1968. Reprinted by permission of Prentice-Hall, Inc., Englewood Cliffs, N.J.

Educational Psychology: The Study of Educational Growth. revised edition, by J. M. Stephens. Copyright © 1951, 1956 by Holt, Rinehart and Winston. Reprinted by permission of Holt, Rinehart and Winston.

Contents

Part two

Development 94

Part three

Learning 220

Part four

Skills, memory, and transfer   *388*

Preface

The existence of texts and courses in educational psychology is based on the assumption that psychologists have learned many things that can be of value to teachers. Those who write books on the subject or who teach psychology courses in professional education programs are therefore eager to communicate what they know to students who are contemplating a career in education. At the same time, educational psychologists are more aware than most of their colleagues of research-substantiated information regarding forgetting and transfer. They realize that they must do everything possible to help students acquire scientific information that relates to teaching, retain it, and be predisposed to apply what they have learned when they take charge of classrooms. The first two editions of this book were written to achieve the goals just listed, and the changes in the third edition have been made in an effort to meet those goals more effectively.

To help students understand and master the information presented in this book, the Key Points that call attention to especially significant sections of the text have been made more detailed. In addition, the Key Points are now listed at the beginning of each chapter in the order in which they appear in the text, instead of being grouped under headings as was the case with the first two editions. To make it possible for readers to review and interrelate Key Points, the end-of-chapter summaries stress only information emphasized in these points. The first part of the Study Guide for the third edition is designed to help students master the Key Points, particularly when preparing for examinations. All of these features relating to the Key Points are intended to help students learn and remember an organized set of ideas in educational psychology.

Several features of the third edition are intended to encourage continual application of what is discussed. The Suggestions for Teaching have been expanded, made more detailed, and are listed in a special index printed inside the front cover so that student teachers and first-year teachers can quickly find specific ideas to use in solving instructional problems. A feature new to this edition is the recommendation that the reader develop a personal Handbook by developing a list of teaching suggestions custom-designed to fit particular teaching assignments and personality traits. To permit students to select suggestions that are appropriate to a particular grade level, points and examples offered in the Suggestions for Teaching stress techniques that might be used by either an elementary or a secondary school teacher. In place of write-in spaces, which were included in the first two editions, Handbook Headings are printed in the margins of this edition. The reader is urged to obtain a three-ring binder and to record personal suggestions for teaching under these headings and thereby compile an individualized guidebook for teaching. The second part of the Study Guide is designed to facilitate the preparation of the personal Handbook. Headings and suggestions are printed on separate, punched sheets that can be inserted in the three-ring binder. The sheets are designed for use by preschool, elementary, or secondary grade teachers.

The Handbook Headings also serve as the basis for end-of-chapter sections titled "Becoming a Better Teacher: Questions and Suggestions." Even if a student conscientiously learns the Key Points and prepares a comprehensive personal Handbook, it may be difficult for a student teacher or first-year teacher to apply what has been learned because so many instructional problems must be dealt with for the first time. To help the novice educator avoid feeling confused and overwhelmed, ideas mentioned under Becoming a Better Teacher: Questions and Suggestions focus attention on specific instructional problems. Each problem is stated in the form of questions a new teacher might ask herself or himself. Following each question at least one suggestion for dealing with the problem is noted, also in the form of a personal reminder. The reader is urged to add additional suggestions after perusing the Suggestions for Teaching. The intention is to encourage and assist the future student teacher or first-year teacher to first prepare for teaching and later carry out an on-going analysis of teaching effectiveness by analyzing one problem at a time and planning how to take specific steps to at least partially solve that problem.

In recognition of the likelihood that readers will be eager to find detailed information about certain aspects of educational psychology, the Suggestions for Further Study at the end of each chapter have been revised, expanded, and brought up to date. To make these annotated bibliography sections more useful, an index to topics covered in the Suggestions for Further Study is printed inside the back cover.

Approximately two-thirds of the material presented in the third edition is either new or substantially rewritten. Some of the changes have been made in order to incorporate new information and trends in psychology and education, other changes were prompted by feedback from students and instructors. The general historical overview and outline of contemporary trends in education that opened the second edition has been replaced in the third edition with an expanded discussion of the nature, values, and limitations of science. The outline of positions on learning that appeared in Chapter 2 of the previous edition has been replaced by a chapter describing what public school teaching is like. The intention is to help the reader make the transition from student to teacher, think about the realities of public school teaching, and analyze why teaching conditions are the way they are. Recent criticisms of education are evaluated from the point of view of an "insider"—a teacher who is on the receiving end of the criticisms and who must cope with certain unavoidable conditions and limiting factors.

The discussion of techniques and problems of studying development that was included in Chapter 3 in the second edition has been dropped to make way for expanded coverage of different theoretical conceptions of development, including the social learning theory view and Maslow's third force view. Chapter 4, "Age-Level Characteristics," presents information about significant aspects of behavior at three grade levels, rather than the five levels discussed in the first two editions, and fewer points are discussed in more comprehensive fashion.

Part 3 on learning has been revised and expanded. Stimulus-response learning, the cognitive-discovery approach, and humanistic techniques of teaching are each discussed in a separate chapter. Related aspects of learning are analyzed in Part 4, "Skills, Memory, and Transfer."

Chapters 10 and 11 make up Part 5 on motivation. Although the chapter titles are the same as in the second edition, each of these chapters has been substantially revised. Part 6 on evaluation begins with a comprehensive analysis of criticisms of traditional evaluation procedures, followed by an analysis of the critique. The intention is to acquaint the future teacher with reasons why certain grading procedures have become more or less permanent features of American education. Then, suggestions are offered for improving evaluation procedures, working within the given restrictions. Material presented in separate chapters on exceptional children and need gratification in the first two editions has been combined into a single chapter (14) in this edition. Chapter 15 on classroom control has been expanded to include guidelines derived from Jacob Kounin's (1970) research and observations on group management. The final chapter retains material from the second edition that stressed how teachers might deal with frustrations, but new to this edition is a culminating section on ways to improve teaching effectiveness.

I would like to express my appreciation to Marjorie Roberts for converting drastically edited rough drafts into a final manuscript, and to the following psychologists for offering comprehensive or detailed suggestions for making the third edition of *Psychology Applied to Teaching* an improvement over the second: Elizabeth Akiba, Carolyn Charles, Donald L. Clark, Linda Clark, Lewis Estrine, Richard M. Evans, Elsa T. Falls, William H. Hedley, Douglas Herbster, Lee K. Hildman, Eugene Hittelman, Daniel Lynch, Henry L. Moreland, Sarah C. Portis, Daniel J. Reschly, Charles Ruett, Jr., Max Siegel, Julius Sassenrath, Jack Snowman, Dennis A. Warner, and Gordon B. Wilson.

R.F.B.

**Psychology applied
to teaching**

This book has been written so that it may be used in three ways: (1) as the means for acquiring an organized body of scientific information about teaching, (2) as a source of practical ideas you can refer to during your student teaching and during your first years of professional teaching, (3) as a reference work you can consult whenever you wish to find detailed information on some aspect of teaching. In the first three sections of Chapter 1 you will find explanations of the various ways this book might be used, plus descriptions of features of organization and design intended to help you acquire information easily and efficiently and apply what you learn in a variety of ways. You are urged to read the description of these features with care so that you will gain maximum benefit from them.

Some educators (e.g., Highet, 1957) argue that teaching is an art that cannot be taught in a scientific way, and they even maintain that a scientific approach may interfere with effective teaching. This text is based on a diametrically opposed point of view: Scientific information can be of particular value to future teachers. The nature, values, and limitations of science are briefly discussed in the last sections of Chapter 1, and the suggestion is offered that you strive to act as a teacher-theorist even as you function as a teacher-artisan, or teacher-practitioner.

New teachers looking back on their first months in the classroom often report that they felt unprepared for many aspects of their new profession. To reduce the shock of transition from student to teacher, the first half of Chapter 2 acquaints you with what you will be expected to do as a teacher and with perceptions of advantages and disadvantages of teaching at different grade levels. To help you grasp why certain features of American education are resistant to change, meritocratic, democratic, and technological aspects of our society are analyzed. The last half of Chapter 2 consists of a summary of criticisms of public education and an evaluation of these criticisms. The purpose of the evaluation of the critiques is to help you decide which aspects of public education you will probably have to learn to accept and which aspects you might try to change for the better.

Part One

Background

Chapter 1   Applying psychology to teaching

Chapter 2   What teaching is like

Key points

The nature and values of science

Dealing directly and objectively with facts

Searching for order and relationships

Scientific knowledge is cumulative

Scientific methods: Sampling, control, objectivity, publication, replication

Studying behavior: Complicating factors

Differences of opinion due to selection and interpretation of data

Cognitive dissonance: Rejection of conflicting ideas

Experimenter bias effect: Communication of expectations

Hawthorne effect: Reactions to change and attention

Pygmalion effect, self-fulfilling prophecy

Open education: Learning centers, self-instruction, interaction

Educational "fads" traceable to accumulating knowledge

Accountability: Teachers expected to offer proof of student achievement

The teacher-practitioner and the teacher-theorist

Teacher-practitioner: Enthusiastic commitment

Teacher-theorist: Objective analysis

Chapter 1	# Applying psychology to teaching

As you begin to read this book, you may find yourself speculating about questions such as these:

Am I sure that I want to become a teacher?

What will this book tell me about teaching that I don't already know?

Am I wasting my time taking courses in education?

Will I be able to get a job as a teacher?

You will not get a definite answer to the last question until you either sign a teaching contract or accept a job outside the field of education. By the time you finish reading this book, however, you should have at least partial answers to the first three questions.

Questions about teaching

Are you sure you want to be a teacher?

You will not be able to evaluate accurately your feelings about functioning as a teacher until you have had a chance actually to interact with students for a period of time. You can make a preliminary appraisal of your feelings, though, by examining reports of how others feel about teaching. In the next chapter you will find descriptions of some of the advantages and disadvantages of teaching as perceived by those who have had years of classroom experience. Reading about the perceptions of experienced teachers will supply insights that should help you evaluate your current conception of what a career in education will be like.

You will gain additional insight into your attitudes toward teaching as you read the remaining chapters. When you learn about characteristics of students at different age levels (Chapters 3 and 4) and how you might arrange and evaluate their learning experiences (Chapters 5 through 13), you can speculate not only about how you might teach but also about whether you will enjoy doing it. The descriptions of characteristics of students at different ages, for example, may help you make or affirm a decision to teach at a particular grade level. The outline of different theories of learning and the description of how these might be converted into practice will permit you to form a realistic conception of exactly what you will do if you take a job as a teacher. As you read about students with special needs (Chapters 11 and 14), you may gain insights that could contribute to a decision to seek (or not to seek) a job in an inner-city school or in a class for students with physical, intellectual, or emotional disabilities. The information provided in this book, therefore, should help you find at least part of an answer to the question "Am I sure that I want to become a teacher?" and also perhaps part of an answer to the question "What kind of teaching would I prefer to do?"

What will you learn that you don't already know?

The answer to the question "What will this book tell me about teaching that I don't already know?" depends on several factors including previous experiences with teaching and the number of psychology courses you have taken. You have been actively engaged in the process of formal education for at least twelve years, and you already know a great deal about learning and teaching. You have had abundant opportunities to observe and react to over one hundred teachers. You probably have read several hundred texts. You have finished all kinds of assignments and taken hundreds if not thousands of examinations. You have undoubtedly established strong likes and dislikes for certain subjects and approaches to teaching. Even though you are thoroughly familiar with education from the student's point of view, you probably have had limited experience with education from the teacher's point of view. As you read this book (and as you interact with pupils), you will discover that the teacher's perception of what takes place in classrooms is often substantially different from the perception of students. As a student, for example, you have probably resented certain assignments and examinations. You may have brooded about the weakness of a teacher who was unable to inspire students to learn and had to resort to coercion. However, you probably have not had the experience—yet—of attempting to arouse and hold the interest of one or more groups of students, nor have you been faced with the problem of assigning grades that must be backed up by evidence.

A classroom takes on a different appearance when seen from a teacher's—not a student's—point of view.

James H. Karales from
Peter Arnold

One type of information about teaching that you don't already know, therefore, takes the form of descriptions of classroom practice seen from a teacher's point of view. Such descriptions make up a substantial part of this book, since its primary purpose is to acquaint you with information about teaching that is derived from the discoveries of psychologists. Psychologists use the methods of science to study behavior, and if you have taken any courses in psychology you are already familiar with the nature of knowledge in this field. This book differs from other books in psychology you may have read because it stresses ways you might *apply* psychological knowledge to teaching. Psychologists have discovered many things about human behavior, and they have established principles and theories to summarize and clarify their insights. You may already be familiar with many facts and theories in psychology, but you have probably not made a concerted effort to convert this knowledge into classroom applications. Therefore, the answer to the second question, "What will this book tell me about teaching that I don't already know?" is that you will acquire insights into teaching based on scientific discoveries. Some of these insights are almost certain to differ from those you have derived from experiences as a student (or teacher) or from reading other books on psychology.

Are you wasting your time taking this course?

The third question, "Am I wasting my time taking courses in education?" may be a cause for concern if you are worried about getting a job as a teacher. Chances are you are being asked to take several courses in order to meet requirements for a credential, and you may doubt whether your investment of time, money, and effort will pay off. When faced with a question as perplexing as this one, most of us have a tendency to wonder whether other individuals have made more prudent decisions than we have. The number of individuals currently seeking jobs in teaching is greater than the number of jobs available. This is true at the present time, and it is likely to remain true for the next several years. The same situation, however, prevails in many other occupations. Perhaps a majority of your fellow students who have chosen other degree programs are also wondering if the courses they are taking will eventually lead to a specific kind of employment. Economic and political conditions that prevail in this country and throughout the world today, together with the likelihood of abrupt and unpredictable changes in the future, make it almost impossible to be certain that any kind of career preparation will guarantee obtaining a particular kind of job.

Awareness that students in degree programs outside the field of education are perplexed about the future may not be a completely comforting thought, but it might curb a tendency for you to brood excessively about whether you are doing the right thing. Jobs in teaching are limited, but many new teachers are hired every year, and you may be one of the fortunate ones. Even if you do not seek or secure a job as a teacher, however, it is likely that what you learn in education courses will benefit you as much as, if not more than, what you might have learned in a different degree program. The knowledge you acquire of learning, teaching, and human behavior, for example, may contribute to success in finding many kinds of jobs not directly related to education. In addition, you may be able to use information presented in this book to improve your own learning ability. If you become aware of a career possibility that necessitates acquiring a new set of skills in a short period of time, you may be able to use information provided in these pages to facilitate self-instruction. Furthermore, if you have children, you should be able to understand better the kind of education they receive and also to serve as an effective tutor in school-related and other learning situations.

The various possibilities just mentioned all stress the potential practical value of the information described in this book. As you read these pages you will frequently be urged to think of ways you might use what you learn. A basic reason for stressing applications is to make you aware that what you are being asked to learn is worth learning. One of the difficulties of this application-orientation, however, is that you will not always know what might be of potential significance. Unless you have had quite a bit of experience as a teacher, you may not appreciate the value of many topics. At the moment, for example, you may not see much point in learning about instructional objectives. If you secure a teaching job, however, and find that you will be expected to list at the beginning of the year precisely what you expect your students to learn, your interest in instructional objectives will increase dramatically.

Even if you have done a bit of teaching and feel that you know almost all you want and need to know, you cannot predict what might suddenly become significant at some time in the future. At the moment, for instance, you may feel that you are not attracted to "technological" approaches to teaching. This conviction could cause you to pay little attention to the discussion in Chapters 5, 8, and 9 of forms of teaching (such as programmed instruction) derived from principles of operant conditioning. Suppose, however, that you are offered a good-paying job in a school located in a community you like but that the job stresses a programmed approach to instruction. At that point you would become eager to find ways to apply information about programmed learning to classroom practice.

It will be to your advantage, therefore, to examine information presented in this book not just in terms of your present estimate of how "relevant" it is, but in terms of general understanding. If you do study to acquire general understanding, you may later discover that what you have learned suddenly becomes relevant in unexpected ways. At the same time, there are compelling reasons for you to make a concerted effort to concentrate on specific applications. You will not be able to anticipate *everything* you will need to know, because many aspects of teaching are unpredictable, but you can and should prepare for teaching situations you are almost certain to encounter. Many facets of teaching are essentially universal (or unavoidable), and you should be able to make quite specific plans for dealing with common aspects of instruction.

To help you learn general ideas that will equip you to be a flexible, resourceful teacher capable of adapting to unexpected situations, this book is designed to assist you in mastering general information about educational psychology. To help you anticipate and prepare for *predictable* problems of instruction, this book is designed to be used as a source of ideas you can convert into personal guidelines for teaching. To help you grasp this distinction between general information and specific applications, here is a description of some ways this book can be used.

Uses of this book

This book has been written so that it can be used in three ways: First, it is a text for a course in educational psychology intended to help you master an organized sampling of scientific knowledge about development, learning, motivation, evaluation, individual differences, and adjustments. Second, it is a source of practical ideas and suggestions to be converted into specific techniques you might use during the time you serve as a student teacher and during your first years of teaching. Third, it is a reference work to be consulted when you want to engage in analyses of aspects of instruction before and after you gain experience as a teacher.

Using this book to acquire scientific information

One use of this book is probably already clear to you because an instructor of a course in educational psychology has probably asked you to buy it and has assigned you to read this opening chapter. A tremendous amount of scientific knowledge is of potential value to teachers. This book offers a selection of information from this pool of knowledge organized so that you can learn and remember what you read as easily and effectively as possible. Chances are that your instructor will present lectures, organize discussions, show films, and perhaps arrange field trips that will tie in with what is discussed in assigned chapters of this text. Depending on the purposes and organization of the educational psychology course you are taking, this book may also serve as the basis for examinations and/or other types of evaluation.

The primary reason you are being asked to read this book, learn supplementary information supplied by your instructor, and perhaps complete assignments and examinations is to help you become well acquainted with an organized body of scientific information in the field of educational psychology. If you become familiar with the information and principles presented in this book, you will be equipped to deal with many problems of teaching, including those you cannot presently anticipate and those that develop so quickly you do not have an opportunity to come up with a preplanned response.

Using this book as a source of practical ideas

A second way this book can be used is as a source of practical ideas on how to teach. In addition to acquiring knowledge and learning principles that will serve as a general, all-purpose background for teaching, you should also think of specific ways you might *apply* what you learn. Sooner or later you are almost certain to be required to act as a student teacher. Perhaps you are student teaching at the same time you are taking educational psychology, although it is more likely that you will student teach after you finish this book and will also take one or more additional courses in methods of teaching. Probably your performance as a student teacher will be the single most important factor to be considered when you apply for a teaching position. Some school district personnel directors are impressed by overall grade point averages, some by grades in education courses, some by letters of recommendation; but they usually pay the most attention to reports about how student teachers actually performed in the classroom. Furthermore, once you secure a job as a teacher, how you perform in the classroom will be the major factor to be considered when your supervisors decide if you will be offered a contract for a second year. Therefore, you will be eager to function as a prepared, confident, resourceful student teacher and first-year teacher. This book has been designed to help you get ready for your first teaching experiences, to make it possible for you to find quick solutions to problems as they occur, and to provide guidelines you might use to identify and to compensate for weaknesses in your teaching technique.

Using this book as a reference work

This text is designed not only to help you master information and principles of educational psychology and to serve as a guidebook before and during student teaching and the first years of professional teaching; it is also designed to be used as a reference work. While taking courses and doing student teaching, you are not likely to have the opportunity or the inclination to carry out a great deal of independent study. You may be asked to write a paper or give a report or participate in a panel discussion as part of your course work, but you probably will not be able to engage in much self-selected study. When you are involved in student teaching, you are likely to be preoccupied with problems that demand immediate solutions. The same feeling of urgency may be characteristic of your first months as a full-time teacher. Once you gain experience as a teacher, though, and reach the point where you can handle class routine with ease, you may be eager to analyze some facet of educational psychology in depth. Certain features of this book have been included to help you find detailed information about many subjects in educational psychology, which you can use for independent study and research.

To further explain the three basic ways you might use this book, a description of some of its features will now be presented.

Features of this book

Several distinctive features of this book merit comment, since they are intended to be used in rather specialized ways. These features include: a list of *Key Points* and major headings at the beginning of each chapter, margin notes printed in color that call attention to the Key Points, lists of *Suggestions for Teaching,* summaries of Key Points, margin notes labeled *Handbook Heading,* questions and suggestions presented under the heading *Becoming a Better Teacher,* and *Suggestions for Further Study.* Each feature has been included for reasons that will now be explained.

Stress on structure

In a classic statement on education Jerome Bruner observed, "The first object of any act of learning, over and beyond the pleasure it may give, is that it should serve us in the future. Learning should not only take us somewhere, it should allow us later to go further more easily" (1960, p. 17). Learning most likely to "serve us in the future," Bruner goes on to say, is dependent on mastery of the structure of a field of study. He then observes, "To learn structure . . . is to learn how things are related" (p. 7). When a student is encouraged to grasp relationships, Bruner notes, learning is assisted in four ways: the subject becomes more comprehensible, what has been learned is more likely to be remembered, what has been learned serves as a model for understanding other things like it that may be encountered, and the gap between elementary and advanced knowledge is narrowed.

Several features of this book have been designed to help you grasp the structure of educational psychology. The table of contents at the beginning of the book is printed in abridged form so that you can comprehend the overall organization of the text. A bit later in this chapter a brief outline of the topics to be covered in the following chapters is presented. An introduction to each part outlines what will be covered in the chapters that make up that section of the text. A list of Key Points grouped under major headings is provided at the beginning and a summary at the end of each chapter. Throughout the text basic theories in psychology serve as unifying themes that tie together topics discussed in separate chapters. All these features are intended to help you comprehend the information presented in this book, learn and remember it more easily and completely, and recognize how information you encounter later relates to things you already know. Another feature of this text that is designed to help you achieve these goals (and other goals as well) is the emphasis on particular sections of each chapter.

Key points

At the beginning of each chapter (except Chapter 2) you will find a list of *Key Points*. The Key Points also appear within each chapter, printed in color in the margins. These points have been selected to help you learn and remember the essence of each chapter. One reason for stressing them is based on research on learning and memory (which will be summarized in Chapters 5 through 9). If you were to try to learn everything in this book, you would be working against yourself because some of the information you memorized would interfere with the acquisition of other information. To reduce forgetting due to such interference, you are asked to concentrate on only a few sections in each chapter.

Other reasons for stressing Key Points center on mastery of structure and future value. The Key Points have been selected for emphasis because they will help you grasp and remember significant concepts and also because they are likely to be useful when you begin to teach. To make it possible for you to check on your understanding of the Key Points and also to encourage you to relate and combine them, they are summarized at the end of each chapter.

The table of contents, the stress on structure, and the emphasis on Key Points are all intended to help you learn principles of educational psychology to the point that you can apply them in a variety of ways. All these features are designed to make it possible for you to acquire the all-purpose background for teaching mentioned in the discussion of the first use of this text. Other features of this volume are included to help you use what is discussed on these pages to make specific preparations for student teaching and your first year of teaching.

Suggestions for teaching

Some of the things you learn in this book (computing a mean or median, for example) will be specific skills, and you will know in advance precisely how and when they might be used. Such skills will be used in essentially the same way regardless of the situation. Other things you learn will be more comprehensive, and the way you apply your understanding will depend on particular situations you later encounter. In Chapter 5, for example, you will become acquainted with the principle that a learner is likely to repeat behavior that is reinforced. You might apply this general principle in a variety of ways—by praising students who help you carry out a task, for example, or by writing favorable comments opposite excellent sections of written assignments. The way you make these applications will depend on the characteristics of your students and the subject matter you are presenting. The words you might use to praise a first grader,

An educational principle such as providing detailed individual feedback may be applied by a teacher in different ways, depending on the age and personality of the pupil and the complexity of the material.
Left: Franz Kraus/DPI; right: Ingbert Gruttner

for instance, would be different from those you would use in commenting favorably on the work of high school seniors.

Before you will be able to apply principles, you must understand them thoroughly enough so that you will be able to recognize that they *are* appropriate in different situations. To help you grasp many of the principles described, this book will acquaint you with research upon which they are based. In selecting experiments to describe, an effort was made to choose those that illustrate and clarify as well as substantiate a point.

In many sections of this text you will find descriptions of experiments that serve as the basis for one or more principles or conclusions. The principles or conclusions, in turn, serve as the basis for *Suggestions for Teaching.* Each suggestion is usually followed by a list of examples illustrating how it might be applied. In most cases examples are provided both for the elementary grades and for the secondary grades, since there usually are differences in the way a principle might be applied in dealing with younger and older pupils.

The principles, suggestions, and examples are intended to help you think about how you can apply psychology to teaching. The lists of Suggestions for Teaching and the examples of some of the ways principles might be applied are intended to help you compensate, at least partially, for lack of experience when you begin to teach. Since you often will want to find quick answers with a minimum of difficulty, applications of principles are first listed as sets of related ideas (which you can later refer to as reminders and as an "index" to detailed analyses of each point). Then each point is discussed and illustrated, in most cases, by multiple examples. To permit you to find quickly information relating to particular aspects of teaching, an index to the Suggestions for Teaching is printed inside the front cover.

Developing a personal handbook

The Suggestions for Teaching and the lists of examples of applications are intended to help you prepare for your initial experiences with teaching. It is impossible to supply for each point discussed information that will have direct relevance to all teachers. Therefore, you should not expect to find under every list of Suggestions an example that will be directly applicable to the grade level and subject you hope to teach. Most of the time you will need to devise your own applications of principles. To help you do this and to help reduce the pressure and tension of your student teaching experience and your first years of professional teaching, you are urged to develop your own personal *Handbook*. As you read this text, especially when you examine the lists of Suggestions for Teaching and the examples of applications, think about how you might apply each point being discussed. Record your ideas in a notebook, and leave space for ideas that occur to you later during other courses in professional education, during your student teaching, and during your first years as a full-time teacher. To allow room for expansion, you might purchase a three-ring binder so that pages can be added or dropped. If you feel the urge to be creative, design your own cover (perhaps using the title page of *The Great Didactic*[1] by the famous seventeenth-century Czech educator John Amos Comenius—see Figure 1-1—as your inspiration).

One way to organize your Handbook would be to use the chapter and section headings of this text. To help you organize ideas within a section, frequent suggestions for *Handbook Headings* will be noted in the margins. You might also revise and expand on the lists of Suggestions for Teaching. If you write out your own version of these suggestions, devise your own examples of applications, and prepare an index, you will equip yourself with a custom-designed guidebook that should assist you in coping with many of the problems you will encounter when you first take over a classroom. If you show your Handbook to fellow-students who hope to teach the same grade level and subject and who are also devising their own "great didactic," you ought to be able to pool ideas for your mutual benefit.[2]

[1] The word *didactic* means "intended to instruct." The book by Comenius was intended to tell new teachers everything they needed to know.

[2] A Study Guide to be used in conjunction with this text can be ordered by your bookstore. The Study Guide consists of two parts: (1) questions and comments intended

Figure 1-1

Title page of *The Great Didactic* by John Amos Comenius, first published 1628–1632

Published by Adams and Charles Black Publisher

The Great Didactic

Setting forth

The whole Art of Teaching
all Things to all Men

or

A certain Inducement to found such Schools in all
the Parishes, Towns, and Villages of every
Christian Kingdom, that the entire
Youth of both Sexes, none
being excepted, shall

Quickly, Pleasantly, & Thoroughly

Become learned in the Sciences, pure in Morals,
trained to Piety, and in this manner
instructed in all things necessary
for the present and for
the future life,

in which, with respect to everything that is suggested,

Its Fundamental Principles are set forth from the essential
nature of the matter,
Its Truth is proved by examples from the several
mechanical arts,
Its Order is clearly set forth in years, months, days, and
hours, and, finally,
An easy and sure Method is shown, by which it can
be pleasantly brought into existence.

Becoming a better teacher: Questions and suggestions

The emphasis in this text on structure and on Key Points is intended to help you become familiar with what psychologists have discovered about development, learning, motivation, evaluation, individual differences, and adjustment. The Suggestions for Teaching and the recommendation that you prepare a personal Handbook are intended to stimulate you to think about how what you learn can be applied in classrooms. All the features of this text that have just been discussed are intended to help you prepare to become a teacher. Such preparation for a teaching career may ease some of the trials and tribulations of your first few months in the classroom, but it will not eliminate problems. There are simply too many things to learn and to deal with at once. Furthermore, even if you have thought ahead of time about what you would like to do in a given situation, you may discover that, for one reason or another, it is extremely difficult or impossible to put your ideas into practice. Or, you may become aware that you are so preoccupied with some aspects of teaching, you have slighted other facets of instruction.

---

to help you master the Key Points, particularly when preparing for exams, and (2) headings and suggestions you can use to organize and facilitate the compilation of your personal Handbook.

For all these reasons, during the first months or years of your teaching career, you may find that it will be to your advantage to make a systematic effort to evaluate selected aspects of your instructional technique. Otherwise, you may simply "do what comes naturally" or imitate methods used by teachers you happen to remember, and you may not always remember those who used favorable techniques. Even with this text, a personal Handbook, and other books on teaching to guide you, you will not be able to think of everything at once. To make it possible for you to analyze selected aspects of your teaching style over a period of time, questions and suggestions you might use to improve your teaching are provided at the end of each chapter (except Chapters 1 and 2). These questions are offered partly to summarize what is covered in a chapter, but their primary purpose is to give you specific points to concentrate on when you are eager to improve your effectiveness as a teacher.

A number of questionnaires and observational scales have been developed for identifying strong and weak points of teaching style. Several of these will be described in the last chapter of this book, but each of these approaches to teacher evaluation has limitations. Student responses to questions provide information about general teaching traits, but they do not supply details about precisely what an instructor might do to correct unfortunate habits. Observational instruments yield detailed information about specific teacher actions, but in order to obtain such information it is necessary to enlist the aid of a trained observer. You may be reluctant to do this the first years you teach for two reasons: (1) You will probably be too busy to take the initiative to find a trained observer. (2) You may hesitate to ask someone to "dissect" your teaching style at a time when you are still engaging in trial-and-error attempts to find your own way of doing things. Information provided by observers using a teacher evaluation schedule can be very helpful, but it may also be a bit ego shattering to a beginner. Therefore, during the first year or so of your teaching career you may prefer to concentrate on do-it-yourself evaluations. The questions and suggestions in the *Becoming a Better Teacher* sections are provided to make it possible for you to make such evaluations in a systematic way.

The Becoming a Better Teacher sections, which you will find after the Summary of Key Points for each chapter (starting with Chapter 3), are based on points made in the text opposite Handbook Headings printed in the margin. They are written to call your attention to specific aspects of your teaching technique and to stimulate ideas you might use to improve your instructional skills. To help you relate questions to appropriate sections of the text, each suggested Handbook Heading printed in the margin is listed in the end-of-chapter Becoming a Better Teacher sections. Following each heading is a question you might ask yourself. (The question format is used on the assumption that it is the most direct way to call attention to particular facets of instruction.) Then at least one "answer" to the question is provided, written as if it were a specific suggestion you might make to yourself.

The Handbook Headings, questions, and suggestions provided in the Becoming a Better Teacher sections are offered to give you an organizational framework and some sample entries for your Handbook. You should feel free to omit headings if they do not seem appropriate to the kind of teaching you expect to do, and you might wish to add headings of your own. The questions and suggestions will probably be more meaningful and useful if you revise them to suit your needs, style, and personality. If you prepare your own Handbook, you are urged to peruse carefully the points made in sections of the Suggestions for Teaching opposite the Handbook Headings printed in the margin. Select, modify, and add examples and write suggestions to yourself. For consistency and to enhance usefulness, all your entries might be made in the form of questions or reminders to yourself, followed by answers or suggestions.

If you follow these suggestions for preparing a Handbook, you might use the questions and suggestions you record not only as general guidelines for teaching but also in these two ways: (1) as troubleshooting aids when you are confronted with a specific, identifiable problem and (2) as a basis for systematic-rotation evaluations. To put the latter procedure into operation you might make it a habit during at least the first year of your teaching career to set aside a few moments at the end of each school day for examining the questions at the end of a chapter. If you feel that you might improve your teaching by concentrating on techniques highlighted by a particular question, plan a step-by-step campaign. The next day, peruse the questions at the end of the next chapter, and so on. If you follow this procedure for a few weeks, you should systematically evaluate all aspects of teaching discussed in this book and also become thoroughly familiar with where information on different facets of teaching is to be found. Then, when you become aware of the need for improving some phase of instruction, you will know exactly where to look for help, and you will have your own step-by-step plan for solving a particular problem.

Suggestions for further study

In the chapters that follow, you will find suggestions that cover many facets of teaching. You are likely to conclude, however, that information on particular aspects of teaching is not complete enough. And even though an attempt has been made to provide at least partial solutions to the most common difficulties faced by teachers, you are bound, sooner or later, to become aware of problems that are not discussed in these pages. To allow for instances where you will need additional or supplementary information, an annotated bibliography is provided at the end of each chapter. In the Suggestions for Further Study for each chapter you will find lists of articles and books you might consult for detailed information on many topics. To help you locate such sources, an index to the Suggestions for Further Study is printed on the inside of the back cover. You may want additional data on some aspects of teaching, either while you are taking this course or after you are experienced enough to have time for a detailed look at some facet of education, psychology, or instruction. To locate such data, consult the index inside the front cover for a description of topics, and use information about Suggestion titles and page numbers to find a list of references.

The Key Points, the list of Suggestions for Teaching and the Suggestions for Further Study, the Handbook Headings, and the questions and suggestions in the Becoming a Better Teacher sections all summarize information supplied by psychologists, although sometimes the observations of individuals not classified as behavioral scientists will be mentioned. People with many different kinds of backgrounds have taken an interest in education, and their ideas will be noted at appropriate places in the chapters that follow. The primary purpose of this book, however, is to offer suggestions on ways *psychology* might be applied to teaching. The existence of this text is based on the premise that information reported by scientists can be especially valuable for those who plan to teach. Some of the reasons for this conviction become apparent when the characteristics of science are examined.

The nature and values of science

In a survey of psychology department heads conducted in 1967 (Myers, 1970, p. 1045), B. F. Skinner was chosen as the most influential American psychologist of the twentieth century. A major reason for this honor is that he has been the leading spokesman for the view that the application of science to human behavior should lead to advances equivalent to those produced by applications of science to other fields of endeavor. Skinner's observations on ways scientific knowledge might be used to improve education will be summarized at several places in this text. In addition to describing how psychologists and educators might develop what he calls a "technology of teaching," Skinner has written extensively on science in general, explaining why and how he believes it can be the key to the improvement of civilization.

B. F. Skinner
The New York Times

Characteristics of science

In the second chapter of *Science and Human Behavior* Skinner writes, "[Science] is a unique intellectual process which yields remarkable results" (1953, p. 11). He then lists some of the characteristics of science:

Dealing directly and objectively with facts

It is a disposition to deal with the facts rather than what someone has said about them ... a willingness to accept facts even when they are opposed to wishes ... [an awareness] of the value of remaining without an answer until a satisfactory one can be found ... a search for order, for uniformities, for lawful relations among events in nature. (pp. 12–13)

Searching for order and relationships

Scientific knowledge is cumulative

Skinner points out that cumulative progress is an especially important characteristic of science that sets it apart from most other intellectual processes. The discoveries of one generation of scientists set the stage for more valuable and far-reaching discoveries by the next. The values of science become clear when account is taken of some of the limitations of casual observation (and of unsystematic applications of such observations to behavior) and of how the scientist tries to correct for these weaknesses.

Limitations of unsystematic observation

Those who make unsystematic observations of human behavior may be easily misled into drawing false conclusions. The first plausible explanation that comes to mind may be treated as if it is the only possible explanation. A single episode may lead to a generalization that will be mistakenly applied to superficially similar situations. The reactions of an individual in a given situation may be due primarily to unrecognized idiosyncratic factors that may never occur again. The behavior of one person under certain circumstances may not be compared to that of other persons in the same circumstances. Unsystematic observers are especially prone to note only evidence that fits their expectations and to ignore evidence that does not. Ignorance of what others have discovered may cause each individual to start at the same point when confronted with a problem and to make the same mistakes others made as they struggled to find solutions.

Strengths of scientific observation

Those who study behavior scientifically are more likely to acquire trustworthy information than a casual observer is, and they are likely to apply what they learn more effectively because they follow certain procedures:

Scientific methods:

Sampling

In most cases, a representative sample of subjects is studied so that individual idiosyncrasies are canceled out.

Control

An effort is made to note all plausible hypotheses to explain a given type of behavior, and each hypothesis is tested under controlled conditions. If all factors but one can be held constant in an experiment, the researcher may be able to trace the impact of a given condition by comparing the behavior of those who have been exposed to it and those who have not.

Objectivity

Observers make special efforts to be objective and to guard against being misled by predetermined ideas, wishful thinking, or selected evidence.

Observations are made in a carefully prescribed systematic manner, which makes it possible for observers to compare reactions.

Publication

Replication

Complete reports of experiments—including descriptions of subjects, methods, results, and conclusions—are published in professional journals. This dissemination makes it possible for other experimenters to replicate a study to discover if they obtain the same results.

The existence of reports of thousands of experiments makes it possible to discover what others have done, a discovery that can then serve as a starting point for one's own speculations.

Although the use of scientific methods makes possible correction of many of the limitations of unscientific observation, the application of knowledge acquired in a scientific manner is subject to a number of complicating factors.

Studying behavior: Complicating factors

Selection and interpretation of data

Behavior is complex, changes with age, and is the product of many causes. As a result, psychologists are obliged to concentrate on quite circumscribed types of behavior when they carry out research. In order to control variables adequately and make precise and objective observations, scientists usually must restrict themselves to examining one facet of behavior at a time (although some research techniques make it possible to study the interaction of several variables at once). As a consequence, most reports of research provide specific information about a particular aspect of behavior, and more comprehensive knowledge is acquired by combining and interrelating separate studies. The amount of information available on behavior is so extensive that no individual could examine or interpret all of it. As a result, all descriptions of behavior, even those presented in multivolume encyclopedic accounts, are based on selected information, chosen and interpreted in the writer's own way.

Differences of opinion due to selection and interpretation of data

As you read this book you will discover that there are sharp differences of opinion among psychologists regarding certain aspects of development, learning, and intelligence. Opposing views may be based on equally scientific evidence, but the way the evidence is selected and interpreted will vary. Just because a topic is studied scientifically, therefore, does not necessarily mean that there will be unanimity of opinion about interpretations of data.

Influences on researchers and subjects

Interpretations of data also may differ because of factors that influence observation and research. Once someone, even a scientist who strives to be as objective as possible, has made a decision about something, conflicting ideas are resisted. Leon Festinger (1957) has labeled this tendency *cognitive dissonance* because ideas that are "dissonant" (or in conflict with prevailing ideas) tend to be ignored or rejected. Cognitive dissonance helps account for sharp disagreements among psychologists. A psychologist who has a strong commitment to a particular position may find it difficult to take into account criticisms or opposing views. If you react negatively to discussions of certain techniques of teaching described in this book, your response may be due to the influence of cognitive dissonance. To combat this tendency, which might prevent you from learning and remembering potentially valuable information, do your best to read with an open mind. Sometimes you may find that facts that run contrary to expectations will clarify and enhance understanding—provided you are willing to evaluate them in an unprejudiced way.

Cognitive dissonance: Rejection of conflicting ideas

Experimenter bias
effect: Communication
of expectations

Another factor that may influence a researcher is called the *experimenter bias effect*. This term refers to the subtle and unintentional transmission of the experimenter's expectations to the subjects of a study. The effect, often abbreviated EBE, is illustrated by some of the research of those who have studied it. Robert Rosenthal, the psychologist who first described it, conducted studies, reported in *Experimenter Bias Effects in Behavioral Research* (1966), that supported the view that EBE exists. Theodore X. Barber and five colleagues (1969) replicated some of Rosenthal's experiments and reported that the results did *not* support the EBE hypothesis. These conflicting results could have been due, at least in part, to the experimenters' positive and negative expectations. Some of the inconsistent results of studies you will read about in this book, as well as others you may discover on your own, may be due to the impact of the EBE. One experimenter might have expected support for a hypothesis; another might have expected the same hypothesis to be rejected; and each might have communicated expectations to the subjects, who were then influenced by the experimenter expectations.

Hawthorne effect:
Reactions to change
and attention

Still another reason for variation in results of experiments is the *Hawthorne effect* (Roethlisberger and Dickson, 1939)—so called because the effect was first noticed in a study made at the Hawthorne, Illinois, plant of Western Electric. The investigators discovered that the subjects of their study of working conditions tended to respond to almost any change, apparently because of their appreciation of the attention paid to them. If the Hawthorne effect prevails, an educational psychologist who introduces a program to improve the learning ability of preschool children, for example, might uncover evidence of substantial gains, although much of the improvement might be produced more by the subjects' reactions to novelty or change than to the program's specific techniques. If the same techniques are used for an extended period of time and thereby lose their novelty or if another investigator tries them on children who do not respond to them as new or different, little or no impact may be detected.

Enthusiasm for new ideas waxes and wanes

Such factors as selection of data, the experimenter bias effect, and the Hawthorne effect help account for conflicts in the way scientific information may be interpreted. They also partially explain why techniques of teaching change so rapidly. A series of experiments may lead to the development of a new concept or pedagogical technique that will be highly successful when it is first tried out. Subsequent studies, however, may reveal that the original research was incomplete, or repeated applications of a technique may show that it is less effective once the novelty has worn off. Recent concepts and techniques that initially were accepted or practiced with enthusiasm, but which later proved to have limitations, include the impact of teacher expectations, programmed instruction, and open education.

Impact of teacher expectations   In 1968 Robert Rosenthal collaborated with Lenore Jacobson in writing *Pygmalion in the Classroom*. In this book he reported results of a study that had been inspired by his earlier research on the experimenter bias effect. Rosenthal reasoned that if an experimenter could influence the behavior of subjects by communicating expectations, teachers might do the same to their pupils. To test this hypothesis, Rosenthal and Jacobson administered tests to elementary school students and then told the teachers that on the basis of test results certain pupils in each class were "likely to show unusual intellectual gains in the year ahead." In reality, however, there was no difference between the test performances of these "superior" pupils, who had simply been selected at random, and those of the other children.

Pygmalion effect

Self-fulfilling prophecy

Rosenthal and Jacobson reported in *Pygmalion in the Classroom* that the students who were labeled potential achievers showed significant gains in IQ and that the reason for these gains was the fact that the teachers expected more of them. The authors referred to this phenomenon as the *Pygmalion effect* because they felt that teachers' expectations had influenced the students to become intelligent in the same way that the expectations of the mythical Greek sculptor Pygmalion had caused a statue he had carved to become endowed with life. Another term frequently used to refer to the same phenomenon is *self-fulfilling prophecy,* because a prophecy that is made about behavior may become fulfilled. If teachers communicate the "prophecy" that certain students will behave intelligently, those students may behave in the expected manner.

When *Pygmalion in the Classroom* was first published, it caused a sensation. A number of writers on educational subjects proposed that it provided the key to revolutionizing the education of disadvantaged students. It was argued that the inadequate school performance of many students from poor backgrounds was due to low expectations on the part of teachers. If the teachers would simply communicate high expectations, it was reasoned, student performance would improve dramatically. Unfortunately for those who felt that a significant breakthrough had been achieved, initial enthusiasm about the potency of the Pygmalion effect was soon replaced by doubts and qualifications. A number of psychologists (e.g., Robert L. Thorndike, 1968; Richard E. Snow, 1969) pointed out weaknesses of the Rosenthal and Jacobson study. Other researchers (e.g., William L. Claiborn, 1969; Jean José and John Cody, 1971; and Elyse S. Fleming and Ralph G. Anttonen, 1971) replicated the study but failed to find evidence to support the hypothesis that teacher expectations had a significant effect on pupil performance. However, Rosenthal (1969) argued that

The heroine of G. B. Shaw's Pygmalion, *the cockney flower girl Eliza Doolittle (Audrey Hepburn, in the movie version of* My Fair Lady *makes a grand entrance as a "lady" at a ball. The self-fulfilling prophecy is sometimes called the Pygmalion effect. As Eliza explains to her admirer Colonel Pickering, "The difference between a lady and a flower girl is the way she is treated. I shall always be a flower girl to Professor Higgins, because he always treats me as a flower girl, and always will; but I know I can be a lady to you, because you treat me as a lady, and always will."*

Culver Pictures, Inc.

many of these studies were not exact replications of his work, and Eleanor Burke Leacock (1969), Alfred L. Shaw (1969), and D. H. Meichenbaum, K. S. Gower, and R. R. Ross (1969) found evidence that confirmed some aspects of the original Pygmalion study.

These conflicting reports prompted the publication of *Pygmalion Reconsidered* (1971), edited by Janet Elashoff and Richard E. Snow, which consists of a lengthy critique by the editors, a review of studies on teacher expectancy, six reviews of *Pygmalion in the Classroom*, a reply to the Elashoff and Snow critique by Rosenthal entitled "Pygmalion Reaffirmed," and a reply by Elashoff and Snow to Rosenthal's reply. This interchange of ideas suggests that teacher expectations may influence pupil performance under certain circumstances,[3] but it is not likely that teachers can cause all their students to function as outstanding scholars simply by acting as if they expect them to do so.

Other examples of the way applications of scientific knowledge may lead to rapid changes in educational practice are provided by the fluctuations in enthusiasm for programmed instruction and for the open school approach.

Programmed instruction   In the 1960s B. F. Skinner led the way in describing how principles based on animal experiments could be converted into programmed instruction. Initial use of the technique led to promising results, and it was predicted that in a few years almost all lessons would be presented in the form of programs. Fred S. Keller, for example, wrote an article titled "Good-bye Teacher . . ." (1968) in which he speculated that teachers would no longer present lessons to groups of students but would supervise pupils as they responded individually to sets of programmed questions written by specialists in a given field of study. Initial enthusiasm for programmed instruction faded rapidly, however, when some of its limitations (to be summarized in Chapter 5) became apparent. Today few students learn by responding to the kinds of programs originally devised by Skinner, but many successful techniques of teaching have been derived from the basic idea of programmed instruction. The use of Key Points in this book, for example, is a variation of programmed instruction, and the basis and rationale of using such instructional objectives will be discussed in Chapter 5.

Open education   In the 1970s Charles Silberman (1970) and Joseph Featherstone (1971), among others, wrote enthusiastically about techniques of open education that were becoming popular in the elementary schools of England. This type of schooling was derived from the theory of Jean Piaget, the Swiss psychologist who has described stages of cognitive development. Under the open education approach few formal lessons are presented to the entire class. Instead, students are encouraged to engage in self-selected study at learning centers featuring books and displays in different subjects. They also interact with small groups of classmates and devise many of their own learning materials. The teacher keeps records of each pupil's performance and

Open education:
Learning centers,
self-instruction,
interaction

---

[3] Carl Braun (1976) reviewed seventy-eight articles on the impact of teacher expectation and concluded that the conflicting results of many studies might be explained by the assumption that many variables are involved and that some teachers convey expectations to some pupils in some situations. Specific conclusions and interpretations examined by Braun will be noted at appropriate points later in this book.

works with individuals or small groups of students when it becomes apparent that they need instruction in specific skills and subjects.

Silberman, Featherstone, and other enthusiasts for the open education approach argued that it would revolutionize schooling, and a number of teachers and schools in the United States were impressed enough to give the technique a try. In time, however, some of those who used the method became aware of problems that Silberman and Featherstone had overlooked. Some difficulties stemmed from differences between the organization of British and American schools. Other problems were a function of the amount of planning and effort required to make open education function properly. Still other problems were caused by complaints from parents who were dissatisfied with the school performance of their children. Moreover, not all students reacted positively when offered the opportunity to control much of their own learning. Today, as is the case with programmed instruction, comparatively few teachers in the United States use a pure open education approach, but many of them make use of techniques that are derived from this form of schooling.

Change inevitable as knowledge accumulates

These examples of rapid changes in enthusiasm for particular techniques of teaching are mentioned to prepare you for the certainty that the same process will continue. Techniques you will read about in the next few years will be hailed by some enthusiasts as significant breakthroughs that will revolutionize education. In a short time, however, it is quite likely that unforeseen problems will appear and

An open classroom where students are invited to study at learning centers, instruct themselves by examining self-selected materials, and interact with and learn from classmates.

Bruce Roberts/Photo Researchers

that the "final" answers of one period will be replaced by newer and better answers just a few years later.

The rise and decline of such "fads" in education is partly a function of selection of data, the experimenter bias effect, and the Hawthorne effect. But frequent shifts in emphasis in education are also a function of the basic nature of science. In his analysis of scientific methods, B. F. Skinner stressed that the quality of science that sets it apart from other intellectual processes is that the discoveries of one generation of scientists set the stage for more complete and far-reaching discoveries by the next. At the present time more researchers are studying aspects of education than at any previous time in history. Thousands of reports of scientific research are published every month, and as our knowledge accumulates, it is inevitable that interpretations of how children learn and how we should teach will continually change. Fads in education are not necessarily evidence of confusion, therefore; they may simply reflect the fact that thousands of individuals are engaged in a continual search for something better. We know more about development, learning, and teaching today than ever before, but because of the nature of some of the factors just discussed—and the complexity of human behavior—answers to many questions are tentative and incomplete.

Educational "fads" traceable to accumulating knowledge

Impact of cultural, political, and economic changes

Other reasons for shifts in thinking about teaching are traceable to the impact of rapid cultural, political, and economic changes. Conditions in our society and the world alter at such a rapid pace that it is necessary continually to revise applications of knowledge to meet new conditions. In the late 1950s, for example, the Russians stunned the world when they successfully launched the first humanly created object to orbit the earth. American leaders and educators reacted by seeking ways to improve instruction in this country in mathematics and science. Curricula in the sciences were developed and stressed in the public schools, science fairs became popular, and outstanding students of scientific subjects were awarded generous scholarships. In a short time all these developments produced a bumper crop of capable young scientists. But when they had done their work and collaborated in landing an American on the moon, the need for some types of scientists diminished to the point that many highly trained individuals were unable to find work in their area of special interest. The schools responded by cutting back on science programs, and students turned to other fields of study.

In the late 1960s and early 1970s, at a time when stress was placed on individual freedom in many aspects of American life, a number of so-called free schools were formed as alternatives to public schools. Those who favored free schools argued that public education in the

United States was too regimented and repressive. Accordingly, the curriculum in some alternative schools was determined almost entirely by students. Many public schools, influenced by the same spirit of personal freedom, introduced student-centered approaches to education that permitted students wide scope for selecting and managing their own learning. At the college level, the number of required courses was reduced or eliminated, and at some institutions students were allowed to devise their own degree programs.

Although such methods were successful with well-motivated individuals with clear goals, many students appeared to find it difficult to select appropriate topics to study or to persevere in completing what they had intended to accomplish. For these, and many other reasons as well, students (on the average) in the early 1970s appeared to know less about many subjects than earlier generations of pupils. Average scores on most standardized tests were consistently lower than they had been a decade or so earlier (Harnischfeger and Wiley, 1976). Professors in colleges and universities reported that students were poorly prepared, and in many institutions literacy requirements were established and remedial programs were initiated to help high school graduates learn basic skills they had failed to acquire earlier. School board members in many communities became alarmed and expressed skepticism about the effectiveness of teachers who did not teach but seemed simply to wait for their students to learn on their own.

This attitude, coupled with the sudden surplus of teachers and the financial problems of most school districts, led many parents and school board members to conclude that teachers should be required to prove that they were having an impact on their students. This requirement came to be referred to as *accountability:* teachers were to be held accountable for what happened in their classrooms. If teachers could not offer tangible proof that their students knew more at the end of a report period than they did at the beginning, it was argued, they should be fired. Since there are many teachers looking for jobs, some contemporary critics of education maintain that schools should hire and retain only those who know what they want their students to learn and are capable of achieving what they set out to do. If teachers are going to call themselves professionals and engage in collective bargaining to win higher salaries and better working conditions, it is reasoned, they should prove that they are earning their salaries and that better working conditions lead to improved student performance.

Partly because of the effectiveness of collective bargaining by teacher organizations, you will probably earn a higher salary when you begin your teaching career than that earned by first-year teachers at any previous time in history. But because of current stress on accountability, you will probably be expected to be quite specific about what you intend to arrange for your students to learn, and you are likely to be asked to offer tangible proof that your students know

Accountability:
Teachers expected to
offer proof of student
achievement

more when they leave your classroom than they did when they entered it.

On the last few pages you have been asked to consider some of the values of science, the strengths of scientific observation, and a few of the factors that complicate the scientific study of behavior and also lead to frequent changes of emphasis in teaching techniques. These points have been offered for your consideration to explain why this book stresses how psychology might be applied to teaching and to support the position that information reported by scientists can be especially valuable for those who plan to teach. At the same time, the intention has been to acquaint you with a few of the limitations and sometimes unsettling by-products of science. The purpose of this book is to help you take advantage of the benefits of science when you teach; it is not to convert you into a "scientific teacher." Science has much to offer to teachers, but a scientific approach is not always appropriate in the classroom, and in some situations certain techniques of scientific observation may actually interfere with effective teaching. This interference may occur because of conflicts between theory and practice.

The teacher-practitioner and the teacher-theorist

Some educators have argued that teaching is an art that cannot be practiced—or even studied—in an objective or scientific manner. For example, Gilbert Highet, a distinguished professor of literature, explains the title of his book *The Art of Teaching* as follows:

[This book] is called *The Art of Teaching* because I believe that teaching is an art, not a science. It seems to me very dangerous to apply the aims and methods of science to human beings as individuals, although a statistical principle can often be used to explain their behavior in large groups and a scientific diagnosis of their physical structure is always valuable. But a "scientific" relationship between human beings is bound to be inadequate and perhaps distorted. Of course it is necessary for any teacher to be orderly in planning his work and precise in his dealing with facts. But that does not make his teaching "scientific." Teaching involves emotions, which cannot be systematically appraised and employed, and human values, which are quite outside the grasp of science. . . . "Scientific" teaching, even of scientific subjects, will be inadequate as long as both teachers and pupils are human beings. Teaching is not like inducing a chemical reaction: it is much more like painting a picture or making a piece of music, . . . like planting a garden or writing a friendly letter. You must throw your heart into it, you must realize that it cannot all be done by formulas, or you will spoil your work, and your pupils, and yourself. (1957, pp. vii–viii)

As a reaction to Highet's statement, you might find this comment by Paul Woodring (*A Fourth of a Nation*) interesting:

The fact that teaching is held to be an art rather than a science does not mean . . . that methodology cannot be taught. Every artist learns his methods from another artist who acts as teacher. The genius will develop his own methods, but it cannot be expected that all of the more than a million American teachers will be geniuses.

The fact that Highet has taken time out from a busy life to write an excellent book on *The Art of Teaching* would seem to indicate that he agrees that this art can, at least in some small part, be learned from books. (1957, p. 52)

It seems difficult to argue with Woodring's observation. Even artists with tremendous creative potential are almost certain at the beginning of their careers to learn some basic techniques from an experienced artist who serves as teacher. And the most fervent advocates of unstructured schooling must believe that the followers of "artistic" or "intuitive" methods of education can learn from others, judging by the number of books they publish. The question remains, however: Are there certain characteristics of science that might hinder rather than help teachers?

The educational psychologist J. M. Stephens offers a scientist's view of the same basic question raised by Highet. He observes:

The professional educator must have considerable faith in the educational process. . . . He must hope and believe that it will accomplish great things. . . . Teaching is often such a warm, emotional, enthusiastic process. It calls for devotion and commitment to a given course of action. It is possible that a cold, analytic attitude of suspended judgment would prevent the teacher from stimulating students and would make for poor rapport.

These convictions and emotional commitments which may be so necessary in the practice of education are obvious handicaps in the careful and precise study of education. Enthusiastic feelings or warm hopes should not influence our decisions as to what is so. . . .

To understand a process, we must try to put our feelings and wishes in cold storage for a time, and having done so, we must try to face the facts with an open mind. But although we must face facts, we need not become the slaves of facts. (1956, pp. 21–22)

Stephens suggests that to remain aware of this distinction you think of yourself as two prospective teachers within the same individual—a *teacher-practitioner* and a *teacher-theorist.* He notes:

The requirements of the teacher-practitioner and of the teacher-theorist are both very real and very important. They are, however, somewhat different, and the differences in these requirements are nowhere more striking than in the matter of caution versus confidence. There are times, unquestionably, when the teacher-practitioner should not be assailed by doubts or qualifications, when he should carry out with confidence and with decision any course of action that he has undertaken. At these times, any large measure of doubt, uncertainty, or hesitation may seriously reduce his effectiveness.

The hesitation or uncertainty which might work against the practitioner

Teacher-practioner:
Enthusiastic
commitment

Teacher-theorist:
Objective analysis

J. M. Stephens urges you to be enthusiastic and committed when you are interacting with pupils in the classroom but objective and unemotional when you analyze your performance and student behavior at the end of a school day.

Bohdan Hrynewych

presents no handicap to the theorist. On the contrary, caution, admission of uncertainty, willingness to withhold judgment are of the utmost importance when the teacher-theorist is forming his opinions about the nature of the educational process. The teacher-theorist, therefore, must receive training in this very necessary practice of entertaining doubts and qualifications. (1956, pp. v–vi)

From these comments you can draw an excellent set of precepts for teaching: Have faith in yourself, and keep in mind that teaching should be a warm, emotional, enthusiastic process. But when you *theorize* about education, put your feelings in cold storage for a time, and try to face facts with an open mind. Remain alert to the pitfalls of unsystematic observation as you seek understanding of a process or relationship, for such alertness may protect you from drawing erroneous conclusions.

This book has been written to equip you with information you will be able to use in a great variety of ways as you function as both a teacher-practitioner and a teacher-theorist, and to help you find information with a minimum of difficulty. Even though specific concepts and interpretations may change as scientific knowledge accumulates and as world and local conditions fluctuate, certain basic kinds of information will always be of value to teachers. This basic core of knowledge is reflected by the contents of this book.

The contents of this book

Young children respond to instruction differently than older children. Accordingly, it is important for teachers to know something about the nature of human development and the characteristics of children at different age levels. This information is provided in Part 2. In Chapter 3 you will find an outline of principles and theories of development. Chapter 4 lists characteristics of children at different age levels. For most characteristics, implications for classroom practice are listed, and you are invited to add (in your Handbook) supplementary ideas of your own.

Teachers are hired to help pupils learn, and learning is discussed in Part 3. In Chapters 5, 6, and 7 you will be introduced to different views of the learning process. First, key experiments will be described, and the way these serve as the basis for principles and theories will be outlined. Then, for each view, suggestions for teaching will be summarized, followed by specific examples of applications. Part 4 supplies information about skills, memory, and transfer. In Chapter 8 you will be offered suggestions for helping students acquire psychomotor abilities and learn and retain information. Chapter 9 consists of suggestions you might use to help students master and remember concepts, principles, and techniques that will make them better problem solvers.

Probably, you are enthusiastic about certain preferred subjects, but you know from personal experience that not all subjects or courses are equally appealing. The same will be true of the young people who will enter your classroom. Regardless of the age of your students or the subject or subjects you teach, it is certain that not all your students will respond with equal interest to all the topics you ask them to learn. Consequently, you will often have to take steps to arouse and sustain their interest. Techniques you might use in accomplishing this goal are described in Part 5 on motivation. Chapter 10 provides information about theories of motivation and how they might be applied. Chapter 11 offers specific suggestions for teaching students from disadvantaged backgrounds, who are likely to have special difficulties sustaining interest in school subjects.

In order to find out if you have been successful in your efforts to help students learn, you will have to make an evaluation of their performance, the topic covered in Part 6. You will also, in all probability, be required to make some sort of evaluation of student achievement, either in parent conferences or on report cards. Some possible explanations of why some students perform much more successfully on tests than others are noted in Chapter 12, which includes a review of interpretations of factors that contribute to a person's general learning ability. Techniques you might practice in evaluating pupil performance, with special emphasis on how you might use examinations to contribute to improved learning, are featured in Chapter 13.

Finding ways to allow for differences in student learning ability will be a basic task you will face as a teacher, but you will also seek ways to adapt learning situations to students who differ in other ways. In Chapter 14, the first of the two chapters that make up Part 7, you will learn about techniques you might use for teaching especially fast or slow learners and for arranging classroom experiences for students with different kinds of physical handicaps. Chapter 14 also includes information about students who are experiencing adjustment problems, together with suggestions you might follow in helping them cope with their difficulties. Chapter 15, Maintaining Classroom Control, is devoted to techniques you might use in dealing with students who disrupt class activities.

The Epilogue offers observations on how you might deal with personal problems you experience as a teacher and on what you might do to improve your effectiveness as a teacher.

Mention of personal problems of teachers and the effectiveness of teachers calls attention to an aspect of instruction that you have undoubtedly recognized since the early grades: A dissatisfied teacher is usually a poor teacher. If you hope to become an effective instructor, you will need to feel reasonably satisfied with what you do in your classroom. Even if you know a great deal about your subject and are aware of techniques of teaching, you are not likely to be an effective teacher if you are unhappy with what you are doing. That brings us back to the first question you were asked at the beginning of this chapter: Are you sure you want to become a teacher? To help you come up with a preliminary answer to that question, the next chapter contains a brief account of the kinds of things teachers at different grade levels typically do, a summary of what experienced teachers consider to be the advantages and disadvantages of their jobs, and an analysis of criticisms of public education.

SUMMARY OF KEY POINTS

B. F. Skinner has characterized science as a "unique intellectual process which yields remarkable results." Those who use scientific methods deal with facts directly, evaluate them in an objective manner, and search for order and relationships. A distinctive feature of science is that it shows cumulative progress. The discoveries of one generation pave the way for the even greater discoveries of the next.

To overcome limitations of unsystematic observation, psychologists use scientific methods of study. They study a sample of subjects, endeavor to control conditions as much as possible, strive to be objective, and publish descriptions of how they proceeded and what they discovered so that others can replicate their work and further test their hypotheses.

Although use of scientific methods makes it possible for psychologists to accumulate trustworthy information, there are still differences of opinion about what that information means because of the way data are selected and interpreted. Those who report and analyze scientific data may be influenced by such factors as cognitive dissonance (the tendency to reject conflicting ideas), the experimenter bias effect (communicating expectations to subjects), and the Hawthorne effect (subjects may react more to change and attention than to actual conditions).

Some new concepts and techniques are greeted as revolutionary breakthroughs of great significance when they are first announced, but they are sometimes found to be not so impressive when additional study is carried out. The Pygmalion effect, for example, was initially considered to be the key to making all students successful. Subsequent research on self-fulfilling prophecy reactions revealed that although what teachers expect may sometimes influence pupils, merely conveying the expectation that a child will do well does not guarantee superior achievement. Open education, with stress on learning centers, self-instruction, and interaction among students, was hailed by some educational writers as an even greater panacea than the Pygmalion effect. After extensive use, the open education approach now appears to be appropriate only in certain situations. Such fads in education should not be taken as signs of muddled thinking, since the constant replacement of ideas is an outgrowth of the cumulative nature of scientific knowledge.

Trends in psychology and education are influenced by cultural, political, and economic conditions in a society. The current surplus of teachers, together with evidence of declining pupil achievement, has led to interest in accountability: Teachers are to offer proof that their students have accomplished specific goals.

Some individuals maintain that teaching is an art and that a scientific approach to instruction will lead to negative consequences. Instead of feeling that you must choose between being an artist-practitioner or a scientist, you are urged to play two roles simultaneously. When you present lessons, you should be an enthusiastic, committed teacher-practitioner. When you analyze your own performance and that of your students, you should function as an objective, dispassionate teacher-theorist.

SUGGESTIONS FOR FURTHER STUDY

1-1
Professional Journals

In order to gain some direct experience with the raw material of psychology—the building blocks that are eventually combined to establish a principle or theory—you might examine one or more of the professional journals in psychology, which consist primarily of reports of experiments. Listed below are titles of such journals likely to be found in a typical college library.

American Educational Research Journal

Behavioral Science

Child Development

Developmental Psychology

Educational and Psychological Measurement

Exceptional Child

Genetic Psychology Monographs

Harvard Educational Review

Journal of Abnormal and Social Psychology

Journal of Applied Behavior Analysis

Journal of Educational Psychology

Journal of Educational Research

Journal of Educational Sociology

Journal of Experimental Child Psychology

Journal of Experimental Education

Journal of Experimental Psychology

Journal of Teacher Education

Merrill-Palmer Quarterly of Behavior and Development

Mental Hygiene

Psychological Monographs

Psychological Review

Psychology in the Schools

Society for Research in Child Development Monographs

To develop awareness of the nature of research in psychology, examine recent issues of some of these journals. To gain some experience as a teacher-theorist, you might select an article describing an experiment that intrigues you or appears relevant to your own interests, grade level, and subject. Then write an abstract of the article following the outline below:

Author of article

Title of article

Journal in which article appears (including date, volume number, and page numbers)

Purpose (or description of problem)

Subjects

Procedure (or methods)

Treatment of data

Results

Conclusions

Are there any criticisms that you can make of the procedure or of the conclusions?

What inferences for your own teaching can you draw from this experiment?

Would you be willing to change your methods of teaching on the strength of this one article?

1-2

Journals of Abstracts and Reviews

Unless you are familiar with research in a particular aspect of educational psychology, you may find it difficult to fit an individual study reported in a journal into a general framework or relate it to other similar research. In most cases, it is prudent to find out what other experiments of a similar type have revealed about a particular point before making generalizations from the results of a single study. A variety of journals and reference works exist to assist you in doing this. The journals listed below consist of abstracts (brief summaries of results) of articles that appear in the type of journal listed in the preceding section.

Child Develoment Abstracts and Bibliography

Exceptional Child Education Abstracts

Psychological Abstracts

The following encyclopedias contain reviews and analyses of research reported in the journals listed in this and the preceding section:

The Encyclopedia of Education (1971), edited by Lee C. Deighton

Encyclopedia of Educational Research (1969), edited by Robert L. Ebel

Second Handbook of Research on Teaching (1973), edited by R. M. W. Travers

Review of Research in Education (1973), edited by Fred N. Kerlinger

The Teacher's Handbook (1971), edited by Dwight W. Allen and Eli Seifman

The journal *Contemporary Psychology* provides reviews of new books in psychology, and the *Annual Review of Psychology* provides information reflected by the title—a specialist in each of several areas of psychology reviews significant studies that have appeared during a given year.

The *Review of Educational Research* features articles that describe, relate, and analyze reports of studies on a particular theme.

To discover the nature of these journals and reference works, examine some of them and perhaps prepare a brief description of the most promising titles to save for future reference. Or select a topic of interest, search for reports of experiments, and summarize the conclusions you reach.

In addition to descriptions of actual experiments, "discussion" articles are published in some professional journals and in many teachers' magazines. Listed below are journals of this type.

Journals consisting of general discussions of trends, developments, and techniques The following journals consist of descriptions of trends, developments, and techniques, as well as interpretations of research data. In some articles, research studies are cited; in others, interpretations of approaches to teaching are offered without reference to specific data. Many of these journals also feature sections on tricks of the trade, and most provide book reviews.

Change (higher education)

Clearing House (junior and senior high school teaching)

Elementary School Journal

Exceptional Children

Journal of General Education

Journal of Higher Education (college and university teaching)

Junior College Journal

Phi Delta Kappan

Teachers College Journal

Teachers College Record

Theory into Practice

Journals consisting of brief commentaries on trends, developments, and techniques The following journals consist of short (usually less than five pages) articles on trends, developments, and techniques in education.

Childhood Education

Education

Educational Forum

Educational Leadership

Educational Record (college and university teaching)

Educational Technology (programmed instruction, behavior modification)

High School Journal

Journal of Education

School Review

Note: *Education Digest* is made up of condensations of articles selected from the types of journals listed in this and the preceding section.

Magazines for teachers The following publications provide articles, usually in magazine format, with emphasis on journalistic style, abundant illustrations, and colorful graphic design:

Grade Teacher   *Psychology Today*

Instructor   *Today's Education*

Learning

If you look through some recent issues of several of these journals, you will discover the nature of typical trend and technique articles on psychology and education. For future reference, you might read an article that you feel is relevant to your own interests, grade level, and subject and then write a synopsis of the author's arguments. If any of these arguments are pertinent to your own theorizing about teaching, briefly analyze your thoughts, perhaps by following an outline such as this one:

Author of article

Name of article

Journal in which article appeared (including date, volume number, and page numbers)

Synopsis of arguments presented

Your reaction to the arguments

1-4

Specialized
Publications for
Teachers

Almost every field of study in education has one or more journals devoted to reports of research, reviews of related experimental studies, discussions of teaching techniques, descriptions of tricks of the trade, and analyses of subject matter. The following list of journals may help you discover what is available in your area or areas of interest:

African Studies Bulletin

Agricultural Education Magazine

American Biology Teacher

American Business Education

American Music Teacher

American Speech

American String Teacher

American Vocational Journal

Arithmetic Teacher

Art Education

Athletic Journal

Audiovisual Instructor

Business Education World

Coach and Athlete

Coaching Clinic

Education and Training of the Mentally Retarded

Educational Theatre Journal

Elementary English

Elementary School Guidance and Counseling

English Language Teaching

English Studies

Forecast for Home Economics

French Review

Geographical Teacher

German Review

Gifted Child Quarterly

Hearing and Speech News

History Today

Improving College and University Teaching

Industrial Arts and Vocational Education

Industrial Arts Teacher

Instrumentalist

Journal of Industrial Teacher Education

Journal of Negro Education

Journal of Nursing

Journal of Reading

Journal of Research on Science Teaching

Journal of School Health

Journal of Secondary Education

Journal of Special Education

Reading Specialist

Marriage and Family Living

Mathematics Teacher

Music Education Journal

Music in Education

Music Journal

National Business Education Quarterly

National Elementary Principal

Physical Educator

Physics Teacher

Recreation

Safety Education

Scholastic Coach

School Arts

School Counselor

School Musician

School Musician Director and Teacher

School Science and Mathematics

School Shop

Science Educator

Science Teacher

Swimming Technique

Teaching Exceptional Children

Tennis

Theatre Arts

Theatre World

Today's Speech

Track Technique

To discover what is available, check titles in the above list that sound promising, spend some time in the periodicals section of your college library, and examine some recent issues. You might select an article you find interesting and write an abstract of it, together with your own interpretation. Or you might prepare a brief description of journals that impress you as worthy of attention. This list could serve as a source of information on what journals to consult after you begin your teaching career.

1-5

Educational Resources Information Center (ERIC)

As a number of journals listed on the preceding pages indicates, thousands of articles are published each year on every conceivable aspect of educational psychology and education. To assist psychologists and educators to discover what has been published on a specific topic, the Educational Resources Information Center (ERIC) has been established by the U.S. Office of Education. ERIC publishes three sources of information:

Current Index to Journals in Education—Annual Cumulation contains an index of articles in over three hundred education and education-oriented journals published in a given year. There are four sections in each volume: Subject Index (which lists titles of articles organized under hundreds of subject headings), Author Index, Journal Contents Index (which lists the table of contents for each issue of journals published that year), and Main Entry Section (which provides the title, author, journal reference, and a brief abstract of articles published in journals covered by the index).

Research in Education lists curriculum guides, catalogues, and the like, and papers, reports, and monographs not published in journals. The Document Résumé section presents descriptions of the documents arranged according to the ERIC classification scheme, together with information about where each can be obtained. There is also a Subject Index (titles of documents listed according to the ERIC classification), an Author Index, and an Institution Index (titles of articles listed with reference to source).

ERIC Educational Documents Index lists titles of documents noted and abstracted in *Research in Education* and also in *Office of Education Research Reports*. Each document is classified under up to five *Major Descriptors* (general categories) and perhaps also under *Minor Descriptors* (more specific categories).

As these descriptions indicate, for information on what is available in journals, you should refer to *Current Index to Journals in Education—Annual Cumulation*. For information about curriculum guides, pamphlets, and reports not published in journals, consult the *ERIC Educational Documents Index* for titles and *Research in Education* for descriptions and information about how to obtain such documents.

You are urged to examine a recent issue of these publications to discover what is available in the ERIC network and how you might obtain information.

1-6

Views of the Art of Teaching

Whereas psychologists are primarily interested in ways to encourage a scientific approach to teaching—even as they seek ways to allow for artistic elements—those outside of science may do the opposite. A comprehensive presentation of the view that teaching is an art that may be spoiled by overemphasis on science is found in Gilbert Highet's *The Art of Teaching* (1957). Highet explains why he considers teaching to be an art, describes what he believes are the qualities of a good teacher, discusses basic methods of instruction, and provides a brief account of some of the great teachers of history and the methods they used. In *The Immortal Profession* (1976) Highet comments on a variety of aspects of teaching and education.

A more complete account of teaching techniques used by famous teachers of history is provided in *The Master Teachers and the Art of Teaching* (1967) by John E. Colman. In the first chapter, Colman outlines "The General Approach" and then devotes a chapter to each of nineteen different approaches to teaching—including the Socratic method, the Jesuit method, and Communist methods. The last chapter is titled "Be an Artist!" and concludes with this statement: "Teaching is nothing less than the vibrant contact of one mind with another mind. And that is an art. Be an artist . . . And so teach!"

Original discourses on the art of teaching by many of the famous teachers described by Highet and Colman may be found in *Three Thousand Years of Educational Wisdom* (1954) by Robert S. Ulich.

1-7
Debates in Psychology and Education

Because of the impact of personal involvement and the nature of cognitive dissonance, the Hawthorne effect, and the experimenter bias effect, a new development in education is often presented as the best way to solve a particular problem of teaching, and criticisms or alternate techniques are ignored or minimized. A person who has devoted several years to perfecting a novel technique naturally begins to think of it as a "cause" and to defend it against criticism and reject counterproposals made by others. This tendency to favor a certain point of view often leads to a polarization of arguments. Throughout the text, an effort has been made to give both sides of key issues so that you can make up your own mind. (It must be noted, however, that the author is not immune to the human frailties that lead to personal affinities for certain ideas in education; consequently, you may find that some points of view are favored over others in the way the discussion in the text is presented.)

As you read about new developments in education, remain aware of the polarizing or dichotomizing tendencies that stem from the psychological mechanisms mentioned above. If a theorist argues in favor of one approach, keep an eye out for counterarguments. (In the text and in these Suggestions, you are referred to many articles or books setting forth a point of view different from that emphasized.) *Today's Education* often presents one or more educators arguing for a position and also one or more arguing against it. And quite often, after an article appears, critical observations from the "other side" are printed in the form of either letters to the editor or articles presenting follow-up critiques. To get experience with this aspect of theorizing about education and psychology, you might read one of the differences-of-opinion articles in *Today's Education* or browse through a bound set of some other teachers' journal for a given year looking for letters or articles that summarize counterarguments to ideas presented earlier. If you make such a comparison, you might list the arguments for and against the subject being debated and then write down your own position on the subject.

1-8
Pygmalion Effect (Self-fulfilling Prophecy)

The publication of *Pygmalion in the Classroom* (1968) by Robert Rosenthal and Lenore Jacobson stimulated several psychologists to attempt replications of the original experiment, others to write critical analyses of the book, others to analyze the nature of the experimenter bias effect from which the Pygmalion effect was derived, and still others to write articles attempting to explain discrepancies between studies and interpretations. If you would like to sample a variety of views on the Pygmalion effect, examine *Pygmalion Reconsidered* (1971), edited by Janet D. Elashoff and Richard E. Snow. For a comprehensive review of research, look for the article "Teacher Expectations: Sociopsychological Dynamics" by Carl Braun in the *Review of Educational Research,* vol. 46(2), 1976, pp. 185–213.

Key points

Note: Because this chapter is intended to help you make a personal analysis of your feelings about education and teaching, no Key Points are indicated in the margins and no Summary of Key Points is presented at the end of the chapter.

Chapter 2

What teaching is like

A POINT often made in books on education—including this one—is that teachers should constantly try to see things from their students' point of view. In this chapter and throughout the rest of this text, you are also asked to reverse that procedure. You presently see things from a student's point of view. Now you are urged to empathize with teachers, put yourself in their position, and see things from *their* point of view. If you fail to do this, you may discover that the abrupt transition from student to teacher causes many problems. As noted in Chapter 1, your present perceptions of what takes place in classrooms will vary significantly from the perceptions you will gain when you close the door to a classroom and face your first group of pupils. This chapter describes education seen from the teacher's vantage point, and it is designed to give you a preview of things that are likely to impress you if you pursue a career in education.

Another reason you are urged to read this chapter is to develop awareness of some of the realities of life in classrooms. The information presented here may help you make up your mind about whether you want to become a teacher. And if you decide that you *do* want to serve as an educator and if you secure a job, this chapter may also make your first year of teaching a less traumatic experience. Many first-year teachers become disenchanted because they begin their careers ignorant of classroom routine and the common frustrations they must face. If you become aware of some of the unpublicized and unglamorous aspects of teaching and of some of the givens and conditions, you should be better prepared to make the abrupt change from student to teacher.

Some facts and figures

To focus your thoughts on what you will be expected to do if you become a teacher, consider the following facts and figures:

Most teachers are expected to provide instruction six hours a day, 180 days a year.

Preschool, kindergarten, and elementary school teachers typically instruct the same group of students all day and all year. Many preschools and some elementary schools, however, use a split-session approach. Other schools use team teaching and/or departmentalized approaches. In such cases the teacher is expected to instruct two or more groups of students. In a self-contained classroom a teacher at these grade levels will instruct between 25 and 30 students. In split-session, team, or departmentalized schools, the number of students to be taught may amount to a hundred or more. Teachers at this level also may be asked to supervise students during recess periods and at lunch time.

Junior and senior high school teachers typically teach five different classes of 30 students each and are allowed one preparation period. Class periods are usually forty to fifty minutes long with a five-minute break between classes. In many secondary schools teachers offer courses that extend throughout the entire 180-day year. In other schools, courses may be 90 days in duration (or even less). Secondary

Frank Siteman/Stock Boston

school teachers who teach five classes a year will have responsibility for instructing approximately 150 pupils. Those who teach five classes of shorter duration may have a total of over 300 students in their classes during a school year. Teachers at this level also may be expected to supervise cocurricular activities after school hours.

Most schools schedule four report periods each year. Over 70 percent of all elementary schools use report cards with a classified scale of letters.[1] Almost 60 percent of such schools use parent conferences, sometimes in conjunction with report cards, sometimes as the exclusive means of evaluating student progress. About 25 percent of all elementary schools use a written description instead of letter grades. This description usually takes the form of a letter to parents. Elementary school report cards may include from as few as five to as many as thirty categories (covering several aspects of academic performance and perhaps attitudes and behavior also). If there are 30 pupils in a self-contained classroom, and if a report card has ten categories (which is common), and if there are four report periods, a teacher will need to record twelve hundred judgments of pupil performance each school year.

Over 80 percent of all secondary schools use report cards with a classified scale of letters; 20 percent use parent conferences. If a secondary school teacher has five classes of 30 pupils, and if there are four report periods, he or she will need to assign six hundred grades per year. (If two courses per year are offered, the teacher will need to assign more than one thousand grades.)

Grades in elementary school may determine the kinds of courses a student may take in junior and senior high school. Grades in secondary school will be of major significance if a high school graduate applies for admission to a college or university. Grades and degrees earned at a college or university may be the key factor leading to acceptance by a graduate school, and they are often of significance when individuals compete for desirable jobs. Students and their parents are therefore concerned about grades, and teachers are often required to defend grades.

Most states require teachers to cover certain subjects at different grade levels. In many cases these requirements stress a sequence of subjects and courses leading to different secondary school programs, such as college preparatory or vocational. Most school systems supplement state requirements with local guidelines. Each school within a district may request teachers to follow a uniform syllabus. Most school systems use texts that are selected by state and local committees.

The decision about whether a teacher will be retained is typically made by administrators. A principal is likely to observe first-year

[1] All figures on types of report cards are based on a nationwide survey summarized in the *NEA Research Bulletin*, "Reporting Pupil Progress," October 1969.

teachers perform in the classroom and is also likely to take into account informal or formal evaluations by colleagues, students, and parents.

American public schools are controlled by school boards selected by the voters in a district. School boards make decisions about the curriculum, the budget (how much money will be allotted to salaries, texts, supplies, teaching aids, athletics, and so on), and school rules, such as dress codes and smoking regulations. They also make the final decision if a teacher who has been dismissed files a grievance.

Although state agencies, school boards, and administrators make many decisions, details of how guidelines will be interpreted and applied are made by personnel in individual schools. In many cases specific applications are arrived at through participatory-democracy procedures. This means frequent before- and after-school faculty meetings.

A typical elementary school usually has one or two classes at each grade level. The total student enrollment may vary from 150 to around 300 pupils, and there may be from seven to fifteen teachers, a principal, one or two secretaries, a custodian, and perhaps cafeteria personnel. Elementary school teachers often know most of the students in the school and have close contact with all other teachers, the principal, and the nonteaching staff.

It is more difficult to describe "typical" secondary schools, since they vary in size and organization much more than elementary schools. Most of them, however, may have from 500 to 2,000 students, from twenty to seventy teachers. Both junior and senior high schools usually have several administrative officers and an extensive office, custodial, and cafeteria staff. Faculty members have contact with students for less than an hour a day and are likely to interact primarily with colleagues who teach the same subject or who occupy adjacent rooms.

To become aware of some of the implications of these facts and figures, consider some of the things you will be expected to do as a public school teacher.

What you will be expected to do

Six hours a day, 180 days a year

If you expect to teach in the elementary grades, you will need to plan a six-hour schedule each day. You will be expected to teach all subjects (if you are in a self-contained classroom), or several subjects (if you are in a team-taught or departmentalized classroom). You will need to take into account the immaturity of your pupils, encourage them to concentrate on school work, and make provision for their short attention span.

If you expect to teach in a secondary school, you will need to pace yourself. If you teach five sections of the same class, you will have only one preparation a day but will face the problem of maintaining your enthusiasm as you present the same material five times in succession. If you teach two or more different classes, you will have greater variety but more work. Fifty minutes may seem like an eternity if you are not prepared, and you will more or less be compelled to schedule films and discussion and activity periods along with lectures and demonstrations. (It takes an enormous amount of stamina to stand and talk for five hours.)

Report cards

At any grade level or in any type of school, almost all teachers are expected to report on student achievement. Consequently, you must find ways to evaluate student performance as objectively as possible and must be prepared to defend your evaluations. This is especially true if you plan to teach high school students. You will therefore need to devote much time and effort to preparing, administering, and grading projects, papers, and exams and to engaging in parent conferences and making out report cards. Elementary school teachers need to establish a basis for evaluating student performance in several subjects. Secondary school teachers, to cite just one of the many factors to consider, need to work out assignments so that they are not confronted with exam papers from 150 students on the same day.

Requirements, bookkeeping, regulations

In most public schools, teachers are required to use particular texts, cover certain topics, and follow established procedures. The degree to which teachers are asked to follow prescribed guidelines varies considerably from one school district to another, but virtually all school systems establish some requirements. Generally speaking, the larger the system is, the more detailed the guidelines will be. In some schools almost the entire curriculum will be spelled out in advance. In other systems, teachers are expected to use particular materials, but they are also given freedom to devise supplementary assignments of their own. Quite often, however, it is necessary to obtain approval before introducing units or topics that supplement or replace the standard curriculum. For example, a high school English teacher who wants to substitute a recent novel for *David Copperfield* will probably have to ask for approval from one or more administrators.

A different aspect of requirements involves record keeping. Almost all public school teachers must spend at least a few minutes every day filling out forms of various kinds and engaging in book-keeping. All public schools are expected to keep accurate attendance records, and at the beginning of each day or period, teachers must take roll. It also is essential to keep track of school property, such as texts and specialized equipment. There may be lockers to be assigned, playground equipment to be accounted for, and lunch money to collect. If you want your class to go on a field trip, you will have to obtain signatures from parents. If you want to obtain an assortment of materials for a special project, you will need to make out a requisition form—probably in duplicate or even in triplicate.

A related facet of life in schools involves regulations. Not so many years ago public school teachers in this country were told how they should behave not only in the classroom but also in their private lives. Female teachers were often forbidden to smoke in public, for example, and male teachers were enjoined from patronizing any local bar. Although such out-of-school control has been largely eliminated, the in-school behavior of teachers is often guided by sets of regulations ranging from signing in and out to dress codes.

In addition to abiding by regulations, teachers are expected to enforce them and are sometimes assigned specifically to that task. Elementary teachers take turns overseeing the playground before and after school and during lunch time. Secondary teachers may be required to stand hall duty or attempt to hold down the chaos in the cafeteria. In some school systems teachers may also be expected to enforce dress codes, smoking regulations, and the like. Such regulations are considered essential because teachers act *in loco parentis,* in place of parents, when children are at school. Parents supervise the at-home activities of their children and may establish certain rules, such as no smoking. When their children are required to leave the home and go to school, parents expect teachers to supervise activities and enforce rules similar to those they have instituted in the family.

Retention and tenure

Most school systems award tenure to teachers after they have been recommended for retention for three years. Once a teacher achieves

tenure, the contract with a school system is automatically renewed every year, unless an individual is charged with unprofessional conduct. The granting of tenure is obviously a major decision, since it amounts to a lifetime contract. You should expect, therefore, to be evaluated carefully during the first years of your teaching career. Because the principal of a school usually has the most to say about who will be retained, such decisions may be influenced by the personality and preferences of one individual. As a teacher, you can often reduce the impact of such idiosyncratic factors if you provide evidence that your students have learned. (In many job situations probationary employees may be fired without being given the chance to offer proof of their effectiveness.) This evidence does not necessarily have to take the form of test scores, but it should be tangible enough to serve as proof that you and your students have accomplished something. Consequently, you may feel obliged to stress subject matter more than such intangibles as interpersonal relationships or personal fulfillment, particularly during your probationary period of teaching.

School boards

Americans endorse democratic governing procedures, where citizens have a voice in selecting leaders and determining the policies they establish. This endorsement is the primary reason public school teachers are expected to abide by decisions made by school boards. Nevertheless, within the limits established by school boards, most teachers have opportunities to introduce personal variations. Occasionally a pressure group in a community will persuade a school board to institute excessive restrictions governing the content of a text or course. In most cases of this type, however, teacher organizations have been successful in reinstituting a high degree of academic freedom. Even so, you may be required to use texts and follow curriculum outlines that must be approved by elected representatives of the citizens of the school district in which you teach. And the school board is likely to make decisions about school policies and how they should be enforced.

Faculty meetings

Even allowing for national, state, and local requirements and the control of school boards, teachers in most American schools have quite a bit to say about what happens in their classrooms. They do not operate in a vacuum, however, and that is the major reason for faculty meetings. Many of the things you do in your classroom may have an impact on what other teachers do in their classrooms, and vice versa. Accordingly, it is necessary for teachers to get together at frequent intervals to reach agreement on standard procedures and to work out compromises. In an elementary school, for example, what happens in one grade will have a substantial impact on what will occur in the next highest grade. At the secondary school level, to note just one factor, all teachers of the same subject should come to agreement about grading standards. Otherwise, pupils in one class may be assigned grades higher or lower than those given to students doing equivalent work in similar classes. You should expect, therefore, to spend many hours before and after school hammering out policies and procedures with your colleagues. This is one price you will have to pay for democracy in education.

Advantages and disadvantages of teaching

The facts, figures, and implications you have just examined have been offered to help you estimate how you will react to common aspects of teaching. Another way you can evaluate your feelings is by examining reports of what teachers like and dislike about their jobs. As you examine the following list of advantages and disadvantages (many of which are based on interviews with first-year as well as veteran teachers), estimate how you feel about each point.

Teaching, like other jobs, has both positive and negative aspects. A factor that may be thought of as an advantage by some individuals in some situations may be perceived as a disadvantage by other individuals under slightly different circumstances. The following lists contrast pros and cons of the same basic aspects of teaching. In the left-hand column in each set of points, you will find positive factors that might develop from a particular characteristic of students, subjects, or school organization. In the right-hand column, potential negative aspects of the same factors are listed. The first set of advantages and disadvantages relates to teaching in all public schools at any grade level. The second and third sets summarize positive and negative features of teaching in elementary and secondary schools.

Teaching any grade

ADVANTAGES

1. You will be attempting to help young people become more skilled, knowledgeable, mature, capable, sensitive, and aware. Teaching is important; and when you are succesful, you will have contributed to the development of something of value and significance.

DISADVANTAGES

1. Some aspects of teaching are tedious and dull. You will have to do quite a bit of paperwork and busywork. You may occasionally wonder if there is any point in teaching, particularly if you fail to detect signs of student progress.

2. You will have the opportunity to develop close personal relationships with young people. Observing and attempting to understand human behavior can be a source of never ending fascination, since every pupil is unique, every group of students is different.

2. Having close relationships with some young people may cause you anxiety and anguish. Sometimes the problems of pupils become *your* problems. You may be frustrated if you understand some of the reasons for a student's unhappiness or poor performance (relationships with parents, for example) and are unable to do much of anything about it. If some of your students are disagreeable, nasty, sullen, hostile, or make it clear that they dislike you, you will still have to do your best to teach them.

3. You will be able to spend some or most of your time dealing with subjects that are of personal interest to you. Presumably you chose to major in certain subjects in college because you enjoy them. You can continue to pursue your interests as part of your job. You will be in a position to encourage students to share your interests and enthusiasms. Awakening an interest in others can be a most rewarding activity, particularly when you are paid for doing it.

3. If students fail to respond when you try to encourage them to share your interests, you will be disappointed and hurt. You may lose some of your own enthusiasm and begin to wonder if a favorite topic really *is* interesting. You will often have to make an effort to try to convince your students that all topics you present are interesting, even though you may not really believe that they are.

4. You will be your own boss most of the time. Even though you must meet certain requirements and take into account the wishes of school boards, committees, and colleagues, the fact remains that when you close the door of your classroom, you are in charge. Whether you are innovative and creative is up to you.

4. There may be times when you will feel cut off and alone because you are the only adult in a classroom. Your attempts to be innovative and creative may be squelched by restrictions. You may have to hold yourself back to adjust your teaching to that of less capable and enthusiastic colleagues.

5. You will be a person in and of authority, and you will have control over many others. Students

5. If you do not assert your authority in the right way, students may become either apa-

Teachers' instructional problems

In 1974 B. R. Bartholomew asked readers of Today's Education to react to a series of statements summarizing common problems faced by teachers. The respondents were asked to indicate if they perceived each problem to be negligible, moderate, serious, or critical. Bartholomew summarized the responses in the following way:

Considerable

Parents apathetic about their children's education*

Too many students indifferent to school*

Physical facilities limiting the kinds of student programs*

The wide range of student achievement

Working with too many students each day

Too many noninstructional duties

The values and attitudes of the current generation

Diagnosing student learning problems

The lack of instructional materials

The quality of instructional materials

Disruption of classes by students

Little help with instruction-related problems from school administrators

The psychological climate of the school*

The mandated curriculum not appropriate for students

Evaluating student achievement

Chronic absence of students from school*

Feeling under pressure too much of the time

The inflexible routine of their situation

The diversity of ethnic-socioeconomic backgrounds of students

Student health and nutrition problems that affect learning

Too few opportunities to improve professional skills

The rapid rate of curricular change

Lack of freedom to teach the way they want

Not assigned to teach what they are qualified to teach

Relatively little　　Student use of drugs

— Effect on teachers' work —

* Problems that appear to affect secondary teachers more than elementary teachers

will be expected to follow your orders, and you may find, in spite of yourself, that it is enjoyable to experience a sense of power. You will know more about most or all subjects than your students, and your superior knowledge is likely to be a source of satisfaction to you and probably will earn you the admiration and respect of many pupils.

thetic or rebellious. You may sometimes get the feeling that your primary role is that of police officer. Even though you will know more than your students, they may not be willing to acknowledge this fact, which will lead to a variety of frustrations.

6. You will have continual opportunities to perform. Even though you may not presently picture yourself as a performer, you will be on stage whenever you stand in front of a class. Being the center of attention may not sound appealing to you now, but you may discover that it is quite enjoyable.

6. Performing before a critical or unresponsive audience is not very enjoyable. There may be times when you will wish that you did not have an audience watching your every move, particularly if you are not prepared or if you say or do something foolish.

7. You will have the opportunity to schedule a substantial amount of your own time. You are expected to be on duty in the classroom nine months a year. You will have extensive vacations at Christmas, Easter, and during the summer. Even though you may have to do school work out of school or sometimes work at another job to earn extra money, you are in a position to decide *when* you will do it. By planning (and saving) ahead, you can devote three months to any activity you like without having to wait until you retire.

7. You will probably have to do some or much work after or out of school. Correcting papers can be tedious; attending PTA meetings may be bothersome; advising an after-school club may seem like an imposition.

8. Once you attain tenure, you will have security. You will not have to worry about sudden dismissal. It is likely that your school district will have an

8. Although teaching is a secure job, it is not a highly paid job. Salary increments are often small, and it may take you fifteen years to reach the top bracket in

excellent retirement plan. If you join a teachers' organization, you may benefit from insurance programs, the power of collective bargaining, and legal assistance if you have a grievance.

a salary scale. You may envy friends and neighbors who spent less time than you did preparing for their jobs but earn substantially more money. Even though you may not aspire to acquire material goods, you may find it hard not to feel envious of those who own expensive homes, cars, or boats and take extravagant vacations.

9. In most cases you will have pleasant working conditions and interesting and intelligent colleagues. Generally speaking, classrooms can be quite agreeable places. You probably will be free to make your room attractive, if you are willing to do it. Your coworkers will all be college graduates and will share many of your interests and perhaps introduce you to others.

9. You may be bothered and limited by inadequate teaching aids, equipment, and supplies. At a time of inflation, high taxes, and high unemployment, many citizens clamor for austerity in school budgets. What school boards consider to be frills you may consider to be essentials.

Teaching elementary grades

ADVANTAGES

1. Elementary school children, particularly those in the lower grades, are usually eager to learn. They may be bored by some subjects and find it difficult to concentrate for more than a few minutes at a time, but they do want to learn most things. You will have a chance to make the most of their initial eagerness and to be in a position to establish their basic attitudes toward school and learning.

DISADVANTAGES

1. Elementary school children are immature. Even though they may be eager to learn, they are likely to find it an effort to concentrate. There may be times when you will lose your patience and be dismayed about their slow rate of progress.

2. Much of the learning of elementary school children is apparent. If you teach first grade pupils, for example, and help nonreaders become readers, you

2. You will be teaching simple skills and knowledge. You may find it difficult to talk constantly in terms your pupils can understand. You may be frustrated by

will *know* that you have accomplished something. Even at the upper elementary grades, student achievement will be apparent, and young children do not attempt to disguise the fact that they are excited and pleased when they learn many things.

3. You will have variety in your teaching, since you will present several subjects. When you and your pupils become bored with one subject, you can switch to another.

4. Younger elementary grade pupils often worship their teachers. Even if older elementary grade pupils do not continue to admire teachers as much as they did earlier, they probably still

their inability to grasp subtle aspects of the topics you discuss.

3. You are not likely to be enthusiastic about teaching all subjects. It may require special effort to show enthusiasm when you teach lessons you detested when you were a student.

4. Sometimes the admiration of pupils may lead to problems in the form of crushes, jealousy, or excessive attempts to gain attention. You may be bothered by the possessiveness of some pupils.

One of the advantages of teaching at the elementary grade level is that pupils often reveal that they admire if not worship their teachers.

George Roos from Peter Arnold

respect them. If your students like you, they are likely to express their admiration openly through comments, spontaneous hugs, cards, presents, and the like.

5. You will have the same children all year, so a sense of group identity is likely to develop. You can develop close relationships with students and may have a substantial impact on their behavior and attitudes.

5. The fact that you have the same children all year may be a disadvantage if you become aware of personality clashes. One or more children may show that they dislike you, or certain pupils may possess characteristics you can barely abide, but you are still stuck with each other for nine months.

6. The atmosphere of elementary schools is often informal and relaxed. At one time or another you may get to know at least half and perhaps almost all pupils in the building. You will probably have at least some contact with the principal and most of your fellow teachers every day. Consequently, a sense of belonging and of personal involvement with others is likely to develop.

6. If you find it difficult to get along with your principal or with one or more of your colleagues, it may be impossible to avoid contact with them. It is difficult to keep to yourself in most elementary schools.

Teaching secondary grades

ADVANTAGES

1. Junior and senior high school students are capable of understanding abstract and complex concepts. They can usually express their ideas well enough to engage in quite sophisticated discussions. You may discover that you will gain new insights as you listen to your students express their opinions and observations.

DISADVANTAGES

1. Some secondary students may have strongly entrenched negative attitudes about school. If they have had a history of failure, they may be convinced they cannot learn. They may resent being forced to attend school and be hostile toward anyone in authority. Even when students do learn something significant because of your instruction, you

2. When you help more mature students acquire complex skills or grasp difficult concepts or discover new ideas, they may experience a sense of excitement about learning that is deeper and more meaningful than they have ever experienced before. In some cases, because of your influence students may make decisions that will alter the course of their lives.

3. You will probably teach most or all courses in one particular area of interest. You will therefore have opportunities to specialize and to perfect lessons, units, lectures, demonstrations, and examinations.

4. Every fifty minutes or so a different group of students will come into your room. Each group will have its own idiosyncrasies, and you may find it stimulating to adapt and vary teaching techniques for each group.

may not be aware of it, either because they keep it to themselves or because the impact of what has been learned occurs after they have left your classroom. Students may be excited about what you teach and admire and respect you as a person, but they may fail to say anything about it or may hide their interest behind a façade of boredom.

2. Despite your efforts to encourage students to learn for the joy of learning, many of them will be primarily interested in earning the highest grade with the least amount of effort. You will need to take precautions to limit cheating, and you may have to engage in frequent arguments about grades.

3. If you are excited about your subject and take a great deal of time and trouble to prepare interesting lessons, you may be terribly disappointed by lack of student response. You may have to be satisfied if only a few students in each class react with occasional sparks of interest.

4. You will probably find that some classes are much more responsive than others. It may require substantial effort to exude enthusiasm with some classes and to maintain a high level of interest as you present the same material over and over again as the day wears on. Repeating a lecture or demonstration or rewatching a film can become exceedingly tedious.

5. Because most secondary schools have hundreds or thousands of students and dozens of teachers who are specialists, you may teach in a room specifically designed for your particular subject and have opportunities to interact with colleagues who share your special interests. Or, if you prefer, you may take advantage of the characteristics of school size and complexity and keep to yourself.

5. The size and nature of most secondary schools cause them to resemble large business concerns in some respects. You may develop close relationships with only a few students and colleagues. You, your students, and your colleagues may have to abide by numerous regulations that are issued and enforced by comparative strangers. You may occasionally feel isolated, insignificant, and ignored.

These lists of advantages and disadvantages of teaching have been presented to help you estimate how you will respond if you pursue a career in education. If, as you perused them, you began to wonder about some of the causes leading to some of the disadvantages, you may be pondering questions such as these: Why is public school teaching the way it is? Are all the conditions described earlier unavoidable, or is it possible to modify or change some of them? To help you come up with some partial answers to those questions, information relating to each of them will be presented in the remaining pages of this chapter.

Some explanations of features of public education

To understand many features of American public schools it is necessary to consider some of the distinguishing characteristics of our society. Three characteristics that have had a significant influence on public education are summed up by the words *meritocracy, democracy,* and *technology.*

The impact of a meritocratic society

Many immigrants were attracted to the United States because it was a meritocracy—a society where a person's place in life was determined to a large extent by personal merit. When the largest number of immigrants were coming to America, most European countries were societies of hereditary privilege and rigid class structure. In such nations it was extremely difficult for individuals born into lower-class

In the 1840s Horace Mann of the Massachusetts Board of Education expressed the hope that children from diverse backgrounds would enter public school classrooms so that education could function as a "great equalizer."

Brown Brothers

families to achieve wealth, prestige, and social status, no matter how talented or ambitious they were. In America, these restrictions were largely eliminated.

In the early 1800s it was concluded that the fairest way to make it possible for any individual—regardless of background—to have the opportunity to become successful was to provide education for all children. Horace Mann, a lawyer and secretary of the Massachusetts Board of Education and one of the most influential spokesmen on education in the 1830s and 1840s, wrote that education would become "the great equalizer of the conditions of men—the balance wheel of the social machinery" (Cremin, 1961, p. 9). In order for schools to serve this equalizing function, early American educators concluded that attendance should be made compulsory. Otherwise, they reasoned, not all parents would be willing to take the trouble to send their children to school, and many young Americans most in need of the chance to make something of themselves would be denied the opportunity.

Mann and others who spoke so glowingly about education as an equalizer failed to take into account the inevitable by-products that develop in any meritocratic approach. In *Excellence,* John Gardner describes these:

In a society of hereditary privilege, an individual of humble position might not have been wholly happy with his lot, but he had never had reason to look forward to any other fate. Never having had prospects of betterment, he could hardly be disillusioned. He entertained no hopes, but neither was he nagged by ambition. When the new democracies removed the ceiling on expectations, nothing could have been more satisfying for those with the energy, ability and emotional balance to meet the challenge. But to the individual lacking in these qualities, the new system was fraught with danger. Lack of ability, lack of energy or lack of aggressiveness led to frustration and failure. Obsessive ambition led to emotional breakdown. Unrealistic ambitions led to bitter defeats.

No system which issues an open invitation to every youngster to "shoot high" can avoid facing the fact that room at the top is limited. (1961, pp. 18–20)

Since the room at the top *is* limited, it is necessary to sort out individuals so that the most capable can be identified and given the opportunity to make the most of their abilities. In America, the public school system is the primary agency for carrying out the preliminary sorting-out process. This policy is defended on the grounds that since all children attend school, every child is provided with an opportunity to achieve success. In order to make the process of selection as fair as possible, however, it is necessary to measure student performance precisely and objectively. As a consequence, considerable emphasis is placed on grade point averages and test scores.

Several features of American education are traceable to the desire to give all children an opportunity to benefit from schooling in a meritocracy:

American public schools attempt to educate *all* children.

Attendance must be made compulsory. Otherwise, many of the children most in need of education would not go to school.

Since the number of desirable and remunerative jobs is limited and since these occupations usually require specialized and advanced education, it is necessary to carry out a process of elimination in the schools and select the most deserving and qualified students for advanced study.

The fairest way to sort out students is to evaluate them as objectively as possible. This means that teachers must give tests and assign grades.

Students who are energetic, capable, and ambitious thrive on competition; they enjoy earning high grades and reap the benefits of scholastic success. Those who do not possess these qualities may feel frustrated, pressured, inferior, angry, defeated, and bitter about schooling. Students who become convinced they can gain no benefit from education often actively resent being forced to stay in school.

While using the schools to perform the sorting-out function is probably the fairest way to carry out this process, it unfortunately may lead to the feeling that education is a means to an end, not an end in itself. Consequently, students may approach many courses, particularly at the high school level and beyond, with the attitude that the primary purpose is to earn a particular grade with the least possible effort. This leads to several unfortunate by-products: lack of interest in a subject for its own sake, a tendency to study just enough to pass, an inclination to cheat, an urge to forget what has been learned as soon as a final examination is written.

The impact of a democratic form of government

A second characteristic of the United States that has had a pervasive impact on the nature of public schools is its democratic form of government—and the fact that public schools are supported by all taxpayers. Early immigrants came from societies where most schools, particularly those beyond the elementary level, were private. Parents who could afford to pay tuition were able to send their children to such institutions; those who were poor never even thought of the possibility. Scholarships were unknown or uncommon. To provide opportunities for all children to benefit from education, America has established the most extensive network of public schools, colleges, and universities anywhere in the world. These schools are financed by taxes; and in most cities, counties, and states, the amount of tax funds spent on education is greater than that spent for any other purpose. Because all taxpayers, not just those who have children, are required to finance public education, it seems only fair to give every voter an opportunity to have at least some say about what takes place in the schools. Accordingly, school boards made up of elected representatives are given the primary responsibility for making decisions about school policies.

Features of American schools that can be traced to our commitment to free public education in a democracy include the following:

Most American schools are quite well equipped, and all students are provided with books and supplies free of charge. In most states, older students can attend public colleges and universities and pay only token tuition. But citizens who pay for the buildings, books, supplies, and equipment demand the right to have some say about what is taught and how it is taught.

Most American public school teachers are paid decent salaries and are provided with excellent retirement plans and other benefits. But the taxpayers who supply the money for these salaries and fringe benefits want to have at least an indirect voice in decisions about who will teach American children.

The impact of technology

A third characteristic of our society that has had a substantial and far-reaching impact on public education is summed up by the word *technology*, but free enterprise, business methods, efficiency, and the assembly line also should be mentioned. All these words and phrases reflect what many people consider to be the distinctive essence of America. Americans enjoy an unprecedented standard of living. Part of the explanation is that America is blessed with abundant natural resources. Many Americans, however, are convinced that our prosperity is primarily the result of energy, ingenuity, and efficiency at making the most of those resources. American inventors designed labor-saving devices that were mass produced at affordable prices through assembly-line methods. Production was broken down into a series of steps, and workers were trained to specialize in a particular part of the process. Small businesses merged into huge corporations, which then competed with other corporations to improve their products and manufacture and merchandise them with ever increasing efficiency. These various aspects of our technological society have influenced education in a variety of ways.

First of all, the fact that America *is* a technological society means that its citizens must possess many skills necessary for everyday living as well as attitudes and interests that will help them live fulfilling lives and coexist with millions of others. From time to time individuals and groups have described qualities that would be desirable for American children to acquire as they progress through our educational system. Here is a typical list prepared by the 1955 White House Conference on Education:

1. The fundamental skills of communication—reading, writing, spelling, as well as other elements of effective oral and written expression; the arithmetical and mathematical skills, including problem solving. . . .

2. Appreciation for our democratic heritage.

3. Civic rights and responsibilities and knowledge of American institutions.

4. Respect and appreciation for human values and for the beliefs of others.

5. Ability to think and evaluate constructively and creatively.

6. Effective work habits and self-discipline.

7. Social competency as a contributing member of his family and community.

8. Ethical behavior based on a sense of moral and spiritual values.

9. Intellectual curiosity and eagerness for life-long learning.

10. Esthetic appreciation and self-expression in the arts.

11. Physical and mental health.

12. Wise use of time, including constructive leisure pursuits.

13. Understanding of the physical world and man's relation to it as represented through basic knowledge of the sciences.

14. An awareness of our relationships with the world community. (U.S. Committee for the White House Conference on Education, 1956)

Before you dismiss this list as nothing but an assortment of empty phrases, examine it again and estimate how desirable if not essential these skills, attitudes, and interests are for someone who hopes to live successfully and happily in the United States during the last quarter of the twentieth century.

One way technology influences the schools is in the determination of what students must be taught. But *how* students are taught and the organization and functioning of the schools also reflect the technological character of our society. Some school practices might be traced, at least in part, to the technological and business orientation of the United States:

The assembly line: dividing the curriculum into courses and awarding a degree after a specified number of units is successfully completed; arranging courses into sequences; requiring students to master one course before going on to the next; having teachers specialize

Business methods: merging small schools into large unified schools in order to increase efficiency, cut costs, and permit specialization by students and teachers; using computers to arrange schedules, correct exams, record grades, figure grade point averages

Competitive free enterprise: having students compete for high grades, scholarships, and openings in prestigious colleges and professional schools; holding teachers accountable for the amount of learning they produce; firing teachers who are not productive

Now that you have examined brief accounts of what public school teaching is like, what teachers like and dislike about it, and some of the reasons why public schooling is the way it is, you may be wondering whether it has to stay that way or whether there are things that can be done to improve public education.

A sampling of criticisms of public education

Few, if any, Americans are completely satisfied with our educational system, and you may have done quite a bit of thinking about how you would like to change things for the better if you were given the chance. Therefore, it should be instructive to analyze some of the most common criticisms of public education and note prescriptions for reform recommended by the critics. Then, the prescriptions (some of which may coincide with your own ideas on reform) can be related to the previous analysis of how and why public education became the way it is. In this section you will find a summary of some of the most widely read recent critiques of American public education, together with the critics' suggestions for reform.

Holt: Schools make children fail

John Holt is probably the most prolific critic of American education. By far the best of Holt's many polemics on American education is his first brief analysis, *How Children Fail* (1964). Since his more recent books make essentially the same points in a more extreme but less effective way, this summary of Holt's criticisms will stress only points made in *How Children Fail.*

John Holt argues that "there are few children who do not feel, during most of the time they are in school, an amount of fear, anxiety, and tension that most adults would find intolerable."

Roger Malloch/Magnum

Holt explains the title of his book in the foreword, where he observes, "Most children in school fail. . . . They fail because they are afraid, bored, and confused. They are afraid, above all else, of failing, of disappointing or displeasing the many anxious adults around them, whose limitless hopes and expectations for them hang over their heads like a cloud" (1954, p. xiii). *How Children Fail* is divided into four parts. In the first, "Strategy," Holt describes techniques students use to cope with a teacher's questions. One technique is to mumble something and hope the teacher will think it is correct. Another is the guess-and-look technique in which a student gives part of an answer and watches the teacher's face for clues indicating whether she or he is on the right track. In addition to describing such strategies, Holt argues that schools give encouragement to producers (those who supply right answers) but discourage thinkers.

In Part 2, "Fear and Failure," Holt amplifies the theme stated in the foreword. He offers many examples to make this point: "There are very few children who do not feel, during most of the time they are in school, an amount of fear, anxiety, and tension that most adults would find intolerable" (pp. 63–64).

Part 3, "Real Learning," consists primarily of descriptions of the use of Cuisenaire rods (a set of wooden sticks of different lengths and colors) to teach mathematics. Toward the end of this section (p. 104), Holt argues that real learning or understanding occurs when students can state an idea in their own words, use it, give examples, or foresee consequences. He maintains that this kind of learning is rare in public schools.

In the last part, "How Schools Fail," Holt observes that "the test-examination-marks business is a gigantic racket, the purpose of which is to enable students, teachers, and schools to take part in a joint pretense that the students know everything they are supposed to know" (p. 135). He also observes that schools are quite similar to concentration camps or jails in the sense that students feel compelled to withdraw and act stupid under "the relentless, insatiable pressure of their elders" (p. 156). In a final summary Holt argues that public schools destroy the intelligence and creativity of most pupils because they resort to so much coercion and fear. As an alternative Holt recommends a "Smörgåsbord of intellectual, artistic, creative, and athletic activities from which each child could take whatever he wanted, and as much as he would or as little" (p. 180).

Goodman and Friedenberg: Control and distrust

In the mid 1060o Paul Goodman and Edgar Z. Friedenberg described what they considered to be wrong with American secondary schools. In *Compulsory Miseducation* (1964) Goodman argues that American public high schools are "an arm of the police" and that they provide "apprentice-training for corporations, government, and the teaching profession itself" (p. 18). More specifically, he criticizes the physical constraint and the size and standardization of the system (p. 28). He maintains that "the compulsory system has become a universal trap, and it is no good. Very many of the youth, both poor and middle class, might be better off if the system simply did not exist, even if they then had no formal schooling at all" (p. 31).

To correct for the weaknesses and dangers of public high school education, Goodman offers these proposals: Have no classes and no school buildings for some students. Make class attendance voluntary. Abolish grades. Develop smaller schools modeled after the old one-room schoolhouse. Send some students to farms. Provide many kinds of vocational instruction. Have students work in hospitals and as janitors and the like.

In *Coming of Age in America* (1965) Edgar Z. Friedenberg avers that the basic purposes of American high schools are to keep students off the streets and to keep them out of the labor market (p. 7). He maintains that the fundamental pattern—even in better schools—is one of "control, distrust, and punishment" (p. 36). As for the quality of education provided, he observes: "Every high school student can ... be virtually certain that he will experience successive defeat at the hands of teachers with minds of really crushing banality" (p. 181). To improve education Friedenberg offers these suggestions (pp. 249ff.): Eliminate compulsory attendance. Provide a wider range of courses. Upgrade and reduce the number of teachers. Make use of programmed instruction so that teachers can have more time to interact with small groups of students.

Postman and Weingartner: Questions and social action

In 1969 Neil Postman and Charles Weingartner wrote *Teaching as a Subversive Activity,* which they intended to shock American students and educators because "The fact is that our present educational system is not viable and is certainly not capable of generating enough energy to lead to its own revitalization" (1969, p. xv). Postman and Weingartner argue that in most American classrooms students spend most of their time sitting and listening to the teacher. They are required to believe in authority, to memorize, and to supply right answers. According to the authors, students are rarely encouraged to ask questions or given any say about what they will study. Instead of requiring students to answer questions asked by others, Postman and Weingartner argue, the basic method of education should be the *inquiry method.* They describe the method by noting what inquiry teachers do and do not do (pp. 34ff.). They do *not* tell students what they should know, use a syllabus of any kind, accept single statements as answers to questions, or summarize what has been said at the end of a lesson. Instead, they spend most of their time listening to students ask questions, encouraging student-student interaction, and letting lessons develop from responses by students. Postman and Weingartner defend the inquiry method by arguing that learning occurs when individuals develop their own perceptions of things, which means that attempts by teachers to inflict their perceptions (or those of "experts") on others will be ineffective.

In order to rid schools of ineffective pedagogues and replace them with inquiry teachers, Postman and Weingartner recommend a moratorium on the use of textbooks, transferring all elementary school teachers to secondary schools and vice versa, eliminating all courses and all course requirements, abolishing tests and grades, making every course an elective, and withholding a teacher's check if students do not attend class (pp. 135ff.). The authors have special recommendations for city schools (described in Chapter 9 of *Teaching as a Subversive Activity* and in an article by Postman printed in *Kaleidoscope,* edited by Kevin Ryan and James M. Cooper, 1972, pp. 155–158). They propose that instead of studying the usual high school curriculum, city students should provide services of different kinds, such as cleaning the streets, directing traffic, painting subway stations, repairing appliances, offering musical and dramatic programs, and working in hospitals and on sanitation crews.

Teaching as a Subversive Activity was addressed primarily to teachers and future teachers. Apparently, Postman and Weingartner concluded that their book had not impressed entrenched educationists because in 1971 they published *The Soft Revolution,* subtitled *A Student Handbook for Turning the Schools Around.* The basic theme of the book is summed up in "An Open Letter to a Faculty Member from One of His Revolutionary Students" (pp. 18–30). The letter argues that American education is based on the assumption that professors are smarter than students. This premise is rejected on the grounds that although professors may be smarter in the sense of knowing more subject matter (which is probably of little or no real value—in the opinion of Postman and Weingartner), they are not smarter in the sense of being better than students at identifying and solving political and social problems. This is the main point of the open letter and of the book: Schools should be "institutes for social action" (p. 28). Other sections of the book offer restatements of points made in *Teaching as a Subversive Activity* and several analyses of the rights of students.

Silberman: Mindlessness and docility

In 1966 Charles Silberman was asked by the Carnegie Corporation to prepare a report on American education. After spending three years reading about education, interviewing educators, and observing teachers in action, Silberman summed up his impressions in *Crisis in the Classroom* (1970). He concludes that the basic problem with American education is *mindlessness* (p. 10). It seems to Silberman that educators do too many things without thinking about why they do them. He sums up other basic characteristics of schools with these three words: *compulsory, collective, evaluative* (p. 121). Silberman comes to the conclusion reached earlier by Friedenberg: American schools seem to be preoccupied with order and control. To Silberman, many teachers appear to function primarily as traffic managers and timekeepers. He feels that emphasis on lesson plans causes teachers to become obsessed with routine and that preoccupation with order and efficiency turns them into disciplinarians (p. 128). He also agrees with Friedenberg that an atmosphere of distrust in American schools (p. 133) causes students to become dependent on teachers and to doubt that they can control their own behavior.

Silberman concludes that most teachers mean well but that they are trapped by the monolithic nature of the system and by the

A number of critics of American education (such as Goodman, Friedenberg, and Silberman) have argued that too many teachers are preoccupied with order and control.

Van Bucher/Photo Researchers

demands of parents that they be disciplinarians (p. 145). As a result of these various factors, the primary educational goal of students is survival, which is achieved by giving teachers what they want and by earning high grades. Some students, in order to survive, must cheat and suppress their feelings. Silberman concludes that the most effective student survival techniques are docility and conformity (p. 152). When asked for their opinions about the way schools are run, most students report that rules are necessary and that the prevailing system is acceptable (p. 157).

In a chapter titled "How Schools Should Be Changed," Silberman recommends that American elementary schools use the open education approach. This kind of teaching, widely used in British primary schools, is characterized by informality, openness, and freedom. Open education is based on the theories of Jean Piaget, who believes that children learn by absorbing and revising impressions and that they go through a series of stages of cognitive development. In the open education approach, children are encouraged to discover many things through their own activities, and the teacher's task is to provide opportunities for learning that are at the child's level of cognitive development. The teacher arranges situations so that children can make their own discoveries, and supplies an abundance of objects and experiences for children to explore.

Silberman's recommendations for improving secondary education are not as specific. He suggests that teachers help students achieve a sense of identity and develop knowledge and skills they need to "make sense out of experience" (p. 336). He also recommends that teachers think more about purposes and goals—what they are trying to do and why—and that they try to bring students to the point where they can educate themselves.

How valid are the criticisms?
How realistic are the prescriptions?

Now that you have examined a sampling of criticisms of American education and prescriptions for reform recommended by the critics, you are invited to make a critical evaluation of the criticisms as well as the proposals for reform.

Holt: Are pupils afraid most of the time?

When John Holt observed elementary school pupils, he became convinced that most of them, most of the time, experienced "an amount of fear, anxiety, and tension that most adults would find intolerable"

(1964, p. 64) because of apprehension they would fail. To check on this perception you are urged to visit a public school and observe pupils on the playground, in the halls, and in classrooms. Do most of them give you the impression they are in a state of constant terror, or do quite a few of them appear relaxed and happy much of the time?

Holt's impressions may have been influenced by the fact that much of his teaching was done in small private schools. Children who know that their parents are spending a considerable amount of money to send them to a private school may also realize that the reason for doing this is to assure their admission to a prestigious university. These children probably do sometimes feel that the "limitless hopes and expectations" of their parents "hang over their heads like a cloud" (p. xiii). Another way to check on Holt's observations is to recall, as best you can, your own reactions to elementary and secondary school. You may be able to remember using some of the strategies Holt describes, and you may have a few vivid recollections of being terrified if you had to take an exam, give a report when you were totally unprepared, or enter the classroom of a cruel and vindictive teacher. But did you feel as if you were in a concentration camp or in jail, and were you in a constant state of terror?

Goodman and Friedenberg:
Are students better off out of school?

Both Goodman and Friedenberg argue that secondary school students should not be required to attend school, which the authors perceive to be an institution that emphasizes control, distrust, and punishment. Both recommend that attendance be made voluntary. Goodman suggests that grades be abolished, that students be sent to farms, and that more vocational training be made available. Friedenberg is in favor of using programmed instruction so that teachers can spend less time presenting subject matter and more time interacting with students in small group discussions.

Imagine for a moment that all twelve- to eighteen-year-olds were allowed to make their own decisions about attending or not attending junior and senior high school classes. What types of individuals would be most likely to attend classes? What would those who elected to stay away from school do with themselves? What are some complications that might ensue if a twelve-year-old boy elected to stay out of school for four or five years and then changed his mind and asked to attend classes with his agemates? What would be the chances that a young person who stopped attending classes at the age of twelve could find a job during the teen years? What kinds of jobs would school dropouts be able to get? If school dropouts failed to get jobs, what would they do with themselves?

Postman and Weingartner:
Will parents pay colearners?

Postman and Weingartner argue that in order for "real learning" to take place, students must develop their own perceptions. Therefore, asking students to read or listen to what others have discovered, they say, is largely a waste of time. They also argue that students know as much about bringing about social and political changes as teachers do—if not more. Since schools are considered to be institutes for social action, students and teachers are equals. For both these reasons, Postman and Weingartner recommend exclusive use of the inquiry method and enjoin teachers to have most if not all lessons emerge from and consist primarily of questions asked by students.

To evaluate the proposals of Postman and Weingartner, imagine this situation. When the parents of a high school student receive their city, county, and state tax bills, information is enclosed indicating that the largest part of the budget for each governmental unit is devoted to education. Both parents work, and after spending eight hours on the job they visit the local high school on back-to-school night. They discover that all teachers are following the recommendations of Postman and Weingartner. None of the teachers uses a course outline, books, or exams. All teachers spend every class period joining with students in discussing questions based on what the participants already know about social problems. Isn't it possible that the parents would wonder why the largest part of their taxes is being used to pay adults ten to fifteen thousand dollars a year simply to sit in classrooms exchanging ideas with children and adolescents? If those who call themselves teachers really do not know any more than pupils, why not let the children ask each other questions in someone's living room or back yard? Why spend money on school buildings, supplies, and teachers' salaries?

Postman and Weingartner's suggestion that high school students in large cities spend all their time painting subways, collecting garbage, serving as hospital orderlies, and acting as entertainers and the like leads to this question: If high school students spend most of their school time collecting garbage and emptying bedpans, will they end up doing the same thing the rest of their lives?

Silberman: Is self-directed learning the answer?

Silberman joins Goodman and Friedenberg in decrying the extent to which American schools are characterized by order and control. He argues that lesson plans cause teachers to become obsessed with routine. At the same time, however, he strongly criticizes mindlessness and lack of purposeful planning. He also deplores the extent to which students have to struggle to survive by giving teachers what they want, even if many students are thus forced to cheat.

Silberman's most specific recommendations for improving American education are based on the British open school approach. Many American teachers, schools, and school systems have experimented with open education in the last ten years. In some cases the open approach seems to work exceptionally well, in other cases it leads to disaster (Barth, 1972). The open education approach stresses a considerable amount of student interaction and students' selection of their own activities. The teacher's task is to arrange a variety of learning centers, provide instruction in specific skills and areas of knowledge, and maintain extensive records of individual pupil progress. This approach appears to be most successful when pupils, parents, and teachers are willing to accept the fact that learning may be fitful and somewhat disorganized. Furthermore, many teachers report that the time and effort required to arrange for small-group instruction and maintain detailed records of individual progress are greater than that demanded in traditional approaches.

The open school approach at its best leads to learning that is informal, active, and often enjoyable. It appears to be most appropriate at the upper elementary school level. One premise of open education is that while adults often think in abstract terms, younger children think in concrete terms; therefore, a pupil may be able to explain some things to another pupil better than a teacher can. Primary grade children, however, need to learn how to read and write. They are too immature to engage in extensive mutual instruction. After the age of twelve, students become progressively more capable of reasoning in abstract terms and hence more adult in their thinking, but they are also asked to deal with more complex and often sequential subject matter. For these reasons it may not be logical to expect students to educate themselves or each other in most primary or secondary school classrooms. High school students and teachers think the same way, but it usually takes a knowledgeable and experienced person to present a complex subject in an understandable and organized way so that it will set the stage for later learning. Yet Silberman praises high schools that offer a maximum of self-direction, even as he decries the mindlessness of American education. He wants high school students to achieve a sense of identity and to develop knowledge and skills they need to "make sense out of experience," but he is most enthusiastic about schools that have no formal program.

As for Silberman's complaints about preoccupation with order and control, it might be interesting to see what would happen if he were responsible for using an informal approach to scheduling and traffic management in a typical high school of 1,500 students. Remember, students must move from one room to another every fifty minutes and somehow end up at the right place at the right time. It is possible

Silberman would answer, "Have small high schools." Such an answer fails to take into account that school boards cannot simply vote to abandon large school buildings. Neither does it take into account that a primary reason for large schools is to make it possible for students and teachers to specialize. Silberman wants students to have as much free choice as possible. If students are to be allowed to choose from a wide variety of courses taught by competent specialists, however, it is essential to bring together large numbers of students and teachers on one campus.

After reforms are tried, return to "tradition"

Each of the critics whose views have just been evaluated called attention to genuine weaknesses in American education. It seems fair to say, however, that most of their recommendations for reform do not appear to be very realistic or workable. Some of the proposals made do not take into account unavoidable realities of public education and are virtually impossible to put into practice. Other recommendations *have* been tried, but the results have been unimpressive (or the techniques have led to unexpected problems), and educators who were initially enthusiastic about new ways of teaching have returned to "traditional" forms of instruction.

In the 1960s, many schools experimented with student selection of courses and relaxed grading standards. Although these policies are still in force in a few institutions, it appears that most school systems have returned to more traditional lists of required courses and stricter grading standards. Another popular innovation of the late 1960s was the open school approach. Perhaps the most distinguishing characteristic of this form of education is that students are given opportunities to engage in self-selected activities. Many open education programs foundered when they were introduced without prior consultation with parents or when insufficient emphasis was placed on teacher direction and evaluation. In *Open Education and the American School* (1972), Roland S. Barth describes what happened when seven enthusiastic but inexperienced young teachers made an all-out effort to use an open education approach in two elementary schools. They encountered so much resistance from students, parents, and administrators that the following year only two of them were still teaching—one in an independent school, the other in a university laboratory school. In analyzing what went wrong, Barth concludes: "The fact of the matter is that *most* parents' concepts of quality education are along the lines of the traditional, rigorous, transmission-of-knowledge model. *Most* parents care deeply about their children and rely heavily upon 'school' to bring them success, wealth, and satisfaction" (1972, p. 205).

The most successful open education programs appear to be those

where parents give their children permission to volunteer to participate, where teachers make sure that the standard curriculum is mastered, and where students are evaluated. Teachers in such programs
typically report that an open education approach requires considerably more effort (because of individualized instruction) than traditional teaching but that it is worth it.

It appears, then, that public school education is not likely to
change in ways recommended by the critics. Most parents seem to
prefer traditional approaches, and they are upset if innovations are
introduced in an abrupt and extreme manner. To understand why the
prescriptions proposed by the critics have not been widely adopted on
a permanent basis and why parents tend to prefer traditional
approaches, consider the following hypothetical situation.

Serving as a tutor

Imagine that you have just graduated from college and have earned a
teaching credential. (You majored in history and did your student
teaching in eighth grade social studies.) You decide to reward yourself with a trip to Europe before looking for a job. On the flight home
you happen to sit next to a man and his two children. You begin to
converse, and it turns out that he is a Nobel Prize–winning chemist
from East Germany. The main reason he had stayed behind the Iron
Curtain was that his wife wanted to be close to her family, but she was
recently killed in an accident, which prompted him to defect. He has
been offered a high-paying position at a famous American university
but confesses that he is concerned about the problems his children
may encounter adapting to our society and our schools. When he
discovers that you are a college graduate and that you have a teaching
credential, he asks you to serve as a private tutor to his children at a
salary of $1,000 per month. You accept the offer, but it is agreed that
either party can terminate the arrangement at the end of any month.
The older child is a sixteen-year-old boy who is eager to follow in his
father's footsteps and become a research chemist. The younger child
is a six-year-old girl. The boy speaks English quite well, but the girl
speaks only German. You are expected to provide instruction from
8:30 A.M. until 3:30 P.M. Monday through Friday.

Imagine what would happen if you followed the advice of the
various critics whose books have just been reviewed. The first month
on the job you place books, records, microscopes, paints and brushes,
musical instruments, sports equipment, and the like around your
"schoolroom" (the living room of the chemist's home). This provides a
"smörgåsbord of intellectual, artistic, creative, and athletic activities"
from which the children can take whatever they want. To teach the
six-year-old English, you use no formal instruction. You simply talk

about things and describe them and assume that she will eventually pick up the language in this "natural" way. You tell both children that they are not required to study or even to come to the schoolroom. You also tell the sixteen-year-old that he will never have to complete assignments or write exams and that you do not plan to use any texts or present formal lessons of any kind. If he has questions he would like to raise, you will be happy to discuss them with him, but you and he will converse as equals. When the sixteen-year-old announces that he plans to spend most of his class time carrying a "Don't Buy Grapes" placard back and forth in front of a supermarket, you express approval since your "school" will function as an "institute for social action." Your pleasure turns to anxiety, however, when you receive a call from the local hospital. It turns out that during the time you were responsible for your student, he engaged in a scuffle with some young farmers, and his arm was broken.

At the end of the first month, when the chemist gives you a check for $1,000 he asks you to think about whether you are satisfied that you earned it. He also points out that he has two primary educational goals for his children: He wants the girl to learn to read and write English as rapidly as possible so that she can play with agemates and join them when they go to school. He wants the boy to qualify for admission to a university that has a highly regarded department of chemistry. He then asks you to serve as tutor for another month.

Will you make any changes in your teaching approach? That is undeniably a loaded question based on stacked evidence, but this extreme example does call attention to the unrealistic nature of many suggestions for reforming American education as well as to the reasons parents favor traditional approaches.

Consider the salary of $1,000 a month. If teachers' salaries are figured on a nine months per year basis, $9,000 is the approximate amount you can expect to earn the first year of your teaching career. That amount of money will not be handed to you directly by the parents of your students (and it will be substantially reduced by withheld income tax, retirement contributions, health and other insurance premiums, and similar deductions), but they will be reimbursing you for your professional services every time they pay taxes. Is it reasonable for them to expect you to *provide* professional services?

Parents of primary grade children are eager for their offspring to learn to read and write, not only because reading and writing are probably the most tangible forms of school learning but also because these skills are so important. Parents expect teachers to have learned ways to help children acquire these skills. If a first grader fails to keep up with classmates in learning how to read and write, that child is almost sure to experience learning and perhaps also social difficulties in later grades. The initial weeks in the first grade are usually an exciting experience, but as the novelty wears off and the intellectual effort needed to master advanced skills becomes more demanding, children inevitably find it difficult to study. If given free choice, they would rather play than study. Is it surprising, then, that parents expect teachers to have learned how to instruct their children and want them to encourage pupils to concentrate on learning tasks?

Parents of many high school students often encourage their children to continue their education and strive to become established in one of the professions. In some cases they are motivated by the desire to build up themselves at the expense of the accomplishments of their offspring, but many parents are motivated by a sincere desire to help their children find jobs that are interesting and rewarding. In order to become research chemists or the equivalent, however, young people must overcome a long series of hurdles. They must prove that they have the intellectual ability and self-discipline to engage in concentrated study. Among other things, they must learn to take examinations, since the fairest way to select the most promising candidates for almost any kind of endeavor is to present them with identical questions and evaluate their answers as objectively as possible. Whether they like it or not, students must compete against others who have similar goals and interests. Does it seem likely that fourteen- to seventeen-year-old adolescents can comprehend the reasons for all these conditions and work toward remote goals entirely on their own? Or does it seem reasonable to expect teachers to supply support and guidance?

To call attention to other weaknesses of the critics' prescriptions for reform, pretend once again that you are involved in the imaginary tutorial position. You become aware of some of the points just made after conducting a post-mortem at the end of your first month of tutoring. You decide that to earn your salary you should teach the six-year-old how to speak, read, and write English and that you should offer a regular high school curriculum, with emphasis on chemistry, to the sixteen-year-old. You discover, however, that your background in history and your student-teaching experience have not prepared you very adequately for these tasks.

When you read *Teaching as a Subversive Activity* as an undergraduate you tittered appreciatively when you came across Postman and Weingartner's suggestions that no texts be used and that elementary and secondary school teachers switch jobs. Now, as you spend all of your evenings and weekends in the nearest college library reading books on foreign language and reading instruction and preparing lessons for high school college preparatory courses in English, literature, math, biology, physics, chemistry, and social studies, you become increasingly disinclined to titter. On the first day that you offer a lesson in chemistry (which you almost flunked in high school and avoided in college), you discover that your pupil knows approximately one hundred times as much as you do, and you comprehend with vivid clarity why most high schools are quite large, why most secondary school teachers specialize, and why there are usually sequences of courses. Furthermore, when you obtain catalogues from several universities that have highly regarded chemistry departments, you are reminded of a fact of academic life you had failed to take into account when you found yourself agreeing with critics who recommend that tests be abolished: All applicants are expected to take college entrance exams. You suddenly realize that you had better give the sixteen-year-old practice in taking American-style multiple-choice tests, since he will not only need test-taking expertise to get *into* college, he will need it to *stay* there.

There is no denying that not all teachers are skilled reading instructors and that not all children acquire reading skills in the primary grades. There is no denying that the competitive nature of secondary schooling causes many problems, particularly for less capable students. There is no denying that some teachers are preoccupied with control and order, particularly if they are lazy and incompetent and are unable to arouse the interest of their students. But it simply does not make sense to suggest that the basic solution to these problems is to not teach. The critics concentrate on what they perceive to be negative aspects of schooling, but when their proposals for reform are examined, it seems clear that they have few if any practical suggestions to offer for improving education.

Since most prescriptions for reform are so unrealistic, it is worth speculating about why this is the case. If you think about possible reasons that complaining about the schools is a national pastime, you may be less bothered by criticisms if you obtain a job as a teacher. Remember, you are thinking about moving from the giving to the receiving end of discussions of "What's wrong with the schools?" Therefore, it should be informative to analyze the possible motives of those who may complain about what you will do as a teacher.

Criticism as an occupational hazard

Perhaps the basic reason people criticize the schools so much is that teaching is an extremely demanding profession and few practitioners do a first-rate job. In that sense, many of the complaints are justified, but few of the complainers are thoroughly familiar with the conditions and demands of prolonged public school teaching. Holt, Postman, and Weingartner had brief careers as elementary or secondary school teachers. Goodman, Friedenberg, and Silberman had no public school experience.

To be a really good teacher, a person must first of all possess personality traits such as patience, positive feelings about others, and self-confidence (to note only a few). Equally important, the effective teacher has to work at it—all of the time. This effort means not only long hours but constant searching for better ways to handle all facets of the job. As you can no doubt attest from personal experience, not too many individuals possess the ideal combination of personality traits, dedication, and imagination that lead to excellent teaching. What most people fail to acknowledge is that the same shortcoming applies to most people in any profession or job. It seems reasonable to assume that there are just as few really good doctors, lawyers, carpenters, or plumbers, as there are really good teachers. Because most of us do not have the chance to make comparisons among such practitioners, we do not have much of a basis for rating them. By the time students get into high school, though, they have seen enough teachers to be able to form judgments of relative effectiveness. If you get a job as a teacher, you can more or less count on being critically evaluated. If your students go to a dentist, their parents will hardly ever say, "Did you rate him as good, average, or poor?" But they are quite likely to say at one time or another, "Well, what do you think of your new teacher compared to your other teachers?"

A related factor is that everyone has had experience with school. Most of us rarely have contact with lawyers or congressmen, and we may not learn about some of their less admirable qualities until we read about scandals. But everyone is an expert at evaluating teachers. Furthermore, students have ample opportunities to draw up lists of teacher deficiencies. Elementary school children watch their teachers in action six hours a day, five days a week. Secondary school students have the opportunity to form judgments for almost an hour a day, every day of the week. How many entertainers, sports heroes, TV stars, or other public idols would still be admired if they performed for that length of time that often? Familiarity may not always breed contempt, but it does give opportunities to pick out weaknesses and form judgments.

Students not only have opportunities to pick out weaknesses, they also have motives for doing so. Teachers are responsible for telling students (and their parents) many things they would prefer not to know. No one likes to be told that he or she is ignorant or incompetent, but every time a teacher hands back a paper with a low grade on it, that message is conveyed. All of us have limitations and weaknesses, and school is the first place we really find out about many of them. Frequently, the only way we can learn is to become aware of mistakes, but even if the teacher is sensitive and sympathetic, it is still hard for pupils to acknowledge that they have erred. Quite often students who put out the least effort and do totally unsatisfactory jobs are most vocal about what is wrong with teachers. Sometimes their parents join in the chorus. Children may not do well in school primarily because their parents never spend any time with them, fail to satisfy their needs for security and love, neglect to provide encouragement, or do not supply things like books and educational objects and experiences. But if such children fail to respond to instruction in school, the teacher is often saddled with the blame.

At a more general level, the schools are often made the scapegoat for national problems. When the Soviet Union surged ahead of the United States in space, the schools were blamed for failing to teach science properly. The schools responded by stressing math and science courses. When delinquency and crime rates soared and thousands of students became alienated and dropped out, the schools were blamed for spending too much time emphasizing technology and not enough time helping students seek personal fulfillment and become better human beings. The schools responded by reducing requirements and introducing courses stressing self-direction and exploration. When high school graduates of the early 1970s were found to be more ignorant and less literate than their predecessors, the schools were blamed for wasting too much time on nonacademic courses. "Return to the basics" is a current battle cry. It is a virtual certainty that whatever ails our society five years from now will be blamed by some individuals on the preoccupation of the schools with the basic subjects.

Another explanation for frequent criticisms of the schools is that they are the most convenient and vulnerable of all tax-supported institutions. Taxpayers may be incensed about the behavior of senators and representatives, for example, but they may have to wait up to six years to do anything about it, and casting a vote rarely gives one a direct sense of satisfaction. But an irate parent gets attention if she or he charges into a principal's office, and a single individual may be able to spearhead a drive to have books removed from a high school library.

Still another explanation for frequent criticism of schools and teachers is that journalists and writers realize that it is profitable. Millions of disgruntled ex-students serve as an eager audience for diatribes about what is wrong with the schools. Reading an article or book by Holt or Silberman or other school critics may give the reader a sense of retaliation for real or imagined mistreatment at the hands of teachers.

The foregoing analysis is not intended to imply that all criticisms of the schools are invalid. Even in the most extreme attacks, there is some truth. And just as students cannot improve unless they admit

Parents not only pay taxes to finance the schools, they are understandably eager to secure the best education for their children. Consequently, they often attend meetings to express their feelings about educational matters.

James H. Karales from Peter Arnold

their mistakes, public education will not improve unless teachers and administrators acknowledge weaknesses and destructive practices. But before you make your personal effort to bring about improvements, take into account the points described in the earlier explanation of features of American education as well as the analyses of the critics' prescriptions for reform. In doing that, you may find it helpful to make a distinction between conditions that appear to be unavoidable and those that can be changed.

What must you accept? What might you change?

If you teach in an American public school you can be reasonably certain that you will encounter certain givens and conditions:

You will be expected to try to educate all children. The pupils you

Nonpublic schools

This chapter describes public education in America because the ratio of public to nonpublic school teachers is approximately ten to one. (The Digest of Educational Statistics for 1975 reports that in 1974 there were 2,168,000 public school teachers and 226,000 nonpublic school teachers.) Nonpublic schools can be classified into three basic types: (1) private schools that specialize in preparing students for college, (2) schools financed by various religious groups, (3) free or alternative schools, many of which are patterned more or less after Summerhill, the famous institution founded by A. S. Neill in England.

Your chances of finding employment in such schools may depend in part on your background. Exclusive preparatory schools, for example, tend to prefer teachers who graduated from certain highly regarded colleges. Religious schools may prefer to hire teachers who are members of that church.

Most private schools are smaller than public schools and are not directly affected by governmental bureaucracy. Disadvantages of public education stemming from size and red tape, therefore, are minimized. On the other hand, many private schools may require teachers to follow a curriculum that is more rigid than that of public schools, and academic pressure, particularly in exclusive college preparatory schools, may be greater. Finally, since parents are usually paying tuition in addition to paying taxes for public education, they may insist on participating in decisions regarding curriculum, policies, and the retention of teachers.

Under A. S. Neill's leadership, Summerhill survived for fifty years. Few American free schools, by contrast, have managed to stay in existence for more than a few years. This is a major factor to consider if you ever look for a job teaching in a free school. Some of the characteristics of these schools seem very appealing, particularly at first glance. They are almost always small, informal, and more relaxed places than public schools. There are typically few guidelines or restrictions, particularly since students are given freedom to choose what they will study. There is likely to be little or no emphasis on tests or grades. On the other side of the ledger, the existence of such institutions is usually precarious. Many of them were formed on the spur of the moment by a particular group of individuals who happened to share similar views. If some of the leaders move or lose interest when their children graduate, replacements may fail to appear and the school may founder.

If you would like information about free schools, particularly locations and job possibilities, a "Directory of Organizations and Periodicals on Alternative Education" compiled by Gary F. Render, Charles E. Moon, and Donald J. Treffinger begins on page 469 of Humanistic Education Sourcebook (1975), edited by Donald A. Read and Sidney B. Simon.

have in any class will vary in intelligence and learning ability, even if steps have been taken to group those of approximately equivalent ability. Part of individual differences in learning ability will be due to inherited factors; part will be due to experiences, particularly those provided by parents in the home. Even though some pupils in any class will be more or less favored by heredity and background, you will still be expected to help all of them learn. In most cases, parents of slow-learning children will be reluctant to acknowledge that lack of ability or poor home background are significant causes of poor performance. You may not always get credit for what you accomplish as a teacher, but you will often be blamed for lack of pupil achievement.

The pupils in your classes will be there because the law compels them to attend school. Hardly any elementary school students will brood about this point. They accept as a matter of course that they will go to school, and although they may sometimes be reluctant to enter a classroom and may often grumble about assignments or examinations, they do not make an issue of compulsory education. Some secondary school students, however, will actively resent the fact that they are compelled to be in your classroom. Their attitude may disappoint and frustrate you, and potential dropouts may exert a disruptive influence on others. For the most part you will simply have to deal with them as best you can.

As students progress through the grades of any American school system, a sorting-out process takes place. Despite frequent demands or suggestions that the schools stop comparing pupils and occasional experiments in noncompetitive education, pupils discover either formally or informally that some individuals are better at a particular skill than others are. Because of the organization of higher education in our society and the law of supply and demand, some students are going to "win" scholarships and places in prestigious colleges and universities. Inevitably, many students will "lose" every time comparisons are made. It is easy to understand the appeal of fantasies about a society, such as the one envisioned by Charles Reich in *The Greening of America,* that "rejects the whole concept of excellence and comparative merit . . . and refuses to evaluate people by general standards" (1970, p. 243). But college admissions officers, personnel directors of business concerns, and those who administer civil service exams are going to continue to compare applicants and select those who have proven that they are more capable than others. In fact, emphasis on excellence and comparative merit has been reaffirmed, not rejected, since the publication of *The Greening of America,* primarily because of the employment situation and competition among graduate school applicants.

Because the educational system in a meritocracy serves a sorting-out function, because taxpayers want proof that they are getting something for their money, and because few pupils possess the self-motivation to learn all that they are asked to learn, you should expect to be required to assign grades and make out report cards. In order to do that in a fair, objective, and defensible way, you will need to make up and score examinations and similar exercises.

For a variety of reasons, some traceable to features of our society, some that are a function of the expectation that school personnel will act in loco parentis, teachers are expected to meet requirements, keep records, and enforce regulations. The number and nature of these vary from school to school, but it is doubtful that any teacher can avoid them completely. Teachers are expected to abide by decisions made by elected representatives of the citizenry; and as participants in a complex and interrelated enterprise, they are also expected to decide among themselves how they will conduct and coordinate many aspects of their work. Accordingly, public school teachers must take into account the wishes and rights of others.

The critics mentioned earlier, many parents and students, and perhaps you as well have concluded that the givens and conditions just noted have led to school practices that vary from ineffective to harmful. Even the most enthusiastic backer of American public education is probably willing to admit that there is ample room for improvement. Unfortunately, however, virtually all the recommendations for reform made by the critics mentioned earlier (and by most other critics) are based on conditions that are for the most part unchangeable. The critics argue that American education can be improved only if attendance is made voluntary, exams and grades are abolished, and formal instruction is eliminated. No matter what the critics say, American students will, in all probability, continue to be required to go to school, they will continue to be evaluated, and teachers will always be expected to instruct them. These policies were established for valid reasons, and they remain in force for valid reasons. The sensible way to seek to improve education is to accept what cannot be changed and concentrate on aspects of teaching that can be changed. This book has been written to help you bring about improvements within the system.

Holt is correct when he points out that many children fear failure, that they use strategies to avoid academic pressure, and that many tests are pointless exercises that do more harm than good. But his smörgåsbord approach is not a workable solution. It is more sensible and realistic to seek ways to reduce pressure, help as many students as possible do superior work, and use examinations as learning devices. Techniques for doing all these things will be described later in this book.

Goodman, Friedenberg, and Silberman are correct when they argue that there is often an unnecessary degree of control, distrust, and punishment in American schools. But their recommendations that attendance be made voluntary and that students be allowed to direct their own education are unrealistic and impractical. It makes more sense for teachers to invite students to establish some of their own classroom regulations, enforce these as infrequently and as fairly as possible, and reinforce desirable forms of behavior instead of punishing negative forms of behavior. Methods for carrying out all these activities will be detailed on the pages that follow.

Postman and Weingartner are correct when they maintain that too many teachers fail to give students sufficient opportunities to ask questions or express their own ideas. But the recommendations of Postman and Weingartner are intended more to titillate or infuriate than to be put into actual practice. Instead of seeking to provoke a snicker of smug but unfounded approval from students by telling them they are smarter than their teachers, it makes more sense to concentrate on specific and workable techniques for encouraging students to participate in learning activities. Chapters 5 through 11 of this book are devoted to such descriptions.

Many American teachers, it is true, fail to think about what they do that makes children fear failure, use exams more to punish than to instruct, and must concentrate on controlling students because they fail to motivate them. But it is equally true that some teachers who operate under all the conditions and restrictions described earlier succeed in helping students learn and develop positive feelings about themselves and about school. Such teachers, unfortunately, are the exception rather than the rule, but this may be an advantage for you. Really good teachers are as rare as really good practitioners in any profession. Consequently, an excellent teacher is almost sure to arouse a positive response from pupils, since they are likely to react favorably to someone who does an out-of-the-ordinary job of instructing. Because of the givens and conditions described earlier, however, it takes ingenuity, perseverance, and above all, effort, to become a really good teacher. If you aspire to become such a teacher, you would be prudent to avoid looking for a secret to easy success. You will make more progress by recognizing that it takes effort.

Several features of American education that might be traced to the technological orientation of our society were mentioned earlier. Another factor that merits mention at this juncture is a belief that American technologists can solve any problem if they devote sufficient time, energy, and money to it. American inventors, scientists, and engineers have a record of so many remarkable accomplishments that it is often assumed there are no limits to what can be achieved. When this line of reasoning is applied to education, it usually takes the form of a search for a panacea, an innovation that will revolutionize schooling and guarantee that all pupils will learn. This tendency is strengthened by newspaper and magazine writers who are always on the alert for trends in education that can be described in exaggerated terms as significant breakthroughs. As a result, every few years some new technique, organizational arrangement, or concept is hailed as *the* answer to the problems of education. In the last twenty years this treatment has been awarded to teaching machines and programmed instruction, TV, team teaching, the concept of the impact of teacher expectations, computer-assisted instruction, and the open school approach. All these developments and conceptions have contributed something to education, but they are used in only limited ways today. Reports of pupil achievement—or lack of it—offer incontrovertible proof that writers who predicted a few years ago that students of the next decade would learn twice as much as those of earlier decades had no understanding of the complexities of education.

Successful teaching will never be based exclusively on some gadget, specific technique, or isolated insight. Teaching may occasionally be improved by any and all of the innovations just mentioned. But the fundamental reason children respond to instruction is that well-trained, sensitive, thoughtful, hard-working professionals seek dozens of ways—every day—to interpret the behavior of individuals and groups of pupils and arrange experiences to help them learn. It is an extremely demanding job, and there are many frustrations and disappointments that must be endured; but when a person is a successful teacher, the hours of preparation, the frustrations, and the disappointments don't seem to be very important.

SUGGESTIONS FOR FURTHER STUDY

2-1

Reactions of First-Year Teachers

One way to examine your feelings about becoming a teacher is to read personal accounts of teachers' impressions of life in classrooms. The initial reactions of first-year teachers are recorded in several books. In *Becoming a Teacher* (1969) by Elizabeth M. Eddy and *Teachers Talk* (1969) by Estelle Fuchs, the impressions of first-year teachers in inner-city schools are summarized. In *Don't Smile Until Christmas* (1970) by Kevin Ryan, six first-year teachers record their impressions in twenty-page reminiscences. An exceptionally insightful, and enjoyable, account of the experiences of a first-year teacher is presented in fictionalized form in Bel Kaufman's *Up the Down Staircase* (1964).

2-2

Examining Your Feelings About Teaching

Another way to examine your attitudes toward teaching is to assess, as best you can, how you feel about different aspects of a career in education. If you did not make a systematic appraisal of how you react to the advantages and disadvantages listed in this chapter, you might do so now. Or, record how you feel about the points listed below by putting a check in the appropriate column.

	Important	Neutral	Not important
A salary of at least $20,000 per year			
No interference from supervisors			
Freedom to do what I want to do			
Not having to work with others			
Not having to abide by regulations			
Doing something valuable and important			
Job security			
Good retirement provisions			
Chance for extended vacations			
Serving as a leader and authority			
Pleasant working conditions			
Chance for interpersonal relationships			

If you rated the first five points as important, you might anticipate problems adjusting to public school teaching. To put things into perspective, though, make a point-by-point comparison of alternative job possibilities. If you compare teaching to a job that pays a higher salary, for example, will you sacrifice some of the desirable aspects of life in the schools, for instance, its comparative noncompetitiveness? Or, if you decide to seek independence by becoming self-employed, will you lose the advantages of job security, retirement provisions, and extended vacations?

2-3

How Teachers Feel About Their Profession

To gain some awareness of teachers' attitudes toward education, ask a teacher in a public school to respond to these questions. (If the teacher you interview says it is difficult to decide one way or another, ask, "Which way do you lean, toward agreement or disagreement?") Record this information about each teacher interviewed: sex, approximate age, grade presently teaching, number of years taught, socioeconomic level of school in which presently teaching. Ask all the teachers you interview to indicate whether they agree or disagree with each of these statements. Also record any unsolicited comments they make.

1. The grading system in public schools should sort out students according to academic ability so that the best students are admitted to the best colleges and universities.

2. The grade of F should be eliminated. If a student fails a course, this should not be indicated on his or her record.

3. Parents should be allowed to use the amount of money now spent on each pupil in public schools to send their children to any school of their choice.

4. All teachers should be hired on one-year contracts, and if they are unable to prove that students in their classes have learned, they should not be rehired.

5. Educational techniques that allow students to have considerable choice in what they study and how they study are a good idea.

6. Having students compete for high grades is a good policy.

7. Busing to get a balance of students from upper- and middle-class backgrounds and from lower-class backgrounds in all classrooms is a good policy.

8. The best way to bring about equality of educational opportunity is to see that all school districts spend the same amount per pupil.

9. A merit pay system should be established in the schools so that superior teachers earn a higher salary.

You might also ask these questions:

What do you like the *most* about teaching?

What do you like the *least* about teaching?

What do you like the *most* about your students?

What do you like the *least* about your students?

What item do you think should be given top-priority attention in order to improve education?

What do you wish you had learned more about in your teacher-training classes in college?

2-4

How Elementary Grade Students Feel About Schooling

If you are thinking about teaching in the elementary grades, you might find it of interest to get some reactions from children similar to those you will teach. To gain some awareness of present-day elementary students' attitudes toward education, ask one or more pupils in an elementary school to respond to the questions that follow. (Record the age, grade, and sex of all pupils you interview.)

1. What school subject do you like the best? What school subject do you like the least? Why do you like your favorite subject? (If the answer is "I don't know," say, "There must be a reason. Just tell me a reason why you like it.") Why do you dislike your least favorite subject?

2. What do you (or did you) like the most about your favorite teacher? What do you (or did you) dislike the most about your least favorite teacher?

3. How often do you feel afraid in school? Most of the time? Some of the time? Hardly ever? What things about school make you feel afraid?

4. How often do you have to take tests? Do you think the tests you take are fair? Are you tempted to cheat? Do you think any of your classmates cheat?

5. Do you have report cards or parent conferences or both in your school? How do you feel about grades—should they be done away with? Would you like to go to a school where no one ever gets any grades?

6. Do you think you would like to go to a school where you could study anything you wanted to and never had to study what the teacher told you to learn? If you *did,* what would you study?

2-5

How Secondary School Students Feel About Schooling

To gain some awareness of secondary school students' attitudes toward education, ask one or more pupils in a public junior or senior high school to respond to these questions. (If the students interviewed say it is difficult to decide one way or the other, ask, "Which way do you lean, toward agreement or disagreement?") (Record the age, grade level, and sex of the pupils you interview.)

1. Which school subject do you like the best? Which school subject do you like the least? Why do you like your favorite subject? Why do you dislike your least favorite subject?

2. What do you like the most about your favorite teacher? What do you dislike the most about your least favorite teacher?

3. Do you think that school attendance should be made voluntary? What do you think would happen if students below the age of sixteen were not required to go to school?

4. How do you think you would respond if all classes were based on your asking questions and discussing things with classmates and if teachers never used texts, gave lectures, or showed films?

5. Do you think that there are too many regulations in your school? If you were in charge, which regulations would you keep? Which ones would you eliminate?

6. Do you wish you had more freedom to choose courses? Do you think that required courses have any advantages?

7. Do you think grades should be abolished? How do you feel about pass/fail and credit/no credit grading?

8. How do you feel about the tests your teachers give you? Are some tests fairer than others? How? Are you tempted to cheat in some classes? Why? Do you think some of your classmates cheat?

2-6

How Parents and Citizens Feel About Schooling

To gain some awareness of parents' and citizens' attitudes toward education, ask some person over thirty to respond to these questions. (Note: If the person interviewed says it is difficult to decide one way or the other, ask, "Which way do you lean, toward agreement or disagreement?'') Record this information about each person interviewed: sex, approximate age, number of children now in school, highest grade completed in school. Ask all people interviewed to indicate whether they agree or disagree with the following statements.

1. The grading system in public schools should sort out students according to academic ability so that the best students are admitted to the best colleges and universities.

2. The grade of F should be eliminated. If a student fails a course, this should not be indicated on her or his record.

3. Parents should be allowed to use the amount of money now spent on each pupil in public schools to send their children to any school of their choice.

4. All teachers should be hired on one-year contracts, and if they are unable to prove that students in their classes have learned, they should not be rehired.

5. Educational techniques that allow students to have considerable choice in what they study and how they study are a good idea.

6. Having students compete for high grades is a good policy.

7. Busing to get a balance of students from upper- and middle-class backgrounds and from lower-class backgrounds in all classrooms is a good policy.

8. The best way to bring about equality of educational opportunity is to see that all school districts spend the same amount per pupil.

9. Children who attend schools in upper- and middle-class neighborhoods get a better education than those in lower-class neighborhoods.

10. Education today is too soft and permissive.

You might also ask this question:

If you were a member of a school board in this city, what single change would you want to make in the schools?

2-7
"Efficiency" in American Education

Many schools in this country emphasize efficiency and economy. This emphasis sometimes leads to educational practices that are improvements from one point of view, but their undesirable by-products may make life difficult for teachers. The impact of citizens' demands for efficiency and economy in education is discussed in *Education and the Cult of Efficiency* (1962) by Raymond E. Callahan. In the last chapter Callahan sums up his views and remarks on factors that tend to cause difficulties and misunderstandings.

In *The Organization Man* (1956), William H. Whyte, Jr., describes the effect of American business methods on our way of life. Part 1, "The Ideology of Organization Man," gives a general overview of his analysis. Chapters 7 and 8 concentrate on the impact of business on education, and Part 5, "The Organization Scientist," tells how an organization approach to science and technology tends to limit creativity. The last chapter sums up the case against the organization. If you have ever brooded about the influence of the establishment on the American way of life—and education—you will find sections of *The Organization Man* highly provocative.

2-8

Background of Present Developments in Education

Callahan and Whyte give their interpretations of the impact of business on American education (and other aspects of our culture). For a more comprehensive analysis of earlier trends that influenced current educational practice, see *The Transformation of the School* (1961) by Lawrence A. Cremin or one of these books by Paul Woodring: *Let's Talk Sense About Our Schools* (1953), *A Fourth of a Nation* (1957), or *Introduction to American Education* (1966).

2-9

Life in a Meritocracy

Numerous arguments have been presented in favor of merit pay or merit advancement, each individual's career depending on objective assessment of his or her abilities, with the most capable people in positions of influence and the less capable in jobs appropriate to their lower level of functioning. In many respects, our society is already moving in this direction; it is very common for organizations to use tests to decide among candidates for a given job. The English sociologist Michael Young has written a fascinating interpretation of what might happen if a society became a pure meritocracy. In *The Rise of the Meritocracy* (1959), he emphasizes the difficulties that may arise if concern with measurement of abilities gets out of hand.

2-10

Advantages and Disadvantages of Competition

The pros and cons of competition in the schools have been energetically debated in recent years. Excessive competition obviously has many disadvantages; most disturbing is the amount of threat involved, which tends to lead to anxiety, hostility, and jealousy. But competition has values too, and certain dangers would follow if all competitive effort were eliminated. John Gardner, former Secretary of Health, Education and Welfare, has analyzed the problem of encouraging and maintaining constructive striving in the United States in three short books. *Excellence* (1961) stresses the importance of high standards. *Self-Renewal* (1965) examines ways individuals and societies might resist the negative impact of apathy and lowered motivation. *No Easy Victories* (1968) describes the difficulties of achieving and maintaining excellence and self-renewal.

2-11

Critiques of American Education

If you would like to read books by the critics mentioned in this chapter in order to draw your own conclusions about their analyses of American education, here are authors and titles:

John Holt: *How Children Fail* (1964), *How Children Learn* (1967), *The Underachieving School* (1969), *What Do I Do Monday?* (1970), *Freedom and Beyond* (1972), *Instead of Education: Ways to Help People Do Things Better* (1976).

Paul Goodman: *Growing Up Absurd* (1956), *Compulsory Miseducation* (1964), *Like a Conquered Province* (1967), *New Reformation: Notes of a Neolithic Conservative* (1969).

Edgar Z. Friedenberg: *The Vanishing Adolescent* (1959), *Coming of Age in America* (1965).

Neil Postman and Charles Weingartner: *Teaching as a Subversive Activity* (1969), *The Soft Revolution* (1971).

Charles Silberman: *Crisis in the Schools* (1970).

The primary reason teachers are needed is that there are pupils to be taught. It seems logical, therefore, to begin to examine what psychologists have learned that may be of value to teachers by considering what has been discovered about the characteristics of pupils at different age levels. It is important for you to begin to think about age-level differences because your most recent school experiences have occurred in the company of individuals who are all physically mature. You would probably find it quite difficult to identify students you encounter on campus as sophomores or seniors. If your professors treat first-year students differently than graduate students, they probably do so because of differences in amount of experience and knowledge in a particular subject, not because of chronological age. A fifty-year-old freshman may be less mature academically than a twenty-year-old junior.

If you expect to teach in a public school you will need to prepare yourself to deal not only with academic maturity but also with physical, social, emotional, and intellectual maturity. Academic performance will depend not only on experience but also on each individual's level of development. It is obvious that first graders must be taught in substantially different ways than high school seniors. It may not become apparent until after you have had a few months of teaching experience that some first graders or high school seniors need to be taught in different ways from their classmates. To be an effective teacher, you must adjust your teaching to the general level of development of pupils in your classes and must allow for individual differences in maturity.

In this part you will find information intended to help you accomplish both these goals. Chapter 3 consists of descriptions of several theoretical analyses of development. Many of these analyses take the form of lists of stages of different facets of development. Taken together the descriptions of theories will equip you with an overall conception of the process and sequence of development. Chapter 4 consists of descriptions of characteristics of pupils at three levels of schooling: preschool and kindergarten, primary and elementary grades, secondary grades. Some of the characteristics noted in Chapter 4 are derived from the theoretical descriptions provided in Chapter 3; some of them do not relate to any particular theory. In both chapters you are urged to think about how you can apply what you learn to adapt your teaching to the characteristics of the pupils you will have in your classes.

Part Two

Development

Chapter 3   Development: Principles and theories

Chapter 4   Age-level characteristics

Key points

Erikson: Stages of psychosocial development

Epigenetic principle: Each stage has time of special ascendancy

2 to 3 years: Autonomy vs. shame and doubt

4 to 5 years: Initiative vs. guilt

6 to 11 years: Industry vs. inferiority

12 to 18 years: Identity vs. role confusion

Preschool years: Freedom with guidance

Elementary grades: Noncompetitive accomplishment

Identity: Goals, recognition, acceptance of body

Confusion about sex roles and occupational choice

Psychosocial moratorium: Delay of commitment

Negative identity: Rejection of accepted roles

Secondary grades: Urge formulation of goals

Havighurst: Developmental tasks

Developmental tasks must be achieved for satisfactory development

Teachable moments: Instruction presented at optimum time

Piaget: Stages of cognitive development

Organization, adaptation, equilibration

Assimilation, accommodation, scheme

Egocentric and socialized speech and thought

Conservation, decentration, operation

Preoperational thought, concrete operational thought, formal thought

Moral realism, moral relativism

Give pupils opportunities to explain thoughts

Unrestrained theorizing by novice formal thinkers

Primary grades: Encourage activity and student interaction

Secondary grades: Teach problem-solving skills

Bruner: Systems of representation

Enactive, iconic, and symbolic stages

Stimulus-response theory

Tabula rasa (blank slate) view

Behaviorism, Pavlovian conditioning, operant conditioning

Significance of identification, imitation, and modeling

Supply rewards systematically

Maslow: Third force psychology

Children enjoy growing

Individuals determine much of their own behavior

Permit pupils to choose, satisfy their needs

Chapter 3

Development: Principles and theories

To UNDERSTAND human development it is necessary to take into account information on physical, biological, intellectual, social, emotional, and other types of behavior. Each type of behavior changes as the child develops, and the changes are the product of genetic factors, biological conditions, past experiences, present experiences, and the culture of the times. Determining exactly how these various factors interact is usually impossible. It is not surprising, therefore, that instead of a single, widely accepted view of development, there are several theories, each of which emphasizes a particular interpretation or type of behavior.

Each individual who has proposed a developmental theory has been influenced by many factors in her or his own development and by the kind of data selected to serve as the basis for the theory. Some theories list stages in which certain types of behavior appear; others focus on general assumptions about behavior. On the following pages are accounts of the speculations of several developmental theorists, which provide an overview of the developmental process that should help you tie together the more specific types of behavior described in the next chapter. The theorists to be discussed are Erik H. Erikson, Robert Havighurst, Jean Piaget, Jerome Bruner, the American stimulus-response theorists, and Abraham H. Maslow. Following the description of each theory, you will find a discussion of its implications for teachers.

Erikson: Stages of psychosocial development

Sigmund Freud's psychoanalytic theory of development provided insights about human behavior that had a substantial impact on many subsequent theorists. While Freud called attention to the significance of biological drives, parent-child relationships, and unconscious thoughts and feelings, some of his followers and most of his critics concluded that he failed to allow for the impact of cultural factors or social interactions between peers. Erik H. Erikson, one of Freud's outstanding pupils, came to this conclusion after comparing the behavior of individuals in many different cultures. Accordingly, he proposed a theory that is derived from psychoanalysis but stresses psycho*social* rather than the oral, anal, phallic, and genital psycho*sexual* stages described by Freud.

Factors that influenced Erikson

Erik Erikson was a late bloomer. He was an indifferent student in high school and after graduating spent several years wandering around Europe attending various art schools. At the age of twenty-five he became friends with someone who later secured a job tutoring the children of an American woman who was being psychoanalyzed by Freud. When some acquaintances of the woman asked if their children also could be given instruction, the friend decided to start a school and requested that Erikson come to Vienna to assist him. Eventually Erikson was introduced to Freud, who was impressed by the young man and invited him to prepare for a career as a psychoanalyst. Erikson completed his training just at the time Hitler came to power, and to escape from the tension building up in Europe, he

Erik H. Erikson
Clemens Kalischer

decided to come to America. He taught at Harvard, Yale, and the University of California at Berkeley, did private counseling, became interested in studying American Indian tribes, did research on normal and abnormal children, and served as a psychotherapist for soldiers during World War II. These experiences led Erikson to conclude that Freud's tendency to stay in Vienna and interact with only a small and very select group of individuals had prevented the founder of psychoanalysis from appreciating how social and cultural factors influence behavior. Erikson decided to formulate a theory of development that would be based on psychoanalytic principles but would take into account such influences.

Erikson bases his description of personality development on the *epigenetic principle*. In fetal development certain organs of the body appear at certain specified times and eventually "combine" to form a child. The personality, says Erikson, develops in a similar way: "Anything that grows has a ground plan, and . . . out of the ground plan the parts arise, each part having its time of special ascendancy, until all parts have arisen to form a functioning whole" (1968, p. 92). Erikson hypothesizes that just as the parts of the body develop in interrelated ways when the human organism is in utero, the personality of an individual forms as the ego progresses through a series of interrelated stages. All these ego stages exist in the beginning in some form, but each has a critical period of development.

> Epigenetic principle: Each stage has time of special ascendancy

In Erikson's view, personality development is a series of turning points, which he describes in terms of dichotomies of desirable qualities and dangers. Erikson does not mean to imply by this scheme that only positive qualities should emerge and that any manifestation of potentially dangerous traits is undesirable. He emphasizes that a *ratio* in favor of the positive is to be sought. Only when the positive quality is outweighed by the negative do difficulties in development arise.

Stages of psychosocial development

The following designations, age ranges, and essential characteristics of the stages of personality development are proposed by Erikson in *Childhood and Society*.

Trust vs. mistrust (birth to 1 year)   The basic psychosocial attitude to be learned by infants is that they can trust their world. Trust is fostered by "consistency, continuity, and sameness of experience"[1] in the satisfaction of the infant's basic needs by the parents. The "quality of the maternal relationship" is more important than "absolute quantities of food or demonstrations of love." If the needs of infants are met and if the parents communicate genuine affection, children will think

[1] All quotations are from Chapter 7 of *Childhood and Society,* 2nd ed. (1963).

of their world as safe and dependable. If care is inadequate, inconsistent, or negative, the children will approach their world with fear and suspicion.

Autonomy vs. shame and doubt (2 to 3 years)   Just when children have learned to trust (or mistrust) their parents, they must exert a degree of independence. If children are permitted and encouraged to do what they are capable of doing at their own pace and in their own way—but with judicious supervision by parents and teachers—they will develop a sense of autonomy. If parents and teachers are impatient and do too many things for children, they will doubt their ability to deal with the environment. Furthermore, adults should avoid shaming children for unacceptable behavior, since this is likely to contribute to feelings of self-doubt.·

2 to 3 years: Autonomy vs. shame and doubt

Initiative vs. guilt (4 to 5 years)   The ability to participate in many physical activities and to use language sets the stage for initiative, which "adds to autonomy the quality of undertaking, planning, and 'attacking' a task for the sake of being active and on the move." If children are given freedom to explore and experiment and if parents and teachers take time to answer questions, tendencies toward initiative will be encouraged. If children are restricted and made to feel their activities and questions are pointless or a nuisance, they will feel guilty about doing things on their own.

4 to 5 years: Initiative vs. guilt

Industry vs. inferiority (6 to 11 years)   A child entering school is at a point in development when behavior is dominated by intellectual curiosity and performance. "He now learns to win recognition by producing things . . . he develops a sense of industry." "The child's danger at this stage lies in a sense of inadequacy and inferiority." If the child is encouraged to make and do things, allowed to finish tasks, and praised for trying, industry results. If the child's efforts are unsuccessful or if they are derided or treated as bothersome, inferiority results.

6 to 11 years: Industry vs. inferiority

Identity vs. role confusion (12 to 18 years)   As young adults approach independence from parents and achieve physical maturity, they are concerned about what kind of person they are becoming. "The growing and developing youths, faced with [a] physiological revolution within them, and with tangible adult tasks ahead of them are now primarily concerned with what they appear to be in the eyes of others as compared with what they feel they are. . . . In their search for a new sense of continuity and sameness, adolescents have to refight many of the battles of earlier years." The goal is development of ego identity, "the accrued confidence of sameness and continuity." The danger of

12 to 18 years: Identity vs. role confusion

this stage is role confusion, particularly doubt about sexual and occupational identity. If adolescents succeed (as reflected by the reactions of others) in integrating roles in different situations to the point of experiencing continuity in their perception of self, identity develops. If they are unable to establish a sense of stability in various aspects of their lives, role confusion results.

Intimacy vs. isolation (young adulthood) "The young adult, emerging from the search for and insistence on identity, is eager and willing to fuse his identity with others. . . . He is ready for intimacy." "The danger of this stage is that intimate, competitive, and combative relations are experienced with and against the selfsame people," which may lead to isolation.

Generativity vs. stagnation (middle age) "Generativity . . . is primarily the concern of establishing and guiding the next generation." Those unable to engage in this guiding process become victims of stagnation and self-absorption.

Integrity vs. despair (old age) Integrity is "the acceptance of one's one and only life cycle as something that had to be and that, by necessity, permitted of no substitutions." "Despair expresses the feeling that the time is now short, too short for the attempt to start another life and to try out alternate roads to integrity."

Implications of Erikson's theory

Erikson's description of psychosocial development calls attention to interpersonal relationships and perceptions of self that are of special significance at different age levels.

Preschool years: Freedom with guidance

Preschool and kindergarten Preschoolers at the age of three years are at the stage of autonomy vs. shame and doubt; those four and five years old are at the initiative vs. guilt level. Autonomy develops when children are permitted to do what they are capable of doing. Shame may be experienced if a child feels that weaknesses have been noticed by others. Doubt may develop if children attempt to do too much, which may cause them to lack confidence in their ability to deal with the environment. If you will be teaching younger preschool children, you might take account of Erikson's theory and permit pupils to engage in considerable free experimentation to encourage the development of autonomy but provide some guidance to reduce the possibility that their weaknesses will be exposed or that they will have doubts about their capabilities. If a three-year-old girl shows signs of becoming frustrated because she is attempting something beyond her capabilities, for example, you might subtly encourage her to try something you know she can accomplish.

Kindergarten children may be more concerned about initiative than autonomy. Erikson notes, "Initiative adds to autonomy the quality of undertaking, planning, and 'attacking' a task for the sake of being active and on the move" (1963, p. 255). Accordingly, at this stage you might permit a maximum of self-initiated activity and perhaps intervene only when a child infringes on the rights of others. At the same time, it would be advantageous to help children plan and undertake tasks that will permit them not only to be "on the move" but also to experience a sense of accomplishment. To minimize feelings of guilt, Erikson emphasizes, parents and teachers of four- and five-year-olds should try to limit or divert jealousy aroused by siblings or peers who have already accomplished what a child is attempting. One way is to avoid making public comparisons of relative ability; another way is to urge children to work at improving their performance without being concerned about what others are doing.

Primary and elementary grades During most of the primary and elementary school years, children are at the stage of industry vs. inferiority. Playing down comparisons between pupils is even more important at this stage than it was earlier. If elementary school pupils are forced to compete against classmates and are publicly compared with others, it is inevitable that only a small proportion will feel successful. Under competitive conditions, most pupils will experience a sense of inadequacy and inferiority at the beginning of their school careers, which could create a self-fulfilling prophecy leading to poor performance during the remainder of their years in school. Since children at this age are typically eager to make use of their sense of industry, they should be given opportunities and encouragement to experience "the pleasure of work completion by steady attention and persevering diligence" (p. 259). This might be accomplished by providing a variety of assignments described in terms of specific objectives so that students will *know* when they have completed tasks. Such tasks might be arranged so that each pupil proceeds at his or her own rate and is provided with remedial instruction as soon as it becomes apparent that difficulties are being encountered. (Several specific techniques for setting up classroom experiences to stress individual mastery will be discussed in later chapters.)

Secondary grades Secondary school pupils are at Erikson's stage of identity vs. role confusion. Since this stage is more complex and difficult to grasp than earlier stages, a more complete description of Erikson's views on adolescence will serve as a firmer base for noting its implications.

The terms *identity* and *identity crisis* have become so popularized

Elementary grades:
Noncompetitive
accomplishment

that it is important to review Erikson's original meanings. Here is how Erikson described the basic concept of identity: "An optimal sense of identity . . . is experienced merely as a sense of psychosocial well-being. Its most obvious concomitants are a feeling of being at home in one's body, a sense of 'knowing where one is going,' and an inner assuredness of anticipated recognition from those who count" (1968, p. 165). Erikson suggests adolescence is a critical period in development for the following reasons:

> Adolescence is the last stage of childhood. The adolescent process, however, is conclusively complete only when the individual has subordinated his childhood identifications to a new kind of identification, achieved in absorbing sociability and in competitive apprenticeship with and among his age mates. These new identifications are no longer characterized by the playfulness of childhood and the experimental zest of youth; with dire urgency they force the young individual into choices and decisions which will, with increasing immediacy, lead to commitments "for life." (p. 155)

The danger in adolescence is *role confusion:* having no clear conception of appropriate types of behavior that others will react to favorably. Sex roles are particularly important because they establish a pattern for many types of behavior. Up until recently, there was little confusion about appropriate characteristics and activities for males and females in our society. Such certainty provided a clear code of behavior for those who possessed or were eager to develop those characteristics, while it created problems for those who did not. Sex stereotypes also led to the kinds of abuses and forms of discrimination objected to by feminists. With recognition of these abuses has come a blurring of sex roles and a trend toward unisex views. This trend may remove pressure from those who reject or are unable to develop "traditional" male and female traits, but it may create problems for the adolescent trying to develop a clear sense of identity.

Sex-role confusion does cause problems for many adolescents, but Erikson stresses that occupational choice is perhaps the major decision leading to a sense of identity. The occupation we choose influences other aspects of our lives perhaps more than any other single factor. Our job determines how we will spend a sizable proportion of our time; it determines how much money we earn; and our income, in turn, determines where and how we live. The last two factors determine, to a considerable extent, the people we interact with socially. All these factors together influence the reactions of others, and these reactions lead us to develop perceptions of ourselves. The choice of a career, therefore, may be the biggest commitment of a person's life. Erikson notes that occupational choice is particularly difficult in America because of our belief in technology, the efficiency of the assembly line, and corporate organization, all of which limit individuality. Other complicating factors are the amount of training needed for many jobs in a technological society, the rapidly changing job

Identity: Goals, recognition, acceptance of body

Confusion about sex roles

Confusion about occupational choice

market, and the fact that many individuals compete against each other for desirable jobs.

Confronted with the realization that the time has come to make a career choice, that many careers pose a threat to personal identity, and that the job market fluctuates rapidly, the young person seeking to avoid role confusion by making a firm vocational choice may feel overwhelmed and unable to act. Because of this, Erikson suggests that for many young people a *psychosocial moratorium* may be desirable. A psychosocial moratorium is a period marked by a delay of commitment. Such a postponement occurred in Erikson's own life. After graduating from high school Erikson spent several years wandering around Europe without making any firm decision about the sort of job he would seek. Under ideal circumstances, a psychosocial moratorium should be a period of adventure and exploration, having a positive, or at least neutral, impact on the individual and society.

In some cases, however, the young person may engage in defiant or destructive behavior. A young person who is unable to overcome role confusion—or to postpone choices leading to identity formation by engaging in a positive psychosocial moratorium—may attempt to resolve inner conflict by choosing what Erikson refers to as a *negative identity.*

> The loss of a sense of identity is often expressed in a scornful and snobbish hostility toward the roles offered as proper and desirable in one's family or immediate community. Any aspect of the required role, or all of it—be it masculinity or femininity, nationality or class membership—can become the main focus of the young person's acid disdain. (1968, pp. 172–173)

An adolescent boy, for example, whose parents have constantly stressed how important it is to do well in school may deliberately act in an unscholarly way or quit school and join a commune. Erikson explains such choices by suggesting that the young person finds it easier to "derive a sense of identity out of total identification with that which he is least supposed to be than to struggle for a feeling of reality in acceptable roles which are unattainable with his inner means" (p. 176). If the young person who chooses a negative identity plays the role only long enough to gain greater self-insight, the experience may be positive. In some cases the negative identity may be "confirmed" by the way the adolescent is treated by those in authority. If forms of behavior adopted to express a negative identity bring the teen-ager into contact with excessively punitive parents, teachers, or law enforcement agencies, for example, the "young person may well put his energy into becoming exactly what the careless and fearful community expects him to be—and make a total job of it" (p. 196). (What Erikson refers to as *confirmed identity* is essentially the same as the self-fulfilling prophecy described by Rosenthal.)

Erikson notes that one reason for the tendency to develop a nega-

Psychosocial moratorium: Delay of commitment

Negative identity: Rejection of accepted roles

tive identity is that the adolescent is capable of imagining many possibilities. The number of possible choices of groups, interests, and activities available to the contemporary American youth may seem overwhelming to a young person who lacks a sense of identity. When confronted with so many choices, the adolescent may develop what Erikson refers to as a *historical perspective,* the fear that earlier events in one's life are irreversible and may limit the choices available.

Erikson's observations may help you understand several aspects of adolescent behavior. Many high school students are probably bothered by the realization that they must make decisions that are no longer "playful." They may be confused about sex roles and reluctant to make a specific career choice. Disinterest in class work may be interpreted in some cases as evidence that a student is engaging in a psychosocial moratorium and lacks enthusiasm for school because of a sense of aimlessness about preparing for a specific career (or even just graduating). Some types of impertinent or disruptive behavior may be less likely to arouse you to counterattack if you allow for the possibility that those involved are acting out a negative identity.

To encourage students to achieve a positive identity you might remind yourself of the three components of identity noted by Erikson: "feeling at home in one's body, ... knowing where one is going, ... assuredness of anticipated recognition from those who count." If you become aware that some students are dissatisfied with their appearance, you might call attention to the fact that even highly publicized beauties often look decidedly plain when they have not had the benefit of several hours of intensive work by a team of make-up artists. Perhaps the main point to stress, though, is that rapid physiological changes at adolescence cause everyone to be concerned about appearance, but that once growth is completed, most adults report that they are quite satisfied with their faces and figures. (Research leading to this conclusion will be reported in the next chapter.) To help students "know where they are going," urge them to explore career possibilities; and if they are unable to make a firm long-term choice, suggest that they concentrate on short-term goals (such as graduating from high school and perhaps entering some sort of college). If your students respect you, you will be someone who counts, which will mean that if you recognize them as individuals and commend them for accomplishments, your positive reactions will cause them to think positively about themselves.

In addition to taking account of the three components of identity described by Erikson, keep in mind the special stress he places on sex roles and occupational choice. Students may be less confused about changing views of sex roles if you suggest that each individual should develop her or his own view of appropriate behavior for females and males. Occupational choice may appear less threatening to your students if you stress that many people change jobs and that preparing

Secondary grades: Urge formulation of goals

for a particular occupation rarely locks a person into a rigid career pattern. To make this point you might describe individuals of your own acquaintance (perhaps yourself) who made several trials and errors before finding a congenial career, or you might ask students to describe someone they know. Students might be urged to talk to a number of individuals who seem happy with their jobs and ask them how and when they decided on that particular career. If they do this, they are likely to discover that chance experiences frequently open up unexpected possibilities. (The way Erikson came to meet Freud is an excellent example.)

The stages Erikson stresses as being of significance during the school and college years are summarized in Figure 3-1. For suggestions you might refer to in order to take advantage of his observations, examine the points listed below. These suggestions might also serve as the nucleus of a section to be inserted in your Handbook.

Figure 3–1

Summary of Erikson's theory

Epigenetic principle: Personality forms as the ego progresses through a series of inter-related stages. All stages exist in the beginning in some form; each has a critical period of development.

Birth to 1 year	Trust vs. mistrust	Consistency, continuity, and sameness of experience lead to trust. Inadequate, inconsistent, or negative care may arouse mistrust.
2 to 3 years	Autonomy vs. shame and doubt	Opportunities to try out skills at own pace and in own way lead to autonomy. Overprotection or lack of support may lead to doubt about ability to control self or environment.
4 to 5 years	Initiative vs. guilt	Freedom to engage in activities and parents' patient answering of questions lead to initiative. Restrictions of activities and treating questions as a nuisance lead to guilt.
6 to 11 years	Industry vs. inferiority	Being permitted to make and do things and being praised for accomplishments lead to industry. Limitation on activities and criticism of what is done lead to inferiority.
12 to 18 years	Identity vs. role confusion	Recognition of continuity and sameness in one's personality, even when in different situations and when reacted to by different individuals, leads to identity. Inability to establish stability (particularly regarding sex roles and occupational choice) leads to role confusion.

Suggestions for teaching: Applying Erikson's theory in the classroom

Handbook heading
Ways to Apply
Erikson's Theory
(Preschool and
Kindergarten)

Handbook heading
Ways to Apply
Erikson's Theory
(Elementary Grades)

Handbook heading
Ways to Apply
Erikson's Theory
(Secondary Grades)

1. Keep in mind that certain types of behavior and relationships may be of special significance at different age levels.

2. With younger preschool children allow plenty of opportunities for free play and experimentation to encourage the development of autonomy, but provide guidance to reduce the possibility that the child will experience doubt. Avoid shaming children for unacceptable behavior.

3. With older preschool children encourage activities that will permit the use of initiative and provide a sense of accomplishment. Avoid making children feel guilty about well-motivated but inconvenient (to you) questions or actions, and try to help jealous children gain satisfaction from their own behavior.

4. During the elementary school year help children experience a sense of industry by presenting tasks they can complete successfully. Arrange such tasks so that students will *know* they have been successful. Play down comparisons and encourage self-competition to limit feelings of inferiority.

5. At the secondary school level remember the significance of each student's search for a sense of identity. Encourage identity by helping pupils accept their personal appearance, by urging them to select short-term goals if delayed career choices seem too threatening, and by showing them that you recognize them as persons of worth. In addition, emphasize that each individual should decide what is

Choosing an occupation may seem less threatening to high school students if they are reminded that many 30- to 50-year-olds change jobs and that a person rarely gets "locked into" a particular career.

Constantine
Manos/Magnum

appropriate behavior for members of each sex and that it is not necessary to make a final commitment to a particular job, since many people change careers.

6. Keep in mind that the aimlessness of older students may be evidence that they are engaging in a psychosocial moratorium. If possible, encourage such individuals to focus on short-term goals.

7. Try to be patient if you suspect that disruptive behavior on the part of some students may be due to acting out a negative identity. If you must control negative behavior in order to preserve a satisfactory learning environment for other students, try to do it in such a way that the troublemaker is not "confirmed" as a troublemaker. One way is to make clear that you do not hold a grudge and that you have confidence in the student's ability to make positive contributions in class. (If possible, arrange opportunities for former troublemakers to carry out assignments that will be positive and constructive.)

Havighurst: Developmental tasks

Erikson's theory of development stresses the importance of certain types of behavior and relationships at different age levels. Robert J. Havighurst was impressed by Erikson's analysis of stages but concluded that the same basic rationale could be applied in a different way to shed light on other facets of development. Erikson describes stages in terms of dichotomies of positive and negative qualities. Havighurst lists what he calls *developmental tasks* for different age levels.

In his explanation of the concept of developmental tasks, Havighurst quotes Erikson's interpretation of the epigenetic principle, stressing that each aspect of personality development has a time of special ascendancy until all parts combine to form a functioning whole. Havighurst also calls attention to Erikson's observation that a child's failure to acquire an early aspect of development may cause problems during subsequent stages. This point is emphasized in Havighurst's definition of developmental tasks:

Developmental tasks must be achieved for satisfactory development

The tasks the individual must learn—*the developmental tasks* of life—are those things that constitute healthy and satisfactory growth in our society. They are the things a person must learn if he is to be judged and to judge himself to be a reasonably happy and successful person. *A developmental task is a task which arises at or about a certain period in the life of the individual, successful achievement of which leads to his happiness and to success with later tasks, while failure leads to unhappiness in the individual, disapproval by the society, and difficulty with later tasks.* (1952, p. 2; italics in original)

Havighurst suggests that developmental tasks have two values for educators: (1) They help focus attention on the purposes of education. (2) They call attention to *teachable moments*—optimum times to stress certain skills or attitudes. In *Developmental Tasks and Education* (1952) he lists developmental tasks for seven stages of life from infancy through later maturity. Here is a list of the tasks for stages occurring during the time children and adolescents are in school. After Havighurst's description of each task (printed in italics), explanatory notes and/or suggestions for teachers are appended. (Many of these notes are based on comments made by Havighurst in *Developmental Tasks and Education*.) Listing the developmental tasks for the grade level you expect to teach would be a potentially valuable addition to your Handbook.

Preschool and kindergarten

Handbook heading

Allowing for Developmental Tasks (Preschool and Kindergarten)

1. *Forming simple concepts of social and physical reality.* These concepts include things like *mother, father, school, teacher,* and everyday objects. Basic ways to help children acquire such concepts are to expose them to many objects and experiences and to be patient in answering their questions.

2. *Learning to relate oneself emotionally to parents, siblings, and other people.* This is often done by imitating others, which means that teachers should strive to serve as desirable models.

3. *Learning to distinguish right and wrong and developing a conscience.* Detailed suggestions for encouraging moral development will be given in Chapter 7.

Elementary grades

Handbook heading

Allowing for Developmental Tasks (Elementary Grades)

1. *Learning physical skills necessary for ordinary games.* Most of these skills are acquired as children interact with their peers. Children who seem to be having trouble developing coordination and skill might be given encouragement and instruction. Techniques for teaching skills will be summarized in Chapter 8.

2. *Building wholesome attitudes toward oneself as a growing organism.* Emphasize the values of cleanliness, a good diet, regular health habits (e.g., brushing teeth after every meal).

3. *Learning to get along with agemates.* If some children seem to antagonize others, seek subtle ways to help them control or eliminate disagreeable behavior. Help shy children make friends.

4. *Learning an appropriate masculine or feminine role.* Avoid using curriculum materials or class experiences that lead to the conclusion that females are passive or dependent. Call attention to the fact that both females and males engage in a great variety of occupations. At the same time, it might be valuable to call attention to the complementary nature of many male-female relationships (e.g., husband-wife, father-mother).

5. *Developing fundamental skills in reading, writing, and calculating.* Suggestions for helping students accomplish this task are provided in most of the chapters of this book, particularly Chapters 5 through 8.

6. *Developing concepts necessary for everyday living.* Such concepts are more sophisticated and advanced variations and combinations of those acquired earlier. Ways to help children achieve this task are noted in subsequent chapters and also in the next section of this chapter, which summarizes the theories of Jean Piaget.

7. *Developing conscience, morality, and a scale of values.* This task will be discussed in Chapter 7.

8. *Achieving personal independence.* Encourage and allow children to make many decisions about classroom routine and topics to be studied; encourage self-management of learning.

9. *Developing attitudes toward social groups and institutions.* Encourage children to respect the rights of others; explain the necessity and desirability of rules. Detailed suggestions for doing this will be summarized in Chapter 8.

Secondary grades

Handbook heading

Allowing for
Developmental Tasks
(Secondary Grades)

1. *Achieving new and more mature relations with agemates of both sexes.* Allow pupils to interact in class; use democratic procedures in the classroom; offer guidance to students who find it difficult to get along with others.

2. *Achieving a masculine or feminine social role.* Suggestions for helping adolescents achieve this task were noted in the discussion of Erikson's analysis of the significance of sex roles in the achievement of identity.

3. *Accepting one's physique and using the body effectively.* This task is similar to the need, emphasized by Erikson, for a young person

to "feel at home in one's body." Comments made in relation to Erikson's point apply here as well.

4. *Achieving emotional independence of parents and other adults.* Perhaps the basic way to help adolescents achieve this goal is to help them develop a positive sense of identity by using techniques described in the discussion of Erikson's theory.

5. *Achieving assurance of economic independence and selecting and preparing for an occupation.* These two tasks are similar to the occupational choice that Erikson argues is a significant element in the achievement of identity. Remarks made in discussing short- and long-term goals in the previous section apply here as well.

6. *Preparing for marriage and family life.* Probably the best way to help students achieve this task is by offering specific courses in marriage and the family.

7. *Developing intellectual skills and concepts necessary for civic competence.* Encourage students to take an active part in school, local, and national governmental affairs. Urge them to register to vote and to function as well-informed voters.

One of the developmental tasks Havighurst lists for high school students stresses socially responsible behavior.

Ginger Chih from Peter Arnold

8. *Desiring and achieving socially responsible behavior.*   Encourage consideration for others. If appropriate, call attention to the needs of less fortunate individuals. Comment favorably on behavior that reveals a sense of personal responsibility.

9. *Acquiring a set of values and an ethical system as a guide to behavior.*   Suggestions for doing this will be offered in Chapter 7. The most effective single technique is to set a good example for students to imitate.

Several of Havighurst's developmental tasks emphasize that if pupils fail to acquire basic academic and intellectual skills at appropriate times, repercussions causing problems in later aspects of development may result. One of the key questions about teaching such skills centers on timing—or, to use Havighurst's phrase, the determination of *teachable moments.* If certain concepts are presented too early, they may confuse children, and failure to understand what is presented could lead to feelings of inferiority rather than industry. If concepts are presented too late, students may be deprived of necessary skills that could have contributed to mastery of other learning experiences, or they may be bored by lessons that impress them as too childish. The Swiss psychologist Jean Piaget has spent sixty years charting the sequence of cognitive development (studying how children of different ages think), and his observations are of great value to those eager to take into account teachable moments as they plan educational experiences for children.

Teachable moments: Instruction presented at optimum time

Piaget: Stages of cognitive development

Factors that influenced Piaget

Piaget was born in the small university town of Neuchâtel, Switzerland, in 1896. His father was a professor of history who specialized in medieval literature, and young Jean was brought up in a scholarly atmosphere. His main boyhood interest was observation of animals in their natural habitat, an interest he pursued with considerable energy and sophistication. He published his first "professional" paper at the age of eleven. (He had seen an albino sparrow in a park and reported this in a nature magazine.)

When he entered school, Piaget concentrated on the biological sciences. A series of articles on shellfish so impressed the director of the natural history museum in Geneva that fifteen-year-old Jean was offered the post of curator of the mollusk collection. Since he had not finished high school, he felt obliged to decline this offer. A vacation

Jean Piaget
Yves de Braine/Black Star

with his godfather, a scholar specializing in philosophy, who urged Jean to broaden his horizons and study philosophy and logic, resulted in Piaget's fascination with *epistemology,* the branch of philosophy concerned with the study of knowledge.

After graduating from high school, Piaget entered the University of Neuchâtel and earned undergraduate and graduate degrees in natural science—he was awarded the Ph.D. at the age of twenty-one. At that point he became intrigued with psychology, which he studied in Zurich, where he was introduced to Freudian theory and wrote a paper relating psychoanalysis to child psychology. From Zurich he went to Paris to study abnormal psychology. Shortly after he arrived, he obtained a position preparing a French version of some reasoning tests developed in England. As he recorded the responses of his subjects, Piaget found that he was much more intrigued with wrong answers than correct ones. He became convinced that thought processes of younger children are basically different from those of older children and adults. His lifelong fascination with biology and his interest in studying the nature of knowledge led him to begin to speculate about the development of thinking in children.

In 1921, an appointment as director of research at the Jean Jacques Rousseau Institute in Geneva permitted Piaget to concentrate full time on the study of cognitive development. He engaged in active study at the Institute until 1975, and he continues to analyze cognitive development in "retirement."

Basic principles of Piaget's theory

Organization: Tendency
to systematize

Adaptation: Tendency
to adjust

The conception of intellectual development Piaget has arrived at after
a lifetime of study reflects his basic interests in biology and epistemology. He postulates that human beings inherit two basic tendencies:
organization (the tendency to systematize and combine processes into
coherent systems) and *adaptation* (the tendency to adjust to the environment). Piaget believes that just as the biological process of diges-
tion transforms food into a form the body can use, intellectual
processes transform experiences into a form the child can use in
dealing with new situations. And just as the biological processes must
be kept in a state of balance *(homeostasis),* Piaget believes intellectual

Equilibration: Urge to
maintain consistency in
thinking

processes seek a balance through the process of *equilibration.* Equilibration is a form of self-regulation that stimulates children to bring
coherence and stability to their conception of the world and to make
inconsistencies in experience comprehensible.

Organization, adaptation, and equilibration are basic tendencies,
but the fundamental way a child transforms experiences into knowledge takes place through two complementary processes, assimilation
and accommodation, that make adaptation possible. *Assimilation*
refers to the process by which elements in the environment are *incorporated* into the child's cognitive structure. *Accommodation* refers to

Assimilation:
Incorporation of
experiences

Accommodation:
Modification of
concepts

Scheme: Organized
pattern

the way children *modify* their conception of the world as new experiences are incorporated and alter their responses to things. When children assimilate and accommodate experiences to the point that an
organized pattern emerges, Piaget says they have developed a *scheme*
(also referred to as *schema,* the plural of which is *schemata*). In some
situations schemes may refer to actions taken by the child in specific
situations. Piaget says, for example, that an infant acquires a scheme
for sucking. But schemes may also represent a change in *cognitive*
structure that underlies behavior. When children learn to talk, for
example, their utterances are based on schemes of objects, situations,
and relationships.

These various tendencies and principles can be illustrated by the
example of an infant's experiences with balls of different kinds. From
interaction with objects previously encountered, the child of six
months or so will have *organized* the separate skills of looking and
grasping into the capability of visually directed reaching. Therefore,
when a ball is encountered for the first time, the child benefits from
past experience when reaching for it and trying to pick it up. If no
previous attempts have been made to pick up an object that rolls, the
first efforts may be unsuccessful, so the child will need to *accommodate* to the new object—altering grasping techniques already mastered. As success in doing this is achieved, the new skill will be
assimilated into a scheme for picking up objects. If the first ball is

small and hard, the child will think these characteristics are typical of all balls until other balls of different sizes and qualities are encountered. When this happens, the need to maintain equilibration will cause the child to make an effort to reduce inconsistencies between the original and later experiences with balls by assimilating (incorporating) and accommodating (modifying) the earlier scheme for *ball*. In time, a cognitive conception of *ball* will be developed that will permit the handling of all types of balls and an understanding of their common qualities.

Stages of cognitive development

As children develop, the way they organize and adapt to environmental experiences is reflected by a succession of stages of thought and behavior. Each of these stages involves a period of formation and attainment; each is an attainment in itself but also serves as the starting point for the next. The rate at which a particular child proceeds through these stages varies to some extent, but Piaget believes the sequence is the same in all children.

Infants and young children up to the age of two years are preoccupied with their senses and motor activities, and so in Piaget's terms they are at the *sensorimotor* stage. By the end of this stage, children have organized their experiences to the point where they can attempt new ways to deal with unique situations rather than using only schemes that worked on roughly equivalent earlier situations.

In order to understand why Piaget refers to the next two stages of children's thinking as *preoperational* and *concrete operational,* it is first necessary to become acquainted with differences between egocentric and socialized thought and with the principles of conservation, decentration, and operation.

The thinking of the three- to five-year-olds centers on mastery of symbols, which permits them to benefit more from past experiences and to manipulate mentally things that they previously manipulated physically. Piaget believes that symbols are derived from mental imitation and involve both visual images and bodily sensations. Because symbols are derived from the child's own experiences, they have qualities that are unique for each child. Rather than standing for things in a direct way, they represent one person's knowledge of things. All children probably have some similarities in their conception of a bicycle, for example, but each child will also have a unique idea of a bicycle, for personal experiences with bicycles will have been different for different children.

When children first learn to use words as symbols, the same reservation applies: each word will have a personal meaning for each child. Piaget believes that one of the most distinctive features of the speech

Egocentric thought: Assumption that others think the same way

and thought of young children is that it is primarily *egocentric*;[2] that is, children are unable to take into account another person's point of view. They interpret and use words in terms of their own experiences, not yet grasping the possibility that other children and adults may have had different experiences and may have different conceptions. The ability to take into account the views of others—called *socialized* speech and thought—does not develop until about the age of seven or eight years. At that point in development the child becomes capable of understanding that others may have different conceptions because their experiences with objects and situations have been different.

Socialized thought: Realization that others have different views

The egocentric speech and thought of preschoolers results not only from their personal interpretation of words and concepts but also from their inability to think about more than one thing at a time, a limitation that also influences the way they reason about things. This is illustrated most clearly by Piaget's experiments to determine the degree of understanding of the principle of *conservation*—the idea that mass or substance does not change when the shape or appearance of an object is transformed. In a typical conservation experiment children are shown water (or juice, or beans, or whatever) being poured from one of two identical jars into a tall, thin jar, and water from the other into a short, squat jar. Preschool children, who can think of only one quality at a time, will maintain that the tall jar contains the most water because they concentrate solely on height. Not until children have organized and adapted to experiences over a period of two or three more years do they become capable of *decentration*—the ability to center their attention on more than one quality. When children can take into account both height and volume, they are able to understand that the amount of water remains the same even when the shape of the water is altered. However, being able to understand the conservation of quantity does not permit the six-year-old to understand immediately and apply a general principle. Children typically do not completely grasp the conservation of weight until they are nine or of volume until they are twelve. Children must organize and adapt to still more experiences before they can generalize.

Conservation: Substance same even when appearance is changed

Decentration: Think of more than one quality at a time

Operation: Mental action that can be reversed

Piaget uses the concept of *operation* to explain the way conservation is mastered. The most distinctive feature of an operation is its *reversibility*—awareness that conditions can be mentally reversed. That is, the child can imagine what conditions were like before they were altered. An operation can be defined, therefore, as a mental action that can be reversed. In the case of the jar experiment, the interiorized action permits children to reverse mentally the pouring of

[2] It is sometimes difficult for Piaget's translators to find English words that convey the exact meaning of the French words used by the Swiss psychologist. *Egocentric* is commonly used in English to convey conceit or selfishness. As used by Piaget's translators, *egocentric* is intended to imply lack of awareness of the views of others because the young child's thinking is ego-(or self-)centered.

water from one jar to another (when the jars are actually in front of them).

Now that you are familiar with what Piaget means by *operation* and with related characteristics and principles, you are prepared to grasp the basic difference between *preoperational* and *concrete operational* thinkers. Three-year-olds are egocentric thinkers. They are unable to conserve or decenter, and they cannot mentally reverse actions, which means they are *preoperational*. Between the ages of three and seven, children gradually become more aware of the

Preoperational thought: Cannot mentally reverse actions

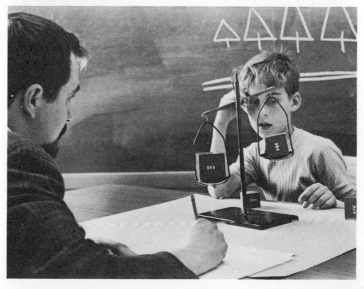

Teachers can determine if pupils have reached the stage of formal thought by observing how systematically individual students set about solving problems—such as how to balance weights.

The New York Times

thoughts of others. They come to comprehend that a substance retains certain qualities (such as volume) even when other qualities (such as shape) are changed, because they can think of more than one quality at a time. When children reach the point (typically around the age of seven) where they can solve problems by mentally reversing actions, Piaget says they are at the *concrete operational* stage of cognitive development. The term *concrete* emphasizes that the kinds of operations engaged in by seven- to eleven-year-olds are limited to objects that are actually present or that they have experienced concretely and directly, since they are unable to manipulate abstract ideas.

Starting around the age of twelve, children move into the final stage of cognitive development, which Piaget calls *formal thought*. As pupils move through the secondary grades, they become increasingly capable of dealing with abstractions and of formulating and testing hypotheses. Formal thinking is characterized by a systematic approach to problem solving, consideration of several variables at the same time, and the ability to generalize by applying principles to many different situations. (The term *formal* reflects the development of *form* or structure of thinking. It might also be thought of as emphasizing the ability of the adolescent to *form* hypotheses.) Comprehension of abstractions leads to a tremendous widening of intellectual horizons. Adolescents can form ideals and speculate about contrary-to-fact propositions. As they gain more experience with formal operations, they may become so fascinated with possibilities that they will fail to take into account some aspects of reality. This failure sometimes leads to difficulties if the theorizing is not related to practical difficulties (as in solutions to social and political problems, for example). And although mastery of formal operations makes it possible for adolescents to adapt to a great variety of problems and to be flexible in their thinking, it also leads to complications because their ability to explore mentally the pros and cons of various future possibilities, such as career choices, can cause considerable anxiety.

Moral realism and relativism

In addition to studying language, thought, reasoning, and intelligence, Piaget analyzed moral development and judgment. Just as the speech of preoperational children is egocentric and their thinking is limited by an inability to decenter, their judgment is influenced by the fact that they cannot take into account the point of view of others and can think of only one thing at a time. This leads to what Piaget calls *moral realism*. He studies and illustrates it with the responses of children asked to assess the guilt of the two children in the following situation: One child, wishing to be helpful, tries to fill a fountain pen but makes a big blot on the tablecloth when opening the ink bottle; another, playing with a pen—after having been told not to do so—makes a small

Concrete operational thought: Reasoning based on actual experiences

Formal thought: Can deal with abstractions and formulate and test hypotheses

Moral realism:
Consequences; literal
and specific rules

blot. In their responses, younger children concentrate on the amount of damage, not the motives, and argue that the child who made the bigger blot is more guilty, despite praiseworthy intentions. This view is called moral realism because of the focus on the "realistic," observable consequences of actions. Moral realism is also reflected in literal interpretation of rules. Because egocentrism prevents them from understanding that other people have different points of view, primary grade children tend to think of rules as "sacred" judgments. The moral realist, unable to generalize, also needs a specific rule for each situation.

At around eleven or twelve, children become capable of *moral relativism*. They are now able to decenter and think of several qualities at once, and they have overcome their egocentrism by becoming aware that other people may have different points of view. Consequently, they take into account motives and circumstances in making moral judgments. Even if a person does something that turns out badly, older children allow for good intentions. And they are more flexible about rules, since they realize that rules are simply agreements among individuals as to forms of conduct appropriate to given situations. Furthermore, they are able to apply a general rule to many situations.

Moral relativism:
Intentions; flexible and
general rules

A summary of Piaget's theory is presented in Figure 3-2.

Implications of Piaget's theory

Piaget's analysis of stages has been used by educators to develop curriculum materials at appropriate levels of difficulty for children at different grade levels. His conclusion that children should be allowed to organize and adapt experiences in their own way serves as one of the fundamental assumptions upon which the open education movement is based. Advocates of open education agree with Piaget that children should be allowed to choose many of their own learning experiences, which is why they arrange activity centers in different parts of the classroom. They also believe that children at a particular level of cognitive development may be able to teach some things to each other more effectively than an adult can. (Children who are at the concrete operational level, for example, talk the same language. Teachers, who are at the formal thought level, may not always be able to explain concepts in terms their pupils can understand.) Accordingly, pupils are encouraged to discuss books and ideas with their peers and to devise their own curriculum materials. In recognition of the idiosyncratic nature of each child's thinking (as exemplified by egocentric speech and thought), instruction and evaluation are individualized as much as possible. Pupils may be encouraged not just to supply answers but to explain the reasoning behind them, which provides clues to the level and nature of their thinking.

Figure 3–2

Summary of Piaget's theory

Basic principles

Equilibration	Form of self-regulation leading to desire to bring order and stability into perceptions of world and to reduce inconsistencies
Organization	Tendency to combine experiences into coherent systems (schemes)
Adaptation	Tendency to adjust to environment
Assimilation	Tendency to incorporate novel experiences into existing schemes or to form new schemes
Accommodation	Tendency to revise schemes to include new experiences
Operation	Interiorized (mental) action that can be reversed
Conservation	Realization that mass or substance does not change when appearance is changed
Decentration	Ability to keep from centering attention on just one quality

Stages of cognitive development

Birth to 2 years	Sensorimotor	Development of schemes primarily through sense and motor activities
2 to 7 years	Preoperational	Gradual acquisition of ability to conserve and decenter, but not capable of operations (reversibility)
7 to 11 years	Concrete operational	Capable of operations, but restricted to concrete experiences; not able to generalize to hypothetical experiences
11 to 14 years	Formal operational	Able to deal with abstractions, form hypotheses, consider possibilities

Types of speech, thought, and morality

Egocentric speech and thought	Up to the age of seven or eight years, children tend to assume all others see things as they see them
Socialized speech and thought	After the age of seven or eight, children are able to take into account that others may have a different point of view
Moral realism	Up to the age of eleven or twelve years, children are concerned about only one aspect of a moral situation, concentrate on material outcomes, are rigid and literal in interpreting rules
Moral relativism	After the age of eleven or twelve, children may take into account circumstances in analyzing moral situations, weigh motives and intentions, and be flexible in interpreting rules

    Some specific educational implications of Piaget's theory are noted below. The implications are arranged with reference to different grade levels.

Preschool, kindergarten, primary grades   Preschool and kindergarten children (and most first and some second graders as well) are at the *preoperational level.* They will be capable of using symbols to stand for objects, which makes mental manipulation possible. Their use of language will be egocentric, however. Words will have different meanings for different children, and most kindergartners will not be able to take into account the fact that other people have different points of view. During the preoperational period, the child gradually becomes capable of *decentration* and eventually can think of more than one quality at a time.

In order to grasp the fact that the language and thought of the preoperational child are qualitatively different from your own, you might ask kindergarten pupils to explain more fully what they mean by certain words—particularly if you are a bit baffled by their statements. To gain insight into the impact of lack of ability to decenter, try some of Piaget's simple experiments with individual pupils. (Detailed instructions are provided in the Suggestions for Further Study at the end of this chapter.) As background for your experiments, you should bear in mind that children typically go through a three-stage process in their understanding of any aspect of conservation: At first, they simply do not grasp the concept. Then they pass through a transition period in which they can understand it only in some situations. Finally, they grasp the idea completely enough to supply correct answers in all situations involving a particular kind of conservation.

The child's earliest awareness of conservation is of mass or substance. If you try the jar experiment or show four-year-olds two clay balls of the same size and then flatten one of them as they watch, they are likely to indicate that the taller jar or the flattened piece of clay has a greater volume. By age five most children comprehend that the mass is the same regardless of the shape, but they may reveal incomplete comprehension by even a slight change of procedure—such as pouring water from the tall jar into a vase, then asking if the amount is the same or if there is more water in the vase. Awareness of conservation of weight typically takes place between the ages of seven and ten; complete understanding of volume, between ten and twelve. The fact that a child can understand one type of conservation but is unable to generalize to other types illustrates a key difference between concrete operations and formal operations. Below the age of twelve, most children lack the capacity to deal with objects abstractly—hence the use of the term *concrete* to describe their operations, or mental acts. Because they are limited to dealing with actual experiences, they are unable to generalize or deal with hypothetical situations or weigh possibilities.

Grades four to nine Around the fifth or sixth grade, children shift from the level of concrete operations to the stage of formal operations. Concrete operations require reasoning, as illustrated by the solving of conservation problems, but children's thinking at this stage is still tied to direct experience. Even though children may not have to manipulate objects in order to understand relationships among them as at the

"Class standards" proposed by sixth graders

Although upper elementary grade pupils are sometimes capable of moral relativism, they still frequently think as moral realists. An example of this is provided by their interpretation of rules. One fifth grade teacher who asked his pupils to suggest class rules had to call a halt when the list reached sixty—with no end in sight. (One reason for the length of the list was that specific rather than general rules were suggested—for example, "Don't run in the hall," "Don't run in the classroom," "Don't run on the way to lunch," "Don't run on the way back from lunch.")

Mrs. Ann Bliss, a sixth grade teacher in Reseda, California, asked her pupils to propose "class standards." The following list—which illustrates how budding moral relativists still think in literal, specific terms—was reprinted in the February 27, 1971, issue of Saturday Review.

Listen to the teacher when she is talking or yelling.

Keep your shoes on in school.

Don't say shut up if the teacher doesn't like it.

Don't stay in the restroom all day.

Don't go to the bathroom all the time.

The bathroom isn't a meeting place and classes aren't held there.

Don't hide in the bathroom on hot days.

Don't play with thing.

Leave your treshures at home.

Stand when you walk into class.

Be ploite to all the teachers, not just yours.

Don't be a taital tail.

Don't lend back of your chair.

Don't scrap your chair.

Stay in your set.

Stay in your sit.

Try not to hit your classmates.

Be good to the little people.

Don't ride on another girl's back, you could get hurt.

No pooping bags at lunch.

Don't spit on the playground.

If the teacher says something funny, don't pound on your desk.

Don't bother the Princable.

Youse are time wisley.

Four people don't have to take one hurt person to the office.

Don't fall out of your chairs.

Don't crew gum or candy.

Don't crawl on floors.

Witch your mouth.

Wash your language.

preoperational stage, thinking at this stage is limited to actual experiences. In areas about which children have acquired no direct knowledge, they reason by analogy to something they *have* experienced.

When they reach the stage of formal operations, however, students can construct theories and make logical deductions about their consequences without having had previous direct experience with the subject. They can deal with abstractions and mentally explore similarities and differences because they have mastered reversibility and decentration. They can think their way through new problems, moving forward and backward and taking into account as many or as few qualities as seem relevant.

If you will be teaching any grade from fourth through ninth, you should keep in mind the differences between concrete and formal operations. It is likely that your students will sometimes function one way, sometimes another. Consequently, it would be well to give *all* your students plenty of opportunities to explain their thoughts, particularly with regard to abstractions, so that you can discern and take into account the level of awareness they have reached on various ideas.

When children reach the point of being able to make some consistent generalizations, they have shown that they are capable of formal thought. Incomplete grasp of this kind of thinking is revealed by the way they set about solving problems. If asked to explain how to predict what will happen if objects of varying sizes and weights are placed on a balance, eleven-year-olds are likely to proceed in a disorganized manner. They may make wild guesses before they begin to experiment and then proceed to engage in haphazard trial and error in searching for a solution. Not until they have gained sufficient experience with formal thought will they be able to plan mentally a systematic approach to solving the problem. Only after a considerable amount of experience will they be able to carry out a plan evolved entirely in their minds and accurately predict the results before they actually balance objects.

High school grades   Ginsburg and Opper (1969, p. 203) note that a significant aspect of formal thought is that it causes the adolescent to concentrate more on possibilities than on realities. (This is the ability that Erikson suggests leads to problems at the stage of identity vs. role confusion. When older adolescents reach the point where they can anticipate the results of a decision to prepare for a particular job and what it might be like to be employed, they may feel so threatened and confused that they postpone the final choice; or young people who try to weigh all the possibilities available may find it difficult to choose among them.)

While mastery of formal thought equips the older adolescent with impressive intellectual skills, it may contribute to role confusion. It

Give pupils opportunities to explain thoughts

may also lead to a tendency for the burgeoning formal thinker to become preoccupied with abstract and theoretical matters. Ginsburg and Opper interpret some of Piaget's observations on this point in this way:

> [The adolescent] constructs elaborate political theories or invents complex philosophical doctrines. He may develop plans for the complete reorganization of society or indulge in metaphysical speculation. Having just discovered capabilities for abstract thought, he then proceeds to exercise them without restraint. Indeed, in the process of exploring his new abilities the adolescent sometimes loses touch with reality, and feels that he can accomplish everything by thought alone. In the emotional sphere the adolescent now becomes capable of directing his emotions at abstract ideals and not just toward people. Whereas earlier he could love his mother or hate a peer, now he can love freedom or hate exploitation. The adolescent has developed a new mode of life; the possible and the ideal captivate both mind and feeling. (1969, pp. 204–205)

Unrestrained theorizing by novice formal thinkers

David Elkind suggests that unrestrained theorizing about ideals without complete understanding of realities tends to make the young adolescent a militant rebel with little patience with parents or other adults who fail to find quick solutions to personal, social, and other problems. Only when the older adolescent begins to grasp the complexities of interpersonal relationships and of economic and social problems does more tempered understanding appear. Elkind also suggests that the egocentrism of early childhood that gave way to socialized speech and thought at the end of the elementary grade years reappears in a different form as *adolescent egocentrism*. This occurs when high school students turn their new powers of thought upon themselves and become introspective. The strong tendency to analyze self is projected upon others. This helps explain why adolescents are so self-conscious: they assume their thoughts and actions are as interesting to others as to themselves. The major difference between the egocentrism of childhood and of adolescence is summed up in Elkind's observation: "The child is egocentric in the sense that he is unable to take another person's point of view. The adolescent, on the other hand, takes the other person's point of view to an extreme degree" (1968, p. 153).

Elkind believes that adolescent egocentrism also explains why the peer group becomes such a potent force in high school. He observes:

> Adolescent egocentrism ... accounts, in part, for the power of the peer group during this period. The adolescent is so concerned with the reactions of others toward him, particularly his peers, that he is willing to do many things which are opposed to all of his previous training and to his own best interests. At the same time, this egocentric impression that he is always on stage may help to account for the many and varied adolescent attention-getting maneuvers....

Toward the end of adolescence, this form of exploitative egocentrism gradually declines. The young person comes to realize that other people are much more concerned with themselves and their problems than they are with him and his problems. (1968, p. 154)

Now that you are familiar with some of the educational implications of Piaget's theory, you can formulate specific classroom applications. You might use the suggestions offered for the grade level you expect to teach as the basis for a section in your Handbook.

Suggestions for teaching: Applying Piaget's theory in the classroom: Preschool and primary grades[3]

Handbook heading
Ways to Apply Piaget's Theory (Preschool Through Primary Grades)

Primary grades: Encourage activity and student interaction

1. Become thoroughly familiar with Piaget's theory so that you will be aware of how your students organize and synthesize ideas. You may gain extra insight if you analyze your own thinking, since you are likely to discover that in some situations you operate at a concrete rather than at an abstract level.

2. If possible, assess the level and the type of thinking of each child in your class. Ask individual children to perform some of the Piaget experiments and spend most of your time listening to each child explain her or his reactions.

3. Remember that learning through activity and direct experience is essential. Provide plenty of materials and opportunities for children to learn on their own.

4. Arrange situations to permit social interaction so that children can learn from each other. To facilitate this, placing some advanced thinkers with less mature thinkers seems preferable to homogeneous grouping.

5. Plan learning experiences to take into account the level of thinking attained by an individual or group; that is, encourage children to classify things on the basis of a single attribute before you expose them to problems that involve relationships among two or more attributes. Ask many questions and give your students many opportunities to explain their interpretations of experiences so that you remain aware of their level of thinking.

6. Keep in mind the possibility that pupils may be influenced by egocentric speech and thought. Allow for the possibility that each child may assume that everyone else has the same conception of a word he or she has. If confusion becomes apparent or if a child becomes impatient about failure to communicate, request an explanation in different terms. Or ask several children to explain their conception of an object or situation.

[3] Many of these suggestions are derived from points made in Chapter 7 of *Young Children's Thinking* (1966) by Millie C. Almy, E. Chittenden, and P. Miller.

One of the principles of instruction that emerges from Piaget's theory of cognitive development is that pupils should be allowed and encouraged to learn from each other.

Ingbert Gruttner

Suggestions for teaching: Applying Piaget's theory in the classroom: Secondary grades

Handbook heading
Ways to Apply Piaget's Theory (Secondary Grades)

Secondary grades: Teach problem-solving skills

1. Become well acquainted with the nature of concrete operational thinking and formal thought so that you can recognize when your students resort to either type or a combination of the two.

2. To become aware of the type of thinking being used by individual students, ask them to explain how they arrived at solutions to problems, either as part of the curriculum in your classes or in response to experimental situations similar to those devised by Piaget. Sample problems are described in the Suggestions for Further Study at the end of this chapter.

3. Teach students how to be more systematic about solving problems. Suggestions for doing this are provided in Chapter 9.

4. Keep in mind that some high school students may be more interested in possibilities than realities. If class discussions become unrealistically theoretical and hypothetical, call attention to facts and practical difficulties. If students are contemptuous of unsuccessful

attempts by adults to solve school, local, national, and international problems, point out the complexity of many situations involving conflict of interests, perhaps by summarizing arguments from both sides.

5. Allow for the possibility that younger adolescents may go through a period of egocentrism that will cause them to act as if they are always on stage and to be extremely concerned about the reactions of peers.

Do attempts to accelerate lead to superficial learning?

Piaget's analysis of cognitive development is endorsed by many psychologists and educators, but some theorists prefer to apply his ideas in ways he does not fully support, and others have proposed alternative descriptions of mental growth. Instead of allowing freedom for children to assimilate and accommodate and develop schemes at their own pace, which is the approach Piaget prefers, many American psychologists (notably J. McV. Hunt, 1961) believe that children should be taught how to move through the stages of cognitive development as rapidly as possible. Several attempts (e.g., Smedslund, 1961) have been made, for example, to teach children to grasp the concept of conservation at an earlier age than they would if left to discover it by themselves. Some psychologists (e.g., Engelmann, 1969) believe that the attempts have been successful and argue that all children should be given instruction designed to accelerate their progress through Piaget's stages. Other psychologists (e.g., Ginsburg and Opper, 1969; Kamii and Dermon, 1972) maintain that efforts to speed up intellectual growth lead to superficial rather than genuine learning. That is, children are able to supply correct answers to questions identical to those they have studied, but they are unable to solve problems that are similar but different. The approach Piaget himself prefers is summed up in this statement:

In the realm of education . . . students should be allowed a *maximum* of activity on their own, directed by means of materials which permit their activities to be cognitively useful. In the area of logico-mathematical structures, children have real understanding only of that which they invent themselves, and each time that we try to teach them something too quickly, we keep them from reinventing it themselves. Thus, there is no good reason to try to accelerate this development too much; the time which seems to be wasted in personal investigation is really gained in the construction of methods. (Almy et al., 1966, p. vi)

It is a great mistake to suppose that a child acquires the notion of number and other mathematical concepts just from teaching. . . . When adults try to impose mathematical concepts on a child prematurely, his learning is merely verbal, true understanding of them comes only with his own mental growth. (1953, p. 76)[4]

[4] Piaget makes a book-length analysis of the points summarized in these brief excerpts in *Science of Education and the Psychology of the Child* (1970).

Piaget's background and views of development help explain these statements. Consider his belief in the inherited tendencies of organization and adaptation (reflecting his interest in biology), his conviction that children and adults think in fundamentally different ways, his emphasis on the need for children to develop their own conception of the world. Piaget distinguishes between "merely verbal learning" and "true" learning. The latter involves the acquisition of a new structure of mental operations that permits the child to assimilate new experiences and to generalize from novel situations. It can occur only after the child has developed the necessary mental equipment.

An American psychologist who has been one of the major critics of Piaget's view is Jerome Bruner, who not only questions the Swiss theorist's conclusions but proposes an alternative conception of cognitive growth.

Bruner: Systems of representation

Stages of representation

Bruner suggests that intellectual development runs the course of three stages of cognitive development (which he refers to as *systems of representation*). He calls the first *enactive* representation because the young child defines events and objects in terms of the actions she or he takes toward them. By the age of three or so, what Bruner terms *iconic* representation appears. This system of thought depends on visual or other sensory organization, with the child using highly concrete visual imagery. Bruner refers to the most advanced form of representation as *symbolic*. At this point children are able to develop abstract images because they are able to translate experience into language and use language as an instrument of thinking.

Enactive, iconic and symbolic stages

The significance of language

Bruner's general description of stages of representation parallels Piaget's description of sensorimotor, concrete operations, and formal operations stages, but Bruner differs from Piaget in his interpretation of the role of language in the development of thought. Piaget theorizes that thought and language are closely related—but different—systems. He believes the thinking of the child is based on a system of inner logic that evolves as a child organizes and adapts to experiences. He also believes the symbols of the younger child are based on visual images and imitation. This hypothesis is based primarily on observations that two-year-old children are able to engage in accurate imitations of complex behavior at a time when their language skills are quite prim-

Jerome S. Bruner

itive. Bruner, however, maintains that thought is internalized lan
guage and that syntactical rules of language rather than logic can be
used to explain mastery of conservation and other principles. He
bases his hypothesis on experiments carried out by his students and
colleagues, which are reported in Chapters 9 and 10 of *Studies in
Cognitive Growth* (written in collaboration with Rose R. Olver and
Patricia Greenfield).

Bruner modified the jar experiment devised by Piaget by having
the water poured behind a cardboard screen that permitted the child
to see only the tops of the jars and not the amount of water. When
children were asked if there would be the same amount of water in tall
and short jars, most were able to give the correct answer, although
many of the same children were unable to conserve when the screen
was removed and they could actually watch the jars being filled.
Bruner explains that children who see the water being poured are
impelled by the visual presence of the pouring to concentrate on
visual cues, whereas children who are asked to describe what has
happened without seeing it use symbolic representation, which
"frees" them from the concrete.

Bruner sums up his views, as compared with Piaget's, in this way:

At the Institute in Geneva, cognitive development is seen as almost purely a
matter of maturation, maturation that takes place by a process of internalization of logical forms; logic, first expressed motorically, is gradually internalized until it can be used symbolically—at which time physical action
becomes no longer necessary for thought. . . . At the Cognitive Center at Har-

vard, cognitive development is conceived more in terms of the internalization of technologies from the culture, language being the most effective technology available. (1966, p. 214)

Piaget is convinced that formal operational thought can be used only by those who have assimilated and accommodated experiences—first in preoperational terms and then in the form of concrete operations. Bruner believes that the most advanced kind of thinking a child can be helped to engage in is the most appropriate. Piaget maintains that whatever kind of thinking a child uses on his or her own is the most appropriate kind and that attempts to impose more sophisticated kinds of thoughts are ill advised.

Bruner also differs from Piaget in his estimate of the degree to which some environments can slow or stop the sequence of development. He believes that spurts are touched off when certain capacities begin to develop, and he describes the overall sequence as basically the development of a series of prerequisites. As he puts it, "some capacities must be matured and nurtured before they can be called into being" (1966, p. 27). This view is similar to Piaget's to the extent that it stresses a hierarchical sequence, but Bruner does not share Piaget's views on allowing children to discover things through their own experiences.

Teaching readiness

In the 1930s a number of researchers (notably Arnold Gesell, 1928) emphasized the concept of *readiness*—the belief that children should not be asked to learn something unless they had matured sufficiently to benefit from instruction. In regard to this view, Bruner writes:

The idea of "readiness" is a mischievous half-truth. It is a half-truth largely because it turns out that one *teaches* readiness or provides opportunities for its nurture; one does not simply wait for it. Readiness, in these terms, consists of mastery of those simple skills that permit one to reach higher skills. (1966, p. 29)

Although Bruner labels the theory of readiness "a mischievous half-truth," in some situations *lack* of allowance for readiness may be just as "mischievous." For example, two kindergarten teachers discovered that they shared a concern about some of their pupils. Each teacher had about a half dozen boys who were among the youngest children in the class and who appeared to be slow maturers. These boys were unable to do many simple tasks that their classmates accomplished with ease, and they also seemed a bit intimidated by the greater maturity and confidence of their older classmates. The teachers were apprehensive that if the boys were promoted to the first grade, they might be doomed to a torturous academic career. However, when the teachers suggested that the boys repeat kindergarten so that they would be the most mature rather than the least mature pupils in the class, the parents were almost unanimously opposed. They were afraid that the slower start would permanently handicap their children.

In this particular situation, allowing for natural development without concern for "making" these boys ready would seem to be a desirable course of action. Although Bruner's argument that we should *teach* readiness rather than wait for it has merit, differences in rate of development cannot be ignored. Moreover, the idea that children should be *made* ready may cause parents and teachers to be apprehensive about those who don't progress as rapidly as others; and this fear may lead, in turn, to unintentional pressure on some children, causing them to feel even more insecure and tense. All this suggests that "a mischievous half-truth" may be implicit in *both* sides of the readiness argument.

Perhaps the central question in the readiness debate is this: Is it better to surround children with stimuli and partly structured experiences and allow them considerable freedom to choose *what* they find meaningful *when* they find it meaningful? Or is it better to note what appear to be characteristic, progressive patterns, or stages, in child

Bruner's description of iconic and symbolic stages of representation calls attention to the desirability of stressing visual imagery when teaching younger pupils.

Roger Malloch/Magnum

development and then systematically lead all children through this sequence?

American psychologists tend to favor the second view. Bruner, for example, is eager to do what he can do *teach* readiness. But as you will discover in Chapter 6, he prefers to do this by arranging learning experiences that allow students to discover many things on their own. Bruner recommends the discovery approach because he is critical of methods of instruction where a teacher (or a book or a program) asks specific questions (which function as stimuli) and students supply specific answers (responses). Such stimulus-response learning is advocated by most American psychologists, and some reasons for its popularity in the United States can be understood by examining a conception of development based on the same principles. Before turning to the stimulus-response theory of development, however, a summary of some of the educational applications of Bruner's views will be noted. These applications might be converted into a list of points in your Handbook.

Suggestions for teaching: Applying Bruner's theory in the classroom

Handbook heading
Ways to Apply Bruner's Theory (Preschool and Primary Grades)

1. With preschool, kindergarten, and lower primary grade children, allow for iconic representation by encouraging children to learn through visual and sensory experience. (Help children *visualize* concepts—use blocks and rods to teach fractions, for example.)

2. If you favor Bruner's suggestion that we try to teach readiness, devise the curriculum so that concepts and skills necessary for advanced learning are presented in systematic fashion. Bruner has written, "If you wish to teach the calculus in the eighth grade, then begin it in the first grade by teaching the kinds of ideas and skills necessary for its mastery later" (1966, p. 29).

3. If you favor Bruner's view that attempts should be made to speed up cognitive development, encourage young children who may be too dependent on visual imagery to verbalize their thoughts as they seek solutions to problems.

4. Remember that students in the elementary grades may sometimes use iconic forms of representation and at other times use symbolic thinking. To allow for this state of affairs, you might present some parts of a lesson by stressing symbols and visual imagery, other parts by stressing language. In addition, allow many opportunities for verbal interchange among students.

Handbook heading
Ways to Apply Bruner's Theory (Secondary Grades)

5. When students become capable of symbolic representation, help them master concepts and principles and call attention to the structure of an area or field of study by emphasizing interrelationships.

Stimulus-response theory

Jean Piaget believes that it is unwise to try to speed up cognitive development. Jerome Bruner agrees with Piaget that there are recognizable stages of cognitive development, but he is convinced that children should be exposed to experiences specifically designed to prepare them for later learning. Many American psychologists agree with Bruner that we should *teach* readiness, but they do not support his suggestion that teachers concentrate on arranging experiences so that students will make their own discoveries. They feel that this is much too inefficient and recommend that students be helped to learn in the most systematic way possible, particularly by arranging stimulus situations planned to arouse specific types of responses. This view of learning is often referred to as stimulus-response theory, and it is endorsed by many American psychologists. Some of the basic assumptions of stimulus-response theory are derived from points originally proposed by Aristotle and John Locke.

Philosophical bases for stimulus-response theory

At one time or another Aristotle seems to have tried to find answers to almost every kind of question. When he speculated about ways children acquire ideas about things, he came to this conclusion:

Mind is in a sense potentially whatever is thinkable, though actually it is nothing until it has thought. What it thinks must be in it just as characters may be said to be on a writing-tablet on which as yet nothing stands written: this is exactly what happens with mind. (*De Anima,* Book 3, Chapter 4, section 430)

Tabula rasa (blank slate) view

This conception of the nature of the mind is referred to as the *tabula rasa* (blank slate) view. In 1690, John Locke, the English philosopher, also speculated about the mind of a newborn child, and he came to the same conclusion as Aristotle. In his famous *Essay Concerning Human Understanding,* Locke wrote:

Let us then suppose the mind to be, as we say, white paper, void of all characters, without any ideas; how comes it to be furnished? Whence comes it by that vast store which the busy and boundless fancy of man has painted on it with an almost endless variety? Whence has it all the materials of reason and knowledge? To this I answer in one word, from experience; in that all our knowledge is founded, and from that it ultimately derives itself. (1690, Book 2, Chapter 1, paragraph 2)

In addition to reaffirming Aristotle's tabula rasa view, Locke urged philosophers and scientists to follow the empirical approach and base their conclusions on observations of actual behavior.

When psychology departments were established in American universities during the early decades of this century, faculty members were apparently influenced by certain characteristics of American culture. Many immigrants came to the United States because they wanted to get away from societies where a person's place in life was often determined more by hereditary position than by actual ability. Because America was a new world, individuals had greater opportunities to determine their own position in life than did citizens of well-established, stratified societies. The ideal of the self-made man or woman appears to have influenced American psychologists when they began to seek explanations for human behavior. They were attracted to points of view that placed emphasis on ways individuals could improve themselves and were skeptical about theories that stressed inherited predispositions. American psychologists were probably also influenced by the success of American technology. By applying scientific discoveries to everyday problems, Americans had succeeded in establishing in this country an unprecedented standard of living. The first American psychologists reasoned that if it is possible for human beings to conquer nature, fight disease, and make their lives more and more comfortable, they should be able to improve human behavior. One of the earliest and most energetic proponents of this point of view was John B. Watson.

Watson: Behaviorism, Pavlovian conditioning

As a graduate student in 1903, Watson wrote a dissertation *Animal Education: The Psychical Development of the White Rat.* In American psychology at that time, an experimenter who had finished observations of animal subjects was expected to speculate about the state of the animal's consciousness. Watson objected to this, arguing that it was more sensible and scientific to concentrate on overt behavior, which could be observed and described objectively. He spent several years developing his arguments and eventually presented them in a paper entitled *Psychology as the Behaviorist Views It* (1913). He called himself a *behaviorist* to emphasize his main point that psychologists should base their conclusions exclusively on observations of overt behavior.

Behaviorism: Observe only overt behavior

In addition to stressing the doctrine of behaviorism, Watson eagerly sought ways to control human behavior. When the Russian scientist Ivan Pavlov published reports of his experiments in conditioned responses, Watson concluded that the key to behavior manipulation had been found. Pavlov demonstrated how a dog learns when it associates a stimulus with a response. In his most famous experiment he induced a dog to salivate when a bell was rung by building up an association between the bell and food. On the basis of this and similar experiments, he proposed that the association was established

Pavlovian conditioning: Association of stimuli and responses because presenting food just after the bell was rung *reinforced* the response. If reinforcement was not supplied from time to time, he discovered, the response would disappear, or *extinguish*. Pavlov also pointed out that a dog conditioned to salivate at the sound of the bell would tend to salivate at other sounds, such as a whistle; he referred to this tendency as *stimulus generalization*. Such generalized responses could be overcome by supplying reinforcement after the bell was rung but never after a whistle was sounded. When this occurred, he said, *discrimination* had taken place.

Watson decided to try to establish a conditioned response in a human subject. In a now classic experiment (Watson and Rayner, 1920), he demonstrated that human behavior *could* be conditioned. He encouraged an eleven-month-old boy named Albert to play with a white rat.[5] When Albert began to enjoy this activity, Watson suddenly hit a steel bar with a hammer just as the child reached for the rat. In observations of infants, Watson had discovered that a sudden, loud sound frightened most children. When Albert came to associate the previously attractive rat with the frightening stimulus, he not only responded with fear but generalized this fear to anything white and fuzzy.

Watson was so elated with his success at conditioning Albert that he made this statement:

Give me a dozen healthy infants, well-formed, and my own specified world to bring them up in and I'll guarantee to take any one at random and train him to become any type of specialist I might select—doctor, lawyer, artist, merchant-chief and, yes, even beggarman and thief, regardless of his talents, penchants, tendencies, abilities, vocations, and race of his ancestors. (1925, p. 82)

Shortly after he made this rash claim, Watson was accused of immoral behavior with a student. Even though the accusation turned out to be groundless, he felt obliged to resign his academic position, and he took a job with an advertising agency. He was quite successful at conditioning consumers to buy particular products, and you probably choose certain brands of goods because of advertising techniques first introduced by Watson.

If Watson had continued his career as an experimental psychologist, he undoubtedly would have discovered what other researchers soon reported: Pavlovian conditioning applies only to essentially involuntary reflex actions (such as salivation or responding with fear). Such reactions are not very common or significant types of behavior, and psychologists therefore sought other ways to build associations between stimuli and responses. B. F. Skinner of Harvard eventually

---

[5] In a later repetition of this experiment (reported and illustrated in *Psychological Care of Infant and Child* [1926]), Watson used a rabbit instead of a rat. Therefore, you may encounter some accounts of this experiment that mention a rat, others that mention a rabbit.

discovered a technique for controlling almost any kind of behavior engaged in by an organism (not just involuntary reflex actions), and he became just as energetic as Watson had been earlier in proclaiming the values of behavior control.

Skinner: Environmentalism, operant conditioning

In Chapter 1 Skinner's description of the values and characteristics of science was presented. Skinner's observations on learning and teaching will be described in Chapter 5. At this juncture his views on a scientific conception of behavior and development will be outlined.

On the opening pages of *Science and Human Behavior* (1953), Skinner makes a statement that sums up the essence not only of that book but of almost all his other publications as well. He writes: "The methods of science have been enormously successful wherever they have been tried. Let us then apply them to human affairs" (1953, p. 5). In order to apply science to human affairs, Skinner argues, it is essential to endorse Locke's arguments that the mind of a newborn child is a blank slate and that all that is learned is acquired through experience. When both these assumptions are accepted, it follows that those who arrange experiences control behavior and shape personality.

The key to behavior control is reinforcement. In a series of experiments with rats and pigeons placed in an ingenious apparatus, Skinner demonstrated that actions followed by a reward of some kind are likely to be repeated, actions that go unrewarded are not likely to occur again. The *Skinner box*, as the original apparatus came to be called, is a small enclosure that contains only a bar (or lever) and a small tray. Outside the box is a hopper holding a supply of food pellets that are dropped into the tray when the bar is pressed under certain conditions (for example, when a tone is sounded). A hungry rat is placed in the box, and when—in the course of exploring its new environment—it approaches and then touches the bar, it is rewarded with a food pellet. A similar device designed for pigeons features a disk (to be pecked) rather than a bar. On the basis of principles derived from his experiments with rats and pigeons, Skinner developed a theory of *operant conditioning*. He chose the term *operant conditioning* to stress that an organism "operates" on the environment when it learns. This type of learning is also referred to as *instrumental conditioning* because what the organism does is instrumental in securing reinforcement.

Skinner points out that Pavlovian conditioning is extremely limited, since an originally neutral stimulus (a bell or a white rat) simply comes to arouse an essentially involuntary action (such as salivation or responding with fear). He argues that the kind of learning demonstrated by a rat or pigeon in a Skinner box is much more common and

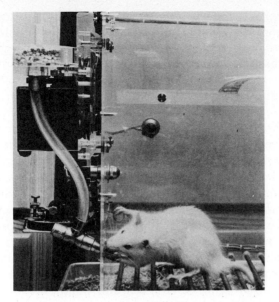

A rat in a Skinner box. When the animal presses the bar, a food pellet is automatically supplied and the behavior is recorded on a graph.

Courtesy of Pfizer, Inc.

Operant conditioning: Strengthen responses by supplying reinforcement

versatile, since a voluntary action (pressing the bar or pecking the disk) could be strengthened by reinforcing the behavior under preselected conditions (when a tone was sounded after a move in a given direction).

Skinner's view of development stresses that children initiate behavior on their own, but the tendency to repeat certain acts is a function of which acts are rewarded. If those in contact with children do not provide reinforcement in a systematic way, Skinner argues, their development will be left to accidental or chance reinforcement. Skinner does not ignore inherited factors, but he points out that these cannot be changed. He prefers to concentrate exclusively on environmental experiences that *can* be arranged and altered.

Sears, Bandura: Identification, imitation, modeling

Significance of identification, imitation, and modeling

Skinner's theory of reinforcement accounts for quite a few types of behavior, but several critics and some of his fellow stimulus-response theorists point out that other aspects of behavior cannot be traced to reinforcing experiences. Robert R. Sears and Albert Bandura, for example, have demonstrated that children do not necessarily have to be reinforced in order to acquire certain types of behavior; they may simply imitate the actions of others, particularly when they identify with them. In two extensive investigations Sears called attention to ways child-rearing practices influence behavior (Sears, Maccoby, and Levin, 1957), and he showed how the extent to which a child identifies with her or his parents may influence moral and other types of development (Sears, Rau, and Alpert, 1965). In an ingenious experiment (Bandura, Ross, and Ross, 1963), Bandura demonstrated how children will imitate aggressive acts they observe being performed by adults, children, and cartoon characters, who function as models.

In addition to calling attention to the impact of imitation (or modeling), Bandura took the lead in proposing that S-R psychologists be more flexible in allowing for conscious control of one's own behavior. Watson was stimulated to propose behaviorism when he was asked to speculate about what was taking place in the mind of a rat. He felt that this was unscientific and urged psychologists to concentrate on measurable actions and avoid analyses of thoughts, which could not be observed. Bandura concluded that many S-R theorists embraced behaviorism so enthusiastically that they came to endorse the view that reinforcement influences human behavior without the conscious involvement of the individual. Bandura suggests (1974) that human beings are capable of choosing how they will respond to many situations because many types of human behavior are under *anticipatory control*. That is, children and adults are capable of observing the effects of their actions, and they are also able to anticipate what will happen under certain circumstances. As a result, they are able to control their own behavior to a significant extent by choosing between different situations and experiences and by deliberately *producing* preselected consequences.

Principles established by stimulus-response theorists apply most directly to learning, and these will be analyzed in detail in Chapter 5. But some of their discoveries also have implications for understanding development. For your Handbook, you might pick out points listed below that impress you as potentially valuable and perhaps add others you derive from the preceding discussion.

Suggestions for teaching: Applying stimulus-response theory in the classroom

Supply rewards systematically
Handbook heading
Ways to Apply S-R Theory

1. Remain aware that behavior is shaped by experiences and that those who arrange experiences for children are in a position to shape their growth and development.

2. Recognize that if behavior is not reinforced, it tends to disappear. If possible, ignore pupil behavior that you would prefer not to have repeated.

3. Keep in mind that behavior is strengthened by reinforcement. Instead of permitting reinforcements to occur in accidental or haphazard ways, be systematic in supplying rewards, first by selecting desired behavior and then by taking steps to strengthen it.

4. Remember that children learn many types of behavior by imitating

others, particularly those they identify with. Since many of your pupils may identify with you, strive to be a worthwhile model.

Stimulus-response theory is endorsed by many but not all American psychologists. Some psychologists in the United States feel that the theories of Freud and his followers are too vague and are not based on scientific evidence. They have also come to the conclusion that the behavioristic view has limitations. Consequently, they have sought an interpretation of behavior that serves as a compromise between the views of Freud and Skinner. To some students of development, the observations of Abraham H. Maslow provide a better framework for understanding child behavior than psychoanalysis or S-R theory.

Maslow: Third force psychology

Children enjoy growing

When Maslow studied psychoanalysis early in his career, he was impressed by Freudian theory. Eventually, however, Maslow came to the conclusion that Freud had been influenced too much by contact with neurotic patients and that Freud sometimes made the child appear to be a helpless, timid creature dominated by unconscious drives. Maslow wondered whether a different view of the child might

Abraham H. Maslow

Abraham H. Maslow (1908–1970). Taken in April 1970. Photographer Wm. Carter emerge if, instead of basing a theory of behavior on observations of abnormally maladjusted individuals, he made observations of especially well-adjusted individuals. After following this plan Maslow concluded:

Maslow: Children enjoy growing

Observation of children shows more and more clearly that healthy children *enjoy* growing and moving forward, gaining new skills, capacities and powers. This is in flat contradiction to that version of Freudian theory which conceives of every child as hanging on desperately to each adjustment that it achieves and to each state of rest or equilibrium. . . .

While this Freudian conception is continually confirmed by clinicians as largely true for insecure and frightened children, and while it is partially true for all human beings, in the main it is *untrue* for healthy, happy, secure children. In these children we see clearly an eagerness to grow up, to mature, to drop the old adjustment as outworn, like an old pair of shoes. (1968, pp. 23–24)

Children make their own choices

Maslow also was dissatisfied with the same aspects of stimulus-response theory that troubled Albert Bandura, particularly the implication that a child is merely a passive organism shaped almost entirely by external forces. Maslow found it difficult to endorse the environmental view that almost all behavior is determined by experiences. He offered this explanation of behavior to serve as an alternative:

Individuals determine much of their own behavior

Life is a continual series of choices for the individual in which a main determinant of choice is the person as he already is. . . . We can no longer think of the person as "fully determined" where this phrase implies "determined only by forces external to the person." The person, insofar as he *is* a real person, is his own main determinant. Every person is, in part, "his own project" and makes himself. (1968, p. 193)

Principles of third force psychology

To overcome what he considered to be disadvantages of both Freudian and stimulus-response theories, Maslow proposed a view that he dubbed *third force* psychology (the first two "forces" being psychoanalysis and S-R theory). Maslow's view is also referred to as *humanistic* psychology (because the behaviorist stricture that only overt behavior be observed is rejected and such "human" qualities as thoughts, feelings, and attitudes are attributed to human subjects). In Chapter 15 of *Toward a Psychology of Being* (2nd ed., 1968), Maslow describes forty-three basic propositions that summarize his views. Some of the most significant of these propositions are: Each individual is born with an essential inner nature. This inner nature is shaped by experiences and by unconscious thoughts and feelings, but it is not ordinarily *dominated* by such forces. Individuals control much of

their own behavior. Children should be allowed to make many choices about their own development. Parents and teachers play a significant role in preparing children to make wise choices by satisfying their physiological, safety, love, belonging, and esteem needs, but they should do this by helping and *letting* children grow, not by attempting to shape or control the way they grow.

Maslow's writings were instrumental in the emergence of what is commonly called *humanistic education*. This approach to teaching will be described in detail in Chapter 7. Furthermore, his views on motivation will be featured in Chapter 10. At this point it will suffice to note the following implications of Maslow's view of behavior. You might outline these points in your Handbook.

Suggestions for teaching: Applying third force psychology in the classroom

Handbook heading

Ways to Apply the
Third Force View
Permit pupils to choose,
satisfy their needs

1. Children enjoy growing and seek new experiences. Therefore, parents and teachers should not feel that they must protect children. Instead, they should provide opportunities for children to explore things on their own.

2. The behavior of children is not determined exclusively by external forces. Each child is his or her own main determinant. Therefore, parents and teachers should allow freedom for children to control much of their own behavior.

3. The most significant influences adults have on children are to satisfy their needs for safety, love, belonging, and esteem and to help them make wise choices.

SUMMARY OF KEY POINTS

Erik H. Erikson's description of psychosocial stages of development is based on the *epigenetic principle,* which emphasizes that each stage of development has its own special time of ascendancy. During the preschool years, two- to three-year-olds are at the stage of *autonomy vs. shame and doubt,* four- to five-year-olds are at the stage of *initiative vs. guilt.* Teachers of two- to five-year-olds who take into account these stages might strive to allow freedom but supply guidance. Six- to eleven-year-olds are at the stage of *industry vs. inferiority,* and elementary school teachers might recognize the nature of this period of development by setting up learning experiences to permit noncompetitive accomplishment. Twelve- to eighteen-year-olds are at the stage of *identity vs. role confusion.* Secondary school teachers can allow for significant aspects of this stage by urging students to formulate goals. Goals are crucial during adolescence because the young person seeks to establish a sense of identity. Identity is most likely to be experienced if adolescents have clear goals and if they accept their appearance and are recognized by those who count. Role confusion may develop if there is uncertainty about sex roles or occupational choice. Some adolescents who experience role confusion engage in a *psychosocial moratorium* (delay of commitment). Others adopt a *negative identity* by rejecting accepted roles and behaving in ways opposite to those held up as desirable.

Robert J. Havighurst agrees with Erikson that certain types of behavior are of special significance at different age levels. Instead of describing stages in terms of dichotomies of positive and negative qualities, Havighurst lists *developmental tasks:* tasks that must be achieved if development is to proceed satisfactorily. A significant point about the timing of developmental tasks is that teachers should try to identify *teachable moments:* points in development when children are ready and eager to learn particular skills.

Basic principles of Jean Piaget's theory of cognitive development reflect his early interest in biology. Piaget proposes that human beings possess a built-in urge *(equilibration)* to maintain a state of mental balance that is similar to the biological urge to maintain homeostasis. Equilibration is maintained by two basic tendencies: *organization,* the tendency to systematize experiences and ideas; and *adaptation,* the tendency to adjust to the environment. Piaget believes that children transform experiences into knowledge by *assimilating* (incorporating) and *accommodating* (modifying) their conceptions of *schemes* (organized patterns of thought).

Piaget has demonstrated that younger children think in fundamentally different ways than older children or adults. Up until the age of eight, children are called *egocentric* because they assume that everyone else thinks of things as they do. Older children are capable of *socialized* thinking because they realize that others have different conceptions of objects and experiences. Preschool children are at the *preoperational* stage: They are unable to grasp that a substance remains the same even when its appearance is changed *(conservation).* They are incapable of thinking of more than one quality at a time *(decentration),* and they cannot mentally reverse actions *(operation).* Seven- to eleven-year-olds are at the *concrete operations* stage because they can solve problems by mentally reversing actions, but only if objects are actually present or if they have had direct experience with similar situations. Starting at the age of twelve, children become increasingly capable of *formal thought:* They can deal with abstractions and formulate and test hypotheses systematically.

The moral thinking of children is influenced by the same factors that affect problem solving. Up to the age of twelve, children tend to be *moral realists:* They concentrate on consequences, interpret rules in literal ways, and need a specific rule for every situation. Beyond the age of twelve, children think as *moral relativists:* They take into account intentions, are flexible in interpreting rules, and can apply general moral principles to a variety of situations.

Teachers of preschool and elementary grade children can take account of Piaget's description of cognitive development by encouraging and permitting pupils to be active as they learn and to interact with their classmates. Teachers of grades four through nine might allow for the transition from concrete to formal operations by giving pupils plenty of opportunities to explain their thoughts. Secondary school teachers might be prepared for the tendency for burgeoning formal thinkers to engage in unrestrained theorizing. Perhaps the best single guideline for teachers of secondary school students is: Give instruction in problem-solving skills.

Jerome Bruner has proposed a three-stage theory of cognitive development that is similar in many respects to Piaget's four-stage theory. The first stage in Bruner's description is called *enactive* because the child's thinking is based on actions. The second stage is labeled *iconic* because concrete images (icons) are the basis for thinking. The last stage is called *symbolic* because abstract symbols serve as the basis for thinking.

Piaget is convinced that cognitive development takes place because children possess built-in tendencies to learn. Many American psychologists disagree with this assumption because they are convinced that the mind of an infant is a *tabula rasa* (blank slate) and that all learning occurs when stimuli are associated with responses. In the early 1920s John B. Watson urged his fellow American psychologists to function as *behaviorists* by basing their conclusions exclusively on observations of overt behavior. Watson also became convinced that Pavlovian conditioning could be used to shape behavior if stimuli were associated with responses in systematic ways. It turned out that Watson overestimated the potency of Pavlovian conditioning, but B.

F. Skinner later proposed that *operant conditioning*—strengthening the responses of an organism by reinforcement—was the key to behavior control. Skinner urged teachers to supply rewards and to try to shape learning as systematically as possible. Robert R. Sears and Albert Bandura, two other eminent S-R theorists, pointed out that children acquire some types of behavior even without reinforcement. Sears and Bandura demonstrated that children may imitate the behavior of models, particularly when they identify with them.

Although most American psychologists agree with Skinner that behavior is controlled by reinforcement, those who call themselves humanistic psychologists are bothered by the assumption that children must be shaped. Abraham H. Maslow, the leading advocate of this view, argued that children determine much of their own behavior. Maslow was also bothered by extreme interpretations of Freudian theory that pictured children as constantly striving to maintain a tensionless state of adjustment. When Maslow observed healthy children, he became convinced that they enjoy growing and seek new experiences. Instead of urging teachers to be systematic as they shape behavior, Maslow recommends that pupils be given abundant opportunities to make their own choices. At the same time, Maslow urges teachers to do their best to satisfy their pupils' needs for safety, love, belonging, and esteem.

BECOMING A BETTER TEACHER: QUESTIONS AND SUGGESTIONS

The following questions, which are based on points made in the text in sections next to the marginal notes marked Handbook Headings, are intended to be used during your student teaching and your first years of professional teaching. You are urged to use the questions, and the accompanying suggestions, to analyze and improve your teaching effectiveness. The questions and suggestions will probably be of greatest value if you select those most appropriate for the grade level and subjects you expect to teach, record them in your Handbook, and supplement the suggestions offered with ideas of your own. To encourage you to think of your Handbook as a personal guidebook, the questions and suggestions listed here are stated in the form of reminders you might write to yourself.

Ways to Apply
Erikson's Theory
(Preschool and
Kindergarten)

Am I providing plenty of opportunities for younger pupils to develop a sense of autonomy? What else can I do to foster independence? Am I doing my best to minimize the emergence of feelings of doubt or shame? Suggestion: Check on how often I give children ample time to complete something on their own, how often I finish a task *for* a child.

With older pupils, am I making it possible for feelings of initiative and accomplishment to emerge? Do I make pupils feel guilty by imposing unnecessary restrictions or regulations? Suggestion: Keep a record of how much time I spend directing activities, how much time I permit pupils to engage in self-selected activities.

Ways to Apply Erikson's Theory (Elementary Grades)

Am I arranging learning experiences so that pupils can complete assignments successfully and can acquire feelings of genuine accomplishment? What can I do to minimize feelings of inferiority on the part of those who don't do as well as others? Suggestion: Arrange learning situations so that pupils compete against themselves and frequently experience a sense of successful achievement.

Ways to Apply Erikson's Theory (Secondary Grades)

What can I do to foster the development of a sense of identity? Do I take enough personal interest in individual students so that they feel they are being recognized as individuals? Suggestion: Keep a record of the number of times I recognize—say hello to, call on, smile at, talk with—each student in my classes. If I discover I have ignored some students, make it a point to address them by name and comment favorably on their class work.

Is there anything I can do in the courses I teach to help students begin to think about occupational choice? Can I provide specific job skills, or should I concentrate on helping pupils get ready for college, not only by learning subject matter, but by becoming skilled students? Suggestion: Make a list of job skills, academic *and* nonacademic, I can teach in my classes.

Is it appropriate in the courses I teach to encourage analysis of sex roles so that each individual can develop a personal philosophy of how to deal with sex differences? Suggestion: Check to see if it would be appropriate to set up a discussion of male and female attitudes and achievement in the field of study I teach.

Should I explain the concept of psychosocial moratorium to students and point out that there is no reason to panic if they are not positive about occupational choice by the time they graduate? Suggestion: Point out that some of the famous people in almost every field of endeavor floundered around before they settled on that particular career.

How can I be tolerant of students who have chosen a negative identity? What can I do to avoid confirming a student's negative identity by reacting too harshly to impertinent or disruptive behavior? If I really have to put down a troublemaker, do I try to give him or her a chance to do something praiseworthy immediately afterward? Suggestion: Keep a record of what I say, and to whom I say it, when I really criticize students. Then write out some guidelines for doing a more effective, positive job of handling the next incident involving a disruptive student. (Check Chapter 15 for ideas.)

Allowing for Developmental Tasks (Preschool and Kindergarten)

What can I do to help pupils form simple concepts? Am I sure that all my pupils have actually had contact with what I consider to be everyday objects and situations? Am I patient and thorough enough when answering questions? Suggestion: Have an informal question

One of Havighurst's developmental tasks for elementary grade pupils is "learning physical tasks necessary for ordinary games." Some games (such as volleyball) call attention to inept players because the loss of a point can be traced to a particular team member. If you become aware that less skillful players become the center of negative attention, you might urge everyone to play for the fun of it or else switch to games that do not stress individual performance.

EMA/DPI

and answer session at the beginning of a unit—just to find out what pupils know and don't know.

What can I do to help pupils get along with each other? Suggestion: Try to help tactless or abrasive children find ways to be more agreeable and friendly.

How can I induce pupils to trust and admire me as a teacher and begin their educational careers with positive feelings about schooling? Suggestion: Make it a point to notice how pupils admire and look up to me. Then write down ways I might serve as a better model for them to imitate.

Allowing for
Developmental Tasks
(Elementary Grades)

What can I do to help less capable pupils become more skillful at games? Should I avoid games that call too much attention to good and poor performers? Suggestion: Analyze the games I organize to see if they call attention to clumsy or inept participants. If I discover that one team member tends to get blamed for a team loss when certain games are played, switch to games that don't call attention to individual performance.

What can I do to help socially unskilled students develop greater social sensitivity and sophistication? Suggestion: Try to help pupils who seem to antagonize others become aware of the feelings of classmates. Be sure to offer "advice" in a friendly, sympathetic way.

Do I make sure that lessons and curriculum materials do not establish or reinforce sex-role stereotypes? What can I do to prevent the development of the concept that girls are less likely than boys to become successful in many careers? Suggestion: Make sure that at least some books we use depict girls and women engaging in exciting and rewarding occupations.

Allowing for Developmental Tasks (Secondary Grades)

Is it appropriate for me, in the course I teach, to encourage proper habits of health and hygiene and foster acceptance of personal appearance? Suggestion: When making out lesson plans next month, search for legitimate ways to stress health, hygiene, and appearance.

What can I do to help students select an occupation or prepare for further education leading to a career? Suggestion: Describe job opportunities in my field.

Ways to Apply Piaget's Theory (Preschool Through Primary Grades)

Am I remaining aware of the fact that all or most of my pupils may be thinking in preoperational terms, that is, that they tend to think of only one quality at a time and are incapable of mentally reversing actions? What can I do to arrange learning experiences that stress only one thing at a time and also feature physical manipulation of objects rather than mental manipulation of symbols? Suggestion: Ask veteran teachers about teaching materials and techniques that stress manipulation.

What can I do to set up learning experiences so that pupils can learn through their own activities and also explain things to each other? Suggestion: Next week set up some learning centers (tables with books, objects, and instructional material in various areas of study and interest), and invite pupils to make and share discoveries.

How can I avoid having students acquire merely verbal learning, such as memorizing statements that they do not really understand? What can I do to encourage students to concentrate on concepts and ideas they thoroughly comprehend? Suggestion: Give pupils frequent opportunities to explain ideas in their own way.

Should I ask individual pupils to carry out some of the Piaget experiments so that I can determine if they are thinking at the preoperational level and also gain insight into how young children think? Suggestion: Pick out appropriate Piaget experiments that are described in section 3-11 of the Suggestions for Further Study, and obtain and prepare the necessary materials so that I will be equipped to evaluate how my students think.

When confronted by a tattletale or when discussing classroom rules, do I keep in mind that pupils of this age are moral realists and that they need separate rules for different situations and tend to concentrate on consequences rather than intentions? Suggestion: If students get needlessly upset over minor rule infractions, treat the matter lightly; point out that sometimes it is better to change rules slightly, and go on to another topic.

Ways to Apply Piaget's Theory (Secondary Grades)

What can I do to allow for the fact that most pupils shift from concrete to formal thinking around the sixth grade and that they will sometimes think one way, sometimes the other? Should I use some of Piaget's experiments, or class exercises, to estimate how many pupils are capable of formal thinking? Suggestion: Pick out appropriate Piaget experiments that are described in section 3-11 of the Suggestions for Further Study, and obtain and prepare the necessary materials so that I will be equipped to evaluate how my students think.

When students show that they are capable of formal thought, how can I teach problem-solving skills? Suggestion: Make a list of promising ways to teach problem solving after examining the section on that topic in Chapter 9.

Should I avoid presenting far-out hypothetical situations in order to curb the tendency for inexperienced formal thinkers to concentrate more on possibilities than realities? How can I encourage novice theorists to take realities into account? Suggestion: When selecting discussion topics, choose those that require students to deal with actual conditions and realistic problems; avoid those that more or less *force* far-out theorizing.

Ways to Apply Bruner's Theory (Preschool and Primary Grades)

Do I allow for the likelihood that my pupils think in terms of symbols? How can I help students manipulate objects and visualize things? Should I use more demonstrations and activities? Are there ways I can induce students to verbalize their thoughts by having them explain how they try to solve problems? Suggestion: Ask veteran teachers for ideas on how to use objects, symbols, and charts to present lessons on key concepts.

Do I pay enough attention to readiness; that is, do I check periodically to make sure that students are prepared for new learning experiences? If they are not all ready, how can I help those who are not *get* ready? Suggestion: Ask students to describe experiences they have had with objects or topics discussed in texts. If they lack experience with certain things, try to supply it.

Ways to Apply Bruner's Theory (Secondary Grades)

Do I allow for the possibility that younger pupils in this grade span will sometimes think iconically, sometimes symbolically? How can I present lessons so that sometimes I stress visual symbols, sometimes words and other abstractions? Suggestion: Analyze the instructional strategies I plan for each day to make sure I'm using a "mix" of visual, written, and verbal symbols.

If I teach older secondary school students, do I call attention to structure when dealing with complex subjects? What can I do to stress relationships and the organization of knowledge? Suggestion: Do a conscientious job of organizing lesson plans and lectures, and make sure students grasp how points are related.

Ways to Apply S-R
Theory

If pupils frequently engage in undesirable types of behavior, is it because I am inadvertently reinforcing such behavior? Is it possible to trace the causes of types of behavior that are unproductive, extinguish such behavior, and reinforce more productive and preferred forms of behavior? Am I paying enough attention to how what I say and do shapes student behavior? Since my behavior is going to influence student behavior whether I like it or not, can I be more systematic about reinforcing the right kinds of behavior and extinguishing neutral or negative types of behavior? Suggestion: Refer to the discussion of techniques of behavior modification in Chapter 5 and make up a list of guidelines for shaping behavior in positive ways.

Am I working hard enough at being a good model for my students to imitate? What can I do to serve as a better model? Suggestion: Use the ladder scale technique:[6] At the top of a piece of paper describe my conception of an ideal "model teacher." At the bottom record my conception of the worst possible model for pupils to imitate in the classroom. Next, draw a ladder with ten rungs extending from bottom to top. Then indicate which rung I am at now, note the rung I would like to be at a month from now, and list specific things I might do to move up the ladder.

Ways to Apply the
Third Force View

Am I providing sufficient opportunities for pupils to explore things on their own? Even if S-R theorists may argue that I should be efficient when I try to shape student behavior, how can I allow for individuality of expression as I do this? Suggestion: Keep a record of the number of minutes each day I allow students to engage in self-selected study.

What can I do to permit pupils to determine more of their own behavior? Am I giving them a chance to help decide what we will study and how class sessions are organized? Suggestion: The next time we start a new unit, invite class members to offer suggestions.

As I build my students' esteem, how can I make them feel safe and secure and show them that I like them and that they belong in my classroom? Do they act relaxed during class? If not, what can I do to make class sessions less threatening? Do I know the names of all students, and do I take an interest in them as individuals? Do I respond more favorably to attractive, model students, than to unattractive, difficult students? Do I set up lessons so that every pupil can get at least some sense of accomplishment? Suggestion: Make up a list of ways to help pupils feel safe, liked, and successful.

SUGGESTIONS FOR FURTHER STUDY

3-1

Sigmund Freud

Even though his theory is not described in this chapter, Sigmund Freud's speculations influenced the thinking of many of the psychologists discussed. For information about Freudian theory, the best

[6] The ladder scale technique was developed by F. P. Kilpatrick and H. Cantril (1960).

source to consult is *The Life and Work of Sigmund Freud* (1953) by Ernest Jones. Jones was a member of Freud's inner circle of close associates, and his three-volume work is considered to be the definitive biography of Freud. Volume 1, *The Formative Years and the Great Discoveries,* is likely to be of greatest interest to a future teacher. A briefer account of Freud and his theory is offered by Paul Roazen in *Freud and His Followers* (1974).

Several books by Freud himself are available in inexpensive paperback form. Two short volumes that together provide quite complete coverage of his life and theories are *An Autobiographical Study* (1935; paperback edition, 1963) and *An Outline of Psycho-Analysis* (1949). A comprehensive one-volume collection of several of Freud's works is available in *The Basic Writings of Sigmund Freud* (1938), edited and translated by A. A. Brill.

3-2

Erikson's Description of Development

Erik H. Erikson's books are of considerable significance in speculating about development and education. In the first six chapters of *Childhood and Society* (2nd ed., 1963), he describes how studying American Indians and observing patients in treatment led to the development of his Eight Ages of Man (described in Chapter 7). In the final chapters of this book, Erikson analyzes the lives of Hitler and Maxim Gorky with reference to his conception of development. *Identity: Youth and Crisis* (1968) features a revised description of the eight stages of development with emphasis on identity and role confusion. Erikson comments on many aspects of his work in an interview with Richard I. Evans, published under the title *Dialogue with Erik Erikson* (1967).

3-3

Havighurst's Analysis of Developmental Tasks

If you would like to read Robert Havighurst's complete listing and analysis of developmental tasks, look for *Developmental Tasks and Education* (2nd ed., 1952). In this book developmental tasks are grouped by age levels, and educational implications are noted and discussed.

3-4

Piaget's Theory of Cognitive Development

Since Jean Piaget has probably exerted more influence on theoretical discussions of development and on educational practices than any living psychologist, you may wish to find out more about him. Of his own books, you might consult *The Language and Thought of the Child* (1952a), *The Origins of Intelligence in Children* (1952b), and *The Psychology of the Child* (1969), which was written in collaboration with Bärbel Inhelder. An inexpensive paperback that provides a biography of Piaget and an analysis of his work is *Piaget's Theory of Intellectual Development: An Introduction* (1969) by Herbert Ginsburg and Sylvia Opper. Other books about Piaget are *Piaget for Teachers* (1970) by Hans Furth and *Understanding Piaget* (1971) by Mary Pulaski. A brief, highly readable account of Piaget and his theories is David Elkind's "Giant in the Nursery: Jean Piaget," which originally appeared in the May 26, 1968, *New York Times Magazine* and is reprinted in Elkind's *Children and Adolescents: Interpretive Essays on Jean Piaget* (1970).

3-5

Bruner's Observations on Development

The most specific and concise account of Jerome Bruner's description of stages of development appears in Chapter 1 of his *Toward a Theory of Instruction* (1966). The remaining chapters of this book are devoted to discussions of how educators might apply a theory of instruction based on a set of assumptions about development. For an overall view of Bruner's theorizing, examine *Beyond the Information Given* (1973), a collection of his writings edited by Jeremy M. Anglin.

3-6

Watson's Views on Behaviorism

John B. Watson seemed to have a knack for making provocative observations, and his articles and books sometimes outraged his readers. If you would like to sample his style and also learn about his views on behaviorism, perhaps the best book to peruse is *The Ways of Behaviorism* (1928), which is made up of articles originally written for *Harper's* magazine. In Chapter 1 he explains the nature of behaviorism. On pages 57–63 he describes how a child can be conditioned to fear a previously neutral stimulus and then reconditioned to overcome his fear. In the last chapter he explores the question "Can the Adult Change His Personality?" For a more complete and technical discussion, examine *Behaviorism* (1925). The case for the famous claim that he could train any healthy child to become any type of specialist is made in Chapter 5 (p. 82). To discover the kind of child-rearing practices Watson urged parents to use, examine *Psychological Care of Infant and Child* (1926). The introduction acknowledges that behaviorists of that era did not know enough to do a completely satisfactory job of prescribing detailed techniques of child rearing, but it still voices the opinion that parents would do a better job if they made use of principles of behaviorism. Chapter 1 asks parents to consider the question "Isn't it just possible that almost nothing is given in heredity and that practically the whole course of development of the child is due to the way I raise it?" (p. 15) and describes how Watson studied and conditioned infants. Chapter 2 is entitled "The Fears of Children and How to Control Them"; Chapter 3 describes "The Dangers of Too Much Mother Love."

If you are unable to find *Psychological Care of Infant and Child* in your library, you will find excerpts from Chapters 2 and 3 reprinted on pages 232–244 of *The Child* (1965) by William Kessen.

3-7

Skinner on Behaviorism

B. F. Skinner has developed a more sophisticated version of behaviorism than the original conception developed by Watson. The publication of Skinner's *Beyond Freedom and Dignity* (1971) led to almost as much controversy as the appearance of some of Watson's books. *Beyond Freedom and Dignity* appeared in condensed form in the August 1971 issue of *Psychology Today* magazine, and it was widely advertised and offered as a selection by several book clubs. Critical reviews aroused considerable interest, which was intensified by Skinner's numerous television appearances. If you would like to discover for yourself what caused the furor, you are urged to read either the *Psychology Today* condensation or the book itself. Here is an excerpt that summarizes one of Skinner's main points:

In the traditional picture a person perceives the world around him, selects features to be perceived, discriminates among them, judges them good or bad, changes them to make them better (or, if he is careless, worse), and may be held responsible for his action and justly rewarded or punished for its consequences. In the scientific picture a person is a member of a species shaped by evolutionary contingencies of survival, displaying behavioral processes which bring him under the control of the environment in which he lives, and largely under the control of a social environment which he and millions of others like him have constructed and maintained during the evolution of a culture. The direction of the controlling relation is reversed: a person does not act upon the world, the world acts upon him. (1971, p. 211)

Another way to sample Skinner is to read excerpts (particularly the first and last chapters) from *Science and Human Behavior* (1953), his earlier book on behaviorism. The same basic arguments are presented in both books, but some students have reported that the earlier analysis is easier to understand than *Beyond Freedom and Dignity*. Still another way to learn about Skinner's views is to read *About Behaviorism* (1974), which is essentially a reply to critics of *Beyond Freedom and Dignity*, or *The Skinner Primer* (1974) by Finley Carpenter, which interprets Skinner's view as well as the views of his critics.

3-8

Stimulus-Response
Theories

A particularly insightful analysis of stimulus-response theories can be found in Chapters 14, 15 and 16 of Alfred Baldwin's *Theories of Child Development* (1967). Another analysis is offered by Sheldon H. White in "The Learning Theory Tradition and Child Psychology," Chapter 8 of *Carmichael's Manual of Child Psychology* (3rd ed., 1970), edited by Paul H. Mussen (vol. 1, pp. 657–702).

3-9

Social-Learning Theory

Alfred Baldwin offers a concise analysis of social-learning theory in Chapter 15 of *Theories of Child Development* (1967). Albert Bandura and Richard H. Walters explain their interpretation of this version of S-R theory in *Social Learning and Personality Development* (1963). Robert R. Sears gives the rationale for his analyses of child-rearing practices in the first chapter of *Patterns of Child Rearing* (1957), written in collaboration with Eleanor E. Maccoby and Harry Levin. He explains why he studied identification in the first chapter of *Identification and Child Rearing* (1965), written in collaboration with Lucy Rau and Richard Alpert. Albert Bandura summarized his reasons for proposing an alternative to a strict behaviorist interpretation of S-R theory in his presidential address for the 1974 convention of the American Psychological Association. The address, titled "Behavior Theory and the Models of Man," was reprinted in the December 1974 issue of *American Psychologist*. Bandura provides a detailed analysis of how a particular type of behavior is learned in *Aggression: A Social Learning Analysis* (1973).

3-10

Third Force Psychology

Abraham H. Maslow offers observations on third force psychology in *Toward a Psychology of Being* (2nd ed., 1968), the last chapter of which lists forty-three propositions of his view; *Motivation and Personality* (2nd ed., 1970); *The Farther Reaches of Human Nature* (1971); *Religion, Values, and Peak Experiences* (1970); *New Knowledge in Human Values* (1970). A book of Maslow's writings edited by Richard Lowry is *Dominance, Self-Esteem, Self-Actualization: Germinal Papers of A. H. Maslow* (1973).

3-11

Using Piaget's Clinical Method to Assess Cognitive Development

Jean Piaget devised a series of simple experiments to gain insight into the thinking of children at different age levels. You can use similar experiments to determine the level of thinking of pupils in your classes. If you take the trouble to carry out some of the following experiments with at least some of your pupils, you may be surprised by the amount of insight you acquire. You are almost sure to become aware of ways your pupils' thinking differs from yours. In addition, you may understand why some approaches to teaching are—or are not—appropriate with some or all of your students.

The experiments described on the next few pages will help you discover that intellectual development is a gradual and continuous process. Typically, children go through a three-stage process in grasping one of the types of thinking described by Piaget: First, they grasp it only slightly; then they understand it in some but not all situations; and eventually they are able to understand all instances involving that type of thought. Accordingly, it will be a good policy to present pupils with a series of experiments arranged so that they are confronted with some situations they already understand, with some they grasp partially, and with some they only vaguely comprehend. The following experiments are arranged in general order of difficulty. The approximate age and grade levels where you are likely to find children in a transitional state are noted at the beginning of each experiment.

Here are guidelines you might follow for selecting experiments appropriate for different grade levels:

For a kindergarten to second grade child, try Experiments 1, 2, 3, 4, 5, 6, 7, and 8.

For a second to fourth grade child, try Experiments 3, 4, 5, 6, 7, and 8.

For a fourth to sixth grade child, try Experiments 4, 5, 6, 7, 8, 9, and 10.

For a sixth grader and above, try Experiments 6, 7, 8, 9, 10, 11, 12, and 13.

It would be to your advantage to try out these experiments now, instead of waiting until you actually begin to teach. You should be able to carry out all the experiments for any age level in a single interview of not more than thirty minutes (if you have familiarized yourself with the materials ahead of time). If you find you do not have time to do all the experiments listed, select those that strike you as most interesting. You will gain more understanding of the processes involved, however, if you conduct all the experiments in a series.

It is not necessary to have a private testing room. You can interview your subject in a hall, a playground, or a school area that is not in a main traffic zone.

After you complete your experiments, you might record your results and conclusions and compare your findings with those of fellow students who interviewed different children.

The experiments described on the following pages can be carried out with easily obtainable objects. You are urged to acquire a complete kit of materials and to gain experience in trying out these experiments so that you will be prepared to test students in your classes. Listed below are materials you will need. You should be able to obtain most of the items in just one trip to a shopping center or a department, drug, or variety store.

KINDERGARTEN AND PRIMARY GRADES

Twenty small blocks, poker chips, or the equivalent

A small package of plasticene or clay

Two plastic or glass tumblers of identical size and either a glass or plastic bowl, or a tall, thin plastic or glass vase (or tall, thin tumbler)

Four pieces of cardboard about $8\frac{1}{2}$ by 11 inches, or approximately thirty 3-by-5-inch cards

A tray of inexpensive watercolor paints and a brush or a box of crayons or colored pencils

ELEMENTARY GRADES

A small package of plasticene or clay

Two plastic or glass tumblers of identical size

Four pieces of cardboard about $8\frac{1}{2}$ by 11 inches, or approximately thirty 3-by-5-inch cards

A piece of string about six feet long and three fishing weights (or the equivalent): one light, one medium, one heavy

JUNIOR AND SENIOR HIGH SCHOOL

Two plastic or glass tumblers of identical size

Two rubber bands of a size that will go around the tumblers

A rock about the size of an egg and a piece of plasticene or clay the same size as the rock (or any two objects identical in size but noticeably different in weight)

A piece of string about six feet long and three fishing weights (or the equivalent): one light, one medium, one heavy

After you obtain these materials, read the descriptions in the equipment sections of the experiments you will be carrying out. These explain how you can convert your acquisitions into full-fledged experimental apparatus. Place cards and the like in clasp envelopes, and store all your materials in a cardboard box of appropriate size. You will then be equipped with a test kit of your own devising.

If you carry out any of these experiments, record the name, age, grade, and sex of your subject, and try to record as much as you can of what the pupil does and says.

Piaget experiment 1—Classification of objects (spontaneous sorting)

Approximate age and grade level: Five to seven years, kindergarten to second grade

Purpose: To discover how the child classifies things. A child who does not grasp the concept of *class* will put together objects in a haphazard or unsystematic way; one who has partial understanding will group some similar objects, fail to group others. A child who understands the nature of classification will put together similar objects in a consistent way.

Equipment: Take some pieces of cardboard or some index cards, and draw six squares approximately two by two inches and six circles two inches in diameter. Cut along the lines, and then cut two of the squares along a diagonal line from one corner to the opposite (to form four triangles); then cut two of the circles in half. With paint, crayon, or colored pencil, color one of each shape in each of four colors.

Procedure: Place the pieces of cardboard in front of the child, and thoroughly mix them up so that they are in a random order. Then say: *Put together things that are alike—that are the same.*

Describe how the child proceeds (for example, confidently or tentatively) and what she or he does. When the child has finished, point to one group of pieces and ask: *How are these the same?* Record the child's answer.

Note: If you do not believe the child has used the same reasoning in making the other groupings, ask for the explanation for each of these as well. Point to another group of pieces and ask: *How are these the same?* Record the child's answer. Point to still another group of pieces and ask: *How are these the same?* Record the child's answer.

Piaget experiment 2—Classification of objects (directed sorting)

Approximate age and grade level: Five to seven years, kindergarten to second grade

Purpose: To discover how children set about classifying things in terms of prescribed conditions. In Experiment 1, pupils are allowed to make their own decisions about how they will classify. In this experiment, they must classify in terms of stated conditions. Younger children are likely to proceed in trial-and-error fashion, moving the objects as they grope for a solution. Older children will be more inclined to think out the problem before sorting. They may engage in mental trial and error, decide on a plan of attack, and then classify in a confident, efficient manner.

Equipment: Three sets of the objects used in Experiment 1—that is, a square, triangle, circle, and half circle, each shape in three different colors.

Procedure: Place the pieces of cardboard in front of the child, and thoroughly mix them up so they are in a random order. Then say: *I want you to sort all of these pieces* (point to pieces) *into three piles where all the pieces in each pile are the same. Put all the pieces that are the same in one way here* (point to a spot in front of the child), *all the pieces that are the same in another way here* (point to another spot), *and all the pieces that are the same in still another way here* (point to a third spot). *Remember, be sure to use all the pieces.* (In order to meet the conditions you have stated, the child must sort by color, since there are four different shapes but only three colors.)

Describe how the child proceeds and what he or she does.

Piaget experiment 3—Inclusion relations

Approximate age and grade level: Five to seven years, kindergarten to second grade

Purpose: To discover if a child is able to think in terms of wholes and parts at the same time. A child of five or so may not be able to think simultaneously in terms of a large collection and of its subdivisions because of the inability to *decenter*. A child of seven, who is not restricted to limiting attention to just one quality, will be able to think of two properties at once. However, even the older child is likely to have trouble if asked to deal with objects not present because of a tendency to think in concrete terms and the need actually to see the objects in order to be able to decenter.

Equipment: Take twenty-one 3-by-5-inch cards, and draw stylized flowers on them, seven of each. (You might draw simple tulips, daisies, and violets.) With paint, pencils, or crayons color three of each type of flower yellow, two red, and two orange (or use other colors of your choice).

Procedure: Place the cards in front of the child, thoroughly mix them up so they are in a random order, and say: *Let's pretend these are flowers—tulips, daisies, and violets.* Point to one of each as you explain: *Put together flowers that are alike—that are the same.*

Describe how the child proceeds (for example, confidently and quickly, or slowly and hesitantly) and what he or she does.

When the child has finished, ask (pointing to one group of flowers): *How are these the same?* Record the pupil's response.

Note: If the other groupings do not appear to have been made on the same basis, ask for an explanation for each of those as well. Then say: *Suppose a little girl* (or boy, depending on the sex of the subject) *takes all the yellow tulips and makes a bunch of them, or else she makes a*

bunch of all the flowers. Which way does she have a bigger bunch?
Record the child's response.

Then say: *Which will be bigger, a bunch of tulips or one of all the
flowers?* Record the child's response.

Finally say: *Suppose the same girl* (or boy) *had several pieces of
candy: three pieces of gum, two pieces of chocolate, two pieces of
licorice. Would she have more gum or more candy?* Record the child's
response.

Piaget experiment 4—Conservation of number

Approximate age and grade range: Four to seven years, kindergarten
to second grade

Purpose: To discover if the child grasps that the number of objects in a
row remains the same even if the distance between them is changed.
Children of four or so will be unable to decenter and are likely to say
that a longer row has more blocks—even though they can count the
blocks in both rows. Older children will be able to understand that the
number is constant, even when the appearance of the blocks is
changed.

Equipment: Twenty blocks, poker chips, or the equivalent.

Procedure: Place the blocks (or whatever) in front of the child, and
space out eight of the blocks about an inch apart in a row. Place the
remaining blocks in a pile close to the child. Then say: *Can you count
the blocks? How many are there?* Point to the blocks you have
arranged in a row. If the child can't count them accurately, give assistance. Then say: *Now take as many of these blocks as you need to
make the same number.* Give assistance if necessary.

Describe how the child proceeds.

Next, take the blocks in the row nearest you, and space them about
three inches apart. Take those in the other row and space them about
one inch apart. Point to the longer row, and say: *Let's say these are my
blocks.* Point to the short row and say: *And these are your blocks. Do I
have more blocks, or do you have more blocks, or do we have the
same?* Record the child's response.

Then ask: *Why do you think so?* Record the child's response.

Finally, take the blocks that were spaced three inches apart, and move
them so that they are one inch apart, just below the other row. Then
say: *Now, do you have more blocks, or do I have more blocks, or do
we have the same?*

Note the child's response and reactions (surprise, confusion, no outward appearance of being bothered).

Piaget experiment 5—Conservation of space

Approximate age and grade range: Four to seven years, kindergarten
to second grade

Purpose: To discover how the child handles a different situation involving conservation. A child who is able to handle the problem presented in Experiment 4 may encounter difficulty when confronted with the same basic problem presented in a different form. In solving the problem in Experiment 4, the child must grasp the fact that the number of blocks stays the same even though the space between them is changed. In this experiment the child must understand that four blocks placed on pieces of paper of equal size take up the same amount of space, even though they are arranged differently.

Equipment: Eight small blocks, poker chips, or the equivalent; two pieces of paper or cardboard at least 8½ by 11 inches.

Procedure: Place the two pieces of paper in front of the child, and arrange the blocks in a pile to one side. Say: *Let's pretend these are fields owned by two farmers. They are exactly the same size, and both farmers have the same amount of space for their cows to graze in. One farmer decides to build a barn (you might say "silo" if you use poker chips) on his field, and we will make believe this is his barn.* (Take one of the blocks and place it near one corner of one piece of paper.) *The other farmer builds a barn on her field, too.* (Put a block on the other piece of paper in the same position as that on the first.) *Do they still have the same amount of space for their cows to graze in?* Record the child's response.

Then say: *Now let's suppose that both farmers make a lot of money and build three more barns. One farmer builds his barns this way* (place three blocks right next to the block already on one sheet of paper), *the other builds her barns this way* (place three blocks several inches apart at different places on the other piece of paper). *Do they still have the same amount of space for their cows to graze in, or does one farmer have more open land than the other?* Record the child's response.

Then ask: *Why do you think so?* Record the child's response.

Finally, take the blocks that were scattered, and place them together so that both sets of blocks are arranged in exactly the same way on each piece of paper. Then ask: *Now, does each farmer have the same amount of space for cows to graze in, or does one have more open land than the other?*

Note the child's response and reactions.

Piaget experiment 6—Conservation of continuous quantity

Approximate age and grade range: Four to seven years, kindergarten to second grade

Purpose: To discover if a child who can understand conservation of number can also grasp conservation of quantity. A child at the level of concrete operations will be unable to generalize from the block experiment and will solve the following problem only if she or he has had sufficient experience with liquids in glasses of different sizes.

Equipment: Two plastic or glass tumblers of the same size, one plastic or glass bowl or vase (or a tall, thin tumbler).

Procedure: Fill one tumbler about two-thirds full of water; the other about one-third full. Put these down in front of the child and say: *Is there more water in this glass* (point to one) *or this one* (point to the other), *or are they the same?* Record the child's response.

Then pour water from the fuller glass into the emptier one until they are equal and ask: *What about now? Is there more water in this glass* (point to one) *or this glass* (point to the other), *or are they the same?* Record the child's response. (If the child says one has more water, invite him or her to pour liquid back and forth from one glass into the other until satisfied that they are the same.)

Next, pour water from one glass into the bowl (or vase) and ask: *Is there more water in this one* (point to the glass) *or this one* (point to the bowl or vase), *or do they contain the same amount of water?* Record the child's response.

Then ask: *Why do you think so?* Record the child's response.

Finally, pour the water from the bowl or vase back into the glass and ask: *Now is there more water in this glass* (point to one) *or this glass* (point to the other), *or are they the same?* Note the child's response and reactions.

Piaget experiment 7—Conservation of substance

Approximate age and grade range: Five to seven years, kindergarten to second grade

Purpose: To discover if a child understands that the amount of a substance remains the same even though its shape is changed. Children who are unable to decenter will be unable to grasp that the amount stays constant, since they will concentrate on only one quality. Older children will be able to allow for both qualities at once. They will be able to mentally *reverse* the action that changed the shape of the substance, which means they are capable of dealing with *operations*. However, if you ask them to deal with an abstract (not actually present) situation of a similar type, they may experience difficulty, indicating that they are at the level of *concrete* operations.

Equipment: A small amount of plasticene or clay.

Procedure: Take a piece of plasticene or clay, and divide it as equally as possible. Roll the pieces into two balls, and ask the child if he or she thinks the two are the same size. If the pupil says that one is bigger than the other, remove as much as necessary from the larger ball until you get agreement that they are identical. Then take one ball, roll it into a sausage shape, and ask: *Is there more clay here* (point to ball) *or here* (point to sausage), *or do they both have the same amount of clay?* Record the child's response.

Then ask: *Why do you think so?*

Then roll the sausage shape back into a ball and ask: *Is there more*

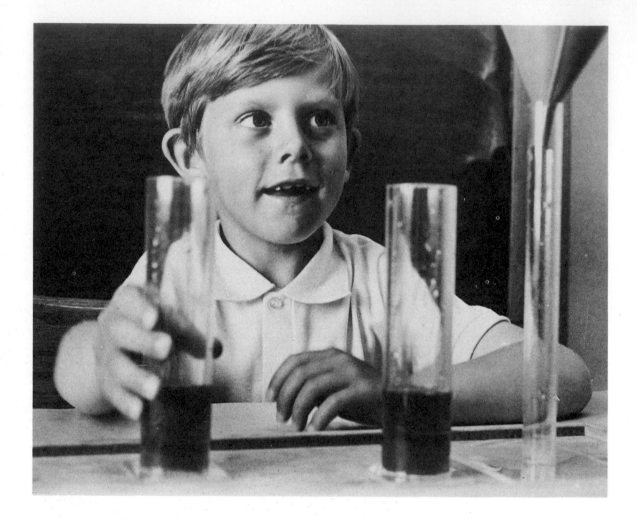

A pupil wrestles with Piaget's conservation problem (described in experiment 6: conservation of continuous quantity).

The New York Times

clay here (point to one ball) *or here* (point to the other ball), *or are they the same?* Note the child's response and reactions.

Next, roll the sausage shape back into a ball and ask the child if the pieces are equal. If she or he says they are not, add or take away clay until the child agrees that they are the same. Then say: *Suppose I put these two pieces on two scales. Would this piece be heavier, or would this piece, or would they both be the same?* Record the child's response.

Then roll one ball into a sausage shape, and ask: *What would happen if I weighed these now? Would this one* (point to ball) *or this one* (point to sausage) *be heavier, or would one be as heavy as the other?* Record the child's response.

Then ask: *Why do you think so?* Record the child's response.

Piaget experiment 8—Conservation of volume (shape)

Approximate age and grade range: Eight to twelve years, second to sixth grade

Purpose: To discover if children understand that equal amounts of a substance will displace the same amount of water even though they are of different shape. Children at the level of concrete operations who are able to handle problems involving conservation of substance are not likely to be able to generalize. They will be able to solve this related problem only if they have had experience with aspects of displacement.

Equipment: Two glasses or plastic tumblers of equal size, two balls of clay or plasticene.

Procedure: Fill the two tumblers about half full of water. Ask the pupil if they appear to have the same amount. If he or she says they do not, pour water back and forth until the pupil agrees that they are equal. Then take two small pieces of clay or plasticene and roll them into balls that appear to be equal in size. (Be sure the pieces are not so large they will cause the water in the glasses to overflow.) Ask the pupil if they appear to be the same size, and if she or he says they do not, take away clay from the larger one until they are equal. Then place the two balls of clay in the glasses, and say: *The water is the same height in each glass, isn't it?*

Then remove both pieces of clay from the glasses, and roll one into a sausage shape. Place the ball next to the sausage, and say: *If I put these back into the glasses, would this one* (point to the ball) *or this one* (point to the sausage) *make the water go up higher, or would they both make the water go up the same amount?* Then record the child's response.

Then ask: *Why do you think so?* Record the response.

Then put the two pieces of clay into the glasses. Note how the child reacts, and if his or her prediction is proven false, ask: *Can you explain why it didn't work out the way you thought it would?* Record the pupil's response.

Piaget experiment 9—Conservation of volume (weight)

Approximate age and grade range: Ten to fourteen years, fourth to tenth grade

Purpose: To discover whether students understand that objects of equal size will displace the same amount of water even though they are of different weights. Students who are able to solve the displacement problem (Experiment 8), where objects equal in size but different in shape are used, may experience difficulty when weight is the key factor. If they are at a transitional point in moving from concrete to formal operations, they will be misled by differences in weight and will not be able to generalize. If they have mastered formal operations (or have had a science class in which displacement was explained), they will be able to discover the key factor in displacement and make an accurate prediction.

Equipment: Two glass or plastic tumblers of equal size, a rock about the size and shape of an egg, a piece of plasticene or clay about the same size as the rock, two rubber bands. (Any two objects equal in size but different in weight may be substituted for the rock and clay.)

Procedure: Fill the two tumblers about half full of water, and put the two rubber bands at the same level as the water. Ask the student if the glasses appear to contain the same amount of water. If she or he says they do not, pour water back and forth until it is agreed they are equal. Then point to the rock and ask the pupil to take the clay and form it into a duplicate of the rock—exactly the same size and shape. When the pupil is satisfied that the two are of equivalent size, ask him or her to pick up one in each hand and gauge the weights of each. Ask: *Which one is heavier, the rock or the clay?*

After the student acknowledges that the rock is heavier, say: *If you were to put the rock into this glass* (point to one of the glasses) *and the clay into this glass* (point to the other), *how far up would each make the water rise? Take these rubber bands* (point to the rubber bands) *and move them to the point where you think the water will go when the rock and the clay are put into it.*

Describe how the student responds (for example, in a puzzled or a confident way) and where the rubber bands are placed.

Next say: *All right, now put the rock and the clay into the glasses.*

Describe the student's reactions when she or he observes how far up the water goes in each glass.

Finally say: *How can you explain why the water went up the same amount even though the rock is heavier than the clay?* Record the student's response.

Piaget experiment 10—Analyzing aspects of formal thought (definitions)

Approximate age and grade range: Ten years and above, fourth grade and above

Purpose: To become aware of the ways children interpret words that stand for abstract concepts.

Procedure: Ask students to write out the Pledge of Allegiance to the Flag. When they finish, ask them to define or explain the words listed below. For each word say: *What does _____ mean?*

> allegiance
>
> republic
>
> indivisible
>
> liberty
>
> justice

For good measure, you might ask the students to define *democracy*.

Piaget experiment 11—Analyzing aspects of formal thought (solving a problem in physical science)

Approximate age and grade range: Twelve years and above, sixth grade and above

Purpose: To discover how students attempt to solve a problem. Children at the level of concrete operations are able to solve problems if they have had actual experience with the kinds of objects and situations involved, but they are unable to handle new and unique situations. In addition, they are likely to approach a problem in a haphazard, unsystematic way. Students at the level of formal operations, on the other hand, can deal with combinations of ideas in a systematic way, propose and test hypotheses, and imagine what might happen in situations they have never before encountered.

Equipment: A piece of string about six feet long and three fishing weights, one small, one medium, and one large. (Any objects of different weights to which a string can be attached may be substituted for the fishing weights.)

Procedure: Take three pieces of string eighteen inches long, and attach one of the weights to the end of each. Pick up the string with the smallest weight and swing it in both these ways: by holding the string at different places and letting the weight drop (when the string is held taut) from different positions and by *pushing* the weight rather than simply letting it fall. Also, call attention to the fact that the strings are equal in length but the weights are different.

Then say: *There are four factors involved here: the length of the string, the difference in weight at the end of the string, the height from which the weight is released, and the force with which the weight is pushed. I want you to figure out which of these factors—or what combination of them—determines how fast the weight swings. Experiment with these pieces of string any way you like, and when you think you have it figured out, tell me what your solution is. Or, if you can, give me your solution without actually handling the strings.*

Describe how the student proceeds.

What solution does the student offer?

Once the solution is given, ask the student to prove it to you. If you detect an oversight, demonstrate the nature of the error and observe the student's reaction. (Note: The *length* of the string is the major determinant of the speed of the swing.)

Piaget experiment 12—Analyzing aspects of formal thought (solving a problem in behavioral science)

Approximate age and grade range: Thirteen years and above, seventh grade and above

Purpose: The problem in the previous exercise involved principles of physical science. Some students may have had courses in science or may have done considerable reading in that subject, which will have given them sufficient background to solve the problem. Accordingly, you may also wish to ask your subjects to wrestle with this *behavioral* science problem.

Procedure: Ask students to explain how they would test this hypothesis: *Because many advertisers make exaggerated claims in their television commercials, the government is beginning to ask them to provide conclusive proof that what they say is true. Suppose a fruit company is planning to use the slogan "An apple a day keeps the*

doctor away." In anticipation of being approached by the government, they ask you to set up an experiment to either prove or disprove
this statement. You have an unlimited budget, and you can proceed
any way you like. How would you go about getting conclusive evidence to prove or disprove the statement "An apple a day keeps the
doctor away"? Tell me all the ideas you get as they come into your
mind.

*Piaget experiment 13—Analyzing aspects of formal thought
(unreality)*

Approximate age and grade range: Thirteen years and above, seventh
grade and above

Purpose: To gain insight into the tendency of students who have
recently mastered formal thought to engage in hypothesizing, which
may center more on possibilities than on realities, and to be somewhat
unrestrained in dealing with abstract and theoretical matters.

Procedure: Ask students to respond to this question: *At the present
time there are between six and eight million unemployed people in
this country. If you had complete power to make laws and establish
and finance programs in this country, how would you try to reduce
unemployment? Tell me all the ideas you come up with as you think
of them.*

Summary of results of Piaget experiments   To gain greater understanding of the implications of Piaget's theory, summarize the results
and conclusions of the Piaget experiments you carried out by noting
examples of behavior that illustrate the points described below. You
are not likely to be able to supply examples for all the types of behavior noted—unless you carried out all the experiments on students of
different ages. Therefore, respond only to questions related to the
levels of thought you observed. Indicate the number of the experiment, and describe the type of behavior observed as specifically as
you can.

What student behavior illustrated the nature of *conservation*, that is,
the child's ability (or inability) to comprehend that a quality stays the
same even though it is changed in appearance?

What student behavior illustrated the nature of an *operation* and of
reversibility, that is, the child's ability to reverse an action or operation mentally?

What student behavior illustrated the transition from *preoperational*
to *concrete operational* thought, that is, partial understanding of
aspects of conservation and reversibility as reflected by tentative or
inconsistent handling of problems involving those factors?

What student behavior illustrated the essence of *concrete operational*
thought, that is, being able to engage in mental manipulations but only
those based on concrete experience?

What student behavior illustrated the transition from *concrete* to *formal* operations, that is, occasional ability to deal with abstractions and hypotheses but primarily in a disorganized, unsystematic, or unrealistic manner?

What student behavior illustrated the essence of *formal* thought, that is, the ability to deal in a systematic way with abstractions, combinations of ideas, or hypothetical situations?

Making a classroom observation to check on Piaget's descriptions of intellectual development   In addition to trying out some of the Piaget experiments described on the preceding pages (or in place of these experiments, if you are unable to find an opportunity to interview students), you might observe in a class at the grade level you expect to teach and look for bits of behavior that illustrate the types of thinking described by Piaget. Use the following outline as a guide, and give a brief description of any behavior you observe that illustrates the points noted.

PREOPERATIONAL STAGE—TWO TO SEVEN YEARS, KINDERGARTEN TO SECOND GRADE

Do you see any indications that the child finds it difficult to comprehend that someone else has a different point of view?

Do you detect any behavior that indicates that a child has a "one-track mind," that is, is unable to decenter and can think of only one thing at a time?

Do you note any examples of an inability to reverse or conserve?

CONCRETE OPERATIONS STAGE—SEVEN TO ELEVEN YEARS, SECOND TO FIFTH GRADE

Do you note any incidents that illustrate growing awareness of the concept that objects stay the same even when altered in some fashion or viewed from a different perspective?

Do you note any examples of a limited ability to generalize, as when a child who can solve a particular problem is unable to handle a slightly different one?

Do you observe any rudimentary attempts to be systematic in solving problems but with incomplete understanding of exactly how to proceed?

FORMAL OPERATIONS STAGE—ELEVEN YEARS AND ABOVE, FIFTH GRADE AND ABOVE

Do you observe any situations where students show their ability to deal with abstractions or imaginary situations or to test hypotheses mentally?

Do you see instances where students are able to handle combinations of ideas and situations by mentally juggling several factors at once?

Do you detect any situations where students seem more intrigued with possibilities than realities or where they engage in theorizing not very closely tied to reality?

Key points

Preschool and kindergarten

Young children have difficulty seeing small objects or print

Shift from parallel to cooperative play between 2 and 5 years

Girls may be conditioned to model selves after housewives

Young children stick to own language rules

Competence promoted by interaction, opportunities, encouragement, appreciation

Competence fostered by models, limits, explanations, warm praise

Primary and elementary grades

Girls taller and heavier from 11 to 14 years

After growth spurt boys have greater strength and endurance

Average age of puberty: Girls—12.5, boys—14

Rigid interpretation of rules in elementary grades

Clinic referrals at a peak from 9 to 15 years

Scholastic and social pressures, impact of puberty may lead to clinic referrals

Girls superior in verbal skills, earn higher grades

Boys superior in mathematical and spatial abilities

Girls have stronger desire to please

Impulsive and reflective thinkers

Analytic and thematic thinkers

Differences in distractability, categorization, divergence, memorization, evaluation

Secondary grades

Primary and secondary sex characteristics appear after puberty

Concern about appearance peaks in ninth grade

Generation gap may be exception rather than rule

Formal thought: Systematic testing of hypotheses

Political thinking becomes more abstract, less authoritarian, more knowledgeable

Chapter 4	# Age-level characteristics

THE THEORIES described in Chapter 3 call attention to many aspects of behavior that are of significance at different stages of development. Other types of behavior of importance to teachers do not fit into any particular theory. These will be described in this chapter. The developmental span is divided into three levels: preschool and kindergarten, primary and elementary grades, secondary grades. Within each of the three major sections of the chapter, physical, social, emotional, and intellectual characteristics are outlined. Under these subheadings specific types of behavior are listed, followed by an analysis of some of the educational implications of each type of behavior.

While it is logical and desirable for you to concentrate on the grade level you expect to teach, you are urged not to ignore the rest of this chapter. One reason for reading about characteristics at all three levels is that even though you expect to teach a particular grade, you may be led by circumstances into teaching younger or older pupils. Another reason for at least examining information about children of all ages is that you may gain awareness of continuities of development and come to realize how some aspects of the behavior of older children were influenced by earlier experiences. Finally, even though a particular type of behavior is discussed at a level where it is considered to be of special significance, it may be important at any age level. The impact on children of authoritative, authoritarian, and permissive child-rearing practices, to note just one example, is discussed in the section on preschool and kindergarten children, but the implications of these different types of control apply to all age levels.

Preschool and kindergarten

Physical characteristics

1. *Preschool children are extremely active. They have good control of their bodies and enjoy activity for its own sake.* Provide plenty of opportunities for the children to run, climb, and jump. Arrange these activities, as much as possible, so that they are under your control. If you follow a policy of complete freedom, you may discover that thirty improvising three- to five-year-olds can be a frightening thing. In your Handbook you might note some specific games and activities you could use to achieve semicontrolled play.

Handbook heading
Active Games

2. *Because of their inclination toward bursts of activity, kindergartners need frequent rest periods. They themselves often don't recognize the need to slow down.* Schedule quiet activities after strenuous ones. Have rest time. Be alert to the possibility that excitement may build up to a riot level if the attention of "catalytic agents" and their followers is not diverted. In your Handbook you might list some signals for calling a halt to a melee (e.g., playing the opening chords of Beethoven's Fifth Symphony on the piano) or for diverting wild action into more or less controlled activity (e.g., marching around the room to a brisk rendition of "The Stars and Stripes Forever").

Handbook heading
Riot-Stopping Signals
and Activities

3. *The children's large muscles are more developed than those that control fingers and hands. Therefore, they may be quite clumsy at, or physically incapable of, such skills as tying shoes and buttoning coats.* Avoid too many finicky activities such as pasting paper chains. Provide big brushes, crayons, and tools. In your Handbook you might note other activities or items of king-size equipment that would be appropriate for the children's level of muscular development.

Handbook heading
Allowing for Large
Muscle Control

Young children have
difficulty seeing small
objects and print

4. *Kindergartners find it difficult to focus their eyes on small objects; therefore, their eye-hand coordination may be imperfect.* If possible, minimize the necessity for the children to look at small things. (Incomplete eye development is the reason for large print in children's books.) Again, avoid too many finicky activities.

5. *Although the children's bodies are flexible and resilient, the bones that protect the brain are still soft.* Be extremely wary of blows to the head in fights between children. If you notice a fight involving such a blow, intervene immediately; warn the class that this is dangerous and explain why.

6. *Although boys are bigger, girls are ahead of boys in practically all other areas of development, especially in fine motor skills, so don't be surprised if boys are clumsier at manipulating small objects.* It may

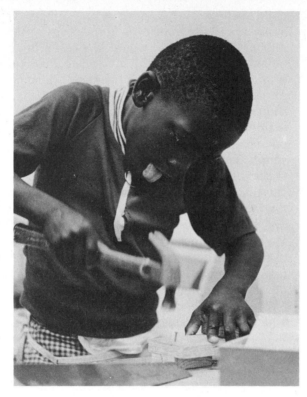

Because of the slow development of the eyes and of muscles controlling the fingers, young children may have difficulty handling small tools. Even when they use a full-size hammer, however, a bit of "body English" and tongue-twisting may come in handy.

Cary Wolinsky/
Stock Boston

be desirable to avoid boy-girl comparisons or competition involving such skills.

7. *Handedness is established in most children, and 90 percent are right-handed.* It is probably unwise to attempt to force a lefty to change. Being right-handed may be more convenient, but it is not that important. Trying to persuade lefties to switch may make them feel odd, guilty, nervous, and upset. The possibility of causing various adjustment problems, such as stuttering, makes the attempt unjustified.

Social characteristics

1. *Most children have one or two best friends, but these friendships may change rapidly. Preschoolers tend to be quite flexible socially; they are usually willing and able to play with most of the other children in the class. Favorite friends tend to be of the same sex, but many friendships between boys and girls develop.* You might make it a habit to notice whether some children seem to lack the ability or confidence to join others. In some cases a child may prefer to be a loner or an observer rather than a participant. But if you sense that a

child really *wants* to get to know others, you might provide some assistance. *Sociometric techniques* are often used to reveal which playmates a shy child would like to get to know. To use sociometric techniques, ask each student to write down (or report orally) the name of the classmate she or he likes best. In some cases you may want to phrase the question more subtly; for example, "Write the name of someone you have fun with" or "Write the name of someone you would like to sit next to." In other cases you could request more than one choice and even negative choices. For most purposes, however, simply asking for the name of the best-liked classmate is most satisfactory, since the task of recording several choices can be a complicated one. Perhaps the simplest and best way to record responses is the *target diagram* (Northway, 1940), illustrated in Figure 4-1.

This diagram is largely self-explanatory. As you see, it focuses attention on the *stars* in the center and the *isolates* outside the circle. If an isolate seems content to be a loner, perhaps you should respect this preference. But in the case of the child who appears eager to join others yet unable to take the first step, you might subtly help by pairing him or her on some activity with the classmate she or he chose when asked to name the child liked best.

Figure 4–1

**Target diagram
showing
sociometric
choices**

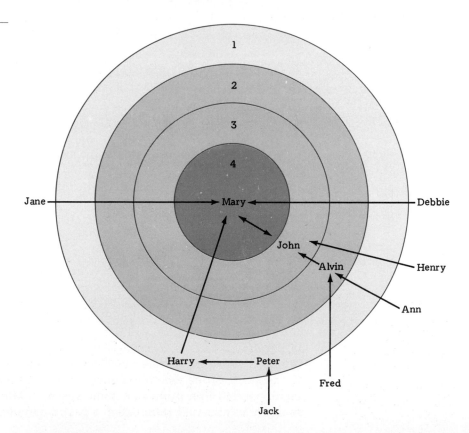

If you would like more information about how to obtain, interpret, and use sociometric techniques, consult *Sociometry in the Classroom* by Norman E. Gronlund or issues of the journal *Sociometry*.

2. *Play groups tend to be small and not too highly organized; hence they change rapidly.* You should not be concerned if children flit constantly from one activity to another. Such behavior is normal for this age group, although it may sometimes drive you wild. You might do some thinking about how much control you will want to exert over your pupils, particularly during free-play periods. At what point does insistence on silence and sedentary activities become justifiable? And should you insist that pupils stick with self-selected activities for a given period of time?

Handbook heading

How Much Control Is
Necessary?

3. *Younger children may play* beside *others; older ones with others.* Mildred Parten (1932) observed the free play of children in a nursery school and noted the types of social behavior they engaged in. Eventually, she was able to write quite precise descriptions of six types of behavior.

Unoccupied behavior—Children do not really play at all. They either stand around and look for a time at others or engage in aimless activities.

Solitary play—Children play alone with toys that are different from those used by other children within speaking distance of them. They make no attempt to interact with others.

Onlooker behavior—Children spend most of their time watching others. They may kibitz and make comments about the play of others, but they do not attempt to join in.

Parallel play—Children play *beside,* but not really with, other children. They use the same toys in close proximity to others, yet in an independent way.

Associative play—Children engage in rather disorganized play with other children. There is no assignment of activities or roles; individual children play in their own ways.

Cooperative play—Children engage in an organized form of play in which leadership and other roles are assigned. The members of the group may cooperate in creating some project, dramatize some situation, or engage in some sort of coordinated enterprise.

Having developed these descriptions, Parten observed a one-minute sample of the behavior of the child selected. At the end of that time, she classified the child's play into one of the six categories. She then repeated this procedure with another child, and so on. Over a period of days she accumulated a record of the type of play engaged

Shift from parallel to
cooperative play
between 2 and 5 years

Handbook heading
Using Time Sampling to
Study Behavior

in, consisting of twenty such samples for each child. An analysis of
these records showed that two-year-olds were most likely to engage in
parallel play (they played *beside,* but not really with, others) but that
older children were more likely to enjoy *associative* or *cooperative*
play (they interacted with others first in somewhat disorganized ways
but eventually engaged in coordinated activities with specifically
assigned roles). This study calls attention to the variety of play activities preschool children engage in, and this knowledge may help you
determine if a child *prefers* solitary play or plays alone because of
shyness or lack of skills for joining in associative or cooperative play.

4. *Quarrels are frequent, but they tend to be of short duration and
quickly forgotten.*   When thirty children are thrown together for the
first time in a restricted environment with a limited number of objects
to be shared, disputes over property rights and similar matters are
inevitable. When possible, it seems preferable to permit the children
to settle these differences on their own and to intervene only if a
quarrel gets out of hand. If you do have to interfere, you might try to
distract the antagonists by suggesting other activities instead of acting
as a referee and forcing a showdown. (Other methods of classroom
control are discussed in Chapter 15.)

Handbook heading
Encouraging Desirable
Forms of Dramatic Play

5. *Preschoolers enjoy dramatic play; most of the plots they invent
stem from their own experiences or TV shows.*   Provide simple
props, perhaps ones that encourage the kinds of plots you consider
desirable. In your Handbook you might note some specific types of
dramatic play you will want to encourage—and *discourage* if you
think there should be restrictions. How do you feel about war games,
for example? Some people argue that games featuring aggression are
desirable because they release tension. Others contend that such
games predispose children to violence and tend to make them unsym-
pathetic to suffering.

6. *Awareness of sex roles begins.*   By the time they enter kindergarten, most children have at least a rudimentary understanding of
behavior once considered appropriate for males and females in our
society. Until recently it was assumed that this behavior was desirable
and should be encouraged, but the policy is now being questioned.
Florence Howe (1971), for example, analyzed teaching materials and
activities used in elementary schools and concluded that boys are
depicted as active, adventurous, self-confident, and ambitious,
whereas girls are represented primarily as homemakers. She argues
Girls may be
conditioned to model
selves after housewives
that starting in kindergarten, girls are conditioned to accept home-
making as their only role and by the end of elementary school the
stereotype is so strong it is difficult to overcome. As a result, girls
dutifully prepare for a role as housewife, only to discover in their

twenties that they want something beyond it. Betty Friedan, in *The Feminine Mystique,* suggests, "A massive attempt must be made by educators and parents . . . to stop girls from growing up wanting to be 'just a housewife' . . . by insisting, with the same attention from childhood on that [is given] to boys, that girls develop the resources of self, goals that will permit them to find their own identity" (1963, p. 351). If you agree with this philosophy, you may want to plan how such a feminine role might be encouraged as soon as children enter school. (Several books you might use for this purpose are listed in suggestion 4-5 at the end of this chapter).

Handbook heading
Avoiding Stereotyped
Sex Roles

Emotional characteristics

1. *Kindergarten children tend to express their emotions freely and openly. Anger outbursts are frequent.*   It is probably desirable to let children at this age level express their feelings openly, at least within broad limits, so that they can recognize and face their emotions. Some kindergarten teachers even urge children to analyze unacceptable bits of behavior. They may say to a child, for example, "Why do you think

you just hit Debbie with the shovel?" You might think ahead about whether you will feel comfortable using this approach. In *Between Parent and Child* (1965) and in *Teacher and Child* (1971), Haim Ginott offers some specific suggestions on how a parent or teacher can help children develop awareness of their feelings. His books may help you work out your own philosophy and techniques for dealing with emotional outbursts.

Suppose, for example, that a boy who was wildly waving his hand to be called on during share-and-tell time later knocks down a block tower made by a girl who monopolized sharing time with a spellbinding story of a kitten rescued by firemen. When you go over to break up the incipient fight, the boy angrily pushes you away. In such a situation Ginott suggests you take the boy to a quiet corner and engage in a dialogue such as this:

You: It looks as if you are unhappy about something, Pete.

Boy: Yes, I am.

You: Are you angry about something that happened this morning?

Boy: Yes.

You: Tell me about it.

Boy: I wanted to tell the class about something at sharing time, and Mary talked for three hours, and you wouldn't let me say anything.

You: And that made you mad at Mary and at me?

Boy: Yes.

You: Well, I can understand why you are disappointed and angry. But, Mary had an exciting story to tell, and we didn't have time for anyone else to tell what they had to say. You can be the very first one to share something tomorrow morning. Now how about doing an easel painting? You always do such interesting paintings.

Ginott suggests that when children are encouraged to analyze their own behavior, they are more likely to become aware of the causes of their feelings. This awareness, in turn, may help them learn to accept and control their feelings.

Anger outbursts are more likely to occur when children are tired, hungry, and/or exposed to too much adult interference (Goodenough, 1931). If you take such conditions into account and try to alleviate them (e.g., by providing a nap or a snack), temper tantrums may be minimized. However, by the time children enter the elementary grades, they should have made a start at learning to control anger themselves. In your Handbook you might jot down any techniques you have observed or can think of that will help children accomplish this goal. If some of the techniques described by Ginott strike you as especially promising guidelines, note these also.

Handbook heading

Helping Pupils
Understand Anger

2. Jealousy among classmates is likely to be fairly common at this age, since kindergarten children have much affection for the teacher and actively seek approval. When there are thirty individuals competing for the affection and attention of just one, some jealousy is inevitable. Try to spread your attention around as equitably as possible; and when you praise particular children, do it in a private or casual way. If a child is given lavish public recognition, it is only natural for the other children to feel resentful. Think back to how you felt about teachers' pets during your own school years. If you have observed or can think of other techniques for minimizing jealousy, jot them down in your Handbook.

Handbook heading
Ways to Avoid Playing Favorites

Intellectual characteristics

1. Kindergartners are quite skillful with language. Most of them like to talk, especially in front of a group. Providing a "sharing time" gives children a natural opportunity for talking, but many will need help in becoming good listeners. Some sort of rotation scheme is usually necessary to divide talking opportunities between the gabby and silent extremes. You might provide activities or experiences for less confident children to talk about, such as a field trip, a book, or a film. In your Handbook you might note some comments to use if pupils start to share the wrong thing (e.g., a vivid account of a fight between their parents) or if they try to "one-up" classmates (e.g., "Your cat may have had five kittens, but *our* cat had a *hundred* kittens"). For titillating topics, for instance, you might say, "There are some things that are private, and it's better not to talk about them to others."

Handbook heading
Handling Sharing

2. Imagination and inventiveness are high at this level. Since most individuals have limited opportunities to be imaginative later in life, you might encourage inventiveness in your pupils as much as possible—in play, storytelling, and painting. However, some children may be so imaginative that they fail to distinguish between reality and make-believe, which can lead to adjustment problems. To handle this without completely squelching imagination, you might encourage children to tell stories during special story times but not during the rest of the day, and you might stress that although making up stories is wonderful, sometimes people must describe *exactly* what happened.

Richard de Mille (1967) observes that sometimes in childhood there seems to be a war between reality and imagination. On the one side are young children letting their imaginations run free. On the other side are adults insisting that reality must be acknowledged. De Mille suggests that since much can be said for either side, parents and teachers should strive to arrange situations so that imagination and reality can coexist. He observes, "Distinctions between reality and imagination are necessary, and it is important that they be learned. But it is also important to teach the distinctions in a way that does not turn off the imagination" (1967, p. 4). In *Put Your Mother on the Ceiling,* he describes thirty games to be played by an adult and a child. The games are built around statements made and questions asked by the adult. The game referred to in the title, for example, starts out with the adult saying, "Mother could climb up a ladder and touch the ceiling, couldn't she? I think so. But could she stand on the ceiling? I never heard of a mother doing that." Then, the adult asks a series of questions intended to encourage the child to imagine that mother *is* standing on the ceiling—and to do all manner of things. The questions are arranged to help the child gradually move from reality to fantasy.

Here is a sample of the kinds of statements the adult is asked to read. (For the sake of brevity, not all of the questions in a particular sequence are included. The / after each question indicates a pause during which the child either silently imagines something or responds verbally.)

"Let us imagine that Mother is standing right there (pointing). / Let's give Mother a hat. What color hat will you give her? / What color dress will you give her? / All right, change the color of her hat. / . . . Change the color of her dress. / Have her go into another room. / . . . Have her riding on an elephant. / . . . Have her riding on a spaceship to the moon. / . . . Have her walking on the bottom of the ocean. / What would you like to have Mother do now? / " (pp. 63–67)

After the child has been given ample time to have Mother do other things, the adult asks, "What was the name of the game we just played?" to signal that fantasy time is over and that it is time to return to the world of reality.

Ideally, the games described by de Mille are to be played with one child at a time, but it is possible to invite several children to participate. For the most part, members of the group are asked to respond silently and to hold up their hands when they have conjured up a response. With some of the questions, though, particularly the open-ended ones at the end of a session, members of the group are asked to exchange ideas. If you will be teaching younger children, you may wish to use the games described in *Put Your Mother on the Ceiling* as the basis for frequently scheduled imagination sessions.

3. *Preschoolers may stick to their own rules in using language.* One of the most intriguing aspects of early language development is the extent to which children stick to their own rules. This tendency is so strong that Roger Brown (1973) has concluded that efforts by parents and teachers to speed up acquisition of correct speech may not always be successful. Evidence to back up this conclusion is provided by an ingenious study by Jean Berko (1958), who found that if four-year-olds are shown pictures and told, for example, "Here is a goose, and here

Handbook heading
Ways to Foster
Imagination

Young children stick to
own language rules

are two geese," and then asked to complete the sentence "There are two _____," most will say "gooses." Further evidence of the degree to which children stick to their own view of language is provided by this conversation (reported by Cazden, 1968), in which a mother attempts to supply subtle instruction:

Child: My teacher holded the baby rabbits and we patted them.

Mother: Did you say your teacher held the baby rabbits?

Child: Yes.

Mother: What did you say she did?

Child: She holded the baby rabbits and we patted them.

Mother: Did you say she held them tightly?

Child: No, she holded them loosely.

You should not be surprised if some preschoolers fail to respond to your efforts to encourage them to use adult forms of grammar.

4. *Competence is encouraged by interaction, interest, opportunities, urging, limits, admiration, and signs of affection.* Studies of young children rated as highly competent (Ainsworth and Wittig, 1972; White and Watts, 1973) lead to the conclusion that those who desire to encourage preschoolers to make the most of their abilities should follow these guidelines:

Handbook heading
Encouraging
Competence

Competence promoted
by interaction,
opportunities,
encouragement,
appreciation

1. Interact with the child often and in a variety of ways.

2. Show interest in what the child does and says.

3. Provide opportunities for the child to investigate and experience many things.

4. Permit and encourage the child to do many things independently.

5. Urge the child to try to achieve mature and skilled types of behavior.

6. Establish firm and consistent limits regarding unacceptable forms of behavior; explain the reasons for these as soon as the child is able to understand; listen to complaints if the child feels the restrictions are too confining; give additional reasons if the limits are still to be maintained as originally stated.

7. Show that the child's achievements are admired and appreciated.

8. Communicate love in a warm and sincere way.

Some of the reasons why such techniques seem to lead to competence in children are revealed by an analysis made by Diana Baumrind (1971) of authoritative, authoritarian, and permissive child-rearing approaches. Baumrind found that parents of competent children were *authoritative.* They had confidence in their abilities as parents and therefore provided a model of competence for their children to imitate. When they established limits and explained reasons for restrictions, they encouraged their children to set standards for themselves and to think about *why* certain procedures should be followed. And because the parents were warm and affectionate, their positive responses were valued by their children as rewards for mature behavior. *Authoritarian* parents, by contrast, made demands and wielded power, but their failure to take into account the child's point of view, coupled with lack of warmth, led to resentment and insecurity on the part of the child. Children of authoritarian parents may do as they are told, but they are likely to do so out of compliance or fear, not out of a desire to earn love or approval. Permissive parents, as defined by Baumrind, were disorganized, inconsistent, and lacked confidence, and their children were likely to imitate such behavior. Furthermore, such parents did not demand much of their children, nor did they discourage immature behavior.

You might refer to these observations on authoritative, authoritarian, and permissive approaches not only when you plan how to encourage competence but also when you think about the kind of classroom atmosphere you hope to establish.

Competence fostered by models, limits, explanations, warm praise

Primary and elementary grades

Physical characteristics

1. *Elementary school children are still extremely active. Because they are frequently required to participate in sedentary pursuits, energy is often released in the form of nervous habits, for example, pencil chewing, fingernail biting, hair twirling, general fidgeting.* You will have to decide what noise and activity level should prevail during work periods. A few teachers insist on absolute quiet, but such a rule can make the children work so hard at remaining quiet to avoid the wrath of the teacher that they cannot devote much effort to their lessons. The majority of teachers allow a certain amount of moving about and talking. Whatever you decide, be on the alert for the point of diminishing returns because of too much or too little restriction.

You may be able to minimize fidgeting if you avoid situations in which your pupils must stay glued to their desks for long periods. Have frequent breaks, and try to work activity into the lessons themselves (e.g , have children go up to the board, bring papers to your desk, move their desks into different formations). In your Handbook you might jot down other techniques for encouraging your pupils to be active while doing classwork.

Handbook heading
Building Activity into Classwork

Elementary grade pupils often find it difficult to sit still for extended periods of time.

Paul Fusco/Magnum

2. Children at the primary grade levels, in particular, still need rest periods; they become fatigued easily as a result of physical and mental exertion. Schedule quiet activities after strenuous ones (e.g., story time after recess or lunch), relaxing activities after periods of mental concentration (e.g., art after reading or spelling).

3. In younger elementary school pupils, large-muscle control is still superior to fine coordination. Many children, especially boys, have difficulty manipulating a pencil. Avoid requiring much writing at one time. If drill periods are too long, skill may deteriorate and the children may develop a negative attitude toward writing or toward school in general.

4. The eyes don't fully accommodate until most children are about eight years old. Consequently, many primary grade pupils may have difficulty focusing on small print or objects. Quite a few children may be far-sighted because of the shallow shape of the eye. Avoid requiring too much reading at one stretch. Be on the alert for signs of eye fatigue (e.g., rubbing the eyes, blinking). Encourage your pupils to read books with large print. When preparing class handouts, be sure to print in large letters or use a primary grade typewriter.

Handbook heading
Avoiding Concentrated
Writing or Reading

5. In the upper elementary grades, fine motor coordination is quite good; therefore, the manipulation of small objects is easy and enjoyable for most children. As a result, arts and crafts and music activities

are popular. Encouraging active participation in drawing, painting, model making, ceramics, and so on is an excellent way to make the most of upper elementary graders' newly developed manipulative skills. Ideally, such activities should center on originality and creativity rather than on copying or assembling prefabricated kits or filling in sections on paint-by-number pictures or the equivalent. You might encourage the playing of musical instruments by holding amateur hours or concerts or by inviting individual pupils to perform during music periods. In your Handbook you might note other activities that would encourage your pupils to use skills in creative ways.

Handbook heading
Encouraging Creative
Expression

6. *At this age children tend to be extreme in their physical activities. They have excellent control of their bodies and develop considerable confidence in their skills, with the result that they often underestimate the danger involved in their more daring exploits. The accident rate is at a peak in the third grade.* You might check on school procedures for handling injuries but also try to prevent reckless play. For example, during recess encourage class participation in "wild" but essentially safe games (e.g., relay races involving stunts) to help the children get devil-may-care tendencies out of their systems. In your Handbook you might list other games to use for this purpose.

Handbook heading
Safe but Strenuous
Games

7. *Bone growth is not yet complete; therefore bones and ligaments can't stand heavy pressure.* If you notice pupils indulging in strenuous tests of strength (e.g., punching each other on the arm until one person can't retaliate), you might suggest that they switch to competition involving coordinated *skills.* Also, in team games encourage rotation of especially tiring positions, for example, the pitching position in baseball.

Girls taller and heavier
from 11 to 14 years

8. *A growth spurt occurs in most girls and starts in early-maturing boys. On the average, girls between the ages of eleven and fourteen are taller and heavier than boys of the same age.* Because girls mature at a more rapid rate than boys, they experience their growth spurt about two years earlier (Tanner, 1970). Some girls begin their spurt as early as seven and one-half years, but the average age is eleven (Maresh, 1964). In a unisex society, the fact that the average eleven-year-old female is taller and heavier than the average male of the same age might not make any difference. But in the prevailing American culture, where differences in sex roles are often recognized (despite the women's liberation movement), the larger size of females between the ages of ten to fourteen may lead to problems. In our society (and most others as well), boys want to engage in activities that permit them to demonstrate their strength and physical prowess. The epitome of "a real boy" in the elementary grades is the disheveled good athlete. (The importance of physical prowess to boys was

emphasized by Paul H. Mussen and Mary Cover Jones [1957], who found that boys who matured early and were physically advanced were more popular and better adjusted than slow-maturing, smaller and weaker boys.)

The stereotyped view of the "ideal girl" of the same age stresses "sugar, and spice, and everything nice." Feminists may dismiss this as a false and treacherous caricature, but many elementary grade girls seem eager to model their behavior on such a conception of femininity. Consequently, a certain amount of anguish may be caused by the temporary sex reversal of physical superiority. The self-concept of a fifth or sixth grade boy who has prided himself on his virility may be rudely shattered if an early-maturing girl in his class suddenly becomes taller than he and sends him to ignominious defeat in ten consecutive games of tetherball. If the girl just described has engaged in fantasies about being demure, petite, and attractive to the opposite sex, however, the taste of victory may quickly sour because of guilt and confusion about her physical superiority over males. If she is a budding feminist, though, she may exult in her victory, but her triumph may be short-lived because her victim is likely to surpass her in size in a few years.

An elementary school girl who prides herself on her athletic ability, particularly when competing with and against boys, may face an adjustment by the time she enters high school. At the present time there is considerable pressure to allow prepubescent females to join males in team sports such as Little League baseball. An eleven-year-old girl athlete who is a fast maturer may be two years ahead of male teammates in physical development and, because of her advanced maturity (coupled with skill), may surpass many boys of the same age in athletic prowess. J. M. Tanner (1972, p. 5) reports that girls until adolescence are equal to boys in strength but that girls between twelve and a half and thirteen and a half, on the average, have larger muscles than boys of the same age. After the growth spurt, however, the muscles in the average boy's body are larger, as are the heart and lungs. Furthermore, the body of the mature male has a greater capacity than that of the female for carrying oxygen to the blood and for neutralizing the chemical products of muscular exercise, such as lactic acid. All these characteristics equip the average male with greater strength and endurance than the average female. A girl who is the star of a Little League team, therefore, is likely to discover that she cannot compete with the best male athletes in high school, which might lead to problems with feelings of self-esteem—unless she adjusts to the idea of being the star of all-girl athletic teams.

After growth spurt boys have greater strength and endurance

If you become aware that pupils are upset about sudden growth (or lack of it), you might try to help them accept the situation by explaining that things will eventually even out after the period of rapid development. To reduce unhappiness due to conflicts between physi-

Handbook heading

Helping Pupils Adjust to the Growth Spurt

cal attributes and sex roles, you might try to persuade pupils that being male or female should not in itself determine what a person does.

9. *Many girls reach puberty. Concern and curiosity about sex are almost universal, especially among girls.* The average age of puberty for girls in the United States is between twelve and thirteen (Tanner, 1970); the range is from nine to sixteen years. For boys the average age of puberty is fourteen years; the range is from eleven to eighteen years. Since sexual maturation involves drastic biological and psychological adjustments, children are concerned and curious. It seems obvious that giving accurate, unemotional answers to questions about sex is desirable. However, for your own protection you should find out about the sex education policy at your school. Some school districts forbid discussion of sex in class even on an informal basis. If no restrictions exist but you yourself feel uncomfortable about leading a discussion, you might make use of one of the many excellent films or pamphlets available. You might also consider asking the school nurse to lead a class discussion.

Average age of puberty: Girls—12.5, boys—14

Social characteristics

1. *At this level children become somewhat more selective in their choice of friends. They are likely to have a more or less permanent best friend and may also pick out a semipermanent "enemy."* You might use sociograms to gain some insight into friendships and then give tentative assistance to children who have difficulty in attracting friends. Also, be on the alert for feuds, which can develop beyond good-natured quarreling.

2. *Children during this age span often like organized games in small groups, but they may be overly concerned with rules or get carried away by team spirit.* Keep in mind that, according to Piaget, children at this age are still *moral realists:* they find it difficult to understand how and why rules should be adjusted to special situations. When you divide a class into teams, you may be amazed at the amount of rivalry that develops (and the noise level generated by screaming participants). One way to reduce both the rivalry and the noise is to encourage the idea that games should be fun. Another technique is to rotate team membership frequently. If you remember or observe any especially good—but not excessively competitive—team games, you might note them in your Handbook.

Rigid interpretation of rules in elementary grades

Handbook heading
Enjoyable Team Games

3. *Quarrels are still frequent. Words are used more often than physical aggression, but many boys (in particular) may indulge in punching, wrestling, and shoving.* Occasional fights are to be expected, but

if certain children, especially the same pair, seem to be involved in one long battle, you should probably try to effect a truce. If you can discover the reason for the animosity, that would, of course, be so. much the better.

If you have observed or can think of some effective techniques for breaking up a fight or for arranging things so that a fight can have a reasonably satisfactory (noninjurious) conclusion, you might jot them down in your Handbook. Consider, for example, how you feel about having two boys settle their differences via a formal, private boxing match complete with overstuffed gloves.

4. *Boys and girls may begin to show different interests, both in schoolwork and in play. The degree of this sex cleavage, as it is sometimes called, varies considerably. In some classes, if the children clearly recognize that different roles have been assigned to boys and girls in our society, a battle of the sexes results.*   To discourage such antagonism, play down comparisons between boys and girls. Eliminate unwelcome boy-girl combinations when possible, for example, by permitting children to choose their own desks.

5. *In the upper elementary grades, the peer group becomes powerful and begins to replace adults as the major source of behavior standards and recognition of achievement.*   During the early school years, parents and teachers set standards of conduct, and most children try to live up to them. By the end of elementary school, however, children may be more eager to impress their friends than to please the teacher. Unfortunately, some children may try to impress their classmates by defying or ignoring the teacher.

As peer groups become more important, children sometimes organize themselves into more or less exclusive, all-boy and all-girl cliques. Generally speaking, these groups operate most actively outside of school. However, occasionally a battle between two groups may lead to trench warfare in class, for example, exchanging venomous notes. If this occurs, a sometimes effective device is to place members of opposing factions on cooperative committees. Such committees will need close supervision, especially during the first few days, but this stratagem may enforce a truce.

Another aspect of group behavior at the elementary level is the tendency to devise what amount to initiation rituals, for example, demonstrations of nerve, such as shoplifting. In some cases, however, such illegal activities simply stem from a desire to get back at authority for placing so many restrictions on behavior. If you encounter thefts in class or a chip-on-the-shoulder attitude, keep in mind the growing independence of children at this grade level and their need for understanding rather than punishment.

Emotional characteristics

1. Children of this age are becoming alert to the feelings of others. Unfortunately, this sometimes permits them to hurt others deeply by attacking a sensitive spot without realizing how devastating their attack is. Occasionally, teasing a particular child who has reacted to a gibe becomes a group pastime. Be on the alert for such situations. If you are able to make a private and personal appeal to the ringleaders you may be able to prevent an escalation of teasing, which may make a tremendous difference in the way the victim feels about school.

2. Primary grade pupils, in particular, are sensitive to criticism and ridicule and may have difficulty adjusting to failure. They need frequent praise and recognition. Because they tend to admire or even worship their teachers, young children may be crushed by criticism. Provide positive reinforcement as frequently as possible, and reserve your negative reactions for nonacademic misbehavior. It is important to avoid ridicule and sarcasm *scrupulously.*

Handbook heading
Avoiding Sarcasm and
Extreme Criticism

3. Many elementary grade children are eager to please the teacher. They like to help, enjoy responsibility, and want to do well in their school work. In some cases, you may become aware that a pupil has a crush on you. The time-honored technique for satisfying the urge to "help" is to assign jobs (e.g., eraser cleaner, wastebasket emptier, paper distributor) on a rotating basis. In your Handbook you might

Since most elementary school pupils eagerly strive to obtain "helping" jobs around the classroom, it is usually wise to arrange a rotating schedule of such jobs.

Anna Kaufman Moon

Handbook heading
Spreading Around
Responsibilities

note other techniques for equal distribution of helping opportunities. (Do you remember, for example, any particular responsibilities you enjoyed as a pupil?)

If you realize that a particular pupil absolutely adores you, an excellent technique to use is to mention your husband or wife, or boy friend or girl friend, thereby revealing that you are already spoken for. However you handle a crush, remember that the child may be completely serious about the infatuation, and you should avoid ridicule or even a humorous treatment of the situation.

4. *In the upper elementary grades, conflict between the group code and adult rules may cause difficulty, including juvenile delinquency.* If you establish classroom control in a fair, consistent manner, head-on collisions between conflicting standards of behavior usually can be avoided. Encouraging children to make suggestions on rules of deportment for the class is one way to achieve a compromise. (Chapter 15 is devoted to a comprehensive analysis of constructive classroom control.)

If severe problems develop despite your efforts, it may help you to know that case histories reveal that "career delinquents" often commit their first serious offense at this age and that a common motive is to gain the approval of the peer group. Theoretically, providing recognition in class for such children might reduce their need to take matters into their own hands.

5. *Behavior disorders are at a peak at the upper elementary grade level, but most children find their own ways to adapt.* An extensive survey (Rosen, Bahn, and Kramer, 1964) of referrals to psychiatric clinics in all parts of the country revealed that the highest referral rates occur during the nine-to-fifteen age span, with peaks at nine and ten and at fourteen and fifteen. The referral rates and peaks varied for males and females: Boys were twice as likely as girls to receive psychiatric treatment; peak referral years for boys were nine and fourteen; peak years for girls were ten and fifteen. The records of psychiatric clinics provide detailed data regarding behavior disorders, but such figures should be interpreted with caution because of the impossibility of making allowance for selective factors of various kinds. The data on referral peaks are supported, however, by teacher evaluations made for an extensive mental health survey of Los Angeles County (1960). Ten- and eleven-year-olds were rated as emotionally disturbed more frequently than those at other age levels.

Several hypotheses have been proposed to account for the high rate of behavior disorders at the upper elementary grade level. E. James Anthony notes, "Among the factors responsible [for high referral rates during the age span of ten to fifteen years] have been men-

Clinic referrals at a
peak from 9 to 15

Scholastic and social pressures, impact of puberty may lead to clinic referrals

tioned scholastic, family, and other social pressures, psychosocial development problems, and variation in adult tolerance of behavior and therefore referral tendency" (1970, p. 681). In regard to the last point, variation in "adult tolerance," it might be reasoned that elementary school students are intellectually mature and sensitive enough to recognize conflicts and pressures but not independent enough to cope with them completely on their own. (A preschool child may be unaware of many problem situations; a high school student may take the initiative in requesting assistance from a school counselor.) Another explanation for the high clinic referral rate between ten and fourteen years is that during these years almost all children experience their growth spurt and many achieve sexual maturity.

Estimates of the prevalence of behavior disorders are difficult to make because of the problem of determining a precise point at which a particular form of behavior becomes "abnormal" or "severe," but a number of surveys have been made. R. Lapouse and M. Monk (1958) carried out intensive interviews with the mothers of a large representative sample of apparently normal six- to twelve-year-olds. They found that mothers reported 80 percent of the children had temper tantrums; approximately half manifested many fears and worries; about one-third had nightmares and bit their nails; and between 10 to 20 percent sucked their thumbs, wet their beds, or showed tics and other physical signs of tension. The researchers concluded that their findings might be interpreted more as an indication of the pressures of meeting the demands of a complex, modern society than as a sign of widespread psychiatric disorders. In another study (Stennett, 1966), data accumulated on a sample of fifteen hundred children between the ages of nine and eleven (a peak period of clinic referrals) led to the estimate that between 5 and 10 percent had "adjustive difficulties" severe enough to warrant professional attention and that 22 percent might be classified as emotionally handicapped.

Jean Walker Macfarlane, Lucile Allen, and Marjorie Honzik (1954) issued a report of behavior problems shown at different age levels by a randomly selected group of one hundred children. During the years from six to twelve the following types of behavior were noted in one-third or more of the cases: overactivity, oversensitiveness, fears, temper tantrums, jealousy, and excessive reserve. At all age levels boys were found to be more likely than girls to show these problems: overactivity, attention demanding, jealousy, competitiveness, lying, selfishness in sharing, temper tantrums, and stealing. Girls were more likely than boys to suck their thumbs; be excessively modest and reserved; fuss about their food; be timid, shy, fearful, oversensitive, somber; and to have mood swings. (The researchers comment that these differences were undoubtedly due to untraceable interactions between biological and cultural factors.)

Even though behavior problems were common, Macfarlane, Allen, and Honzik concluded their report by observing:

May we pay our respects to the adaptive capacity of the human organism, born in a very unfinished and singularly dependent state into a highly complex and not too sensible world. Unless handicapped by inadequate structure and health and impossible and capricious learning situations, he threads his way to some measure of stable and characteristic patterning. We see, even in the raw frequency figures presented in this report, the variety of coping devices he uses for his complex set of tasks. He starts out with overt expression of his needs and feelings and attempts immediate and direct solutions to his problems. Many of his overt and direct problem-solving attempts are not tolerated, so he learns when necessary to side step, to evade, to withdraw, to get hurt feelings and, also, to submit overtly even while his releases and problem-solving continues internally until controls are established. If he is under fairly stable and not too discontinuous pressures and secures enough approval and support to continue his learning and enough freedom to work out his own compromise overt-covert solutions, he becomes, to use the vernacular, "socialized," and even without this optimum combination, he frequently arrives at a stable maturity. When we look at the hazards of the course, we are not sure that we have begun to understand how or why. (1954, pp. 220–221)

Handbook heading
Helping Pupils Adapt

In their observations, Macfarlane, Allen, and Honzik offer some suggestions for helping children adapt: Provide a stable environment. Try to minimize pressures. Supply support and approval. Give freedom for children to work out their own compromises.

Intellectual characteristics

1. *Elementary school pupils are usually eager to recite—whether they know the right answer or not.*   Most children in these grades like to engage in class discussion so much that you may have to control participation by letting children speak up only when called on. Reminders to take turns and be good listeners may be necessary. And even if you are successful in this area, you may feel a bit unsettled to find that a child, after wildly waving her or his hand to be recognized,

Handbook heading
Ways to Handle Wrong Answers

will often supply a hopelessly wrong answer. You may want to develop some phrases that gently and/or humorously indicate that an answer is erroneous or irrelevant. If you can think of some now, you might jot them down in your Handbook.

2. *Concepts of right and wrong begin to develop. Usually these are concerned with specific acts at first and only gradually become generalized. The idea of fairness looms large, and "It's a gyp" is a frequent complaint. The tendency to tattle on others may be part of this whole concern for rules.*   During the elementary grade years, most children move from moral realism to moral relativism (to use Piaget's terms). Moral realists think in rigid, literal terms and may therefore

Some characteristics of classroom recitation

H. V. Baker (1942) took notes on class discussions in second, fourth, and sixth grades and classified each recitation into one of three categories. Here are his results:

Contribution	Grade 2	Grade 4	Grade 6
New topic not obviously related to what any earlier speaker had said	*87%*	*33%*	*23%*
New topic but apparently suggested by something said by a previous contributor	*8%*	*24%*	*33%*
Logical continuation of a topic previously introduced	*5%*	*43%*	*44%*

Source: Table form adapted from Arthur Jersild, Child Psychology, 6th ed., copyright © 1968 (Englewood Cliffs, N.J.: Prentice-Hall, 1968). Data adapted by Jersild from H. V. Baker, Children's Contributions in Elementary School Discussion, Child Development Monographs, no. 29 (New York: Teachers College Press, Teachers College, Columbia University, 1942). Reprinted with permission of Prentice-Hall, Inc., and Teachers College Press.

These results might be offered as support for Piaget's contention that a child moves from egocentric to socialized speech at around the age of seven or eight.

An additional reason for the apparently unrelated contributions of the second graders is their intense desire to recite. Saying something unrelated to what the preceding reciter said might mean that the child wasn't taking into account the topic of the moment. It might also mean that the child's hand had gone up five minutes before, when what she or he wanted to say was relevant but that several other contributors had been recognized first and had nudged the discussion away from the original point. Such an occurrence leaves the reciter with three choices: (1) The reciter can say, "Never mind." (2) The reciter can forget about what he or she was going to say and make a lame effort to say something that is related to what the preceding speaker said. (3) The reciter can go right ahead and say what she or he has spent the last five minutes preparing to say.

The results of the Baker study suggest that older pupils are more likely to resort to the first and second alternatives. But it might be argued that the third also has considerable merit. If you insist that everything said in class recitation be a logical continuation of what was said before, will you be helping or hindering intellectual exploration? As you think over how you might handle "irrelevant" remarks, consider the implications of the three alternatives open to the child.

have difficulty grasping that sometimes there are extenuating circumstances to be taken into account. Moral relativists are better able to understand that it is occasionally necessary to interpret rules to meet special situations, but they may be disturbed when they become aware that not all people abide by even flexible rules. (A child who makes a special effort to be honest and considerate finds it difficult to know how to deal with people who are dishonest and inconsiderate.)

Handbook heading
Encouraging Moral
Relativism

A particularly effective way to assist children in becoming moral relativists is to discuss with them specific acts as they occur. For example, you could have the class talk about the positive things that occurred when a pupil found and returned an object lost by someone else, or you could discuss reasons why children should obey traffic laws when walking or riding bicycles to school. In addition, you might read stories or describe situations to stimulate discussion of common ethical problems children face. Finally, when you are teaching pupils to be considerate and sympathetic as well as honest and fair, always keep in mind the powerful effect of your own example. (More complete suggestions for encouraging moral development are offered in Chapter 7, "The Humanistic View of Learning.")

At these grade levels you may encounter pupils who will make it a point to tell you about incidents of rules being broken. Such behavior may sometimes be due to jealousy or malice, but more often it probably will be a function of cognitive development. If a child calls your attention to the misbehavior of others, and you respond by saying only, "Don't be a tattletale," the child may be hurt and confused. On the other hand, if you thank the child too enthusiastically and then proceed to punish the culprit, you may encourage most members of the class to begin to inform on each other. Perhaps the best policy is to tell an informant that you already are aware of the errant behavior and that you intend to do something about it. Then you might follow up on your statement by talking to the offending parties. You can probably head off a great deal of tattling by explaining why some exceptions are acceptable, by nipping rule breaking in the bud, and by inviting the class to discuss why certain regulations are necessary.

3. *Elementary grade children often are curious about almost everything. Collections of things abound, and a child may suddenly drop one to start another.* Obviously, curiosity is an asset and should be capitalized on. Encourage children to find answers themselves rather than always supplying them, but remember that this can be overdone: A coy "Why don't you find that out for yourself?" will sometimes kill interest.

If a child asks a question you are unable to answer, remember that bluffing is foolish. Your pupils will not expect you to know everything, but they will lose faith in you if you attempt to cover up ignorance. And if a child obviously knows more about a given topic (e.g., birds, flowers, buildings in Washington, D.C.) than you do, the smart thing to do is to encourage his or her contributions and let the class benefit from expert knowledge.

If children flit from one interest to another, this does not necessarily mean they lack mental discipline and should be forced to persevere. At this age children should sample many different activities so that later they can specialize in the ones they like best. If they are forced to stick to something that no longer intrigues them, they may develop such a distaste for it that they will later resist exposing themselves to other hobbies and pursuits. Nevertheless, it is obviously an advantage—if not an actual necessity—for pupils to learn some perseverance. The trick seems to be to encourage students to keep at a job until they do it well without causing them to dislike it by feeling they are being badgered.

Handbook heading
Encouraging
Perseverance

4. *Some elementary grade children may set unrealistically high standards for themselves and tend to be perfectionists. Frequently, the inability to live up to such standards leads to feelings of frustration and guilt.* It is desirable, of course, to encourage children to do their best, but when children set impossibly high standards, they are doomed to fail. One way to help pupils develop realistic goals is to have them start out with simple tasks and work up to difficult ones. In doing so, they not only test their capabilities but also have some experience with success, and the latter makes it easier for them to accept failure when they reach their limits. If you suspect that pressure from home (e.g., in the form of a bribe) is the cause of outlandishly high goals, you, the principal, or the school psychologist might try to reason with the parents.

5. *There are sex differences in specific abilities and in overall academic performance.* Helen L. Bee (1974) and Eleanor L. Maccoby and Carol N. Jacklin (1974) analyzed sex differences in cognitive functioning and found evidence that during the elementary school years girls, on the average, are superior in verbal fluency, spelling, reading, and mathematical computation and that they earn higher grades. Boys, on the average, are superior in mathematical reasoning and in tasks involving understanding of spatial relationships. One possible explanation for boys' superior ability in mathematical reasoning is that they have a greater tendency, on the average, to concentrate on specific aspects of a situation without being confused by background information (Witkin, Dyk, Faterson, Goodenough, and Karp, 1962). Possible explanations for the verbal superiority of females are that girls interact more with their mothers—and therefore engage in more verbal interplay—and that they are more likely to use words than actions to express their needs.

Girls superior in verbal
skills, earn higher
grades

Boys superior in
mathematical and
spatial abilities

Females earn higher grades in school, but males are more likely to achieve at a higher level in many activities later in life. Lois Wladis Hoffman (1972) suggests that the girls' school achievements may be due, in part at least, to their desire to please. Boys, by contrast, appear more interested in working on tasks that interest them and less concerned about earning approval. Because of these tendencies, girls may

Girls have stronger
desire to please

Researchers have reported a consistent tendency for girls to be more eager than boys to earn the approval of teachers.

Terry McKoy

try to earn high grades to get a positive response from parents and teachers and boys may engage in more self-motivated study. If a boy does not find a particular subject interesting, he may not make much of an effort to learn it, which will lead to poorer overall evaluations on report cards. But the tendency for a boy to study something for its own sake may pay off later in life when prolonged self-directed study is called for.

Hoffman speculates that girls may be motivated by a desire to please because they are not encouraged to strive for independence early in life. On the basis of research carried out by Howard Moss (1967), she suggests that mothers tend to think of male infants as sturdy and active and female infants as delicate dolls (despite the fact that female infants are more mature and better able to cope with many forms of stress than are male infants). As a result, mothers overprotect female infants and treat them as dependent, and this process continues throughout childhood. Hoffman also hypothesizes that a girl may find it more difficult to develop autonomy and independence because she identifies more completely with the primary caretaker (almost always the mother) and her first teachers (almost all of whom are women) and also experiences less conflict with them. If you feel that this explanation seems plausible, you might want to try to encourage girls to be independent and to have confidence in their ability to do things on their own.

Handbook heading
Encouraging Girls to Be
Independent

Impulsive and reflective thinkers

6. *Differences in cognitive style become apparent.* In addition to sex differences in general and specific learning abilities, there are also differences in cognitive style that are not related to sex. Jerome Kagan (1964a, 1964b), for instance, found that some children seem to be characteristically *impulsive,* whereas others are characteristically *reflective.* He notes that impulsive children have a fast conceptual tempo; they tend to come forth with the first answer they can think of and are concerned about giving quick responses. Reflective children, on the other hand, take time before they speak; they seem to prefer to evaluate alternative answers and to give correct responses rather than quick ones. Kagan discovered that when tests of reading and of inductive reasoning were administered in the first and second grades, impulsive pupils made more errors than reflective pupils. He also found that impulsiveness is a general trait; it appears early in a person's life and is consistently revealed in a great variety of situations.

Jerome Kagan found that some students are impulsive thinkers who tend to react quickly when asked a question. Other pupils are reflective thinkers who prefer to mull things over before answering.

Charles Harbutt/Magnum

Analytic and thematic
thinkers

Kagan has also described *analytic* and *thematic* styles of conceptualization. He reports that analytic students tend to note details when
exposed to a complex stimulus, whereas thematic students respond to
the pattern as a whole. Kagan found that these styles are just as permanent and generalized as impulsiveness and reflectivity.

Awareness of these varying styles of conceptualization may help
you understand (in part, at any rate) the wide individual differences in
the way your pupils react to different approaches to teaching. An
impulsive boy, for example, may ruin class discussion by blurting out
the first thing that pops into his head, upstaging the reflective types
who are still in the process of formulating more searching answers. To
minimize this possibility, you may want to have an informal rotation
scheme for recitation or sometimes require that everyone sit and think
about a question for two or three minutes before answering.

Samuel Messick (1976) summarizes research on other cognitive
styles. He notes that some students more than others seem to experience things vividly and also are aware of many more aspects of a
situation at a given moment. Some students are more likely than
others to be distracted by conflicting ideas. Other students appear to
place things in broad categories compared to classmates who classify
experiences into many separate categories. Still other pupils seem to
have a tendency to "level" memories by merging similar recollections,
as contrasted with peers who retain distinct recollections of separate
experiences. J. P. Guilford (1967) has concluded that some individuals
appear to be *convergent* thinkers—they respond to what they read and
observe in conventional, typical ways. Others are *divergent*
thinkers—they respond in totally unexpected or idiosyncratic ways.
Some pupils memorize much more easily than others; some are more
capable than others of grasping ideas and evaluating their accuracy or
appropriateness in a particular situation.

These differences in cognitive style first become apparent in the
lower grades, but they continue to influence student reactions
throughout their school careers. The existence of such differences
means that you should expect wide variations in the way individual
pupils react to learning situations. You should also not be surprised if
a student does well in one kind of learning activity but poorly in
another. In some cases, you will probably be well aware of the comparative strengths or weaknesses of pupils in one or more areas of
cognitive functioning. Many times, however, the way cognitive styles
influence pupil performance will be impossible to assess. The surest
way to allow for differences in cognitive styles, therefore, is to present
a variety of instructional activities so that every pupil will occasionally be asked to do school work that happens to fit her or his way of
thinking. (This point will be emphasized again in several later chapters, and specific suggestions for organizing learning experiences for
pupils with different cognitive styles will be outlined.)

Differences in
distractability,
categorization,
divergence,
memorization,
evaluation

Handbook heading
Allowing for
Differences in Cognitive
Style

Secondary grades

Physical characteristics

1. *Most girls complete their growth spurt at the beginning of this period. A boy's growth spurt, however, usually is not completed before the eighth or ninth grade, and it may be precipitous. Some boys add as much as six inches and twenty-five pounds in a single year.*

The accelerated period of growth that begins for some children in the late elementary grades involves almost all pupils in junior high. The variation between individual students is tremendous. Some early-maturing, ninth grade girls look as if they could almost be the mothers of some late-maturing, seventh grade boys.

H. E. Jones (1954) compared peer ratings and the actual behavior of early and late maturers. Early-maturing boys were found to be self-confident and assured and likely to be chosen as leaders. Boys who were immature for their age, however, were not very popular with their peers and often engaged in attention-getting behavior. Presumably, their immaturity prevented them from achieving status through sports, so they seemed driven to make sometimes desperate attempts to gain recognition in other ways. Such antics tended to make their immaturity even more apparent; and when asked to write and interpret stories, they revealed that they suffered from deep feelings of inadequacy and anticipated rejection by their peers later in life (P. H. Mussen and M. C. Jones, 1957). (When the same boys were contacted as adults, the researchers found that many of the early-maturing boys had retained their self-assurance and leadership qualities, but that the late maturers' anxiety about rejection later in life had been exaggerated. They had overcome much of their earlier sense of inadequacy, although they were still regarded as likely to seek the aid and encouragement of others. However, they were rated as more sensitive and insightful than the early-maturing subjects of the study—perhaps because of the anguish they had suffered earlier [M. C. Jones, 1957].)

If you become aware that late-maturing boys in your classes are either driven to seek attention or inclined to brood about their immaturity, you might try to give them extra opportunities to gain status and self-confidence by succeeding in school work or other nonathletic activities.

2. *Puberty is reached by practically all girls and by many boys.* The sex organs (primary sexual characteristics) mature rapidly, and secondary sex characteristics appear: breast development, rounded hips, and the appearance of a waistline in girls, broadening of the shoulders, replacement of fat with muscle tissue in boys. In both sexes, pubic, axillary, facial, and body hair appear; the texture of the skin changes (often with temporary malfunctioning of the oil-producing

Primary and secondary sex characteristics appear after puberty

glands, which leads to acne), and the voice changes. All these changes have a profound impact on the appearance, biological functioning, and psychological adjustment of the young person who is reaching puberty.

The remarks previously made about sex education in the elementary grades apply even more directly to this age group. You should check on school policy and act accordingly. Girls, particularly, need accurate information, since the changes associated with menstruation may produce fear if the process is not understood.

3. *There is likely to be a great deal of concern about appearance. Both boys and girls take pains with their grooming; and what they may lack in finesse, they may make up for in imagination and verve.* The timing of puberty and the development of characteristics signaling sexual maturation are extremely important to both boys and girls for many reasons, but an especially compelling one is concern about appearance, particularly attractiveness to members of the opposite sex. During the elementary school years, children tend to prefer the company of peers of the same sex. If boys and girls do engage in similar activities, such as neighborhood games, they are more likely to judge each other on the basis of skill than any other quality. But the growth spurt, sexual maturity, and the discovery that particular members of the opposite sex arouse feelings never before experienced lead many recently pubescent boys and girls to think seriously for the first time about male-female relationships. A boy who delighted in provoking the girls in his sixth grade class by a well-phrased gibe may strive to win their approval by what he says and does in high school. A girl who treated boys with ill-concealed contempt in the fifth grade may take great pains to make herself appear attractive to them in junior high school. Suddenly, physical appearance becomes extremely important.

Manufacturers and advertising agencies spend millions of dollars doing their best to convince young people that being attractive to the opposite sex is *the* most important aspect of their lives. If you count the number of TV commercials intended to foster this belief or examine ads in magazines catering to interests of young males and females, you will appreciate the extent of the bombardment. These ads may have an especially strong impact on adolescents who have just achieved puberty, partly because such young people are not sophisticated enough to recognize the manipulative techniques being used, partly because they may still dream that their appearance will change. The growth spurt pushes the young person quite far in the direction of ultimate adult appearance, but further changes in face and figure are yet to come. Realizing this, the junior-high-age boy or girl who is less than satisfied with the reflection seen in a mirror may hope that—with a bit of assistance from the beauty aids advertised so alluringly on television and in magazines—a final metamorphosis from ugly duckling to beautiful swan may take place. The older high school student, on the other hand, who has achieved close to final physical maturity, may accept the fact that no further changes are forthcoming and become more fatalistic about appearance. There is still interest in making oneself attractive, in building muscles or taking off fat, and in using beauty aids to enhance appearance, but the older adolescent is more likely to think when gazing into a mirror, "I'll just have to make the best of it." This may account for the studied sloppiness of some older adolescents. If they are dissatisfied with their appearance and recognize that there is little they can do about it, they may try to convince themselves and others that concern about looking attractive is childish or unsophisticated.

Evidence indicating that appearance is of greatest concern to the adolescent at the time puberty is achieved was provided by a study carried out by Arthur Jersild (1952). He asked students from the fourth grade through the college years to write a composition on the theme "What I Dislike About Myself" and then classified their responses under a variety of headings. In the fourth grade, 11 percent of the boys and 16 percent of the girls mentioned physical characteristics and appearance. In the sixth grade, 17 percent of the boys and 31 percent of the girls stressed appearance, which might be explained by the timing of the growth spurt and age of menarche in girls. Concern about appearance reached a peak in the ninth grade when 32 percent of the boys and 53 percent of the girls wrote on that topic. The percentages gradually declined through high school, and by the twelfth grade 10 percent of the boys and 30 percent of the girls concentrated on appearance in their themes. (At all ages, the most frequently mentioned disliked personal qualities were classified by Jersild under the heading: "Personality, character, inner resources, emotional tendencies.")

Additional evidence relating to sex differences and concern about appearance was supplied by Herbert R. Stolz and Lois Meek Stolz (1944), who gave physical examinations every six months during the adolescent years to approximately one hundred boys and girls. During these physicals, Stolz and Stolz noted worries expressed by their subjects. About one-seventh of the boys indicated concern about their physique or lack of muscular growth. Almost 40 percent of the girls, however, expressed concern about their bodies. More than one-fifth of the girls were worried about becoming too tall, and an equal number were dismayed about being too fat. Dissatisfaction was also expressed about facial features, having to wear glasses, and being flat-chested.

Evidence such as this substantiates Erik Erikson's belief that "feeling at home with one's body" is a significant aspect of identity. If appropriate in the courses you teach, you might discuss the desirability of making the most of one's features and also point out that indi-

Concern about
appearance peaks in
ninth grade

viduality in face and figure is to be desired (e.g., try to persuade a tall girl that she should not brood because she is above average in height).

4. *According to Kinsey (1948), the male sex drive is at a peak at the ages of sixteen and seventeen.* A strong sex drive and severely limited opportunities to satisfy it are sources of much concern to many young people. On the one hand, the two most common forms of direct satisfaction, masturbation and premarital intercourse, sometimes evoke disapproval. On the other hand, biological urges are intensified by curiosity and the feeling that one must indulge in sexual activity to be adequate and "normal."

Glandular changes often lead to physical symptoms such as acne, which frequently can be alleviated by improved diet and special medical treatment.

Social characteristics

1. *The peer group becomes the source of general rules of behavior. There is sometimes a conflict between the peer code and the adult code, owing partly to the drastic cultural changes that have taken place over the last twenty-five years, although a generation gap is not inevitable.* Some parents enforce family rules more strictly than other parents, which leads to the "Mary's mother says *she* can go" sort of argument. And since many parents are influenced by such arguments more than they are willing to admit and tend to give in a bit here and there, the ultimate result is that adolescents themselves establish many of the ground rules for social behavior.

In a sense, developing a code of behavior is a groping toward adult independence and therefore is to be desired. You might try to make the most of this movement toward independence by encouraging your students to help develop a set of class rules and by making clear that the test of their readiness for such a privilege is whether they are responsible enough to abide by their decisions.

The term *generation gap* is frequently used to emphasize that rapid cultural change may lead to substantial differences between the views of parents (and older teachers) and those of their adolescent offspring. Although such a gap probably exists in some families (and classrooms), it is not inevitable and may be the exception rather than the rule. Daniel Offer (1969) discovered this when he made a comprehensive study of seventy-three normal adolescent boys and their families. Offer felt that too many conclusions about adolescence were based on extreme cases, and he deliberately chose subjects who were *not* identified as maladjusted. He and his associates conducted six forty-five-minute interviews with each subject over a period of three years, administered projective and other tests, and also interviewed parents.

Handbook heading
Permitting Pupils to
Establish Regulations

Generation gap may be
exception rather than
rule

They found that disagreements with parents reached a peak in the seventh and eighth grades but even at that time were not severe. The boys were most rebellious at twelve and thirteen; they argued with their parents about hair and clothes at thirteen and fourteen and about the car at sixteen. Eighty-eight percent of them felt home discipline was fair, and there were few strong complaints about parents (inconsistent discipline was one of the most common factors mentioned). Offer found that by and large the boys endorsed the same values as their parents. Most parents were pleased with the behavior of their sons, particularly because they felt that pressure on adolescents had increased since their youth. Offer concluded that there was little evidence of parent-child conflict or a generation gap. Apparently, parents recognized cultural changes influencing the behavior of their teen-age sons and adjusted their attitudes accordingly.

Although Offer's results and conclusions may have been significantly influenced by his deliberate choice of "normal" subjects (who might have emphasized their normality because of their awareness that he was a psychiatrist), it does seem reasonable to say that conflict between adults and teen-agers is not inevitable. At the start of your teaching career you will probably be quite close to your students in age and values. The Offer study suggests that even though the age gap separating you and your pupils will steadily increase, you are likely to adjust your values as new cultural trends emerge.

2. *Secondary school students feel a need to conform because they want to feel they belong.* Adolescents often find it reassuring to dress and behave like everyone else because they lack confidence and need tangible evidence that they "belong." To counteract this tendency, you might try to encourage individuality and creative nonconformity in class. You might give open-ended assignments, for example, or merely show a willingness to accept offbeat approaches to problems. The difficulty here is to distinguish between an approach that is different merely for the sake of being different and a genuine expression of individuality. Although giving the student the benefit of the doubt is probably a good idea, you might want to point out that *sometimes* it is necessary to be predictable.

Handbook heading
Encouraging
Individuality

Emotional characteristics

1. *At this age students may be moody and unpredictable—partly because of biological changes associated with sexual maturation and partly because of confusion about identity.* Perhaps the only thing a teacher can do is be consistent in handling the class and treat students as responsible young adults whenever possible. The latter usually involves a certain amount of trial and error—in offering privileges and having them misused—before a satisfactory compromise is reached.

2. *Adolescents tend to be intolerant and opinionated, partly because of lack of self-confidence, partly because of lack of experience as formal thinkers. It is reassuring for them to think that there are absolute answers and that they know them.* In class discussion, stress the importance of considering another person's point of view in order to improve your own ideas—and practice this yourself. Also, remind budding formal thinkers of the importance of taking realities into account. Be on the alert for very pushy, opinionated students who intimidate their classmates so that no one dares to disagree with them.

Handbook heading
Encouraging
Open-mindedness

If you can think of graceful ways to convince such students that allowing others to express their ideas doesn't mean that they have capitulated, you might note them in your Handbook. (Detailed suggestions for leading group discussions will be offered in Chapter 6.)

3. *In searching for a sense of identity and in their efforts to become independent, many adolescents experience moments of confusion, anxiety, and anger. They may express their frustration by turning to drugs or alcohol or by otherwise rejecting established values.* In *Identity: Youth and Crisis,* Erik Erikson offers observations on factors in our society that may push students in unfortunate directions, particularly the tendency, resulting from role confusion, to adopt a negative identity. Kenneth Keniston has provided a different analysis in *The Uncommitted* (1965). This book is based on in-depth analyses of a small group of Harvard undergraduates selected for study because of extreme alienation, that is, an unwillingess to accept the values of our technological society. Many of Keniston's observations were later stressed by Alvin Toffler in *Future Shock* (1970) and Charles Reich in *The Greening of America* (1970). Although the Keniston work is not as superficially titillating as the other two, it discusses the same subjects on a much deeper and more thought-provoking level. He points out that chronic social change (treated at length in *Future Shock*) has led to a generational discontinuity whereby identification with parents is replaced by partial identification with other groups and that many young people thus commit themselves to change itself—a major theme of *The Greening of America*. In commenting on the difficulty of making an occupational decision (as stressed by Erikson), Keniston maintains that the development of our technological society has led to a fragmentation of tasks that forces individuals to become specialists and also to subordinate feelings. Awareness that parents and other adults find it difficult to become involved in such work, which they see as primarily a means for earning money to spend while not working, causes many young people either to postpone occupational decisions as long as possible or to try to avoid them entirely. Those who plan on a career may expect little personal fulfillment; those who avoid one try to postpone binding commitments and seek identity in private experience.

To understand the plight of many young people, Keniston suggests we consider the goals of the alienated. "Though their goals are often confused and inarticulate, they converge on a passionate yearning for openness and immediacy of experience, on an intense desire to create, on a longing to express their conception of the world, and, above all, on a quest for values and commitments that will give their lives coherence" (p. 386). This description is basically similar to what Erikson means by identity. It is also an extremely difficult set of goals to achieve, particularly for students—and teachers. It appears that some aspects of contemporary education seen as major contributing influences to the technology trap make matters worse. In observations (1970) made after the publication of *The Uncommitted,* Keniston offered the hypothesis that academic pursuits have been unsuccessful in helping students to achieve the kind of meaning sought by the alienated and that many have sought it on their own—often through drugs.

Keniston interviewed and observed college students at a time when searching questions were being asked about the values of our society. American involvement in Vietnam led young people, in particular, to question many aspects of American life. Almost any older person in authority—not just governmental figures but teachers as well—was distrusted or discounted. This was also a time when interest in consciousness raising and self-fulfillment was at a peak. Partly to show contempt for rigid authority, partly to seek new experiences, many young people experimented with drugs. They also proclaimed their rejection of the American way of life, with its stress on success and accumulation of material wealth, by joining communes in unprecedented numbers.

In just a few years, many of the attitudes prevalent when Keniston and Reich described their perceptions of alienation and expanded consciousness have substantially changed. The resolution of American involvement in Vietnam, more liberal drug laws, inflation, and unemployment, as well as many other causes, have contributed to an apparent return to many "traditional" values. There are still many young people who experiment with drugs and some who prefer to live an ascetic existence, but a substantial number of contemporary high school students appear to be more concerned about preparing for and finding a job than about psychedelic experiences or communal living. They are also concerned about male-female relationships. Because increasing numbers of young women are eager to establish themselves in careers (instead of becoming "just housewives"), new conceptions of marriage are emerging. This change may lead to greater adjustment difficulties for males than for females, since the husband may no longer be the sole, or even the most successful, wage earner in a family. Because of the availability of birth-control devices, the option of abortion, and the stress on zero population growth, many couples

The increasing tendency for women to do what was formerly "men's work" has many advantages, but it may contribute to role confusion.

Courtesy of AT&T Photo Center

no longer automatically assume they will have children when they get married. Personal fulfillment may be considered more important than raising a family.

For all these reasons, you may find that Erikson's observations on identity are especially relevant today. High school students of this era seem to be especially concerned about developing a satisfactory personal conception of appropriate sex roles and about occupational choice. Therefore, the points made in discussing Erikson's theory in the preceding chapter merit repetition: Whenever appropriate, offer opportunities for high school students to discuss the roles of males and females in contemporary American society. Do everything possible to help adolescents prepare for and think about careers.

Handbook heading

Encouraging Thinking about Sex Roles and Careers

Intellectual characteristics

1. *Secondary school students gradually acquire the capability of engaging in formal thought, but they may not always make use of this capability.* In explaining the nature of the transition from concrete to formal operations in the preceding chapter, the reactions of children to a problem involving a pendulum were described. This simple situation is a prototype of other more complex problems, and the way adolescents try to solve it reveals much about their style of thinking. The younger adolescent is likely to begin by guessing about what might happen and then search for a solution by proceeding in a haphazard trial-and-error manner. The older adolescent is likely first to plot a course of action, then to test hypotheses in a systematic manner by observing and perhaps recording the results of different actions, and finally to draw logical conclusions. Older adolescents are able to take into account how separate qualities might interact and combine. And because they have built up an immense repertoire of schemes, they can bring to bear on a problem a versatile array of techniques and an impressive amount of information. Consequently, they are not likely to have much difficulty accommodating new experiences, which are rarely seen as revolutionary enough to require a substantial revision of their views of things. The blasé statement "So what else is new?" reflects the worldly sophistication of young people who are no longer surprised by unique events.

Even though older adolescents know a great deal and are capable of formal thought, they may not always function as sophisticated formal thinkers. Therefore, if appropriate in the courses you teach, you may wish to provide instruction in problem-solving skills and give your students plenty of opportunities to use them. (Detailed suggestions for doing this are presented in Chapter 9.)

2. *In adolescents, between the ages of twelve and sixteen, political thinking becomes more abstract, liberal, and knowledgeable.* Joseph Adelson (1971, 1972) used an interview approach to obtain information about the development of political thought during the adolescent years. At the start of the interviews, the subjects were requested to imagine that a thousand people ventured to an island in the Pacific for the purpose of establishing a new society. The respondents were then asked to explain how these people might establish a political order, devise a legal system, and deal with other problems of public policy.

The analysis of the interview responses showed no significant sex differences in understanding political concepts and no significant differences attributable to intelligence and social class, although brighter students were better able to deal with abstract ideas and upper-class

Formal thought:
Systematic testing of
hypotheses

students were less likely to be authoritarian. The most striking and consistent finding was the degree to which the political thinking of the adolescent changes in the years between twelve and sixteen. Adelson concluded that the most significant changes were: (1) an increase in the ability to deal with abstractions, (2) a decline in authoritarian views, (3) an increase in political knowledge.

Political thinking becomes more abstract, less authoritarian, more knowledgeable

The increase in the ability to deal with abstractions is a function of the shift from concrete to formal operational thought. When thirteen-year-olds were asked, "What is the purpose of laws?" a typical answer was "So people don't steal or kill" (1972, p. 108). A fifteen- or sixteen-year-old, by contrast, was more likely to say, "To ensure safety and enforce the government" (p. 108). The young adolescent who thinks in concrete terms concentrates on individuals and finds it difficult to take into account society as a whole. When asked about the purpose of laws to require vaccination of children, for example, the twelve-year-old is likely to say it is to prevent sickness in the child who receives the treatment. The fifteen-year-old, who has mastered formal thought, is likely to take into account how it will protect the community at large. Thinking in concrete terms also causes the twelve-year-old to concentrate on the immediate present because of the inability to analyze the significance of past events or project ideas into the future. And as Piaget noted in his comparison of moral realists and relativists, the younger child is not likely to take motives into account. When asked to explain why many prisoners are recidivists, for example, only older adolescents would mention such motives as having a grudge against society. Adelson and his colleagues found that when twelve-year-olds were asked how prisoners should be treated, many of them recommended that they be punished and taught a stern lesson. Adelson speculates that the tendency for younger adolescents to be punitive and authoritarian might be attributed to several factors: preoccupation with wickedness, the inability of the young adolescent to grasp the concept of rights, and the conviction that laws are immutable. By fourteen or fifteen, the adolescents interviewed by Adelson were more likely to consider circumstances and individual rights and to recommend rehabilitation rather than punishment.

If you will be teaching courses in social studies, you may find this information useful in lesson planning. It may also help you understand why your students respond to discussions of political or other abstract matters in different ways.

3. *High school students are engaged in the process of establishing a personal value system. Teachers may participate in this process, but the rights of parents and the students themselves should be acknowledged.* Partly because they have become capable of formal thinking, partly because they are on the verge of becoming independent of their parents, high school students seek to develop their own personal set of

values. It is generally agreed that this is a significant aspect of the process of maturation. One of the goals of education listed by the White House Conference Committee, for example, was "ethical behavior based on a sense of moral and spiritual values." One of the developmental tasks of adolescence is "acquiring a set of values and an ethical system as a guide to behavior" (Havighurst, 1952, p. 62). Even though almost everyone agrees that the development of values is important at this stage of development, there is lack of agreement about exactly what role teachers should play in this process. Many parents, for instance, feel that it is their prerogative to instill values in their children. If they choose to have others participate in this process, they may prefer that clergymen, Boy or Girl Scout leaders, or the equivalent handle the task, rather than classroom teachers who cannot be selected by the parents. Since adolescents are often obliged to make many of their own decisions (about premarital sex, for example, or using drugs), parents may actively resent any attempt on the part of a high school teacher to inculcate attitudes or beliefs. Accordingly, you should avoid any kind of teaching that smacks of indoctrination. Students are a captive audience, and it is unethical and unprofessional for an instructor to take advantage of this situation and force pupils to reflect particular opinions or risk getting a low grade.

Even if you strive to avoid teaching values, you will still influence your students. Some young people in your classes may identify with you and be eager to emulate your behavior and share your beliefs. The *way* you teach may influence attitudes as much as what you teach. Furthermore, you may wish to use techniques (such as values clarification, to be discussed in Chapter 7) to help students become aware of their values. The most important point to remember about the development of values, though, is that it should be a *personal* experience, where adolescents are free to elect or reject points of view in accordance with their own preferences.

4. *Adolescents need to develop feelings of self-esteem, competence, self-definition, and individuality.* In *The Vanishing Adolescent* Edgar Z. Friedenberg offers a conception of adolescence that reflects points emphasized also by Robert Havighurst and Erik Erikson. He suggests that the central developmental task of adolescence is self-definition and that the major factor leading to self-definition is the development of competence. Friedenberg observes, "In a world as empirical as ours, a youngster who does not know what he is good *at* will not be sure what he is good *for;* he must know what he can do in order to know who he is" (1959, p. 17). He suggests that schools place greater emphasis on intellectual competence, and he points out.

Handbook heading
Encouraging
Competence

It is essential, however, that the adolescent think of this competence as his own and make it his own. The school must bring itself to recognize and respect a far wider variety of competence than it now does; more particularly, it must learn to accept the student's pride in his own distinction as well as to cultivate his participation in the things it thinks are important. (p. 143)

You will find suggestions for helping students become competent in individual ways in most of the remaining chapters of this book.

SUMMARY OF KEY POINTS

Young children have difficulty focusing their eyes on small objects or print, a fact that kindergarten teachers should keep in mind when arranging lessons and activities. Two-year-olds tend to play beside others (parallel play), while five-year-olds are more likely to play with others (associative or cooperative play). Because even three-year-olds are aware of physical differences between the sexes, preschool teachers might begin to take steps to prevent girls from modeling their behavior after that of a stereotyped conception of a housewife.

A number of investigators have analyzed techniques of care used by parents of children rated as highly competent. Teachers who wish to encourage competence in preschool pupils might use techniques similar to those practiced by effective parents: strive to interact with children often, provide opportunities for them to investigate and experience many things, encourage them to do things independently, show appreciation for accomplishments. It has been suggested that parents who use such techniques encourage competence in their children because they serve as models of competence to be imitated. When they establish limits and explain reasons for restrictions, effective parents encourage children to set standards for themselves and to think about why certain procedures should be followed. Because effective parents are warm and affectionate, positive responses are highly valued by their children.

Toward the end of the elementary school years, a growth spurt occurs in most children. Because girls mature at a more rapid rate than boys, they experience their spurt earlier, and are taller and heavier than boys, on the average, from eleven to fourteen years. Up until puberty, boys and girls are approximately equal in strength, but after the growth spurt, boys, on the average, have greater strength and endurance than girls. The average age of puberty for girls is 12.5 years, for boys it is 14.

Up to the fifth or sixth grade, elementary school pupils tend to be moral realists who interpret rules in rigid ways. Around the age of twelve, children begin to think as moral relativists: They are flexible in interpreting rules and take into account circumstances.

Older elementary school and junior high school pupils appear to be more likely to suffer adjustment problems than children of any other age and grade levels—the highest referral rates to psychiatric clinics occur between nine and fifteen. Children of this age may experience behavior disorders severe enough to merit referral to a clinic because of scholastic and social pressures, and because of physiological and psychological problems associated with changes due to puberty.

Analyses of grades and achievement test scores reveal that girls are superior in verbal skills and earn higher grades, on the average, while boys are superior, on the average, in mathematical and spatial abilities. One explanation for the higher overall achievement of girls is that they are more eager than boys to please adults. Other differences in pupil performance are not a function of sex differences, but of cognitive style. Some children are impulsive thinkers, others are reflective. Some are analytic thinkers, others are thematic. There are also variations among students in distractability, categorization, divergence, memorization, and evaluation.

During the secondary school years almost all students achieve puberty. At the time of sexual maturity primary and secondary sex characteristics appear, which have a profound impact on appearance, biological functioning, and psychological adjustment. Young people in the process of achieving maturity are understandably preoccupied with appearance, with ninth graders expressing peak concern about how they appear to others.

There is a popular belief that a generation gap exists between most adolescents and their parents, but this may be the exception rather than the rule because many parents seem to revise their values as new trends emerge.

Older secondary school students are capable of formal thought. They can deal with abstractions, state hypotheses, and test them systematically. They are quite sophisticated thinkers, as revealed by changes in political thinking that take place between the ages of twelve to sixteen. During that span of time, adolescents show an increasing ability to deal with abstractions, a decline in authoritarian views, and a substantial increase in political knowledge.

BECOMING A BETTER TEACHER: QUESTIONS AND SUGGESTIONS

Active Games

Preschool and kindergarten[1]
What games and exercises can I use to permit pupils to be active in

---

[1] An excellent book describing many techniques for teaching preschoolers is *Teachers of Young Children* (2nd ed., 1975) by Robert D. Hess and Doreen J. Croft. An accompa-

reasonably controlled ways? Suggestion: Ask veteran teachers for energetic but safe game ideas.

Riot-stopping Signals and Activities

What signals can I use to gain immediate attention, even when the noise and activity level is excessively high? What activities and games can I use to calm down pupils when they begin to get carried away? Suggestions: Pick out some piano chords to use as an "Attention!" signal. Select two or three calming activities to use.

Allowing for Large-Muscle Control

Am I requiring pupils to spend too much time working at finicky activities? Are the pencils, crayons, brushes, and tools in the classroom large enough, or do pupils seem to have difficulty manipulating them? Suggestion: Make an inventory of objects that are held in the hand and see if some seem hard for children to manipulate.

Using Sociometric Techniques

Should I use sociometric techniques to become more aware of isolates? Should I try to help isolates develop skill and confidence in social situations by pairing them with popular children? Suggestion: Make lists of children I think are popular and those I think are isolates. Then ask children, individually, to tell me whom they like best, and compare the sociometric responses to my predictions.

How Much Control Is Necessary?

Am I exerting too much control over my pupils? If I keep insisting on quiet play, am I doing it primarily for my own convenience? Should I stipulate that once a child gets out some blocks, finger paints, or the equivalent, he or she must play with these materials for at least a specified period of time? How can I help children become conscientious about cleaning up after they have engaged in activities that involve equipment? Suggestion: Keep a record of the amount of time pupils spend in particular self-selected activities, and note what they do when they switch from one activity to another.

Using Time Sampling to Study Behavior

Can I use the time-sampling technique to obtain information that may help me understand pupil behavior or plan learning activities? Should I obtain samples of social behavior, leadership behavior, quarrels, favorite activities, games? Suggestion: Carry out a time-sampling study of activities children engage in during free play. Perhaps use the results to plan rotation schemes or additional activities.

Encouraging Desirable Forms of Dramatic Play

If pupils show a preference for war or gangster games, should I try to divert their attention to other activities? What kind of dramatic play should I encourage? Should I collect props and costumes to encourage students to engage in preferred forms of dramatic play? Suggestion: Make a list of props and costumes likely to lead to desirable forms of dramatic play.

Avoiding Stereotyped Sex Roles

Are there books in our classroom library that depict girls or older females as weak and submissive and destined to become only house-

nying *Activities Handbook* provides detailed instructions for arranging all kinds of learning experiences.

wives? If so, should I dispose of them? Are there plenty of books that depict females engaging in a wide variety of careers? If girls in the class persist in playing house, should I try to encourage them to engage in other activities? Suggestion: Carry out a time-sampling study to determine the proportion of girls and boys who engage in sex-stereotyped activities (e.g., girls playing with dolls).

Helping Pupils Understand Anger	The last time a pupil became angry about something or hit someone, or the like, did I simply intervene and punish, or did I try to help the child understand the behavior? Should I use Ginott's technique of taking the child aside and asking questions intended to help him or her realize why the anger outburst occurred, and, if possible, should I suggest less destructive ways of letting off steam? Suggestion: Make a resolution to try Ginott's technique the next time I deal with an angry child.
Ways to Avoid Playing Favorites	Am I reacting more positively to some pupils than others and inadvertently causing jealousy and resentment? Do I respond more favorably to attractive, obedient pupils who show that they like me and less favorably to unattractive, trouble-making, or indifferent pupils? What can I do to be more positive to pupils I find difficult to like? Should I make a systematic effort to spread my smiles and praise around more equitably so that all pupils get approximately the same number of positive reactions? Suggestion: Keep a record of the number of times I respond positively to each child in the class. If some children don't have a check mark opposite their names after one week, make sure they do by the end of the next week.
Handling Sharing	Do all pupils get to participate in sharing? If not, how can I encourage shy children to gain some experience talking in front of others? Am I prepared in case someone starts to share the wrong thing? Suggestion: Keep a record of sharing participation: who speaks up, what they say, how long they talk, how confident they are.
Ways to Foster Imagination	How can I teach distinctions between reality and imagination in a way that does not turn off the imaginative? Suggestion: Get hold of a copy of Richard de Mille's *Put Your Mother on the Ceiling,* and try out one of the games.
Encouraging Competence	Am I using techniques likely to lead my pupils to develop feelings of competence and self-confidence? How often and successfully do I:

Interact with individual pupils?

Show interest in what children say and do?

Permit and encourage independence?

Urge pupils to strive for more mature and skilled ways of doing things?

Establish firm and consistent limits?

Explain why restrictions are necessary?

Show pupils that their achievements are admired and appreciated?

Communicate sincere affection?

Serve as a model of competence?

Suggestion: List these points on a sheet of paper, and try to keep a tally of the number of times I behave in the way described. Then concentrate on one or two points and make a deliberate effort to do a better job of using that type of behavior.

Primary and elementary grades

Building Activity into Classwork

Am I forcing students to sit still too long? What can I do to give pupils legitimate reasons for moving around as they learn? Suggestion: Keep a record of the amount of "seat time" pupils have to put in before they are given the chance to move around.

Avoiding Concentrated Reading or Writing

Am I asking pupils to engage in too much writing or reading at a stretch? Do children seem to get restless, tired, or sloppy after a few minutes of writing? Am I conscientious about presenting printed material in large-size letters? Suggestion: Ask pupils to help me decide how long they should work on reading and writing.

Encouraging Creative Expression

Do I give my pupils chances to engage in art and craft activities and to display their work? How can I encourage pupils to work at original craft and art projects? Are there ways I can encourage students to sing, act, dance, or play an instrument if they want to do so before an audience? Suggestion: Consider setting up a Friday afternoon amateur hour.

Safe But Strenuous Games

Am I encouraging pupils to engage in safe but strenuous games during recess? When I am on playground duty, do I remain alert for reckless play? Have I found out the procedure to follow if a child is injured? Suggestion: Keep a time-sampling record of recess activities.

Helping Pupils Adjust to the Growth Spurt

Do any pupils seem to be upset about the timing of the growth spurt—fast-maturing girls or slow-maturing boys, in particular? Is there anything I can do to help them adjust (e.g., explain about the spurt; point out that things will eventually even out; urge them to engage in activities that do not depend on size or strength)? Suggestion: Pick out the three most mature and three least mature girls and boys, and check to see if they seem bothered by their atypical maturity or immaturity.

Enjoyable Team Games

At recess time do students engage in frequent arguments about rules? If so, what team games might be used to arouse interest but minimize quarrels? Should I ask pupils for their favorite games or consult books describing team games of various kinds? Should I find out what teachers of other grades do during recess in order to avoid duplication of recess activities? Suggestion: Ask the class to suggest games they would like to play.

Handling Feuds and Fights	Am I alert for the possibility of feuds in the classroom? If I discover that some pupils seem to delight in antagonizing each other, what can I do to effect a truce? Have I thought about how to handle an honest-to-goodness fight? Suggestion: Keep a record of arguments and fights. If some pupils get into an excessive number of altercations, try to persuade them to find other ways to let off steam.
Minimizing Competition Between the Sexes	Am I unwittingly causing boys versus girls competition in the way I present lessons or organize activities? If the pupils have started to engage in a battle of the sexes on their own, how can I stop it? Suggestion: Set up class activities to encourage, but not force, girls and boys to work together.
Avoiding Sarcasm and Extreme Criticism	Do I tend to use sarcasm with pupils who may take what I say too literally? Have I recently been excessively critical of individual pupils or the entire class? Have I ever ridiculed or publicly humiliated a pupil? If so, what can I do to prevent myself from engaging in such activities in the future? Suggestions: At the end of each day analyze all extreme or critical statements I have made. If I can't remember all critical remarks, make it a policy to write them down. Ask myself if my anger was justified. Try to remember how the victim (or victims) reacted.
Spreading Around Responsibilities	Do I use a fair rotation scheme so that all pupils—not just favorites—get a chance to handle enjoyable responsibilities? Do I give pupils enough chances to help out? What other classroom responsibilities can I add to those already assigned? Suggestion: Ask the class to suggest ways to spread around enjoyable responsibilities.
Helping Pupils Adapt	Am I reducing the likelihood that behavior disorders will develop by providing a stable classroom environment? Am I putting my pupils under unnecessary pressure in any way? Do I supply support and approval for all pupils in the class? Do I give students a chance to find their own solutions to conflict situations? Suggestion: Make a list of ways to make the classroom environment more stable and relaxed. Ask pupils to write a brief description of "Things We Do in Class That Make Me Tense and Nervous." Analyze their responses, and then ask them to suggest ways to reduce tension and anxiety.
Ways to Handle Wrong Answers	Have I used an effective technique recently for handling hopelessly wrong answers? If not, what should I say the next time this occurs? Suggestion: Ask veteran teachers how they handle wrong answers.
Encouraging Moral Relativism	Am I helping my students understand why rules are necessary? Do I encourage them to talk about what might happen—to others as well as themselves—if they ignore rules and laws (e.g., riding their bicycles on the wrong side of the street or in a reckless manner)? Do I take advantage of object lessons that occur spontaneously? Am I setting the best possible example as an honest, considerate, thoughtful person? How should I handle a tattletale? Suggestion: Pick out a type of "illegal" or

inconsiderate behavior (such as parking bicycles in front of doors instead of in the racks), and ask the class to discuss why having rules helps people become aware of the rights and safety of others.

Encouraging Perseverance

How can I help students develop perseverance without nagging them excessively? Should I arrange what is to be learned into a series of short assignments? Suggestion: Urge pupils to set goals for themselves and gradually increase the amount of time and effort they spend working toward these goals.

Encouraging Girls to Be Independent

Am I treating girls as if they are more delicate and need more protection than boys? Is there anything I can do to encourage girls to be more independent and less eager to win my approval? Suggestion: Keep a record of how I treat boys and girls and how often they ask for my approval.

Allowing for Differences in Cognitive Style

What can I do to allow for differences in cognitive style? Suggestion: Follow the procedure described in Suggestions for Further Study, section 4-6, Becoming Aware of Differences in Cognitive Style.

Permitting Students to Establish Regulations

What can I do to be a democratic rather than a dictatorial leader? Suggestion: Make it a point to invite students to participate in making decisions about class regulations, assignments, and topics.

Secondary grades

Encouraging Individuality

How can I give students more opportunities to express their individuality? Suggestions: Allow freedom of choice when making assignments. Award bonus points for projects that are judged high in originality. Perhaps ask the class to select the most original project submitted as part of some assignment by voting on an unannounced, secret ballot.

Encouraging Open-mindedness

How can I encourage students, particularly those who are especially pushy, to be tolerant of the opinions of others? Suggestion: Before discussions begin, make the point that we can't improve our own thinking unless we listen to ideas proposed by others. At the end of a discussion, call attention to the ways separate ideas can be combined to produce a conclusion that is superior to any single view expressed.

Encouraging Thinking About Sex Roles and Careers

How can I help adolescents develop a sense of identity by thinking about sex roles and careers? Suggestion: Describe and ask the class to discuss how attitudes have changed toward female participation in careers associated with the subject I teach. Encourage students to think and write about what they intend to do after they graduate from high school.

Encouraging Competence

What can I do to help students develop areas of competence that they feel are due to their own efforts? Suggestion: Don't base grades entirely on work I assign. Give students opportunities to develop skills and earn grades by engaging in self-selected study.

SUGGESTIONS FOR FURTHER STUDY

4-1
Developmental
Psychology

The selected coverage of developmental psychology outlined in this chapter barely skims the surface of a highly complex field. If you would like to become more knowledgeable about what has been discovered about development, you might take a course in developmental psychology. Or read a text in this field. There should be dozens of such books in your library. Titles you might look for include *Child Development: An Introduction* (1976) by Robert F. Biehler, *Child Development and Personality* (4th ed., 1974) by Paul Mussen, John Conger, and Jerome Kagan, or *Childhood and Personality* (3rd ed., 1973) by L. Joseph Stone and Joseph Church. An excellent text on adolescent development is *Adolescence and Youth: Psychological Development in a Changing World* (2nd ed., 1977) by John Janeway Conger.

4-2
Time Sampling

Observing social behavior can be quite fascinating; and if you would like to make a systematic record of some aspect of interactions between children, the time-sampling technique is easy and enjoyable. One way to proceed is to use Parten's classifications of the social behavior of nursery school children. (For details of her descriptions and techniques, see her article "Social Participation Among Preschool Children," *Journal of Abnormal and Social Psychology,* 1932, 27, 243–269.) Or select some form of behavior that is of interest (e.g., elementary school playground interaction, high school between-class behavior). To develop your own list of observational categories, simply observe children of the age you have selected as they engage in a particular type of behavior, and write down what they do. Eventually, you should be able to describe five or so categories that cover most aspects of their behavior. At that point, pick out a pupil to observe for ten seconds. At the end of that time, put a check mark in the appropriate column opposite the pupil's name. Then select another pupil, observe him or her for ten seconds, record the behavior, and so on. If you sample behavior on several different occasions, you will have a record of the types of behavior engaged in by different pupils. Parten's technique is just one of many types of time sampling. A summary of several variations of the basic technique is presented on pages 92–104 of "Observational Child Study" by Herbert F. Wright, Chapter 3 in *Handbook of Research Methods in Child Development* (1960), edited by Paul H. Mussen.

4-3
New Views of the
Feminine Role

The traditional family roles of woman as mother and housewife and man as breadwinner have been questioned more in the last ten years than in any time in history. If you would like to become acquainted with the views of the women's movement as background for deciding what you consider appropriate roles for males and females in contemporary society, these books and articles are recommended: *The Second Sex* (1952) by Simone de Beauvoir; *The Feminine Mystique* (1963) by Betty Friedan; *Occupation: Housewife* (1971) by Helena Z.

Lopata; *Woman's Place* (1970) by Cynthia Fuchs Epstein; *Psychology of Women: A Study of Bio-Cultural Conflicts* (1971) by Judith M. Bardwick.

4-4
Sex-Typing and Socialization

For a concise review of studies on how social factors determine sex-role behavior, see "Sex-typing and Socialization" by Walter Mischel, Chapter 20 in volume 2 of *Carmichael's Manual of Child Psychology* (3rd ed., 1970), edited by Paul H. Mussen. Mischel reviews studies of sex-typed behavior, sex-role stereotypes (and how valid they are), consistency and specificity in sex-typed behavior, the acquisition of sex-typed behavior, the extent to which children exhibit sex-typed behavior, and the impact of child-rearing practices on sex roles.

A more comprehensive discussion of sex differences is provided in *The Psychology of Sex Differences* (1974) by Eleanor E. Maccoby and Carol N. Jacklin. They survey all available research on the subject and provide an annotated bibliography of 1,400 research studies published since 1965. In their conclusions they describe *myths* about male-female differences (girls are more social, more suggestible, and lack motivation to achieve), *well-established differences* (males are more aggressive and excel in visual, spatial, and mathematical ability; girls have greater verbal ability), and *open questions* (the possibility that there are sex differences in competitiveness, dominance, compliance, and passivity).

4-5
Helping Girls Resist Sex Stereotypes

A number of publications have been prepared for those who would like to encourage young girls to overcome, at least partially, the stereotyped view of females presented in movies, TV shows and commercials, books, and magazines. Perhaps the best-known book of this type is *Free to Be You and Me* (1973) by Marlo Thomas and several associates. A similar publication is *What I Want to Be When I Grow Up* (1975) by Carol Burnett, George Mendoza, and Sheldon Secunda. Two publishers that specialize in books written to persuade girls they have all kinds of capabilities are: Feminist Press (Children's Series), Box 334, Westbury, N.Y.; and Lollipop Power, Inc., P.O. Box 1171, Chapel Hill, N.C. 27514. A comprehensive list of books and toys for girls is provided on pages 77–81 of *The New Woman's Survival Sourcebook* (1975), edited by Susan Rennie and Kirsten Grimstad.

4-6
Becoming Aware of Differences in Cognitive Style

When you begin to teach, you may be baffled by the extent of the differences in the way your pupils respond to class activities. To gain awareness of the range of individual differences, make it a point to look for variations among students when you observe or participate in a classroom. Such awareness may prepare you for the wide range of reactions your students will display when you take over a classroom and may also help you make plans to allow for such variations. Listed below are pairs of terms that summarize essentially opposite types of thinking, perceiving, and reacting. They are based on descriptions of cognitive styles noted in this chapter with reference to the work of

Jerome Kagan, Samuel Messick, and J. P. Guilford. Observe students in a public school or college class, and try to pick out—for as many of the opposites as you can—a student who exemplifies each extreme. Then give a brief description of the behavior that led you to select that student as a model of that particular style. Finally, speculate about what, if anything, you might do to allow for such differences when you begin to teach.

Impulsive—tendency to give first answer, to be eager to respond quickly

Reflective—tendency to think things over, to be deliberate and cautious in responding

Analytic—tendency to note details, preference for specifics

Thematic—tendency to respond to whole pattern, interest in "big picture"

Attentiveness to detail—tendency to recognize and respond to many aspects of a situation

One-track responding—tendency to concentrate on only one aspect of a situation at a time

Concentrated attention—tendency to concentrate on a particular task or idea and to resist distractions or interruptions

Distractability—tendency to be diverted from one task or idea when conflicting or different activities or ideas are present

Resistance to change—reluctant to accept unexpected or unconventional views or evidence

Flexibility—high degree of adaptability to new, different, or unexpected points of view

Conventionality—tendency to seek or provide one right answer, or a conventional answer

Individuality—tendency to respond in nonconventional, unexpected, or individual ways

On the basis of your observation, are there any procedures or techniques you might want to try in your classes to allow for the differences you noted?

4-7

Impact of Puberty and the Growth Spurt

To appreciate the nature and magnitude of changes that take place at the time of puberty, arrange to visit a seventh grade and a ninth grade classroom. Observe the students not only in class but also in the halls and after school. Describe differences in physical appearance and in behavior between the seventh and ninth graders, paying particular attention to differences between boys and girls. You might also try to pick out the most and least mature children in a group and concentrate on their behavior in and out of the classroom. If you make an observation of this type, note your reactions and comment on the implications of differences you detect.

4-8

Early and Late
Maturation

If you would like more detailed information about the impact of early and late maturation, a description of the attitudes and self-conceptions of the fast- and slow-maturing boys of the Berkeley Growth Study is provided in an article by Paul H. Mussen and Mary Cover Jones in *Child Development,* 1957 (vol. 28), on pages 243–256. A follow-up study, reporting the attitudes of the same individuals at adulthood, appears in an article by Mary Cover Jones in the same issue of *Child Development,* 1957 (vol. 28) on pages 113–128. A report by Jones and Mussen of the impact of early and late maturation on girls can be found in *Child Development,* 1958 (vol. 29) on pages 491–501.

4-9

Biological and
Physiological Aspects of
Adolescence

For more complete information about biological changes at adolescence, consult *Growth at Adolescence* (2nd ed., 1962) by J. M. Tanner, whose condensed versions of the material in this book can be found in Chapter 3 of *Carmichael's Manual of Child Psychology* (3rd ed., 1970), edited by Paul H. Mussen, and Chapter 1 of *Twelve to Sixteen: Early Adolescence* (1972), edited by Jerome Kagan and Robert Coles.

4-10

Age Differences in
Satisfaction with
Appearance

Arthur T. Jersild found that concern about appearance reached a peak in junior high school and that it tended to taper off in high school and college. (For details, see *In Search of Self* [1952].) If you would like to discover how older individuals feel about their appearance, read "The Happy American Body: A Survey Report" by Ellen Berscheid, Elaine Walster, and George Bohrnstedt in *Psychology Today,* November 1973, pages 119–131. As the title implies, most older Americans say they are quite satisfied with their appearance. You might speculate about the reasons for and implications of changes in concern about appearance at different ages, either with reference to the Jersild and *Psychology Today* descriptions or simply in terms of your own observations. Why do young people say they are so concerned about how they look while older people say they are not? Might these differences cause problems because of different emphases during courtship and during later married life?

4-11

Blos on Adolescence

On Adolescence (1962) by Peter Blos is widely acknowledged as the outstanding psychoanalytic interpretation of this period of development. In Chapter 1, Blos gives a brief outline of the Freudian view of adolescence. In Chapter 2 he gives an outline of the psychosexual development leading up to and culminating in puberty, stressing the need to take into account earlier experiences in order to understand adolescence. (This serves as an excellent brief summary of the overall Freudian view of development.) The nature and significance of the latency period is described on pages 52–57, preadolescence on pages 57–71, early adolescence on pages 75–82 (in which friendships and crushes are discussed), and adolescence proper on pages 87–138. In this last section Blos describes tender love (pp. 101ff.), homosexuality (pp. 105ff.), asceticism and intellectualization (pp. 111ff.)., and uniformism (pp. 118ff.). Later adolescence as a time of consolidation and crisis is described on pages 128–158. Chapter 5 is called "The Ego in Adolescence"; Chapter 7 is entitled "Two Illustrations of Deviate

Adolescent Development." (Psychoanalytic, as well as other theories of adolescence, are analyzed by Rolf E. Muus in *Theories of Adolescence* [2nd ed. 1969].)

4-12
Erikson on Adolescence

Blos presents an orthodox Freudian view of this period of development. Although Erik H. Erikson received the same psychoanalytic training as Blos, his later experiences led him to propose a psychosocial (rather than psychosexual) view of development. The special significance of the stage of identity vs. role confusion in Erikson's scheme is explained in *Identity: Youth and Crisis* (1968). In the preface, Erikson notes that identity is unfathomable and all pervasive; and therefore, he says, "I will not offer a definitive explanation of it in this book" (p. 9). (The explanation he offers on page 165 may not be definitive, but it is quite clear.) In Chapter 1, he describes how he first came to use the phrase *identity crisis* and gives a general description of what he means by it. In Chapter 2 he explains how his anthropological studies and treatment of war veterans led him to reinterpret Freud's original explanations of development. Chapter 3 is an overview of all his stages of psychosocial development and emphasizes how they lead up to the stage of identity vs. role confusion. Chapter 4 presents brief descriptions of identity crises experienced by George Bernard Shaw, William James, and Freud, and the meaning of *psychosocial moratorium* is explained (pp. 156–158). *Negative identity* is described on pages 173–176.

The primary reason children attend school is to learn. Teachers are hired because it is assumed they possess skills that will enable them to arrange school experiences so that learning will take place. The topic of learning, therefore, should be thoroughly analyzed in any book that describes how psychology might be applied to teaching. The main question to be faced is: How should this information be organized? Thousands of experiments on learning have been performed, and dozens of theories have resulted. A great variety of teaching techniques based on these experiments and theories have been proposed and put into practice. In the three chapters that make up this part of the text, related experiments, theories, and techniques have been grouped as three major sets of ideas that parallel the conceptions of behavior and development described in Chapter 3. The following analysis of these three conceptions, therefore, will serve as a review of points covered earlier as well as a preview of what is to be covered in this part of the text.

The first conception is the behaviorist-environmentalist-associationist position championed by B. F. Skinner and his followers.

They stress that scientists should base their conclusions on observations of overt behavior (behaviorism). They argue that the mind of a newborn child is like a blank slate, that all learning comes from experience, and that hereditary factors are of little significance, since they cannot be changed (environmentalism). They also believe that most learning can be explained by tracing relationships between stimuli, responses, and reinforcements (associationism). Accordingly, they recommend that teachers present lessons by carefully arranging sequences of questions (stimuli) to arouse correct answers (responses). (Because its proponents place such stress on stimuli and responses, this view of learning is often referred to as S-R psychology.) When students either realize on their own or are told that an answer is correct, they are reinforced and are therefore likely to remember and repeat the answer. This is the essence of programmed instruction, and Skinner and his followers believe that the best learning environment is one where students work individually on programs.

The second view is not as clearly defined, but it might be referred to as the cognitive-discovery approach. The leading American spokesman for this set of ideas has been Jerome Bruner, although the originators were several German psychologists who were fascinated by ways organisms perceive things. Advocates of the cognitive view argue that it is not always possible to gain complete understanding of behavior by restricting oneself to observations of overt actions. They therefore reject the strict behaviorist conception of science and seek information about ways individuals think (or engage in cognitive activity) and perceive situations. They seek to analyze a person's thoughts, even though thoughts cannot always be measured in objective ways. Cognitive psychologists maintain that learning takes place when individuals grasp new relationships. When this occurs, the person gains insight or sees things in a new light. Instead of urging teachers to supervise students as they work individually on programs and acquire what others have described, cognitive psychologists recommend that teachers present background information and pose questions intended to stimulate students to discuss topics until they experience the feeling they have discovered things for themselves.

One of the clearest examples of the cognitive-discovery view of learning is the open school approach. This type of education is derived most directly from the cognitive theory of Jean Piaget, but it is also partly based on, or at least in harmony with, concepts introduced by the German psychologists who studied perception. Piaget and the German psychologists analyzed different types of behavior and recommended self-discovery for different reasons, but even though they arrived at their conclusions via different paths, they agree that children should be encouraged to learn many things on their own

and by interacting with each other. Piaget believes that "children have real understanding only of that which they invent themselves" (Almy, 1966, p. vi). (Where Piaget's translator uses the word invent, cognitive theorists would probably substitute the words perceive or discover.) As noted in Chapter 3, Bruner disagrees with Piaget about some of the ways children acquire knowledge, but both theorists urge teachers to avoid trying to shape child behavior in carefully predetermined ways.

The third conception of behavior, development, and learning is even less clearly defined than the second, but it is often referred to as the humanistic view, although the terms sensitivity training, existential psychology, and growth psychology (among others) are sometimes used to refer to the same basic ideas. Two of the most influential advocates of this view have been Abraham H. Maslow

Part Three

Learning

and Carl R. Rogers. Maslow, who was primarily interested in motivation, wanted to find ways to help children develop their inherited potentialities, and he urged teachers to concentrate on satisfying the needs of pupils so that they might make wise choices and become self-actualizers. In contrast to Skinner, who pays little attention to inherited tendencies because they cannot be appreciably changed by experiences, Maslow bases much of his theorizing on the assumption that "we have, each one of us, an essential inner nature which is instinctive, intrinsic, given, 'natural,' i.e., with an appreciable hereditary determinant, and which tends strongly to persist" (1968, p. 190). Maslow goes on to point out, however, that "these are potentialities, not final actualizations." He feels that perhaps the primary goal of parents and teachers is to help children make the most of—or self-actualize—their inherited abilities.

Rogers, who is America's best-known psychotherapist, based his approach to therapy (called client-centered or nondirective) on the premise that clients should be helped to treat themselves. Instead of analyzing the behavior of patients as Freud did, Rogers uses subtle questions and suggestions to help clients understand their own behavior and eventually solve their own problems. When clients are successful, they acquire confidence in their ability to control their own destinies, which helps them to solve problems later without the aid of a psychotherapist. After analyzing his own experiences as a teacher, Rogers came to the conclusion that the same basic approach should be used in education. He became convinced that the programmed approach proposed by Skinner made pupils too dependent on their teachers. He agrees with advocates of the cognitive-discovery approach that pupils should be helped to control much of their own learning, but, in addition, he stresses the significance of interpersonal relationships.

Other psychologists who are classified as humanists emphasize additional aspects of behavior. They agree with Maslow that children should be allowed to make many of their own choices and with Rogers that students should become capable of directing their own learning and of developing close relationships with others. But they maintain that teachers should also help students understand and express their emotions, clarify their attitudes and values, and become more aware of themselves and others.

Humanistic psychologists and educators, therefore, recommend that teachers try to develop close relationships with their pupils and permit them to direct much of their own learning. Teachers are also urged to arrange learning situations that permit students to analyze their emotions, engage in fantasy activities, examine their values, participate in forms of physical expression, and share feelings with others.

When you read defenses of any of these views of behavior by the originators or their followers, you may be told, either explicitly or implicitly, that it is desirable if not necessary to be completely faithful to a particular approach in order to reap maximum benefits. This suggestion may have merit for a person attempting to establish a comprehensive theory in the abstract, but it may be poor advice for someone interested in applying psychology as effectively as possible in public school classrooms. One reason for this is a function of the goals and conditions of American education described in Chapter 2. Because of the nature of these goals and conditions, it is highly unlikely that you could teach in a manner that would be completely consistent with any one of the views just outlined, even if you wanted to. Instead, you are likely to spend part of your time helping students master specific subject matter, part of your time arranging situations and discussions to promote student discovery, and part of your time trying to establish interpersonal relationships likely to enhance learning and perhaps also contribute to self-fulfillment and self-awareness. Consequently, you are urged to read the three chapters that follow, not to decide which view is the best (which might lead to cognitive dissonance and the

tendency to ignore contrasting ideas) but to think about the kinds of teaching situations in which each view is most appropriate.

Another reason for seeking ways to benefit from each view—as opposed to choosing one "best" view—is highlighted by research on the impact of various approaches to teaching. When comparisons have been made (e.g., Stephens, 1967) of the effectiveness of different factors, methods, and procedures in teaching (including class size, school size, individualized instruction, ability grouping, discussion versus lecture, and group-centered versus teacher-centered approaches), the usual conclusion is that essentially the same amount of learning occurs regardless of the approach.

One implication of these findings is that teachers should feel free to choose from a variety of techniques of instruction, since it appears that no particular method is significantly better than any other. But if explanations for this state of affairs are sought, a more important implication emerges. One explanation for the conclusion that different teaching techniques yield the same results, on the average, might be that teachers can arouse a positive response in some pupils some of the time, but they can't satisfy all pupils all of the time. Some students, for example, seem to thrive on step-by-step programmed approaches; others respond more favorably to small-group discussion of open-ended questions; still others enjoy sessions intended to sensitize them to interpersonal relationships. For every child who registers delight when any one of these techniques is about to be used, there may be one who reacts with dismay.

Preferences for different types of learning might be traced to such causes as personality factors, cognitive style, and favorable or unfavorable experiences. Children who enjoy programmed approaches, for example, may prefer working by themselves because they are shy introverts. They may also be analytic thinkers who have had humiliating experi-

ences when asked to recite in front of the whole class. Students who prefer class discussion, on the other hand, may be self-confident extroverts who love to perform. They may be impulsive thinkers who often come up with quick answers in discussions and thereby gain the admiration of teachers and classmates.

The implication of this explanation is that because of factors such as these, you may do some of your pupils an injustice if you make almost exclusive use of techniques you happened to like when you were a student. Some of your pupils are certain to share your enthusiasm for a particular approach, but others are just as certain to dislike that teaching technique to the point that they will fail to learn very much or will perhaps dread coming to class. If you hope to reach all your students some of the time, therefore, you should make occasional use of techniques derived from each of the basic conceptions of learning to be described in this part of the text

In order to gain maximum benefit from these three chapters on learning, you should make an effort to be as open-minded as possible. Because of the factors just discussed, you probably have personal preferences for certain approaches to teaching. Because of things you have studied or read in other courses or books on psychology, you may have already developed a perception of some theories as negative or threatening, others as positive and exhilarating. Many people, for example, seem to harbor negative feelings about B. F. Skinner because he asks us to acknowledge that we may not have as much control over our behavior as we think we have. The views of Maslow and Rogers may be more attractive to us, perhaps because they appeal to our vanity. It is flattering to be told, "You are intrinsically wise and good and the master of your destiny." It would be unfortunate to approach the discussion of Skinner's ideas on education with a negative set, however, because he has proposed techniques that can be of substantial benefit to any teacher. It may also be unfortunate if you approach the discussion of Maslow's and Rogers's ideas in an uncritical way, because some of their suggestions fail to take account of certain realities of public school teaching.

In an effort to help you evaluate in an objective but critical way each of the three views of learning discussed in these chapters, each conception will be analyzed in detail, including mention of the following five elements: (1) a brief outline of basic assumptions, including mention of when and why they were proposed, (2) a description of key experiments or observations that led to the establishment of basic principles, (3) an outline of applications to education recommended by proponents, (4) a critique of assumptions and techniques, (5) a list of suggestions for putting each view into practice in your classroom.

You are urged, for two reasons, not to skip over the discussion of basic assumptions, the description of experiments or observations, or the critiques of each view in your eagerness to get to the list of teaching suggestions. First, your versatility in making applications will be enhanced if you grasp underlying principles. Second, if you understand why certain procedures are recommended, you may be able to evaluate them more objectively. If you comprehend the reasoning behind programmed learning, to cite just one example, you will probably be less likely to dismiss it—as some poorly informed critics have—as an insidious form of brainwashing.

Key points

Basic assumptions of the S-R view

Skinner's strict scientific view: World acts on person

Bandura's modified scientific view: Anticipatory control

S-R view: Attempt to shape behavior systematically

Experimental evidence underlying S-R theory

Reinforcement, extinction, spontaneous recovery

Generalization, discrimination

Schedules of reinforcement

Pavlovian conditioning: Involuntary action aroused by previously neutral stimulus

Operant conditioning: Voluntary behavior strengthened by reinforcement

Shape behavior by supplying step-by-step reinforcement

Educational applications of S-R theory

Programmed learning: Reinforce small steps

Linear and branching programs

Vanishing prompts (reducing cues)

Keller's Personalized System of Instruction

Computer-assisted instruction

Behavior modification

Criticisms of S-R theory

Human beings need to feel they can control their own behavior

Controllers may choose goals that benefit *them*

Well-written programs exception, not rule

Immediate feedback not always desirable

Performance contracting not successful

Supplying brief answers becomes tedious

Extensive use of behavior modification may reduce effectiveness

Teachers may be tempted to shape docility

Applying S-R theory in the classroom

Lowest common denominator effect

Premack principle (Grandma's rule)

Individual reward menu

Chapter 5

The S-R view of learning

CHAPTER 3 PRESENTED some possible explanations of why John B. Watson proposed behaviorism, He was reluctant to spend time trying to fathom the thought processes of rats and wanted to find ways to improve human behavior by using the methods of science. Even though many of his colleagues were bothered by Watson's rather flamboyant style, they agreed with his basic views on science; and ever since the publication of *Psychology as the Behaviorist Views It* in 1913, a majority of American psychologists have concentrated on making objective observations of overt behavior. In addition to stressing objectivity in research, they have also tended to suggest that the principles they have established be *applied* in an objective way.

In the account of B. F. Skinner's contributions to the S-R view of behavior and development in Chapter 3, this statement by Skinner was quoted: "The methods of science have been enormously successful wherever they have been tried. Let us then apply them to human affairs" (1953, p. 5). After making this statement Skinner hastened to add:

If we are to use the methods of science in the field of human affairs, we must assume that behavior is lawful and determined. We must expect to discover that what a man does is the result of specifiable conditions and that once these conditions have been discovered, we can anticipate and to some extent determine his actions. (1953, p. 6)

Basic assumptions of the S-R view

Skinner acknowledged that his proposal would be difficult for many people to accept because the view of man as a free agent capable of controlling his own destiny was both well established and appealing. Nevertheless, he continued to stress this argument, and almost twenty years after he made the statement quoted above, he reaffirmed it in these terms:

In the traditional picture a person perceives the world around him, selects features to be perceived, discriminates among them, judges them good or bad, changes them to make them better (or, if he is careless, worse), and may be held responsible for his action and justly rewarded or punished for its consequences. In the scientific picture a person is a member of a species shaped by evolutionary contingencies of survival, displaying behavioral processes which bring him under the control of the environment in which he lives, and largely under the control of a social environment which he and millions of others like him have constructed and maintained during the evolution of a culture. The direction of the controlling relation is reversed: a person does not act upon the world, the world acts upon him. (1971, p. 211)

Skinner's strict scientific view: World acts on person

While these statements summarize Skinner's basic reasoning in an extreme form, the assumptions of the S-R view may be more understandable and acceptable to you if they are phrased in less emphatic terms. First of all, when Skinner describes the "scientific picture," it would be more accurate to say "the scientific picture as seen through the eyes of a behaviorist and fervent supporter of the environmental view of determinism." Other scientists, including some who classify themselves as behaviorists and associationists, do not endorse Skinner's extreme environmentalistic interpretation. As noted in the brief account of S-R theory presented in Chapter 3, Albert Bandura (1974) maintains that human beings are capable of choosing how they will respond to many situations because many types of human behavior are under *anticipatory control*. We are able to observe the effects of actions and anticipate what will happen under certain circumstances. As a result, we can control our own behavior to a significant extent by choosing between different situations and experiences and by deliberately *producing* preselected consequences. The argument that the world acts on us, therefore, does not necessarily mean that we have no control whatever over our behavior. It is simply a way of stressing that we are not always aware of the extent to which we have been influenced, and are being influenced, by experiences.

Bandura's modified scientific view: Anticipatory control

You may believe, to cite just one illustration, that you chose to enter a teacher education program entirely of your own free will. Actually, your decision was influenced by positive and negative experiences with teachers and subjects, parental attitudes, opinions of friends, and dozens of other factors. To a certain extent, you had no control over many of these. For example, if you were assigned to a room where you met the teacher who inspired you to follow in his or her footsteps, you had no choice in the matter. In a sense, then, the world has acted on you and caused you to engage in certain types of behavior. Even so, you have some control over your own destiny because you are able to weigh alternatives and anticipate what might happen. (This is the point stressed by Bandura.) If you decide, after reading this book and imagining what it will be like to serve as a public school teacher, that you would prefer to seek a position in a particular type of school, your choice will be influenced by experiences, but it will not be completely beyond your control.

The underlying philosophy of the S-R view stresses that scientists have been most successful when they have traced the causes of events and have found ways to alter behavior in predictable ways. To apply science to human behavior, therefore, Skinner argues that we must constantly analyze causes. If we can discover what makes people behave in a desirable manner, we should be able to arrange conditions to produce that kind of behavior. If we do not search for causes and attempt to arrange experiences, we will leave things to chance. In an uncontrolled situation some lucky individuals will have a favorable chain of experiences that will equip them with desirable attitudes and skills; others will suffer an unfortunate series of experiences that will lead to difficulties and grief. In a controlled situation it may be possible to arrange experiences so that almost everyone acquires desirable traits and abilities.

Even if you feel a bit uncomfortable about the idea that human behavior is shaped by experiences over which the individual has incomplete control, Skinner argues that you will be a better teacher if you endorse this assumption. If you reject the proposal completely, you may not become aware of how you are influencing your pupils in undesirable ways, and you may fail to arrange experiences that could benefit them. S-R theorists stress the point that what you do as a teacher—whether you acknowledge the fact or not—is going to have an impact on your students. Therefore, they recommend that you make systematic efforts to influence student behavior in efficient, consistent, and positive ways.

S-R view: Attempt to shape behavior systematically

Skinner reasoned that applying science to human behavior could be as enormously successful as applying science in other ways if we were objective and could trace specifiable conditions. Therefore, he set out to discover the kinds of experiences that determine behavior. He felt that he had made a major step toward achieving this goal when he invented the Skinner box and carried out a series of experiments with rats placed in this apparatus.

Experimental evidence underlying S-R theory

Experiments with the Skinner box

The Skinner box was mentioned briefly in Chapter 3. To grasp the way this device is used, imagine the following situation (which might occur in a bad dream or be presented in a science-fiction drama on TV or in a film). Instead of waking up in your bedroom one morning, you find yourself confined in a tiny, dimly lit jail cell. You have no contact with anyone else, and although you are allowed to drink all the water you want, you are not given any food for two days. Without warning, on the third morning a voice from a hidden loudspeaker orders you to stand in front of the door to your cell and walk through when it slides open. Since the voice sounds very authoritative and since you are eager to do anything to escape from your cell, you obey the order and find that you have entered a room that seems quite large and brightly illuminated compared to the cell you have just left. While your eyes are adjusting to the unaccustomed brightness, the door through which you have entered slides shut.

When you are able to see clearly, your first impression is that the room contains nothing but yourself. Suddenly, you notice that there is something on one wall—a sort of handle over what looks like the delivery slot of a vending machine. Since you have been confined in your cell and since the handle and slot are the only objects in the entire room, you walk over to investigate them. You tentatively push the handle and are startled and delighted by the sudden appearance of a small food bar (made up of dried fruit, nuts, and cereal) in the slot. Because you have not had anything to eat for two days, you eat the bar voraciously and push the handle as you chew. Sure enough, another food bar appears. You push the handle again even as you reach for the bar, and still another bit of nourishment appears. Because you are starving and the food bars are quite small, you push the handle about thirty times and obtain a bit of food each time. Then, just when the handle pushing has become almost automatic, the food bars suddenly stop appearing. Your first reaction is to push the handle several times in rapid succession. When that fails to produce food, you try slow, deliberate pushes. When that technique also fails to activate the mechanism, you slam the handle down as hard as you can. Still no food bar. Disappointed and disgusted, you slump to the floor and rest with your back against the wall next to the handle. A few minutes later, just as you are dozing off, the voice tells you to get up and walk to the door. Since you have concluded that there is no point in staying in the big room anyway, you comply with the order; and when the door opens, you return to your cell.

The next morning, when your hunger pangs are becoming more and more noticeable, the voice once again orders you to move to the cell door. You obey with alacrity; and as soon as the door opens and you enter the large room, you grope your way toward the handle and slot, even before you can clearly see where you are going. You push the handle and are terribly dismayed to discover that no food bar appears. Close to a state of panic, you push the handle several times in quick succession, and after several frantic pushes, you are delighted to hear the familiar clunk as the food appears in the slot. You manipulate the handle again several times, and after a series of pushes, the coveted bit of food is delivered. In a matter of minutes you discover that you must push the handle ten times in order to get a food bar, and so you quickly develop a pattern of ten rapid pushes followed by a few seconds to eat, followed by ten rapid pushes. As you eat one of the food bars, you notice for the first time a series of small colored light bulbs recessed high on a wall. You note that the green bulb is illuminated but are much more interested in pushing the handle in order to get food. You try several ten-push sequences without success before the voice orders you to the door.

Soon the procedure of being told to stand by the door of your cell and move into the larger room becomes a daily routine. But the procedure to follow in order to get the food bars is never routine. One day you discover that it does not make any difference how many times you push the handle. It is the timing of the push that leads to the payoff. The first push after a three-minute interval of time is followed by food; all other pushes are superfluous. So, you consult your watch (which fortunately has a sweep second hand) and impatiently wait for three minutes to pass before operating the handle. You also notice that the red bulb on the wall is illuminated when timed handle pushing leads to a payoff. After it goes out, no more food bars appear, even though you first push the handle dozens of times, then in sequences of ten pushes, then in timed pushes. The next day you are unable to discern any pattern. The food bars seem to appear at unpredictable intervals, and so you are obliged to push the handle almost constantly. As you do this, you notice that the blue bulb on the wall is lit. To keep yourself occupied, you decide to count the number of pushes you

The steadiest amount of output is produced when an organism is placed on an intermittent reinforcement schedule.

Elliott Cruitt/Magnum

make, and you have reached 4,372 before the voice tells you to move to the door.

After a few days you get into the habit of looking at the light bulbs before you begin to manipulate the handle. You push the handle in a given way depending on which bulb is illuminated, and you quickly change your behavior when one bulb goes dark and another blinks on.

If John B. Watson were alive, he would be dismayed by this description because you have just been asked to imagine what it would feel like to be a rat in B. F. Skinner's laboratory. The experiences of your fantasy illustrate the first principles Skinner established when he perfected the Skinner box. The unknown person who spirited you away and who arranged conditions in the jail cell and the big room did not resort to force or coercion but was highly successful in controlling your behavior. You pressed the handle according to patterns preselected by your controller because behavior you instituted (or *emitted*, to use Skinner's terminology) on your own was rein-

Reinforcement

forced. When your handle-pushing behavior was *reinforced* several times in succession, you were strongly inclined to continue that activity. When the reinforcement was abruptly withdrawn, however, the

Extinction

tendency to push the bar quickly diminished, or was *extinguished*, to use S-R terminology. Even though your handle pushing was extinguished the first day, your initial act when you moved in front of the handle the second morning was to manipulate it again. In the parlance

Spontaneous recovery

of S-R theory this behavior is referred to as *spontaneous recovery* because you went back to the previously extinguished behavior of your own accord. You not only retained the once extinguished tendency to manipulate the handle; you also expected the original pattern of receiving a food bar after every push to be maintained. This

Generalization

expectation illustrates *generalization*,[1] since you assumed that what was true the first time in a given situation would continue to be true. When you discovered that the pattern of handle pushing varied each day and that it was linked to the color of the light bulb that was

Discrimination

illuminated, you learned to *discriminate*. You recognized that different kinds of handle pushing were appropriate under different conditions. Your behavior was influenced by the way reinforcements were supplied, and you altered your handle-pushing activities when

Schedules of reinforcement

you were rewarded after ten pushes (referred to by Skinner as a *fixed-ratio schedule*) or every three minutes (a *fixed-interval schedule*). You engaged in the greatest amount of handle pushing when you were never sure when you would obtain a food bar (*intermittent schedule*).

[1] S-R theorists often distinguish between *stimulus generalization*, where the same response is made to similar stimuli, and *response generalization*, where varied responses are made to the same stimulus. Since the basic principle is the same, and there does not seem to be any pedagogical value in distinguishing between the two types in a discussion intended to lead to applications, in this text the word *generalization* will be used to refer to either or both.

Classical and operant conditioning: Similarities and differences

The first four principles just described (reinforcement, extinction, spontaneous recovery, generalization) are similar to those originally established by Ivan Pavlov after he had conducted his famous series of experiments with dogs. By ringing a bell just before food was presented and repeating this stimulus several times, Pavlov conditioned dogs to salivate when a bell rang. The salivation response was reinforced by the food, and it tended to extinguish if the bell was sounded several times without reinforcement. Typically, however, dogs would exhibit spontaneous recovery and salivate the first time a bell was rung a few hours after the response had extinguished. Once a dog had been conditioned to salivate when the bell rang, it would tend to generalize and salivate when it heard a similar sound. But, if food was presented after the bell but never after the other sounds, the dog would learn to discriminate.

As noted in Chapter 3, John B. Watson was one of the first psychologists to demonstrate that children could be conditioned (Watson and Rayner, 1920). He induced eleven-month-old Albert to fear a white rat by making a loud, sudden sound just as the boy reached for the animal. Albert not only developed the fear response very quickly, he also generalized it and acted afraid of any white, furry animal or object. The dramatic success of his experiment with Albert led Watson to conclude that he could condition children to acquire all kinds of behavior. It soon became apparent, however, that the kind of conditioning first demonstrated by Pavlov and later employed by Watson was limited to essentially involuntary reflex actions (such as salivating or reacting with fear). Furthermore, attempts by Watson and other psychologists to build sequences of conditioned responses were rarely successful.

The kind of learning that takes place in a Skinner box is similar to that demonstrated by Pavlov and Watson in several ways: Both types of learning are forms of conditioning based on the establishment of associations between stimuli and responses, and the principles of reinforcement, extinction, spontaneous recovery, generalization, and discrimination can all be demonstrated. But, there is a significant difference. Pavlov and Watson caused an originally neutral stimulus (a bell or white rat) to arouse an essentially involuntary action (salivation or fear). Skinner, by contrast, caused actions voluntarily and spontaneously made by an organism to become strengthened. Since this is the case, *any* kind of behavior that an organism engages in (or *emits,* to use Skinner's terminology) can be conditioned by using the methods developed by Skinner. To call attention to this distinction, Pavlovian conditioning is often called *classical,* since it was based on a classic experiment, while Skinner's version is called either

Pavlovian conditioning: Involuntary action aroused by previously neutral stimulus

Operant conditioning: Voluntary behavior strengthened by reinforcement

operant (since the organism operates on its environment) or *instru-mental* (since what the organism does is instrumental in bringing about reinforcement).

While the principles of reinforcement, extinction, generalization, and discrimination account for many types of learning when operant conditioning techniques similar to those used in a Skinner box are applied to animals or humans, Skinner concluded that behavior might be altered even more extensively if other forms of conditioning were discovered. Accordingly, he developed an apparatus basically similar to the original Skinner box for the purpose of carrying out a series of experiments with pigeons. To grasp how he proceeded, imagine that you have another dream (or that you watch another TV or film drama).

Skinner's experiments in shaping behavior

You are back in your jail cell and receive no food for two days. On the third day the voice from the loudspeaker orders you to walk through the door. When you comply, you discover that you are in an enclosure that appears to be completely empty. The handle and the dispensing tray that were features of the room in your previous dream are nowhere to be found. You wander aimlessly in circles for a few moments, and then, suddenly, just as you turn in a particular direction, a previously undetected light blinks on, a buzzer sounds, and a small, concealed trap door opens up in the wall under the light. Behind the open door is a food bar. As soon as you take the bar, the door snaps shut. After eating the bar you begin to feel the wall around the trap door. As your fingers move up and away from where the bar appeared, the light and buzzer precede the opening of the door once again. You grab the bar and the door snaps shut. For the next few minutes you finger the wall without success, but just after you happen to push against a tiny spot on the wall with your thumb, the light and buzzer and trap door are activated, and you receive another food bar. After the door snaps shut and as you eat the food, you push your thumb against the tiny spot. The door opens, and it continues to open and deliver a food bar every time you repeat the action. After about thirty repetitions of this action, the voice tells you to stand in front of and pass through the door you entered, and you return to your cell. As you think about what has just happened, you realize that without any verbal or written instructions of any kind, you have learned to carry out a highly specific act. You speculate about how long it might have taken you to accidentally push your thumb against that tiny spot on one part of the wall if the progressive movements you made toward that ultimate action had not been rewarded with food.

The next day when the voice tells you to move through the door, you immediately go over to the wall and push the tiny spot with your thumb. Nothing happens. You push until your thumb is sore, and you feel so disappointed about your failure to arouse any response that you sit down in the middle of the floor. After a few minutes you get up. As you do so, the light and buzzer precede the opening of the trap door, behind which is a food bar. After eating the food you move back to the center of the room, but nothing happens. You sit down. Nothing happens. You get up. Nothing happens. You start to turn to your right and are delighted when the light and buzzer precede the opening of the trap door. By the time the trap door has opened thirty times, you have developed a well-established ritual of sitting down, getting up, turning in a circle to the right, turning in a circle to the left, raising your left arm, then raising your right arm. You have learned this rather elaborate sequence because the trap door opened only after you had carried out a progressively complex series of actions. After you learned a two-step sequence, you had to add the next step before you were rewarded, and so on. After ten repetitions of the final sequence, you carry out the actions so quickly and automatically it is essentially a dance routine. After the voice orders you back to your cell and you think about what has happened, you smile ruefully to yourself as you ponder, "I never thought I could dance, yet there I was acting like a member of a chorus line."

This imaginary situation is similar to experiments Skinner carried out with pigeons placed in an apparatus related to the original Skinner box, which was designed for use with rats. Instead of a bar to be pushed, the pigeon is confronted with a disk to be pecked (the pigeon equivalent of thumb pushing in humans). After shaping the pecking behavior of pigeons placed in the special apparatus, Skinner used the same basic technique to train pigeons to, among other things, peck out tunes on a toy xylophone and play a game similar to table tennis. The pigeon-musicians acquired their skill by pecking first one key, then two, then three, and then four in sequence. At first, pecking one key was reinforced with food. Eventually, food was supplied only when all four bars on the xylophone were pecked in the correct sequence. (If you would like to attempt roughly similar feats with a pet dog or cat, read Skinner's article "How to Teach Animals" in the December 1951 issue of *Scientific American*, pp. 26–29.)

Shape behavior by supplying step-by-step reinforcement

The basic principle of learning derived from such experiments is that movements can be shaped if actions that move progressively closer to the desired *terminal behavior* (to use Skinner's terminology) are rewarded. The key to success is to take one step at a time. The movements must be gradual enough so that the organism becomes aware that each step in the sequence is essential. If the trainer tries to go too fast, the organism is likely to become confused part of the way through the performance and engage in confused trial-and-error behavior.

Skinner enjoyed such success shaping the behavior of pigeons that he reacted in much the same manner as John B. Watson, the originator

The trainer of this porpoise first decided on the terminal behavior (jumping through a hoop) and then shaped that behavior by supplying reinforcement when movements leading to the appropriate action were carried out.

Joel Gordon/DPI

of behaviorism, had after he conditioned Albert to fear the rat. Watson boasted that he could cause a child to become anything he chose; Skinner argued that what had previously occurred by chance could now be produced. To make his point, Skinner wrote *Walden Two* (1948), a novel in which he described a utopia based on principles of operant conditioning. All children born to couples who live at Walden Two, a large commune, are placed in the hands of child-rearing specialists. These specialists use the same methods Skinner employed to train pigeons to shape the personality traits of their charges. The leader of Walden Two, who speaks for Skinner, defends this procedure by arguing that highly successful and creative people get that way not because of inherited tendencies but because of a lucky series of reinforcements. Instead of just hoping that such traits as perseverance and self-control will be reinforced, the child-rearing specialists of *Walden Two* arrange situations to make sure that this happens.

Robert P. Hawkins was so impressed with this idea that he later proposed (1972) that only couples who have demonstrated their ability to use techniques of operant conditioning to shape behavior should be allowed to have children. He observed:

To paraphrase Skinner it is not a matter of whether parents will use [operant conditioning] techniques to manipulate their children, but rather whether they will use these techniques unconsciously with unknown, unchosen and unhappy results, or use them consciously, efficiently and consistently to develop the qualities they choose for their children. (1972, p. 40)

This statement sums up a basic principle of Skinner's theory: If it is assumed that all behavior is the result of reinforcing experiences, it is logical to try to arrange reinforcing experiences to produce desirable types of behavior.

About the time Skinner was working on *Walden Two*, his daughter was a student in public school. When he asked her what the class had done each day and examined the books and assignments she brought home, Skinner became increasingly appalled about the kind of education his child was receiving. He concluded that traditional teaching techniques were terribly confused and inefficient and also primarily negative, in the sense that most children study to avoid negative (or *aversive*, as Skinner calls them) consequences. It appeared to Skinner, for example, that his daughter studied most diligently to avoid being embarrassed or punished or to avoid a low grade. When he analyzed teacher-pupil behavior with reference to principles of operant conditioning, he was especially bothered by the fact that there was almost always a substantial interval between when pupils answered questions and when they received feedback as to whether their responses were correct or incorrect. Skinner realized that it was physically impossible for a teacher responsible for thirty students to respond to more than a few answers at a time, but he was still bothered by this situation. Finally, he noticed that lessons and workbooks were often poorly organized and did not seem to lead students to any specific goal. Skinner became convinced that if the principles of operant conditioning were systematically applied to education, all these limitations could be either reduced or eliminated. With characteristic energy and ingenuity, he proceeded to perfect programmed instruction and the use of teaching machines.

Educational applications of S-R theory

Programmed instruction and teaching machines

The experiments in which the behavior of a pigeon is shaped by reinforcing the bird's movements in the right direction illustrate the key idea behind Skinner's technological approach to teaching: The learning of students in school should be *shaped* by presenting them with programs of stimuli designed to lead them to a predetermined end result. The basic technique is described by Skinner in these terms:

[The two basic considerations of programmed learning are] the gradual elaboration of extremely complex patterns of behavior and the maintenance of the behavior in strength at each stage. The whole process of becoming com-

Programmed learning:
Reinforce small steps

petent in any field must be divided into a very large number of very small steps, and reinforcement must be contingent upon the accomplishment of each step.... By making each successive step as small as possible, the frequency of reinforcement can be raised to a maximum, while the possibly aversive consequences of being wrong are reduced to a minimum. (1968, p. 21)

Skinner argues that in the typical classroom situation, a teacher cannot supply reinforcement quickly enough or often enough. Accordingly, he recommends the use of teaching machines, which he maintains possess these advantages.

The important features of the device are these: reinforcement for the right answer is immediate. The mere manipulation of the device will probably be reinforcing enough to keep the average pupil at work for a suitable period each day, provided traces of earlier aversive control can be wiped out. A teacher may supervise an entire class at work on such devices at the same time, yet each child may progress at his own rate, completing as many problems as possible within the class period. If forced to be away from school, he may return to pick up where he left off....

The device makes it possible to present carefully designed material in which one problem can depend upon the answer to the preceding problem and where, therefore, the most efficient progress to an eventually complex repertoire can be made. (1968, p. 24)

Though the machine is the mechanical means used to provide reinforcement, the crucial factor in programmed learning is the program that is fed into the machine. The creation of truly successful programs is not easy, and Skinner himself has said, "It must be admitted that a

---

Figure 5-1

Part of a program in elementary grade spelling

1. **Manufacture** means to make or build. *Chair factories manufacture chairs.* Copy the word here:

   ☐ ☐ ☐ ☐ ☐ ☐ ☐ ☐ ☐ ☐ ☐

2. Part of the word is like part of the word **factory.** Both parts come from an old word meaning *make* or *build.*

   m   a   n   u ☐   ☐   ☐   ☐ **u   r   e**

3. Part of the word is like part of the word **manual.** Both parts come from an old word for *hand.* Many things used to be made by hand.

   ☐   ☐   ☐   ☐ **f   a   c   t   u   r   e**

4. The same letter goes in both spaces.

   m ☐ **n   u   f** ☐ **c   t   u   r   e**

5. The same letter goes in both spaces:

   m   a   n ☐ **f   a   c   t** ☐ **r   e**

6. **Chair factories** ☐ ☐ ☐ ☐ ☐ ☐ ☐ ☐ ☐ ☐ ☐ **chairs.**

Source: B. F. Skinner, "Teaching Machines," *Science,* vol. 128 (October 24, 1958), pp. 969–977, figs. 1 and 2, with permission of the American Association for the Advancement of Science and B. F. Skinner.

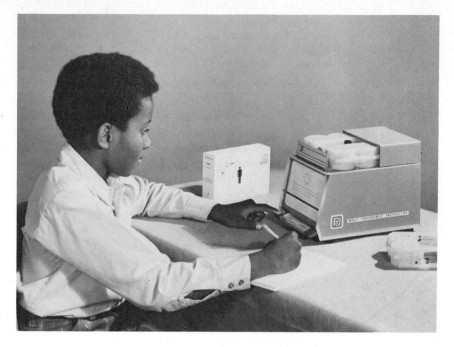

A student using a teaching machine.

Courtesy of Mast Development Company

considerable measure of art is needed in composing a successful program" (1968, p. 49). To get an idea of what a program looks like, look at Figure 5–1, a set of six frames from a program designed to teach spelling to third and fourth grade pupils.

Suppose a boy takes a turn at a teaching machine containing this program. After he has printed his answer to the first question, he moves a knob on the teaching machine, which pulls a transparent cover over what he has written (so he can't erase) and at the same time uncovers the information revealing whether or not his response is correct. He moves the knob again, pulling the transparent cover over this second response and revealing the correct answer. At that point he turns another knob, which uncovers a new frame—and so it goes.

A section of a more elaborate program designed for a high school physics course is reproduced in Figure 5-2. To "take" the course, cover the words in the right-hand column, and check your responses after you mentally fill in the blanks. (For additional frames in this course see *The Technology of Teaching*, pages 45–47.)

When developing such a program, the first step is to define precisely what is to be learned (the terminal behavior). Then terms, facts, or principles must be arranged in a sequence designed to lead the student to the desired end result. This requires first making the steps small enough that the frequency of reinforcement will be maximized, then putting them in the proper order and arranging them so that students will be adequately prepared for each frame, or numbered problem, when they reach it.

Figure 5-2

Part of a program in high school physics

Sentence to be completed	Word to be supplied
1. The important parts of a flashlight are the battery and the bulb. When we "turn on" a flashlight, we close a switch which connects the battery with the _____.	bulb
2. When we turn on a flashlight, an electric current flows through the fine wire in the _____ and causes it to grow hot.	bulb
3. When the hot wire glows brightly, we say that it gives off or sends out heat and _____.	light
4. The fine wire in the bulb is called a filament. The bulb "lights up" when the filament is heated by the passage of a(n) _____ current.	electric
5. When a weak battery produces little current, the fine wire, or _____ does not get very hot.	filament
6. A filament which is *less* hot sends out or gives off _____ light.	less
7. "Emit" means "send out." The amount of light sent out, or "emitted," by a filament depends on how _____ the filament is.	hot

Source: B. F. Skinner, "Teaching Machines," *Science,* vol. 128 (October 24, 1958), pp. 969–977, figs. 1 and 2, with permission of the American Association for the Advancement of Science and B. F. Skinner.

Figure 5-3

Part of a branching program on instructional objectives

A course *descripton* tells you something about the content and procedures of a course. A course *objective* describes a desired outcome of a course. Perhaps the sketch below will help make the distinction clear:

Instruction

PREREQUISITES	**DESCRIPTION**	**OBJECTIVES**
what a learner has to be able to do to qualify for a course	*what the course is about*	*what a successful learner is able to do at the end of the course*

Whereas an objective tells what the learner is to be like as a result of some learning experiences, the course description tells only what the course is about.

The distinction is quite important because a course description does not explain what will be accepted as adequate achievement. Though a course description might tell students which field they will be playing on, it doesn't tell them where the boundary lines are, where the goalposts are located, or how they will know when they have scored.

It is useful to be able to recognize the difference between an objective and a description, so try another example.

Which of the following statements looks most like an *objective?*

In at least two computer languages, be able to write and test a program to calculate arithmetic means.   Turn to page 15.

Linear and branching
programs

In arranging the sequence of steps, programmers may use a *linear* program, which tries to insure that every response will be correct, since there is only one path to the terminal behavior. Or they may use a *branching* program, in which there is less concern that all responses be right; if a wrong answer is supplied, students are provided with a branching set of questions to enable them to master the troublesome point. Since it would be impossible to provide supplementary frames for all the wrong answers that might be written in by a student, branching programs are often multiple choice. Students thus select their answers from a small number of alternatives, and a branch is supplied to correct wrong responses. Another type of branching program provides students with a more complete explanation of the misunderstood material and then urges them to go back and study the original explanation more carefully. The latter type of branching program is illustrated in Figure 5-3.

Skinner prefers the linear approach, which was used in writing the frames reproduced in Figures 5-1 and 5-2, because it requires students to supply their own responses and because it maximizes reinforcement. Other psychologists, notably N. A. Crowder (1963), favor

---

Discusses and illustrates principles and techniques of modern computer programming. *Turn to page 17.*

Page 15: You said, "be able to write and test a program to calculate arithmetic means in at least two computer languages" was a statement of an objective.

Correct! The statement describes an outcome—something the student is expected to be able to do—rather than the procedure by which the student will develop that skill.

Since you can tell the difference between a course description and a course outcome, it's time to move on.

Turn to page 19.

Page 17: Well . . . no. The collection of words which led you to this page is a piece of a course description—and not a very good description, at that. Look at it again:

Discusses and illustrates principles and techniques of modern computer programming.

Notice that the statement seems to be talking about what the course or the instructor will be doing. There isn't a word about what the student will be able to do as a result of the instruction. I hope you are not being misled by the fact that college catalogs are full of statements like this one. They are *not* statements of learning outcomes, and they are not what we are concerned with here.

Let me try to explain the difference this way. A course description outlines various aspects of a *process* known as instruction. A course objective, on the other hand, is a description of the *results* of the process known as instruction. It's sort of like the difference between bread and baking. Baking is what you do to get the bread, but it isn't the same as bread. Baking is the process; bread is the result. Similarly, instruction is the process; student competence is the result.

Turn to page 6, and read the material again.

Source: From the book *Preparing Instructional Objectives*, 2nd ed., by Robert F. Mager. Copyright © 1975 by Fearon Publishers, Inc. Reprinted by permission of Fearon Publishers, Inc.

branching programs because students are able to advance in larger steps and because the machine can "talk back" to them and thus come closer to approximating a human tutor.

In composing a program, the writer strives to reduce progressively the degree of *prompt*, or the number of cues necessary to elicit the correct answer. In the parlance of programming, the prompt is *vanished*. But in reducing cues, it is important to remember Skinner's experiments with pigeons and not to go too far too fast. In the program for teaching spelling (Figure 5-1), notice how the degree of prompt is gradually reduced. This type of prompt is called *formal* because it hints at the physical *form* of the response. In the physics unit (Figure 5-2), however, *thematic* prompts are used; answers are deduced from themes or associations previously learned.

Although the kinds of programs just described are the basic tool of a technology of teaching, other programmed techniques derived from S-R theory have been developed by Skinner and his associates. One such technique (described in *Handwriting with Write and See* by Skinner and Sue Ann Krakower) is used to teach handwriting to primary grade pupils. The various letter shapes are printed on a chemically treated paper, and the child traces over them with a special pen. Suppose a first grade girl is working with these materials. When she traces accurately, the pen produces a gray line. When she strays off the letters, the pen produces a yellow line. At first the printed prompt consists of the entire letter shapes. As the child progresses, parts of the letters are gradually vanished until only a few dots and dashes provide the prompt.

Sophisticated devices resembling jukeboxes have been used to develop a musical sense in children. The child tries to match beats and sounds produced by the machines, and correct responses are reinforced by candy or tokens. Other machines have been developed to help preschool children learn to discriminate between shapes and patterns by looking at a sample reproduced in one window and selecting an equivalent shape from other windows. More elaborate machines, developed to establish reading readiness, present auditory as well as visual patterns, which are often followed by a programmed reading series.

Skinner believes that operant conditioning can even be used to teach thinking (by conditioning the student to develop techniques of self-management, e.g., paying attention and studying efficiently), to foster creativity (by inducing greater amounts of behavior and reinforcing what is original), and to encourage perseverance (by systematically widening the ratios of reinforcement).

Though Skinner, his students, and his followers have developed the specific techniques just described, principles of operant conditioning have been applied in a variety of ways by other psychologists.

These include the Personalized System of Instruction, computer-assisted instruction, and behavior modification.

Personalized System of Instruction

Keller's Personalized System of Instruction

Fred S. Keller (1968), a colleague of Skinner, was so impressed by the educational potential of principles of operant conditioning that he developed a technique of teaching referred to as the *Personalized System of Instruction* (PSI) or as the *Keller Plan*. Keller first wrote a series of thirty units for a course in psychology that consisted of sections of the required text supplemented by a programmed version of the material. Students were provided with the first unit and told to study until they felt they thoroughly understood it, at which point they were asked to take a short quiz of ten fill-in questions and one short-answer essay on the material. Immediately after writing the answers, students took the test to a proctor (a student who had earned an A in the course the previous semester) to be corrected. For marginal answers, the proctor asked for further clarification. If the students met a predetermined criterion with or without any clarifying comments, their success was indicated on a wall chart and they were given the next unit. If they failed the exam by only one or two answers, the proctor called attention to sections of the text that should be read over and told those students to study for another thirty minutes. Then they were given another chance at the test. If they missed four or more questions, they were told they were not ready and they should study the material more intensively. Students who passed the first three units by a certain date were told they would have the privilege of attending a lecture or demonstration, a procedure that was followed for subsequent units. Thus all the presentations by the instructor served as vehicles of motivation and reinforcement. At the end of the semester, a final examination consisting of questions based on the quizzes was given.

The Personalized System of Instruction is clearly a direct application of principles of operant conditioning (state the terminal behavior; arrange instruction in step-by-step stages; provide immediate reinforcement). At the same time, this method fits many aspects of open education: It makes it possible for students to study independently and learn at their own pace. It makes provision for them to learn from each other. It presents material in a structured and organized fashion. It uses tests to diagnose and aid learning.

Variations of the Keller Plan have been developed by other psychologists. S. N. Postlethwait (1967) uses independent study sessions featuring tapes and films and has student proctors give oral quizzes and tutorial assistance. Harry C. Mahan (1967) favors Socratic-type programming involving tape-recorded interchanges between instructor and students. C. B. Ferster and M. C. Perrott (1968) use an interview technique in which students are asked to explain sections of the text.

Computer-assisted instruction

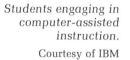

Computer-assisted instruction

The emergence of programmed instruction coincided with the development of computers capable of printing messages on screens similar to those on television sets. Dozens of psychologists who grasped the compatibility of programming and computers developed various forms of *computer-assisted instruction* (CAI). In some variations of CAI, the frames of a program are recorded on tape, and students respond to questions presented on the computer screen by typing out answers. In other variations, examinations on either programmed or nonprogrammed material are presented via computer. In either approach, various kinds of comments can be inserted to make the computer "talk" with the student. A section of a "conversational" computer exam developed by Glenn Cartwright of McGill University for test materials for an earlier edition of this text is reproduced in Figure 5-4.

A different computer-presented version of the same materials has been perfected by Richard M. Evans (1976). In the Evans approach, students are awarded three points if they select the correct answer on a multiple-choice question on the first try, two points if they select it on the second try, and one point if they choose it on the third try. They also have the opportunity, as in the Cartwright system, of requesting an explanation of why one answer is considered more correct than the

Students engaging in computer-assisted instruction.
Courtesy of IBM

Figure 5–4

Section of a print-out from a computer-assisted examination

Good afternoon, Joe, and welcome!

It's good to see you again. In this quiz, I will give you the opportunity after each question of requesting further explanation. You may do this whether or not you get the question right. I am leaving the choice up to you. You decide! So after each question I will type the word "EXPLANATION?" You simply type yes or no as you see fit. If you type yes I will be pleased to give you the explanation. If you type no, I will pick another question for you at random. And don't forget to tell your instructor if you prefer this system. We're doing our best to help you master the material.

Thank you for your attention, Joe! Now let's begin the quiz!

If you were to put into practice the key idea emphasized by Rosenthal and Jacobson in "Pygmalion in the Classroom," which of the following practices would you be most likely to follow in the classroom?

1. Do your best to be objective so that you don't produce the equivalent of an experimenter bias effect.

2. Give your students practice in taking tests, so that they will earn higher scores.

3. Make an effort to avoid stereotyping your pupils, particularly those, who for one reason or another, you tend to think of as lacking promise.

4. Tell all of your students their test scores in an effort to motivate them to improve.

Please type 1, 2, 3 or 4.

?

3

Good! You got it right!

Explanation?

?

No

Jerome Bruner has suggested a three-stage theory of intellectual development. A child who makes considerable use of visual imagery as he organizes his thoughts Bruner would place at the:

1. Concrete operations stage.

2. Enactive stage.

3. Iconic stage.

4. Preoperational stage.

Please type 1, 2, 3 or 4.

?

2

Not quite!

Explanation?

?

Yes

Why that choice? I'll tell you.

Bruner's series of stages is described on page 84. He selected the word iconic to emphasize the importance of visual imagery to a primary grade child. (Keep in mind that an icon is an image or a symbol.) His enactive stage stresses actions. The other two stages listed are from Piaget's classification.

others. In both approaches, students are encouraged to take alternate forms of exams to improve their performance. Evans reports that when students are given multiple chances to select the right answer, they are more inclined to analyze a question as well as the explanation of the answer. As a result, they are more likely to earn higher scores when they take alternate forms of an examination.

Until recently, most computers were quite cumbersome and expensive. Today, however, portable computers that sell for less than five thousand dollars are on the market. This means that many school systems can afford to establish a computer room, and you may have an opportunity to present lessons or exams via computer. To do this, you would first either purchase or prepare tapes for lessons, units, or chapters. Then, students could be instructed to sign up for appointments with a computer as soon as they feel ready to study a unit or take an exam.

If you secure a teaching position in certain large school systems, you may encounter elaborate computer-assisted approaches, such as the Program for Learning in Accordance with Needs (PLAN) developed by J. C. Flanagan (1971). Under PLAN, units of instruction are arranged in two-week modules, and for each unit there are several alternate sets of materials and procedures. Considerable stress is placed on having students select from among alternatives and direct their own learning. The computer handles test scoring, record keeping, scheduling, and analysis of student progress. In another program, Individually Prescribed Instruction (IPI), developed by W. W. Cooley and Robert Glaser (1969), the entire curriculum in a subject is broken down into units. (A math curriculum, for example, features 430 specific objectives and 88 units of study.) Students in IPI take a placement test that identifies their initial level of understanding, and they are then provided with a unit of appropriate difficulty. They work their way through the unit (taking computer-presented exams) until they meet the objectives; then they go on to the next unit. (For more complete information on uses of computers, see *Computer Assisted Instruction: A Book of Readings,* edited by R. C. Atkinson and H. A. Wilson.)

Behavior modification

Behavior modification

Although used in many ways, the term *behavior modification* basically refers to the use of operant conditioning techniques to—as the phrase indicates—modify behavior. In some cases, the behavior change is brought about by a literal application of the techniques Skinner uses on rats and pigeons. In one case (Wolf, Mees, and Risley, 1964), an autistic boy who had been born with cataracts and who frequently exploded into violent temper tantrums could not be induced to wear corrective glasses even though he was doomed to permanent blindness without them. First of all, therapists extinguished his temper tantrums by making sure that they were never followed by reinforcing circumstances. Then the boy was deprived of food and put in a room with several empty eyeglass frames scattered about. Every time he picked up a frame, he was given something to eat. In time, his behavior was shaped so that he put the frames on his face in the proper position. At that point lenses were inserted in the frames, and his sight was saved. Literal applications of Skinner's methods in controlling the behavior of hungry pigeons have been used by Lindsley (1960) and by Ayollon and Azrin (1965) in dealing with psychotic patients.

More frequently, behavior modification does not involve inducing hunger to increase the impact of food as a reinforcer, but rather it consists primarily of reinforcing desirable responses while ignoring undesirable ones. In classroom settings, reinforcement may consist of praise, opportunities to engage in desired activities, candy or money, or tokens that can be traded in for prizes. Kinds of classroom behavior modified through such techniques vary from overall academic performance (Evans and Oswalt, 1967) to reducing classroom noise (Schmidt and Ulrich, 1969) and eliminating disruptive behavior (Thomas, Becker, and Armstrong, 1968).

This brief survey of some of the educational innovations derived directly or indirectly from S-R theory should make it clear that Skinner has had a wide-ranging influence on education.

Criticisms of S-R theory

While many American psychologists and educators are enthusiastic about applications of S-R theory to teaching, others have called attention to some of the limitations and disadvantages of such applications. Some critics have questioned basic assumptions of S-R theory; others have criticized specific techniques.

Criticisms of basic assumptions

Some of Skinner's critics have found fault with the basic assumptions Skinner considers essential if science is to do for human behavior what it has accomplished in other fields. When Skinner re-emphasized his earlier assumptions in *Beyond Freedom and Dignity,* published in 1971, the book became a best seller, partly because of the number of outraged responses it stimulated. Most reviewers stressed points that had been made previously by critics of Skinner's earlier publications. Arthur Combs and Donald Snygg, for example, had criticized Skinner's environmental view of determinism because they felt it led to the assumption that human beings are similar to rats in a Skinner box. They observed:

Man is not a puppet bandied about at the mercy of the forces exerted upon him. On the contrary, he is a creature of discretion who selects his perceptions from the world he lives in. He is not the victim of events but is capable of perceiving, interpreting, even creating events. (1959, p. 309)

Combs and Snygg also pointed out that the Skinner approach to shaping behavior "requires that someone must know what the 'right' goal is in order effectively to manipulate the required forces" (p. 311).

Carl R. Rogers (1951) felt that Skinner's view of human behavior was a threat to efforts to improve mental health. In all his therapeutic sessions Rogers endeavored to help his clients develop a conviction diametrically opposed to Skinner's view: "I am not compelled to be simply the creation of others, molded by their expectancies, shaped by their demands. I am not compelled to be a victim of unknown forces within myself. . . . I am increasingly the architect of self. I am free to will and choose" (1963, pp. 268–269). Rogers engaged in a debate with Skinner (reported in *Science,* 124 [1956], pp. 1057–1066) and wrote an essay *Learning to Be Free* (1963), in which he took issue with the environmental view of determinism.

Abraham H. Maslow was bothered by the extent to which basic assumptions of S-R theory led to the conclusion that inherited characteristics were of no significance and that parents and teachers should try to shape behavior. He made this plea: "It is necessary in order for children to grow well that adults have enough trust in them and in the natural processes of growth, i.e., not interfere too much, not make them grow, or force them into predetermined designs, but rather let them grow and help them grow" (1968, p. 199).

Many of Skinner's critics argue that teachers who become too concerned about manipulating the classroom environment and student behavior risk practicing control for the sake of control. This point can be clarified by considering Skinner's experiments with animals. Many operant conditioning enthusiasts follow the practice of taking to a psychology class a hungry rat or pigeon in a Skinner box and asking students to specify what they would like the animal to do—for example, walk a figure-eight pattern. They supply food pellets when the animal moves in the desired direction and shape the desired behavior in a matter of minutes. It is an impressive demonstration, and the psychologist and students are reinforced by the extent to which the behavior of the animal has been controlled. Teachers who take a course in behavior modification and find that their first attempts to shape student behavior are successful are often equally impressed as well as excited about the possibilities of further control. It seems possible, however, that teachers who make substantial use of operant conditioning techniques might—without realizing it—tend to use such

Human beings need to feel they control their own behavior

methods not only because they want to produce behavior they have carefully preselected as likely to benefit students but also because they want to make life easier for themselves—and perhaps because they are reinforced by the degree to which they can control others. In such cases, learning may be limited rather than enhanced. In analyzing this possibility, consider some differences between animal and human behavior.

The pigeon whose behavior is shaped by an experimenter does not really benefit by being induced to walk in a figure-eight pattern. All it needs is food, and it could obtain this with less effort by not walking in circles. However, neither does it suffer, because even its spontaneous behavior would consist of random movements of various kinds. In a sense, then, only the experimenters benefit, because they have demonstrated their ability to produce such behavior; and even if the pigeon is manipulated, it makes no difference.

Those who use operant conditioning techniques with human beings do so because they believe they can produce behavior that will benefit those who are controlled. Unlike pigeons, though, human beings are capable of engaging in self-directed behavior that *might* be more beneficial to them than behavior selected by others. The manipulation of one human being by another might make a difference,

A basic criticism of the S-R view is that instructors who use programmed instruction and behavior modification techniques may become preoccupied with power and control.

Movie Star News

because it raises the question of who is to decide what will be beneficial—the controller or the individual. This point is raised by Combs
and Snygg when they state that such an approach "requires that
someone must know what the 'right' goal is in order effectively to
manipulate the required forces" (1959, p. 311). In deciding on "right"
goals, teachers might inadvertently choose those that will benefit them
more than their students, perhaps because of a desire to establish a
class routine that will simplify instruction, perhaps because shaping
the behavior of others gives them a sense of power. (If, because all
rewards are dispensed by a teacher, students seldom feel that their
own behavior is reinforcing, it is difficult for a teacher *not* to feel a
sense of importance and power.)

Controllers may choose
goals that benefit them

In deciding on "right" In *Beyond Freedom and Dignity* Skinner observes:

> In the prescientific view . . . a person's behavior is at least to some extent his
> own achievement. He is free to deliberate, decide, and act, possibly in original
> ways, and he is to be given credit for his successes and blamed for his failures.
> In the scientific view . . . a person's behavior is determined by a genetic
> endowment . . . and by the environmental experiences to which as an indi-
> vidual he has been exposed. (1971, p. 101)

This view is summed up by the statement "A person does not act upon
the world, the world acts on him" (p. 211). When Skinner maintains
that the "world" acts on the individual, he speaks of "environmental
experiences." However, he does not make explicit the fact that, in the
operant conditioning view, not an amorphous "world" but those who
arrange experiences are actually responsible for the behavior of the
individuals they manipulate. In this sense, the experimenter or
teacher deserves the credit for success that the "prescientific" view
attributes to the individual. (The teacher, in this view, is also blamed
for failure, which may be one explanation for current interest in
accountability.)

Skinner deserves full credit for what he induces his rats and
pigeons to do, since they would never be able to perform on their own
the feats he has conditioned them to perform. But do teachers deserve
similar credit when their students learn? With considerable effort a
child may be trained to score fifteen points higher on an intelligence
test, to master aspects of conservation a month ahead of schedule, to
finish a program on some subject, or to line up for recess with precision. If the child accomplishes these things, it is the individual who
provided the training or wrote the program or supplied reinforcement
who is responsible and deserves the credit, not the "world" or
"experiences." Even though she or he might not say it, the teacher in
such situations may think, "*I* made this child intelligent," or "*I* taught
this child how to think," or "Wow! Look at 'em jump into line when I
give the signal."

But, unlike the rat or pigeon, children can use language and thought to enhance exploration of ideas on their own and organize and adapt to experiences that make them potentially capable of even more impressive and personally valuable accomplishments if left to their own devices. Skinner notes, "To refuse to control (as in permissiveness) is to leave control not to the person, but to other parts of the social and non-social environments" (p. 84). He implies that the "other parts" of the environment will influence the individual in the same way and to the same extent as those that are deliberately arranged. Those who favor the views of Combs and Snygg, Maslow, and Rogers, however, believe that the individual will have greater freedom to *choose* from nonarranged "other parts" than from experiences that are highly structured by others.

The points just noted question some of the basic assumptions of S-R theory. Other questions about Skinner's technological approach to education take the form of evidence that techniques of teaching and behavior control based on operant conditioning have failed to live up to their early promise.

Evidence of the ineffectiveness of applications of S-R theory

When programmed instruction became popular in the 1950s, it was hailed by some educators as *the* ideal form of instruction. Schools were envisioned in which each pupil would be assigned to a cubicle and spend most of her or his time manipulating teaching machines, watching televised lectures and demonstrations, and doing independent study. America's leading electronics manufacturers vied with each other to produce elaborate teaching machines, some of them capable of reinforcing the student with recorded vocal responses that approximated the effect of a warm, friendly teacher. Foundation grants and state and federal pilot programs multiplied at a rapid rate. School superintendents, attuned to the business approach to education and eager to show that they were abreast of current developments, competed with one another to acquire both machines and grants.

Initial enthusiasm was followed by disappointment in many circles as some of the limitations of a primarily technological approach to education became apparent. For one thing, it soon became apparent that Skinner had been correct when he observed "a considerable measure of art is needed in composing a successful program" (1968, p. 49). Many of the programs issued during the boom period were boring, ineffective, or both. For another, the elaborate computerized teaching machines that had seemed especially promising cost so much that school systems were unable to buy them without some sort of subsidy, and most foundation and government grants were reserved for short-term pilot studies. Furthermore, a study of comprehensive applications of programmed instruction in four cities (Fund for the

Well-written programs are exception, not rule

Advancement of Education, 1964) led to the conclusion that although programs were often effective in helping students master specific topics (such as using a slide rule), they were not appropriate for many parts of the curriculum. Among problems that became apparent when programmed techniques were applied in a comprehensive way were difficulties in finding or preparing satisfactory materials, adapting programs to differences in student background and abilities, and creating programs that were not boring and impersonal in the eyes of the students.

In addition, not all of Skinner's original assumptions about programmed learning have been substantiated by research. The need for students to make an overt response (e.g., by writing an answer) and find out if it is correct does not seem to be as essential as Skinner believed it to be. R. A. Goldbeck and V. N. Campbell (1962) found that for simple or familiar material, students appeared to learn as much by simply reading through a program as by writing down answers and receiving feedback about the correctness of each answer. A number of studies (P. Sturges, 1972; W. J. McKeachie, 1974; J. M. Sassenrath, 1975) have revealed that immediate feedback is not always desirable. It appears that Skinner failed to take into account significant differences between rats, pigeons, and human beings when he developed programmed instruction. Animals learn simple tasks most effectively when they receive immediate feedback for each response, presumably because they are unable to store or process information in sophisticated ways. But human beings, who are able to memorize all kinds of information and associate past and present memories and experiences, may find that a response-feedback, response-feedback routine becomes tedious, annoying, or unnerving. A student taking a program may quickly grasp a point and be eager to learn something else, only to be asked to respond, find out if the response is correct, respond, and so on. When human beings are asked to deal with complex ideas, they may benefit from an *incubation* period (for reasons to be discussed in Chapters 6, 8, and 9), and immediate feedback may interfere with their attempts to process information in personally meaningful ways. It appears, therefore, that some of the features of programmed instruction that Skinner argued were its greatest strengths may actually be weaknesses in certain situations.

Perhaps the most damaging blow to the programmed instruction movement in education occurred in the early 1970s when the government sponsored a number of so-called *performance contracting* arrangements. Some critics of American education had argued that instruction might be improved if it were put on a contractual basis. It was reasoned that business firms are paid only when they fulfill the terms of a contract; therefore, teachers might be motivated to do a better job if they were paid only if their pupils reach a specified level of performance at the end of a given period of time. (This was one of

Immediate feedback not always desirable

the first and most extreme variations of accountability.) Accordingly, the government selected several cities where large numbers of students were below average in academic performance and offered to sign a contract with any company that agreed to produce specified types of improvement (e.g., a grade level higher in reading skill) within a year. If the contract specifications were exceeded, the company would be paid a bonus; if the company did not meet the specifications, however, they would not receive any money for their efforts.

Educational technologists headed most of the companies that won contracts. Thoroughly convinced of the values of operant conditioning in education, they set up learning situations that maximized applications of Skinner's teaching techniques. Materials were programmed in the most scientific manner possible, and traditional reinforcement in the form of the student's satisfaction in having provided correct answers and being given praise was supplemented with tangible rewards such as candy, money, or the chance to play games (such as pinball or pool).

By their very nature, performance contracts supply direct information about their effectiveness: If a majority of students exceeds the agreed-upon criterion, the contracting company makes money; if most fail, the company is not paid. The first comprehensive report on the results of performance contracting appeared in 1972 in a pamphlet published by the Office of Economic Opportunity (OEO), *An Experiment in Performance Contracting: Summary of Preliminary Results.* Despite the care and consistency in planning and the use of rewards as reinforcement, the OEO report reveals that almost all the performance contracts funded by the government failed to produce the agreed-upon amount of learning. Several companies went out of business. Thus, operant conditioning techniques, tried out under close to optimum conditions and evaluated with great objectivity and sophistication, were proved less successful than had been hoped.

Performance contracting not successful

A similar pattern of great enthusiasm followed by disappointment and doubts has characterized interest in behavior modification. In 1972 *Psychology Today* devoted most of its November issue to articles stressing the tremendous success and potential of behavior modification. Some of the most impressive evidence marshaled in support of applications of operant conditioning stressed successful shaping of the behavior of psychotics in institutions and inmates in reformatories and prisons. By the mid-1970s, however, confidence in behavior modification had been shaken, partly because initial successes were not always repeated, but also because of attacks by advocates of civil liberties. Governmental financing of several behavior modification programs in prisons, for example, was withdrawn when the complaint was made that they were designed to brainwash inmates so that they would become obedient, passive, and easier to control.

Instead of concluding from the evidence just summarized that programmed learning and behavior modification are worthless, it will be more constructive and instructive to consider possible explanations why problems have developed. Then it will be possible to make an effort to avoid or minimize disadvantages.

Explanations of the limited effectiveness of S-R theory

One way to discover possible reasons why programmed instruction has not become the basic means of instruction in public schools is to re-examine the sample programs depicted in Figures 5-1 and 5-2 and imagine you are asked to complete them. The first few minutes of operating a teaching machine and supplying responses to frames such as those illustrated might be intriguing and enjoyable. But would you want to spend four or five hours a day, 180 days a year, responding to such programs? After a few days—perhaps after a few hours or even a few minutes—supplying one-word answers would probably become boring if not irritating. If you grasped a point quickly, you might detest the needless repetition and yearn to skip ahead to something new. Sooner or later you would probably resent being asked to supply only the answer specified by the program writer. You might come to the conclusion that the primary purpose of education seemed to be to supply a brief response on cue, and you might wonder if you were not beginning to behave like a dog or seal trained to bark on command. The chance to work alone and at your own pace might seem desirable at times, but eventually you would probably yearn for opportunities to interact with other human beings.

Another way to examine the reasons why programmed instruction has not been an unqualified success is to evaluate the technique with reference to common criticisms of American education. Some critics of public schooling (e.g., John Holt, 1964, 1967) are bothered by the extent to which pupils become producers primarily interested in supplying correct answers. Many critics are convinced that learning is too controlled. Still others (e.g., Charles Silberman, 1970) are upset about preoccupation with order, which leads to student docility and conformity. All these points might apply in some circumstances to programmed instruction and behavior modification. The basic purpose of programs is to induce students to supply correct answers. The step-by-step routine of a program requires controlled learning in an ordered sequence. The basic purpose of behavior modification is to control behavior.

Not all students respond negatively to programs, and some programmed instructional techniques reduce the disadvantages stressed by the critics. Even so, the kinds of factors just outlined probably account for the failure of programmed instruction, teaching machines,

Supplying brief answers becomes tedious

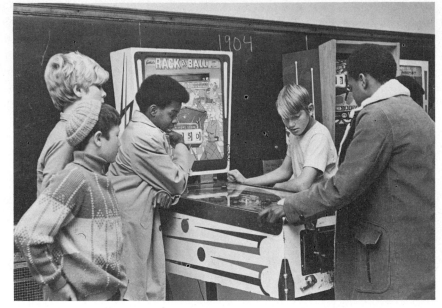

A reward room in a junior high school where instructors used a performance contracting approach based on S-R principles.

Courtesy of Dr. Joan Webster, Grand Rapids Public Schools, Director, Contract Learning Projects

and behavior modification to dominate education to the extent predicted by Skinner and his followers in the 1950s.

Since most performance contracting companies made use of programmed instruction, their failure might be attributed, in part at least, to the kinds of factors just noted. Another explanation for the inability of contractors to meet their goals (and for the ineffectiveness of programmed techniques) is the rapid decline of interest after initial enthusiasm. Think of a fifth grade boy who has never been successful in school and who is two grade levels below average in all basic skill areas. Imagine that his teacher, faced with the responsibility of working with thirty pupils and unable to provide individualized remedial instruction, reluctantly has decided to more or less ignore him, since previous efforts to help have been rebuffed. One day the boy is told that he is to participate in a special program to be offered in a special room. The fact that he has been *selected* for this program arouses pleasurable interest. The first day in the new classroom the boy is impressed by the enthusiasm of his teachers and is first incredulous and then delighted when told that each time he completes an assignment he will get a reward. It may be money, a poker chip to be traded in for candy or a phonograph record or other desirable objects, or the chance to play the pinball machine in an adjacent room. The initial reaction to this setup is almost sure to be enthusiastic. If the boy is far below grade level and has made little effort to learn for years, he is almost certain to make quick progress when he first tries to earn a reward. The novelty of getting *paid* for learning or being allowed to play pinball in school is sure to have immediate appeal. But what happens when the initial spurt of success is followed by the realization that further learning is going to require a great deal of effort? What happens when the new teachers and new techniques become familiar and routine? And what happens when the student begins to speculate, "Is concentrating on this stuff for an hour really worth twenty-five cents or a couple of games on the same old pinball machine?"

This description is pure conjecture, but it may account, in part at least, for the lack of success of performance contracting and also of behavior modification, which was the basic approach used by most performance contractors.

Many individuals who have used behavior modification techniques report a high degree of success. Most of the reports, however, offer immediate results as proof of effectiveness. Rarely do they discuss what happens after the same techniques have been used for an extended period of time. Furthermore, many of the most successful applications of behavior modification have taken place in mental institutions, prisons, or factories or with young children. Inmates or employees are in a subservient position, and young children are not always able to recognize what is happening when they are being manipulated. These factors account for the criticisms of civil libertarians who argue that behavior modification is unethical and perhaps illegal. The main point they make is that the behavior that is shaped is too often chosen primarily because it is convenient for the shaper. Institution orderlies and prison guards want inmates to obey orders. Employers want workers to do their jobs and not make trouble. Teachers may want students to keep quiet and do as they are told. Evidence supporting this last point is reported in a study by R. A. Winett and R. C. Winkler (1972), who analyzed articles on classroom management reported in the *Journal of Applied Behavior Analysis* (which is devoted to uses of behavior modification) between 1968 and 1970. Winett and Winkler subtitled the article "Be Still, Be Quiet, Be Docile" to reflect their conclusion that most teachers who use behavior modification in the classroom are interested in shaping submissive behavior.

While almost all of the articles noted by Winett and Winkler reported success in shaping behavior, the continued efficacy of the techniques described might be doubted for reasons noted in the previous analysis of performance contracting. A teacher's first efforts to shape behavior may be successful, but if the same techniques are used too often, they are likely to self-destruct. Even young pupils will soon catch on to the fact that they get praise or rewards only when they do what the teacher wants them to do. Some will resent this and perhaps misbehave out of spite. Others may weigh the amount of effort required to earn a favorable comment or a privilege and decide the

Teachers may be tempted to shape docility

Extensive use of behavior modification may reduce effectiveness reward is not worth the trouble. Older and wiser students may try to outshape teachers by responding with interest when a teacher moves toward the door and by yawning and acting bored when a teacher picks up a piece of chalk and approaches the board. Even if behavior modification is successful and if teachers avoid the pitfalls just noted, an almost inevitable by-product is the development of the attitude "What's in it for me?" Students may come to think of learning as something that one does to earn a reward—only a means to an end, never an end in itself. This not only reduces the likelihood that students will later learn some things just for the joy of it; it also means that learning may come to an abrupt halt when no one is around to supply rewards.

Now that you have considered the basic assumptions of S-R theory, become familiar with key experiments, learned about how Skinner feels principles based on these experiments can be applied to education, and examined some criticisms of the assumptions and recommendations, you are in a position to decide when and how you might apply S-R theory in your classroom. A summary of suggestions is given below to help you grasp the relationships between points and also to facilitate later reference and applications. Then each point is discussed, and examples of applications are offered.

Suggestions for teaching: Applying S-R theory in the classroom

1. Remain aware that behavior is the result of particular conditions.

2. Use reinforcement to strengthen behavior you want to encourage.

   a. When students are dealing with factual material, do your best to give feedback frequently, specifically, and quickly.

   b. When students are dealing with complex and meaningful material, consider using delayed feedback.

   c. Use several kinds of reinforcers so that each retains its effectiveness.

3. Use awareness of extinction to combat forgetting and to reduce the frequency of undesirable forms of behavior.

4. Be alert for generalization. When it occurs, use reinforcement (or lack of it) and explanations to bring about discrimination.

5. Take advantage of knowledge of the impact of different schedules of reinforcement to encourage persistent and permanent learning.

   a. When students first attempt a new kind of learning, supply frequent reinforcement. Then supply rewards less often.

   b. If you want to encourage spaced-out spurts of activity, use a fixed-interval schedule of reinforcement.

6. Use actual programs, either by writing your own or by obtaining a published program.

7. Use programmed approaches to teaching by describing terminal behavior, organizing what is to be learned, and providing feedback.

a. Describe the terminal behavior. That is, list exactly what you want students to learn after they have completed a given unit of study.

b. If appropriate, arrange the material to be learned into a series of steps or into an outline of points.

c. Provide feedback so that correct responses will be reinforced and so that students will become aware of and correct for errors.

8. If possible, use variations of the Personalized System of Instruction or of computer-assisted instruction.

9. When students must struggle to concentrate on material that is not intrinsically interesting, use special forms of reinforcement to motivate them to persevere.

a. Select, with student assistance, a variety of reinforcers.

b. Establish, in consultation with individual students, an initial contract of work to be performed to earn a particular reward.

c. Once the initial reward is earned, establish a series of short contracts leading to frequent, immediate rewards.

10. To reduce the tendency for pupils to engage in undesirable forms of behavior, first try withholding reinforcement and calling attention to rewards that will follow completion of a task. If that does not work, consider the possibility of taking away a privilege or of resorting to punishment.

11. Remain aware of criticisms and disadvantages of controlled education.

12. Make judicious and selective use of operant conditioning techniques.

1. Remain aware that behavior is the result of particular conditions. Even though you may not accept Skinner's environmental view of determinism to the point that you endorse his assumption that people are not free, it may be helpful to acknowledge that behavior *is* the result of particular conditions. Skinner and his followers believe that it should be possible to specify the conditions leading to any act of behavior if observations are made systematically. That is why they argue that you have two choices: Either shape behavior systematically, or do it in a haphazard way. This argument does not take into account that in a classroom (as contrasted with a Skinner box) many

causes of behavior may not be observable or traceable (except, possibly, through explorations of the unconscious, as in psychoanalysis). Furthermore, it is clearly impossible for a classroom teacher to handle teaching routine and also minutely observe and analyze the behavior of thirty pupils. You might as well accept the fact, therefore, that quite often you are going to be a haphazard shaper of behavior. Nevertheless, there will be times when you and your pupils may benefit if you say to yourself, "Now, there *have* to be causes for that behavior. Can I figure out what they are and do something about changing things for the better? Am I doing something that is leading to types of behavior that are making life difficult for some or all of us in the room?" When

Handbook heading
Checking on Causes of
Behavior

In some situations, teachers inadvertently cause disruptive behavior because they unintentionally reinforce such behavior. Sometimes, however, the disruptive behavior may be beyond the teacher's control, and the S-R theorist's advice that the behavior will "extinguish" if it is ignored may only make matters worse than if the teacher responded in some way.

engaging in such speculations, keep in mind that reinforcement strengthens behavior. Check to see if you are inadvertently rewarding pupils for misbehavior (by calling attention to them, for example) or failing to reinforce those who engage in desirable forms of behavior.

EXAMPLES

If you become aware that it takes a long time for your students to settle down at the beginning of a period and that you are reacting by addressing critical remarks specifically to those who dawdle the longest, ignore the dawdlers, and respond with interest to those who are ready to get to work.

Assume that you give students thirty minutes to finish an assignment. To your dismay, few of them get to work until toward the end of the period, and you find that you have to do a lot of nagging to hold down gossip and horseplay. When you later analyze why this happened, you conclude that you actually encouraged the time-killing behavior because of the way you set up the lesson. The next time you give a similar assignment, tell the students that as soon as they complete it, they can have class time to work on homework, a term project, or the equivalent and that you will be available to give help or advice to those who want it.

2. Use reinforcement to strengthen behavior you want to encourage. The four basic principles of operant conditioning are reinforcement, extinction, generalization, and discrimination. Awareness of each of these can be of value when you arrange learning experiences. The most important and significant of these principles is reinforcement, and there are several techniques of teaching that can be derived from knowledge of the impact of rewards on behavior.

When you think about how and when to supply reinforcement, though, keep in mind the research on feedback mentioned earlier. Skinner became convinced of the need for immediate feedback after each response just after he had completed experiments with rats and pigeons and had listened to his daughter describe her experiences in elementary school. If a pigeon is to be induced to peck a disk or if a third grader is to learn to read, spell, or do math problems, immediate feedback for each response is desirable. But when older students are asked to deal with complex and meaningful material, occasional and/or delayed feedback may be preferable. Therefore, as you decide how and when to supply feedback, take into account the kind of learning you are dealing with and the intellectual capacities of your students.

a. When students are dealing with factual material, do your best to give feedback frequently, specifically, and quickly. Elementary grade students spend much of their time learning specific bits of information—the alphabet, how to spell *house*, the product of six times six, and so on. Furthermore, they are at the concrete operations stage of cognitive development. For both these reasons, it usually makes sense to provide frequent and immediate feedback as often as possible when instructing elementary grade pupils. If a child misspells a word or supplies the wrong answer to an arithmetic problem, it is important to call attention to the error as specifically and quickly as possible. When a pupil supplies a correct answer, it is just as important to reinforce the response so that it will be strengthened. Accordingly, you should strive to supply frequent, detailed, and immediate feedback when teaching most subjects to elementary school children or when teaching factual information to older students.

EXAMPLES

After giving a problem, go over the correct answer immediately afterward.

Have pupils team up and give each other feedback.

Have some pupils go to the board while others work at their desks. Give a problem, and have those at their desks compare their answers to one at the board you identify as correct.

Meet with students in small groups (as in an open education approach) so that you can give more individual feedback per pupil.

When you assign reading or give a lecture or demonstration, have a short self-corrected quiz or an informal question and answer session immediately afterward.

Handbook heading

Ways to Supply
Specific and Immediate
Feedback

In your Handbook, you might note other techniques you could use to supply specific and immediate reinforcement for correct responses.

b. When students are dealing with complex and meaningful material, consider using delayed feedback. The techniques listed above are intended to supply immediate feedback. Although quick knowledge of correctness is desirable in many types of learning, as noted earlier, when students are dealing with meaningful material there may be advantages to supplying delayed feedback. (This is especially true of older students who are formal thinkers.) To see why this may be true, think about how you feel when you are asked to answer a comprehensive essay question on an exam or write a term paper. You are almost sure to come up with ideas over a period of time, and some of these may occur after you have handed in an assignment. Have you ever experienced the frustration of thinking of a terrific point just *after* leaving an examination room or dropping off a term paper? If so, you can grasp why immediate feedback is not always necessary or desirable. Sometimes students will think more about a subject and come up with their own "corrections" if there is an interval of time between writing an answer and receiving an evaluation of it. (Just after you finish an exam, do you examine your notes and the text to check on certain questions? If so, you are engaging in self-feedback, which might mean more to you than an answer supplied immediately by a teacher or program.) Consequently, you should not feel that supplying corrections of student work several days or even weeks after it was completed will necessarily be ineffective.

EXAMPLES

Hand back and discuss all exams. Even though students may have written their answers a week or more earlier, they will still be getting feedback when they look at the answer they wrote as you discuss it.

On written work, correct spelling and grammatical errors (if you can), and make brief favorable comments when a section is particularly well phrased or when an important point is emphasized. Make general favorable comments—if deserved—at the end of the paper.

Before handing back a term paper, essay exam, or the equivalent, you might ask students to jot down additional points they thought of after they completed the work. Or you might announce, "If you realized after you completed your work that you had made a mistake, make a note of it and mention how you would correct it if you were to do the assignment over again now. Then we can see if your evaluation agrees with mine." If you try out this idea, you might make some sort of allowance (perhaps in the form of some bonus points) for corrections made by students before they examine your corrections.

Handbook heading
Ways to Supply
Delayed Feedback

If you can think of other ways to supply delayed feedback, note them in your Handbook.

   c. Use several kinds of reinforcers so that each retains its effectiveness.   In many learning situations the correct answer to a problem serves as the reinforcer. In other situations, however, the reinforcer will take the form of a comment or a smile from you, a mark or a grade or other symbol of achievement, or the chance to engage in a desired activity. Some enthusiasts for behavior modification urge teachers to try to shape their own praising behavior by first making a record of the number of favorable comments, smiles, and so on, emitted before behavior control is instituted (called the *baseline period* by behavior modification specialists) and then engaging in a systematic effort to increase the frequency of each type of reinforcement. (If this idea sounds appealing to you, you will find instructions and sample forms to use on pages 485–490 of *Teaching: A Course in Applied*

Psychology [1971] by Becker, Engelmann, and Thomas.) It seems possible, however, that if you are too methodical about supplying reinforcement, you might cause students to think that you are insincere. If you try to increase your praising ratio from ten to twenty per period, for example, you might have to work extra hard at projecting enthusiasm and genuine appreciation. On the other hand, if you do not pay any attention to how you dispense reinforcement, you may be inefficient or actually work against yourself. Perhaps the best policy is to think frequently about how and when you use different types of reinforcement but not to the point of keeping a tally of techniques (which might cause you to act in robot fashion).

Handbook heading
Ways to Supply
Different Types of
Reinforcement

EXAMPLES

*One of the basic
principles of instruction
highlighted by S-R
theory is that teachers
should provide
reinforcement for
correct responses.*

Phil Mezey/DPI

When a student gives a correct answer or makes a good point in class discussion or does something helpful, say things like: "Good." "That's right." "Terrific." "Great." "Very interesting point." "I hadn't thought of that." "I really appreciated what you did." "That was a big help." (If you believe in being prepared, you might list in your Handbook similar statements to use as verbal reinforcers. In addition to making such comments, smile and show that you are sincere.)

Walk over to and stand near a pupil who seems to be having a hard time concentrating.

With younger pupils, give a pat on the back after an especially good achievement.

Encourage students to keep a private chart of their achievements and to record their progress, perhaps with colored ink, gold stars, or the like. (Before you dismiss gold stars or the equivalent as infantile or silly, glance through several issues of a local newspaper and count the number of pictures or articles reporting awards that have been made. If the most improved junior varsity football player is given a two-foot-high trophy, for example, why shouldn't a math student get a similar—though less impressive—symbol of achievement?)

Announce in advance how many points a particular assignment will count toward a final grade. Award bonus points for work completed ahead of time or for extra work.

3. Use awareness of extinction to combat forgetting and to reduce the frequency of undesirable forms of behavior.   Many of the techniques just described are intended to combat extinction. When dealing with knowledge, extinction is equivalent to forgetting. Consequently, you will want to supply occasional reinforcement to maintain responses that have been learned. (A variety of techniques for doing this, many of them based on principles of operant conditioning, will be discussed in Chapter 8.) When dealing with nonacademic forms of behavior, you will sometimes want to use knowledge of extinction to reduce the frequency of misconduct or disruptive activities. The basic rule to follow is: consistently ignore behavior that you would prefer to have weaken or disappear. It is not always possible to do this, of course, and sometimes your lack of response will be offset by positive responses from students, but you can still exert a degree of control by studiously ignoring behavior you want to discourage.

EXAMPLES

If a boy experiments with knocking his books off his desk in an effort to arouse a response, pay no attention and continue with the lesson.

If a student says something transparently provocative in class discussion, don't comment, and immediately call on someone else.

4. Be alert for generalization. When it occurs, use reinforcement (or lack of it) and explanations to bring about discrimination.   Regardless of the grade level or subject you teach, your students will tend to apply what they learn in one situation to what they perceive to be similar situations. Sometimes this is desirable. In other cases, how-

ever, it will cause problems. When you become aware that pupils are generalizing in ways that lead to errors or misconceptions, encourage them to discriminate by using selective reinforcement or by calling attention to differences.

EXAMPLES

When a kindergartner says, "I saw two gooses," explain that even though that seems like the logical way to say it, the word for more than one goose is *geese*.

If a high school language student conjugates an irregular verb by applying rules for regular verbs, point out that the verb *is* irregular and should simply be memorized.

5. Take advantage of knowledge of the impact of different schedules of reinforcement to encourage persistent and permanent learning.

   a. When students first attempt a new kind of learning, supply frequent reinforcement. Then supply rewards less often. Keep in mind the impact of different schedules of reinforcement by taking into account Skinner's experiments with rats and pigeons. When Skinner wanted to encourage rats and pigeons to learn bar pressing and disk pecking, he first reinforced every response. While this was the most efficient way to train the animals initially, the behavior extinguished rapidly as soon as reinforcement stopped. After the animals had learned the basic skill, they were more likely to continue to respond at a steady rate when put on a fixed-ratio or intermittent schedule of reinforcement. You can also use the same techniques of reinforcement in your classroom.

EXAMPLES

When introducing new material, give a point for every correct response. Then specify that a point can be earned only if five questions are answered correctly.

When students first try a new skill or type of learning, praise almost any genuine attempt, even though it may be inept. Then, as they become more skillful, reserve your praise only for especially good performances.

Avoid a set pattern of commenting on student work.

Make favorable remarks at unpredictable intervals.

If students in a gym class catch on that the instructor walks methodically up and down checking to see if everyone is doing calisthenics, they may do their pushups (or whatever) only when they know they

Sometimes consistent generalizing leads to problems

In Chapter 4 mention was made of the fact that preschoolers tend to stick to their own rules in using language, as when saying that the teacher "holded the baby rabbits." In many respects, children who first learn to form the past tense of a verb by adding ed (as when scold becomes scolded) are generalizing more consistently than those who concocted verb forms for the English language. When dealing with the generalizations of young children, therefore, it would be wise to allow for the possibility that three-year-olds may be more consistent in their thinking than the venerable British linguists who originally proposed verb forms. You should also remember that children are eager to maintain cognitive equilibrium. The tendency for children to generalize and their urge to accommodate new ideas into already existing schemes are illustrated by the following anecdote.

A three-year-old girl was looking at a picture in a book titled Three Billy Goats Gruff. *She carefully pointed to each goat and said: "Look! Three billy goats eated." Her mother, busily working near her, simply said, "Ate."*

The girl once again counted the figures in the picture and said, "Three billy goats eated." Her mother responded again by mechanically saying, "Ate."

At that point the little girl shrugged her shoulders and said, "OK! Eight billy goats eated!"

Source: Reported by Dennis A. Warner of Washington State University in a personal communication.

are being watched. To encourage steady exercise, it would be better to follow an unpredictable pattern when observing this kind of behavior.

Handbook heading
Ways to Use Schedules
of Reinforcement

If you can think of other ways to use fixed-ratio or intermittent schedules of reinforcement, note them in your Handbook.

b. If you want to encourage spaced-out spurts of activity, use a fixed-interval schedule of reinforcement. Occasionally you will want to encourage students to engage in spurts of activity, since steady output might be too demanding or fatiguing. In such cases, supply reinforcement at specified periods of time.

EXAMPLES

Schedule a quiz every Wednesday.

When students are engaging in strenuous or concentrated activity, circulate and provide praise and encouragement by following a set pattern that will bring you in contact with each student at predictable intervals.

Experimenting with schedules of reinforcement is probably worthwhile, but don't be surprised if your pupils fail to respond in the predicted manner. What happens in the classroom is not always identical to what happens in a Skinner box. There is a film on operant conditioning, for example, that first shows some pigeon experiments depicting various schedules of reinforcement, then a classroom situation in which a boy is called on several times in a row when he raises his hand. Calling on the boy reinforces his eagerness to recite, but the response is rapidly extinguished when the teacher abruptly stops calling on him. Several experienced teachers who saw this film tried to duplicate the experiment in their own classrooms. They reported that as far as they could tell, varying the reinforcement schedule applied to hand raising in actual classrooms made no difference. The same pupils put up their hands at the same rate regardless of the reinforcement supplied. The moral of this experience is obvious but worth noting: Children are not pigeons.

An animal that has no life outside a Skinner box and only a limited repertoire inside it may have its behavior shaped by a specific change in its environment precisely because its environment is so restricted. If all a pigeon sees are food pellets, sudden failure of the pellets to appear is a cage-shaking experience. But children are infinitely complex, and their behavior at any given moment may be influenced by countless stimuli within their environment and countless others outside it. If a boy happens to be paying attention and wants more than anything in the world to please his teacher, he might be upset if he is not reinforced when he raises his hand. But if he is engrossed in examining the profile of the girl in front of him or in dreaming about the Little League game that evening, he won't care at all about not being reinforced. In fact, he won't even *realize* that he isn't being reinforced.

6. Use actual programs, either by writing your own or by obtaining a published program. Composing a program from scratch requires considerable time, care, and expertise. If you feel inclined to try, you will need to consult one or more books written for novice programmers. Three of the best are *A Guide to Programmed Instruction* by Jerome P. Lysaught and Clarence M. Williams, *Good Frames and Bad: A Grammar of Frame Writing* by Susan Meyer Markle, and *Practical Programming* by Peter Pipe.

But even with the aid of these books, be prepared for some frustrations. For one thing, initial attempts to write a program are usually unsuccessful because of the difficulty of anticipating the different ways in which children will react. Remember, it is essential that almost all questions be answered correctly (Skinner sets the minimum at about 95 percent) in order to make the most of reinforcement, avoid aversive consequences, and maintain continuity. Almost invariably, original programs will "lose" many students because the programmer cannot anticipate how all children will respond and will fail to ask the right questions in exactly the right sequence.

Since programmed instruction provides detailed and permanent feedback in the form of answers supplied by the pupils, it would seem that a teacher could easily correct a program by examining these answers. One problem here is time. Obviously, only a painstaking analysis of all responses can reveal every programming error. Moreover, such an analysis sometimes has to be repeated several times, and this often produces subsidiary problems: The children may become bored when they are presented with the same program again, or their responses may not be valid because of their previous exposure to the questions.

In addition to the sheer amount of work involved in writing and testing programs, there is the problem of allowing for individual differences in ability. Skinner argues that programs do allow for differences because each child proceeds at her or his own rate, but this is not a complete answer. Every teacher, even one who deals with homogeneously grouped students, must pace a presentation so that it is not too fast for the slow learners and not too simple for the fast ones. The most common solution is an almost automatic tendency to concentrate on the slow students. When teachers do this, they can be reasonably sure that they are getting through to the less able students, even though the brighter ones may be bored.

Lowest common denominator effect

Program writers have the same problem and usually arrive at the same solution. Markle (1969) notes that in order to insure that approximately 95 percent of the answers will be correct, as Skinner suggests, programmers are forced to keep revising programs for the *lowest common denominator*—the slowest students in the group. This eventually leads to programs that most students can complete fairly easily, but it also leads to programs that are oversimplified and repetitious. Slow students won't be bothered by this, but bright pupils may become bored and absent-minded, just as they would if they were listening to an overly simple lecture. If they can supply answers automatically, they may gain only superficial understanding or slide over a key point. And if they are irritated by the simplicity of the program, they may not even be willing to backtrack to find their errors. Of course, you could cope with the problem of ability differences by writing two or more sets of programs, but this would be possible only if you had an unlimited amount of time, which you will not have.

In view of all these problems, it is probably more realistic to assume that you will have to depend on using published materials if you wish to use programs.

Hundreds of programs have been published. They cover all sorts of subjects, and they vary considerably in quality. You can consult several journals to discover what is available: *The Journal of Programed Instruction, Programed Instruction* (the bulletin of the Center for Programed Instruction), and *Programed Instructional Materials* edited by Kenneth Komoski. If you have complete freedom to choose a program, in order to make sure you pick out a fairly decent one consult the book *A Guide to Evaluating Self-Instructional Programs* by Paul Jacobs, Milton Maier, and Laurence Stolurow.

You should realize, however, that even if you find a program that seems appropriate for your curriculum, that is rated as adequate, and that your school district can afford, you still face complications. It has been found, for example, that programs perfected on one group of children may not succeed with another group. This sometimes occurs because the curriculum in the standardization school was atypical in subtle ways and prepared the children for some of the questions. Children who are products of a different curriculum may be unable to answer these questions, and if they get off the track just once or twice, the entire program may be ineffective.

You may also be faced with the task of holding down competition so that pupils don't race to see who can finish first. It seems logical to assume that children who skim through a program are less likely to absorb it thoroughly than those who take their time. You may want to disguise, as much as possible, the rates at which individual students are learning.

The fact that pupils finish the program at different times—which Skinner sees as in *advantage* of machine instruction—creates still another problem. Unless you are able to assign individual students one program after another, which is unlikely, you will be faced with the task of organizing activities for an ever increasing number of pupils. Finding ways to occupy the time of rapid learners who complete an assignment early is not a problem unique to programmed learning, but the nature of machine instruction may require you to be especially ingenious in devising supplementary exercises until the entire class is ready to go on to another assignment.

7. Use programmed approaches to teaching by describing terminal behavior, organizing what is to be learned, and providing feedback.   Skinner taught pigeons to peck tunes on a xylophone and play table tennis by reinforcing a series of approximations to the desired terminal behavior. His success in doing this led him to propose that programmed instruction, based on the same principles and techniques, should become the basic form of instruction used in schools. As noted in the analysis of criticisms of the S-R view, it is highly unlikely that you will be able to use an all-programmed approach in your classroom. It is almost certain, however, that some of the lessons

you present will be more effective if you take account of some of Skinner's suggestions.

Regardless of the grade level or subject you teach, there are likely to be some types of knowledge that can be specifically defined. In order to learn how to read, primary grade pupils need to master letters and words. In order to learn how to spell and do mathematics, elementary grade students need to memorize combinations of letters and numbers. In order to comprehend discussions of most subjects, junior high students need to acquire understanding of facts and principles. In order to learn a foreign language, high school students need to memorize thousands of words and verb forms. Whenever you want to help students master information of this type, consider using the following procedure.

Handbook heading
Describing Terminal
Behavior

a. Describe the terminal behavior. That is, list exactly what you want students to learn after they have completed a given unit of study.

EXAMPLES

List all the mathematical concepts to be learned during a report period or year.

Pick out fifty frequently misspelled words.

Select ten or so facts or principles that you consider to be the key points in a chapter of a text.

b. If appropriate, arrange the material to be learned into a series of steps or in an outline of points.   In some cases there will be no logical way to organize the points you have listed. It rarely makes any difference, for example, how a list of spelling words is arranged. Most of the time, though, you can help your students master material by arranging ideas in sequence or by organizing points so that one emerges from or is related to others.

EXAMPLES

Select a series of readers for use in the primary grades where the words learned in the first book make it simpler to read those in later books.

Have language students use a conversational approach so that they grasp sentence structure as they memorize vocabulary and verb forms.

In a science class, group related facts and concepts and present them as separate units.

Before giving a lecture or demonstration or showing a film, hand out a sheet of paper listing in organized form the points that will be covered, leaving space under each for student notes.

c. Provide feedback so that correct responses will be reinforced and so that students will become aware of and correct for errors. Since the key principle of operant conditioning is reinforcement, it is essential to provide feedback to strengthen correct responses and inform students when their responses are incorrect. Therefore, you should follow procedures noted under point 2 in this list of suggestions to supply frequent, specific, and prompt feedback. In addition, use techniques such as those listed below.

EXAMPLES

Immediately after students read a chapter in a text, give them an informal quiz on the key points you listed. Then, have them pair off, exchange quizzes, correct and discuss them.

As soon as you complete a lecture or demonstration, ask individual students to volunteer to read for the rest of the class what they wrote about the points they were told to look for. Indicate whether the answer is correct; and if it is incorrect or incomplete, ask (in a relaxed and nonthreatening way) for additional comments. Urge students to amend and revise their notes as they listen to the responses.

8. If possible, use variations of the Personalized System of Instruction or of computer-assisted instruction. If you are systematic and thorough in carrying out the procedure just described, you may be able to use variations of Fred Keller's Personalized System of Instruction, with or without the aid of computers. To carry out the Keller Plan, you should devise a series of short units and quizzes on a given subject. Perhaps the simplest way to do this is to identify key points for each chapter in a text and prepare multiple-choice or completion exams to measure understanding of these points. Then schedule a series of exam days. As soon as students complete their exam on a given unit, score them yourself on an individual basis, or have student proctors who have already passed the exam do it for you. (If you use multiple-choice or completion questions, exams can usually be scored in less than a minute.) Finally, invite students to refer to their texts or notes so that they can write out more complete explanations to themselves of points they missed. Ideally, you should then give anyone who wants it a chance to take a different exam on the same material. This will serve to motivate students to read the text over in order to correct errors and omissions. It will also help them master the material more thoroughly.

Handbook heading
Using the Personalized
System of Instruction

If you happen to have access to a computer room, you can put the questions on tapes and instruct students to sign up for appointments as soon as they feel ready to take an exam. (If your school does not own a computer, you might be able to persuade them to purchase one if you can prove that you would make steady use of it.)

To encourage students to analyze their answers and request feedback, you might try the graded scoring technique developed by Richard Evans: give three points of credit if the correct answer on a four-item multiple-choice question is chosen on the first try, two points if selected the second try, one point if selected on the third try. The computer approach is much more effective if, in addition to indicating if an answer is correct or incorrect, you also explain why the answer identified as correct is preferable to the other options.

9. When students must struggle to concentrate on material that is not intrinsically interesting, use special forms of reinforcement to motivate them to persevere.   In discussing uses of reinforcement in earlier points in this list of suggestions, the stress was on providing feedback or taking advantage of knowledge of the impact of different schedules of reinforcement. You can also use reinforcement to motivate students to complete difficult tasks. In order to master almost any skill or subject, a certain amount of tedious and disagreeable effort is usually necessary. Hardly any students shout with joy, for example, when they are requested to learn spelling words, practice addition or multiplication, memorize chemical symbols, do calisthenics, and so on. Furthermore, some students—for a variety of reasons—may have an extraordinarily difficult time concentrating on almost anything. Accordingly, you may sometimes find it essential to use techniques of behavior modification to help students stick to a task. If and when that time comes, you might follow these procedures, based on Skinner's experiments with pigeons in which successive approximations to the terminal behavior were reinforced.

a. Select, with student assistance, a variety of reinforcers.   A behavior modification approach to motivation appears to work most successfully when students are aware of and eager to earn a payoff. Because students react differently to rewards and because any reward is likely to lose its effectiveness if used to excess, it is desirable to list several kinds of rewards and permit students to choose. Some behavior modification enthusiasts (e.g., Homme and Tosti, 1971) even recommend that you make up a *reinforcement menu* for each pupil. Such a menu might consist of such time-honored rewards as gold stars, marks on a chart, or points leading to a grade. But a type of reward prefered by many S-R psychologists is based on what is sometimes called the *Premack principle,* sometimes referred to as *Grandma's rule.* The Premack principle (Premack, 1959) states that any higher probability behavior will reinforce any lower probability behavior upon which it is contingent. Put in terms that Grandma might have used, the principle can be stated: If you will do something you'd rather not do first, I'll let you do something you really like to do as a reward.

Handbook heading
Ways to Have Students
Suggest Reinforcers

Premack principle
(Grandma's rule)

(This is called Grandma's rule because it is based on a technique used by generations of grandmothers when they said things like "Eat all of your mashed potatoes and peas and you can have your dessert.")

Individual reward menu

If all your pupils are allowed to prepare individual reward menus, they should be instructed to list school activities they really enjoy doing. It would be wise, however, to stress that entrées on anyone's menu must be approved by you in order to make sure they will not conflict with school regulations or interfere with the rights of others. It would not be possible, for example, for a pupil to go home early, practice a guitar, or smoke in the classroom. A student's reward menu might consist of activities such as these: read a book of my own choice, work on an art or craft project, use earphones to listen to a tape or record, explore a general interest corner, go to the library, view a film or a filmstrip in another room. (If you have the space and the resources, you might even establish a *reinforcing event area* made up of toys and games that almost all children enjoy. This technique was used by many performance contractors who were able to purchase pool tables and pinball machines. For the most part, though, it seems preferable to use actual school activities as rewards.)

b. Establish, in consultation with individual students, an initial contract of work to be performed to earn a particular reward. Once you have established a list of payoffs, you should consult with students (on an individual basis, if possible) to establish a certain amount of work that must be completed in order to obtain a reward selected from the menu. The first contract should not be too demanding, to ensure that the student will earn the reward.

Handbook heading
Ways to Set Up
Learning Contracts

EXAMPLES

Successfully spell at least seven out of ten words on a list of previously misspelled words.

Correctly complete twenty addition problems made up of two-digit numbers.

Outline twenty pages in the text, and correctly answer at least seven out of ten questions based on the key points.

c. Once the initial reward is earned, establish a series of short contracts leading to frequent, immediate rewards. The results of many operant conditioning experiments lead to the conclusion that the frequency of reinforcement is of greater significance than the amount of reinforcement. Therefore, having students work on a series of brief contracts leading to frequent payoffs provided immediately after the task is completed is preferable to having them work toward a delayed, king-size reward.

EXAMPLES

Ask students to learn how to spell a list of fifty tough words by rewarding themselves after they have mastered batches of five or ten.

Have students accumulate points toward a final grade by completing an exam or project every week, instead of scheduling one or two comprehensive exams and a blockbuster term paper.

10. To reduce the tendency for pupils to engage in undesirable forms of behavior, first try withholding reinforcement and calling attention to rewards that will follow completion of a task. If that does not work, consider the possibility of taking away a privilege or of resorting to punishment.   Students often engage in types of behavior that are disruptive in one way or another. Theoretically, such behavior will tend to extinguish if it is not reinforced. Therefore, as noted in point 3, your first reaction might be to ignore it. Unfortunately, however, you will not be the only reinforcing agent in the classroom. You may ignore a wisecrack, for example, but classmates sitting around the culprit may respond enthusiastically and strengthen the tendency to wisecrack. Furthermore, in some cases you simply cannot ignore behavior. If a pupil is on the verge of destroying school property or injuring a classmate, you may be held responsible if you fail to respond. Accordingly, you may need to follow a sequence something like this when confronted by undesirable behavior, such as two boys engaging in a scuffle when assigned to work together on a chemistry experiment. (Assume that the scuffling behavior becomes more violent after each phase.)

Handbook heading
Ways to Use Behavior
Modification to
Maintain Control

First, ignore the behavior.

Second, remind the class that those who finish the experiment early will earn five bonus points and be allowed to see a film.

Third, approach the boys and tell them (privately and nicely) that they are disturbing others and making life difficult for themselves because if they do not complete the experiment in the allotted time, they will have to make it up at some other time.

Fourth, resort to punishment by informing the boys (in a firm but not nasty way) that they must leave the classroom immediately and report to the vice principal to be assigned to a study hall for the rest of the class period. Tell them they will have to complete the experiment when the rest of the class has free experiment time.

Finish by pointing out that once the work is made up, they will be all caught up and in a good position to do above average work the rest of the report period.

This sequence is based on studies (e.g., Hall and others, 1971) leading to the conclusion that punishment is most effective when it occurs immediately after a response, cannot be avoided, is as intense as seems necessary, and provides the individual with an alternative and desirable response.

Constructive classroom control will be discussed more completely in Chapter 15, but in this outline of applications of S-R theory it is appropriate to call attention to a few undesirable by-products of punishment. Even though punishment may be effective in inhibiting student behavior, there is the risk that the individual will come to associate anxiety, shame, and anger aroused by the act with the punisher and the situation. A student may come to fear and hate a teacher, a classroom, a subject of study, or the whole idea of school, particularly if punishment is excessively harsh, protracted, or embarrassing. This may be especially true if the punishment is perceived as unfair or if there is no escape from it.

A final point regarding punishment is that it differs from what Skinner refers to as *negative reinforcement*. Skinner describes punishment as the use of an aversive stimulus intended to inhibit the response that preceded it. Negative reinforcement, on the other hand, is designed to strengthen an escape response. The sequence outlined above ended with punishment—the scuffling boys were required to endure the aversive consequences of being banished to a study hall. Instead of resorting to punishment in such a situation, suppose you say, "If you don't stop that fooling around and finish that experiment, I'll give you both an F for this unit." That would be an application of negative reinforcement because if the boys responded as planned they would do the experiment not to gain a reward but to avoid negative consequences.

Negative reinforcement is sometimes effective, but it may be risky because it is not always possible to predict the kind of escape behavior that will be used. In this case, your intention would be that the boys would try to escape the low grade by working diligently on the experiment. If the boys resented the threat, though, or were fooling around because they did not know how to get started on the experiment, they might literally escape from the whole situation by not coming to class for several days. Consequently, it is preferable to use positive reinforcement and stress the rewards that will follow desired activities.

11. Remain aware of criticisms and disadvantages of controlled education. Even if you were skeptical about how much you might use techniques of teaching based on principles of operant conditioning when you began this chapter, you have probably made a mental note to try at least some of the methods you have just read about. If you do experiment with some of these techniques and if they turn out to be successful, you may need to guard against being shaped into a demon behavior controller. The discovery that you can shape some of the

behavior of students in a predictable manner may cause you to try to shape almost all their behavior. Such a reaction would be unfortunate for at least two reasons: (1) You will tend to make your students dependent, passive, docile, calculating, and materialistic. (2) The more you use operant conditioning techniques, the more likely they are to become ineffective.

The first point refers to the fact that programmed techniques require students to supply answers—usually very short answers—that have been selected by someone else. When pupils are being asked to learn factual material, this may not be a disadvantage, provided they spend only part of the school day or class period engaging in such study. If students spend most of their time interacting with actual programs or programmed exercises, or listening to programmed lectures, however, they are likely to think of education as consisting entirely of supplying brief answers on cue. As a result, they may fail to retain or develop such traits as independence, initiative, and self-direction. Furthermore, if excessive use is made of reinforcing events, students may approach every task by thinking in terms of its payoff value. This may lead to the conviction that learning is always work and that it should never be engaged in unless it is followed by a specific reward.

The second point can be illustrated by referring to the suggestion made by some behavior modification enthusiasts that you try to shape

© 1965 United Feature Syndicate, Inc.

your own praising behavior. If you succeed in increasing the number of positive responses you make from, say, ten an hour to thirty an hour, your praise is almost sure to become so automatic and frequent it will lose its effectiveness. The same reasoning applies to most other behavior control techniques—doing everything for a reward gets boring; reinforcing events may become unrewarding.

Finally, if you experiment with techniques of behavior modification to establish and maintain classroom control, your successes may shape you in undesirable ways. To guard against this possibility, you might frequently ask yourself: "Am I doing this because it's good for the pupils or the learning atmosphere, or am I doing it because it makes life easier for me or gives me a sense of power?"

For reasons such as these, you are more likely to get positive results if you make occasional and selective use of operant conditioning principles.

12. Make judicious and selective use of operant conditioning techniques. Since programmed techniques require students to supply specific answers, such methods are most useful when students are being asked to learn factual material. One way to estimate how appropriate a programmed approach might be is to take a stab at describing the terminal behavior for a unit. If you find that you have listed a number of facts, concepts, or specific techniques, consult the preceding list of suggestions before you plan lessons.

Handbook heading
Deciding When to Use a
Programmed Approach

Another way to estimate if programmed approaches are appropriate is to evaluate student background and confidence. When they first encounter a subject, most students need reassurance that they are learning. Students who are insecure and/or who are experiencing learning problems may need almost continuous evidence that they are making progress. Because programmed techniques stress step-by-step learning and supply frequent evidence that learning is taking place, they are particularly effective when students need tangible proof that they are getting somewhere.

Now that you have examined a description of S-R views and are acquainted with techniques of programmed instruction and behavior modification, you probably realize that you are certain to use some of the techniques described. No matter what grade level or subject you teach, there will be times when you will want to present lessons that are organized to lead students to a predetermined goal. No matter how enthusiastic and skilled you are as a teacher, there will be times when you will need to offer rewards to induce students to concentrate on assigned work, or take steps to limit or eliminate disruptive behavior. Because of some of the limitations and criticisms noted, however, you will not be able to make exclusive use of teaching techniques based on the stimulus-response view. There will be times when you will want to encourage students to engage in discussions with classmates or arrange lessons to assist pupils to gain insights that will be at least partly unpredictable. For ideas about how you might teach in this manner, the observations of cognitive psychologists are likely to be of greater value than the writings of Skinner and his followers. The cognitive view will be discussed in the next chapter.

SUMMARY OF KEY POINTS

Views of learning are derived from basic conceptions of behavior. The behaviorist-environmentalist-associationist position stresses study of overt behavior, the assumption that behavior is determined primarily by experiences, and the principle that learning occurs when stimuli are associated with responses. Proponents of this view urge teachers to present lessons in the form of questions (stimuli) to arouse correct answers (responses).

B. F. Skinner maintains that in order for the S-R view to be as effective as it might be, it is essential to assume that experiences shape behavior (or that the world acts on the person). Albert Bandura offers a less extreme interpretation of environmental determinism than Skinner, suggesting that many experiences are under anticipatory control. Regardless of how strictly they interpret the environmental view of determinism, S-R theorists urge teachers to shape behavior systematically, since they maintain that the alternative is to engage in haphazard control.

Principles of S-R theory are illustrated by experiments carried out by Skinner with rats and pigeons for subjects. If an organism is *reinforced* after a response, that response will be strengthened. If the reinforcement is withheld for a period of time, *extinction* may occur, although the response may temporarily reappear (or recover itself spontaneously) after an interval. A response in one situation may be *generalized* to similar situations, and it may be necessary to use selective reinforcement to teach the organism to *discriminate* between one learning task and another. The responses of organisms can be shaped by the timing and frequency of reinforcements.

The principles of S-R theory demonstrated by Skinner are similar to those originally described by Ivan Pavlov, but there is a key difference between the conditioning studied by the two men: In Pavlovian conditioning, an involuntary reaction (e.g., salivation) is aroused by a previously neutral stimulus (e.g., a bell). In operant conditioning, voluntary behavior (e.g., pushing a bar) is strengthened by reinforcement (e.g., a food pellet). When principles of operant conditioning are applied to teaching, the basic rule that emerges is: Shape behavior by supplying step-by-step reinforcement.

Perhaps the best-known application of S-R principles to education takes the form of programmed instruction: A unit of study is presented in small steps, and reinforcement is supplied after each correct answer. When programs are written, they may take a *linear* form, where all students follow the same sequence. Or students may arrive at the final learning destination by different routes, or *branches*. One of the most important skills to be mastered by a program writer is to gradually *vanish prompts* (reduce cues) so that the learner eventually becomes self-sufficient.

One comprehensive application of programmed instruction is Fred S. Keller's Personalized System of Instruction: A course of study is divided into units, and students are invited to take exams on each unit as soon as they feel prepared. A similar approach involves the presentation of information and examinations with computer assistance. The application of principles of operant conditioning to the control of behavior is referred to as *behavior modification*.

The S-R view is endorsed by many American psychologists, but it has been criticized on a number of counts. The psychotherapist Carl Rogers argues that Skinner's strict view of environmental determinism, with stress on the idea that the world acts on people, leads individuals to believe they are unable to control their own behavior. Other psychologists have pointed out that too often behavior controllers choose to shape behavior that benefits *them* rather than the individuals they reinforce. Other criticisms of the S-R view take the form of evidence of weaknesses or ineffectiveness. To be effective, programs must be exceptionally well written, and few of them merit that description. Furthermore, some of Skinner's original assumptions, such as the need for immediate feedback, have not been supported by experimental evidence. The failure of performance contractors to meet their goals might be interpreted as evidence of the ineffectiveness of both programmed instruction and behavior modification.

The fact that programmed approaches have not lived up to the claims for them made by Skinner and other S-R enthusiasts might be attributed to a number of factors: Supplying brief answers becomes tedious. Extensive use of behavior modification may reduce the value of the technique because reinforcements lose their potency. Teachers may be tempted to shape submissive behavior that is of little or no benefit to the learner.

Those who apply S-R theory in the classroom must make allowance for the *lowest common denominator effect,* or they may find themselves presenting lessons primarily to the slowest students in a class. One effective way to use reinforcement is to practice the *Premack principle* (or Grandma's rule) by urging students to reward themselves with a favorite activity after they have completed an arduous assignment. Perhaps the best way to use the Premack principle is to encourage pupils to draw up their own *reward menu.*

BECOMING A BETTER TEACHER:
QUESTIONS AND SUGGESTIONS

Checking on Causes of Behavior

Did I do anything today that shaped undesirable forms of student behavior? Suggestion: The next time the class is listless or uncooperative or a student is rebellious, analyze what I said and did before and after I noticed the behavior to try to determine if I inadvertently shaped it. If it appears that I *did* cause problems for myself, make a resolution to avoid repeating the mistake.

Ways to Supply Specific and Immediate Feedback

The last time I asked the class to learn factual material, did I supply specific and immediate feedback? Suggestion: The next time I plan a lesson that requires students to supply many right answers, make it a point to arrange things so that feedback is frequent, specific, and immediate.

Ways to Supply Delayed Feedback

Am I taking into account that with meaningful material it may be preferable to supply delayed feedback? Suggestion: The next time I ask students to wrestle with thought questions, give them a chance to reason out, revise, and augment their answers before giving feedback.

Ways to Supply Different Types of Reinforcement

Am I overusing certain types of reinforcement, thereby causing them to become ineffective? Suggestion: Make a list of dozens of different ways I can supply reinforcement. Then try to recall at the end of a day which ones I used and did not use in an effort to become a versatile rather than a mechanical reinforcer.

Ways to Use Schedules of Reinforcement

Am I taking advantage of the impact of different schedules of reinforcement? Suggestion: When planning lessons, ask myself if I want spurts of effort (studying for exams) or steady output (continuous effort during a practice period), and plan to supply either intermittent or fixed-interval reinforcement.

Describing Terminal Behavior

Am I being systematic enough about describing precisely what students should achieve when they complete an assignment or a unit? Suggestion: The next time I draw up lesson plans, describe the terminal behavior, and figure out what students will need to know or do in order to achieve it.

Using the Personalized System of Instruction	Is it appropriate for me to use the Personalized System of Instruction? Suggestion: Pick out a unit, and set it up so that students are expected to carry out a series of steps at their own pace. Or for the next report period, try making up a pair of quizzes on short sections of the text. Give an exam every Friday, and let students take any quiz a second time if they would like to try to improve their performance.
Ways to Have Students Suggest Reinforcers	Am I taking advantage of the Premack principle (Grandma's rule)? Suggestion: Invite students to draw up their own reward menus, and then let them reinforce themselves after they have completed tedious tasks or tough assignments.
Ways to Set Up Learning Contracts	Is it feasible and appropriate for me to use learning contracts? Suggestion. When we start the next report period or a new unit, explain the contract system and ask if any students would like to work on individual projects instead of carrying out standard assignments.
Ways to Use Behavior Modification to Maintain Control	Can I do a more effective job of controlling the class if I use behavior modification techniques? Suggestion: Pick out a common type of discipline problem (e.g., two students scuffling), and plan how to handle it by using behavior modification techniques. Then, the next time that kind of trouble occurs, try out the planned techniques, and make any adjustments that seem necessary.
Deciding When to Use a Programmed Approach	Am I being systematic about deciding when and how I will use programmed approaches? Suggestion: As I make out lesson plans, begin by describing the terminal behavior. Then decide if it will be effective to work toward the goal by proceeding step by step. Consider using programmed approaches when introducing new material and when working with students who lack confidence or are disappointed by their apparent inability to improve.

SUGGESTIONS FOR FURTHER STUDY

5-1 *The Technology of Teaching*	*The Technology of Teaching* (1968) is B. F. Skinner's most concise and application-oriented discussion of operant conditioning techniques related to pedagogy. There are several sections of this book you might want to sample. For an overview of programmed learning and teaching machines, see Chapter 3. In Chapter 5, "Why Teachers Fail," Skinner describes what he perceives to be common mistakes made by many teachers. In Chapter 8, "The Creative Student," he discusses determinism and the issue of personal freedom. If you read any of these chapters, or another of your choice, you might record your reactions to general or specific arguments in the book.
5-2 Dialogues with Skinner	*B. F. Skinner: The Man and His Ideas* (1968) is a series of dialogues with Skinner (originally filmed for educational television) recorded by Richard I. Evans. In Chapter 1 you will find "Reactions to Various

Psychological Concepts," including the theories of Pavlov and Freud. Chapter 2, "Aversive Versus Positive Control of Behavior," deals with the incentive system in the Soviet Union and gives Skinner's reactions to criticisms of his utopian novel, *Walden Two*. Chapter 3, "The Formal Educational System," includes some of Skinner's observations on overconformity and the changing role of the American woman. If you are intrigued by Skinner and his theories, you may find it enjoyable to read and react to one or more of the dialogues recorded in this book.

5-3
Skinner's Utopia

In *Walden Two* (1948) B. F. Skinner describes his conception of a utopia based on the application of science to human behavior. To get the full impact of the novel and of Skinner's ideas, you should read the entire book. (As a matter of fact, it may be hard to put down once you begin it.) However, if you cannot read the whole thing at this time, Chapters 12 through 17—in which the approach to child rearing and education at Walden Two is described—may be of special interest to you as a future teacher. Reading from page 95 to at least page 148 will give you a good sample of life in Skinner's utopia. Then record your reactions, including perhaps an opinion as to whether you might like to join a society based on the ideas of Walden Two. You might also take a stab at sketching out a utopia of your own—perhaps you will be able to improve on Skinner's version.

5-4
Negative Utopias

Aldous Huxley in *Brave New World* (1932), George Orwell in *Animal Farm* (1946) and *1984* (1949), and Ray Bradbury in *Fahrenheit 451* (1967) present conceptions of what might be characterized as negative utopias. *Brave New World*, in particular, is founded on the principles of conditioning. Whereas Skinner describes how such principles could be used to set human beings free, Huxley shows how they could be used to enslave human beings. If you read *Brave New World*, ask yourself whether any of the predictions Huxley made in 1932 have come true. (For example, is our behavior conditioned by TV commercials? How many people make habitual use of pain relievers or tranquilizers?) Or if you read the accounts of Orwell or Bradbury, you might note techniques they describe that are in use today and that might be abused.

5-5
Writing a Short Program

To gain some direct experience with programmed instruction, select a topic from this chapter or from a book you might use when you begin to teach, and write a short program. Use the following suggestions offered by Peter Pipe in *Practical Programming* (New York: Holt, Rinehart and Winston, 1966) as a guide, or make use of those found in other books on programming listed below.

Prepare yourself by following these steps:
1. Select your topic.
2. Write a general statement.
3. Define your objectives in behavioral terms.
4. Define prerequisite skills, again in behavioral terms.

5. Write a criterion test.
6. Develop the content outline. (Pipe, p. 19)

Divide your program into these five phases:
1. An introduction that describes in familiar terms what is to be accomplished in this section of the program.
2. A review of any concepts that are essential to the task in hand. This review might call on the student to demonstrate certain important skills, or it might merely summarize ideas for him.
3. A step-by-step development of new concepts, one at a time, in language which does not interrupt communication.
4. A "weaning" stage in which the student is gradually encouraged to display the full competence called for by the objectives.
5. A final summary and criterion test. (Pipe, p. 34)

Other books you might consult for suggestions on writing programs are *Good Frames and Bad: A Grammar of Frame Writing* (2nd ed., 1969) by Susan Markle or *A Guide to Programmed Instruction* (1963) by Jerome Lysaught and Clarence Williams.

5-6
Trying a Program Yourself

A good way to find out about a pedagogical technique is to try it yourself—from the *student* point of view. To clarify your thoughts about programmed instruction, record your reactions to any programmed books, units, or courses you have taken; or if you have never been exposed to this technique, seek out a programmed unit and work through it. To find a suitable program, ask your instructor for assistance, check with classmates who have used one in the past, browse through a college bookstore, or consult with the person in charge of the curriculum and materials section of the library.

5-7
Examining Research on the Effectiveness of Programmed Instruction

P. C. Lange reviewed 112 studies in which programmed approaches were compared to other forms of instruction. In an article titled "What's the Score on Programmed Instruction?" published in the February 1972 issue of *Today's Education,* he reported that in 41 percent of the studies programmed instruction was found to be superior, in 49 percent of the studies there were no significant differences, and in 10 percent of the cases traditional instruction was superior. If you are curious about these conclusions, you might examine the Lange article as well as selected references listed in the article. This might be beneficial for two reasons: (1) You might find data relating to the effectiveness of programmed instruction in subjects you will be teaching. (2) You might evaluate the possibility that programmed instruction was rated more effective in some cases because the multiple-choice questions used to measure student understanding were similar to those used in some programs.

5-8
The Personalized System of Instruction

If you are intrigued by the Personalized System of Instruction, you might read the initial description of this technique by its originator—that is, Fred S. Keller's article "Goodbye Teacher . . ." in the *Journal of*

Applied Behavior Analysis, 1 (1968), pages 79–89. For a comprehensive review and analysis of studies of variations of Keller's original technique, examine *PSI—Keller's Personalized System of Instruction: An Appraisal* (1974) by Bruce A. Ryan. Ryan reviews dozens of articles and also supplies an appendix in which specific references are listed relating to different aspects of the personalized approach (e.g., preparing course objectives and study guides, preparing unit tests, managing the system).

5-9

Computer-Assisted Instruction

For more information on computer-assisted instruction, examine *Computer-Assisted Instruction: A Book of Readings* (1969), edited by R. C. Atkinson and H. A. Wilson. For details of Individually Prescribed Instruction, look for "The Computer and Individualized Instruction" by W. W. Cooley and R. Glaser in *Science,* 166 (1969), pages 574–582. For a report on the Program for Learning in Accordance with Needs (PLAN), see "The PLAN System for Individualizing Education" by J. C. Flanagan in *Measurement in Education,* 2 (1971), pages 1–8.

5-10

Behavior Modification

If the possibilities of behavior modification seem attractive, you may wish to examine issues of the journal *Educational Technology* or read one or more books on the systematic application of principles of operant conditioning to classroom problems, perhaps for the purpose of drawing up your own list of guidelines for future use. If you browse through the education and psychology sections of your college bookstore, you are likely to find a number of books on behavior modification. Or you might look for these titles in the library: *Instructional Product Development* (1971), edited by Robert L. Baker and Richard E. Schutz; *An Empirical Basis for Change in Education* (1971), edited by Wesley C. Becker; *Teaching: A Course in Applied Psychology* (1971) by Wesley C. Becker, Siegfried Engelmann, and Don R. Thomas; *Behavior Technology: Motivation and Contingency Management* (1971), edited by Lloyd Homme and Donald Tosti; *Behavior Modification in Education* (1973) by Donald L. Macmillan; *Changing Classroom Behavior: A Manual for Precision Teaching* (1969) by Merle E. Meacham and Allen E. Wiesen; *Reinforcing Productive Classroom Behavior: A Teacher's Guide to Behavior Modification* (1971), edited by Irwin G. Sarason and others; *Learning Is Getting Easier* (1972) by S. R. Wilson and D. T. Tosti.

5-11

Experimenting with Behavior Modification

If you have the opportunity to work with students on an individual or group basis, you might try your hand at behavior modification. First describe a type of behavior you would like to modify. Then write down a procedure for shaping it in a desired direction. Next, try it out, and finally, record your results and conclusions. In developing your approach, keep in mind the basic techniques used by Skinner in his experiments with rats and pigeons, and also make use of these guidelines:

Pay no attention to undesired behavior.

Decide on a reinforcer or a series of reinforcers. (For example, list such techniques as smiling, praising, giving tokens or candy.)

Reinforce students when they engage in the desired behavior.

Remember Grandma's rule: Observe students until you discover an activity they prefer. Then use that activity as a reinforcer for the desired behavior.

Make up a record card, and give a check mark each time a particular student exhibits the desired behavior. When ten check marks are accumulated, reward that student with the opportunity to engage in a favorite activity.

To record your experiment, supply information under these headings:

Description of type of behavior to be modified

Procedure you decided in advance to use in attempting to modify it

What happened when you tried out your procedure

Conclusions

Key points

Basic assumptions of the cognitive-discovery approach

Cognitive view of motivation: Built-in desire to learn

Hypothesis: Self-discovered learning is more meaningful

Perceptions are influenced by the way stimuli are arranged

Perceptions are influenced by experiences and interests

Life space: Everything one needs to know about a person at a particular time

Gestalt: Form, pattern, relationship

Structure aids learning, remembering, mastery of principles

Discovery approach: Arrange for pupils to find own solutions

Hypothesis: Students develop confidence and become problem-solvers

Experimental demonstrations of cognitive-discovery principles

Insight: Perception of new relationships

Developing own mediators advantageous

Advance organizers serve as mediating links

Educational applications of the cognitive-discovery approach

Inducing discovery by using contrast, guessing, participation, and awareness

Inducing discovery by switching, disturbing, and permitting mistakes

Inquiry training: Pupils learn to ask questions

Criticisms of the discovery approach

It is impossible for students to discover all they need to know

Discovery is rare, inefficient, and time consuming

One or two students may make most discoveries in a class

Parents may object if teachers fail to teach

Applying the discovery approach in the classroom

Open education: Activity, learning areas, cooperative and individualized planning

Contract approach: Individual pupils agree to complete a project

Closure: Tendency to complete a perception or a task

Individuals may succumb to group pressure

Chapter 6

The cognitive-discovery view of learning

Since the 1920s when John B. Watson was at the peak of his fame, the majority of American psychologists have endorsed the behaviorist-environmentalist-associationist point of view. One explanation for the popularity of the S-R view in America is that it reflects many aspects of our society. Americans have always been characterized as individuals who are interested more in tangible results than in theoretical speculations. This point of view is reflected by the stance of the behaviorist, who observes overt behavior and does not try to fathom the intangible and invisible workings of the mind. America was founded by individuals who wanted to escape from societies based on the principle of hereditary privilege. The environmental view of determinism reflects this rejection of emphasis on heredity and stresses that whatever a person becomes is the result of experiences. One of the most distinguishing characteristics of our way of life is preoccupation with technology, particularly the assembly line. Associationism, with emphasis on the gradual accumulation of associations between stimuli and responses, is essentially an assembly-line conception of learning. It seems fair, therefore, to say that developments in American psychology were influenced by basic features of our society.

It is always difficult for individuals who are deeply committed to and involved in a particular point of view to see things from the perspective of an outsider. American psychologists who became enthusiastic supporters of the behaviorist-environmentalist-associationist position did not at first recognize some of the potential dangers and limitations of this set of ideas. Other individuals, particularly those who were not scientists, began to call attention to possible problems as early as the 1930s. Aldous Huxley wrote *Brave New World* in 1932 to dramatize what might happen if the behaviorist-environmentalist view was applied in an extreme way. More recently, Lewis Mumford (1967, 1970) and Arthur Koestler (1968), to mention only two of the most prolific critics, have repeatedly called attention to some of the damaging by-products of scientific and technological approaches to managing human affairs. But novelists and social critics have not been the only ones to detect weaknesses in the behaviorist-environmentalist-associationist position. Some American psychologists of the 1920s were not impressed by Watson's justification for behaviorism, and many contemporary learning theorists and educators have called attention to what are perceived to be limitations and inconsistencies in the arguments and techniques of teaching proposed by B. F. Skinner.

A substantial number of American psychologists who have been dissatisfied with the views of S-R theorists have been attracted to sets of ideas that were originally proposed by Europeans. Just as aspects of our culture influenced the thinking of those who developed behaviorism, environmentalism, and associationism, aspects of European society appear to have influenced psychological theorists in that part of the world.

First of all, Europeans seem more inclined to speculate about non-observable and unmeasurable forms of behavior than down-to-earth Americans. Sigmund Freud, for example, did not hesitate to propose that our behavior is influenced by forces that are not only unobservable but also unconscious. And Jean Piaget has devoted his lifetime to the analysis of children's thinking. Secondly, even though most European countries no longer strictly adhere to the policy of hereditary privilege, they still place a great deal of emphasis on blood lines (as in royal families, for example). Accordingly, European psychologists seem more inclined than their American counterparts to acknowledge the impact of inherited predispositions. Finally, while American universities offer courses and degrees in applied as well as academic fields and faculty members frequently engage in research intended to lead to practical applications, European universities tend to concentrate almost exclusively on professional training and pure research.

These differences between European and American social structure and university characteristics may account for differences in the conceptions of learning developed on either side of the Atlantic. American psychologists have studied learning primarily by observing the overt behavior of rats and pigeons placed in highly controlled situations where the subjects are induced to carry out simple and specific tasks. European psychologists, particularly graduates of German universities, first studied learning by placing higher-order animals (such as apes) in loosely structured situations where the subjects were expected to come up with their own solutions to fairly complex problems.

Many American psychologists who were dissatisfied with aspects of the behaviorist-environmentalist-associationist point of view were attracted to the speculations of European theorists, and over a period of time an alternative to the Watson-Skinner conception of behavior and learning has emerged. This set of ideas is often referred to as the *cognitive-discovery* view because it stresses thinking (cognition) and ways we discover relationships. The nature of the cognitive-discovery view will become clear as you examine some of its basic assumptions.

Basic assumptions

Many aspects of the cognitive-discovery view are illustrated by principles proposed by Jean Piaget, whose theory of cognitive development was outlined in Chapter 3. Piaget has spent over fifty years studying children's thinking and he has concluded that human beings possess an innate tendency *(equilibration)* to bring coherence and stability to their perception of the world. Children develop coherent and stable conceptions as they incorporate *(assimilate)* experiences into their cognitive structure and modify *(accommodate)* their conceptions as they encounter new experiences. Because each child has different experiences, each child's conception of the world is unique, although there are many similarities between the cognitive structures of children from similar environments.

This conception of behavior and learning differs markedly from the behaviorist-environmentalist-associationist view. Skinner and his followers trace motivation for learning to primary drives, such as hunger. Rat or pigeon subjects, for example, are starved for a few days before they are placed in a Skinner box, which makes them eager to secure food pellets. To account for human learning, which rarely takes place when children are starved, S-R theorists have proposed the concept of *secondary reinforcement,* which states that anything associated with a primary drive may come to have reinforcing value of its own. Pupils in school may feel reinforced by the teacher's smile, for instance, because their mothers smiled at them when they were fed during infancy. The teacher's smile, it is argued, arouses a pleasurable sensation similar to that originally caused by eating.

These associationistic assumptions about motivation lead to the conclusion that teachers should stimulate students to learn and reinforce them when they supply correct responses. The principles proposed by Piaget lead to a much different conception of motivation. Piaget urges teachers to assume that children have a built-in desire to learn because they are more or less impelled to make sense of what they observe and experience. He also maintains that learning is its own reward. A child who modifies a conception so that it makes sense will not need to be given a reward, since achieving equilibration will yield a feeling of satisfaction. Instead of asking pupils to complete programs or the equivalent in order to earn a reward, therefore, Piaget

Cognitive view of motivation: Built-in desire to learn

Hypothesis:
Self-discovered learning
is more meaningful

recommends that teachers permit children to interact with objects, situations, and each other. As children do this, they can form their own self-rewarding conceptions of things, which cognitive theorists believe are more meaningful and permanent than ideas acquired by memorizing material arranged and presented by others.

Piaget's observations explain many aspects of the *cognitive* part of the cognitive-discovery view. To understand why discovery is stressed along with thinking, it is essential to consider elements of what is called *field theory*.

Principles of field theory

Perceptions are
influenced by the way
stimuli are arranged

For reasons noted earlier, when German psychologists became interested in studying learning, they concentrated on analyzing how organisms solve problems. The German theorists were also fascinated by perception—the ways we interpret things that we sense and observe. When they asked subjects to react to illusions of various kinds, they discovered that individuals interpret what they see in terms of the arrangement of stimuli. When you look at the two vertical lines in Figure 6-1, the converging lines at the end of line A cause it to appear longer than line B. Yet, all the lines in A and B are exactly the same length. The way they are *arranged* causes them to look different. The converging lines at the ends of line A "draw" the vertical line outward; those at the end of line B seem to shorten it.

Perceptions are
influenced by
experiences and
interests

The German psychologists also discovered that our perceptions are influenced by past experiences and current interests. Several individuals may look at the same word, yet their interpretations of the identical assortment of letters will differ. What do you think of, for

Figure 6-1

Different arrangements of lines of identical length alter perceptions

The vertical lines shown here are the same length, as are the diagonal lines attached to the end of the vertical. But the arrangement of the diagonal lines causes line A to appear longer than line B.

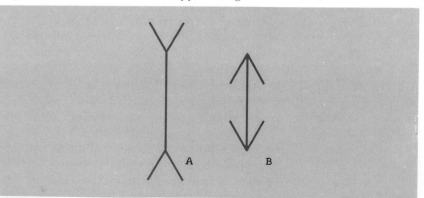

Figure 6-2

Magnetic field surrounding two bar magnets

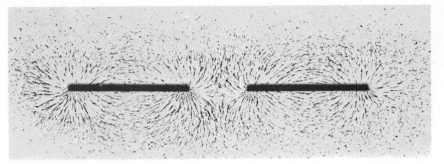

If the magnets were placed in different positions, the magnetic field would be altered. Field theory in psychology stresses that psychological fields are altered in similar fashion as positive and negative forces act on human beings.

example, when you see the word *field*? If you are a sports enthusiast, you may think of a football field, of a baseball player who fields a grounder, or of field events at a track meet. If you are a biology major, you may think of a field trip. If you had difficulty choosing a major, you may think of a field of study. If you come from a rural area, you may think of a field of corn or wheat. If you are a history major, you may think of a field of battle. If you are interested in weaving or painting, you may think of a bright design on a subdued field or background. A physicist or a psychologist who endorses the cognitive-discovery approach probably would think of a field of forces.

In attempting to explain how various kinds of physical forces operate, physicists developed the concept of a field of forces, which can be illustrated by placing iron filings and magnets on a table and then tapping the table. As shown in Figure 6-2, the filings arrange themselves in clearly differentiated and symmetrical patterns around the magnets. Early German psychologists felt that the same basic idea could be used to explain behavior, and that is why their school of psychology is often referred to as *field theory*. The psychologist who developed the field of forces idea most comprehensively was Kurt Lewin.

Lewin's life space concept

Lewin developed a system for diagramming how human behavior is influenced by positive and negative valences (forces) and by the direction of these forces (vectors). His diagrams are similar to those physicists use to depict magnetic and other forces. He also proposed the concept of the *life space*. As Lewin defined it, the life space of an individual consists of everything one needs to know about a person in

Life space: Everything one needs to know about a person at a particular time

order to understand his or her behavior in a specific psychological environment at a specific time.

The diagrams and the concept of the life space are intended to call attention to ways a slight alteration in a situation may cause an individual to perceive things differently. Lewin demonstrated this in an intriguing experiment (Barker, Dembo, and Lewin, 1941). He first permitted preschool children to play individually with an assortment of rather dingy old toys. After the children played with the hand-me-downs for a few minutes, a partition was removed, and they were allowed to investigate a marvelous assortment of brand-new toys in another part of the room. After a few moments of ecstatic interaction with these wonderful playthings, the children were led back to the old toys, and a wire screen was lowered between them and the superior playthings. When the old toys were the only ones available, most children played quite contentedly and constructively with them. But after tasting the thrill of manipulating the new and exciting playthings, the children found the old toys worthless or even disagreeable because they could compare the old toys (visually, at least) to the inaccessible new ones. In these circumstances the behavior of most children regressed to less constructive types of play. The before and after life spaces of the children in this experiment are depicted in Lewin-type diagrams in Figure 6-3. (Think of the toys as magnets to grasp the similarity between psychological and magnetic fields of forces.)

The life space concept calls attention to the fact that it is not always possible to draw accurate conclusions simply by observing overt behavior, which the behaviorist maintains is the preferred approach. Someone who merely observed the children in the second part of the Lewin experiment and was not aware of the reasons why their play was immature would not really understand what was taking place. In order to do that, the observer would have to take into account how the children perceived the situation at a particular moment. The field theorist maintains that to understand behavior it is essential to be "subjective" in the sense that the observer must try to see things from the subject's point of view at a given moment.

Gestalt psychology

Many of the principles that make up field theory are also referred to as *Gestalt psychology,* and you are likely to encounter that term if you do any additional reading on the work of the early German psychologists. The German word *Gestalt* is sometimes translated *form* or *pattern,* sometimes *configuration.* These words call attention to the significance of *relationships.* The S-R theorist conceives of learning as the adding together of associations. The separate frames of a program, for example, are combined in sequence to lead to the terminal behavior.

Gestalt: Form, pattern, relationship

Figure 6-3

Lewinian-type diagrams depicting changes in attraction

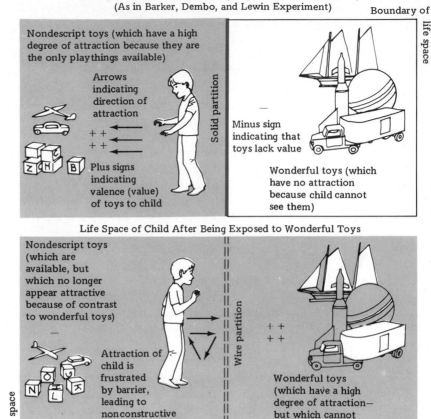

Life Space of Child Before Being Exposed to Wonderful Toys
(As in Barker, Dembo, and Lewin Experiment)

Boundary of life space

Nondescript toys (which have a high degree of attraction because they are the only playthings available)

Arrows indicating direction of attraction

Plus signs indicating valence (value) of toys to child

Solid partition

Minus sign indicating that toys lack value

Wonderful toys (which have no attraction because child cannot see them)

Life Space of Child After Being Exposed to Wonderful Toys

Nondescript toys (which are available, but which no longer appear attractive because of contrast to wonderful toys)

Attraction of child is frustrated by barrier, leading to nonconstructive indecision

Wire partition

Wonderful toys (which have a high degree of attraction— but which cannot be reached)

Boundary of life space

The Gestalt view calls attention to the fact that many things are learned when we arrange ideas into patterns. We don't just add together impressions; we grasp how they are related. The early German psychologists demonstrated that we tend to perceive things as more simple, regular, and complete than they really are. In some cases these tendencies will be an advantage to a student; in other cases they may lead to difficulties. Teachers may endeavor to make the most of patterning tendencies by calling attention to the organization of a presentation and by helping pupils grasp relationships.

Piaget and the Gestalt psychologists proposed principles that serve as the basis for the cognitive view. The psychologist who is usually acknowledged as the leading spokesman for the discovery view in America is Jerome Bruner, formerly of Harvard but now a professor at Oxford University. Bruner studied children's thinking and proposed a theory of cognitive development that is very similar to that of Piaget.

He has also been an outspoken critic of the behaviorist-environmentalist-associationist conception and has recommended an approach to education that serves as an alternative to programmed instruction.

The importance of structure and discovery

Bruner's interest in the cognitive-discovery approach was initiated when he studied and wrote a book on perception (1951) and then one on thinking (Bruner, Goodnow, and Austin, 1956). His interest in finding ways to apply to education what he had discovered about these two areas of study was given impetus when he was asked to serve as director of the Woods Hole Conference on Education. This conference was called in 1959 for the purpose of finding ways to improve science education in the public schools at the time Russia had demonstrated its superiority in space technology. Bruner summarized his perception of the main points brought out in the conference in *The Process of Education* (1960). This book, which has achieved the status of a classic statement on education, triggered an interest in school learning in general, which Bruner discussed in *Toward a Theory of Instruction* (1966) and *The Relevance of Education* (1971). He also developed a set of materials for teaching social studies in the elementary grades which is called *Man: A Course of Study* (often abbreviated MACOS).

One of the major points emphasized in *The Process of Education* is that students should be assisted in grasping the structure of a field of study. (*Structure* is still another way to translate *Gestalt,* and it emphasizes the significance of relationships.) Bruner's arguments in favor of structure were noted in Chapter 1 as explanations for some of the features of this book. He suggests that when students are helped to grasp the overall pattern of a field of study, they are more likely to remember what they learn, comprehend principles that can be applied in a variety of situations, and be prepared for mastering more complex knowledge. Another point stressed by Bruner is that too much school learning takes the form of step-by-step study of verbal or numerical statements or formulas that the student can reproduce on cue but is unable to use outside of the classroom. When students are presented with programmed materials, Bruner argues, they become too dependent on others. Furthermore, they are likely to think of learning as something that is done only to earn a reward.

Instead of using techniques that feature preselected and prearranged materials, Bruner urges teachers to practice the *discovery approach* by confronting children with problems and urging them to seek solutions either independently or by engaging in group discussion. This is essentially the same approach advocated by those who have used the theory of Piaget as the basis for open education, and the arguments to substantiate student-directed learning are the same in

Structure aids learning, remembering, mastery of principles

Discovery approach: Arrange for pupils to find own solutions

both cases. Piaget and Bruner both argue that conceptions that children arrive at on their own are usually more meaningful than those proposed by others and that students do not need to be motivated or rewarded when they seek to make sense of things that puzzle them. Bruner maintains, in addition, that when children are given a substantial amount of practice in finding their own solutions to problems, they not only develop problem-solving skills, they also acquire confidence in their own learning abilities plus a propensity to function later in life as problem-solvers.

Hypothesis: Students who make discoveries develop confidence and become problem-solvers

To illustrate some of the assumptions on which the cognitive-discovery view is based, here are descriptions of a classic experiment in field theory as well as typical experiments carried out by Bruner and by David P. Ausubel, another leading cognitive theorist.

Experimental demonstrations of cognitive-discovery principles

A classic experiment demonstrating insight

As noted in contrasting American and European approaches to science, B. F. Skinner and his fellow S-R psychologists chose to observe the behavior of simple animals in highly controlled situations. Gestalt psychologists, by contrast, chose to study the way higher-order animals behave in loosely structured situations. The most famous experiment of this type was supervised by Wolfgang Köhler in 1916 and featured a chimpanzee named Sultan.

Sultan was put in a large cage with a variety of objects, including some short sticks. In the process of manipulating objects in his cage, Sultan discovered that he could use a stick to rake things toward him when he was feeling lazy. One day Köhler put a banana and a very long stick outside the cage; both objects were too far for Sultan to reach with his arm, but the stick was closer than the banana. Sultan first picked up one of the short sticks in the cage and tried to rake in the banana. The stick wasn't quite long enough, and he threw it down and stomped off to another part of the cage in a fit of pique. As he sat brooding, his eyes suddenly focused on the two sticks and the banana, all arranged in a row. He jumped up, ran over to the small stick, used it to rake in the larger stick, and triumphantly raked in the banana. Köhler suggested that this learning experience involved a rearrangement of Sultan's *pattern* of thought. The ape had previously raked things, but the idea of using one stick to rake another stick and then using the longer stick to rake the banana involved a new application of his prior activity.

This experiment illustrates the essence of learning as viewed by a

A re-enactment of Köhler's most famous experiment. The ape solves the problem by perceiving the relationship between the sticks and the food. Insight occurs when the animal realizes that the short stick can be used to rake in the longer stick.

Yerkes Regional Primate Research Center of Emory University

Insight: Perception of new relationships

field theorist: *the perception of new relationships.* Sultan did not solve the problem by being conditioned; he solved it by gaining insight into the relationship between the two sticks and the banana. Field theorists usually concede, however, that Sultan's previous experience with the essentials of the problem had been necessary in order for insight to develop and that insight had been facilitated by the arrangement of the environment. Sultan had previously raked things, and the sticks and banana were placed fairly close to each other. Apes that had not had any raking experience or happened to face away from the sticks and banana failed to solve the problem.

Bruner: The values of self-selected mediators

To illustrate the impact of relationships as well as the values of having children develop their own—as opposed to ready-made—conceptions, Bruner (1961) carried out this simple experiment. He presented pairs of words to three groups of twelve-year-olds. The first group was simply asked to memorize the pairs of words. The second group was told to memorize the words by producing a word or idea (called a *mediator*) that would tie the pair together in some way that made sense. (For the pair *chair-forest*, for example, one child said to himself, "Chairs are made from trees in the forest.") The third group was told to memorize the pairs by using mediators selected from those proposed by the children in the second group. The children who supplied their own mediators were able to remember up to 95 percent of a list of thirty pairs when tested shortly after they had studied them. Those who were not instructed to use any mediators rarely remembered more than 50 percent. The percentage remembered by the children who used mediators proposed by others was about halfway between the percentages of the other two groups.

Developing own mediators advantageous

Ausubel: The values of advance organizers

David P. Ausubel (1960) performed an experiment to demonstrate the value of *advance organizers* in the learning and retention of meaningful verbal material. He had college seniors spend twenty minutes studying a short passage on an unfamiliar subject. Then they were given a short, multiple-choice test to measure the degree of learning. On the basis of this test, two matched groups were formed. One group was given a short passage on quite abstract material about metals and alloys, emphasizing major similarities and differences, their respective advantages and limitations, and the reasons for making and using alloys. The control group was not given introductory material. Then both groups were asked to study a somewhat longer and more detailed passage on steel. (Care was taken not to include any information *directly* related to the material on metals and alloys studied by the one group.) Three days later a multiple-choice test on the material was administered, and the group that had studied the advance information did significantly better.

Advance organizers serve as mediating links

Ausubel attributes the superior performance of the group that read the introductory material to the impact of *advance organizers,* which functioned as mediating links at a high level of abstraction. This permitted the students to integrate and relate the material they later studied. He suggests that teachers consider offering fairly general and abstract introductory material before presenting detailed information. Done properly, this will provide students with some structure to aid them in learning specific information.

Educational applications of the cognitive-discovery view

Skinner and his fellow S-R psychologists assume that behavior is the result of experiences and that the most common kind of learning occurs when a response to a stimulus is reinforced. Accordingly, they urge teachers to do everything possible to decide in advance precisely what should be learned and to arrange stimuli and supply reinforcements to lead students to the predetermined terminal behavior. Cognitive psychologists assume that behavior is significantly influenced by the way organisms perceive things and that learning occurs when an individual gains insight or becomes aware of a new pattern of relationships. Those who endorse this view urge teachers to arrange learning situations to help students develop new insights. Because every student will have had different previous experiences, it is impossible to predict exactly how any particular individual will develop insight. Consequently, cognitive-discovery psychologists reason that learning situations should be arranged to allow for variety in the ways students gain understanding.

Bruner: The discovery approach

Jerome Bruner became interested in applying principles of cognitive psychology to teaching after he wrote *The Process of Education*. One of his first efforts consisted of a technique for teaching geography in the elementary grades. Bruner objected to teaching this subject by having pupils memorize facts. Instead, he gave fifth grade students blank outline maps and asked them to try to figure out where the major cities, railways, highways, and so on were located. Thus geography was presented "not as a set of knowns but as a set of unknowns" (1960a). The students were not permitted to consult books for other maps; they had to figure out locations on their own by asking questions. A few years later, Bruner developed the much more comprehensive MACOS materials for teaching elementary school social studies. These are described in Chapter 4 of *Toward a Theory of Instruction* and are available from Curriculum Development Associates, Inc., 1211 Connecticut Avenue, N.W., Washington, D.C. 20036. Here is Bruner's brief description of the MACOS curriculum: "The content of the course is man: his nature as a species, the forces that shaped and continue to shape his humanity. Three questions recur throughout: What is human about human beings? How did they get that way? How can they be made more so" (1966, p. 74)?

In seeking answers to these questions, pupils study subjects considered to be significant in human social behavior: social organization, the management of prolonged childhood, parenthood, group relationships, and the concept of culture. To give you an idea of how these subjects are studied, here is a brief account (from a pamphlet describing the MACOS materials) of a unit on baboons:

Infant rearing, food gathering, defense against predators, intergroup relationships and communication are studied as background against which to examine human social behavior. Baboon behavior raises some interesting questions about the functions of dominance, aggression, sharing and reciprocity, territoriality and exchange, and various interpersonal relationships within small groups, human and non-human alike. As the only other ground-adapted primates, baboons offer an unusually provocative contrast for examining the child-rearing practices and social behavior of man.

Techniques used in presenting the MACOS curriculum include:

Inducing discovery by using contrast, guessing, participation, and awareness

1. *Emphasizing contrast* (e.g., contrasting human beings with animals, the modern human with the prehistoric, the adult with the child)

2. *Stimulating informed guessing* (e.g., asking students to hypothesize how Eskimos decide which breathing holes to stalk in hunting seals and then showing a film to illustrate how they actually *do* decide)

3. *Encouraging participation* (e.g., arranging for pupils to function as anthropologists by making observations, collecting data, formulating and testing hypotheses)

4. *Arousing awareness* (e.g., having students analyze *how* they are attempting to solve problems)

Bruner's approach to teaching—implicit in this description of a unit on human beings—is summarized in the following statement:

To instruct someone in [a] discipline is not a matter of getting him to commit results to mind. Rather, it is to teach him to participate in the process that makes possible the establishment of knowledge. We teach a subject not to produce little living libraries on the subject, but rather to get a student to think mathematically for himself, to consider matters as an historian does, to take part in the process of knowledge-getting. Knowing is a process, not a product. (1966, p. 72)

Bigge: Reflection level teaching

While Bruner has been the most widely read proponent of the discovery approach, Morris L. Bigge offers a comprehensive treatment of ways the cognitive view might be applied in the classroom in *Learning Theories for Teachers* (3rd ed., 1976). In this book he distinguishes three levels of learning and teaching. Bigge assigns the name *memory level* learning and teaching to the committing of facts to memory by students. He argues that although facts learned this way may eventually be used to solve problems, pure memorization is often ineffective because in the absence of meaning, facts are quickly forgotten.

Understanding level learning and teaching, in Bigge's terminology, involve the perception of relationships instead of memorizing an assortment of facts. Students gain an understanding of a smaller number of principles that they can use in solving future problems. As Bigge defines it, understanding level learning and teaching involve control by the teacher. Students are essentially passive and are told what the principles are and how they might be used.

Bigge argues that although the understanding level is to be preferred to the memory level, *reflection level* learning and teaching are even better. In this approach, students are required to participate actively in developing insight by attacking a problem posed by the teacher. Bigge suggests three general techniques for producing especially effective discussion:

Inducing discovery by switching, disturbing, and permitting mistakes

1. *Switch the subject matter* (e.g., try to convince students in a political science class that the federal government should not interfere with the economy, and when they have accepted the idea, ask them whether they favor protective tariffs for specific products).

2. *Introduce disturbing data* (e.g., show a movie that depicts ideas contrary to those the students take for granted).

3. *Permit students to make mistakes* (e.g., allow something to go wrong in a problem or experiment, and then ask the students why it happened).

Bigge admits that the reflective level approach requires free discussion and lots of time and therefore is inappropriate to a rigid schedule. But he maintains that if the proper conditions can be met, the approach is usable in most subject areas, at most grade levels, and with children of all levels of ability. He also offers evidence that students who successfully use the reflective method are highly motivated, tend to score higher than others on standardized achievement tests, show a gain in critical insight, and use their learning outside of class. It should be noted that these results are from studies done by people who *believed* in the reflective approach, so contagious enthusiasm may have affected student performance in a Hawthorne effect.

Suchman: Inquiry training

Another psychologist who has put cognitive principles into practice is J. Richard Suchman (1961), who advocates *inquiry training*. He illustrates the technique by showing fourth and fifth grade children short films on such simple physics demonstrations as the following: A bimetallic knife is held over a flame, and it bends down; then it is put in water, and it straightens out; next it is turned over and held over the flame again, and it bends up; finally it is put in water again, and it straightens out. The children are encouraged to find out "why" by asking questions that can be answered only by yes or no. Tape recordings of all sessions are made and later analyzed so that in subsequent sessions the teacher can help the children ask more effective questions. This is done by pointing out that the most valuable questions are those that identify questions or events, that narrow the focus of inquiry, that "manipulate" the conditions of the experiment and lead to certain outcomes, that test hypotheses of cause and effect, and that check on the validity of conclusions. By the time the students in

Inquiry training: Pupils learn to ask questions

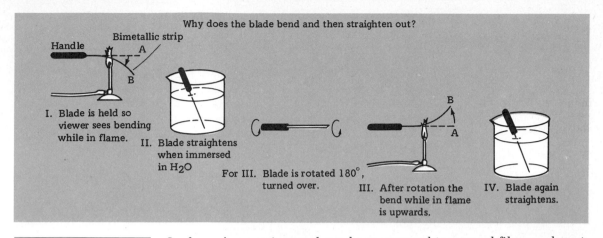

Why does the blade bend and then straighten out?

Handle   Bimetallic strip

I. Blade is held so viewer sees bending while in flame.

II. Blade straightens when immersed in H₂O

For III. Blade is rotated 180°, turned over.

III. After rotation the bend while in flame is upwards.

IV. Blade again straightens.

Figure 6-4

Suchman's bimetallic knife

Reproduced with permission of Dr. J. Richard Suchman

Suchman's experiments have been exposed to several films and post-mortem sessions, they have become more adept at these techniques.

Now that you have been acquainted with arguments in favor of the discovery approach and a description of techniques of teaching advocated by enthusiasts for this method of instruction, you may gain some perspective by examining criticisms of the discovery approach.

Criticisms of the discovery approach

One of the most complete critiques of the discovery approach is offered by B. F. Skinner in *The Technology of Teaching* where he observes:

[The method of discovery] is designed to absolve the teacher from a sense of failure by making instruction unnecessary. The teacher arranges the environment in which discovery is to take place, he suggests lines of inquiry, he keeps the student within bounds. The important thing is that he should tell him nothing.

The human organism does, of course, learn without being taught. It is a good thing that this is so, and it would no doubt be a good thing if more could be learned in that way. Students are naturally interested in what they learn by themselves because they would not learn if they were not, and for the same reason they are more likely to remember what they learn in that way. There are reinforcing elements of surprise and accomplishment in personal discovery which are welcome alternatives to traditional aversive consequences. But discovery is no solution to the problems of education. A culture is no stronger than its capacity to transmit itself. It must impart an accumulation of skills, knowledge, and social and ethical practices to its new members. The institution of education is designed to serve this purpose. It is quite impossible for the student to discover for himself any substantial part of the wisdom of his culture, and no philosophy of education really proposes that he should. Great thinkers build upon the past, they do not waste time in redis-

It is impossible for students to discover all they need to know

covering it. It is dangerous to suggest to the student that it is beneath his dignity to learn what others already know, that there is something ignoble (and even destructive of "rational powers") in memorizing facts, codes, formulae, or passages from literary works, and that to be admired he must think in original ways. It is equally dangerous to forego teaching important facts and principles in order to give the student a chance to discover them for himself. Only a teacher who is unaware of his effects on his students can believe that children actually discover mathematics, that (as one teacher has written) in group discussions they "can and do figure out all the relationships, facts, and procedures that comprise a full program in math."

There are other difficulties. The position of the teacher who encourages discovery is ambiguous. Is he to pretend that he himself does not know. . . . Or, for the sake of encouraging a joint venture in discovery, is the teacher to choose to teach only those things which he himself has not yet learned? Or is he frankly to say, "I know, but you must find out" and accept the consequences for his relations with his students?

Still another difficulty arises when it is necessary to teach a whole class. How are a few good students to be prevented from making all the discoveries? (1968, pp. 109–111)

All these criticisms may be true in certain situations. As noted in Chapter 2 in the critique of the inquiry method favored by Postman and Weingartner, when students are expected to devote most class time to making their own discoveries, the teacher becomes a colearner. While this absolves the teacher of blame if students fail to learn, it also raises the question "Is the teacher necessary?" Skinner's point that it is impossible for students living in a technological society to discover for themselves all that they need to know also seems valid. It has taken millions of thinkers thousands of years to accumulate knowledge about natural and human phenomena, and it is absurd to assume that a group of children can even begin to come up with equivalent insights. As noted in Chapter 1, one of the major strengths of scientific observation is that knowledge is cumulative. Exclusive use of the discovery approach would, in effect, cancel out everything that has been learned by other people.

Discovery is rare, inefficient, and time consuming

Even for a teacher who is outstandingly effective and competent in using the discovery method, occasional failure is inevitable simply because not all discovery sessions are likely to be productive. Skinner has pointed out the undeniable truth that genuine discovery is rare inside or outside the classroom. The most ardent believers admit that discovery is often inefficient and time consuming and that learning frequently proceeds fitfully. Since mastery of minimum amounts of material is a prerequisite for higher education in the United States, students who are exposed only to the discovery approach may not learn enough to qualify for admission to most colleges and universities. Even when this somewhat arbitrary requirement imposed by our educational system is disregarded, it seems reasonable to question whether students would learn much through exclusive use of the discovery method. And is there really anything wrong with having an enthusiastic person tell others what she or he has learned?

It seems clear that Skinner is also correct when he points out that many interpersonal problems arise when the discovery method is used. For one thing, students may become frustrated if teachers refuse to tell what they obviously know, especially on days when discussion has been disorganized and unproductive. For another, it is highly likely that, as Skinner suggests, one or two pupils will tend to monopolize the discoveries, since a whole class will rarely experience insight at the same moment. Also, it seems probable that this situation would create jealousy, resentment, or feelings of inferiority in students who never come up with a discovery of their own. When a *teacher* presents a perceptive explanation, this problem doesn't exist.

Another interpersonal difficulty arises from the fact that only one person can speak at a time. There are techniques, such as dividing the class into small groups, that teachers can use to distribute recitation opportunities; but no matter what they do, one pupil will inevitably function as a lecturer, and the rest of the group will be forced at least temporarily into the role of listeners. As listeners, they may be less involved—and enlightened—than they would be if they were working

One or two students may make most discoveries in a class

One of the potential disadvantages of the discovery approach is that an insight explained by a student may interest the class less than information presented by the teacher.

Paul Conklin

on a teaching machine, especially if the speaker is inarticulate and long-winded or given to prefacing every phrase with "I mean . . . you know." (Some college students complain about discussion courses because they say that they can listen to and argue with their classmates any time. In the classroom they prefer to hear what the teacher has to offer.)

Still another criticism of the discovery approach might be traced to current stress on accountability stemming from evidence that students of the mid-1970s perform less well on measures of academic achievement than students of a decade ago. Many advocates of the cognitive-discovery view of learning have considered the MACOS materials developed by Bruner to be a prime example of what education should be. Yet, the MACOS curriculum has been vigorously attacked by members of Congress (who want to withdraw federal funds supporting the project), by parent groups (who argue that it is a waste of time), and by a few psychiatrists (who maintain that it is detrimental to mental health). A reporter who investigated and analyzed these various charges (Schaar, 1975a, 1975b) speculated that perhaps the basic reason MACOS has been castigated is that parents feel that they no longer have enough control over what their children are being taught. This point is stressed by Onalee McGraw, national coordinator of a group called the Coalition for Children. Schaar reported that in commenting on MACOS, McGraw asked, "What's happened to teaching the basics?" and then stated, "Leave the development of the child's social values to the parents, in the home where they belong." McGraw also asserted that "the idea of MACOS teaching children 'to understand themselves' and 'be aware of themselves' is a bunch of garbage." These criticisms may strike you as illogical and extreme—many parents of children who have used the MACOS materials are more than satisfied with the results, and many psychiatrists fail to see how the curriculum can harm children. Nevertheless, McGraw's criticisms reflect the dissatisfaction of some parents with school exercises that purport to encourage children to make their own discoveries while the teacher stands or sits in the background.

A final criticism of the discovery approach is that even though its advocates claim many things—that students learn and remember more, that confidence and problem-solving skills are increased, that later learning is more likely to occur—they rarely offer evidence to substantiate these claims.

Most of these criticisms become significant only if the discovery method is used as the more or less exclusive means of instruction. While some enthusiasts make this recommendation and while group discussion may be the most frequently used technique in particular classes, chances are you will find that you will make selective use of the discovery approach. Here are some guidelines you might follow when you do this.

Parents may object if teachers fail to teach

A subject matter switch

To illustrate some of the strengths and weaknesses of the S-R view and the discovery approach, here is a description of a discovery unit and a programmed unit, together with some speculations about what might happen if the same subject were taught by the opposite method.

Robert B. Davis (1966) has used the discovery approach in teaching math to culturally deprived junior high school pupils with low IQs. In one of his exercises, students are asked to solve quadratic equations such as:

$$(\Box \times \Box) - (5 \times \Box) + 6 = 0$$

Davis points out that the only method available to these students is trial and error, and he puts forth many claims for this method. First of all, he argues that in making their trials and errors, "pupils get a great deal of experience using variables and signed numbers, and in a situation they do not regard as drill" (p. 116). Second, he says that when students eventually discover the rules for solving such equations, they are so excited about uncovering a secret their friends do not yet share, they feel sufficiently rewarded for their efforts. Finally, he says that his method "brings history into the classroom" in the sense that students come to understand why modern math is the product of a long series of trials and errors. To help them understand this process even more clearly, he advocates torpedoing, that is, providing a challenge by presenting slightly different equations that cannot be solved by the original rule.

Now suppose that B. F. Skinner created a program to teach the same thing. In it the students would be shaped systematically to achieve awareness of the rule. Like Davis's pupils, they would get "a great deal of experience using variables and signed numbers" in a situation they would "not regard as drill," but their trials would rarely result in errors. Furthermore, all pupils would be more or less guaranteed success. (Davis gives the impression that most of his pupils were highly enthusiastic. He does not speculate about how a student might feel if he hadn't yet discovered the correct rule and his classmates were chortling with delight about their "secret." Nor does he mention what happened when his slower students were torpedoed.) Which technique is better? Or do they both have strengths and weaknesses?

To look at this question from the other side, consider the physics program reproduced in Chapter 5 (Figure 5-2). Suppose Bruner wanted to create a discovery unit on the same subject—the relationship between heat and light. He might encourage his students to talk about matches, candles, campfires, and light bulbs. Then he might wave around a flashlight and ask them to guess why the bulb lights, what part the filament plays, why it glows, and so on. In this case the students would learn about heat and light by carrying on a lively class discussion instead of by writing responses and moving knobs on a machine. Which teaching technique is better, do you think? Or do they both have strengths and weaknesses?

Suggestions for teaching: Applying the discovery approach in the classroom

1. Take advantage of the tendency for children to want to find answers to problems that have personal significance.

2. Keep in mind Piaget's suggestion that conceptions that children develop on their own are idiosyncratic (or egocentric). Give your students frequent opportunities to explain how they see things.

3. Remember that a student's behavior at any given moment will be a function of forces in his or her life space. Try to see things from the student's point of view.

4. Call attention to and take advantage of structure. Stress relationships in what you present, use advance organizers when appropriate, and urge students to seek patterns and develop mediators of their own.

5. Make use of techniques of open education.

6. If you intend to use any kind of discussion approach, first establish a relaxed atmosphere.

7. Arrange the learning situation so that discovery is likely to take place.

   a. Ask students to discuss familiar topics or those that are matters of opinion.

   b. Provide necessary background information by asking all students to read all or part of a book, take notes on a lecture, or view a film.

8. Structure discussions by posing a specific question, by presenting a provocative issue, or by asking students to choose topics or subtopics.

   a. In some cases, encourage students to arrive at conclusions already reached by others.

   b. In other cases, present a controversial topic for which there is no single answer.

   c. If the subject is complex, ask the class to suggest subtopics.

9. If time is limited and if only one topic is covered, ask students to form a circle and have an all-class discussion.

   a. Ask questions that stimulate students to apply, analyze, synthesize, or evaluate.

   b. Allow sufficient time for initial responses, and then probe for further information (if appropriate).

   c. When selecting students to recite, use techniques likely to sustain steady but nonthreatening attention. At the same time, guard against the temptation to call primarily on bright, articulate, assertive pupils.

10. If abundant time is available and if a controversial or subdivided topic is to be discussed, divide the class into groups of five or so, and arrange for all members in each group to have eye contact with every other group member.

a. Have students choose to be members of a group, or divide the class by rows or by a counting-off procedure.

b. Ask the students to move chairs or desks to form circles in different parts of the room.

11. Consider appointing or having the group elect a moderator and a recorder.

12. Consider asking all pupils to spend three minutes or so individually writing out their initial reactions to the discussion topic before they begin to share ideas.

13. As the groups engage in discussion, observe benignly but silently. Intervene only if it seems necessary to keep the discussion proceeding in a constructive manner.

a. If the group has strayed from the topic, if one individual is dominating the discussion, or if the group is pressuring one individual to alter an opinion, use subtle remarks to try to correct the situation.

b. In most cases, avoid answering questions or participating actively in the discussion.

14. Ask the groups to share conclusions after they have had ample time to discuss the topic.

a. Allow time at the end of the period for a spokesperson for each group to report on conclusions on specific points. Perhaps list these on the board and invite comments from the entire class.

b. Consider asking each group to write a brief outline of their conclusions or prepare a project or demonstration, and combine these into a notebook or culminating event.

15. Consider the possibility that the discovery method is most appropriate for bright, confident, highly motivated pupils and for topics that lack clear terminal behavior.

1. Take advantage of the tendency for children to want to find answers to problems that have personal significance. Many of the most common criticisms of American public education focus on the extent to which learning is controlled and regimented. Too often, students spend almost all of their time in school learning only what others require them to learn. You can avoid this kind of situation in your classroom by scheduling frequent periods when students can engage in individual or group analyses of topics they select them-

Handbook heading
Ways to Permit
Students to Engage in
Self-Selected Study

selves. When students engage in such study they are usually self-motivated, and they are more likely to remember what they learn. (Be prepared, though, for the possibility that some students may not come up with *any* ideas that intrigue them when you invite them to engage in self-study.)

EXAMPLES

Provide time for students to do projects or write papers on topics of their own choice.

Invite members of the class to suggest topics to be studied within a particular part of a unit or course.

Perhaps schedule occasional "Personal Puzzle Times" when students are encouraged to first describe something that puzzles them and then seek a solution.

2. Keep in mind Piaget's suggestions that conceptions children develop on their own are idiosyncratic (or egocentric). Give your students frequent opportunities to explain how they see things. Piaget maintains that the tendencies for children to assimilate and accommodate cause them to develop personal conceptions of the world. Ideas about the very same thing will vary from child to child, therefore, because of differences in experiences. Furthermore, children at the preoperational, concrete operational, and formal thought stages respond to experiences in different ways. Consequently, you should not be surprised if some of your students reveal that they have developed conceptions dissimilar to those you expected them to acquire as the results of a lesson. Idiosyncratic views of things may develop because, in their search for meaning, children try to fit new ideas into what they already know. As they do this, they tend to simplify, and they also strive to develop conceptions that are regular and complete. Accordingly, what makes sense to them may not make sense to you.

Handbook heading

Ways to Permit Students to Explain What They Are Thinking

One of the clichés about problems in interpersonal relationships is, "It was just a lack of communication." The same cliché often applies in the classroom. You can save yourself and your students many problems if you frequently invite them to explain—to you and to each other—what *they* got out of a lesson.

EXAMPLES

As much as possible, use exercises and examinations that permit students to explain their answers.

After showing a film, ask the class to comment on what impressed them and what they thought certain sections were intended to convey.

Ask students to read part of a book, and then divide them into small groups so that they can exchange interpretations of what was covered.

Whenever a pupil gives a "wrong" answer that baffles you, ask him or her, privately and in a nonthreatening way, to explain the reasoning behind the answer.

3. Remember that a student's behavior at any given moment will be a function of forces in his or her life space. Try to see things from the student's point of view. You may sometimes be able to understand why confusing or irritating student behavior occurs if you think in terms of Lewin's life space concept. Keep in mind his experiment with the old and new toys and his diagrams of forces acting on individuals. Instead of reacting with anger when students behave in a surprising or bothersome way, think a bit about how things seem to them.

EXAMPLES

If you have just asked elementary school students to concentrate on a difficult assignment and another class goes howling out to recess—which makes your pupils begin to watch the clock for the time *their* recess begins—switch to a less demanding kind of activity. Come back to the tough assignment some other time when distractions are at a minimum.

If all the boys in a high school class routinely get distracted when a curvaceous and provocative coed undulates into the room to pick up attendance slips, tape the attendance slips to the outside of the door. In this way you may be able to maintain your status as a plus value in their life spaces.

If a shy, slow boy with a speech handicap tends to fall asleep almost every time you have a full-class discussion, don't humiliate him into staying awake. Instead, try to imagine how you would feel in his place, and arrange small-group discussions, placing him with a small number of patient, sympathetic classmates.

Handbook heading
Helping Students Take Advantage of Structure

4. Call attention to and take advantage of structure. Stress relationships in what you present, use advance organizers when appropriate, and urge students to seek patterns and develop mediators of their own. Several principles of field theory can be of value when you plan lessons and make presentations. The major point to remember is that *Gestalt* means *pattern*. Whenever you present a topic, call attention to the way ideas are related. If the topic is organized and complex, use advance organizers to give a preview and provide structure. In considering this suggestion, however, you should keep in mind Piaget's observations on intellectual development. The use of advance organizers involves comprehension at the level of formal operations (or the symbolic mode, to use Bruner's description). Ausubel used college seniors as subjects. Less mature students may be confused

Older students may be aided by advance organizers presented in the form of a lecture outline or the equivalent. Younger pupils are more likely to benefit if a particular point is explained and illustrated in a simple and graphic way.

Bohdan Hrynewych

rather than helped by abstract generalizations presented at the beginning of a unit. For younger students, it may be preferable to work up to bigger ideas or at least to limit the use of relationships to material at a relatively low level of abstraction.

An additional point to consider has been noted by V. K. Kumar (1971), who emphasizes the desirability of taking account of student interests. He suggests that since an instructor cannot be certain of choosing advance organizers that will prove relevant to everyone, students might be invited to list what they consider to be the key points in an outline of material to be covered. The instructor could then perhaps provide individualized or small-group discussion in accordance with the points selected.

A final suggestion stems from emphasis on structure and concerns aspects of memorization and forgetting. Point out to your students that rote memorization is the hardest kind of learning, and suggest that organizing ideas and searching for meaning lead to faster acquisition of knowledge and better memory of what is learned. Keep in mind Bruner's experiment featuring groups of students asked to memorize pairs of words. Remind students at frequent intervals to develop their own ways of tying ideas together.

EXAMPLES

At the beginning of a unit or course, hand out an outline of topics to be covered. Then, as you present information, call attention to the ways one point emerges from or is related to others.

When introducing a complex topic, give a general overview of the material to be covered. Point out that you don't expect that everything you mention will be remembered. Emphasize that it is a preview.

If students must memorize material that is not intrinsically meaningful, urge them to develop personal mediators. (Additional suggestions on memorization featuring mediators will be offered in Chapter 8.)

Handbook heading
Using Techniques of
Open Education

5. Make use of techniques of open education. Many techniques of open education are congruent with the discovery approach. In *Open Education: Promise and Problems,* Vito Perrone gives information about specific practices. He points out that there are many interpretations of this approach but that most open classes feature the following common attributes:

Open education:
Activity, learning areas,
cooperative and
individualized planning

Activity Typically, many activities are going on at one time, and children are free to move from one activity to another. The classroom atmosphere is relaxed, and students are encouraged to talk to each other.

Learning areas Open classrooms usually are divided into separate learning areas by screens, bookcases, and planters. At the elementary level, it is common to find special areas for art, reading, language arts, science, math, drama, woodworking, and so on.

Cooperative planning At the beginning of the day in an elementary level open class, students commonly are permitted to engage in free, self-selected examination of materials in the various learning areas. After an hour or so, the class will be called together for a planning session. The teacher may describe some activity or call attention to additions to learning centers, and students are invited to describe books or activities they have found especially interesting. Then each student draws up a personal plan for the day. These plans may include designated times when selected students will meet with the teacher in small groups for instruction in specific skills, for example, using reference materials or taking advantage of context in reading. At the end of the day, the students come together again and describe the activities they have found especially interesting or instructive.

Individualized planning The teacher attempts to concentrate on the learning of individual pupils. She or he observes individuals, converses with them, keeps records of their progress (to the point of writing something about each child every day), and collects records that pupils keep of their own activities, as well as actual exercises or reports they have prepared. (This description emphasizes an important point about open schooling: It usually requires more effort than traditional teaching. However, many teachers who have switched from traditional to open education seem to agree that the effort is worth it.)

To date, most open education methods have been developed for the elementary level. As noted in the discussion of Piaget's theory in Chapter 3, an approach that stresses direct experience and interaction with peers is especially appropriate for students who are functioning at the stage of concrete operations. For students who are capable of formal operations, using such assumptions as a basis for an open approach is no longer completely consistent. However, you may occasionally wish to use the same basic techniques at the secondary level as a means of permitting greater student initiative and avoiding some of the disadvantages of controlled education.

If you will be teaching at the secondary level, you might provide for more student activity and interaction by structuring discovery sessions through use of the techniques described in these suggestions, by organizing small group discussions, or by inviting pairs or small groups of students to exchange views on text materials or outside reading. You might experiment with activity areas if you are teaching a subject that lends itself to such an approach. For example, in a science class it would be possible to set up different demonstrations and apparatus, arrange displays, and establish a library corner. Cooperative, individualized planning could be instituted by using a *contract approach*, whereby each student meets with you at the

Contract approach: Individual pupils agree to complete a task

beginning of a report period to agree on a project that might consist of a term paper, several book reports, an experiment, or the like. Such projects might be presented to the rest of the class either in small group, round-robin fashion, or as more formal presentations.

You might select or devise organized sets of materials so that students can work individually at their own pace, using tests primarily to discover weaknesses or misinterpretations. Then you might meet with small groups of students who are experiencing a common difficulty (e.g., understanding a particular concept, finding references in the library) and help them overcome it.

To individualize instruction, you might set aside certain class periods for tutorial sessions. Instead of requiring written reports, invite students to sign up for ten-minute blocks of time on designated days to give you an oral report. This will not only save the student the trouble of writing or typing a report and you the trouble of reading a report; it will also give you the opportunity to interact with each of your students on a person-to-person basis and to probe more deeply into interpretations.

To increase the amount of information about individuals, encourage students to keep their own records to supplement those you maintain.

(These first five suggestions relate to general applications of principles proposed by Piaget, Lewin, and Bruner. Teaching techniques that are most congruent with the assumptions of the cognitive discovery view, though, feature student discussion. The remaining points offer suggestions you might follow when you decide to use this form of instruction.)

6. If you intend to use any kind of discussion approach, first establish a relaxed atmosphere. For the discovery method to work properly, pupils must feel free to express ideas without fear of ridicule or failure. When you want to use this technique, therefore, you should do your best to convince your students that they are free to play with ideas. Regardless of how pointless or silly some contributions may seem, you should avoid ridiculing those who make them. And if one or more students laugh at or belittle something that is said by a classmate, do your best to gloss over the incident by noting that the idea is worth exploring or by saying something like, "Remember, they laughed at Columbus, too. We can't come up with new ideas if we aren't willing to go out on a limb a bit."

Handbook heading
Ways to Arrange for
Discovery to Take Place

7. Arrange the learning situation so that discovery is likely to take place. This is the crux of the discovery approach. The basic idea is to *arrange* things so that insight will take place, just as Köhler arranged the sticks and banana so that Sultan would perceive the relationship between them. In some cases, you may present a topic that is a matter of opinion or one that all students are sure to know something about. In other cases, you can structure the discussion by exposing all participants to the same background information.

a. Ask students to discuss familiar topics or those that are matters of opinion.

EXAMPLES
What are some of the techniques that advertising agencies use in TV commercials to try to persuade us to buy certain products?

What do you think is the best book you ever read, and why do you think so?

b. Provide necessary background information by asking all students to read all or part of a book, take notes on a lecture, or view a film.

EXAMPLES

After the class has read *Great Expectations* say, "What do you think Dickens was trying to convey when he wrote this novel? Was he just trying to tell a good story, or was he also trying to get us to think about certain kinds of relationships between people?"

"After I explain some of the principles of electrical currents, I'm going to ask you to suggest rules for connecting batteries in series and in parallel. Then, we'll see how well your rules work."

"This film shows how beavers live. After it's over, we'll discuss ways that beaver behavior is similar to human behavior."

8. Structure discussions by posing a specific question, by presenting a provocative issue, or by asking students to choose topics or subtopics. As the examples just noted indicate, it is important to structure a discovery session by giving students something reasonably specific to discuss. Otherwise, they may simply engage in a disorganized and desultory bull session. Some enthusiasts for the discovery approach assert that *any* discussion has value and thereby strengthen Skinner's argument that the method is set up to make instruction unnecessary. If you are going to function as a teacher, you should organize experiences so that more learning takes place under your direction than would occur if you left children entirely to themselves. You might supply direction in the following ways.

a. In some cases, encourage students to arrive at conclusions already reached by others. Bruner's MACOS materials illustrate this approach. Thousands of books provide detailed answers to the questions "What is human about human beings? How did they get that way? How can they be made more so?" But Bruner believes that answers mean more when they are arrived at by the individual, not supplied ready-made by others. As you look over lesson plans, therefore, you might try to select some questions that you will ask students to answer by engaging in discussion, as opposed to reading or listening to what others have already discovered. In searching for such topics, you might take into account the techniques described by Bruner—and also those discussed by Bigge. Here is a combined list of these techniques, together with an example of each one. In your Handbook you might describe similar applications you could use when you begin to teach. In thinking about possibilities, keep in mind that the gaining of insight depends on appropriate previous experience.

Handbook heading
Ways to Set Up
Discovery Sessions

Emphasize contrast   In a sixth grade social studies unit say, "When you watch this film on Mexico look for customs and ways of living that differ from ours. Then, we'll talk about what these differences are and also why they may have developed."

Stimulate informed guessing In a junior high unit on natural science you might say, "Suppose we wanted to figure out some kind of system to classify trees so that we could later find information about particular types. What would be the best way to do it?" After students have developed their own classification scheme, show them schemes developed by specialists.

Encourage participation In a high school political science class, illustrate the jury system by staging a mock trial.

Stimulate awareness In a high school English class, ask the students to discuss ways the author developed the plot.

Switch the subject matter In a fifth grade unit on conservation, ask students to list the disadvantages of nuclear power plants. Then, after

Staging a jury trial is one way to encourage participation when using the discovery approach.
Kenn Goldblatt

they have convinced themselves that such plants should be prohibited, ask them to list disadvantages of other types of energy production, such as strip mining of coal.

Introduce disturbing data   In a junior high math class, give a series of problems that can all be solved the same way. Then insert a problem that looks similar but which must be solved a different way. After students have struggled with the problem for a few minutes, ask them to try to figure out how it differs.

Permit students to make mistakes   In a high school cooking class, don't say anything if you notice that two students fail to put baking powder in their cake batter. Then, when they remove their flat cake from the oven, ask them to speculate about what went wrong.

b. In other cases, present a controversial topic for which there is no single answer.   Other types of discussion topics might center on provocative issues about which there are differences of opinion. One caution here is to avoid topics (such as premarital sex or legalizing marijuana) that parents may feel should not be discussed in school, either because they are convinced it is their prerogative to discuss them with their children or because they feel that students may be pressured to endorse your opinion because you assign grades. Remember that some parents argue that Bruner's MACOS materials, which are intended to achieve the seemingly innocuous goal of helping students relate our culture to other cultures, usurp their prerogative to inculcate values. You should not avoid controversy, but neither should you go out of your way to agitate pupils and their parents.

Another caution is to avoid selecting issues to provoke more than instruct. You may be tempted to present a highly controversial topic and then congratulate yourself at the end of the period if most students engaged in heated discussion. But if they simply argued vociferously about something that had nothing to do with the subject you are assigned to teach, you could not honestly claim to have arranged an instructive exchange of ideas. A final caution relates to a characteristic of formal thought described in Chapter 3: There may be a tendency for secondary school students to engage in unrestrained theorizing when they first experience the thrill of being able to deal with hypotheses and possibilities. You may find that it is necessary to remind some students to take into account realities when they discuss controversial issues involving tangled background circumstances or conflicts of interest.

EXAMPLES
In a junior high school science class, ask students to list arguments for and against attempting to alter the genetic code of human beings.

In a high school political science class, ask students to list arguments for and against the Equal Rights amendment.

c. If the subject is complex, ask the class to suggest subtopics.   In some cases, you may wish to ask the class to discuss a topic that has many facets. When dealing with such material you might first ask students to list subtopics. Use this information to divide the class into groups, and have each prepare a report of some kind.

EXAMPLES

Instead of structuring sixth grade sessions on the nature of human beings by using Bruner's MACOS materials, ask the students themselves to describe humanizing forces such as toolmaking, language, and social organization.

In a high school history class, ask students to list key figures of a certain era.

9. If time is limited and if only one topic is to be covered, ask students to form a circle and have an all-class discussion.   In some situations you may find it necessary or desirable to have the entire class discuss a topic. Such discussions are most likely to be successful if all students have eye contact with each other. The simplest way to achieve this is to ask all students to form a circle. Next invite responses to the question you have posed. As students make remarks, serve as moderator more than leader. Try to keep the discussion on the topic, but avoid directing it toward a specific predetermined end result. If one or more students tend to dominate the discussion, say something like, "Mary and Jack have given us their ideas. Now I'd like to hear from the rest of you." If an aggressive student attacks or belittles something said by a classmate, say something like, "It's good to *believe* in a point of view, but let's be friendly as we listen to other opinions. This is supposed to be a discussion, not an argument or a debate."

In some instances, whole-class discussions work beautifully. A contribution by one student will spark a related one by another, and almost everyone will follow what is said with interest. On other occasions, however, the outcome can be deadly, disorganized, or both. Sometimes the first thing said by the first student will annihilate the topic and the discussion. (An opinionated young man may say, for example, "There's absolutely no point in talking about that question. We can't change anything, so why waste time talking about it?") At other times, your bright and enthusiastic question, "Well, what do you think about that?" will be followed by complete silence, which in turn will be followed by nervous shuffling, much gazing out the window, and the like. (Just in case that happens, you might always have some sort of back-up activity planned for discussion periods.) Factors that lead to successful or unsuccessful discussions are often idiosyn-

Handbook heading
Ways to Supervise
Discovery Sessions

cratic, but there are certain procedures you might follow in order to increase the likelihood of success.

   a. Ask questions that stimulate students to apply, analyze, synthesize, and evaluate.   When you first structure a discussion session and also when it is under way, take care to ask questions likely to arouse thoughtful responses. If you ask students to supply information (e.g., "When did the Civil War begin?"), the first correct response will lead to closure, and you may end up asking a series of questions leading to brief answers that will be the equivalent of a program or a fill-in exam. M. D. Gall (1970) reviewed dozens of studies of classroom recitation sessions and found consistent evidence that up to 80 percent of all questions asked by teachers stressed facts and knowledge. In some situations, such as a review session before an exam, asking a series of questions for the purpose of testing knowledge is logical and desirable. But when the intention is to encourage pupils to make their own discoveries or to develop skills as deductive thinkers, it is preferable to ask questions likely to tap higher levels of thinking.

EXAMPLES
"You just learned how to calculate the area of a circle. Think of as many different ways as you can of how you might be able to use that bit of knowledge if you were a do-it-yourself home owner." (Application)

"What are possible reasons the Civil War took place when it did? Try to think of as many different possible causes as you can, and I'll list them on the board." (Analysis)

"Last month we read a novel by Dickens; this month we read a play by Shakespeare. What are some similarities in the way each author developed the plot of the story?" (Synthesis)

"We just read five short poems by Emily Dickinson. I'd like you to tell me which one you liked the best and then explain why you preferred it to the others. What qualities did your favorite poem have that the others did not have, at least to the same extent?" (Evaluation)

   b. Allow sufficient time for initial responses, and then probe for further information (if appropriate).   Mary Budd Rowe (1974) found that many teachers fail to allow enough time for pupils to respond to questions. She discovered that quite often instructors would wait only one second before repeating the question or calling on another student. When teachers were advised to wait to least three seconds after asking a question, student responses increased in frequency, length, and complexity. Furthermore, students seemed to be more confident (as reflected by the way they spoke and the kinds of statements they made), and more members of the class were inclined to participate.

One possible explanation for improved student recitation when teachers wait longer for a response is that reflective thinkers have an opportunity to figure out what they want to say. But even impulsive thinkers probably welcome a few more seconds of thinking time. It seems logical to expect that snap answers would be more superficial than answers supplied after even a few seconds of reflection. Therefore, instead of setting up question sessions so that students compete to see who can supply the fastest answer, you might make it a habit to say something like this before asking a question: "Now, before you put your hand up and ask to be called on, I want everyone to think about this question, and perhaps even jot down a brief answer on a piece of paper."

In addition to giving students ample time to make an initial response, you should also encourage them to pursue an idea. If it seems appropriate, probe for further information or clarification of a point by asking pupils who give brief or incomplete answers to explain how or why they arrived at a conclusion or to supply additional comments.

EXAMPLES

"Well, Mary, I'm sure a gardener might sometimes need to figure the area of a circle, but can you give a more specific example? If you can't think of one right away, put up your hand as soon as you can describe a specific situation where it would help to know the area of a circular patch of lawn or soil."

"Yes, John, it seems certain that differences of opinion about slavery had a lot to do with the Civil War. But let's pursue that a bit further. What were some of the economic and agricultural differences between the North and the South that influenced feelings about slavery?"

c. When selecting students to recite, use techniques likely to sustain steady but nonthreatening attention. At the same time, guard against the temptation to call primarily on bright, articulate, assertive pupils. In addition to asking questions during class discussions, you will need to decide *who* will recite. The way you moderate student contributions may not only determine how successful the discussion will be; it may also influence how pupils feel about themselves and each other. Jacob Kounin (1970) has pointed out that when a teacher first names a student and then asks a question, the rest of the class may tend to turn their attention to other things. The same tendency to "tune out" may occur if a teacher follows a set pattern of calling on students (e.g., by going around a circle). To keep all the students on their toes, therefore, you should ask questions first and then call on volunteers in an unpredictable sequence, frequently switching from one part of the room to another. As you look around the room before selecting a volunteer from those holding up their hands, remember Skinner's criticism that a few students may make all the discoveries, and guard against the temptation to call primarily on students you expect to give good or provocative answers. Repeatedly ignoring pupils who may be a bit inarticulate or unimaginative may cause them and their classmates to conclude that you think they are stupid. If that occurs, those who are never given opportunities to express opinions or volunteer information are likely to lose interest in participating in discussions, to the point of totally ignoring what is taking place.

A related question has to do with voluntary vs. required recitation. Most advocates of the discovery approach stress the importance of trying to establish a relaxed atmosphere so that students will express themselves freely. But some students, as you may know from personal experience, are uncomfortable to the point of being terrified if they are forced to speak up in front of an entire class. If you follow a procedure of asking a question and then scanning the room before calling on someone to answer, you may establish an atmosphere that will be perceived by some students as the equivalent of being selected to stand in front of a firing squad. (If you ever had a sadistic teacher who took delight in calling on students who seemed most timid or afraid, you know from personal experience how much tension can build up during classroom discussions.) To encourage free interchange of ideas in a nonthreatening atmosphere, it seems preferable to call on students only if they first indicate that they are eager or willing to recite. (An exception to this general rule might be rapid-fire recitation, as in a foreign language class. You can reduce anxiety in such situations, though, by asking questions very rapidly, by directing the easiest questions at the most timid and insecure pupils, and by using a light touch so that it seems more like a game than an oral examination.)

Even if you use the techniques just described, all-class discussions are often hard to control because so many variables are involved. And even under the best of conditions, not all students will be able to participate. Therefore, you may find that it will often be advantageous to divide the class into small groups when you want to encourage students to make discoveries through discussions.

10. If abundant time is available and if a controversial or subdivided topic is to be discussed, divide the class into groups of five or so, and arrange for all members in each group to have eye contact with every other group member.   A major limitation of any kind of discussion is that only one person can talk at a time. This difficulty can be reduced by dividing the class into smaller groups before asking them to exchange ideas. A group of about five seems to work best. If only two or three pupils are interacting with each other, the exchange of ideas

may be limited. If there are more than five, not all members will be able to contribute at frequent intervals.

Two factors to consider in forming small groups are how to form them and how to arrange them.

Handbook heading
Techniques for
Arranging Small Group
Discussions

a. Have students choose to be members of a group, or divide the class by rows or by a counting-off procedure. One way to form groups, particularly if students have suggested subtopics, is to ask them to list in order their first three subject preferences. (Some later arguments may be avoided if you mention at the start that it is unlikely that all the students in the class will get their first choice.) Then you can divide the class by referring to the lists. One advantage of this technique is that students embark on a discovery session with the feeling that they have chosen to do so. Another advantage is that you can do a certain amount of arranging of group membership, since students won't know how many of their classmates listed a particular topic as first choice. You might break up potentially disruptive pairings (e.g., two boys who often engage in wrestling matches, two girls who get the giggles whenever they are together, a high school couple who are passionately in love with each other) and also spread around talkative, creative, and thoughtful students.

Another way to divide the class, particularly if all groups are to discuss the same topic, is to ask all pupils in a row to form a group. Or have the class count off from one to five. That is, ask the first pupil in the first row to say "One," the next pupil "Two," and so forth, until the fifth pupil counts off. Then, start over again at one. After all students have counted off, ask all "ones" to move to one part of the room, "twos" to another part, and so on. There are often advantages to having different assortments of students discuss different topics. You can accomplish this goal by asking students to count off in different ways each time you divide the class.

b. Ask the students to move chairs or desks to form circles in different parts of the room. Once the groups are formed, assign each one a particular part of the room. If the students do not form a circle of their own accord, urge them to arrange themselves so that they are all facing each other.

11. Consider appointing or having the group elect a moderator and a recorder. Two of the most common problems of group discussion, regardless of the number of participants, are that one person will do most of the talking and that the members will wander away from the original topic and engage in a gabfest. When the class is divided into groups, both these difficulties can be minimized if a moderator and a recorder are appointed or elected. Perhaps the simplest way to select them is to have students draw straws. Sometimes elections or

Small group discussions arranged so that all participants have eye contact with each other encourage the exchange of ideas.

Marion Faller/Monkmeyer

appointments lead to hurt feelings, suspicion of favoritism, and the like.

The moderator should be instructed to keep the discussion on the topic and to make sure that everyone has a chance to speak. One way to avoid the possibility that a moderator will get too bossy is to suggest that he or she ask the members of the group to vote on whether they are wandering away from the point. To make sure that everyone in the group has a chance to speak up and also to shut off a verbose or pushy talker, you might wait twenty minutes or so after the groups form and then say, "I think it is time for moderators to make sure that those who haven't said anything so far be given the chance to contribute ideas."

The role of the recorder is to list major points that the members of the group agree are important. When Bruner used his MACOS materials, he sometimes instructed the recorder to write out points on 3-by-5-inch cards. Then, when the time came to organize these into a final report, points could be easily arranged into a logical sequence. If you do not ask a group to keep some sort of record of what is said or prepare some sort of answer to the question under discussion, the interchange of ideas is likely to dissolve into a bull session.

The aim of the discovery approach is to produce some relatively specific insight in the minds of most, if not all, class members—in other words, to impel students to reorganize their perceptions in some fairly definite way so that they grasp new relationships. Therefore, completely open-ended discussions that trail off without any kind of conclusion are usually undesirable—unless, of course, the students are dealing with personal opinions and have been exposed to a variety of stimulating ideas.

The Gestalt principle of *closure* emphasizes this idea. In Figure 6-5 you will find the type of designs used in several experiments conducted by field theorists. When subjects are shown the bottom set of figures for a few seconds and asked to reproduce them from memory, they depict the designs quite accurately. But most subjects do not produce faithful copies of the upper figures; they tend to close the gaps and depict *complete* designs. The principle behind this perceptual tendency also applies to behavior. People tend to want to close discussions and activities, to find solutions to problems. Therefore, if discovery sessions repeatedly fail to provide any closure at all, your students may become frustrated and develop a distaste for the technique. In a sense, programmed learning is effective in providing closure, for even if a student does not finish a program, the completion of even a few frames may give a sense of accomplishment. However, this aspect of programmed learning may also be undesirable because of a phenomenon related to closure.

B. Zeigarnik (1927) first demonstrated the tendency for students to recall unfinished tasks and to forget completed ones. The explanation she offered was that a "tension system" builds up within an individual until a task is finished. Thus the feeling of accomplishment engendered by filling in separate frames on a program may lead to forgetting when the task is finished, whereas a sense of dissatisfaction induced

Closure: Tendency to complete a perception or task

Figure 6-5

Closure

After looking at the top three figures briefly, one sees them as complete. This perceptual tendency illustrates the Gestalt principle called closure. The bottom figures, however, are too incomplete for closure to take place.

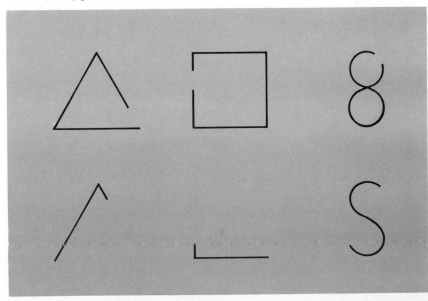

by an incomplete discovery session may predispose students to
remember and want to return to the subject. In fact, Postman and
Weingartner (1969) urge teachers to cut off discussions deliberately
before closure is achieved, on the assumption that the participants
will be more likely to remember what has been analyzed and more
inclined to complete the learning experience on their own.

Bruner (1966, p. 119), however, suggests that the Zeigarnik effect
holds only if a task has structure, that is, a specific beginning, a recognizable sequence, and a clear-cut end result. You should keep this in
mind if you attempt to take advantage of the Zeigarnik effect; do not
expect your students to remember a discussion or feel impelled to
seek answers out of class simply because you end a disorganized
discovery session at some arbitrary point. You will have to establish
structure and help students make considerable progress toward finding a solution before you cut off discussion.

The suggestion that you structure discovery sessions implies that
you should have some idea of what you want your students to learn
before you start. However, you need to be flexible enough to allow
your students to take a somewhat different tack or go beyond what
you figured out by yourself. This is what Bigge means by reflection
level teaching. If you give your students a chance, you may be amazed
at how much you can learn from them. This is an important advantage
of the discovery approach as opposed to programmed learning.

12. Consider asking all pupils to spend three minutes or so individually writing out their initial reactions to the discussion topic before
they begin to share ideas.   This suggestion is based on research on
cognitive styles, which was summarized in Chapter 4. The discussion
approach is ideal for impulsive thinkers who enjoy reacting to a
question with quick answers. Reflective thinkers, on the other hand,
may become frustrated if they carefully reason through a point only to
discover that it is no longer relevant because an impulsive thinker has
already tossed out a less clearly articulated but related idea or is
monopolizing the discussion. Asking everyone to write out initial
reactions gives the reflective thinkers a chance to marshal their ideas
and may also reduce the tendency for impulsive types to spout out
opinions without doing much deliberating. It may also help shy students gain confidence about reciting, since they can refer to their
notes. This approach can be used as a prelude to either all-class or
small-group discussions.

13. As the groups engage in discussion, observe benignly but silently.
Intervene only if it seems necessary to keep the discussion proceeding
in a constructive manner.   Generally speaking, it seems preferable
for the instructor to avoid participating in small-group discussions.
Because of your roles as class leader, expert, and evaluator, whatever

you say is likely to be accepted as the "right" answer. Consequently, you may wish either to observe from your desk (perhaps while you correct exams or prepare a lesson) or to wander around the room, being careful not to hover around any group for a long time.

a. If the group has strayed from the topic, if one individual is dominating the discussion, or if the group is pressuring one individual to alter an opinion, use subtle remarks to try to correct the situation. If the moderator is unable to cope with such problems, you might demonstrate to her or him (and also to all others in the group who may serve as moderators in the future) how to keep a discussion on the track. You might ask to look at what the recorder has written down, for example, or solicit the opinion of a student who has been pushed into the background.

Individuals may succumb to group pressure

In an ingenious experiment, S. E. Asch (1956) demonstrated the extent to which group members may exert pressure on an individual to accept their view. He arranged for seven students who were his confederates to unanimously agree that certain lines on a purported test of perception were the same length, even though they were quite obviously different lengths. When unsuspecting individuals were introduced into this group and asked about the lines, most of them briefly resisted the group opinion, then acted confused and uncomfortable, and finally agreed that the lines were equal. Sometimes in group discussions it is desirable to ask the members to reach consensus on a common group of points. In other cases, however, it may be preferable for each individual to develop her or his own opinion. In such cases, you might offer some support to an individual who is being pressured by others to accept their view. You might say something like, "It's a good idea to listen to what others have to say, but make up your own mind, and don't be bothered if your conclusions aren't exactly the same as other people's."

b. In most cases, avoid answering questions or participating actively in the discussion. After arranging many discovery sessions, Lawrence Shulman (1970) concluded that if a teacher answers a question posed by a member of a group, the ensuing interchange is likely to take the form of an "ask the expert" session. If you can keep a discussion going by answering a question, it is logical to do so, but for the most part it seems better to urge students to find their own answers. You should also try to control the tendency to lecture. If groups find that doing their own thinking is an effort, they may attempt to entice you into doing it for them. They may smile and act interested when you make a remark and shape your behavior to the point that you supply most of the information and ideas.

14. Ask the groups to share conclusions after they have had ample time to discuss the topic.

a. Allow time at the end of the period for a spokesperson for each group to report on conclusions on specific points. Perhaps list these on the board and invite comments from the entire class. When all groups have been discussing the same topic, you may wish to pool ideas contributed by separate groups. One way to do this is to stand at the board and ask the recorder from group one to give a point from their list, then the recorder from group two to do the same, and so forth. Stress that each spokesperson should mention points not already noted and continue inviting comments in order until all points are listed. Then use the final list as the basis for a class discussion.

Handbook heading
Techniques for Sharing
Conclusions

b. Consider asking each group to write a brief outline of their conclusions or prepare a project or demonstration, and combine these into a notebook or culminating event. When each group has been working on its own project, you will want to arrange for all members of the class to learn about what others have discovered. In some cases, you might ask each group to prepare a written, illustrated report to be incorporated into a homemade textbook. Then a copy could be reproduced for each member of the class. In other cases, you might ask each group to prepare a display or demonstration or skit to be presented on a particular day or days. If appropriate, you might treat the culmination as a gala occasion, complete with programs and refreshments.

15. Consider the possibility that the discovery method is most appropriate for bright, confident, highly motivated pupils and for topics that lack clear terminal behavior. Although many advocates of the discovery method maintain that it can be used at all grade levels, with pupils of all levels of ability, and with all subjects of study, it is clearly more appropriate in some situations than in others. There is a strong possibility, for example, that very young children do not derive full benefits from the method. This is suggested by Piaget's observation that such children may still be at the egocentric level of speech and may experience difficulty taking into account what others say, which may prevent them from staying on the track in class discussion. In addition, it seems reasonable to conclude that although bright, confident pupils who are excited about school and learning might thrive on a steady diet of discovery, slow pupils—after repeatedly observing their classmates beaming with satisfaction at the moment of insight— might become discouraged. Furthermore, pupils who aren't particularly interested in school, for whatever reason, and those who have a strong need to feel that they have accomplished something might be better off working on teaching machines.

As for subject matter, some topics, such as the nature of human beings or personal reactions to literary works, are tailor-made for discussion. Other topics, such as how to operate a power saw or a theory in chemistry, are simply not suitable. It seems absurd deliberately to avoid telling pupils something others have already learned or figured out, merely for the sake of letting them try to discover it on their own. And, as noted earlier, students may prefer the teacher's insight to that of a classmate. Most important of all, you may find that by disclosing information in an efficient way, you can produce many more experiences of insight than the pupils could if left to themselves.

Now that you are familiar with the discovery approach and open education, both of which are based on the cognitive-discovery view, you probably realize that you will want to use some of the techniques just described when you teach. Programmed methods of instruction are excellent when you want to present specific subject matter systematically and efficiently or to assign students to individualized study. But some topics are more appropriate for group discussion, and the opportunity for pupils to participate actively in finding solutions to problems will be a refreshing change of pace—for you and your students—from teacher-directed lessons. Some psychologists and educators, however, are critical of the cognitive-discovery view precisely *because* it emphasizes thinking and perception. They argue that teachers should not only be concerned with the mental development of their pupils; they should also encourage the fruition of such human qualities as feelings, emotions, attitudes, values, relationships with others, and self-understanding. This is the essence of humanistic psychology, and it will be discussed in the next chapter.

SUMMARY OF KEY POINTS

Cognitive psychologists, who are interested in ways we think and perceive, suggest that human beings have a built-in desire to learn because they are eager to maintain a cognitive equilibrium and that what children learn on their own has more personal meaning than what they are told by others.

Cognitive psychology is derived from principles of field theory stressing that our perceptions are influenced by ways stimuli are arranged, by experiences, and by interests. Kurt Lewin emphasized this view with his concept of the life space, which consists of everything one needs to know about a person to understand her or his behavior in a specific psychological environment at a particular time.

Some principles of cognitive psychology were proposed by Gestalt psychologists. Gestalt means form, pattern, or configuration, and Jerome Bruner has pointed out that stress on the structure (or overall pattern) of a field of study aids learning and remembering. Bruner also claims that grasp of structure leads to mastery of principles that can be applied in a variety of ways, which paves the way for more complex learning.

The basic instructional technique advocated by cognitive psychologists is the discovery approach, which is put into practice by arranging for pupils to find their own solutions to problems. When students find their own answers, it is argued, what they learn has personal meaning, they develop self-confidence, and they acquire problem-solving skills.

Principles of cognitive psychology and the essence of the discovery approach were demonstrated by Wolfgang Köhler, who arranged for the ape Sultan to gain insight by perceiving new relationships. Jerome Bruner demonstrated that pupils learn more effectively when they develop their own mediators. David P. Ausubel showed how advance organizers serve as mediating links.

The discovery approach can be used in the classroom in a variety of ways. Bruner recommends setting up group discussions by emphasizing contrast, stimulating guessing, encouraging participation, and arousing awareness. Morris L. Bigge urges teachers to switch subject matter, introduce disturbing data, and permit mistakes. Suchman advocates inquiry training to teach pupils how to ask questions.

The discovery approach has many advantages, but critics have called attention to weaknesses. B. F. Skinner argues that it is foolish and impossible to expect students who live in a technological society to discover everything for themselves, particularly because the discovery approach is inefficient and time consuming. Furthermore, interpersonal problems may arise if one or two pupils routinely make most of the discoveries. Finally, parents and school administrators may object if the impression is that students are expected to educate themselves.

One of the most completely developed applications of principles of discovery learning is found in the open education approach, which stresses activity, learning areas, and cooperative and individualized planning. A related technique used with individual pupils is the contract approach, consisting of an agreement that a student will complete a specified project. Group and individual searches for answers to problems may be aided by the urge to achieve closure, or the tendency to complete a perception or task. One problem teachers may encounter with all-class or small-group discussions is the possibility that individual pupils will succumb to group pressure and alter or withdraw an opinion that is at variance with the view of the majority.

BECOMING A BETTER TEACHER:
QUESTIONS AND SUGGESTIONS

Ways to Permit
Students to Engage in
Self-Selected Study

Am I giving my students opportunities to participate in deciding what we will study? Suggestion: At the beginning of the next unit or report period, spend the first class period inviting the class to discuss what we will study and how we will do it.

Ways to Permit Students to Explain What They Are Thinking	Do I give my pupils sufficient chances to explain how much they know? Suggestion: Give an ungraded quiz just after introducing a new unit to find out how well students understand basic concepts and ideas.
Helping Students Take Advantage of Structure	How well did I call attention to the structure of the last unit I presented? Suggestion: When working on lesson plans for the next unit of study, concentrate on how to emphasize the organization of points, either by preparing an outline to be mimeographed or printed on the board, or by calling attention to advance organizers.
Using Techniques of Open Education	Are there ways I can take advantage of techniques of open education? Suggestion: Next week experiment with ways to permit more pupil activity, set up learning areas, schedule group and individual planning sessions. Also, ask pupils if they would like to try the contract approach.
Ways to Arrange for Discovery to Take Place	When I set up discovery sessions, do I arrange the situation so that it helps students gain insight? Suggestion: The next time I plan a discovery session, think about how to present background information or otherwise arrange things so that students are likely to grasp new relationships.
Ways to Set Up Discovery Sessions	Do I occasionally check Bruner's and Bigge's lists of discovery techniques for ideas on how to set up class discussions? Suggestion: Make up a list of the techniques used by Bruner and Bigge, and glance over it the next time I plan how to stimulate an all-class discussion.
Ways to Supervise Discovery Sessions	Am I doing an effective job supervising all-class discussions? Suggestion: Make up a check list of steps to follow in supervising discovery sessions that involve the entire class. Include such things as how to arrange desks and chairs, what sorts of questions to ask, a reminder to wait at least three seconds for students to respond, phrases to use when probing for more complete or revealing answers, a strategy for calling on students so that everyone remains alert but no one feels threatened or ignored.
Techniques for Arranging Small-Group Discussions	Am I doing an effective job arranging small-group discussions? Suggestion: Make up a check list of steps to follow in setting up and supervising small-group discussions. Include ideas on how to organize the groups and select a moderator and recorder, on what to do while the groups interact, and on guidelines for when to intervene.
Techniques for Sharing Conclusions	The last time we had small-group discussion, did the whole class learn about what each group had concluded? Suggestion: Make out a detailed plan for organizing the culmination of the next small-group discussion session. Decide how much time to allow, how the conclusions will be reported, who will list ideas on the board, how reports, projects, or demonstrations will be presented to the rest of the class.

SUGGESTIONS FOR FURTHER STUDY

6-1

Gestalt Psychology

The evolution and impact of Gestalt psychology is traced in Chapter 23 of *A History of Experimental Psychology* (2nd ed., 1950) by Edwin G. Boring.

6-2

Kurt Lewin and Field Theory

Lewin presents extensive analyses of field theory in *Principles of Topological Psychology* (1936) and *Field Theory and Social Science* (1952). A concise summary of his theory is presented in Chapter 15, "Behavior and Development as a Function of the Total Situation," of *Manual of Child Psychology* (2nd ed., 1954), edited by Leonard Carmichael. An educational psychology text based on Lewin's views is *Between Psychology and Education* (1974) by David E. Hunt and Edmund V. Sullivan. Alfred J. Marrow has written a biography of Lewin titled *The Practical Theorist: The Life and Work of Kurt Lewin* (1969).

6-3

Ausubel's Cognitive View

David P. Ausubel provides quite technical interpretations of the cognitive view of learning in *The Psychology of Meaningful Verbal Learning* (1963) and *Educational Psychology: A Cognitive View* (1968). In these books he explains the use of advance organizers and many other points.

6-4

Bruner on Education

Toward a Theory of Instruction (1966) is Jerome Bruner's most concise and application-oriented book on teaching. Chapter 1, "Patterns of Growth," and Chapter 3, "Notes on a Theory of Instruction," provide general descriptions of Bruner's views on teaching and learning. Chapter 4 describes how the MACOS materials were used to structure a discovery approach.

6-5

Bigge on Learning

Morris L. Bigge provides one of the most systematic and practical analyses of the discovery approach explained in terms of principles of field theory in *Learning Theories for Teachers* (2nd ed., 1975). Much of the same material is covered in *Psychological Foundations of Education* (3rd ed., 1976) by Bigge and Maurice P. Hunt.

6-6

Analyzing Experiences with the Discovery Approach

In this chapter you read about techniques developed by Jerome Bruner and Morris L. Bigge for structuring discovery sessions. At least once in your recent experiences as a student, you have probably been involved in a class session where the instructor made use of one of these techniques. Describe such a situation, and then comment on how you and your fellow students reacted, or note what might have been done differently to make the situation more successful or how you might use a similar technique yourself. (If you can remember more than one type of discovery session, describe as many types as you can recall.) To assist you in selecting an experience, here is a list of the techniques suggested by Bruner and Bigge.

Emphasizing contrast—Did the instructor invite you to *compare* different people, reactions, or events?

Stimulating informed guessing—Did the instructor present a problem for you to try to solve and then provide information about how others actually solved it?

Encouraging participation—Did the instructor ask you to engage in a provocative activity or discussion?

Stimulating awareness—Did the instructor encourage you to think about *how* you might attack a problem, where you might find information, how to check on hypotheses, and so on?

Switching subject matter—Did the instructor first permit or encourage you to conclude that a point of view was sensible and then confront you with evidence to weaken or disprove it or lead you to see aspects of the problem you had overlooked?

Permitting mistakes—Did the instructor permit you to set about solving a problem the wrong way or to come to a false conclusion and then ask you to think about how and why this error occurred?

6-7

Thelen on Group
Discussion

Thorough analyses of small-group discussion are offered by Herbert A. Thelen in *Education and the Human Quest* (1960) and *Classroom Grouping for Teachability* (1967).

6-8

Open Education

One of the most comprehensive descriptions of open education in Britain is presented in *Children and Their Primary Schools* (1967) (usually called the Plowden Report, after Lady Plowden, who headed an educational commission asked to investigate primary education in Britain). Accounts of the British approach written by teachers who have practiced it include *Inside the Primary School* (1971) by John Blackie; *Primary Education in Britain Today* (1970), edited by Geoffrey Howson; and a series of twenty-three booklets being issued by Citadel Press under the title *Informal Schools in Britain Today*. Descriptions of open education by American educators include *Schools Are for Children: An American Approach to the Open Classroom* (1971) by Alvin Hertzberg and Edward Stone; *Homework: Required Reading for Teachers and Parents* (1971) by Gloria Channon; *The English Infant School and Informal Education* (1971) by Lillian Weber; *Children Come First* (1971) by Casey and Liza Murrow; *Open Education: Promise and Problems* (1972) by Vito Perrone (dean of the Center for Teaching and Learning at the University of North Dakota, center of the open education movement in the United States); *Open Education: A Sourcebook for Parents and Teachers* (1972), edited by Ewald B. Nyquist and Gene R. Hawes; *Schools Where Children Learn* (1971) by Joseph Featherstone; and *Crisis in the Classroom* (1970) by Charles E. Silberman. Most of these books concentrate almost exclusively on the advantages of open education. For information about problems that may develop when this approach is used, examine *Open Education and the American School* (1972) by Roland S. Barth.

Key points

Basic assumptions

Third force view: Trust children to make their own choices

Learner-centered teaching: Trust, sincerity, prizing, empathy

Humanistic teacher: Facilitator, encourager, helper, friend

Humanists stress emotions, fulfillment, relationships

Humanists strive to merge thinking, feeling, and action

An experiment in humanistic education

Summerhill theory: Child is innately wise, needs no help from adults

Summerhill practice: Voluntary lessons

Techniques of humanistic education

Humanists want students to become more aware of feelings

Role playing, psychodrama, simulation games, creative expression popular with humanists

Confluent education: Affective and cognitive elements flow together

Values clarification: Encourage pupils to choose, prize, and act on beliefs

Criticisms of humanistic education

Humanistic view is based on vague propositions

Achievements of Summerhill students unimpressive

Summerhill graduates not atypically creative

Graduates wanted own children to attend Summerhill only briefly

Some humanistic educators affect holier-than-thou attitude

Values clarification may not have a significant impact

Humanists offer testimonials, not evidence, to justify lavish claims

Some humanistic techniques resemble compulsory psychotherapy conducted by "amateurs"

Impossible to maintain close personal relationships with pupils

Applying the humanistic view in the classroom

Cardinal principle of humanistic education: Give pupils choices

Cardinal principle of communication: Talk to situation, not personality

Taxonomy of Educational Objectives: Affective Domain

Analyzing actual moral situations more effective than memorizing principles

Kohlberg: Levels of moral thinking

Using moral dilemmas to encourage moral development

Chapter 7   # The humanistic view
of learning

IF you were to ask ten randomly selected educational psychologists to describe the S-R and cognitive-perceptual views by listing basic assumptions, referring to key experiments, and noting teaching techniques derived from each position, their responses would probably stress many of the same points. If you asked them to do the same for the humanistic view, however, their responses probably would differ to such an extent that you might wonder whether they were talking about the same thing. The disparity would be likely because the phrases *humanistic psychology* and *humanistic education* are used in a variety of ways and because even those who identify themselves as humanistic psychologists and educators stress different ideas. One reason for this diversity of opinion is that humanists in psychology and education come from varied backgrounds and do not share a common interest as do those who endorse the views of Skinner (learning) or Bruner (cognitive and discovery). Even though the humanistic view is not well defined, it does involve a cluster of assumptions and techniques that are sufficiently different from the two views already discussed to merit mention in a text on how to apply psychology to teaching.

Basic assumptions

The humanistic view is not based on experimental data, such as reports of the behavior of rats in a Skinner box or apes in problem situations; instead, it is based on observations, impressions, and speculations. To structure this discussion of assumptions, the experiences and observations of the "elder statesmen" of humanistic psychology—Abraham H. Maslow, Carl R. Rogers, and Arthur Combs—will be summarized.

Maslow: Let children grow

Maslow earned his Ph.D. in a psychology department that supported the behaviorist-associationist position. After he graduated, however, he came into contact with Gestalt psychologists, prepared for a career as a psychoanalyst, and became interested in anthropology. As a result of these various influences, he came to the conclusion (noted in the discussion of the third force view of behavior in Chapter 3) that American psychologists who endorsed the behaviorist position had become so preoccupied with overt behavior and objectivity that they were ignoring some of the most important aspects of human existence. This conclusion was reinforced when his first child was born. Maslow observed later: "All the behavioristic psychology that I'd learnt didn't prepare me for having a child. A baby was so miraculous and so wonderful . . . all the work with rats . . . just didn't help at all" (quoted in Wilson, 1972, p. 146). (B. F. Skinner, by contrast, found that his work with rats *did* help him bring up his children. He designed an ingenious combination crib-playpen for his daughter. Superficially, the Air Crib, as it is called, resembles a Skinner box. But it is not intended to shape a child's behavior. Instead, it serves as a controlled environment in which an infant can sleep, explore, and play in safety and comfort.)

Maslow became convinced that a strict Freudian view of behavior, which led to the conclusion that human beings desperately strive to maintain control of themselves, also had limitations, primarily because much of it was based on the behavior of neurotic individuals. When he observed the behavior of especially well-adjusted persons— or *self-actualizers,* as he called them—he concluded that healthy children *seek* fulfilling experiences. As an alternative to the behavioristic and psychoanalytic interpretations of behavior, Maslow proposed *third force* psychology. This view, as noted in Chapter 3, is based on the assumption that if children are given free choice, they will choose what is good for them. Parents and teachers are therefore urged to trust children and to let and help them grow instead of interfering too much and trying to shape their behavior.

Third force view: Trust children to make their own choices

Rogers: Learner-centered education

Carl R. Rogers had experiences quite similar to those of Maslow, and he came to similar conclusions. Rogers began his career as a psychotherapist who used psychoanalytic techniques. Eventually he came to a conclusion identical to that of Maslow: The psychoanalytic view sometimes made troubled human beings appear to be helpless individuals who needed the more or less constant help of psychotherapists to cope with their problems. Over a period of years Rogers developed a new approach to psychotherapy. He called it *client-centered* (or *nondirective*) therapy to stress that the client, rather than the

Carl R. Rogers
Photo by Lilo

therapist, should be the central figure. (Or, as the term *nondirective* indicates, the therapist was not to tell the patient what was wrong and what should be done about it.) This view of therapy is a departure from psychoanalysis, where the analyst is the central figure who makes interpretations and offers prescriptions. It is also based on rejection of the strict behaviorist view of determinism, since it is assumed that the client will learn how to control his or her own behavior (and not merely be shaped by experiences).

As he practiced client-centered therapy, Rogers came to the conclusion that he was most successful when he established certain conditions (1967, pp. 53–54). He did not attempt to put up a false front of any kind. He established a warm, positive, acceptant attitude toward his clients, and he was able to empathize with clients and sense their thoughts and feelings. Rogers concluded that these conditions set the stage for successful experiences with therapy because clients became more self-accepting and aware of themselves. Once individuals acquired these qualities, they were inclined and equipped to solve personal problems without seeking the aid of a therapist.

In addition to functioning as a therapist, Rogers also served as a professor. As he analyzed his experiences as an instructor he came to the conclusion that the principles of client-centered therapy could be applied just as successfully to teaching. He proposed that education become *learner-centered* and that teachers try to establish the same conditions as client-centered therapists. Rogers sums up the qualities of a teacher who wants to use a learner-centered approach in this way:

Learner-centered teaching: Trust, sincerity, prizing, empathy

One of the requisites for the teacher who would facilitate this type of learning is a profound trust in the human organism. . . . If we trust the capacity of the human individual for developing his own potentiality, then we can permit him the opportunity to choose his own way in his learning. . . .

Another element of the teacher's functioning which stands out is his sincerity, his realness, his absence of facade. He can be a real person in his relationship with his students. He can be angry. He can also be sensitive and sympathetic. . . . Thus he is a *person* to his students. . . .

Another attitude which stands out . . . is a prizing of the student, a prizing of his feelings and opinions. . . .

Still another element in the teacher's attitude is his ability to understand the student's reactions from the inside, an empathic awareness of the way the process of education and learning seems to the student. (1967, pp. 59–60)

Rogers argues that the results of learner-centered teaching are similar to those of client-centered therapy: Students become capable of educating themselves without the aid of teachers.

Combs: The teacher as facilitator

Arthur Combs became an enthusiastic advocate of the humanistic view after having experiences similar to those of Maslow or Rogers. He too became disenchanted with behaviorism and psychoanalysis and sought an alternative. While Maslow based his conception of third force psychology on the study of motivation and Rogers based his view on his experiences as a psychotherapist, Combs uses the cognitive view as a starting point for his speculations. He begins with the assumption that "all behavior of a person is the direct result of his field of perceptions at the moment of his behaving" (1965, p. 12). (This is the same point emphasized by Kurt Lewin's concept of the life space.) From this assumption it follows that a teacher should try to understand any learning situation by speculating about how things seem from the students' point of view. This assumption also leads to the conclusion that to help students learn, it is necessary to induce them to modify their beliefs and perceptions so that they will see things differently and behave differently. Some aspects of Combs's analysis of learning are similar to those of Bruner and other cognitive psychologists, but Combs places less stress on cognitive aspects of learning and more emphasis on the personal perceptions of the learner.

Combs believes that how a person perceives herself or himself is of paramount importance and that a basic purpose of teaching is to help each student develop a positive self-concept. Maslow and Combs both assert that human beings are self-motivated, but Maslow explains motivation in terms of a hierarchy of needs, while Combs proposes that all behavior is due to a single basic need for *adequacy*. If it is assumed that students are eager to become as adequate as possible in any situation, the role of the teacher is seen in a much different light than when it is assumed (as in S-R theory) that behavior is shaped by reinforcing experiences. Combs observes, "The task of the teacher is not one of prescribing, making, molding, forcing, coercing, coaxing, or cajoling; it is one of ministering to a process already in being. The role required of the teacher is that of facilitator, encourager, helper, assister, colleague, and friend of his students" (1965, p. 16). Combs elaborates on these points by listing six characteristics of good teachers: (1) They are well informed about their subject. (2) They are sensitive to the feelings of students and colleagues. (3) They believe that students can learn. (4) They have a positive self-concept. (5) They believe in helping all students do their best. (6) They use many different methods of instruction (1965, pp. 20–23).

Humanistic teacher: Facilitator, encourager, helper, friend

Cognitive and humanistic views: Similarities and differences

In many respects, the assumptions of the humanistic view are similar to those upon which the discovery approach to learning is based. Cognitive psychologists and humanistic educators share the view that extreme interpretations of the behaviorist-environmentalist-associationist position may lead to unfortunate school practices. Humanists agree with Bruner that observing only overt behavior is restrictive and that learning that occurs when stimuli are associated with responses may often be limited and may lack personal meaning. Humanists differ from cognitive psychologists, however, in stressing the significance of emotions, feelings, personal fulfillment, and relationships with others. An example of this difference is provided by the reaction of Richard M. Jones to Bruner's approach to teaching *Man: A Course of Study.* In *Fantasy and Feeling in Education,* Jones argues that Bruner's method of conducting discovery sessions is too sterile and that class activities with the MACOS materials should be arranged to stimulate pupils' "emotional and imaginal responses" (1968, p. 9). He describes his own experiences in presenting MACOS and says that the most meaningful learning took place in a situation of "controlled emotion" (p. 25). He comments on the values—as well as the dangers—of an approach that stresses emotion and imagination and in Chapters 7, 8, and 9 of his book offers suggestions as to how it might be put into practice.

Humanists stress emotions, fulfillment, relationships

A similar point is made by George Dennison, who asserts in *The Lives of Children* that Bruner is too concerned with "control, social engineering, manipulation" (1969, p. 253). Dennison suggests that the discovery approach is most effective when it is arranged so that students can interact with the teacher and each other in situations in which they are free to reveal themselves. He presents his critique and describes ways to improve on the Bruner approach (as well as education in general) in Chapter 12 of his book.

Merging the cognitive, affective, and psychomotor domains

An argument often made by humanistic psychologists is that the tendency for behavioral scientists to subdivide topics and engage in specialized research has led to the assumption that human behavior must be compartmentalized. Many texts in psychology classify types of behavior into three major *domains: cognitive* (thinking), *affective* (emotions, attitudes, and values), and *psychomotor* (physical skills). It is essential to resort to such subdividing schemes when discussing complex topics, but humanistic psychologists and educators maintain that it is a mistake to try to subdivide behavior in classrooms. They recommend that teachers arrange learning experiences so that students think and feel and perhaps also engage in physical activities at the same time, instead of taking separate courses in subject matter, attitude formation, and physical education.

Humanists strive to merge thinking, feeling, and action

Still another point made by humanists is that students should be encouraged to explore their feelings and to engage in many forms of self-expression. The term *humanist* reflects the idea that we should not lose sight of the fact that we are, after all, human. Maslow and Combs acknowledge that the behaviorist's stress on objectivity and precise observation has led to impressive advances in knowledge of human behavior, but they point out that it has also caused S-R theorists to sometimes equate humans with simple animals, machines, or computers. Machines and computers do not fall in love, experience anger or jealousy, or become ecstatic about especially fulfilling experiences. Animals may have such feelings, but they are incapable of analyzing them or of perfecting ways of expressing or communicating them with depth, subtlety, and permanence. The humanistic psychologist or educator believes that the unique qualities of human beings should be developed to the fullest possible degree.

A final point made by several psychologists who identify themselves as humanists is that students should be helped to become aware of and clarify their values. In the opening chapter of *Values Clarification,* Sidney B. Simon, Leland H. Howe, and Howard Kirschenbaum call attention to the fact that young people today are faced by many decisions and must choose from among many alternatives. The authors maintain that "everything we do, every decision we make and course of action we take, is based on our consciously or unconsciously held beliefs, attitudes, and values" (1972, p. 13). In *Personalizing Education: Values Clarification and Beyond,* Leland W. Howe and Mary Martha Howe assert that "If our values are clear, consistent, and soundly chosen, we tend to live our lives in meaningful and satisfying ways" (1975, p. 17). In addition to endorsing the basic assumptions proposed by Maslow, Rogers, and Combs, then, humanistic psychologists and educators support the view that students should not only acquire knowledge and perfect intellectual and motor skills, they should examine their emotions, explore their feelings, learn how to communicate with others, engage in many forms of self-expression, and clarify their attitudes and values.

In the preceding chapters on the S-R view and the cognitive-discovery view, the section following the outline of assumptions consisted of a description of experiments that serve as a foundation for and demonstration of the principles of each theory. It is impossible to insert such a section in this chapter because the humanistic view is not based on experimental evidence. There was, however, what might be thought of as a fifty-year "experiment" in humanistic education, and a brief account of this will be offered as a substitute for a description of systematic research.

An experiment in humanistic education

In 1921 A. S. Neill, who had experienced difficulties and frustrations serving as a teacher in English public schools, established his own school. He called it Summerhill, and after the school had been in operation for forty years, a compilation of his earlier writings was published in 1960 under the title *Summerhill*. It became an immediate best seller and was frequently described as the most important book ever written on education. In the first chapter of *Summerhill* Neill states his basic philosophy, which is essentially the same as that of Maslow, Rogers, and Combs: "My view is that a child is innately wise and realistic. If left to himself without adult suggestion of any kind, he will develop as far as he is capable of developing" (1960, p. 4). Neill amplifies on this point in the third chapter, titled "Summerhill Education vs. Standard Education." In criticizing standard education, he argues, "Every time we show Tommy how his engine works we are stealing from that child the joy of life—the joy of discovery—the joy of overcoming an obstacle. Worse! We make that child come to believe that he is inferior, and must depend on help" (p. 25).

In other parts of *Summerhill,* it becomes clear that Neill himself did not endorse this view in actual practice. There were teachers at Summerhill, and they offered lessons. Pupils were not compelled to attend the lessons, but if a child skipped several classes and then asked the teacher to take time to explain what had been missed, those who had attended regularly had the right to forbid him or her from coming to future sessions. Afternoons were free for both teachers and pupils to do as they wished. Most students spent their time working on art or crafts projects, or writing and producing plays.

Every Saturday night a general meeting was held. Any person who had a grievance against any other individual could bring it up at these meetings, and all members of the school—faculty and students alike—

Summerhill theory: Child is innately wise, needs no help from adults

Summerhill practice: Voluntary lessons

A. S. Neill and a group of pupils at Summerhill.
Wide World Photos

were allowed to vote in determining if the complaint was just. If a majority agreed that a particular action infringed on the rights of others, the offending party had to promise not to repeat the action, and might also be required to pay a fine or give up a privilege. General school policies were also determined at these meetings. On one occasion, for example, Neill argued that children below the age of sixteen should not be allowed to smoke because tobacco is "a drug, poisonous, not a real appetite in children, but mostly an attempt to be grown up" (p. 45). When the vote was taken, Neill's proposal was defeated by a large majority.

Neill proved that a school based on the modified assumption that "children are innately wise and realistic" was workable. A significant point to keep in mind, though, is that Summerhill was a full-time boarding school and parents who sent their children to Neill asked him to serve not only as teacher but also as substitute parent. Accordingly, hardly any of the policies in force at Summerhill can be used in public schools. Few parents of public school children are likely to support the view that children of all ages should select their own curricula, for example, nor are they likely to agree that students should be permitted to outvote teachers and administrators in determining school regulations. Thus, even though Neill successfully carried out a fifty-year experiment in humanistic education, the techniques he developed can be used in pure form only in small, private boarding schools. For information about techniques of humanistic education that might be used in American public schools, it is necessary to turn to books by other advocates of this view.

Techniques of humanistic education

The psychologists who presented the basic arguments that serve as the rationale for humanistic education unfortunately have not supplied many specific suggestions for putting them into practice. Maslow confined himself to the general suggestion that teachers *let* children grow and help them make wise choices. Rogers offered a few guidelines for those who are eager to practice learner-centered teaching, but most of these are rather vague, and some of them simply cannot be used in most public schools. (Rogers perfected the methods he recommends in seminars with selected graduate students or in workshops for professional persons.) Here is a summary of points made by Rogers:

The [learner must] be in contact with, be faced by, a real problem. . . . Instead of organizing lesson plans and lectures, [a humanistic] teacher concentrates on providing all kinds of relevant raw material for use by the students, together with clearly indicated channels by which the student can avail himself of these resources. . . .

[The teacher] does not set lesson tasks. He does not assign readings. He does not lecture or expound (unless requested to). He does not evaluate and criticize unless the student wishes his judgment on a product. He does not give examinations. He does not set grades. (1967, pp. 58–61)

In estimating how successfully you might be able to put these various suggestions into practice, you might keep in mind that Rogers is America's most eminent psychotherapist, that students compete for the privilege of paying substantial fees to attend his seminars, and that he does not need to worry about school or university regulations (such as examinations and grades). What works for him in a one-week seminar might not work for you in a public school class of thirty students, five hours a day, 180 days a year.

Combs is a bit more specific than Rogers in describing how teachers might use a humanistic approach to education. He elaborates on the characteristics of effective teachers in various books and articles (1962, 1965, 1975) and offers suggestions ranging from general to specific in regard to how the points described might be put into practice. Only rarely, however, do these suggestions take the form of detailed descriptions of techniques of teaching.

Since Maslow, Rogers, and Combs do not offer specific guidelines for teaching practice, and since Neill's approach to education cannot be used in public schools, to find out what you might actually *do* if you want to function as a humanistic educator it is necessary to turn to books comprised of articles by enthusiasts for this approach. One such volume is *Humanistic Education Sourcebook* (1975), edited by Donald A. Read and Sidney B. Simon. The sourcebook contains fifty-six articles and, as its title indicates, is intended to serve as a source of ideas for teachers who would like to put humanistic education into practice. Here is an account of articles in the sourcebook that contain the most specific suggestions for educators.

An assortment of humanistic educational techniques

In the first article, Carl Rogers offers a slightly different version of the ideas summarized in the quotations from his 1967 article presented above. (He makes essentially the same points in another article reprinted in the sourcebook on pages 39–49.) In the second article, Alfred S. Alschuler describes "psychological education." Its goals are developing "a constructive dialogue with one's own fantasy life" (p. 24), using nonverbal exercises (such as pantomime and dance), "developing and exploring individuals' emotional responses to the world" (p. 25), and emphasizing "the importance of living fully and intensely 'here and now'" (p. 25). (Alschuler makes essentially the same points in a later article that appears in the sourcebook on pages 62–71.) In an article titled "Values and Valuing," Louis E. Raths, Merrill Harmin, and Sidney B. Simon list seven criteria (to be described later in this chapter) for helping students clarify values. In an article titled "Education and Therapy," Walter M. Lifton offers suggestions for leading group discussions. Arthur Combs (pp. 255ff.) describes the characteristics of good teachers listed earlier. Howard Kirschenbaum (pp. 315–320) explains the nature of "sensitivity modules"—exercises intended to make students more sensitive to the feelings of others (e.g., "spend a morning making the rounds with a visiting nurse" [p. 316]). Orvis A. Harrelson (pp. 325–328) and Kent Owen (pp. 329–332) describe how films, such as "Living with Love," which depicts relationships between a temporary foster mother and children waiting to be adopted, can be used to structure class discussion of emotions.

> Humanists want students to become more aware of feelings

Other articles in the sourcebook stress the values (and limitations) of encounter groups and sensitivity training, the virtues of free expression through movement (e.g., "touch or be touched on all exposed body surfaces by self, others, or objects" [p. 346]) and of role playing (pp. 363–369, 421–432). Another chapter urges the reader to make use of "depth unfoldment experiences," defined as a "small-group technique for helping people to break down interpersonal estrangement in order to facilitate communication and participation" (p. 391). Still other chapters describe sociodrama and psychodrama (e.g., two students act out the roles of a teacher and a student caught cheating, then reverse the roles) (pp. 409–414); and creative dramatics (e.g., all members of the group imagine that they are ice cubes in the process of melting) (pp. 439–450). Additional recommended techniques include simulation games (e.g., six students act out the roles of leaders of countries) (pp. 451–456) and "Magic Circle" discussions

> Role playing, psychodrama, simulation games, creative expression popular with humanists

(e.g., elementary grade pupils sit in a circle and finish and explain statements such as "I felt good when...") (pp. 457–459). Finally, methods are described for encouraging a positive self-concept (e.g., have students describe a successful accomplishment they achieved before they were ten years old; have all members of a group "bombard" a selected individual by listing all the strengths they see in him or her) (pp. 460–468).

Confluent education

Confluent education: Affective and cognitive elements flow together

The *Humanistic Education Sourcebook* consists of short articles by different authors. Additional insight into the techniques of humanistic education is provided by books that are highly regarded by enthusiasts for this approach. One such book is *Human Teaching for Human Learning: An Introduction to Confluent Education* (1971) by George Isaac Brown. Brown uses the term *confluent education* to stress the point that the techniques he describes are intended to cause affective and cognitive elements in learning to flow together. To illustrate what he means he describes a situation where a class of first graders were alerted to watch a TV program depicting, among other things, how birds eat turtle eggs. The next day their teacher asked them to act out the roles of bird and turtle, talk about what they had seen and done, and write stories about similar situations. In the third chapter of his

Some humanistic educators advocate encounter group sessions where individuals are encouraged (or required) to share highly personal thoughts and feelings.

Sepp Seitz/Magnum

book Brown describes several *affective techniques* (e.g., have students pair off and explore each other's faces with their hands, blindfold half of the students in the class and have a nonblindfolded partner take them on a "trust walk"). In the fourth chapter he describes classroom applications, several of which feature units for use in a tenth grade English class for slow learners. In one unit, the class read *Lord of the Flies,* discussed it, imagined that they were in a similar predicament to that described in the novel (left to cope after a plane crashes on an uninhabited island), spent a few minutes each day engaging in meditation with their eyes closed, and listened to a recording of Stravinsky's "Rite of Spring" after having been encouraged to "enter into the music." The remainder of the book consists of anecdotal reports by teachers who felt they had enjoyed success using techniques of confluent education.

Values clarification

The most explicit instructions available to those who would like to use humanistic techniques of teaching are to be found in books on *values clarification*. This term, which is sometimes capitalized and sometimes abbreviated V.C., was originally applied to techniques proposed by Louis Raths for helping children become more aware of their values. In the first book on the subject, *Values and Teaching* (1964) by Raths, Merrill Harmin, and Sidney B. Simon, the basic strategies of values clarification were described. The authors proposed that students are likely to develop a set of values that will help them make confident and consistent choices and decisions if they engage in the following activities:

Choose their beliefs and behaviors by first considering and then selecting from alternatives.

Prize their beliefs and behaviors by cherishing and publicly affirming them.

Act on their beliefs repeatedly and consistently.

Values clarification: Encourage pupils to choose, prize, and act on beliefs

Seventy-nine strategies for helping students engage in such activities are described in *Values Clarification: A Handbook of Practical Strategies for Teachers and Students* (1972) by Sidney B. Simon, Leland W. Howe, and Howard Kirschenbaum. Students are asked to choose their beliefs freely and from carefully considered alternatives, for example, in strategy 5, "Either-Or Forced Choice" (pp. 94–97). The teacher institutes this strategy by asking students, "Which do you identify with more, a Volkswagen or a Cadillac?" Pupils indicate their preference by walking to one side of the room or the opposite; they then team up with a classmate who made the same choice and explain the reasons for the choice. Students are encouraged to cherish and publicly affirm their beliefs by engaging in activities such as that presented in strategy 12, "Public Interview" (pp. 139–162). In this strategy a student volunteers to be interviewed by the rest of the class and publicly affirms and explains her or his stand on various issues. Pupils are urged to act repeatedly and consistently on their beliefs when the teacher uses strategies such as number 42, "Letters to the Editor" (pp. 262–263), and asks each student in the class to write at least one letter to the editor of a newspaper or magazine. Copies of the letter and clippings from the paper or magazine (if available) are posted on a bulletin board, and at the end of the month pupils read their letters to the rest of the class and explain their reasons for speaking out on the issue they selected.

In addition to strategies that are clearly intended to encourage students to choose, prize, and act on their beliefs, *Values Clarification* also includes many strategies that are difficult to fit under any of these categories. Several of these ask students to explore their interests; others are intended to help them build positive self-concepts; still others are designed to make them sensitive to the feelings of others. Furthermore, the strategies are not arranged in any clearly discernible order. Consequently, *Values Clarification* is essentially a grab bag of humanistic education techniques, and it is difficult to determine how to use the strategies in any coordinated way.

Several values clarification enthusiasts recognized the lack of organization in *Values Clarification* and set out to remedy the situation. Merrill Harmin, Kirschenbaum, and Simon wrote *Clarifying Values Through Subject Matter* (1972). As the title indicates, the authors explain how values clarification strategies might be incorporated into the presentation of subject matter. Kirschenbaum and Simon collaborated in editing *Readings in Values Clarification* (1973), which consists of thirty-seven articles written by different authors. While some of these describe values clarification techniques, others touch on aspects of humanistic education not directly related to the process originally described by Raths.

In recognition of the fact that the term *values clarification* was coming to be used to refer to almost any form of humanistic education, Leland W. Howe and Mary Martha Howe compiled *Personalizing Education: Values Clarification and Beyond* (1975). In the preface to their book, they express the fear that values clarification may become a fad that is used by teachers only when they need a game to liven things up on Friday or when students get bored or restless. In the opening chapter they acknowledge that they have included strategies that stress not only values clarification but other aspects of humanistic education as well. They also explain what they mean by *personalized education*. Their description indicates that what they mean by personalized education is essentially the same as humanistic education as described by others.

Howe and Howe group the strategies in their book under the following chapter titles (a list that summarizes many techniques of humanistic education):

4. Developing a Climate of Acceptance, Trust, and Open Communication

5. Building Students' Self Concepts

7. Helping Students Become Aware of, Prize, and Publicly Affirm Their Values

8. Helping Students Choose Their Values Freely, from Alternatives, After Weighing the Consequences

9. Helping Students Learn to Set Goals and Take Action on Their Values

11. Developing Curriculum to Serve Student Concerns

12. Adapting Curriculum to Serve Student Interests, Needs, Concerns, Goals, and Values

15. Goal Sheets and Learning Contracts: Facilitating Student Self-Directed Learning

16. Developing and Managing a Choice-Centered Classroom

17. Discipline in the Choice-Centered Classroom

18. Using Values Clarification in the Choice-Centered Classroom (1975, pp. 5–6)

Now that you are familiar with the assumptions and techniques of humanistic education, it is time to subject them to a critical evaluation.

Criticisms of humanistic education

One of the most fundamental criticisms of the humanistic view is that it is not based on empirical data or on a consistent set of principles. Programmed instruction and behavior modification are based on a substantial amount of experimental evidence. The cognitive-discovery view is derived from concepts of Gestalt psychology and field theory. As a consequence, it is possible to apply both the S-R and the cognitive view in the classroom by reasoning logically from a clearly stated theoretical position. Programmed approaches should feature a series of steps designed to lead the learner to a specific goal; discovery sessions should be structured to encourage awareness of new relationships. Humanistic psychology, by contrast, is derived from an assortment of vaguely stated assumptions and observations. Proponents argue that teachers should trust children and let them grow without interference. But what, exactly, does that mean? How does one go about putting that philosophy into practice, and what happens if children *are* self-educated? One way to seek an answer to these

Humanistic view is based on vague propositions

questions is to evaluate Neill's Summerhill, since his school was the most consistent embodiment of the humanistic point of view.

How successful was Summerhill?

Neill maintained that "a child is innately wise and realistic. If left to himself without adult suggestion of any kind, he will develop as far as he is capable of developing" (1960, p. 4). If taken literally, Neill's basic philosophy would mean that children should be expected to ignore all that adults of any kind have learned and try to discover everything for themselves. This is obviously an impossible task, which Neill himself recognized. He paid lip service to the joys of completely self-directed learning but hired teachers to provide lessons. Attendance at classes was voluntary, but peer pressure might have caused it to become at least partly compulsory. Furthermore, in describing some of the private lessons he provided, Neill reveals that many Summerhill pupils sought and welcomed help from teachers.

Neill defended self-directed learning by arguing that his students learned as much as public school students and that they were much more likely to go into creative work after they left Summerhill. Neill's personal impressions were not supported by more objective observations made by others. A team of inspectors from the British Ministry of Education visited the school and wrote a report reprinted in *Summerhill*. They concluded, "On the whole the results of [the self-directed learning] system are unimpressive. It is true that the children work with a will and an interest that is most refreshing, but their achievements are rather meager" (p. 80). The inspectors added that they felt the system would have worked better if the teachers had been more inclined to supervise, integrate, stimulate, and guide the pupils.

Other evidence on the impact of Summerhill was provided when a young American named Emmanuel Bernstein interviewed fifty graduates of the school. He reported (1968) that the occupations of the fifty were typical of the general population and did *not* include a disproportionate number of creative individuals. When he asked the former Summerhillians for their general opinion of the school, ten of the fifty had nothing but praise. They felt that their experience at the school "had given them confidence, maturity, and had enabled them to find a fulfilling way of life" (p. 38). On the other hand, seven of the fifty felt Summerhill had been harmful to them. Most of these felt that their experience at the school had "led them to find more difficulty in life than they might have otherwise experienced" (p. 40). An interesting point that emerged from the interviews was that those who had stayed at Summerhill for the *fewest* number of years tended to feel that they had benefited the most; those who had attended the longest "appeared most likely to have difficulty and tenacious adjustment problems" (p.

Achievements of Summerhill students unimpressive

Summerhill graduates not atypically creative

40). Perhaps the most significant point of all was the finding that "the majority of Summerhillians had only one major complaint against the school: the lack of academic opportunity and inspiration, coupled with a dearth of inspired teachers" (p. 41). Few of the graduates who had children of their own sent them to Summerhill. Some who did not have children at the time they were interviewed indicated that they might send their offspring to the school but only for a few years before the age of ten or so.

Graduates wanted own children to attend Summerhill only briefly

It appears, then, that when teachers are enjoined to trust children and let them grow, it is appropriate to add, "But don't expect them to make all the decisions themselves and give them help when they need it." Maslow himself recognized this when he made a distinction (to be explored more completely in Chapter 10) between *bad choosers* and *good choosers.* He suggested that only children who have their needs well satisfied and who enjoy close to optimal adjustment can be expected to make wise choices. Most children do not possess these desirable qualities and, if they are not guided by adults, will often make choices that are destructive.

"Humanistic teachers" do not have a monopoly on positive qualities

Some humanistic educators affect holier-than-thou attitude

A criticism that is related to the idealistic, unrealistic, and vague nature of humanistic education probably deserves to be called a holier-than-thou attitude. Those who write on humanistic education sometimes describe themselves and those who endorse their views in ways that imply that all other types of educators are *in*human. Humanistic teachers are characterized as *real* persons who *trust* children. They *prize* students, *believe* in them, and are *sensitive* to their needs. They want to *help pupils do their best,* and they do not prescribe, coax, or cajole but serve as *facilitators* and *helpers.* By implication, educators who do *not* endorse the views of Maslow, Rogers, and Combs are phony, distrustful, negative, dictatorial, insensitive pedagogues who don't care whether students learn and who fail to facilitate learning. The latter description may apply to a few nonhumanistic teachers, but a teacher who uses techniques of programmed instruction or the discovery approach can be just as real, trusting, and sensitive as a teacher who favors values clarification sessions or self-expressive activities. In terms of the results of learning experiences, it is probably reasonable to say that a teacher who gives a well-organized lecture on how to compute percentages, for instance, is being more of a facilitator and helper than one who leans against a windowsill and watches students engage in interpretations of melting ice cubes.

In addition to assuming a holier-than-thou stance, some humanists also offer what might be classified as elaborate rationalizations for

Simply because a teacher takes the lead in organizing classroom activities does not, as some humanistic educators imply, mean that he or she is distrustful, dictatorial, insensitive, or inhuman.

Rich Smolan/Stock Boston

what they do. Suppose two teachers in an elementary school occasionally devote thirty minutes to interpretive dance. One, who has read several books on humanistic education, explains, "This is confluent education in which affective and cognitive elements flow together. It is intended to permit students to engage in a constructive dialogue with their fantasy lives, explore emotional responses to the world, break down interpersonal estrangement in order to facilitate communication and participation, and allow each unique individual to live fully and intensely here and now." The other teacher, who has not read any books on humanistic education, says, "The kids like to do this every now and then because it's fun and gives them a chance to move around and let off steam. Also, it saves me the trouble of preparing a lesson."

Humanistic educators claim too much

Humanistic educators make themselves vulnerable to criticism because they claim so much for the techniques they espouse. They aspire not to teach subject matter, but to create students who will be happy, well-adjusted self-actualizers with a firm sense of identity and a clear set of values. In *Personalizing Education,* Howe and Howe assert that "if our values are clear, consistent, and soundly chosen, we tend to live our lives in meaningful and satisfying ways" (1975, p. 17). The Howes use the phrase "soundly chosen," but they join other values clarification advocates in stressing that "Values Clarification is not an attempt to teach students 'right' and 'wrong' values. Rather, it is an approach designed to help students prize and act upon their own freely chosen values. Thus, V.C. is concerned with the process by which students arrive at their values, rather than the content of these values" (p. 19). There is no reason to assume, however, that students will automatically make sound choices when they engage in values clarification sessions. It is quite possible that when students are encouraged to develop clear and consistent values, they will choose those that focus on material possessions, power, self-indulgence, and the like. Considering the nature of high-pressure advertising in America and the kinds of individuals who achieve notoriety in our society, it would be surprising if such values were not favored by many young people. Simply because a person's values are made more consistent as a consequence of values clarification sessions, therefore, does not guarantee that the individual will live in a "meaningful and satisfying way." It is just as likely that the opposite could be the case.

Furthermore, if Piaget's description of cognitive development is taken into account, there is reason to doubt that very many pupils will actually develop a consistent value system as a result of engaging in values clarification exercises. Many values clarification strategies are designed to be used with elementary school children who are at the concrete operations stage of cognitive development and unable to grasp abstract concepts or generalize. To cite just one example, when they are asked to indicate if they prefer ice cream, Jell-o, or pie for dessert (a question featured in a values clarification strategy intended to give children practice in choosing between alternatives), young children will probably react in a quite literal way. They will think about their favorite dessert but not about the principle of choosing between alternatives. There is no reason to believe that when they are faced with a choice involving values they will see any connection between picking a dessert and making a moral or ethical decision.

The same tendency to respond in literal ways is likely to be characteristic of many secondary school students as well, since the transition to formal thought is a gradual process. But even high school students who are capable of dealing with abstractions and hypothetical situations may not develop a realistic or workable set of values, because novice formal thinkers tend to overlook realities. Secondary school students are also eager to impress others. If a high school girl volunteers to be interviewed by the class, for instance, she may supply glib and idealistic answers and be so preoccupied with making a good impression on classmates that there will be no carry-over to behavior outside of class. Simply because students can talk about positive values in discussing hypothetical situations, they will not necessarily act that way when the chips are down. Because of factors such as these, it is unrealistic to expect that use of values clarification strategies will equip students with a value system that will lead to a "meaningful and satisfying life."

Those who call themselves humanistic teachers may describe their

Values clarification may not have a significant impact

philosophy of teaching in glowing (but vague) terms and make lavish claims about what they are doing to foster the development of better human beings. In actual practice, they are likely to make occasional use of games or strategies such as those described in books on values clarification. Many of these strategies are provocative and likely to arouse a positive response, but there is no substantive evidence that they have the intended effect. Typically, humanistic educators offer "proof" of the effectiveness of the techniques they recommend by providing diaries and impressions written by individuals who have had positive experiences with the methods described. Testimonials from selected students or teachers, however, do not prove anything. They are particularly unimpressive when one considers the claim that humanistic education leads students to live more meaningful and satisfying lives. Furthermore, in an era of accountability and low test scores, most parents, administrators, and school boards are not likely to be favorably impressed if teachers say that the primary goal of their instruction is to help students "explore or express themselves" or engage in "meaningful interpersonal relationships."[1] You are reminded that in her criticism of Bruner's MACOS materials, Onalee McGraw delivered the opinion that "teaching children 'to understand themselves' and 'be aware of themselves' is a bunch of garbage." She went on to say, "By what authority are these people getting involved in the psychological development of the child? And what right have teachers to probe into the delicate reaches of the child's mind and unleash the child's emotions?" (Shaar, 1975, p. 5). Not all parents are as extreme or as outspoken as McGraw, but many of them endorse, at least partially, the view that teachers should concentrate on helping children learn skills and subject matter and not try to set themselves up as psychotherapists in the classroom.

> Humanists offer testimonials, not evidence, to justify lavish claims

Some humanistic techniques may be misguided therapy

Several forms of humanistic instruction are closer to psychotherapy than to education, and criticisms that humanistic educators sometimes function as misguided analysts have a certain amount of validity. The use of such approaches in public schools amounts to *compulsory* psychotherapy. Studies of the impact of encounter groups made up of individuals who chose to participate under the guidance of leaders with at least some training as psychotherapists indicate that the results varied from mildly successful to definitely harmful (Back, 1972; Coulson, 1972; Lieberman, Yalom, and Miles, 1973). Thus, it

---

[1] Harry S. Broudy (1972, p. 127) has speculated that if accountability becomes a feature of American education, parents might take humanistic educators to court if their children use drugs, engage in premarital sex, or say disrespectful things about our country. Following this line of reasoning, one might also anticipate that students who had teachers who stressed values clarification might sue their instructors if they do not later live in "meaningful and satisfying ways."

Some humanistic
techniques resemble
compulsory
psychotherapy
conducted by
"amateurs"

seems likely that the results would be even less impressive if pupils were forced to participate in encounter groups led by teachers with no training in psychotherapy. Attempts at psychotherapy by "amateurs" may do much more harm than good. It seems reasonable to speculate about their motives when classroom teachers elect to persuade their classes to function as encounter groups. Without realizing it, teachers might use such techniques in an effort to try to win friends, bargain for popularity, or even function as gurus.

In *Fantasy and Feeling in Education,* Richard M. Jones emphasizes this point when he observes, "If the confrontation of emotions in classrooms is not made in the primary interests [sic] of achieving educational objectives, both the means and ends may suffer" (1968, p. 161). Even if the goal is achievement of educational objectives, the fact that there is a "confrontation of emotions" means that humanistic techniques are usually appropriate only for short-term or sporadic use. It is impossible for human beings to exist in a state of aroused emotion for any length of time without suffering physical and psychological damage. Those who have tried to teach by building up

Impossible to maintain
close personal
relationships with
pupils

extremely close personal relationships with all pupils in a class have been unable to continue this kind of education for more than a year or two. Herbert Kohl, for example, described in *36 Children* how he used a highly personal, humanistic approach to teaching in an inner-city elementary school. After two years of that kind of instruction, he felt obliged to move to Spain to recuperate. George Dennison, one of the most outspoken advocates of humanistic education, established his First Street School as a demonstration project. The school went out of existence after two years for reasons Dennison explains this way: "It was not merely lack of money that closed the school. We ourselves were not strongly enough motivated to make the sacrifices that would have been necessary to sustain it" (1969, p. 273). He then notes that he returned to a full-time career as a writer after the school closed.

Taking all these factors into account, it would seem most realistic to use humanistic approaches to education on a limited basis. If you hope to teach in the elementary grades, you might make *occasional* use of some of the techniques described. If you attempt to practice humanistic teaching most of the time, you are almost sure to be criticized by parents, administrators, and perhaps students themselves. If you will be teaching in the secondary grades, you may feel—depending on the subject you teach—that none of the techniques are appropriate or that particular strategies may be ideal for presenting certain parts of the curriculum. In most cases, therefore, you will probably want to schedule humanistic education sessions at infrequent intervals. Here are some suggestions you might follow as you do so. As you examine them, you will discover that many techniques described in the preceding chapter on the discovery approach are similar to forms of humanistic education. This is because many techniques of humanistic learning overlap with forms of instruction advocated for different reasons by proponents of the cognitive-discovery view.

At appropriate places in the following list of suggestions, strategies described in books on values clarification are mentioned. If you are impressed by any of these, you might consult the source for additional information. If you select strategies that you think you would like to use and list them in your Handbook under headings similar to those given in this list of suggestions, you should be able to make systematic use of the ideas proposed by humanistic educators who specialize in values clarification.

Suggestions for teaching: Applying the humanistic view in the classroom

1. Try to remain aware of the extent to which you direct and control learning. Whenever possible, permit and encourage students to make choices and to manage their own learning.

2. Establish a warm, positive, acceptant atmosphere. Do your best to communicate the feeling that you believe every student in the class can learn and that you want them to learn.

3. When it seems appropriate, function as a facilitator, encourager, helper, and assister. Before attempting to function as a colleague or friend, think about possible complications.

4. If you feel comfortable doing it, occasionally show that you are a "real person" by telling students how you feel. When you express anger, however, comment on the situation, not on the personality traits of your students.

5. If you do not have strong positive feelings about yourself and how you function as a teacher, consider participating in individual or group counseling sessions, and also work at improving your skills as an instructor.

6. Do your best to help your students develop positive feelings about themselves. Empathize with them, and show you are sensitive to their feelings.

7. If appropriate, schedule occasional periods during which students are encouraged to examine their emotions.

8. If appropriate, schedule occasional periods during which students are encouraged to become more sensitive to the feelings of others.

9. If appropriate, schedule occasional periods when students are encouraged to express themselves through movement, physical contact, and creative dramatics.

10. If appropriate, ask students to participate in role playing, psychodrama, or simulation games.

11. Make systematic use of values clarification strategies.

    a. Call attention to the process of values development.

    b. Select and use strategies that cover all seven steps in the process of values acquisition and call attention to ways an exercise illustrates one or more aspects of the sequence.

    c. Use long-term strategies in class, and urge students to continue to use them on their own.

    d. Look for ways to introduce values clarification strategies into lesson plans.

12. Use the Taxonomy of Educational Objectives: Affective Domain to identify specific goals of humanistic education.

13. Do your best to provide learning experiences that will lead to the development of the habits and attitudes you want to foster.

14. Make use of object lessons. When illustrative incidents occur in the course of events, take advantage of them.

15. Set a good example.

16. Be aware of your students' level of moral development, and encourage understanding of subtle aspects of morality by presenting "moral dilemmas."

1. Try to remain aware of the extent to which you direct and control learning. Whenever possible, permit and encourage students to make choices and to manage their own learning.   Humanistic psychology developed as a reaction against strict environmentalistic and psychoanalytic interpretations of behavior. Maslow, Rogers, and Combs ask educators to avoid the pitfalls of assuming that children are entirely shaped by experiences or that they need to be protected and guarded at all times. The cardinal principle of humanistic education is: Give students opportunities to make choices and manage their own learning. For reasons noted in discussing the goals and realities of public education in Chapter 2 and in the critique of Summerhill in this chapter, it is neither logical nor possible to give students complete freedom of choice. Immature children cannot anticipate what they will need to know in order to live in a technological society and cannot be expected to supervise or sustain all their own learning experiences. Furthermore, parents, school boards, and school administrators expect teachers to earn their salaries and produce tangible results. Even so, you should be able to offer your students many opportunities to participate in decisions about what will be studied, how it will be studied, and how classroom order will be maintained. As you plan lessons, you might ask yourself, "Am I setting up a controlled situation here because it is in the best interests of the students,

Cardinal principle of humanistic education: Give pupils choices

or am I doing it because it's easier, because I like to feel that I'm indispensable, or because it gives me a sense of power?" If you are willing, you can find many ways to give students opportunities to make choices as they learn.

EXAMPLES

Ask the class to select topics to be covered (as noted in the suggestions for arranging group discussions presented in the preceding chapter).

Permit individual students to choose topics to be studied, perhaps by selecting from a suggested list, perhaps by proposing subjects on their own.

Arrange an open classroom situation so that students can engage in self-selected study of subjects of interest.

Invite students to participate in making decisions about class rules.

A number of strategies for providing opportunities for students to participate in decisions about what will be studied are described in *Personalizing Education* by Howe and Howe. In Chapter 11 (pp. 364–393) they describe a ten-step procedure to follow if you would like to have students participate in developing a teaching unit. They also supply an example of a student-developed elementary school unit on crime and law enforcement. The steps in the procedure are:

1. Have students brainstorm (call out as many ideas as possible in a short period of time) about topics of interest, and list these on the board.

2. Ask students to develop a set of criteria for selecting a topic from the list of brainstormed ideas.

3. Help the class prepare a *flow chart* by breaking the main topic down into subtopics.

4. Carry out a *question census;* that is, have the students list all the questions they think are of importance or value in studying subtopics.

5. Ask students to list resources they might turn to in seeking answers to the questions. These might be listed under the following headings: readings, audiovisuals, field trips, people, manipulative devices.

6. Have students pair off and develop activities from one or two of the questions.

7. Analyze the purposes of the unit by having students list objectives under three headings: knowledge, cognitive skills, values.

8. Examine the curriculum plan, and revise it to make it better organized and to eliminate overlap.

9. Invite students to help you decide how the unit should be struc-

tured and taught, what requirements should be established, and how the unit should be evaluated.

10. Carry out the final plan.

Other ways to permit students a degree of choice, particularly when a prescribed curriculum must be covered, are described in Chapter 14 of *Personalizing Education*. One of these is the Student Self-Paced Style. This approach is very similar to the Personalized System of Instruction developed by Fred S. Keller, which was described in Chapter 5. In both approaches, students are asked to study a prescribed topic, but they determine how fast, where, when, and with whom they will study. The major differences between the two versions is that Keller recommends that student-tutors evaluate completed work and the Howes suggest that students correct their own work. For details of the Self-Paced Style, see pages 465–468 of *Personalizing Education*.

Handbook heading
Using Self-Paced and
Self-Selected Styles

An approach that gives students a bit more control over their own learning is called the Student Self-Selected Learning Style. It is similar to the Self-Paced Style, except for the first step: Instead of being given assigned work, students choose their own topics. One way to facilitate this approach is to prepare a large number of activity cards that give suggestions for studying different topics. The Howes suggest that these include the following information: the name of the activity, the purpose, materials needed to complete the activity, steps to be followed, evaluation criteria to be used, suggestions for follow-up activities. Many teachers' journals supply information that might be used in preparing such cards, or you might team up with other teachers and develop a combined set that could be reproduced in some way. Another obvious way to accumulate such cards is to ask students to develop their own and then save the best ones each year.

Still another variation of self-directed learning consists of what is often called the *contract approach*. Students meet with the teacher on an individual basis and agree on a contract of self-selected learning. In *Personalizing Education* the Howes suggest that the contract terms include the payoff to be earned if the contract is completed, the deadline for completion, and the details of the project.

2. Establish a warm, positive, acceptant atmosphere. Do your best to communicate the feeling that you believe every student in the class can learn and that you want them to learn.   These points are related to J. M. Stephens's distinction between the teacher-practitioner and the teacher-theorist that was mentioned in Chapter 1. In their eagerness to persuade teachers to be efficient and objective, some advocates of the behaviorist-environmentalist-associationist view ignore the

impact of the teacher's attitude. Humanistic psychologists join with Stephens in calling attention to the extent to which *how* you teach will influence the response of your students. At times you will want to be efficient and objective, but because successful learning experiences seem to depend to a significant extent on interpersonal relationships, you should not attempt to play the role of an impersonal authority or leader. You are more likely to get a positive response from your students if you exude warmth, enthusiasm, and high expectations. Remember the nature of the self-fulfilling prophecy, and communicate, as best you can, the attitude that every student in the class is capable of learning.

Handbook heading

Ways to Communicate Interest in Pupils as Individuals

EXAMPLES

Learn pupils' names as fast as you can, and take an interest in them as individuals.

Try to show that you are intrigued, fascinated, excited, and enthusiastic about at least some of the things you present to the class.

Urge all students to do their best, and avoid forcing students to compete for a limited number of high grades. (Detailed instructions for doing this will be presented in the learning for mastery section of Chapter 13.)

Show that you are pleased (but not surprised) when students do well; don't act as if it bothers you to give high grades.

Strategy Number 51, "Rogerian Listening," described on pages 295–298 of *Values Clarification* by Simon, Howe, and Kirschenbaum, might be used to establish an atmosphere conducive to humanistic education (as well as discovery-approach discussions). This strategy is based on Carl Rogers's suggestions that good listening involves empathizing with the speaker and suspending one's own value judgments. To help students become better listeners, the class is divided into groups of three. One member of the group expresses her or his views on a mutually agreeable topic. The second member is then required to summarize what was just said. The third person acts as a monitor or cross-examiner, calling attention to points that were missed or misinterpreted.

Chapter 4 (pp. 41–80) of *Personalizing Education* by Howe and Howe describes several strategies for "developing a climate of acceptance, trust, and open communication." Several of these are intended to help students become better acquainted. In one strategy, for example, students meeting as a class for the first time are instructed to mill about and find someone who fits one of the descriptions on a mimeographed list. Typical statements include: someone who plays a musical instrument, someone who loves to go horseback riding. Most of the other strategies in the chapter are similar to or variations of Rogerian listening.

3. When it seems appropriate, function as a facilitator, encourager, helper, and assister. Before attempting to function as a colleague or friend, think about possible complications. Even though you may have been impressed by Combs's argument that you avoid "prescribing, making, molding, forcing, coercing, coaxing, or cajoling" (1965, p. 16), you probably cannot completely avoid these behaviors. In fact, you may find that they are both necessary and desirable. Even if you trust children and are convinced that they are often self-motivated, there are certain to be times when they will need and probably welcome prescriptions. There are also bound to be times when they will need to be coaxed or cajoled into completing even self-selected assignments. On the whole, however, you will probably get a better response from your pupils if they see you as a facilitator, encourager, helper, and assister. This view of education is very similar to that proposed by advocates of the discovery approach, who stress that teachers should arrange lessons to permit students to gain insight. Even though you sometimes prescribe, you can dispel an impression that you are a dicatator or a manipulator by explaining why you are asking your pupils to learn certain things and by inviting students to help plan classroom activities. As for cajoling and coaxing, these could be classified as forms of encouragement, and the chapter on motivation discusses noncoercive techniques to arouse and sustain interest.

Before you make a decision to try to function as your pupils' colleague, consider a point made earlier: Parents and school boards may wonder why they should pay you a salary to be a colearner. And before you make an effort to become a close friend to all of your students, consider some of the problems likely to arise when you are required to assign grades, when you try to prevent jealousy or divide your in-class and at-home time between 30 to 150 "best friends," and when you must drop one crop of "friends" in favor of a new crop each report period or year. Teachers who take a genuine interest in their pupils and show that they like them almost invariably get a better response than those who are cold and aloof, but it is usually not advisable to replace the teacher-pupil relationship with a friend-to-friend relationship.

4. If you feel comfortable doing it, occasionally show that you are a "real person" by telling students how you feel. When you express anger, however, comment on the situation, not on the personality traits of your students. Many advocates of humanistic education believe that students are more likely to examine their emotions if they observe a teacher do the same. In addition, it is reasoned, students

may become more sensitive to ways their behavior may hurt others. Accordingly, they recommend that you not hesitate to show when you are pleased, angry, afraid, disappointed, and the like.

One of the first psychologists to propose this policy was Haim Ginott. In *Teacher and Child* he reasons that because of the realities of teaching, it is inevitable that teachers will become frustrated and angry. When this happens, the teacher is urged to be authentic and genuine (or, as Rogers puts it, a "real person"). Ginott observes, "An enlightened teacher is not afraid of his anger, because he has learned to express it without doing damage. He has mastered the secret of expressing anger without insult" (1972, p. 85). The "secret" is summed up by the cardinal principle of communication: "Talk to the situation, not to the personality and character" (p. 84). Ginott illustrates the secret and the principle by contrasting the response of two teachers who become angry when two boys throw pieces of bread at each other. The first attacks the boys' personalities by saying, "You two slobs! Clean it up now! You are not fit to live in a pigsty. I want to talk to your parents about your disgusting behavior!" (p. 87). The second expresses anger over the situation by saying, "I get angry when I see bread made into bullets. Bread is not for throwing. This room needs immediate cleaning" (p. 87).

The degree to which you use this technique will be a function of your personality, the age of the pupils you teach, perhaps the subject you teach, and many other factors. But if you occasionally reveal your feelings, you may gain release of frustrations, show your students how they might do the same in similar situations, and make them more aware of how their actions may be unfair or damaging to others. If you have a very low level of frustration tolerance and reveal your feelings too often, however, your students may think of you not as a "real person" but as a chronic complainer or perhaps as someone with paranoid delusions of persecution. Whenever you do express anger, try to remember Ginott's cardinal principle and vent your hostility by commenting on the situation, not on the personalities of your students.

5. If you do not have strong positive feelings about yourself and how you function as a teacher, consider participating in individual or group counseling sessions, and also work at improving your skills as an instructor. Humanistic psychologists reason that a person who has a poor view of himself or herself is likely to perceive students in a negative way. Sigmund Freud was the first psychologist to call attention to ways that our own personality traits influence what we see in others. In fact, Freud decreed that all individuals who were to receive his personal endorsement as psychoanalysts must first be analyzed themselves. We are all influenced by the tendency to project characteristics we dislike to acknowledge in ourselves by attributing them to others. If you feel these observations are valid, you should occasion-

Cardinal principle of communication: Talk to situation, not personality

ally assess your feelings about yourself and your reactions to teaching. If you are burdened with personal problems or doubts after you have taught for a few years or if you are having difficulty coping with some of the restrictive aspects of public school teaching, you might consider discussing your problems with others. If you take the trouble to inquire, you probably can find a sensitivity training or encounter group in your vicinity or a therapist who holds group sessions for others who share your concerns. (Further information on this topic will be presented in Chapter 16. A most important caution, to be noted here and re-emphasized later, is that you should make sure that the leader or therapist is qualified and experienced.)

Another way to develop positive feelings about yourself is to work at perfecting your skills as a teacher. If you arrive at school well prepared, plan a variety of activities, and continually analyze your teaching with the aim of improving it, you are likely to develop a strong positive self-concept. Two of the characteristics of effective teachers described by Combs are being well informed and being capable of using a variety of methods of instruction. Your positive regard for yourself as a teacher is likely to be maintained and enhanced if you are knowledgeable and versatile.

6. Do your best to help your students develop positive feelings about themselves. Empathize with them and show you are sensitive to their feelings.   Try to see things from the student's point of view. Reflect on how you felt when you were a student, particularly when you felt insecure, ignorant, or frightened. Remain alert for things that you say or do that might embarrass, threaten, or belittle your students.

Handbook heading

Ways to Help Students Develop Positive Feelings About Themselves

If you suspect that some of your students do not think highly of themselves, you might experiment with techniques for helping them develop positive self-concepts. Methods for doing this are described by John T. Canfield and Harold C. Wells on pages 460–468 of the *Humanistic Education Sourcebook* and in several strategies outlined in *Personalizing Education* (pp. 81–105) by Howe and Howe. One technique is to ask members of small groups to describe a successful accomplishment they achieved before they were ten years old. Another is to ask students to list things they are proud of. Still another is to ask members of a small group to "bombard" a selected classmate with all the strengths they see in her or him. In *Values Clarification*, Simon, Howe, and Kirschenbaum suggest (strategy 11) that students "whip around" the classroom telling what they are proud of, and in strategy 62 they provide words and music so this can be done in the form of a song. (Such techniques may contribute to the development of a better self-concept; however, perhaps the surest way to make students feel good about themselves and proud of their accomplishments is to help them master subject matter and skills.)

7. If appropriate, schedule occasional periods during which students are encouraged to examine their emotions. Most enthusiasts for humanistic education urge teachers to arrange for their students to explore emotional responses. You might do this in the elementary grades by setting aside occasional blocks of time for that purpose. At the secondary level, it would seem that analysis of emotions would be appropriate only in some classes, such as psychology, health, marriage and family, literature, social studies, and the like.

Handbook heading
Ways to Help Students
Examine Emotions

One technique you might use with primary grade children is the "Magic Circle" approach developed by Harold Bessell (1968). Ask seven to twelve children to form a circle and spend twenty minutes discussing questions such as: "I felt good when ..." and "I felt bad when ..." (For more information, see the article by Bessell or the article by William Lefkowitz starting on page 457 of the *Humanistic Education Sourcebook.*) Also at the elementary school level you might show a film from the "Inside/Out" series produced by the National Institutional Television Center. These films are intended to stimulate children to think about various emotions. For information about the films and the accompanying suggestions for instructors, write to National Instructional Television Center, Bloomington, Indiana 47405.

8. If appropriate, schedule occasional periods during which students are encouraged to become more sensitive to the feelings of others. A dramatic example of this approach was developed by Jane Elliott, a third grade teacher in a small town in Iowa, who was so deeply affected by the assassination of Martin Luther King, Jr., that she devised a technique for providing her pupils with direct experience with prejudice. Her basic technique, which is reported in the television documentary "The Eye of the Storm" and in *A Class Divided* by William Peters, could be used as a model for similar learning situations. She divided the class on the basis of eye color, and told the students that brown-eyed people are better, cleaner, more civilized, and smarter than blue-eyed people. The "superior" brown-eyed students were given extra time at recess, allowed to go to lunch first and sit in the front of the room, and were extensively praised for correct answers. The "inferior" blue-eyed students were required to use paper cups rather than the drinking fountain, were not allowed to use the equipment on the playground, and were treated as stupid when they gave wrong answers.

Just a few hours under this regime led to startling changes in the behavior of the students. Brown-eyed pupils became convinced of their superiority, to the point of mistreating blue-eyed classmates and then demanding an apology; formerly confident blue-eyed children became tense, clumsy, and unsure of themselves. The following week, the roles were reversed, and the blue-eyed children were decreed

A scene from "The Eye of the Storm." The blue-eyed children smiling on the right were given special privileges. Brown-eyed children, required to wear paper collars to identify their lower status, were told—and treated as if—they were inferior.

Photograph by Charlotte Button for the ABC News documentary program "The Eye of the Storm"

superior and given all the privileges. Despite the fact that the now inferior brown-eyed children were aware that this was just a temporary "game," they reacted intensely and seemed to become convinced that they now *were* inferior. The only difference between the two phases of the experiment was that the blue-eyed children who had experienced discrimination first were noticeably less vicious in their treatment of their "inferior" classmates. After a few days, the experiment was concluded, and the pupils were asked to discuss it and write about it—which they did with great animation and insight. The experiment was repeated the next year, with slight variations, including the use of paper collars to identify inferior pupils. Even though some of the students were aware of what had taken place the previous year, they still responded as if the changes were genuine.

You should keep in mind that some teachers who have used this technique have encountered criticism from parents, school board members, and other citizens—which suggests that you secure approval from local school authorities and the parents of your pupils before putting such an experiment into practice. If you prefer not to use such a drastic technique or if it would be inappropriate for your grade or subject area, you might devise variations of the Elliott method by asking your students to engage in less extreme forms of role playing. For example, have students play the roles of a boy who has just dented the fender of the family car and his best friend who saw him do it. Explain that the guilty driver is thinking of blaming the accident on a hit-and-run driver, but the friend wants him to tell the truth. After the students act out how they would behave in such a situation, ask them to analyze their reactions.

A technique for making secondary school students aware of the feelings of others has been developed by Howard Kirschenbaum, who recommends use of *sensitivity modules,* assignments designed to make students more aware of the lives and perceptions of other people. An eleventh grade social studies teacher, for example, asked his students to do two exercises of the following type within two weeks:

Wear old clothes and sit in the waiting room of the State Employment Office. Listen, observe, talk to some of the people sitting next to you. Read the announcements on the bulletin board, etc.

Go to the magistrate's court and keep a list of the kinds of cases brought before the magistrate. Who are the "customers"? How are they handled?

Spend a few hours in a prowl car traveling with a team of policemen. Listen to the squad car radio. Ask questions. If the policemen park and walk a beat, walk with them.

Sit in the waiting room of the maternity ward of a city hospital whose patients are mostly charity cases. Strike up a conversation with any other persons in the waiting room.

Spend a morning making the rounds with a visiting nurse. (1975, p. 316)

(If you would like a list of additional sensitivity modules, examine strategy 45 [pp. 266–275] in *Values Clarification* by Simon, Howe, and Kirschenbaum.)

In commenting on sensitivity modules, Kirschenbaum acknowledges that many parents may object to the technique, particularly if risks are involved. He maintains, however, that too many children live sheltered lives and are almost completely unaware of how individuals from other types of backgrounds live and perceive their environments. Even if you agree with this argument, it would be prudent to use the sensitivity module approach (or its equivalent) only in elective classes and only after parents have given their permission.

9. If appropriate, schedule occasional periods when students are encouraged to express themselves through movement, physical contact, and creative dramatics. Some humanistic educators recommend exercises intended to make children more sensitive to physical sensations and movement. Proponents of such techniques maintain that they energize children, break down inhibitions, and permit children to express their emotions. Some of the positive reactions described by proponents of such exercises may be due to the Hawthorne effect. Nevertheless, if you will be teaching elementary school children—who need frequent changes of pace and the chance to alternate between cognitive and physical activity—or appropriate electives at the secondary level, you might use exercises such as these:

Handbook heading
Ways to Encourage
Physical and Dramatic
Forms of Expression

Have children touch each other on all exposed parts of their bodies and verbalize how it feels.

Some high school students enjoy creative dance classes. If all students were required to participate in such activities, however, many of them would probably object.

James H. Karales from Peter Arnold

Ask pupils to move their bodies in a wide variety of ways, in different positions, and at different heights.

Suggest that students explore objects in the environment by touching them and verbalizing how they feel.

Place several objects in a paper bag, and ask children to try to identify them by touch alone.

Most of these suggestions, and others of the same type, are described in an article by Buchanan and Hanson (1972) reprinted on pages 345–352 of the *Humanistic Education Sourcebook*.

A related approach is to encourge creative dramatics. Davis, Helfert, and Shapiro (1973) divide such activities into three types: (1) movement exercises (e.g., have all members of a group act out holding up the roof; do an interpretation of an ice cream machine); (2) sensory and body awareness exercises (e.g., have all members of the group discover all the ways their bodies can be made to swing); pair students, blindfold one member of each pair, and ask that individual to identify objects by touch alone as he or she is led around the room; (3) pantomime and play making (e.g., do imitations of different animals; act out how a particular character would behave at a picnic).

For a more complete list of activities, see the article by Davis, Helfert, and Shapiro that is reprinted on pages 439–450 of the *Humanistic Education Sourcebook*. Before deciding when and how you might use such activities, however, consider these observations. It might be proposed that activities involving creative expression are appropriate in all the elementary grades but should be stressed only in secondary school classes that cover appropriate subject matter, such as art, music, dramatics, dance, and the like. To appreciate this point consider the following situations. If you were to ask all students in a kindergarten class to imagine that they were leaves falling from a tree, they would probably delight in carrying out your suggestion. If you were to ask all students in a high school geometry class to do the same thing, however, you would probably get reactions varying from disbelief to categorical refusal. (If you were to ask high school students who had chosen creative dance as an elective to do an impression of falling leaves, on the other hand, they would probably comply with as much enthusiasm as kindergartners.) If you selected two kindergarten children and asked them to dress up in animal costumes, get down on their hands and knees, and imitate a bear or lion, they would probably be thrilled to perform in front of their peers. If you asked two students in a high school auto shop class to do the same, they might question your sanity. (If you were to ask two students in the dramatics club to imitate animals, however, they would probably revel in performing as much as five-year-olds.)

These examples may be a bit extreme, but they do call attention to differences between younger and older pupils. Primary grade children are not self-conscious, and they expect the curriculum to include a great variety of activities. Secondary school students *are* self-conscious, and they expect to engage in self-expression only when they have volunteered to do so by choosing particular courses. In the lower grades, you might schedule self-expressive activities every day. In the upper elementary grades, however, you might be alert for the development of self-consciousness. If you come to the conclusion that some fifth and sixth graders seem reluctant to perform in front of their peers, perhaps you should not require them to do so. (Remember Combs's argument: Humanistic teachers do not "force, coerce, coax, or cajole.") Instead, you might encourage them to express themselves in private ways—by writing, drawing, painting, weaving, and the like. If you insist that all children engage in public self-expression on the assumption that doing so will break down their inhibitions, you might do just the opposite. And is there anything wrong with being "inhibited" in the sense that a person prefers to not call attention to herself or himself? If we were all performers, there would be no audience.

Handbook heading
Using Role Playing,
Psychodrama, and
Simulation Games

10. If appropriate, ask students to participate in role playing, psychodrama, or simulation games.   Some learning situations can be made more meaningful if students are encouraged to act out, identify with, or become involved in an activity. One way to do this is by asking students to engage in role playing.

EXAMPLES

Have elementary students act out the roles of George Washington, Abigail Adams, Benjamin Franklin, and so on, when they study the Revolutionary War period of American history.

Have junior high school students assume the roles of members of Congress debating some current issue.

In a high school business class, have students make believe they are job seekers and employers interviewing applicants for a position.

For more complete information on this technique see *Role Playing Methods in the Classroom* (1966) by Mark Chesler and Robert Fox.

Psychodrama is a variation of role playing that stresses awareness of interpersonal problems.

EXAMPLES

Have two junior high school students assume the roles of a boy who is playing hooky and the police officer who asks him why he is not in school. Then, ask the participants to reverse roles.

Ask two high school students to assume the roles of a father or mother and a teen-age son or daughter who wants to use the family car to go on a trip. Then, after they have spontaneously acted out what would be said when this question is debated, have them reverse roles.

For more information on psychodrama, consult *Psychodrama* (1946) by Jacob L. Moreno (the originator of the technique) or *Psychodrama* (1976) by Leon Yablonski.

Simulation games feature the same basic technique as role playing and psychodrama but present students with more structured and elaborate situations. A number of such games are available from publishers. One game of this type is "Generation Gap." Four to ten junior or senior high school students spend fifty minutes or so discussing interactions and conflicts between parents and an adolescent son or daughter. "Ghetto," as the name implies, stimulates students to spend two to four hours becoming involved in the problems of inner-city life. "The College Game" helps high school seniors prepare for college. During a period of ninety minutes, they learn about course requirements, schedules, study habits and demands, and typical problems of first-year students.

For more information on such games, consult *Learning with Games* (1973) by C. L. Charles and R. Stradsklev; *The Guide to Simulation/Games for Education and Training* (1973), edited by David W. Zuckerman and Robert E. Horn; or *Contemporary Games* (1973), compiled by Jean Belch.

11. Make systematic use of values clarification strategies.   In the critique of humanistic education presented earlier in this chapter, several questions were raised about the extent to which values clarification achieves the goals claimed by its proponents. Even though there are many reasons to doubt that participating in values clarification sessions will cause children to develop a consistent set of values that will make their lives more meaningful and satisfying, the technique does possess advantages. For one thing, many of the strategies are provocative and interesting, and most students seem to enjoy them. For another, children may gain important insights as they carry out some of the activities. These insights may not merge into a coherent value system or be applied consistently when out-of-school values decisions are made, but they may occasionally influence behavior. Therefore, if you will be teaching in the elementary grades, you may wish to schedule frequent values clarification sessions. At the secondary level, you might endeavor to work values clarification into lesson plans whenever it seems appropriate.

Two of the goals listed in the White House Conference Report quoted in Chapter 2 were "respect and appreciation for human values and the beliefs of others," and "ethical behavior based on a sense of moral and spiritual values." These two statements reflect the point that parents and school boards are eager to have students acquire positive values, and the values clarification approach is probably the most effective technique yet devised for achieving that goal. It would seem that you are most likely to be a successful values educator, though, if you apply values clarification in a systematic way. If you simply select strategies at random, there is little reason to expect that your students will think of the exercises as more than game time. The following suggestions indicate how you might make an organized effort to help your students clarify their values.

a. Call attention to the process of values development.   If students are to become aware of how their values influence the decisions they make, the first step would seem to be to call their attention to the ways we acquire values. To do this, you might explain the process of values development as originally described by Raths and perhaps put a description of the process on permanent display. For that purpose, you might use this outline provided by Simon, Howe, and Kirschenbaum in *Values Clarification:*

Handbook heading
Ways to Set Up Values
Clarification Sessions

PRIZING One's Beliefs and Behavior
1. prizing and cherishing
2. publicly affirming, when appropriate

CHOOSING One's Beliefs and Behaviors
3. choosing from alternatives
4. choosing after consideration of consequences
5. choosing freely

ACTING on One's Beliefs
6. acting
7. acting with a pattern, consistency and repetition (1972, p. 19)

An excellent way to introduce and illustrate this list would be to use the strategy referred to as the "Values Grid" (described on pages 35–37 of *Values Clarification*). The teacher and students select several issues. At the elementary level, these might include such topics as pollution, conserving resources and energy, and being considerate of others. At the secondary level, topics might center on such additional issues as amnesty for Vietnam draft evaders and the Equal Rights amendment. After the issues have been selected, students list them on the left-hand side of a piece of paper and draw seven vertical lines on the right-hand side, numbering the columns from 1 to 7. Then they jot down a few key words that summarize their position on each topic. Next the teacher lists the following directions on the board:

1. Are you proud of (do you prize or cherish) your position?

2. Have you publicly affirmed your position?

3. Have you chosen your position from alternatives?

4. Have you chosen your position after thoughtful consideration of the pros and cons and consequences?

5. Have you chosen your position freely?

6. Have you acted on or done anything about your beliefs?

7. Have you acted with repetition, pattern, or consistency on this issue? (p. 36)

The students are asked to classify their responses under one of the seven categories and then form trios and discuss the issues and their positions.

b. Select and use strategies that cover all seven steps in the process of values acquisition and call attention to ways an exercise illustrates one or more aspects of the sequence.   One way to do this is to examine values clarification publications and select strategies that will lead students to engage in all seven processes. Chapters 6, 7, 8, and 9 of *Personalizing Education* by Howe and Howe consist of strategies grouped more or less under headings that parallel the seven steps listed above. You might refer to that book first and then consult other volumes on the subject for additional ideas. To give you an idea how

Handbook heading
Values Clarification
Strategies to Try Out

you might arrange your own list of values clarification strategies, here are some selected examples.

Prizing and choosing   "Values Lists" (described on pages 119–126 of *Personalizing Education*). Ask students to list twenty-five things they value, prize, or cherish. The items on the list are then classified under such categories as *possessions, persons, character traits,* and *items similar to those valued by parents.* Then students form small groups to discuss the patterns that they discern in their values.

Publicly affirming, when appropriate   "Privacy circles" (described on pages 183–188 of *Values Clarification*). Students are asked to draw a series of five concentric circles. The smallest is labeled *self,* and from there outward, the others are labeled *intimates, friends, acquaintances, strangers.* Then the teacher reads a series of statements and

Educators who favor values clarification techniques urge students to publicly affirm and act on their beliefs.
Jeff Albertson/Stock Boston

asks pupils to write a key word in the circle that indicates with whom they would discuss that topic. Sample statements: Whether or not you have ever stolen something (Key word: *Lifted*). What you dislike about your best friend (Key word: *Friend*).

Choosing beliefs from alternatives "Rank Order" (described on pages 58–93 of *Values Clarification*). The teacher reads a question and a list of three alternatives and prints them on the board. Six to eight students are then asked to rank these in order and explain why they prefer one over the others. Several hundred questions and alternatives are supplied for use with students of all age levels.

Choosing after consideration of consequences "Alternatives Action Search" (described on pages 198–203 of *Values Clarification*). The teacher reads a vignette and asks students to write out what they would do in that situation. Then students form into groups of three or four to compare and discuss their reactions and to decide which solution would be most desirable. Sample vignette: You see a boy younger than you shoplifting when you are in a store. You doubt that he realizes what might happen if he gets caught. What would you do?

Choosing freely The "Free Choice Game" (described on pages 299–302 of *Values Clarification*). The class is divided into groups of five or six, and one person in each group volunteers to describe a choice situation the group is confronted with. The other members of the group ask questions to help the individual make a decision. The questions follow a five-step progression: (1) to gain understanding of the situation, (2) to help the person clarify her or his perception of the problem, (3) to explore alternatives, (4) to analyze consequences, (5) to explore feelings and movement toward a decision.

Acting on beliefs "Values in Action" (described on pages 257–261 of *Values Clarification*). The teacher asks students to make a list of five changes they think would improve some aspect of their school, community, state, or the nation. Then a work sheet is distributed that lists things a person might do to bring about changes (e.g., write a letter, go to a meeting). Students check things they have done and indicate things they would be willing to do. A month later they are asked if they carried through on their intentions.

Acting with a pattern, consistency, and repetition "Taking Action on My Values" (described on pages 316–318 of *Personalizing Education*). Students are given a work sheet that lists a number of things they are to indicate they feel strongly about (e.g., helping others, ecology). They are instructed to select three of these and note (1) how they presently act on it, (2) other things they could do to act on it.

If you browse through books on values clarification to select your own strategies to supplement these examples, keep in mind Piaget's observations on cognitive development. Remember that elementary grade pupils are concrete thinkers and that secondary school students are prone to engage in unrestrained theorizing. For younger pupils, look for strategies that ask them to deal with familiar, concrete situations. For older students, avoid strategies that center on extreme hypothetical situations or issues that are remote from their daily lives. Quite a few values clarification strategies appear to have been devised by individuals who were eager to be imaginative and clever. Asking secondary school students to engage in debates about far-out situations that are totally implausible or to offer solutions to global problems may be a way to use up thirty minutes of class time, but it is not likely to have any impact on their behavior.

c. Use long-term strategies in class, and urge students to continue to use them on their own. While most values clarification strategies take the form of short, one-time exercises, some are long-term projects. These strategies might be more likely than separate exercises to cause students to become aware of and act on their beliefs, and you may wish to introduce them early in the year. Three possibilities to consider are described below.

Handbook heading
Ways to Set Up
Long-Term Values
Clarification Projects

"The Values Journal" or "The Values Data Bank" (described on pages 168–170 of *Values Clarification*). Students are encouraged to reserve a section of a notebook for values. In it they keep copies of work sheets used in values clarification strategies, their reactions to these, and random ideas about values that occur in and out of school.

"Pages for an Autobiography" (described on pages 236–240 of *Values Clarification*). Students are periodically given time to write pages for their autobiography. They are instructed to recall events from their past lives and then look for patterns. They are also urged to analyze how events were influenced by circumstances and to think about factors that they considered when they made decisions.

"Diaries" (described on pages 388–391 of *Values Clarification*). Students keep diaries on different subjects (e.g., disagreements, budget, religion, hostility, and anger). Questions might be asked to help students discern patterns (e.g., how often did you get mad when you disagreed with someone?).

d. Look for ways to introduce values clarification strategies into lesson plans. To limit the possibility that values clarification will be thought of primarily as game time, several enthusiasts for the technique recommend that strategies become an integral part of the curriculum. If you are impressed with values clarification, therefore, you might look for ways to work V.C. strategies into lesson plans. Two

Handbook heading
Ways to Work Values
Clarification into the
Curriculum

excellent sources to consult for ideas about how to do this are *Readings in Values Clarification* (1973), edited by Kirschenbaum and Simon, and *Clarifying Values Through Subject Matter* (1973) by Harmin, Kirschenbaum, and Simon. Separate chapters in each of these volumes offer suggestions for working values clarification into the curriculum when teaching English, history, science, math, home economics, language, health education, and other subjects. The basic procedure recommended is to analyze a unit or course by listing points to be covered under three headings: facts, concepts, and values. If teaching a required unit on the Constitution, for example, Kirschenbaum and Simon suggest you include under the *facts* category the list of the first ten amendments and why they were called the Bill of Rights. Under *concepts,* you might outline a discovery session topic that would call attention to social injustices the Bill of Rights was intended to correct. Under *values,* you might insert a values clarification strategy that would ask students to form small groups and discuss the rights and guarantees they have in their families. (For additional examples of facts, concepts, and values to be taught in such a unit, see pages 114–116 of *Readings in Values Clarification.*)

Devising lesson plans by listing topics and exercises under the headings recommended by Kirschenbaum and Simon is one way to introduce values clarification into the curriculum. A more systematic way to accomplish the same purpose involves the use of a comprehensive classification of educational objectives centering on attitudes and values.

12. Use the Taxonomy of Educational Objectives: Affective Domain to identify specific goals of humanistic education.   Many humanistic educators object to the tendency of psychologists to divide behavior into cognitive and affective domains. Yet the suggestion made by Kirschenbaum and Simon that teachers plan lessons by listing facts, concepts, and values does essentially the same thing. In making plans, it is almost always essential to organize related ideas. And to achieve goals, it is necessary to first define them. Several years before values clarification became popular, a group of psychologists (led by David B. Krathwohl, Benjamin S. Bloom, and Bertram B. Masia) drew up a comprehensive classification of affective objects. They called it the *Taxonomy of Educational Objectives, Handbook II: Affective Domain* (1964). Many of the points in it are similar to those later emphasized in books on values clarification.

If you wish to be systematic in planning how to encourage values, you may find it helpful to consult the taxonomy. As you make up lesson plans, think about affective as well as academic or cognitive goals. In teaching social studies, you might strive to inculcate an open-minded attitude toward the opinions of others, in addition to helping students acquire knowledge. When teaching a skill of any

Taxonomy of
Educational Objectives:
Affective Domain

kind, you might stress pride in doing an excellent job, in addition to showing students how to master techniques. The taxonomy was compiled to help you focus on such goals. A *taxonomy* is a classification scheme, and the following account summarizes the kinds of affective goals you might want to emphasize as you plan lessons.

At first glance, the taxonomy may appear confusing, but if you will examine it carefully, you should begin to grasp its organization. The first major heading, "Receiving (Attending)," stresses awareness, which is similar to values clarification strategies that ask students to list and discuss the values they prize and cherish. The second category, "Responding," is essentially the same as the values clarification emphasis on acting on one's beliefs. "Valuing," the third category, offers a different explanation of the seven-step process of valuing proposed by Raths. The last two categories—"Organization" and "Characterization by a Value or Value Complex"—call attention to ways values might be merged to form a coherent philosophy of life. If you study the taxonomy carefully, you may find ways to present values clarification strategies and other forms of humanistic education in a systematic way.

TAXONOMY OF EDUCATIONAL OBJECTIVES: AFFECTIVE DOMAIN[2]

Receiving (attending)   "The learner [becomes] sensitized to the existence of certain phenomena and stimuli."

> *Awareness*   What sorts of attitudes or awarenesses do you want your students to have? (e.g., "awareness of aesthetic factors in dress, furnishings, architecture," "recognition that there may be more than one acceptable point of view" on a question)
>
> *Willingness to receive*   What sorts of *tolerances* would you like to encourage your students to develop? (e.g., "tolerance for a variety of types of music," "listening to others with respect," "increase in sensitivity to human need and pressing social problems")
>
> *Controlled or selected attention*   What sorts of attributes that untrained observers frequently ignore would you like to encourage your students to recognize? (e.g., listening for rhythm in poetry or prose read aloud, sensitivity to the "importance of keeping informed on current political and social matters," looking for construction details in garments or furniture)

Responding   The learner does something with or about the phenomena.

> *Acquiescence in responding*   What sorts of habits of self-discipline would you like to encourage in your students? What specific

[2] The headings in this summary are exactly the same as those in the complete taxonomy. All other exact quotations are enclosed in quotation marks.

kinds of regulations do you want your students to comply with? (e.g., rules that homework must be completed, playground regulations, health regulations, "rules in an industrial arts shop")

Willingness to Respond   What kinds of voluntary habits relative to your subject would you like your students to adopt? (e.g., voluntarily searching for information, practicing rules of safety, voluntarily reading books and magazines, participating in a variety of construction hobbies and recreational activities)

Satisfaction in response   What kinds of habits that arouse positive feelings of satisfaction would you like your students to develop? (e.g., "pleasure in reading for recreation," "pleasure in good music," "enjoyment of literature, intellectually and aesthetically, as a means of personal enrichment and social understanding")

Valuing   The learner displays consistent behavior reflecting a general attitude.

Acceptance of a value   What sorts of beliefs (emotional acceptance of a proposition) would you like your students to develop? (e.g., desire "to attain optimum health," "increased appetite and taste for what is good in literature")

Preference for a value   What kinds of values would you like your students to develop to the point of their feeling a sense of active identity with a given concept or idea? (e.g., writing letters to agencies, organizations, or newspapers in order to express opinions, initiating group action for the improvement of health regulations")

Commitment (conviction)   What sorts of ideas would you like your students to entertain with considerable conviction? (e.g., "loyalty to the various groups in which one holds membership," "loyalty to the social goals of a free society")

Organization   The value system of the person is internalized.

Conceptualization of a value   What sorts of wide-ranging conceptions would you like to try to develop in your students? (e.g., trying to identify characteristics of an admired art object, "forming judgments as to the responsibility of society for conserving human and material resources")

Organization of a value system   What might you do in your classes to contribute to the formation of a desirable system of values by your students? (e.g., help them "form judgments as to the major directions in which American society should move," help them develop "techniques for controlling aggression in culturally acceptable patterns")

Characterization by a value or value complex   In effect, the attitude and value system becomes a way of life.

Generalized set What could you do in your classes to encourage your students to develop encompassing attributes of character? (e.g., develop a conscience, develop a consistent philosophy of life)

The taxonomy may be more meaningful and useful to you if you concentrate on the first three categories and if you think about how you might use values clarification strategies to achieve goals in the Valuing and Organization categories. Many strategies are designed to help students accept values, become aware of preferences and commitments, and organize their value systems. The development of advanced commitments and beliefs represented by the final categories is likely to occur long after you lose contact with your students. Even so, you may find that points toward the end of the outline will help you identify some affective goals for your classes, although you may never find out whether you have achieved any measure of success in helping students attain them.

Handbook heading
Lists of Affective Goals and Ways to Try to Achieve Them

13. Do your best to provide learning experiences that will lead to the development of the habits and attitudes you want to foster. If you do come up with a list of value and attitude goals, do some specific thinking about how you might encourage such attitudes by using techniques other than values clarification strategies.

EXAMPLES

A kindergarten teacher tried to encourage perseverance by having her pupils begin the year with short-term projects and toward the end of the year undertake more ambitious tasks (e.g., all the children made their own paper chains for the class Maypole).

If you want pupils to respect the rights of others, experiment with a modified Summerhill open meeting where any student can express a complaint about the disruptive or annoying behavior of a classmate.

If you want to encourage students to be sensitive to the skills of artists, novelists, or composers, point out subtle details and particularly effective sections of works.

To make students aware of the joys of good design, encourage them to look for everyday objects that are not only useful but attractive as well.

In your Handbook you might note some specific techniques for encouraging the development of the habits, attitudes, and values you listed earlier. (If you decide, for example, that you would like to encourage awareness of the importance of keeping informed, *how* might you do this?)

14. Make use of object lessons. When illustrative incidents occur in

One of the best ways to encourage a positive attitude toward a form of self-expression such as music is to demonstrate personal interest and help pupils learn to share your enthusiasm.

Paul Conklin

the course of events, take advantage of them.   In attempting to inculcate attitudes and values, you may find that it is sometimes more effective to use natural situations than to devise formal presentations.

EXAMPLES

If a national or international figure demonstrates his or her commitment to a value system (e.g., a government official resigns from a high-paying position to protest an unfair decision), invite the class to discuss the event.

If someone in the class does something especially thoughtful for a classmate (e.g., sends a get-well card), ask the class to consider how pleased the recipient must have felt.

Use current events to illustrate the nature of certain kinds of behavior (e.g., discuss the causes of riots or point out the importance of being informed about propositions on ballots).

15. Set a good example.   Some advocates of values clarification contend that systematic efforts to build attitudes are more likely to be effective than modeling because there is no way to determine which models will be imitated. While there may be a degree of validity to this argument, the fact remains that children acquire many types of behavior by imitating others and you will be one of the adult models they will have extended contact with. Therefore, the example you set may have an impact on your students, and you should make an effort to serve as a good model.

EXAMPLES

If you want your students to become sensitive to the feelings of others, show that you are sensitive to their feelings.

If you want your pupils to be tolerant of different opinions, act that way yourself.

If you want children to be honest and considerate, show that you are honest and considerate in your dealings with them.

If you would like your students to get assignments in on time, be prompt in evaluating and returning their work.

16. Be aware of your students' level of moral development, and encourage understanding of subtle aspects of morality by presenting "moral dilemmas."   The word *values* covers many types of behavior. Before humanistic education and values clarification techniques became popular, it frequently served as a synonym for *morality* and *character*. Many of the decisions individuals must make are based on ethical considerations. If they possess a well-defined set of moral standards and positive character traits, they tend to behave with honesty and integrity. If they do not possess such traits, they succumb to temptation and engage in deceitful or illegal behavior. Because of the amount of dishonesty that has been displayed by contemporary Americans in the public eye, as well as the pervasiveness of dishonesty in everyday dealings with others, some critics of the schools have argued that character education should become an integral part of the curriculum. (Occasionally critics who blame the educational system for failing to inculcate honesty and related virtues also demand that the schools stick to the "basics" and let parents teach their children attitudes and values.)

In a classic study of character training, Hugh Hartshorne and Mark May (1930) found that asking students to memorize platitudes (such as "Honesty is the best policy") was ineffective. They concluded that the best way to encourage children to acquire desirable character traits was to help them analyze the various factors involved in actual situations where moral decisions had to be made. An explanation for this

Analyzing actual moral situations more effective than memorizing principles

finding is offered by Piaget's distinction between moral realism and moral relativism. Children below the age of twelve or so are moral realists. They concentrate on consequences, not motives, interpret rules in literal fashion, and need a specific rule for each situation. Secondary level students, who are capable of thinking as moral relativists, have matured to the point where they can take into account motives and circumstances and can apply a few general principles to many different situations. Asking children, particularly young ones, to memorize a few general moral principles, therefore, is almost certain to be a waste of time. It makes more sense to ask them to examine situations where moral judgments must be made by analyzing the various factors involved. If a variety of situations are examined this way, pupils are likely to begin to follow the same procedure when they must make personal and private moral decisions. Older children may also begin to evolve a personal set of moral principles.

Lawrence Kohlberg (1966) has developed a theory of moral development that is a more elaborate version of Piaget's distinction between moral realism and relativism. He has devised a series of hypothetical situations describing *moral dilemmas,* such as whether a boy should tell his father about a brother's misdeed. The situations are presented to children and their responses rated with reference to three levels of moral thinking: preconventional, conventional, and postconventional. (Each level is subdivided into two stages.)

Kohlberg: Levels of moral thinking

Just as *operations* are the key to Piaget's stages of intellectual development, *conventional* moral thinking is the key to Kohlberg's stages. Children at the *preconventional* level interpret moral situations in terms of physical consequences (e.g., punishment) or out of deference to power or prestige (e.g., the desire to avoid trouble). Children at the *conventional* level interpret moral situations in a conforming (conventional) way, first because of a desire to please others and later because of a desire to show respect for authority and to maintain the social order for its own sake. Adolescents at the *postconventional* level make independent moral judgments; they recognize that the rules of the social order are somewhat arbitrary and make decisions in terms of general ethical principles and personal conscience. (This level is similar to Piaget's *moral relativism* stage).

These stages can be illustrated by reactions to the moral dilemma involving a boy telling his father about a brother's misdeed.:

Preconventional. "He'd better not or he'll get beat up." (Punishment)
"He should keep quiet because his brother might squeal on him." (Avoid trouble)

Conventional. "If my father finds out later, he won't trust me." (Respect for authority)
"We should always tell the truth. Otherwise, no one can trust anyone else." (Maintain the social order)

Postconventional. "I need to think about what my brother did and why he did it." (Consideration of general moral principles)

"He thought he could trust me. I have to consider that." (Coming to terms with one's conscience)

Just as Piaget argues that the child advances through the stages of intellectual development in sequence, Kohlberg maintains that children must pass through lower stages of moral development in order to become capable of postconventional thinking. And just as Piaget urges the teacher to pay heed to the intellectual level of the child in planning learning experiences, Kohlberg recommends that teachers take note of the level of moral development of their pupils in assessing their reactions to moral situations and in planning character education.

The Kohlberg stages are not clearly related to specific age levels, particularly since many individuals never progress beyond the conventional level. However, the switch from preconventional to conventional thought typically takes place around the end of the elementary grades. Consequently, elementary grade pupils may not be capable of interpreting moral situations in terms other than punishment or avoiding trouble. (Kohlberg notes: "It does not seem wise to treat cheating as a genuine moral issue among young children" [1966, p. 26]). Furthermore, they may not be able to respond to efforts at moral education that are beyond their level of understanding.

Using moral dilemmas to encourage moral development

Kohlberg suggests that teachers ask questions and listen to the explanations their students give for moral judgments to gain insight into their level of moral thought. He also suggests that moral dilemmas be presented so that students will be confronted with "a sense of uncertainty as to the right answer to the situation in question" (p. 23). Ideally, these discussions should aim at communicating ideas one level beyond that of the pupils who are participating. In addition, pupils should be encouraged to apply moral judgments to their own actions. Finally, Kohlberg urges teachers to try to avoid being overly concerned about classroom rules and routines, since they tend to apply only to the school environment. To encourage moral development that will permit your pupils to deal with problems unrelated to school routines, you should encourage analysis of "broader and more genuinely moral issues" (p. 26).

Handbook heading

Moral Dilemmas and Ways to Use Them

To put these recommendations into practice, you might set aside certain periods for discussion and analysis of moral dilemmas. To begin, you could describe a situation from your own experience and ask students to write about what they think they would have done. These explanations could be used to assess the general level of moral thinking of the class, and further situations might be described to encourage more advanced thinking. To stimulate your students to apply moral reasoning to their own behavior, you might ask them to write about their own experiences with moral dilemmas and then have them exchange experiences and interpretations in informal small-group discussions.

A number of strategies described in *Values Clarification* and *Personalizing Education* ask pupils to deal with moral dilemmas. "The Fall-Out Shelter Problem" (described on pages 281–286 of *Values Clarification*), for example, asks groups of six or seven students to discuss which six individuals out of a group of ten should be selected to stay in a fall-out shelter during a nuclear attack. Similar strategies described in the same book are "Cave-In Simulation" (pp. 287–289) and "Alligator River" (pp. 290–294). Moral dilemma strategies described in *Personalizing Education* include "Kidney Machine" (pp. 243–245), "Job Openings" (pp. 245–247), "Life Raft" (pp. 247–249), "Value Dilemmas" (pp. 251–279), and "Dear Abby's" (pp. 281–289). (These last two ask students to deal with situations that are most similar to those recommended by Kohlberg. The strategies listed first are so extreme and unrealistic it does not seem likely that students would relate what they discuss to their own behavior.)

SUMMARY OF KEY POINTS

Basic assumptions of humanistic psychology and education have been stated by Abraham H. Maslow, Carl R. Rogers, and Arthur Combs. Maslow's third force view emphasizes that teachers and parents should trust children and let them make many of their own choices. Rogers's learner-centered view of teaching emphasizes trust, sincerity, prizing, and empathy. Combs's humanistic conception of teachers pictures them as facilitators, encouragers, helpers, and friends.

Humanistic psychologists join with cognitive psychologists in suggesting that extreme interpretations of the S-R view may lead to excessive regimentation and control. Humanists differ from cognitive theorists in stressing that emotions, feelings, self-fulfillment, and interpersonal relationships should be stressed along with thinking. Some humanistic educators make this point by arguing that teachers should strive to merge thinking, feeling, and action. Others advocate extensive use of values clarification techniques.

The humanistic view, in contrst to the S-R and cognitive-discovery views, is not based on experimental evidence. Perhaps the closest thing to an experiment in humanistic education was carried out by A. S. Neill at Summerhill. In theory, Summerhill was based on the assumption that children are innately wise and will learn all they need to know without adult intervention of any kind. In practice, adult teachers supplied instruction, but only when students volunteered to attend class.

Specific educational techniques recommended by those who call themselves humanists include exercises intended to encourage pupils to become more sensitive to feelings, role playing, psychodrama, simulation games, forms of creative expression, confluent education (merging affective and cognitive goals), and values clarification (students choose, prize, and act on beliefs).

Humanistic conceptions of education are vulnerable to many types of criticism. Basic assumptions are derived from vaguely stated propositions and observations. Students who attended Summerhill, the epitome of humanistic education, achieved little, did not fulfill Neill's claim that they would be highly creative, and graduates of the school reported that they would not want their own children to attend the school for more than a year or so. Furthermore, some humanistic educators affect a holier-than-thou attitude, falsely implying that they have a monopoly on positive qualities. Humanists also make elaborate but unfounded claims for the techniques they espouse. Enthusiasts for values clarification are particularly prone to make lavish claims, but close examination of their approach leads to doubts about whether the strategies they use actually have any permanent impact on students. Instead of evidence, humanists tend to offer testimonials and subjective reports. Occasionally, they advocate what amounts to compulsory psychotherapy to be conducted by untrained "amateurs." Humanists who urged teachers to develop close personal relationships with pupils were unable to do this themselves for more than a year or two.

The cardinal principle of humanistic education is: Give pupils opportunities to make choices and decisions. A specific technique for communicating with pupils in personal ways is talk to the situation, not a pupil's personality. In planning how to work humanistic goals into the curriculum, it may be helpful to refer to the Taxonomy of Educational Objectives: Affective Domain. When, attempting to encourage moral development, it appears to be more effective for teachers to urge pupils to analyze actual situations than to ask them to memorize principles. Lawrence Kohlberg has provided a description of levels of moral development and has suggested ways that teachers can select and present moral dilemmas intended to help pupils make mature ethical decisions.

BECOMING A BETTER TEACHER: QUESTIONS AND SUGGESTIONS

Ways to Give Pupils
Choices

Am I giving my students plenty of opportunities to participate in making decisions and freedom to choose among alternatives? Suggestion: Try out the ten-step procedure recommended by Howe and

Howe for permitting pupils to participate in the planning of a teaching unit.

Using Self-Paced and Self-Selected Styles

Should I introduce student self-direction by first using self-paced and then self-selected styles of learning? Suggestion: Set up a unit so that students can work at their own pace. (One way to do this is to use Keller's Personalized System of Instruction described in Chapter 5.) Then set up a unit where students can choose from a variety of topics (perhaps presented on activity cards). If the activity cards work out, look for additional activities in teachers' journals and also ask pupils to make up activities to add to an "Independent Project File."

Ways to Communicate Interest in Pupils as Individuals

Am I communicating the feeling to students that I am interested in them as individuals? Suggestion: The next time I schedule a work period or exam, glance around the room and silently try to name every pupil in class. If I can't think of the names of some pupils, work at learning those names that afternoon. The next day make it a point to say something to all "unrecognized" pupils, partly to get practice in using their names, partly to show them that I am aware of their existence and that I am interested in them as individuals.

Ways to Help Students Develop Positive Feelings About Themselves

Have I used any techniques recently to try to encourage students to feel good about themselves? Suggestion: Try out a values clarification strategy that encourages pupils to describe things they have done that they are proud of.

Ways to Help Students Examine Emotions

Would it be appropriate to ask students to analyze emotions in a unit to be presented in the near future? Suggestion: Check over lesson plans, and, if appropriate, schedule a film or discussion that explores emotions. Or ask students to write brief stories with titles such as "The Day I Felt Particularly Happy" and "The Day I Felt Particularly Sad and Depressed."

Ways to Encourage Physical and Dramatic Forms of Expression

Am I missing opportunities to encourage pupils to express themselves through movement or creative dramatics? Suggestions: If appropriate, ask the class if they would like to experiment with some creative movement or dramatic sessions. After describing possibilities, invite pupils to volunteer to participate during free-study or free-activity periods.

Using Role Playing, Psychodrama, and Simulation Games

Should I try out activities that get students actively involved in the subject we are studying? Suggestion: As I make up lesson plans next month, look for ways to work in an exercise in role playing or psychodrama. Also, examine simulation games in a curriculum library to find out if one or more might be appropriate for my classes.

Ways to Set Up Values Clarification Sessions

Should I use any values clarification strategies during the next two weeks? Suggestion: Read the section on values clarification in Chapter 7 and/or one of the recommended books consisting of V.C. strategies, and pick out at least one to try out next week.

Values Clarification Strategies to Try Out	If students respond to the trial values clarification strategy, how can I use other strategies? Suggestion: Peruse recommended books on values clarification, select promising techniques, and write up a description of how to use each on a sheet of paper to be inserted in my Handbook.
Ways to Set Up Long-Term Values Clarification Projects	Would my use of values clarification strategies be more effective if I asked students to carry out long-term projects? Suggestion: Examine descriptions of long-term values clarification strategies in Chapter 7 and in recommended books, and record ways to arrange a long-term project during the next report period.
Ways to Work Values Clarification into the Curriculum	Am I looking for ways that I might work values clarification into the curriculum? Suggestion: From now on when I draw up lesson plans, list things to be covered under three headings: facts, concepts, and values.
Lists of Affective Goals and Ways to Try to Achieve Them	Are there ways other than values clarification I can help students achieve affective goals? Suggestion: Look over the Taxonomy of Educational Objectives: Affective Domain, and list some habits and attitudes I should try to foster. Then describe specific ways I might encourage students to achieve these affective goals.
Moral Dilemmas and Ways to Use Them	Is it appropriate for me, in the classes I teach, to ask students to wrestle with moral dilemmas? Suggestion: Look over what is to be covered during the next report period and decide if moral dilemmas might be included in any units. If it appears that discussion of moral situations is appropriate, set up a class session either by writing a moral dilemma of my own or by asking members of the class to submit dilemmas. (If I try the latter alternative, a couple of weeks before the unit on moral dilemmas is to take place ask students to write brief stories titled "The Most Difficult 'Moral' Decision I Ever Had to Make." Illustrate the kind of story to be written by describing a moral dilemma I had to face.)

SUGGESTIONS FOR FURTHER STUDY

7-1 Maslow on Humanistic Education	If you would like to sample Abraham H. Maslow's observations on humanistic education, perhaps the best single book to read is *The Farther Reaches of Human Nature* (1971). In Part 4 of this book, you will find three articles on education, although articles in other sections may also be of interest to a future teacher. Two other books by Maslow that sum up his final observations on humanistic psychology are *Religions, Values, and Peak Experiences* (1970) and *New Knowledge in Human Values* (1970).
7-2 Rogers on Humanistic Education	Carl Rogers developed the technique of client-centered therapy over twenty years ago and has since applied the same basic idea of growth

of the self to other aspects of living, including education. For a concise description of Rogers's philosophy, look for the essay "Learning to Be Free" in *Conflict and Creativity* (1963), edited by Farber and Wilson, and also in *Person to Person: The Problem of Being Human* (1967) by Rogers and Stevens. The latter volume includes three more essays by Rogers, as well as related discussions by others who share his philosophy. In *Freedom to Learn* (1969), Rogers comments on various aspects of his view of education and presents descriptions of actual classroom applications in the elementary grades and at the college level. If you read one or more sections in any of these books, you might summarize the points made and add your own reactions to keep for future reference.

7-3
Combs on Humanistic Education

Arthur Combs (together with Donald Snygg) explains his rationale for humanistic education in *Individual Behavior* (rev. ed., 1959). Part 1 of this book provides theoretical background; Part 2 consists of a discussion of implications and applications.

7-4
Neill on Humanistic Education

If you have never read any of A. S. Neill's books on education and child rearing, you might want to do so before embarking on a teaching career. In *Summerhill* (1960), probably the most straightforward account of the school of that name, Neill sets forth the philosophy he put into practice for over forty years. In the opening section of the book, Neill gives a complete, although somewhat disorganized, exposition of what the school is like. For a visitor's impression of what Summerhill was like, browse through *Living at Summerhill* (1968) by Herb Snitzer. For opinions of some Summerhill graduates that will provide a frame of reference for sorting out your reactions, read "What Does a Summerhill Old School Tie Look Like?" by Emmanuel Bernstein in the January 1968 issue of *Psychology Today*. Neill comments on a variety of aspects of child rearing and education in *Freedom—Not License!* (1966); he recounts how he was influenced to found Summerhill in his autobiography, *Neill! Neill! Orange Peel!* (1972). If you read any of these accounts of Neill's philosophy and methods, you might summarize the points made and comment on which you endorse and which you find hard to accept.

7-5
Surveys of Humanistic Education

If you would like to sample a variety of descriptions and interpretations of humanistic education, examine *Readings in Values Clarification* (1973), edited by Howard Kirschenbaum and Sidney B. Simon; *Humanistic Education Sourcebook* (1975), edited by Donald A. Read and Sidney B. Simon; or *Will the Real Teacher Please Stand Up* (1972) by Mary Greer and Bonnie Rubinstein. A text in educational psychology written from the humanistic point of view is *Behavior Dynamics in Teaching, Learning, and Growth* (1975) by Don E. Hamachek.

7-6
Values Clarification

For more information on values clarification and detailed instructions for putting values clarification strategies into practice, refer to *Values and Teaching* (1966) by Louis E. Raths, Merrill Harmin, and Sidney B.

Simon; *Values Clarification: A Handbook of Practical Strategies for Teachers* (1972) by Sidney B. Simon, Leland W. Howe, and Howard Kirschenbaum; or *Personalizing Education: Values Clarification and Beyond* (1975) by Leland W. Howe and Mary Martha Howe.

7-7
Confluent Education

George Isaac Brown explains his version of humanistic education in *Human Teaching for Human Learning: An Introduction to Confluent Education* (1971). Chapters include the following: 1 ("Introduction and Rationale"), 3 ("Some Effective Techniques") 4 ("Classroom Applications"), 9 ("Proceed with Caution"), 10 ("The Conclusion for Now").

7-8
Kohlberg's Stages of
Moral Development

If you would like to read a more detailed account of Lawrence Kohlberg's view of moral development, look for "Moral Development in the Schools: A Developmental View" (*School Review*, 1966, 74, pp. 1–30). A more direct way to gain insight into Kohlberg's distinction between preconventional, conventional, and postconventional moral thinking is to ask children of different ages to respond to one or more moral dilemmas. You might present a moral dilemma you once faced or asked younger children to respond to this one:

David and John are brothers. Their father has a home workshop, and he encourages the boys to make things. But, he has made a very strict rule that his power tools are never to be used unless he is present. David decides to build his father a pipe rack for Christmas. When the time comes to drill the holes for the pipes, he uses his father's electric drill. John sees him do it. Should John tell his father that David used the electric drill? Why?

If you interview adolescents, you might present this moral dilemma (if you can't think of one you once faced):

David and John are brothers. David has just passed his driver's license test and offers to drive John (who is two years younger) to a store to pick up a model-airplane kit he has ordered. On the way back, David passes a friend in a sports car. When both cars stop at a traffic light, they have a drag race. David is so eager to make a fast start he almost hits an old woman in the crosswalk. John looks back as the car speeds off and notices that the old woman has fallen to her knees but that she seems able to get up and is apparently not injured. Should John tell his parents about the incident? Why?

7-9
Hartshorne and May's
Studies of Character

A series of studies on character development carried out by Hugh Hartshorne and Mark A. May have never been equaled in terms of ingenuity, thoroughness, or depth. Even though they were done in the 1930s, the results of these studies are still well worth examining. The authors give detailed descriptions of how they developed and administered their various measures, as well as their results and conclusions, in a three-volume series published under the general title *Studies in the Nature of Character*. Volume 1, *Studies in Deceit* (1930), gives the background of the study and then provides a description of the methods and results of the studies of honesty. Descriptions of tests used to measure honesty appear on pages 29–103. Information about how and to whom the tests were administered appears on pages 105–130. In Chapters 6 through 13, the relationships between honesty and age, sex, intelligence, and several other variables are analyzed in detail. Aspects of moral education are discussed in Chapters 15 through 20; general conclusions and problems are presented in Chapters 21 through 23. A summary of general conclusions and implications appears on pages 408–414. Volume 2, *Studies in Service and Self-Control* (1929), describes how cooperative behavior and charitable behavior were measured (Chapters 1 through 4). Factors associated with service are described in Chapters 6 through 14; conclusions and implications of the studies of service are presented in Chapter 15. Tests used to measure self-control are outlined in Chapters 16 through 22; factors associated with self-control are summarized in Chapters 23 through 28. Conclusions and implications of the studies of self-control appear in Chapter 29. Volume 3, *Studies in the Organization of Character* (1930), reports a follow-up study of interrelationships between the types of behavior reported in volumes 1 and 2. Relationships between social intelligence and social attitudes are explained in Part 2; components of character in Part 3, the significance of integration of traits in Part 4; and the conclusions of the entire character-education inquiry are outlined in Part 5. (The final summing up begins on page 382.)

7-10

Neill's Approach to Character Education

A. S. Neill comments on character education in several sections of *Summerhill* (1960). A section called "Religion and Morals" is presented on pages 241–268, but character training is also discussed in several other brief chapters: "Destructiveness" (pp. 138–145), in which Neill gives his answer (on p. 144) to the question: "What would you do if a boy started to hammer nails into the grand piano?"; "Lying" (pp. 146–151); "Responsibility" (pp. 152–154); "Obedience and Discipline" (pp. 155–161), in which the basic rule of Summerhill is explained—"Each individual is free to do what he likes as long as he is not trespassing on the freedom of others" (p. 155); and "Rewards and Punishment" (pp. 162–171), in which Neill gives an explanation of what he would do if a street urchin knocked off his hat with a lump of clay (p. 168).

7-11

Character Training in Russia and America

Urie Bronfenbrenner made a comprehensive analysis of child-rearing methods used in Russia and then compared what he saw with observations of family life in America. In *Two Worlds of Childhood: U.S. and U.S.S.R.* (1970), he notes: "We are experiencing a breakdown in the process of making human beings human" (p. xv). He explains this conclusion in Chapter 3, "The Unmaking of the American Child." Bronfenbrenner maintains that the child is no longer brought up by parents in this country, but by peers—and by television. Therefore, the American child has contact primarily with agemates, which minimizes understanding of and cooperation with individuals of different ages, and that the American child's character is shaped by television.

Bronfenbrenner believes that some aspects of Russian society, such as the use of modeling (where parents, teachers, and peers provide examples of behavior to be emulated) and planned character education in the school, tend to produce individuals with considerable concern for others. If you would like to sample his views, examine these chapters of *Two Worlds of Childhood:* 1 ("Upbringing in the Soviet Family"), 3 ("The Psychological Implications of Soviet Methods of Upbringing"), 4 ("The Unmaking of the American Child"), 5 ("Principles and Possibilities").

In the 1960s the amount of public money spent on education exceeded $30 billion per year. By 1974 the amount had increased to $110 billion. (These figures are based on estimates mentioned by Ralph Tyler in the preface to Update on Education [1966] by Simon S. Johnson.) When legislators, taxpayers, and educators became aware of the rate at which educational expenditures were increasing, they quite naturally began to wonder whether the investment was paying dividends. As the critical books reviewed in Chapter 2 revealed, many individuals were convinced that education was not all that it might be, but these opinions were based on impressions. There was no trustworthy way to determine what students were actually learning—or not learning—in American schools. Accordingly, in 1964 the Education Commission of the States was formed for the purpose of instituting what came to be called the National Assessment of Educational Progress.

The purpose of the National Assessment was to provide information about the knowledge, understanding, skills, and attitudes American children acquire in the public schools. To accomplish this purpose, thousands of individuals at four age levels—nine, thirteen, seventeen, and twenty-six through thirty-five—are tested periodically in ten learning areas: art, career and occupational development, citizenship, literature, mathematics, music, reading, science, social studies, and writing. The results of the tests are recorded in terms of age, sex, race, region of country, parental education, and size and type of community. The program was instituted when groups of teachers, scholars, educators, and laymen formed committees to draw up lists of educational objectives for each of the ten areas. Then specialists in each subject area met to prepare examinations to measure how well these objectives were being achieved. Finally, a rotating schedule for administering the tests was agreed upon and the examinations were administered to representative samples of individuals. As each test was completed, the answers were scored and the results published in a series of reports.

Generally speaking, the results lead to the conclusion that the public schools are not doing a very effective job of meeting either the goals listed in 1955 by the White House Conference Committee (noted on page 64 of Chapter 2) or by the groups that drew up objectives for the ten learning areas chosen by the National Assessment. Here are some excerpts from Update on Education: A Digest of the National Assessment of Educational Progress: "Young adults . . . typically performed less well than 17-year-olds on science tasks, and in a few cases, less well than 13-year-olds. They were especially low in as-

pects of science dealt with primarily in the classroom. However, adults frequently performed better than 17-year-olds in those aspects of science people pick up in daily living. . . .

"The general level of writing skills shown nationally was not very high. At age 9, few individuals have mastered the basics of written English; by age 17, about half the individuals had some mastery of basics, but they rarely attempted anything beyond the simplest constructions or used anything beyond a rather limited vocabulary. At no age did

Part Four

Skills, memory, and transfer

Chapter 8   Helping students acquire skills and information

Chapter 9   Teaching for transfer

Application for Employment

PLEASE TYPE OR PRINT   DATE_____

PERSONAL INFORMATION

NAME
           LAST   FIRST   INITIAL

PRESENT ADDRESS
           STREET & NUMBER   TOWN OR CITY   STATE   ZIP

PERMANENT ADDRESS

SOCIAL SEC. NO.   U.S. CITIZEN: YES NO   HOME TELEPHONE NO.   BUSINESS TELEPHONE NO.

EDUCATION

	NAME AND ADDRESS OF SCHOOL ATTENDED	DATES ATTENDED FROM	TO	DATE OF GRADUATION	DEGREE
HIGH SCHOOL					
COLLEGE OR UNIVERSITY					
POST GRADUATE					

MAJORS AND FIRST MINORS IN COLLEGE: MAJOR: MINORS:

EXPERIENCE

PRESENT POSITION

ADDRESS OF PRESENT POSITION
     STREET & NUMBER TOWN OR CITY STATE ZIP

NAME OF SUPERVISOR

PRESENT SALARY   WHEN CAN YOU BEGIN

BUSINESS AND/OR TEACHING EXPERIENCE

NAME AND ADDRESS OF EMPLOYER	DATES OF SERVICE FROM	TO	POSITION	SALARY
	MO. YR.	MO. YR.		
	MO. YR.	MO. YR.		
	MO. YR.	MO. YR.		

many individuals show much of a flair for writing. . . . Americans seem to have difficulty writing in business situations of even the simplest nature. Only at age 17 did even slightly more than half manage to fill in correctly a simple information form asking for name, address, birth date, and current date. . . .

"The vast majority of young Americans can read fairly simple material, but many cannot; many young Americans are handicapped by deficient reading skills. They cannot follow simple directions, and they find it difficult to draw inferences or conclusions based on what they do understand when they read (1975, pp. 5–8)."

An NAEP Newsletter (August 1975, vol. 8, No. 4), issued after Update on Education was published, reported that only 1 percent of seventeen-year-olds and 16 percent of adults tested knew enough math to balance a checkbook.

On the basis of these facts and figures, it seems fair to say that there is ample room for improvement in American education. Because National Assessment reports sometimes make front-page news, in fact, there may be a demand on the part of parents and taxpayers that teachers do a better job of instruction. Up until recently educators often argued that it was impossible to determine how effective the schools actually were. That is no longer the case, and it seems likely that National Assessment not only developed as a consequence of a demand for accountability in education but also played a major role in increasing interest in accountability. Therefore, it is worth considering some of the implications of National Assessment information and of accountability in education.

One implication of educational accountability that was emphasized in Chapter 2 is that you are not likely to have complete freedom to teach any way you like. Even though you may have felt attracted to techniques of teaching based on the cognitive-discovery and humanistic views of learning described in Chapters 6 and 7, there is little chance that you will be able to make exclusive use of such methods. Techniques of teaching derived from the S-R view are usually more efficient than discovery or humanistic approaches, and you may be obliged to prove your efficiency as an instructor. Furthermore, parents who learn that many graduates of American schools are unable to interpret what they read or even fill out a simple application form are not likely to be pleased if their children report that they are spending large blocks of time every school day engaging in group discussions of hypothetical situations or clarifying their values. (Remember the imaginary situation presented in Chapter 2 involving the chemist who hired you to tutor his children.)

A second outgrowth of accountability is that you probably will be required to list instructional objectives for a unit, a report period, or a year. In some cases, these objectives may be selected for you by state or district school officials if National Assessment reports reveal inadequacies in one or more areas of subjects you teach. (Up to 1974, approximately half of the fifty states were using National Assessment materials, data, or techniques in developing and evaluating instructional programs.) Instructional objectives not only give teachers and students common goals to strive for; they also make it simpler to determine if goals have been met.

A third implication of emerging interest in accountabilty is that you may be expected to teach not only to produce high test scores at the end of a report period but also to produce more lasting forms of learning. National Assessment results reveal that many young adults do not maintain skills they once had when they were in school and do not continue to learn or engage in intellectual and artistic pursuits after they graduate.

The two chapters that make up this part of the text supply information relating to these three implications of accountability. In the first section of Chapter 8, you will learn about different kinds of instructional objectives. In the subsequent sections, techniques you might use to help students acquire skills and learn and retain information are described. In Chapter 9, "Teaching for Transfer," suggestions are offered for inducing students to continue to use what they have learned after they graduate and to function as problem-solvers and creative individuals.

Key points

Using instructional objectives

For specific objectives, describe terminal behavior, conditions, criteria

For general objectives, list learning outcomes by specifying observable behavior

Invite students to participate in stating objectives

Gagné's eight conditions of learning

Gagné's hierarchy of conditions of learning

Problem solving is based on mastery of simpler forms of learning

Taxonomy of Educational Objectives: Cognitive Domain

Taxonomy for the cognitive domain: Comprehensive list of cognitive goals

Developing clear objectives may require experience

Teaching skills

Chaining: Step-by-step progression toward terminal behavior

Beta hypothesis: Exaggerate error, then relearn

Negative transfer: Previous learning interferes

Learning curve: Leveling off after initial improvement

Plateaus: Periods of no apparent improvement

Helping students memorize and remember

Long-term storage depends on coding

Attention getters: Size, color, intensity, novelty, unexpectedness

Meaningfulness a key factor in remembering

Mnemonic devices (mediators)

Advance organizers better for older students

Verbal or physical activity leads to remembering

Imagery and the loci method

Key to memory feats: Ridiculous associations

Disuse leads to fading of brain trace

Some memories are reorganized or distorted

Disagreeable experiences are repressed

New learning interferes with old, and vice versa

Distributed practice: Frequent brief study sessions

Serial-position effect: Beginning and end remembered better than middle

Chapter 8　Helping students acquire skills and information

$\mathbf{O}$NE OF THE BASIC principles of instruction highlighted by the experiments carried out by S-R theorists is that teachers should describe terminal behavior. When B. F. Skinner planned one of his experiments, the first thing he did was to describe precisely what he wanted his rat or pigeon subjects to do. Because Skinner believes that teachers should shape behavior as efficiently as possible (since the alternative is haphazard shaping), he recommends that they follow the same procedure. He asks, in effect, "How can teachers do an efficient job of instruction if they have not thought about what they want their students to do after a lesson or unit is completed?"

In the late 1960s and early 1970s, when open-ended forms of instruction such as the discovery approach and humanistic education became popular, Skinner's recommendation that teachers describe specific goals often went unheeded. Today, for reasons noted in the introduction to this part, there is a great deal of interest in instructional objectives and teaching efficiency. Accordingly, it will be to your advantage to examine ways you might describe instructional objectives so that you, your pupils, their parents, and school administrators will be able to determine if learning goals have been met.

Using instructional objectives

Mager's suggestions for stating specific objectives

A particularly effective explanation of why it is desirable to focus on objectives is presented by Robert F. Mager in *Preparing Instructional Objectives*. (Excerpts from this book were presented in Figure 5-3,

p. 240, to illustrate a branching program.) Mager summarizes the basic message in the opening paragraph of his book:

Once an instructor decides he will teach his students something, several kinds of activity are necessary on his part if he is to succeed. He must first decide upon the goals he intends to reach at the end of his course or program. He must then select procedures, content, and methods that are relevant to the objectives; cause the student to interact with appropriate subject matter in accordance with principles of learning; and, finally, measure or *evaluate* the student's performance *according to the objectives or goals* originally selected. (1962, p. 1)

Mager sums up the techniques for accomplishing this instructional sequence:

1. A statement of instructional objectives is a collection of words or symbols describing one of your educational *intents*.

2. An objective will communicate your intent to the degree you have described what the learner will be DOING when demonstrating his achievement and how you will know when he is doing it.

For specific objectives, describe terminal behavior, conditions, criteria

3. To describe the terminal behavior (what the learner will be DOING):

a. Identify and name the over-all behavior act.

b. Define the important conditions under which the behavior is to occur (givens or restrictions, or both).

c. Define the criterion of acceptable performance.

4. Write a separate statement for each objective; the more statements you have, the better chance you have of making clear your intent.

5. If you give each learner a copy of your objectives, you may not have to do much else. (p. 53)

You are urged to consider Mager's suggestions when you begin to teach. With certain kinds of material you may find that a detailed list of all objectives you want your students to achieve will be ideal. Such a list will permit you to be highly systematic in your approach to instruction; it will lend itself to precise identification of weak areas; it will give your students specific goals to strive for and information about how they are doing; and it will simplify arranging your instruction for accountability—if you are required to prove your productivity. You can give students goals to shoot for and feedback regarding their performance if you follow Mager's recommendations that you state objectives in terms of a *time limit* (e.g., correctly solve at least seven addition problems consisting of three two-digit numbers within a period of three minutes), *a minimum number of correct responses* (e.g., given a collection of twenty rock specimens, correctly identify by labeling at least fifteen), or a *proportion of correct answers* (e.g., correctly spell 90 percent of the words included in the spelling exercises presented during the preceding four days).

Gronlund's suggestions for stating general objectives

In *Stating Behavioral Objectives for Classroom Instruction,* Norman E. Gronlund points out that Mager's objectives are most appropriate for teaching simple skills and specific items of information, since each objective is an end in itself. For more advanced types of instruction, Gronlund recommends stating a general objective first and then clarifying it by noting *samples* of the type of performance that indicates understanding. He notes that using sampling types of objectives leads to emphasizing more general principles and that mastering principles is more likely to lead to learning that involves understanding rather than simple recall.

Gronlund recommends the following procedure for stating objectives:

For general objectives, list leaving outcomes by specifying observable behavior

1. State the general instructional objectives as *expected learning outcomes.*

2. Place under each general instructional objective a list of specific learning outcomes that describes the *terminal behavior* students are to demonstrate when they have achieved the objective.

   a. Begin each specific learning outcome with a *verb* that specifies definite, *observable behavior.*

   b. List a sufficient number of specific learning outcomes under each objective to describe adequately the behavior of students who have achieved the objective.

   c. Be certain that the behavior in each specific learning outcome is relevant to the objective it describes.

3. When defining the general instructional objectives in terms of specific learning outcomes, revise and refine the original list of objectives as needed.

4. Be careful not to omit complex objectives (e.g., critical thinking, appreciation) simply because they are difficult to define in specific behavioral terms.

5. Consult reference materials for help in identifying the specific types of behavior that are most appropriate for defining the complex objectives. (1970, p. 17)

If you are impressed by this set of procedures, you might use as a model Gronlund's description of objectives to reflect understanding of scientific principles.

UNDERSTANDS SCIENTIFIC PRINCIPLES.

1. States the principle in his own words.

2. Gives an example of the principle.

3. Identifies predictions that are in harmony with the principle.

4. Distinguishes between correct and incorrect applications of the principle. (1970, p. 34)

Mager and Gronlund present logical arguments in defense of using behavioral objectives but supply no data to substantiate their claims. Many other psychologists, however, have studied the impact of objectives, and Phillipe C. Duchastel and Paul F. Merrill (1973) reviewed over fifty of the studies. They concluded, "A number of studies have shown facilitative effects. However, an equal number of studies have failed to demonstrate any significant difference" (1973, p. 54). They point out that one interpretation of this conclusion is that, since "objectives sometimes help and are almost never harmful . . . one might as well make them available to students" (p. 63). They also note that while they were concerned in their review only with research relating to facilitation of learning, behavioral objectives also give direction to teaching and curriculum development and provide guidance for evaluation.

Ojemann's suggestions for inviting students to state objectives

One possible explanation for the ineffectiveness of instructional objectives in some situations can be derived from observations by Ralph H. Ojemann (1968), who suggests that while the behaviorist emphasis on overt behavior has been helpful in making descriptions of some types of objectives more useful, it has also contributed to neglect of a different type of objective.

First, Ojemann depicts a *school* or *laboratory* situation (e.g., a reading test) in which students are provided with specific instructional materials, urged to do their best, and induced to cooperate (in the sense that unsuccessful efforts may have to be repeated). He then contrasts it with a *free-to-do,* or *on-their own* situation (e.g., voluntary leisure-time reading) in which students do whatever they wish. Ojemann observes that those who stress stating instructional objectives have ignored the distinction between *controlled motivation* and *on-their-own* behavior. He suggests that recognizing the difference leads to awareness of the importance of including in analyses of objectives those that contribute to the students' feeling that what they are being asked to study will have personal significance or worth. Instead of simply stating terminal behavior in terms that reflect primarily what *you* want, Ojemann suggests that you invite students to begin a learning unit by discussing the potential significance to themselves of what they will be asked to learn. For example, in introducing a unit on specific gravity, Ojemann and Pritchett (1963) asked first grade pupils to discuss "Why should we spend our time trying to figure out why things float?" In another situation, Finder (1965), before having pupils from an inner-city slum embark on the study of English, asked them to discuss reasons why studying English would be worth the trouble.

Ojemann's distinction between types of objectives reflects the differences of opinion between S-R theorists, cognitive psychologists,

Invite students to participate in stating objectives

and advocates of humanistic education that were noted in the preceding three chapters. Skinner was appalled by inefficiency in education and recommended that teachers be as systematic as possible in providing instruction. The obvious first step for those who want to be efficient teachers is to describe, as precisely as possible, the ultimate goal (or terminal behavior) of any learning situation.

Bruner, on the other hand, concluded that telling students exactly what they should learn would limit them to acquiring only information the teacher felt they should acquire. He reasoned that this would prevent students from generating their own ideas. He also believed that what students learned "on cue" would be less likely to be remembered and used than information they acquired through their own efforts. Bruner therefore recommends that teachers arrange learning experiences to achieve general goals (e.g., come up with answers to questions such as "What is human about human beings?") but emphasizes that it is neither possible nor desirable to predict exactly what will be learned. The children who work with the MACOS materials are all exposed to the same films and exercises. The conclusions they draw, however, are a function of idiosyncratic experiences and perceptions, which means that the ultimate conclusions reached by any individual or group will always differ in some respects from those drawn by others.

Humanistic psychologists object to detailed instructional objectives because of the degree of control exerted by the teacher. They argue that prepackaged learning makes students dependent on others and may therefore limit or even prevent future learning. Accordingly, some humanists might disagree with the conclusion of Duchastel and Merrill that instructional objectives are "almost never harmful." If students feel they are being forced to learn material that has no personal meaning or worthwhile purpose, they may experience resentment and make a resolution to avoid a subject in the future. Ojemann's suggestion that teachers invite students to feel that they are engaging in on-their-own behavior would be an excellent way to limit negative reactions to use of instructional objectives.

A question often posed by students is: "What do we have to learn this stuff for, anyway?" Too often the teacher's answer has been: "Because I'm telling you to learn it." In a sense, simply stating objectives in a specific, detailed, and explicit way reflects this answer. Ojemann suggests that a better answer is, "Okay, That's a legitimate question. Why *should* we study this? What are some ways this information might be of interest or of value to you?"

Better yet, don't wait for the question to be asked. Invite students to discuss reasons for learning material before you present objectives—or, in appropriate situations, before you *write* objectives. If you provide a list of objectives after encouraging such a discussion, students would most likely have a different feeling about them from what is usually evoked by lists that are simply presented as something to be accomplished. In some cases, however, it may be difficult for students to anticipate some of the most important values of information. Therefore, it may be desirable for *you* to provide an explanation. Also, since it is impossible to predict how information might be used, you might explain that you are asking your students to learn certain information because experience has shown that it is *likely* to be of value. In discussing the rationale of this book in Chapter 1, the point was made that since you have limited experience with teaching, you may not be able to recognize the value of some of the material you are being asked to learn. You were asked to accept on faith that information selected for emphasis has been chosen because it has high potential payoff value for a teacher. In some cases, you may wish to make a similar statement.

Handbook heading
Ways to Use
Instructional Objectives

As you make out lesson plans and plan learning activities for a report period, consider types of objectives appropriate for each unit of instruction. The following suggestions are offered as guidelines.

Suggestions for teaching: Using instructional objectives

1. Use the contract approach by inviting students to select individual goals and perhaps decide on deadlines and evaluation procedures.

2. If the unit stresses information, simple skills, and the like, consider stating detailed objectives by following the suggestions of Mager; that is, describe what students will actually do when they demonstrate achievement, define the conditions under which the behavior is to occur, and indicate the criterion of acceptable performance (if appropriate).

3. If the unit stresses concepts, principles, complex skills, and the like, consider stating objectives by following the suggestions of Gronlund; that is, describe general goals, and then list detailed learning outcomes by using verbs that specify definite, observable behavior.

4. If the unit is intended to encourage students to develop their own perceptions or if you suspect that pupils may resist learning certain material, invite them to discuss why what they are being asked to learn is worth learning.

5. Try to remain aware of the extent to which you direct and control learning. Whenever possible, permit and encourage students to make choices and to manage their own learning.

6. After listing cognitive objectives for a unit, look for ways to also include affective objectives in lesson plans.

1. Use the contract approach by inviting students to select individual

goals and perhaps decide on deadlines and evaluation procedures. You can permit students to write the equivalent of personal instructional objectives by using variations of the contract approach.

EXAMPLES

At the elementary level, invite students to select a number of activity cards and carry out the instructions.

At the secondary level, announce that students who wish to can meet with you individually and draw up a contract of study for a unit or course.

2. If the unit stresses information, simple skills, and the like, consider stating detailed objectives by following the suggestions of Mager; that is, describe what students will actually do when they demonstrate achievement, define the conditions under which the behavior is to occur, and indicate the criterion of acceptable performance (if appropriate).

Many published learning materials list instructional objectives, present lessons, provide self-test materials, and supply record sheets where students can chart their progress.

Christopher Morrow/Stock Boston

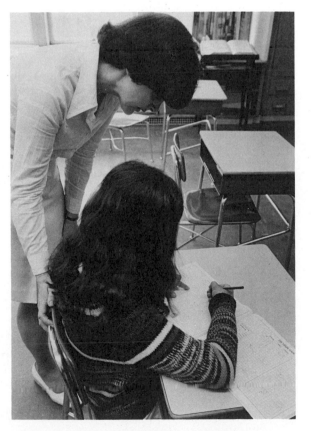

EXAMPLES

In order to earn a "pass" on this unit you will need to spell correctly at least eighteen of these twenty words on the quiz to be given on Friday.

Before you go on to the next unit, you will need to conjugate these five irregular verbs without making any errors.

By the end of this month you should be able to type a 240-word selection in less than six minutes and with no more than five errors.

After you watch this film, you should be able to list five basic kinds of crop and give an example of each.

In order to earn an A in this course, you will need to answer correctly at least twenty of twenty-five questions on each of five exams.

After you take notes on this lecture, you will be asked to list four types of tree and give an example of each.

At the end of this report period, strive to work up to the point where you can do 30 percent more pushups, pullups, and situps than you were able to do yesterday.

3. If the unit stresses concepts, principles, complex skills, and the like, consider stating objectives by following the suggestions of Gronlund; that is, describe general goals, and then list detailed learning outcomes by using verbs that specify definite, observable behavior.

EXAMPLES

The basic goal of this unit is to help you learn to appreciate and enjoy poetry. When you have finished it you should be able to:

　　1. Distinguish between superior and inferior poetry.

　　2. Give reasons for classifying a poem as superior or inferior.

　　3. Explain why you like some poems better than others.

　　4. Find books and magazines that contain poems you are likely to enjoy.

The primary objective of this unit is to help you comprehend and apply the laws of thermodynamics. To earn a passing grade on this unit you will be asked to:

　　1. State the first and second laws of thermodynamics in the same basic terminology used in the text. (Slight alterations will be permitted, provided they do not alter the meaning of the law.)

　　2. Rewrite these laws in your own words.

　　3. Predict what will happen in various energy-producing situations.

　　4. Explain how any energy system works.

At the end of this unit on use of the table saw, you will be expected to:

1. State five safety rules to observe every time you use the saw.

2. Set up the saw for crosscutting and ripping.

3. Use the dado head to cut half-lap joints, tongue-and-groove joints, and box joints.

4. If the unit is intended to encourage students to develop their own perceptions or if you suspect that pupils may resist learning certain material, invite them to discuss why what they are being asked to learn is worth learning.

EXAMPLES

What are some reasons why it is desirable for all of us to know how to spell correctly?

Now that you have voted on music as the topic for our next special unit, what are some things we might study so that we could get more enjoyment out of listening to music?

Since you will be eligible to vote when you are eighteen, the state board of education believes you should know basic facts about our government, including knowledge of the Constitution of the United States. When I planned this unit on the Constitution, I thought the unit would be more interesting if you learned about the men who actually wrote the Constitution and also about some of the conditions in this country in the 1760s and 1770s that influenced them. Are there other topics you think might be of interest or that might help you learn about and remember the main points of the Constitution?

5. Try to remain aware of the extent to which you direct and control learning. Whenever possible, permit and encourage students to make choices and to manage their own learning. This is the identical point made in the first item listed in Suggestions for Teaching: Applying the Humanistic View in the Classroom in the preceding chapter (p. 353). One of the potential problems of becoming involved in instructional objectives is that you might get carried away by the technique and prearrange almost all student learning. While this may be appropriate in some courses, most of the time you will get a better response from pupils if you occasionally or frequently invite them to decide what they will study and how they will do it. If you want students to help you select and arrange instructional objectives, you might follow the ten-step sequence proposed by Howe and Howe in *Personalizing Education*. This sequence was described in the preceding chapter, but the following brief summary of points is offered to strengthen your memory of it: (1) Have students brainstorm ideas. (2) Select the best of these. (3) Prepare a flow chart. (4) Carry out a question census. (5) List

resources. (6) Develop activities from the questions. (7) Analyze purposes under the headings *knowledge, cognitive skills, values.* (8) Revise the curriculum. (9) Decide how the unit will be structured, taught, and evaluated. (10) Carry out the plan.

6. After listing cognitive objectives for a unit, look for ways to also include affective objectives in lesson plans.   Point 11d in Suggestions for Teaching: Applying the Humanistic View in the Classroom offered in the preceding chapter was "Look for ways to introduce value clarification strategies into lesson plans." Humanistic educators argue that too often teachers concentrate exclusively on information, concepts, and skills and fail to pay sufficient attention to attitudes and values. They also argue that what is to be learned should not be divided into "domains." The kinds of objectives recommended by Mager, Gronlund, and Ojemann tend to focus attention on cognitive and psychomotor goals, although Gronlund urges teachers not to forget complex objectives such as appreciation. Accordingly, you may wish to make a systematic attempt to list affective goals for any unit of study.

In *Clarifying Values Through Subject Matter* (1973), Merrill Harmin, Howard Kirschenbaum, and Sidney Simon recommend that teachers list topics for a unit under three headings: facts, concepts, and values. (This suggestion reveals that even though humanistic educators object to dividing what is to be learned into "domains," in their own efforts to plan meaningful lessons they do just that.) But without some sort of classification scheme, you might not be able to do this very effectively. The last point made by Gronlund in his suggestions for stating objectives is that you consult reference materials for help in identifying specific types of objective. In the preceding chapter, you were introduced to the *Taxonomy of Educational Objectives: Affective Domain* and urged to refer to it when deciding how attitudes and values might be incorporated into lesson plans. To list facts and concepts—and also psychomotor skills, which are not mentioned by Harmin, Kirschenbaum, and Simon—you might refer to a description of types of learning arranged in a hierarchy and also to taxonomies of objectives that have been prepared to cover the cognitive and psychomotor domains.

Gagné's eight conditions of learning

In *The Conditions of Learning*, Robert Gagné reviews theories of learning proposed by those who have studied this form of behavior and describes the prototypes that have emerged. He then observes:

These learning prototypes all have a similar history in this respect: each of them started to be a representative of a particular variety of learning situation. . . . Pavlov was studying reflexes. . . . Köhler was studying the solving of problems by animals. By some peculiar semantic process, these examples became prototypes of learning, and thus were considered to represent the domain of learning as a whole, or at least in large part. Somehow, they came to be placed in opposition to each other: either all learning was insight or all learning was conditioned response. Such controversies have continued for years, and have been relatively unproductive in advancing our understanding learning as an event. (1970, p. 20)

This is the same point made in the introduction to Part 3 on learning and also repeated at the end of the preceding chapter on humanistic education: You are more likely to profit from what has been discovered about learning if you make selected use of techniques based on different theories than if you make exclusive use of one approach. To facilitate such a procedure, Gagné describes different sets of conditions under which learning occurs, and then proposes a hierarchy of eight progressively complex types of learning (see Figure 8-1).

Gagné's hierarchy of conditions of learning

Signal learning This is exemplified by the classical conditioning experiments of Pavlov, in which an involuntary reflex is activated by a selected stimulus (e.g., a dog salivates when a bell rings). Since such learning involves *involuntary* responses, it is basically different from the other seven types.

Stimulus-response learning This type of learning is illustrated by Skinner's operant conditioning experiments, in which voluntary actions are shaped by reinforcement (e.g., a pigeon learns to peck a disk when progressively more precise disk-pecking movements are rewarded with food pellets).

Chaining Individual acts previously acquired through S-R learning are combined when they occur in rapid succession, in the proper order, and lead to reinforcement (e.g., a novice driver learns to start a

Figure 8-1

Gagné's conditions of learning

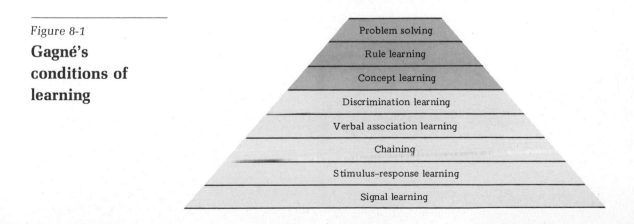

Problem solving

Rule learning

Concept learning

Discrimination learning

Verbal association learning

Chaining

Stimulus–response learning

Signal learning

car by combining the skills and observations already acquired: checking to make sure the gearshift is in neutral, inserting the key in the ignition, turning the key, waiting to hear the motor start, releasing the key, depressing the accelerator).

Verbal association learning   Verbal chains are acquired through a process that includes the following elements: S-R connections already acquired in the form of words, a *coding connection* between old and new words, contiguity of each link with the following one, an indication that the new response is correct (e.g., a high school girl who is studying French learns that *alumette* is the word for *match* because as she learns it and as she correctly answers a question asked by the teacher she says to herself, "A *match* is used to illuminate, so the word for *match* is *alumette*").

Discrimination learning   Pupils learn to vary their responses to verbal association as their store of responses becomes more numerous and complex. The major difficulty to be overcome in this type of learning is *interference* between new and old chains (e.g., students of French may forget previously learned verbal associations when they acquire new words; to prevent interference they will need to thoroughly learn distinctive chains that will permit them to differentiate between words).

Concept learning   The learner responds to things or events as a class (e.g., the child learns the concept *middle* by being presented with many sets of different objects arranged in a line and by generalizing that regardless of size or shape, *middle* always refers to the one between the others).

Rule learning   Pupils learn to combine or relate chains of concepts previously acquired in such a way that they are able to apply what they have learned to a wide variety of similar situations (e.g., a kindergarten boy combines the concepts *round* and *ball* when he learns that round things roll).

Problem solving   Individuals learn to combine rules in a way that permits them to apply the rules to a wide variety of new situations (e.g., a child who understands that round things roll puts a ball in a place where it will not roll away).

Gagné argues that the more advanced kinds of learning can take place only when a person has mastered a large variety of verbal associations, which are in turn based on a great deal of stimulus-response learning. Students are more likely to grasp a concept if they are acquainted with a variety of verbal associations, more likely to

Problem solving is based on mastery of simpler forms of learning

Signal learning, the first condition of learning in Gagné's hierarchy, is illustrated by the more or less reflexive reaction of drivers and pedestrians to traffic signals of various kinds.

Frank Siteman/Stock Boston

Chaining, the third condition in Gagné's hierarchy, is illustrated by the way a person learns to drive a car.

Bonnie Unsworth

Discrimination learning, the fifth condition in Gagné's hierarchy, is illustrated by the way students learn to discriminate between words and phrases in a foreign language laboratory.

Henry Monroe/Black Star

Problem solving, the final condition in Gagné's hierarchy, is illustrated by experiments and projects in a science laboratory.

Burt Glinn/Magnum

understand rules if they have grasped appropriate concepts, more likely to solve problems if they have a large repertoire of rules.

In *The Conditions of Learning*, Gagné offers some examples of the learning structure of mathematics (pp. 175ff.), science (pp. 180ff.), foreign language (pp. 190ff.), and English (pp. 196ff.). He lists hierarchies of things to be learned for selected topics within each of his subject areas, the hierarchies being based on his eight progressive types of learning. This is one way to map a plan for teaching a given subject. If you will be teaching one or more of the subjects outlined by Gagné, you may want to examine his examples. Even with such examples as aids, however, you may find it difficult to list verbal associations, concepts, and rules in that order because such an approach demands awareness of the *entire* structure of a given topic or subject. You have to list rules first and then work backwards. In many subjects the development of a hierarchy of things to be learned is a substantial intellectual feat.

Handbook heading
Taking into Account
the Hierarchical Nature
of Learning

Taxonomy of Educational Objectives: Cognitive Domain

Handbook heading
Using the Taxonomy of
Educational Objectives:
Cognitive Domain

You may find it helpful to augment Gagné's conditions with the *Taxonomy of Educational Objectives, Handbook I: Cognitive Domain* (1956), developed by Benjamin S. Bloom and several associates, which covers the same general types of learning as Gagné's verbal associations, concepts, rules, and problem solving. At this point an outline of the taxonomy of cognitive goals is provided (as an alternative to Gagné's hierarchy of types of learning) to serve as a framework for describing the terminal behavior you may want your students to achieve in a given topic or subject and to help you outline sequences of learning activities.

The preceding chapter introduced you to the Taxonomy of Educational Objectives: Affective Domain and urged you to use it to select attitudes and values to encourage. The taxonomy for the cognitive domain was prepared to help educators draw up academic or intellectual goals, and it represents a comprehensive classification of *all* the cognitive objectives schools should try to achieve in their efforts to produce educated citizens. If you wanted to create a complete curriculum for the entire educational career of a student, you could use the entire taxonomy as a guide. Since you are not likely to be faced with such a master planning problem, you will probably find it more helpful to focus on those sections of the taxonomy that relate to your grade level and subject area.

Taxonomy for the
cognitive domain:
Comprehensive list of
cognitive goals

The following outline will be most useful in drawing up lesson plans during your methods course, your student teaching, and your first years of professional teaching. Since it is likely to be of considerable value, you are urged to obtain the handbook containing the complete list. It is an inexpensive paperback that should be a valuable addition to your professional library. It not only presents a complete description of all the types of learning in the cognitive domain but also supplies for each type some sample test questions that might prove helpful in making up exams.

Before you examine this outline and consider how you might use it, be forewarned that you should not expect to come up with a "perfect" list of objectives on your first try. For simple skills and subjects, you may find it easy to describe terminal behavior. But if your subject matter is fairly complex, you may have to develop a list of goals through a lengthy process of experimentation, in which ideas emerge as you try out a variety of approaches to teaching. Only after you have gained complete familiarity with a given subject are you likely to be able to sit down and write out a reasonably coherent description of terminal behavior. Thus, you may find the taxonomy more meaningful *after* you have taught a year or two.

On the following pages you will find an abridged outline of the taxonomy for the cognitive domain.

Developing clear objectives may require experience

TAXONOMY OF EDUCATIONAL OBJECTIVES: COGNITIVE DOMAIN[1]

Knowledge

Knowledge of specifics

Knowledge of terminology What terms and symbols will your students need to know? (e.g., verb, noun, + −, H_2SO_4)

Knowledge of specific facts What specific facts will your students need to know? (e.g., names of the states, chief exports of Brazil, the properties of H_2SO_4)

Knowledge of ways and means of dealing with specifics

Knowledge of conventions What sets of rules will your students need to know? (e.g., rules of etiquette, rules of punctuation)

Knowledge of trends and sequences What awareness of trends and sequences will your students need to have? (e.g., nature of evolution, changes in attitudes about the role of women in American society)

Knowledge of classifications and categories What classification and category schemes will your students need to know? (e.g., types of literature, types of business ownership, types of government)

[1] In this outline the headings (with the exception of Intellectual Abilities and Skills) are the same as those in the complete taxonomy. The rest of the material is an abridgment.

Knowledge of criteria   What sets of criteria will your students need to be able to apply? (e.g., factors to consider in judging the nutritional value of a meal)

Knowledge of methodology   What sorts of methodology will your students need to master? (e.g., ways to solve problems in math, how to set up an experiment in chemistry)

Knowledge of the universals and abstractions in a field

Knowledge of principles and generalizations   What general principles will your students need to know? (e.g., laws of heredity, laws of motion)

Knowledge of theories and structure   What general theories will your students need to know? (e.g., nature of free enterprise system, theory of evolution)

Intellectual abilities and skills

Comprehension

Translation   Ability to put communication into another form. What sorts of translations will your students need to perform? (e.g., state problems in own words, read a musical score, translate words and phrases from a foreign language, interpret a diagram, grasp the meaning of a political cartoon)

Interpretation   Ability to reorder ideas, comprehend interrelationships. What sorts of interpretations will your students need to be able to make? (e.g., give their own interpretation of a novel or a poem, gather data from a variety of sources and prepare an organized report)

Extrapolation   Ability to go beyond given data. What sorts of extrapolations will your students need to make? (e.g., theorize about what might happen if . . . draw conclusions from given sets of data, predict trends)

Application   Ability to apply principles to actual situations. What sorts of applications will your students need to make? (e.g., take principles learned in math and apply them to laying out a baseball diamond, apply principles of civil liberties to current events)

Analysis   Ability to distinguish and comprehend interrelationships, make critical analyses. What kinds of analyses will your students have to make? (e.g., discuss how democracy and communism differ, be able to detect logical fallacies in an argument)

Synthesis   Ability to rearrange component ideas into a new whole. What kinds of syntheses will your students need to make? (e.g., plan a program or a panel discussion, write a comprehensive term paper)

Evaluation Ability to make judgments based on internal evidence or external criteria. What sorts of evaluations will your students need to make? (e.g., evaluate a work of art, edit a term paper, detect inconsistencies in the speech of a politician or advocate of a given position)

Now that you have become familiar with classification schemes that you might consult as you draw up instructional objectives, it is logical to turn to the types of learning that are at the bottom of Gagné's hierarchy of conditions of learning and begin to work up toward those that are at the top.

In the next two sections of this chapter, suggestions will be offered for teaching chaining, verbal associations, and discrimination. In the next chapter, techniques will be described for teaching concepts and rules that set the stage for problem solving.

Teaching skills

The type of learning Gagné refers to as *chaining* is found most clearly in the acquisition of psychomotor skills. Regardless of the grade level or subject you teach, you are likely, occasionally or frequently, to want to help your students acquire physical skills of various sorts. In the primary grades, for example, you will want your pupils to learn how to print legibly. In many subjects in junior and senior high school, psychomotor skills (e.g., driving a car, operating a sewing machine, manipulating an electric typewriter, using a power saw, swinging a golf club) may be of major if not exclusive importance. A list of psychomotor objectives and some of the research evidence on skill learning will now be examined as a prelude to considering how to teach psychomotor abilities.

Taxonomy of Educational Objectives: Psychomotor Domain

R. J. Kibler, L. L. Barker, and D. T. Miles (1970) have developed a taxonomy of educational objectives for the *psychomotor domain*. If you are asked to develop lesson plans for teaching skills or a unit or course that features psychomotor abilities, you may find it of value. An outline of the taxonomy follows.

TAXONOMY OF EDUCATIONAL OBJECTIVES: PSYCHOMOTOR DOMAIN

Gross body movements Movements that require some coordination with the eye or ear but which emphasize strength or speed

Classroom Questions: What Kinds?

This is the title of a book by Norris M. Sanders in which the Taxonomy of Educational Objectives: Cognitive Domain is used as the basis for structuring classroom activities. Here is an example of the use of the taxonomy in arranging a sequence of learning experiences for a social studies class:

Memory: What is meant by gerrymandering? (Students are asked to recall the definition given to them earlier.) . . .

Application: The mayor recently appointed a committee to study the fairness of the boundaries of the election districts in our community. Gather information about the present districts and the population in each. Determine whether the present city election districts are adequate. (Students are expected to apply principles of democracy studied in class to this new problem.)

Analysis: Analyze the reasoning in this quotation: "Human beings lack the ability to be fair when their own interests are involved. Party X controls the legislature, and now it has taken upon itself the responsibility of redrawing the boundaries of the legislative election districts. We know in advance that our party will suffer."

Synthesis: (This question must follow the preceding application question.) If current election districts in our community are inadequate, suggest how they might be redrawn.

Evaluation: Would you favor having your political party engage in gerrymandering if it had the opportunity? (1966, pp. 3–5)

Sanders notes that some students might find it difficult to cope with these

---

Movements involving upper limbs (e.g., throwing a baseball, swinging a tennis racket)

Movements involving lower limbs (e.g., kicking a soccer ball, running the hundred yard dash)

Movements involving two or more body units (e.g., swimming the breaststroke, carrying out a square dance step)

Finely coordinated movements Patterns or sequences of coordinated movements that usually involve eyes, ears, and body

Hand-finger movements (e.g., buttoning clothing without looking at it)

Hand-eye coordination (e.g., operating a jigsaw, making a woodblock print)

Hand-ear coordination (e.g., playing a violin or guitar in tune)

Hand-eye-foot coordination (e.g., operating a sewing machine, forming a vase on a potter's wheel)

questions and suggests a different approach for students who are not too highly motivated or creative. In this alternate technique, a list of questions is presented, and students are asked to decide which ones would be legitimate questions for collective bargaining. Some of the questions are:

How much should workers of various skills be paid?

How much vacation should workers have?

How fast should the assembly line move?

For what price should the products be offered for sale?

Who should be selected as the officers of a company?

How much should be paid to the owners of the company in dividends? (p. 132)

After studying the complete list of questions, students are presented with this synthesis problem: "What principles or standards can you devise that would help determine which of the above questions should be decided by collective bargaining?" (p. 133). This problem could be tackled on an individual basis or in group discussion.

Classroom Questions: What Kinds? *Contains many other examples of questions and activities for a variety of subject areas and for all grade levels. If you would like some hints on how to structure classroom experiences to develop higher-level cognitive abilities, you are urged to take a look at what Sanders has to say.*

Combinations of coordinated movements (e.g., starting a car, driving it down the street, parking it)

Nonverbal communication sets   Types of learned behavior that are used to communicate messages without the use of words

Facial expressions (e.g., communicating joy, sorrow, fear, and so on, in a dramatic performance)

Gestures (e.g., giving hand signals when acting as a referee)

Bodily Movement (e.g., expressing feelings or actions in a dance performance)

Speech behaviors   Types of learned behavior involved in speech production

Sound production (e.g., producing vowel sounds)

Sound-word formation (e.g., pronouncing words correctly)

Sound projection (e.g., making oneself heard at the back of an auditorium)

Sound-gesture coordination (e.g., using gestures and movement to make speech more comprehensible or to present a song more effectively)

Although this outline may be of some value to you in planning psychomotor learning experiences, you may find that you are more interested in the details of how to achieve these objectives than in listing or classifying them. If you will be teaching tennis, ceramics, sewing, or typing, for example, you will probably not need to refer to the taxonomy to determine the basic skills your students will need to master. You will be aware that you want them to acquire a smooth backhand stroke, throw a pot on the wheel, sew a seam, or type fifty words a minute. You may desire some guidelines, however, when the time comes to figure out exactly how you plan to help your students acquire these skills. For that purpose, analyses of skill learning based on S-R theory may be of value.

Conditions for chaining

The term *efficiency expert* conveys the way S-R theory is applied to skill learning. Most large companies hire psychologists to analyze how workers can be trained to carry out their jobs in the most efficient manner. This is usually done by following the procedure Skinner recommends for programmed instruction. First, the terminal behavior is described, then ways to achieve that end result in step-by-step fashion are delineated. This procedure is illustrated by Gagné's analysis of chaining, the third form of learning in his hierarchy. Here is an example of the chain of actions that need to be carried out in order for a person to operate a drill press. It is based on a description of chaining presented on pages 128–131 of *The Conditions of Learning.*

A student might build up a chain of movements necessary to operate a drill press by carrying out the following sequence of steps:

1. Each individual S-R connection must have been previously learned (e.g., to operate a drill press, the person must select a drill of the correct size, lock it in the chuck, arrange the belt on the pulleys to produce the correct spindle speed, set the depth stop, clamp the object to be drilled on the table, switch on the motor, and rotate the feed handle until it reaches the depth stop).

2. The steps, or links, in the chain must be performed in the proper order. You could teach this either by demonstrating the proper sequence and then inviting the learner to perform or by using verbal instructions as prompts (e.g., "All right, now that you have selected the drill of the correct size and type, how do you make sure that it will turn at the proper speed so that it will cut through this kind of material most efficiently?").

Chaining: Step-by-step progression toward terminal behavior

Handbook heading
Ways to Use Chaining

3. The individual steps must be performed in close succession to establish the chain.

4. Repetition is usually necessary if the act is to be performed easily and efficiently, since it often takes several tries to smooth out clumsy and superfluous movements.

5. The terminal step, or link, must result in success, which provides reinforcement (e.g., the hole must be drilled to the correct depth in the right place in the material).

6. Once a psychomotor skill has been learned, it can be generalized (e.g., the technique for operating one drill press can be appied to a slightly different drill press). However, it may be necessary to teach the student to discriminate if there is a significant difference in the second act (e.g., operating a table-mounted drill press, a floor-mounted drill press made by a different manufacturer, or a radial drill press).

In analyzing the ways chains of responses are learned, psychologists have speculated quite a bit about which kinds of cues are the most helpful. It would appear that *external* cues, provided through verbal instruction and demonstration, are generally better than physical manipulation of the learner, because skills must be learned through a personal process of trial and error. A clear example of this is the baby learning to walk. Toddlers must learn to master their muscles and nervous system by trying to walk, making an error, trying again, reducing the error, and so on until they become expert walkers. The same process is necessary in learning any sensorimotor skill—learners have to do it themselves. If someone else tries to do it for them, the process may be impeded. Consequently, it seems preferable for teachers to take this into account and provide external cues but not physical guidance when assisting students to master psychomotor skills. The basic techniques for providing such cues—demonstration and verbal guidance—will now be discussed.

Suggestions for teaching: Providing demonstrations and guided practice

Here are some suggestions, based on Gagné's analysis of the conditions for learning chains, for how you might put the techniques of demonstration and verbal guidance into practice in teaching skills.

1. If possible and appropriate, analyze the skill to ascertain the specific psychomotor abilities necessary to perform it; arrange these component abilities in order, and help students to master them in this sequence.

2. Provide demonstrations, and as students practice, give verbal guidance to aid in mastery of the skill.

    a. Demonstrate the entire procedure straight through, then describe the links of the chain in sequence, and finally demonstrate the skill again step by step.

    b. Allow ample time for students to practice immediately after the demonstrations.

    c. As students practice, give guidance verbally or in a way that permits them to perform the skill themselves.

    d. Give guidance in a relaxed, noncritical atmosphere and in a positive form.

3. Be alert to generalization and interference.

1. If possible and appropriate, analyze the skill to ascertain the specific psychomotor abilities necessary to perform it; arrange these component abilities in order, and help students master them in this sequence.   When S-R theory is applied to the teaching of a skill, the first step is to analyze the terminal behavior of the skill in order to isolate the links in the chain. The next step is to arrange the links in

the proper sequence, and the final one is to shape the desired behavior. Military and industrial psychologists often use this technique. First, they perform a *task analysis* to isolate the components of a skill; next they arrange the components in the most efficient order; and then they train personnel to follow the chain exactly. Although the technique works fine for disassembling a rifle or assembling a spark plug, it may not function too well with more complex tasks. If learners are required to concentrate too much on the separate steps, focusing of attention may prevent them from linking steps in a natural, fluid way.

For example, some coaches, impressed by the task analysis technique and eager to apply scientific methods to sports, will watch an expert tennis player or golfer and then describe the steps involved in serving or putting. Afterwards they assist novice athletes to follow these movements step by step. In some cases, this method works very well, but in others, learners get so involved in thinking about the steps that they are distracted from developing the smooth, coordinated movement they are trying to acquire. Moreover, some learners may be forced into using a style unnatural to them. If you watch sports on TV, you are well aware of how much variety there is in the way professional athletes hit a baseball or shoot a basketball. And you probably realize that professional athletes are *not* thinking, "Step one, step two, step three," as they perform.

It is told of Yogi Berra, the legendary Yankee catcher, that early in his career he encountered an efficiency-expert coach who wanted to make hitting as scientific as possible. The coach kept urging all the players to analyze what they were doing when they were at the plate. Yogi tried to follow this advice, but after striking out five straight times, he rejected the theory, saying, "How can you think and hit at the same time?" Expert performers may be handicapped if they think too much, but this may not be true of novices—though even beginners may be bothered by too much advice.

Also, some skills appear to be more teachable than others. for example, it has been hypothesized that the primary reason baseball rules were recently changed to favor the hitter more was that pitching, which is preplanned and methodical, can be taught, while hitting, which involves a spontaneous and instantaneous reaction, cannot. Many baseball men argue that hitters are born, not made. Perhaps this explains Yogi Berra's problem. Hitters don't have time to think; they simply react. As you speculate about the possibility of using a task analysis approach, you might ask yourself whether the skill is a mechanical one, which should be performed in a premeditated, unvarying way, or a spontaneous response, which must be performed more or less instinctively.

There are substantial differences of opinion about the desirability of using a programmed approach in teaching many skills. To draw your own conclusions, you might attempt a simple task analysis of a skill you want your students to acquire, then make tentative efforts at shaping their behavior. If a step-by-step approach helps some students, continue to use it with them. But if others seem upset by analytic methods and are obviously "thinking too much," you might present skills as complete coordinated actions. It is possible that the analytic and thematic styles of conceptualization described by Kagan (1964a) also apply to the learning of skills.

Skinner's programmed technique of teaching handwriting (which was described in Chapter 5) illustrates many of the advantages and disadvantages of an S-R approach to teaching skills. With this method students are systematically helped to perform the movements necessary to write each of the letters of the alphabet. They begin by tracing the complete letter and eventually learn to perform the proper movements as the prompts (tracing models of parts of the letter) are gradually vanished, or withdrawn. When the students have mastered all the letters, they put them together into words. Thus they learn to assemble all the links in the chain through repeated activity, which gives immediate reinforcement.

However, some primary grade teachers who watched a film on the skinner technique speculated that the rather jerky movements many students made as they traced the letters, particularly when the tracing models consisted of only parts of the letter, might actually interfere with the acquisition of a smooth, flowing hand. No research evidence on this point is available, but it does seem that some children might respond more favorably to a global approach, which teaches them from the beginning to write each letter in one smooth motion.

If you will be teaching a complex skill such as typing, sewing, or cooking, you will probably be given abundant information about the most efficient techniques when you take a special methods of teaching course. Many complex skills have been analyzed in minute detail by teams of specialists. There are even time-and-motion studies on ways to make a sandwich and wash dishes. If you do not encounter such analyses in a teacher education course, you will probably be able to find detailed descriptions in one of the professional journals in your field.

Whether you use an analytic or global approach, the basic technique of teaching skills is to encourage the students to perform the necessary movements in sequence. In most cases you can do this by providing first a model for the learner to follow (demonstration) and second mediating links in the form of verbal instructions (guidance).

2. Provide demonstratons, and as students practice, give verbal guidance to aid mastery of the skill.

   a. Demonstrate the entire procedure straight through, then describe the links of the chain in sequence, and finally demonstrate the skill again step by step.   First, tell what you are going to do, and then demonstrate the entire procedure, because the resulting overall impression will serve as an advance organizer. If you have any doubts about your ability to perform a skill or conduct a demonstration, practice the night before. If you discover you can't perform the skill very well, have a student do the demonstration. A poorly coordinated and out-of-shape high school basketball coach once explained to the varsity team the advantages of a new way to shoot foul shots. The method sounded logical, and the team was all for it until the coach demonstrated—and missed eight out of ten tries. The players lost confidence in both the coach and the method. Your students won't demand that you be better than they are in all phases of the skill you teach. In many cases it may be preferable to invite one of your better pupils to show a technique you can't perform particularly well yourself.

If you do perform the demonstration yourself, resist the temptation to show off. You may make your students feel too inferior to try the skill, or you may bore or antagonize them to the point that they will stop paying attention. For example, a wood-shop teacher in a junior high school made a practice of demonstrating the use of the various tools with an ostentatiously effortless performance of the limited skills the students would be allowed to attempt. Then as an encore the teacher would do an advanced trick, pointing out that it was much too difficult for beginners but that it was just meant to show what *could* be done by an expert. Instead of working on their own projects, the class had to stand around and "oh" and "ah." After a while, none of the pupils would go to this teacher for assistance for fear they might set off another performance. (The accident rate in this shop was abnormally high.)

After you complete the initial demonstration, describe the links of the chain in the correct order (you will probably want to do a limited task analysis beforehand). Emphasize the crucial links, and point out the tricky points to watch out for. It frequently helps to list such points on the board and refer to them as you demonstrate the skill again step by step. For example, in demonstrating to first graders how to print *p* and *q*, emphasize which side of the letters the vertical line goes on. In teaching biology students how to set up a microscope, list the proper sequence of steps.

b. Allow ample time for students to practice immediately after the demonstrations.   Allow plenty of time for everyone to have a crack at the skill immediately after it has been demonstrated. After arousing pupils' interest by showing them something new, it is illogical—and a bit unfair—to force them to divert their attention to something else. If you don't have enough equipment for all your students, it is probably better to demonstrate to only a half or a third of the class at a time.

Handbook heading
How to Give
Demonstrations

© 1963 United Feature Syndicate, Inc.

Also, in order to maximize reinforcement, you should set up practice sessions in such a way that you are free to circulate around the class and provide specific suggestions on an individual basis.

In planning practice sessions, keep in mind that learning is more likely to take place if your students are active, if you permit them to perform the skill many times, and if you arrange the sessions so that they receive immediate reinforcement for every response. If most of the class has trouble with one particular phase of a skill, review this part and again demonstrate the proper way to do it. In fact, a good policy is to give spontaneous demonstrations whenever you discover even a few individuals making the same mistake. Students are likely to pay closer attention to these popular-demand demonstrations than to the formal, and perhaps somewhat artificial, ones.

c. As students practice, give guidance verbally or in a way that permits them to perform the skill themselves.   It is tempting to give manual assistance in many skills; for example, you may take a first grader's hand in yours and push it around the paper in an effort to improve the child's printing. As noted earlier, this kind of guidance does little good and may even cause added difficulty. Students must learn to master their own muscles and nerves. If they are passive instruments with you at the controls, they gain nothing from the experience. When they are later required to perform the skill, their only resources will be their own brains and muscles. You may get a satisfying feeling that you are speeding up the learning process when you do things for pupils, but you may actually be forcing them to depend on you and cheating them of practice.

d. Give guidance in a relaxed, noncritical atmosphere and in a positive form.   Most students, especially older ones, are self-conscious about trying new psychomotor skills for fear they will make mistakes and look silly. You can minimize this feeling by encouraging a devil-may-care approach. The more relaxed novices are, the more likely they are to give it a try. (A relaxed, unhurried atmosphere should not be reserved only for discovery sessions.)

Emphasizing the right way to perform a skill is usually the most helpful kind of guidance. But when a student has an especially stubborn problem in mastering a particular skill or one aspect of it, deliberate exaggeration of the error may be helpful. This technique, sometimes referred to as the *Beta hypothesis*, was first described by Knight Dunlap (1949). Exasperated by a quirk in his typing technique that caused him to type "hte" for "the," Dunlap deliberately banged out several dozen "hte's" and to his surprise discovered that he was then in a position to relearn the correct movements. On reflection he concluded that he had previously fixated the wrong response to the point that it had become an automatic, unthinking reaction. By delib-

Giving a demonstration and then encouraging pupils to practice is a basic technique for teaching a physical skill.

Terry McKoy

erately *thinking* about the error, he had been able to bring it under his control and relearn the right response. Subsequently, Dunlap applied the Beta hypothesis to the treatment of stuttering. Encouraging children to exaggerate their stuttering seemed to help in many cases.

Coaches have used the Beta hypothesis to help athletes. Divers who habitually make an awkward movement are told to exaggerate the error in practice and then relearn the dive from the beginning. If you encounter pupils who keep doing the wrong thing and can't seem to help themselves, you might have them exaggerate the error and then start all over again to learn the correct technique. In addition, if *you*, the teacher, demonstrate an error in an extreme way, especially when students first encounter the trouble spot, this will help make them aware of the tricky mistake they are making. Doing this in a good-natured way may reduce some of the tension that often accompanies awkwardness.

Handbook heading
Applying the Beta
Hypothesis

3. Be alert to generalization and negative transfer.   Students may encounter difficulty learning a new skill if they generalize by applying specialized movements previously learned in performing a related but different skill (e.g., using a baseball swing to hit a golf ball). When something that has been previously learned interferes with the acquisition of a new skill, psychologists say *negative transfer* has occurred because the carry-over (or transfer) is negative or unfortunate. If you have ever had to alternate between driving a car with a stick shift and one with an automatic transmission, you have had direct experience with negative transfer in the psychomotor domain.

Negative transfer:
Previous learning
interferes

To correct for generalization, the best approach may be to explain to the learner that the new skill requires special movements of its own. To cope with negative transfer, probably the best policy is to help learners remain constantly aware that they are performing a skill in which interference is likely to occur. For example, the driver switching from one type of shift to another might keep thinking, "I'm driving a car with a stick shift." (When Sweden changed from left-lane to right-lane driving, an extensive, systematic campaign was conducted to inform all drivers about the nature of negative transfer and to keep them thinking, "Drive on the right.")

As you observe the attempts of your students to master a new skill, you will probably detect certain general trends in the way they progress. These trends have been studied systematically and have been plotted graphically in the form of learning curves.

Implications of the learning curve

When the progress of an organism in learning a skill is plotted on a graph, the most typical pattern is illustrated in Figure 8-2. This curve is a highly oversimplified presentation of a complex process, and some psychologists argue that learning curves either represent a nonexistent phenomenon or are too unreliable to be of value. But if the concept is not taken too literally, it can be useful in pointing up some trends in skill learning (and also related trends in cognitive learning).

Think back to your own efforts at learning a foreign language or geometry, typing or tennis. You probably got off to a slow start the first week or so. Just how slow the start was depended mainly on how much previous experience in related skills you brought with you. If you took French before Spanish, for example, you had a big jump on

Figure 8-2

A hypothetical learning curve

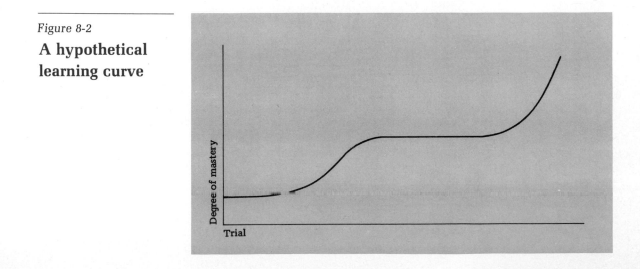

Learning curve:
Leveling off after initial
improvement

your fellow students in Spanish class. Even so, your first efforts were undoubtedly a bit clumsy. After you got the hang of it, though, you probably went through a period of rapid improvement. The first flush of success usually makes a new activity enjoyable to beginners and motivates them to keep trying. It is likely that you eventually reached a leveling-off stage. When that happened, your continued mastery of the activity probably depended on whether it had a special appeal for you or whether you were required to go on using it. If you took Spanish or geometry only to satisfy a college requirement, you undoubtedly forgot most of it. If you periodically used your typing skill to prepare term papers, you probably maintained a fair degree of proficiency. If you enjoyed tennis so much that you played twice a week, you probably came close to achieving your potential.

The learning curve provides some supplementary suggestions for teaching skills.

Suggestions for teaching: Implications of the learning curve

1. When presenting a new skill, give extra assistance and encouragement to the slow starters.

2. Make the most of initial interest and enthusiasm.

3. When a leveling off of interest or improvement occurs, either encourage continued practice to maintain the skill or help students master advanced techniques.

Handbook heading
Implications of the
Learning Curve

1. When presenting a new skill, give extra assistance and encouragement to the slow starters.   The initial rate of learning a skill depends on a person's readiness and innate ability. Pupils who have had considerable previous experience with an activity or have a special affinity for a skill or subject will learn much more rapidly during the first few days than those who do not. Inexperienced pupils may need special attention and encouragement the first few days. Otherwise, the way some of their classmates whiz along may destroy their self-confidence and squelch their eagerness to try.

2. Make the most of initial interest and enthusiasm.   As earlier noted, once students have experienced some success, they are especially susceptible to encouragement, so make the most of their excitement about improving. Eventually, though, a point at which no further improvement is discernible will be reached.

3. When a leveling off of interest or improvement occurs, either encourage continued practice to maintain the skill or help students master advanced techniques.   If the leveling off occurs after satisfactory performance has been attained, occasional practice is usually

sufficient to enable the students to maintain the skill. If you want your pupils to develop *maximum* proficiency, however, you will need to be alert to these *plateaus* in the learning curve—periods of no apparent improvement. They are called plateaus because this is what they resemble on a learning curve diagram—a flat surface at a higher level than the original level of learning.

The phenomenon first received attention in a study of how novice telegraphers learn to send and receive Morse code (Bryan and Harter, 1897). The study revealed that after a few weeks of training most of the students hit a plateau that lasted a week or two and then experienced another spurt of learning. Analysis suggested that the telegraphers had initially reacted to each letter as a separate entity and that after they had developed considerable skill in sending and receiving in this way, their improvement leveled off. Then suddenly, and more or less unconsciously, they started thinking in terms of words rather than letters. They reacted to the word *the,* for example, as one unified burst of dots and dashes instead of three discrete letters.

Perhaps the main point to remember about plateaus is that they are common. Since you will not always be able to identify them or make specific suggestions to your pupils on how to shorten or eliminate them, the best policy is probably to do what you can to encourage continued effort. Without encouragement, a student may quit just when he or she is on the verge of attaining genuine proficiency. If you ever took music lessons, for example, it may be that you were forced to keep practicing during a phase when you wanted to chuck the whole thing. But if you persevered, perhaps you learned to play so well that you could devote your thoughts to the subtleties of interpretation rather than to the proper placement of your fingers and arms. At that point you probably began to enjoy yourself.

Once a skill has been almost perfected, extinction is usually no longer a problem. A person rarely forgets how to swim or ride a bicycle. The most logical explanation for this is that a great many repetitions are necessary to master the skill in the first place and that the exercise of the skill even for a short time provides abundant reinforcement. For example, if you know how to type, consider the number of times you must have hit each key as you practiced. Add to this the number of times you hit each key every time you type a term paper. In view of the thousands or millions of repetitions and reinforcements involved in the mastery and use of a skill such as typing, swimming, and riding a bicycle, it is not surprising that a person who has not used such a skill for several years can quickly get back into the swing of it.

Now that you have examined suggestions for teaching skills, suggestions that are related to or derived from Gagné's description of chaining, it is time to move up his hierarchy. The fourth and fifth types listed by Gagné are *verbal association* and *discrimination* learning.

These two forms of learning are of significance whenever students are asked to memorize and remember information, and the next section of this chapter is devoted to that topic.

Helping students memorize and remember

Much of what we learn has to be memorized. Primary graders must memorize the alphabet and thousands of words when they learn to read, numbers and the multiplication table when they learn math. Throughout the elementary grades pupils continue to memorize new words and commit hundreds of facts to memory. In almost any course at the secondary level, students must memorize key terms and ideas. In some courses, such as shorthand or foreign language, memorizing is the basic technique of learning. Accordingly, you will want to do what you can to help your pupils memorize with a minimum of difficulty and remember what they learn. A logical way to focus attention on ways you might help a student (including yourself) remember what is learned is to consider the structure of memory.

The structure of memory

Psychologists who have studied the nature of remembering and forgetting have postulated that the structure of memory is made up of two storage systems: a short-term store (STM or STS) and a long-term store (LTM or LTS). All of us are continuously bombarded by stimuli and incoming information. There are hundreds of words on this page, for example, and hundreds of thousands in this book. The same is true of all the other texts you are studying this term. When you go to class, you are exposed to other information, presented orally when a professor lectures. You also watch demonstrations and films, read supplementary materials, and engage in discussions with classmates.

Sections of this text (or of a lecture or film or the equivalent) that you attend to or concentrate on are retained in your short-term memory. Information or stimuli that you fail to attend to are not retained. Immediately after you finish reading this section, you will be able to recall ideas that are stored in your short-term memory. But if a bit of information does not impress you for one reason or another, or if you do not make any effort to remember what you can recall a few minutes from now, you probably would not do very well on an exam given two weeks from today. In order to shift what you learn from your short-term store to your long-term store, you need to assimilate it (to use Piaget's term) or code it (to use the memory specialist's term) in some way. Your memory is somewhat analogous to a filing cabinet with a fixed capacity. There are only so many bits of information you can

Long-term storage depends on coding

retain in your memory at one time; and as new items enter the short-term store, they tend to push out items that have not been attended to, assimilated, or coded.

The filing cabinet analogy also calls attention to another significant point about memory: Retrieving or recalling information may be more of a problem than storage. Sigmund Freud's description of levels of consciousness[2] calls attention to the fact that there are many experiences stored in our memories that we may be unable to recall. In dreams, under hypnosis, and when we free associate either intentionally or unintentionally, we recall many "forgotten" memories. (It has also been demonstrated [Penfield, 1969] that when brain pathways are touched with electric probes during neurological operations on epileptic patients, they recall details of events that had apparently been forgotten.)

The memory "filing cabinet" not only has a limited capacity, but also its contents may be arranged as if ideas were filed by a not terribly well organized secretary. We may know the information is in there, but we cannot always go directly to the right section of the right drawer to pull it out. If you have ever remembered the answer to a question just after you handed in an exam, you can appreciate the significance of retrieval of information. In considering ways to help students remember, therefore, it is important to think not only about how information might be stored in long-term memory but also about ways that information can later be retrieved when needed.

The description of the structure of memory and the filing cabinet analogy can be of assistance to you as student and teacher because they lead to the question, What are some of the factors that cause us to attend to or assimilate or encode information during the time it is in our short-term store? Or, to put it in different words, What can I do to memorize and be able to retrieve information that I will want or need to remember later?

Factors that lead to long-term storage

Attention getters: Size, color, intensity, novelty, unexpectedness

One answer to those questions centers on what attracts your attention. Generally speaking, you are more likely to attend to a stimulus if it stands out because of such qualities as size, color, intensity, novelty, or unexpectedness. You are also likely to attend to stimuli that are of personal significance at the moment. (This is a point emphasized by cognitive psychologists and by Kurt Lewin's concept of the life space.

[2] Freud postulated three levels of consciousness. The *conscious* consists of all mental processes a person is aware of at a given moment. The *preconscious* (or *foreconscious*) consists of memories that can be readily recalled, particularly by the association of ideas. The *unconscious*, which comprises the largest part of the mind, is made up of memories that may influence thinking and behavior but cannot be recalled (except under such special circumstances as dreams, hypnotic states, psychoanalysis, or free associations).

Depending on the forces acting on you at any given moment, you may or may not pay attention to a stimulus. Just before lunch, for example, when you are hungry and tired, you may find it much more difficult to stay awake and attentive in class than earlier in the morning.)

Another answer to questions about how to retain information in the long-term store centers on aids to coding or assimilation. Perhaps the most important single factor can be summed up in the word *meaningfulness*. If this discussion of memory helps you grasp how you might improve your abilities as a student and teacher, it is likely—without a great deal of effort or repetition—to become a part of your long-term store. The same will be true of what you teach. If you are successful in presenting subject matter so that it makes sense to your students or can be related to important aspects of their lives, it is likely to be remembered and retrieved. Other factors that lead to assimilation or encoding are summed up in the words *familiarity, associations, mnemonics, patterns,* or *structure, activity* or *involvement,* and *imagery* or *representations*.

In a review of research on meaningful learning, Ronald E. Johnson (1975) concludes that "meaningfulness is potentially the most powerful variable for explaining the learning of complex verbal discourse" (pp. 425–426). In defining meaningfulness, Johnson notes: "Learning may be said to be meaningful to the extent that the new learning task can be related to the existing cognitive structure of the learner, i.e., the residual of his earlier learnings" (p. 427). This observation stresses the point that memories are more likely to be retained in one's long-term store if they can be related to what is familiar—or already remembered. Another way of stressing the same idea is to say that a new idea associated with an old one is likely to be remembered. Johnson emphasizes that the degree of meaningfulness depends on the "associational background of the learner" (p. 427). The use of the word *association* calls attention to the significance of connecting what is to be learned with what one already knows. In making associations, it is desirable to relate ideas of maximum depth and richness, since superficial similarities are not likely to lead to encoding. Sometimes, however, what is to be learned is not logical or sensible, and it may be necessary to resort to mnemonic devices.

Mnemonic devices are jingles or phrases such as "i before e except after c" that we use to tie together ideas. You may recall the description in Chapter 6 of Jerome Bruner's experiment involving the memorization of pairs of words. Children who were encouraged to develop their own mnemonic devices, or mediators, learned and remembered much more successfully than children who did not use such memory aids. Bruner and other cognitive psychologists explain the values of mediators by suggesting that when we learn how things are related, we are able to use one point to help us recall other points. When you present a lesson, therefore, your students are more likely to remember

Meaningfulness a key factor in remembering

Mnemonic devices (mediators)

A carefully prepared lecture outline can function as a helpful advance organizer.

Ron Benvenisti/Magnum

what you emphasize if you call their attention to the organization of points.

If you will be teaching older students, you might consider the use of *advance organizers.* As noted in Chapter 6, David P. Ausubel (1960) found that giving a brief overview of what was to be covered helped students learn and remember a presentation that covered the previewed points in greater detail. He hypothesized that this occurred because the preview served to provide an advance organization of points that students were then able to use to integrate and relate material they later studied. Subsequent research (Barnes and Clawson, 1975) has led to the conclusion that advance organizers are not always effective. One explanation for this finding is that students must be capable of formal operations (to use Piaget's term) or the symbolic mode of thought (to use Bruner's term) in order to benefit from advance organizers, since they must deal with ideas in the abstract.

Advance organizers better for older students

Therefore, some uses of advance organizers may have been ineffective because the students were not capable of formal thinking. Another reason advance organizers may not always help students learn is that the organization chosen by the teacher may not make sense to students. Bruner found that children who were encouraged to develop their own mnemonic devices learned and remembered more than those who used mediators supplied by others. Consequently, you might find that giving a brief overview of a topic and then asking students to help you select major points and arrange them in order will lead to better results than presenting *your* version of advance organizers.

Activity, either verbal or physical, often can be used to help students code material in the long-term storage system. This point was first established when A. I. Gates (1917) discovered that students who spent half or more of their study time actively talking about material remembered more than those who studied silently. It has also been established that physical activity aids memorization. Kunihara and Asher (1965) demonstrated that foreign language students learned vocabulary faster and were more likely to retain it when they acted out the words they were studying. When students were learning to say *sit, stand,* and *walk* in Japanese, for example, they carried out these actions.

A final factor that aids encoding is use of imagery. In *The Mind of a Mnemonist: A Little Book About a Vast Memory* (1968), A. R. Luria describes how a Russian man who had a "photographic memory" used imagery along with other mnemonic devices of many kinds to build up associations. When asked to memorize nonsense syllables (meaningless combinations of letters), for example, the man would associate them with a series of imaginary actions. A related technique is called the *loci method,* first used by Greek and Roman orators before the birth of Christ. *Loci* is the plural of *locus,* which is Latin for *place.* To use this technique, you should think of a particular place, such as the street on which you live. Then imagine that you are walking down the street and visualize an object or a situation to be remembered superimposed on or next to a feature of the familiar location. Other ways imagery can be used to encode information is through concrete words and pictures that make memorable situations or combinations. These can be presented by a teacher or developed by students themselves. When students develop and actually record their own images, the images may be more meaningful and at the same time more likely to be remembered because motor activity (in drawing or writing) accompanies cognitive activity.

Many of the techniques just described for coding material in the long-term storage system are discussed and illustrated in *The Memory Book* (1974) by Harry Lorayne and Jerry Lucas, both of whom have enjoyed notable success as memory experts. They point out that the basic rule of memorization is: Associate what you want to learn with something you already know. The key to performing memory feats is to add a phrase to that basic rule: But make the association "in a ridiculous way" (p. 9). Instead of selecting conventional associations, you should imagine associations that involve incongruous substitutions or exaggerations, preferably combined with action.

To illustrate the Lorayne-Lucas technique, suppose you want to memorize Gagné's eight conditions of learning. If you were to read

Verbal or physical activity leads to remembering

Imagery and the loci method

Key to memory feats: Ridiculous associations

The Conditions of Learning carefully, or if you already have a substantial background in the psychology of learning, you would probably be able to describe all eight conditions by logically classifying types of learning, just as Gagné did when he developed his hierarchy. But in the absence of complete information and if you are pressed for time, you might conjure up the following mnemonic "dramatization."

The first type of learning described by Gagné is *signal* learning. To fix that in your mind imagine Ivan Pavlov dressed up like a Russian peasant (complete with beard, tunic, and boots) ringing a huge bell *signaling* to a thousand salivating dogs that it is chow time. Next, choose a ridiculous, impossible, incongruous way to associate signal with *stimulus-response* learning. Picture an irate rat (also dressed as a Russian peasant) marching around a Skinner box waving a signal flag with the letters *S-R* ("signaling rat") embroidered on it. As it waves the S-R flag, the rat also shouts at B. F. Skinner (who is peering into the box), "Stimulus-response, shtimulus-response. You can stimulate but I'm not going to respond unless I get caviar instead of food pellets." The demand is ignored, so the rat calls to a stool pigeon in a nearby cage and urges it to send a message to the police. The stool pigeon persuades a carrier pigeon to deliver the message, and the police come and take Skinner away after *chaining* him up. Skinner, still in chains, is taken to a courtroom where he is defended by the legal firm of Walk, Jog, Run, Sprint, and Associates. The lawyers who make up this firm take the form of verbs with arms and legs. (Imagine the verbs *walk, jog, run,* and *sprint* with arms and legs attached to them.) Together, they function as a *verbal association* of lawyers. The members of the verbal association argue their case on a huge disk that rotates faster and faster. Walk, Jog, Run, and Sprint are thrown closer and closer to the disk's rim until *discrimination* takes place. When that occurs, the judge declares Skinner guilty and sentences him to ten years in prison. But Skinner is immediately pardoned for good behavior (modification), which makes him an ex-*con*—ex*cept* that he never served time in the slammer. The ex-con ('cept he isn't) is met at the gates of the prison by thousands of psychologists who place a crown of pigeon feathers (plucked from the stool pigeon) on his head, kneel down, and ask him to *rule* over them. Skinner refuses, however, because he says he has a *problem* to *solve*—how to convert a Skinner box to supply caviar instead of food pellets.

To discover if this story helps you remember the eight conditions of learning in order, read it over again and then see if you can remember the hierarchy clearly enough to be able to list all eight conditions in the proper sequence. If you can't, try making up your own chain of associations. Once you have memorized the eight conditions of learning the Lorayne-Lucas way, it would be desirable to examine the sequence logically and relate it to points you remember from the discussion of different types of learning in earlier chapters of this text. (You are reminded that in his review of the role of meaningfulness in learning, Ronald E. Johnson stressed that encoding is more likely to take place if ideas of maximum depth and richness are associated.)

To learn abstract words or phrases that have no apparent meaning, Lorayne and Lucas recommend that you think of something that sounds like or reminds you of what is to be learned and "that *can be pictured* in your mind" (p. 21). To remember Beta hypothesis, for example, you might imagine you are water skiing on the African Bay of Ta when you encounter a scholarly looking hippo (complete with spectacles and pipe) writing a Ph.D. thesis (making it a hippo-thesis) on a huge typewriter. (To remember what the Beta hypothesis is, imagine that the hippo has just typed *hte* instead of *the*.)

To learn names, Lorayne and Lucas recommend that you first make up substitute sounds or phrases for names, preferably substitutes that involve imagery and/or action, and then associate these substitute words with distinctive features of individuals. For *Smith*, picture a blacksmith hammering; for *Morris*, think of *more rice* (perhaps imagine a truckload of rice being dumped on a table.) For *Mary*, think of *marry*; for *Henry*, think of a hen reeling. Lorayne and Lucas supply substitute words for six hundred of the most common names in America on pages 54–65 of *the Memory Book*. If you are serious about wanting to memorize names, you might refer to this list. But keep in mind that Bruner found that self-developed mediators are often more effective than those supplied by others. You may find that you will remember names better if you make up your own substitute words, perhaps after checking the Lorayne and Lucas list for ideas.

Suppose you decide to concentrate on learning first names the first day you meet a class. If the first pupil in the first row is named Mary, you should think *marry* and then select a feature of her appearance that impresses you as distinctive. Once you pick out that feature, you should concoct a ridiculous association between the substitute word and the feature. Assume that Mary has big blue eyes. To remember her name, you might imagine a long parade of brides walking out of her eyes on their way to get married. If a large-eared boy named Henry sits next to Mary, picture millions of hens drunkenly reeling in one of his ears and out the other. After learning first names, you can follow the same procedure to learn last names.

If you will be teaching a subject (such as a foreign language) that requires learning many new words, Lorayne and Lucas recommend that you urge your pupils to associate the word to be learned with the English equivalent by imagining a ridiculous picture of some sort. To learn that the French word for *ham* is *jambon*, for example, think of a French chef jamming a bone into a gigantic ham. To help students remember if nouns are masculine or feminine, Lorayne and Lucas suggest you work singing into all images involving feminine nouns, because sopranos (who are feminine) often sing *la, la, la.* If you recall an image that does not involve singing, assume that it is masculine. Since your French chef is not singing as he jams the bone into the ham, you correctly assume that it is *le jambon.*

Why and how we forget

Here are some explanations of why and how we forget:

Disuse leads to fading of brain trace

Disuse The idea this word denotes is that people forget when the brain trace, which is the physical record of memory, fades away. This fading is analogous to the atrophy of a muscle that is not used. No one has yet come up with a satisfactory explanation of exactly what goes on in the brain when we learn something. There is agreement that *some* sort of change, or connection, takes place, but the exact nature of this process is yet to be pinned down. (Current research suggests that ribonucleic acid is the key.) Even so, it does seem logical to assume that a thought or idea or bit of knowledge that is used frequently becomes more strongly implanted than something that is only briefly considered, that an idea is made more permanent in individual consciousness every time it is activated.

Suppose you are able to learn the names of all the pupils in five different classes the first week of a new year. By the end of the report period, you will probably remember only the names of those pupils who ask to be called on quite often. If a student doesn't ask to be recognized until the end of the report period, you may have to mumble, "Yes?" and hope that this will sound a little bit like the actual name. Frequent repetition of names strengthens the brain trace; disuse, on the other hand, appears to cause names to fade quickly from memory.

Some memories are reorganized or distorted

Reorganization Reorganization (sometimes called *distortion* or *trace transformation*) is more a description of what happens to memories than a cause of forgetting, but it merits mention. Quite frequently we don't forget things completely; a residue remains. When you are asked to supply an answer to a question about some rarely used idea, you may generalize and fill in the gaps with stray bits of related ideas you happen to rememer.

Reorganization is illustrated perfectly—and hilariously—in a book entitled *1066 and All That* (1931) by Walter Carruthers Sellar and Robert Julian Yeatman. This delightful little volume presents English history as a typical ex-student might recall it ten years after graduation. One example: "Joan of Ark was a French descendant of Noah, who, after hearing angel voices singing Do Re Mi, became inspired, thus unfairly defeating the English in several battles." As the authors

A few things you probably never knew

To illustrate the nature of reorganization, as well as the way the mind of a child works, here are a few statements originally handed in to an elementary school teacher, later published in a New York newspaper, and eventually included in an anthology by H. Allen Smith entitled Don't Get Perconel with a Chicken. (An earlier work of the same type was called Write Me a Poem, Baby [1956].)

We don't raise silk worms in the U.S. because the U.S. gets her silk from rayon. He is a much larger animal and gives more silk.

Denver is just below the O in Colorado.

An adjective is a word hanging down from a noun.

They don't raise anything in Kansas but alpaca grain and they have to irritate that to make it grow.

The Mediterranean and the Red Sea are connected by the sewage canal.

Marconi invented the Atlantic Ocean.

Abraham Lincoln was shot by Clare Boothe Luce.

When a man has more than one wife he is a pigamist.

A epidemic is a needle that puts you to sleep.

A spinster is a bachelors wife.

Chicago is nearly at the bottom of Lake Michigan.

The equator is a menagerie lion running around the earth and through Africa.

When you breathe you inspire and when you don't you expire.

A blizzard is the inside of a fowl. (1969, pp. 38–39)

These excerpts also illustrate why it is wise for a teacher to get some feedback from time to time, just to find out what pupils really think.

point out in the preface, "History is not what you thought. It is what you can remember." No doubt you have had the experience of answering a test question not by writing about what the textbook author or the lecturer thought but by putting down what you could remember.

Disagreeable experiences are repressed

Repression   Some things are forgotten because they are unpleasant. This tendency to *repress*, or resist remembering, disagreeable experiences is a key concept in Freud's theory of psychoanalysis.

New learning interferes with old, and vice versa

Interference   In his analysis of discrimination learning, Gagné stresses the impact of interference between old and new verbal associations, a phenomenon called *retroactive inhibition*. You will tend to forget the names of former students when a new report period begins

"Miss Peach" by Mell Lazarus. Courtesy of Mell Lazarus and Field Newspaper Syndicate

and you learn another set of names. A related factor in learning and forgetting is *proactive inhibition,* in which the old interferes with the new. You may have difficulty remembering new names because the old ones are still cluttering up your memory. Such interference is most likely to occur when similar material is involved. Remembering names is just one example. Memorizing spelling words is another; learning Spanish and French at the same time is another; studying for final exams in Psychology and Sociology at the same time is still another. But even dissimilar things compete with each other, since the mind can assimilate just so much at one time. Interference is essentially the same as negative transfer, and sometimes the terms are treated as synonyms. Quite often, though, interference is used to refer to factors that effect recall of verbal learning, while negative transfer is used to refer to factors that complicate the learning of psychomotor skills.

Now that you are familiar with the structure of memory, factors that lead to long-term storage, tricks of memorization, and causes of forgetting, you are prepared to examine suggestions for helping students memorize and remember.

Suggestions for teaching: Helping students memorize and remember

The following suggestions for helping students memorize are based on this analysis of the nature and causes of forgetting as well as the description of the structure of memory.

1. To combat disuse, use repetition, recitation, and review.

    a. Make sure your students learn things well in the first place.

    b. Make use of recitation, examples, and test questions to provide repeated exposure.

    c. Have frequent review sessions. In particular, compensate for "summer loss" and for the forgetting that occurs between the introductory and the advanced course.

2. To prevent reorganization or distortion, stress meaningfulness and encourage discrimination learning.

    a. Emphasize meaningfulness; de-emphasize rote memorization or thoughtless repetition.

    b. If confusion becomes apparent, take up each of the conflicting ideas separately; make sure students master each one thoroughly.

3. To combat repression, make your room and your teaching pleasant and enjoyable.

4. To minimize interference, encourage thorough learning, provide distributed study periods, alternate between intensive and relaxing activities, and make learning active.

a. Help students really master material at the start.

b. Use distributed study periods, especially with drill subjects.

c. Alternate between intensive intellectual activity and relaxing pursuits.

5. Use size, color, intensity, novelty, unexpectedness, or uniqueness to call attention to important points.

6. Do everything possible to help students assimilate, encode, and retrieve information.

a. Stress meaningfulness.

b. Encourage students to associate new ideas with things they already know and to use mnemonic devices.

c. Call attention to structure, pattern, and organization.

d. Arrange for students to be active as they learn.

e. Make use of imagery and the loci method.

1. To combat disuse, use repetition, recitation, review.

Handbook heading
Ways to Make Sure
Students Use What
They Learn

a. Make sure your students learn things well in the first place. Brain traces fade more slowly if they are well established at the start. Therefore, it makes sense to encourage your students to do their original learning thoroughly. You shouldn't force students to repeat things to the point that they become bored or rebellious because this may tend to operate *against* their remembering; but you should keep them at something beyond the point of barely recalling the ideas or information.

b. Make use of recitation, examples, and test questions to provide repeated exposure. A second way to prevent disuse is to have your pupils continue to apply the idea or method learned. This is related to the points made in discussing the teaching of concepts and principles in Chapter 6 (The Cognitive-Discovery View). Continue to present new ideas in as many different ways and situations as possible. One of the most direct ways to get pupils to use ideas is to give them quizzes and exams.

c. Have frequent review sessions. In particular, compensate for "summer loss" and for the forgetting that occurs between the introductory and the advanced course. Another way to prevent disuse is to incorporate frequent review sessions into your lesson plans. Be sure to do this at least before every exam, but use every opportunity to reaffirm or illustrate a previously learned point. (Many of the points noted first in Chapters 5 and 6 are being emphasized again in this chapter to take advantage of the value of repetition, reinforcement, and mediating links.)

If you will be teaching at the elementary level, you must allow for the considerable amount of forgetting that takes place during the summer vacation. Studies (Bruene, 1928: Brueckner and Distad, 1923) suggest that the loss is greatest for specific skills such as spelling and multiplying fractions, rather than for geography and science, and that loss is more severe for incompletely mastered skills. For example, the reading skill of a first grader is more riddled by forgetting than that of a sixth grader. To offset this kind of forgetting, provide special review sessions at the beginning of the school year, devoting most of the time to specific techniques and incompletely mastered skills.

If you will be teaching at the secondary level, you would be wise to give an informal, ungraded quiz at the beginning of every advanced course you teach. This will permit you to discover which key points the students have forgotten since they took the introductory course. If you then devote a few days to review of key ideas, with special emphasis on the forgotten points revealed by the quiz, you may be able to avoid considerable confusion later in the course.

2. To prevent reorganization, or distortion, stress meaningfulness and encourage discrimination learning.

Handbook heading

Ways to Minimize Reorganization

a. Emphasize meaningfulness; de-emphasize rote memorization or thoughtless repetition.   To reduce confusion between similar ideas, which is the most troublesome form of reorganization, emphasize mastery of concepts and principles as much as possible. If your students really understand the idea behind something, it won't matter if they get some of the details a bit garbled. Furthermore, their use of concepts and principles may actually improve retention. In a classic study, R. W. Tyler (1934) found that whereas students suffered almost 80 percent memory loss for names of animal structures learned in a course in Zoology the previous year, they showed a slight *gain* in applying principles and a substantial gain—22 percent—in interpreting new experiments.

On the other hand, if students are forced to learn by rote, frequent distortions are to be expected. What's worse, the meaningless repetition may encourage the student to respond mechanically. A story is told of an elementary school boy who persisted in saying, "I have went." After correcting him a dozen times, his teacher finally exploded and sentenced him to write "I have gone" a hundred times after school. As he reached the ninetieth repetition late that afternoon, the teacher left the room on an errand. When she returned, she discovered that the hapless pupil had finished his task and departed. On the board were a hundred progressively sloppier "I have gone's," together with this note: "Dear teacher, I have wrote 'I have gone' a hundred times and I have went home."

The moral of this tale is, of course, that repetition does little good unless students are helped to *understand* their errors. This story also points up the futility of requiring an excessive number of repetitions. It is usually more effective to ask error makers to do something the correct way a few times and *think about it* than to force them to do it a hundred times, which will be so tedious and distasteful that they will almost certainly think about something else. For example, it is much better for a girl who can't remember how to spell *principal* to write the word five times and make use of a mnemonic device by thinking to herself, "The principal is a pal," than to write it a hundred times and think that her teacher is a louse. Furthermore, excessive repetition may actually encourage reorganization, since the repeated material may begin to look queer. (Try writing your signature twenty-five times in rapid succession and see whether you feel more—or less—sure of what you are doing.)

b. If confusion becomes apparent, take up each of the conflicting ideas separately; make sure students master each one thoroughly. In his hierarchy, Gagné places discrimination learning between verbal association and concept learning to emphasize how new chains will interfere with old ones. To minimize confusion, make sure pupils learn the words in the first primers thoroughly. If you find that your students tend to confuse adverbs and adjectives or the techniques of multiplying and dividing fractions, review the conflicting ideas separately, and make sure that they understand the first one before you take up the other.

Handbook heading

Ways to Minimize Repression

3. To combat repression, make your room and your teaching pleasant and enjoyable. Other things being equal, pupils learn more and remember more in an agreeable atmosphere. The obvious way to avoid the negative influence of repression is to make life in your classroom as enjoyable as possible.

EXAMPLES

Decorate your room with attractive (but not too vivid) displays. Act as if you are enjoying yourself and you like your pupils.

4. To minimize interference, encourage thorough learning, provide distributed study periods, alternate between intensive and relaxing activities, and make learning active.

Handbook heading

Ways to Minimize Interference

a. Help students really master material at the start. Something learned well is less likely to be displaced by new material, so make sure that important ideas are learned thoroughly.

Distributed practice: Frequent brief study sessions

b. Use distributed study periods, especially with drill subjects. If you have a list of fifty spelling words to be learned, it is far better to present ten words a day during short study periods on each of several days than to give all fifty at once. This is called *distributed practice,* and the obvious reason for it is to prevent the words from interfering with one another. You are actually encouraging retroactive and proactive inhibition when you present too much material in one period. To prevent forgetting due to disuse, as you present new words, continue to ask students occasionally to spell words from earlier lists by including them in lists of new words.

Serial-position effect: Beginning and end remembered better than middle

In distributed practice, it is usually necessary to divide the material into small parts, which because of the *serial-position effect* (R. C. Atkinson, 1957) seems to be the best way for students to learn and retain unrelated material (e.g., spelling words). The serial-position effect is the tendency of people to learn and remember the words at the beginning and end of a long list more easily than those in the middle. When you use short lists, you in effect eliminate the hard-to-memorize middle ground.

However, dividing what is to be learned into parts may not be the best way to help students learn and retain meaningful material (e.g., a role in a play). It may be preferable for the learner to concentrate on large amounts of material at once in order to make the most of overall organization. If you asked pupils to learn roles in a play by scheduling short rehearsals, they would be unable to grasp how the entire plot evolved. If you allowed enough rehearsal time to run through an entire act, on the other hand, your students could relate one speech to another because they would comprehend the overall structure of the play. If you will be teaching a subject such as dramatics or music, which requires the memorization of large amounts of material, remember the values of grasp of structure when the time comes to help your students learn a role or a composition, and think of ways to help them grasp the structure.

c. Alternate between intensive intellectual activity and relaxing pursuits. Studies of forgetting reveal that the greatest amount of interference occurs when one intellectual activity is followed by a similar intellectual activity (Gibson, 1941). The least interference comes from sleep or rest (Jenkins and Dallenbach, 1924). Thus, from a theoretical point of view, there are advantages to putting your students to sleep. A more practical approach is to try to schedule things so that periods of intensive intellectual activity are followed by restful or nonacademic activities.

5. Use size, color, intensity, novelty, unexpectedness, or uniqueness to call attention to important points.

EXAMPLES

Ways to Use Size,
Color, Intensity,
Novelty and
Unexpectedness

Print key words or ideas in extra-large letters on the board.

Use colored chalk to emphasize important points written on the board.

When you come to the key part of the lesson, say, "Now really concentrate on this, it's especially important." Then present the idea with intensity and emphasis.

Insert some oddball problems among standard types so that occasional novelty will keep students alert and on their toes.

Start off a lesson with unexpected remarks such as "Imagine that you have just inherited a million dollars and . . . ."

6. Do everything possible to help students assimilate, encode, and retrieve information.

a. Stress meaningfulness. Explain why what is being learned is worth learning, how it might be used, and why it is of personal significance.

Teaching Memory
Techniques

b. Encourage students to associate new ideas with things they already know and to use mnemonic devices. If you will be teaching subjects that require a substantial amount of memorization, you might offer a short unit on how to memorize before presenting subject matter. (Refer to the points made earlier in this chapter or to *The Memory Book* by Lorayne and Lucas for ideas you might use in developing such a unit.) In addition, offer suggested associations as you present information.

EXAMPLES

A rat operates on the bar in a Skinner box, and that's why it's called operant conditioning.

To remember the ways to get students to attend, think SCINU, to stand for size, color, intensity, novelty, and unexpectedness.

c. Call attention to structure, pattern, and organization.

EXAMPLES

Print an outline of a lecture on the board, or give students a page with the outline mimeographed on it.

If students are trying to memorize trees, birds, rocks, or the equivalent, suggest that they group those that have similar qualities.

Suggest that students outline a chapter in a text by listing points under major headings.

Francis P. Robinson (1961) has developed a technique called the Survey Q3R method that is particularly helpful when pupils are asked to master chapters in a text or an organized unit of study. You might try it yourself and also recommend that your students practice it. The title for the technique reflects these steps:

Handbook heading

Using the Survey Q3R Technique

Survey: Glance over headings in a chapter or unit of study to grasp the main points, and read the final summary if there is one.

Question: Convert the first heading into a question.

Read: Read to answer the question.

Recite: Look away from the material and try to answer the question, preferably by jotting down key phrases on a piece of paper.

Repeat these steps for the other headings.

Review: After reading the entire selection, look over your notes on main points, and fill in subpoints verbally or in writing. Then expose each major point, and check your ability to supply the subpoints listed under it.

In addition to suggesting that your students use this technique on their own, you might adapt it for learning sessions with the entire class or small groups of students.

    d. Arrange for students to be active as they learn.

EXAMPLES

Have first graders print letters in the air as they spell out words.

Use Cuisenaire rods (or the equivalent) to teach fractions.

Have sixth graders solve problems in fractions by asking members of the class to move into groups representing relative values.

Have high school language students act out words (when appropriate) as they say them.

    e. Make use of imagery and the loci method.

EXAMPLES

To remember differences between S-R theory and the cognitive-discovery view, imagine that you are actually in a Skinner box and in the cage Köhler used with Sultan.

To remember the four causes of forgetting discussed in this chapter, imagine that you are sorting out the clothes in your bedroom closet.

With younger pupils in particular, it is desirable to make learning as active as possible.

De Wys, Inc.

First you throw out those that are *disused;* then you *reorganize* the remaining garments by putting clothing you wear most often in the most accessible place. Next you hide (or *repress*) an outfit that arouses unhappy memories, and finally you sort out clothing by color so that one part of an ensemble won't *interfere* with another.

Develop your own diagrams or images to help you remember the key points in this book, perhaps by using techniques recommended by Lorayne and Lucas: Think up ridiculous associations. Use substitute words. Link ideas in incongruous, exaggerated, active ways.

So much for suggestions for helping students memorize. Even though such learning is often essential, memorization may be a waste of time if what is acquired is neither remembered nor used. Since this happens too frequently in education, you should find the next chapter on how to teach so that students will *use* what they learn of special interest.

SUMMARY OF KEY POINTS

Several educators have described the values and uses of instructional objectives. Robert Mager recommends that for specific objectives, teachers describe terminal behavior (what the learner will be doing) and define the conditions and criteria for determining when that behavior has been achieved. Norman Gronlund suggests that for more general objectives it is preferable to first state expected learning outcomes, which are then subdivided into specific objectives. Ralph H. Ojemann maintains that students may respond more favorably to some objectives if they are invited to participate in selecting them.

Instructional objectives call attention to the desirability of arranging learning experiences in hierarchical form. The same basic concept is stressed in a more comprehensive way by Robert Gagné, who has described a sequence of eight progressively complex types (or conditions) of learning. A major purpose of Gagné's hierarchy is to call attention to the fact that problem solving, the most complex and valuable condition of learning, depends on mastery of simpler forms of learning.

A more comprehensive list of types of learning arranged in hierarchical order is presented in the Taxonomy of Educational Objectives: Cognitive Domain. The categories in this taxonomy serve as a comprehensive list of cognitive objectives. Because the list is so comprehensive and because it is often difficult to draw up a complete and logical set of educational goals, you may find that the taxonomy will be more meaningful and useful after you have had a year or so of teaching experience.

When you teach skills, you may find it helpful to refer to the Taxonomy of Educational Objectives: Psychomotor Domain. One of the most fundamental ways to teach a skill is to take into account *chaining* (as described by Gagné) and show students how to follow a step-by-step progression toward the terminal behavior. Sometimes, pupils who are quite adept at a skill may develop a quirk in their technique. Techniques based on the *Beta hypothesis* might be used in such situations: First have pupils exaggerate the error. Then have them relearn the correct movements. The learning of some skills is impeded by negative transfer, or interference caused by previously learned skills. When measurements of psychomotor abilities are plotted on a graph, the resultant learning curve indicates that rapid initial learning is usually followed by a *plateau,* or a period of no apparent improvement.

When you seek to help students memorize information, keep in mind that long-term storage of memories depends on coding. Coding is aided by attention-attracting factors such as size, color, intensity, novelty, and unexpectedness. Perhaps the single most important factor leading to long-term storage is meaningfulness. You should therefore do everything possible to stress meaning in your teaching and urge your students to seek meaning as they study. When what is to be learned is not meaningful, it may be necessary to resort to mnemonic (or mediating) devices. The learning of complex material may be facilitated by the use of advance organizers. When students must do a great deal of memorization (as in a foreign language class) verbal or physical activity may be helpful. You may also wish to teach your pupils to use imagery, the loci method, or to form ridiculous associations.

You may be able to prevent forgetting by your pupils if you take into account that disuse leads to the fading of a memory trace, some memories are reorganized or distorted, disagreeable experiences are repressed, and new learning interferes with old learning, and vice versa.

When arranging learning experiences, you should take into account that with drill subjects, distributed practice periods are often effective. One reason for asking pupils to engage in short memorizing sessions distributed over a period of days is that they will be dealing with many short lists of items and be less susceptible to the impact of the serial-position effect. When teaching meaningful material, however, it seems preferable to schedule comparatively long study sessions and to urge students to concentrate on the "big picture" so that they can benefit from the advantages of grasp of structure.

BECOMING A BETTER TEACHER: QUESTIONS AND SUGGESTIONS

Ways to Use Instructional Objectives

Am I making effective use of instructional objectives? Suggestion: When planning teaching units, look over Mager's suggestions for stating specific objectives, Gronlund's ideas on subdividing learning outcomes, and Ojemann's reminder to invite students to participate in goal selection. Then figure out the best way to state instructional objectives for each unit.

Taking into Account the Hierarchical Nature of Learning

When I plan lessons, do I pay enough attention to the fact that mastery of complex knowledge or skills usually depends on grasp of simpler knowledge and skills? Suggestion: The next time I work on a lesson plan, look over Gagné's list of conditions of learning. Take a stab at listing a hierarchy of what needs to be learned. If I want students to learn concepts or rules, for example, am I sure that they understand and can discriminate between basic terms?

Using the Taxonomy of Educational Objectives: Cognitive Domain

Have I consulted the Taxonomy of Educational Objectives: Cognitive Domain when drawing up lesson plans? Suggestion: The next time I plan a unit, refer to the headings and questions listed in the abridged version of the taxonomy for the cognitive domain presented in Chapter 8. Make an attempt to list the kinds of things I would like students to learn, using the headings of the taxonomy to organize them.

Ways to Use Chaining

Should I try to teach skills by using a chaining approach? Suggestion: Each time I plan to teach a skill, look over the description of chaining in Chapter 8 and check to see if it would be beneficial to describe a list of specific steps for students to follow.

Deciding When to Program Skills

Do I check on how individual pupils respond to programmed approaches to teaching skills? Suggestion: If I use a step-by-step approach to teaching a skill, observe how students react and also ask them if they think it helps or hinders to carry out a series of actions. If some students say that it is bothersome to concentrate on steps, let them experiment with a coordinated rather than an analytic approach to learning the skill.

Demonstration Do's and Don'ts

What kind of job did I do the last time I gave a demonstration? Suggestion: Before I actually give my next demonstration, make up (and then pay attention to) a list of dos and don'ts (e.g., do try it out beforehand; don't show off; do tell students what to look for).

Ways to Set Up Practice Sessions

Am I setting up effective practice sessions? Suggestion: When arranging student practice sessions, plan how to let everyone practice just after a demonstration and how to supply immediate feedback to as many students as possible.

Applying the Beta Hypothesis

Should I apply the Beta hypothesis when students develop quirks in the way they perform a skill? Suggestion: The next time a pupil consistently makes the same error, suggest that he or she exaggerate and think about the wrong movements, then try to relearn the right movements.

Implications of the Learning Curve

When I plan and supervise practice sessions, do I take into account implications of the learning curve? Suggestion: Before supervising the next practice session I have scheduled, write down ways to give extra assistance and encouragement to slow starters and techniques to help pupils move beyond plateaus.

Ways to Make Sure Students Use What They Learn

Are my students forgetting some of the things they have learned because of disuse? Suggestion: Figure out how to insert into future lessons key ideas learned earlier in the report period; schedule regular review sessions.

Ways to Minimize Reorganization

Are my students frequently giving garbled answers, indicating that they have reorganized or distorted what they have learned? Suggestion: Make it a point to find out if students really understand what they have learned (e.g., by asking them to explain things in their own words). If it is apparent that some students don't grasp certain ideas, continue to discuss and explain those points until they are thoroughly understood.

Planning and practice ahead of time will make demonstrations before the class easy both to perform and to learn from.

James H. Karales from Peter Arnold

Ways to Minimize Repression	Am I doing enough to make life pleasant and enjoyable for my students? Suggestion: Make a list of ways to make the room more attractive and to establish a relaxed and enjoyable atmosphere. If I have to sharply criticize one or more students, make it a point to convince them that I am not holding a grudge and that bygones are bygones.
Ways to Minimize Interference	Am I inadvertently causing students to forget because of retroactive and proactive inhibition? Suggestion: When I plan the schedule for a day or period, decide when to use distributed practice, when to use the whole method. In addition, make sure that I do not require students to learn too much material at one time.
Ways to Use Size, Color, Intensity, Novelty, and Unexpectedness	Am I doing an effective job of calling attention to important points? Suggestion: Next week use at least one method for emphasizing key points that involves size, color, intensity, novelty, and unexpectedness.

Teaching Memory
Techniques

Would it be appropriate for me to present a short lesson on how to memorize? Suggestion: The next time I ask students to memorize something, explain and illustrate how they might use mnemonic devices, imagery, the loci method, or ridiculous associations to help themselves learn and remember.

Using the Survey Q3R
Technique

Should I urge students to use the Survey Q3R technique? Suggestion: The next time I ask students to read a chapter in a text, ask them to follow this procedure: First survey what is to be covered. Then convert the first heading into a question. Read what is covered under the heading. Write down an answer to the question. Then do the same for all other headings. Finally, review the entire chapter.

SUGGESTIONS FOR FURTHER STUDY

8-1
Writing Instructional
Objectives

To gain some direct experience with instructional objectives, select a unit for a subject or course you expect to teach and write a set of objectives. To assist you in writing effecive objectives, suggestions offered by Robert F. Mager and Norman C. Gronlund are listed below. (For more complete information, refer to the discussion in this chapter or the books by Mager and Gronlund.)

MAGER'S SUGGESTIONS FOR WRITING OBJECTIVES

1. Identify and name the overall behavior act.

2. Define the important conditions under which the behavior is to occur (givens or restrictions, or both).

3. Define the criteria of acceptable performance.

4. Write a separate statement for each objective. (From *Preparing Instructional Objectives*, p. 53)

GRONLUND'S SUGGESTIONS FOR WRITING OBJECTIVES

1. State the general instructional objectives as *expected learning outcomes*.

2. Place under each general instructional objective a list of specific learning outcomes that describe the *terminal behavior* students are to demonstrate when they have achieved the objective.

a. Begin each specific learning outcome with a *verb* that specifies definite, *observable behavior*.

b. List a sufficient number of specific learning outcomes under each objective to describe adequately the behavior of students who have achieved the objective.

c. Be certain that the behavior in each specific learning outcome is relevant to the objective it describes. (From *Stating Behavioral Objectives for Classroom Instruction*, p. 17)

8-2

Reading Gagné's
Description of the
Conditions of Learning

Gagné's *The Conditions of Learning* (2nd ed., 1970) gives the rationale behind his classification of learning (Chapters 1, 2, and 3), explains each type of learning in detail (Chapters 4 through 8), and provides examples of how learning experiences might be guided in a systematic way by a sequence of lessons based on the classification. Gagné discusses learning hierarchies in a variety of subject areas in Chapter 9, readiness and motivation in Chapter 10, and the design of procedures of instruction in Chapter 11. If you like the idea of a carefully planned sequence of learning experiences, read one or more chapters of *The Conditions of Learning,* and summarize how you might use Gagné's suggestions in your own teaching.

8-3

Picking Out Examples
of Gagné's Conditions
of Learning

To gain understanding of Gagné's conditions of learning, select and describe from your own behavior (or the behavior of those you observe) examples of each of his eight types of learning. Write your description by referring to the following explanation of each type. (Note: Do your best to describe examples that differ from those provided by Gagné or mentioned in this chapter.)

Signal learning—An involuntary, "reflex" action is aroused by a new stimulus (as in Pavlov's experiment with the dog).

Stimulus-response learning—Spontaneous or "voluntary" actions are shaped by reinforcement (as in Skinner's experiments with rats and pigeons).

Chaining—A motor skill is acquired by combining previously learned separate actions.

Verbal association learning—New vocabulary is acquired by using a coding connection and gaining awareness of the correctness of a response.

Discrimination learning—Confusion between similar acts, words, or ideas is overcome.

Concept learning—Gaining the ability to respond to the same quality in different situations or sets of objects or events; learning to classify and generalize. (For example, picking out the *middle* object from several different sets of objects.)

Rule learning—Combining concepts in such a way that it is possible to predict or explain what will happen under certain conditions.

Problem solving—Finding a solution to a problem by combining one or more previously learned rules in a new way.

8-4

Taxonomy of
Educational Objectives:
Cognitive Domain

In this chapter you are provided with an abridged outline of the taxonomy developed by Benjamin Bloom and several associates in *Taxonomy of Educational Objectives Handbook I. Cognitive Domain* (1956). To better understand the taxonomy and to gain insight into coordinating objectives and evaluation, examine this book. Chapter 1 is called "The Nature and Development of the Taxonomy," and chapter 2, "Educational Objectives and Curriculum Development." The remainder of the book consists of definitions of the general and specific classifications, followed by illustrations and exam questions.

8-5
Using the Taxonomy of Educational Objectives

To discover how the *Taxonomy of Educational Objectives: Cognitive Domain* might help you develop a teaching unit systematically, select a topic you are almost sure to teach eventually, and list items you will want to cover under the appropriate headings supplied below. (For more complete information, refer to the outline and discussion in this chapter.)

Knowledge of terminology—What *terms* and *symbols* will your students need to know?

Knowledge of specific facts—What specific *facts* will your students need to know?

Knowledge of conventions—What sets of *rules* will your students need to know?

Knowledge of trends and sequences—What awareness of *trends* and *sequences* will your students need to have?

Knowledge of classifications and categories—What *classification* and *category* schemes will your students need to know?

Knowledge of criteria—What sets of *criteria* will your students need to be able to apply?

Knowledge of methodology—What sorts of *methodology* will your students need to master?

Knowledge of principles and generalizations—What general *principles* will your students need to know?

Knowledge of theories and structure—What general *theories* will your students need to know? What awareness of the interrelatedness of ideas will help them learn?

What sorts of *translations* will your students need to perform?

What sorts of *interpretations* will your students need to be able to make?

What sorts of *extrapolations* will your students need to make?

What sorts of *applications* will your students need to be able to make?

What kinds of *analyses* will your students have to make?

What kinds of *syntheses* will your students need to make?

What sorts of *evaluations* will your students need to make?

8-6
Performing a Task Analysis and Teaching a Skill

Select a simple skill that students you eventually expect to teach will need (or a skill you possess that they are not likely to possess), and perform a task analysis of it. Then ask permission to work with a small group of students, demonstrate the entire procedure, describe each step, and then demonstrate the skill again. Immediately afterward, allow time for students to practice the skill and give verbal guidance in a relaxed, noncritical atmosphere. Be alert to generalization and interference, and provide guidance to help overcome it. Finally, note how you might improve your approach if you teach the skill again.

Skill selected:

Description of task analysis:

How you set up the learning situation:

How students reacted:

How you might improve your approach if you teach the skill again:

8-7

Analyzing Demonstrations You Have Witnessed

Demonstrations are a very common pedagogical device. If you would like to sort out your thoughts with regard to this form of teaching, think back to good and bad experiences you have had with teachers who used this method of instruction. Describe the best and the worst demonstrations you can remember. Then analyze why you were favorably or unfavorably impressed, and try to compose a set of guidelines to follow when *you* give demonstrations.

8-8

Analyzing Experiences with Negative Transfer

The negative-transfer effect that a previously learned skill may have on the mastery of a new skill can be exasperating, time consuming, and frustrating. Think back to skills you have learned and try to recollect any problems you encountered due to negative transfer. One boy, for example, had learned to play the violin and then decided to take piano lessons. On his violin music, the numeral 1 appeared over the notes to be played with the first finger. On his piano music, the numeral 1 was placed over the notes to be played with the *thumb*. It was so difficult to overcome the tendency to use his forefinger in response to a 1 in the music that the student gave up piano lessons in disgust. Analyze this situation or a similar one you experienced yourself, and describe how you might help someone to overcome the confusion induced by negative transfer. (If you had been the teacher of the piano student, how might you have helped him use the thumb rather than the first finger?)

8-9

Analyzing Experiences with a Plateau

Many learning curves have plateaus. You will surely recall learning situations in which you reached a point of no apparent improvement, only to go on eventually to a higher level of performance. Describe such an experience, and then indicate what a teacher might have done to help you cope with or overcome the plateau in your curve of learning.

8-10

Using Programmed Techniques in Developing Vocational Instruction

Programmed instruction is rather common in military and industrial situations for teaching skills of various kinds. If you will be teaching a course that involves training in specific skills, you are urged to purchase a copy of *Developing Vocational Instruction* (1967) by Robert F. Mager and Kenneth M. Beach, Jr. The authors have had wide experience in industry, in behavioral research, and in teaching. In their words, "*Developing Vocational Instruction* is designed to aid both the skilled craftsman who is preparing instruction through which to teach his craft, and the experienced vocational or technical instructor who is interested in improving his present course or finds it necessary to prepare a new one." They also point out, however, that the book "is not specific to subject matter or vocation, and it applies to many academic as well as vocational and technical areas." If you will be teaching a craft or vocational skill or if you would like to know how to make a job description, carry out a task analysis, derive course objectives, and develop lesson plans (among other things), read *Developing Vocational Instruction*, and note your reactions.

8-11
Learning More About Teaching Skills

For complete, technical information about skill learning you might consult *Acquisition of Skill* (1966) edited by Edward A. Bilodeau. For concise, application-oriented discussions of teaching athletic skills, see *What Research Says to the Teacher: Physical Education in the Elementary Schools* (1963) by Anna S. Espenschade, *What Research Says to the Teacher: Physical fitness* (1963) by Paul Hunsicker, or *Teaching Physical Education* (1966) by Muska Mosston. (This last book includes a chapter on the use of discovery methods in physical education.)

8-12
Analyzing the Nature of Your Own Forgetting

To gain insight into the nature of forgetting, think back over your recent experiences, and describe an episode where you were the victim of each type of forgetting described below.

Disuse—What did you have trouble remembering recently, probably as a result of not using the relevant information for a period of time? Describe the bit of information, and then state why you attribute your temporary inability to remember it to disuse.

Reorganization—What bit of information did you recently distort or transform because you confused it with some other similar item of information? Describe the reorganized memory, and explain what caused the confusion.

Repression—What did you forget recently because it might have been something you disliked or wanted to avoid?

Interference—What did you have trouble remembering recently because new learning apparently "pushed" the old learning out of your mind or because something you previously learned made it difficult to learn something new?

Assimilating material into your long-term memory storage system— What recently acquired information can you remember because you feel you assimilated it into your long-term storage system? To put it another way, why do you feel you can now remember some item of information but are unable to remember other information you learned at the same time?

8-13
Memory

For more information about how we memorize and why we forget, peruse *Man and Memory* (1970) by D. S. Halacy, *Memory and Atten-*

tion: An Introduction to Human Information Processing (2nd ed., 1976) by D. A. Norman, or *The Memory Book* (1974) by Harry Lorayne and Jerry Lucas. In Chapter 2 of their book, Lorayne and Lucas explain why and how you should think up ridiculous associations; in Chapter 4 they offer suggestions for using substitute words. Techniques for learning foreign and English vocabulary are explained in Chapter 7; ways to remember names and faces are described in Chapter 8.

Key points

The nature and significance of transfer

Transfer: Apply what is learned in class to out-of-class situations

Teachers may be unaware of most valuable kinds of transfer

Aims of education

General goals of education often stated in abstract terms

National Assessment goals specific, data available

Research-substantiated principles of transfer

Maximize similarity between in-class and out-of-class situations

Provide plenty of practice and examples

Make sure principles are understood

Specific and general transfer

Specific transfer: Apply specific skills

General transfer: Apply principles in versatile ways

Abstract principles can be applied only by formal thinkers

Problem solving depends on mastery of background information

Thoroughly understood principles not likely to be forgotten

Encouraging positive attitudes

Positive attitude revealed by approach responses

Students do well at and associate positive feelings with favorite subjects

Ways to encourage transfer

What is relevant today may be obsolete tomorrow

Standard curriculum may be best preparation

Set ways of doing things not always advantageous

Programmed approach to problem solving: Repeated successful experiences

Discovery approach to problem solving: Pose problems, guide searching

Discovery: Preparation, incubation, illumination, verification

Heuristics: Systematic techniques of problem solving

Encouraging Creativity

Choice of an expressive activity depends on abilities and experiences

Help pupils cope with disappointments, encourage practice

Chapter 9

Teaching for transfer

THE KINDS of instructional objectives and the suggestions for teaching skills and helping students memorize and remember outlined in the preceding chapter refer for the most part to specific short-term goals—things you will want students to accomplish by the time they finish a unit, course, or grade. In addition to stressing such objectives, you also should take into account more general, long-term goals. Data collected for the national Assessment of Educational progress reveal that in many areas of knowledge, young adults know less than seventeen-year-olds or even thirteen-year-olds. Although some of this loss of learning can be attributed to the nature of forgetting and to lack of practice in skills and in test taking, it seems likely that part is traceable to ineffective teaching.

Too often teachers think only about what should be accomplished in class. This tendency causes students to perceive study as a means to an end, and as soon as they write exams and earn a grade, they forget most of what they learned. This is not only a waste of time for teacher and students alike, it may also cause pupils to develop a negative attitude toward a subject. If that happens, they may avoid having anything to do with it the rest of their lives. In order to make learning more than a pointless ritual, teachers need to concentrate on finding ways to help students use what they learn, continue to learn, and feel positive about learning. When such learning outcomes occur, psychologists say that *transfer* has taken place, because what is learned in school transfers to out-of-school situations.

Transfer: Apply what is learned in class to out-of-class situations

The nature and significance of transfer

This chapter is devoted to an analysis of transfer and to suggestions about how you might teach for transfer. To become aware of why you should concentrate on encouraging transfer, think for a moment about what you can recall of what you learned in the primary, elementary, and secondary grades.

The fact that you are reading this book and the certainty that you can also write are evidence that the basic skills you learned in the primary grades have transferred. You may not be able to recall precisely how you acquired these skills, and your present proficiency is due in large part to practice since you originally learned them, but it seems safe to say that you have continued to use what you learned in the primary grades. To the extent that lessons in the upper elementary grades helped you perfect basic skills, it can be said that a certain amount of transfer of what you learned at that time also took place. But how much do you remember about the rest of the curriculum? If you memorized information about the presidents of the United States, geography, or science, what details do you recall?

When you think about specific courses taken at the secondary level, how much can you remember? Probably all you can recall about some is the appearance of the teacher or vague recollections of what the room was like. For others, perhaps all you remember are a few scattered facts. If you took chemistry, for example, you may be able to recall the formula for salt or water, but not much else. For a few courses, even though you can't recall factual information, you may have a general positive feeling that what you studied was interesting and enjoyable. Such positive feelings might have caused you to take related courses later or even to engage in out-of-school reading in that area of knowledge. But if you were to take today the exams you took in high school, you would almost certainly flunk nearly all of them.

If you are the introspective sort, you may find yourself dismayed and discouraged when you think about how little you actually remember from your elementary and secondary school days. During your first years of teaching, this realization may cause even greater dismay. You may spend sleepless nights asking yourself, "What's the point of it all? Why slave over lesson plans, get exhausted radiating enthusiasm, and spend entire weekends grading papers if nobody in the class is going to remember what they have learned?" If you find yourself thinking such thoughts at frequent intervals during your first year of teaching, you may take the line of least resistance and resolve just to put in time. If that happens, you can be quite sure that you will fail to have much of a permanent impact on your students. For your own good, as well as that of your students, it is important to think about how you might teach so that students will apply what they learn and be interested in continuing to learn.

It seems possible that one reason many teachers fail to have much of a permanent impact on their students is lack of thinking about the ultimate aims of education. A common complaint made by assembly-line workers is that they do not feel that they contribute in significant ways to the creation of a final product. An auto worker whose job is to tighten two bolts on a chassis may not take any pride or interest in the work because he or she never gets to see the finished car move off the end of the assembly line. You might possibly develop the same feeling about teaching. You may come to think of what you do—presenting lessons, giving exams, making out grades—as the equivalent of tightening a couple of bolts and, consequently, may forget about ultimate aims. Unfortunately, when teachers function that way, their students also forget about what is taught. But because of the nature of education, teachers may have just as much difficulty as assembly-line workers comprehending how what they do contributes to the final product. In fact, the assembly-line workers may have an advantage. If they want to, they can point to the appropriate part of every car they worked on and say, "I assembled that." Teachers, on the other hand, are rarely able to point to former pupils and claim credit for specific characteristics or accomplishments. As a matter of fact, teachers are usually *unaware* of some of their most impressive achievements.

You might teach primary graders to read in such a way that they develop a love for reading and continue to read for pleasure the rest of their lives. You might arouse the interest of older elementary grade students in geography, social studies, or science to the point that they use what they have learned to notice things most people fail to observe. You might do such an inspiring job teaching a particular subject in the secondary grades that some of your students will decide to major in your subject in college primarily because you made it seem so interesting. All these types of learning are especially valuable, but they also have an unfortunate characteristic: You are not likely to ever find out that they are due to your influence.

Many teachers, who are incapable of producing such learning or who are bothered by lack of tangible proof that they are accomplishing something, may concentrate on easily measured forms of learning. Unenlightened stress on accountability might increase this tendency. But when teachers concentrate only on immediate, highly specific goals, they may begin to act and think like assembly-line workers. To avoid doing that yourself, you should frequently speculate about the kind of final product you (and your fellow teachers) hope to "produce." Even though you will rarely discover how well you are succeeding, it is still important to make the effort. Otherwise, you may think only in terms of asking students to complete assignments and take exams. To counter that tendency, frequently ask yourself these questions: What kinds of individuals do American schools hope to produce? What can I do to contribute to the characteristics of such individuals? One way to seek answers to these questions is to examine descriptions of the aims of education. In Chapter 2 you were asked to consider goals of education in order to gain awareness of why teaching is the way it is. In this chapter you are asked to think about general aims in order to make teaching more permanent and effective.

Teachers may be unaware of most valuable kinds of transfer

Aims of education

Human beings have thought about and debated the purposes of education since the beginning of recorded history. The goals of schooling have probably been analyzed and discussed more in America than in any other society because of the extent and nature of our public educational system. When all children are required to go to school and when taxpayers are required to finance education, it is only natural for legislators and citizens to join with educators in being concerned about what students should be like when they graduate. At various times in the history of American education, different basic purposes have been stressed. Some of these goals are still considered to be important; others have been supplanted by newer statements of purpose. To provide background for later discussion and to help you analyze your own views of the purposes of education, here is a review of aims that have been stressed at different times.

General aims of education

Most nations of the world are made up of individuals with a common background, but American citizens originally came from dozens of different countries, and early leaders of our nation reasoned that the school should equip every child with a common language and a common core of basic information. To put it another way, the schools are expected to make heterogeneous individuals become homogeneous enough to all be recognized as citizens of the United States. To put it still another way, the schools of America, particularly in earlier times, were expected to serve as the melting pot that caused all citizens to blend together.

A related purpose of education, but one that is not unique to America (or to other melting-pot nations such as Canada and Australia), is the transmission of culture by the schools. In order to prepare individuals to coexist in a society and to ensure that a society will continue to exist, it is necessary to acquaint young people with the culture in which they live. This involves not only learning about a culture but also acquiring skills considered to be essential for constructive participation in that culture. As noted in Chapter 2, the fact that America is a technological society means that the skills needed by citizens of this country are much more varied and complex than those required of members of simpler cultures.

Another point stressed in Chapter 2 is that America is a meritocratic society. As a consequence, education is supposed to equalize opportunities so that any individual, regardless of background, can achieve success. Success depends on acquiring an employable skill, so the schools are expected to provide vocational training and preparation for later professional specialization. In addition to preparing students for employment, the schools are also expected to introduce them to activities not related to work—appreciation of the arts, the development of interests and hobbies, the inclination and skills to engage in recreational activities, and the like.

In earlier times educators often claimed that their basic aim was to teach "disciplined thinking." More recently some educators have asserted that the primary goal of education should be to make individuals more sensitive to social problems. At almost all times in history the schools have been expected to inculate desirable attitudes and values.

These aims are stated in quite abstract terms, and it is difficult to grasp them all at once. A list of educational goals prepard by the White House Conference Committee was presented in Chapter 2. It is presented again here since it includes all the goals just mentioned (and others as well) in easily digested form.

EDUCATIONAL GOALS PROPOSED BY THE WHITE HOUSE CONFERENCE

1. The fundamental skills of communication—reading, writing, spelling, as well as other elements of effective oral and written expression; the arithmetical and mathematical skills, including problem solving. . . .

2. Appreciation for our democratic heritage.

3. Civic rights and responsibilities and knowledge of American institutions.

4. Respect and appreciation for human values and for the beliefs of others.

5. Ability to think and evaluate constructively and creatively.

6. Effective work habits and self-discipline.

7. Social competency as a contributing member of his family and community.

8. Ethical behavior based on a sense of moral and spiritual values.

9. Intellectual curiosity and eagerness for life-long learning.

10. Esthetic appreciation and self-expression in the arts.

11. Physical and mental health.

12. Wise use of time, including constructive leisure pursuits.

13. Understanding of the physical world and man's relation to it as represented through basic knowledge of the sciences.

14. An awareness of our relationships with the world community. (U.S. Committee for the White House Conference on Education, 1956)

The goals on this list all seem eminently desirable. Some may strike you as more important than others, but a case can be made for each of them. The major difficulty you may encounter with such lists is deciding how to help students achieve the goals. If you will be

General goals of
education often stated
in abstract terms

teaching in the primary grades, you can do something quite definite about helping students begin to learn the fundamental skills of communication. But how, exactly, should you induce them to acquire self-discipline? If you will be teaching in the upper elementary grades, you may help students improve communication skills, understand something of the physical world, and become aware of our place in the world community. But how, percisely, should you inculcate ethical behavior? If you secure a position in a secondary school, you may be able to grasp that what you are teaching leads to mastery of such things as communication skills, awareness of civic rights and responsibilities, or understanding of the physical world. But how might you arouse intellectual curiosity and eargerness for life-long learning or produce social competency?

Objectives proposed by national assessment commitees

One of the purposes of National Assessment is to state in more precise terms some of the rather abstract goals on lists such as that prepared by the White House Conference Committee.The first step in setting up the National Assessment program was to ask committees of teachers, scholars, educators, and laymen to state goals for each of the ten measurement areas. The committees prepared lists of basic objectives and broke these down into more specific objectives, often arranged by age levels. The basic objectives for each of the ten measurement areas are presented below. Next to each heading is the ERIC[1] classification number for booklets or microfiche copies that may be available in your library. It would be to your advantage to examine the complete lists of objectives for subjects and grade levels you expect to teach. (A section of the list of specific objectives prepared by the committee on social studies is presented in Figure 9-1.)

ART OBJECTIVES (ED 051 255)[2]

1. Perceive and respond to aspects of art.

2. Value art as an important element of human experience.

3. Produce works of art.

4. Know about art.

5. Make and justify judgments about the aesthetic merit and quality of works of art.

---

[1] ERIC stands for Educational Resources Information Center. For an explanation of ERIC documents, see Suggestions for Further Study 1-5.

[2] The general objectives listed here are taken from NAEP objectives booklets. The objectives are frequently revised and it is possible that booklets prepared after January 1977 might list different objectives than those reproduced here.

Figure 9-1
Section of National Assessment of Educational Progress list of objectives for social studies

Cycle II social studies objectives for 9-year-olds
I. Develops a knowledge base for understanding the relationships between human beings and their social and physical environment.

A. Acquires knowledge about social organization.

1. Identifies some groups that human beings form (e.g., family, peer, community, national groups) and indicates why these groups form (e.g., for protection, for care of young, for social satisfaction, for pooling of energy to provide food and shelter).

2. Describes some of the functions of family and peer groups in own society and other cultures.

3. Gives examples of some basic institutions in the community (e.g., educational—schools, legal—law enforcement agencies, financial—banks, health care—hospitals, business—stores and factories) and describes some of the functions of these institutions.

B. Acquires knowledge about the relationships between human beings and their social environments and understands some of the consequences of these relationships.
1. Identifies some influences family and peer groups have on individual behavior and attitudes (e.g., choice of clothes, food, language, recreation and attitudes toward other people and institutions such as education).

2. Identifies individuals and groups whose efforts, ideas or inventions have significantly affected the lives of other human beings and describes their contributions.

3. Identifies ideas and inventions that have changed the ways people live, describes the changes that have occurred as a result of these ideas and inventions and evaluates the effect of these changes on the way people live.

4. Describes some ways ideas, customs and inventions have been transmitted and spread to other people.

Source: National Assessment of Educational Progress booklet *Social Studies* (Second Assessment), 1970.

CAREER AND OCCUPATIONAL DEVELOPMENT (ED 059 119)

1. The student should have an understanding of his own abilities, needs, and attitudes relevant to vocational choice and continuing vocational development.

2. The student should possess knowledge and skill in a specific occupational field in the nonprofessional world of work.

3. The student should develop the concept of productivity for personal and social goals.

4. The student should have an understanding of the interaction of people and groups.

5. The student should possess knowledge of a general nature important to all individuals and basic to most occupations.

6. The student should possess information about vocations—their dynamic character, requirements, and environments.

CITIZENSHIP OBJECTIVES (ED 074 010)

1. Show concern for the well-being and dignity of others.

2. Support just law and the rights of all individuals.

3. Know the main structure and functions of their governments.

4. Participate in democratic civic improvement.

5. Understand important world, national, and local civic problems.

6. Approach civic decisions rationally.

7. Help and respect their own families.

LITERATURE GOALS (ED 041 009)

1. Read literature of excellence.

2. Become engaged in, find meanings in and evaluate works of literature.

3. Develop a continuing interest and participation in literature and the literary experience.

MATHEMATICS OBJECTIVES (ED 063 140)

1. Recall and/or recognition of definitions, facts, and symbols.

2. Perform mathematical manipulations.

3. Understand mathematical concepts and principles.

4. Solving mathematical problems—social, technical, and academic.

5. Using mathematics and mathematical reasoning to analyze problem situations, define problems, formulate hypotheses, make decisions, and verify results.

MUSIC OBJECTIVES (ED 063 197)

1. Perform a piece of music.

2. Read standard musical notation.

3. Listen to music with understanding.

4. Be knowledgeable about some musical instruments, some of the terminology of music, methods of performance and forms, some of the standard literature of music and some aspects of the history of music.

5. Know about the musical resources of the community and seek musical experiences by performing music.

6. Make judgments about music and value the personal worth of music.

READING OBJECTIVES (ED 089 238)

1. Comprehend what is read.

2. Analyze what is read.

3. Use what is read.

4. Reason logically from what is read.

5. Make judgments concerning what is read.

6. Have attitudes about and an interest in reading.

SCIENCE OBJECTIVES (ED 072 976)

1. Know the fundamental aspects of science.

2. Understand and apply the fundamental aspects of science in a wide range of problem situations.

3. Appreciate the knowledge of processes of science, the consequences and limitations of science, and the personal and social relevance of science and technology in our society.

SOCIAL STUDIES OBJECTIVES (ED 097 288)

1. Have curiosity about human affairs.

2. Use analytic-scientific procedures effectively.

3. Are sensitive to creative-intuitive methods of explaining the human condition.

4. Have knowledge relevant to the major ideas and concerns of social scientists.

5. Have a reasoned commitment to the values that sustain a free society.

WRITING OBJECTIVES (ED 702 460)

1. Write to communicate adequately in social situations.

2. Write to communicate adequately in business or vocational situations.

3. Write to communicate adequately in scholastic situations.

4. Appreciate the value of writing.,

These goals are quite similar to those advocated by Gronlund (described in the preceding chapter), and it would be possible to plan learning experiences based on specific subobjectives. If you teach in a state or a school district that makes use of National Assessment data, in fact, you might be required to refer to such goals when you make out lesson plans. (An advantage of the National Assessment objectives is that you can obtain frequent feedback about how well they are being achieved.) One way to teach to produce more permanent learning, therefore, is to use National Assessment objectives as guides in setting up goals.

National assessment goals specific, data available

Although these lists provide leads for satisfying some of the general goals of education mentioned earlier, they do not cover them all. If you feel that some aims of education not covered by National Assessment objectives are worth striving for, you will need to work out your own set of specific objectives. In doing that, you may benefit

The initial teaching alphabet

One ingenious approach to the teaching of reading features the use of the Initial Teaching Alphabet, or I.T.A. for short. This alphabet was developed by Sir James Pitman of England and consists of forty-four symbols (see Figure 9–2). A section from a reader printed in I.T.A. is reproduced in Figure 9–3.

The proponents of I.T.A. point out that English is an inconsistent language. A letter can have different sounds in different words (e.g., bone, one, done, gone). Some words are spelled the same but pronounced differently (e.g., tear meaning to rip and tear as in crying). The long i sound can be spelled aisle, height, choir, eye, pie, cry, sigh, buy, guide, island (and at least twelve other ways). The symbols used for lower-case and capital letters differ, and so do those for written and printed letters. Because of these

Figure 9-2

I.T.A. alphabet

Reprinted by permission of Fearon-Pitman Publishers, Inc.

æ	face
b	bed
c	cat
d	dog
ee	key
f	feet
g	leg
h	hat
ie	fly
j	jug
k	key
l	letter
m	man
n	nest
œ	over
p	pen
ɹ	girl
r	red
s	spoon
t	tree
ue	use
v	voice
w	window
y	yes
z	zebra
ʒ	daisy
wh	when
ch	chair
th	three
th	the
ʃh	shop
ʒ	television
ŋ	ring
a	father
au	ball
a	cap
e	egg
i	milk
o	box
u	up
ω	book
ω	spoon
ou	out
oi	oil

inconsistencies and the generalization they produce, learning to read through conventional methods causes confusion.

The fact that English is not a phonetic language complicates things for the beginning reader. According to Pitman, in the regular English alphabet two thousand or more visual patterns are used for the forty-four sounds of English speech. In the I.T.A. he uses just one pattern for each sound, which means that once children have associated the forty-four symbols with their respective sounds, they can read any word. In addition, children can write on their own at a much earlier stage. For further simplification, capital letters are omitted, and there is no difference between written and printed letters. Thus, I.T.A. provides children with a versatile, all-purpose alphabet that encourages transfer.

Figure 9-3

Page from an I.T.A. reader

From the book *The Trick* by Albert J. Mazurkiewicz and Harold J. Tanyzer. Copyright © 1966 by Initial Teaching Alphabet Publications. Reprinted by permission of Fearon-Pitman Publishers, Inc.

timoᴛhy's spook

it woᴢ aulmœst hallœwccn and timoᴛhy woᴢ wurrid. hcc woᴢ wurrid about witᴄheᴢ.

"everywun tauks about ᴛhem," sed timoᴛhy. "everywun tells storiᴢ about ᴛhem. but—ar ᴛhæ real? really real?"

"ie dœn't ᴛhiŋk sœ," sed muᴛher.

"nœbody nœᴢ," sed faᴛher.

"ie wont tω nœ," sed timoᴛhy. "but hou can ie fiend out? whot can ie dω?"

from learning about views of transfer that have been substantiated by research.

Research-substantiated principles of transfer

In *The Transfer of Learning*, Henry C. Ellis provides a concise review and interpretation of research on transfer. He summarizes his analysis with seventeen empirical principles and five guidelines. Six of the principles and all the guidelines are noted below.

EMPIRICAL PRINCIPLES

Over-all task similarity. Transfer of training is greatest when the training conditions are highly similar to those of the ultimate testing conditions. . . .

Learning-to-learn. Cumulative practice in learning a series of related tasks or problems leads to increased facility in learning how to learn.

Insight. Insight, defined behaviorally as the rapid solution of problems, appears to develop as a result of extensive practice in solving similar or related classes of problems. . . .

Task or stimulus variety. In general, variety of tasks, or of their stimulus components, during original learning increases the amount of positive transfer obtained.

Amount of practice on the original task. The greater the amount of practice on the original task, the greater the likelihood of positive transfer; negative transfer is likely to occur following only limited practice on the original task.

Understanding and transfer. Transfer is greater if the learner understands the general rules or principles which are appropriate in solving new problems. (1965, pp. 72–74)

GUIDELINES FOR TEACHING

Maximize similarity between in-class and out-of-class situations

Provide plenty of practice and examples

Make sure principles are understood

Maximize the similarity between teaching and the ultimate testing situation.

Provide adequate experience with the original task.

Provide for a variety of examples when teaching concepts and principles.

Label or identify important features of a task.

Make sure that general principles are understood before expecting much transfer. (pp. 71–72)

These principles and guidelines will be referred to frequently when suggestions for teaching for transfer are made later in this chapter. At this point it is appropriate to offer observations about *why* so much stress is placed on principles. Ellis not only states his conclusions in the form of principles, he also emphasizes the use of principles to encourage transfer. One of the clearest explanations of why this is the case has been provided by Jerome Bruner.

Specific and general transfer

In his widely acclaimed *The Process of Education,* Bruner wrote:

Specific transfer: Apply specific skills

General transfer: Apply principles in versatile ways

The first object of any act of learning, over and beyond the pleasure it may give, is that it should serve us in the future. Learning should not only take us somewhere; it should allow us later to go further more easily. There are two ways in which learning serves the future. One is through its specific applicability to tasks that are highly similar to those we originally learned to perform. Psychologists refer to this phenomenon as specific transfer of training; perhaps it should be called the extension of habits or associations. Its utility appears to be limited in the main to what we usually speak of as skills. A second way in which earlier learning renders later performance more efficient is through what is conveniently called nonspecific transfer or, more accurately, the transfer of principles and attitudes. In essence, it consists of learning initially not a skill but a general idea, which can then be used as a basis for recognizing subsequent problems as special cases of the idea originally mastered. This type of transfer is at the heart of the educational process—the continual broadening and deepening of knowledge in terms of basic and general ideas.

The continuity of learning that is produced by the second type of transfer, transfer of principles, is dependent upon mastery of the structure of the subject matter....

[It involves, in addition] the development of an attitude toward learning and inquiry, toward guessing and hunches, toward the possibility of solving problems on one's own.... To instill such attitudes by teaching requires something more than the mere presentation of fundamental ideas. Just what it takes to bring off such teaching is something on which a great deal of research is needed, but it would seem that an important ingredient is a sense of excitement about discovery—discovery of regularities of previously unrecognized relations and similarities between ideas, with a resulting sense of self-confidence in one's abilities. (1960b, pp. 17-20)

Bruner wrote *The Process of Education* to summarize the deliberations of participants in a conference convened for the purpose of improving public school instruction in mathematics and physics. When the Russians launched Sputnik and demonstrated their superiority in certain aspects of technology, this country reacted by embarking on an all-out effort to produce scientists and engineers. The conference Bruner was asked to direct was one of the initial steps in this effort, and it led to the development of curricula in math and the sciences. You may have been exposed to these curricula during your elementary and secondary school years.

The rise and fall of the new math

Probably the most widely publicized of these programs was called the new math. It was called "new" to emphasize that the "old" stress on memorization and drill was to be replaced by emphasis on under-standing and principles. You may have studied the new math, but it is unlikely that you will teach it. After the new math had been tried out for several years, it became apparent that those who had developed the curriculum had failed to allow for certain characteristics of children.

Some of America's most eminent mathematicians and psycholo-gists collaborated in devising the new math curriculum. Since they had become successful in their fields by mastering principles and structure, they assumed that what was good for them was good for everyone else. They did not take into account that principles are effective only when they have been thoroughly mastered by individu-als who are capable of dealing with abstractions and making general-izations. Garden-variety pupils in elementary schools, who must study several other subjects in addition to math, do not have the time, dedication, or background to thoroughly master the subject. More important, most of them are incapable of grasping abstractions or of making generalizations. Jean Piaget has shown that before the age of twelve, children are concrete thinkers and that they only gradually become capable of formal thought as they progress through the sec-ondary grades. Consequently, it does not make sense to ask younger students to try to learn and apply principles at a high level of abstrac-tion. When the new math approach was found to be ineffective, these points were recognized. Current instruction in elementary school mathematics places less stress on abstractions.

Abstract principles can be applied only by formal thinkers

Drawing by O'Brian; © 1964 by The New Yorker Magazine, Inc.

"Think!"

The need to provide background information

As Bruner's statement from *The Process of Education* indicates, mastery of principles makes learners much more versatile—provided they are mature enough and well-informed enough to use them. Piaget's description of cognitive development calls attention to the various stages of mental maturity. The major implication of his theory has just been noted: Don't expect younger pupils to generalize. Robert Gagné's description of conditions of learning (which was presented in the preceding chapter) focuses attention on how students become well informed. The major implication of this eight-level hierarchy is : Make sure students master background information before you attempt to teach them concepts and principles. To make this implication clear, here is a brief review outline of the eight conditions of learning in Gagné's hierarchy.

Signal learning—exemplified by the classical conditioning experiments of Pavlov

Stimulus-response learning—illustrated by Skinner's operant conditioning experiments

Chaining—illustrated by the description of learning how to use a drill press presented in the preceding chapter.

Verbal association learning—essentially the same as memorization

Discrimination learning—reducing confusion and interference between verbal associations

Concept learning—responding to things as a class

Rule learning[3]—being able to use concepts in a variety of ways and situations

Problem solving—combining rules to solve problems

As this list makes clear, students must master many verbal associations and discriminate between them before they can grasp concepts and rules, which in turn make solving problems possible. Asking students to memorize information, therefore, is not necessarily a waste of time. Some humanistic educators (e.g., A. S. Neill, 1960) argue that students should be asked to learn only what they recognize has personal meaning because they are not likely to forget such information. What this argument fails to take into account is that very few self-directed learners are able to grasp that a great deal of background information must be assimilated before one receives a payoff. Accordingly, you should not assume that you will be wasting time if you ask students to memorize—provided what they memorize is likely

Problem-solving depends on mastery of background information

[3] What Gagné refers to as *rules* is essentially the same as what Bruner and other psychologists call *principles*. The terms are used interchangeably in this chapter.

to contribute to specific transfer or to a grasp of concepts and principles. Even though younger pupils may be concrete thinkers, they can still understand how ideas are related, and they may be able to apply what they learn in one situation to other situations. The major problem is making sure they genuinely understand concepts and principles.

The need for genuine understanding

Too often pupils are taught to state principles on cue, but they reveal by further responses that they do not really understand what they are talking about. The classic illustration of this all too common trap was given by William James in his *Talks to Teachers*:

A friend of mine, visiting a school, was asked to examine a young class in geography. Glancing at the book, she said: "Suppose you should dig a hole in the ground, hundreds of feet deep, how should you find it at the bottom—warmer or colder than on top?" None of the class replying, the teacher said: "I'm sure they know, but I think you don't ask the question quite rightly. Let me try." So, taking the book, she asked: "In what condition is the interior of the globe?" and received the immediate answer from half the class at once: "The interior of the globe is in a condition of *igneous fusion*." (1958, p. 106)

If these students had genuinely understood concepts and principles regarding the composition of the earth, instead of having simply memorized meaningless phrases, they would have been able to answer the question. As Gagné puts it, "The effect of concept learning is to free the individual from control by specific stimuli" (1970, p. 182). In this case, the specific stimulus was the intoning of the exact question by the teacher.

Mastery of a concept is indicated by the student's ability to *generalize* beyond specific stimuli to a variety of situations, such as a question phrased in a different way. Unlike verbal associations, which are vulnerable to extinction, principles that are understood and applied are highly resistant to forgetting—in part because they are likely to be used in a variety of situations and because use functions as reinforcement. In fact, practice may lead to improvement in applying principles months or even years after they are first learned. R. W. Tyler (1934) asked college students to take examinations before, immediately after, and fifteen months after they were enrolled in a course in zoology. Immediately after the course, students were able to name many more parts of animals than they could at the start, but almost 80 percent of that gain was lost in fifteen months. By contrast, there was no loss in their ability to apply principles to new situations, and a 25 percent *gain* in their ability to interpret new experiments. These results might be explained by taking account of the fact that the names of parts of animals were rarely used or reinforced, and so extinction

Thoroughly understood principles not likely to be forgotten

took place. The principles, on the other hand, made sense and could be applied, and each time they were applied, the students gained in understanding and also benefited from the experience of making applications.

It is clear that there are many advantages to teaching principles. It should not be assumed, however, that simply because students *know* principles, they will automatically use them to solve problems. In his statement from *The Process of Education,* Bruner notes that in addition to mastery of structure, students need to develop "an attitude toward learning and inquiry, toward guessing and hunches, toward the possibility of solving problems on one's own." He goes on to suggest that one way to encourage such an attitude is to try to arouse "a sense of excitement about discovery," and the kind of teaching he recommends (described in Chapter 6 and illustrated by his MACOS materials) attempts to lead to that kind of behavior. Another way to encourage students to function as problem-solvers is to teach them techniques of problem solving. These are called *heuristics,* and several different aproaches to teaching such techniques will be described later in this chapter.

That Ellis, Bruner, and Gagné all stress principles and problem solving is quite understandable since all of them are behavioral scientists. Any science is made up of principles, and what is discovered is applied to the solution of problems. But if you will not be teaching a scientific subject or if you will be teaching younger students, you may find it difficult to follow the advice of these three psychologists. In many subject areas, teachers do not share a psychologist's interest in teaching principles to be applied outside the classroom. If you teach nonscientific subjects, your major long-term goal may be to have your pupils acquire a positive attitude toward your subject. You may strive to induce primary graders to *enjoy* reading, for example, or you may strive to persuade secondary pupils to learn to appreciate literature, music, or art to the point that they can continue to enjoy related activities for the rest of their lives. Accordingly, it is worth considering how students come to develop positive attitudes toward a subject.

Encouraging positive attitudes

In *Developing Attitude Toward Learning,* Robert Mager discusses ways you might teach to produce positive feelings about a subject. Mager, you may recall from Chapter 8, is a behaviorist and a leading advocate of stating instructional objectives in specific terms. He defines *attitude* in terms of overt behavior and describes it as an objective in this way: "At the end of my influence over the student, when in the presence of the subject of _____, the percentage of

Positive attitude
revealed by approach
responses

approach responses made by him will be at least as great as it was
when the student first arrived" (1968, p. 15). Mager defines an
approach response as "an action that indicates a *moving toward* the
subject" (p. 21). He gives examples of approach responses as if a
private detective followed a boy enrolled in a biology course and
recorded all his activities. For example: "During the week, the student
went to the library twelve times; spent 70 per cent of time there reading biology books. ... Tuesday evening, student attended meeting of
the university biology club; broke date with favorite girl to attend" (p.
24).

Although you will be eager to increase approach responses, you
also will want to reduce the likelihood of *avoidance responses*. For
example: "On Tuesday, student tried to convince mathematics
instructor that he should excuse him from course. [On Wednesday]
failed to turn in three of four mathematics assignments on time" (p.
27). Mager observes that once avoidance responses develop, they are
not likely to be reversed. Thus, instruction that produces avoidance
tendencies will do considerably more harm than good.

To discover the sorts of experiences that lead to approach and
avoidance tendencies, Mager asked students to describe the subjects
they favored the most and least and then explain the reasons for their
preferences. Before you read the next few sentences, you might jot
down or at least think about your own reactions to these questions:

What subject do you like best?

How and why did the subject become your favorite?

What subject do you like least?

How and why did you come to dislike that subject?

Here is the way Mager describes the results of his interviews:

Students do well at and
associate positive
feelings with favorite
subjects

To summarize the results of the study, we can say that a favorite subject tends
to get that way because the person seems to do well at it, because the subject
was associated with liked or admired friends, relatives, or instructors, and
because the person was relatively comfortable when in the presence of the
subject or activity. A subject least favored tends to get that way because the
person seems to have little or no aptitude for it, because the subject is associated with disliked individuals, and because being in the presence of the
subject is often associated with unpleasant conditions. (p. 37)

On the basis of these results, Mager suggests that to increase the
likelihood of approach tendencies, you should do everything possible
to help students learn well, accentuate positive conditions by providing clear instructional objectives, giving students some choice in
selecting what they will study and some control over length of study
sessions, and treating students as individuals. You should also try to
reduce or eliminate negative conditions such as pain, fear and anxiety,

One way to analyze attitudes is to observe approach tendencies. If a student concentrates on studying a particular subject in the library for hours at a time, day after day, it is reasonable to assume that there is a tendency for that person to be eager to approach that subject.

Peter Travers

frustration, humiliation and embarrassment, boredom, and physical discomfort. Furthermore, you should remain aware of the importance of *modeling;* that is, behave the way you want your students to behave. (If you want your students to be enthusiastic about your subject, act that way yourself.)

One of the points that stands out in Mager's analysis of an individual's favorite course is that "the person seems to do well at it." This point is significant because even though a teacher tries to associate a subject with admired individuals, arranges conditions so that students feel comfortable with it, accentuates positive conditions, and exudes enthusiasm, not all students will become proficient in that subject. In some cases poor performance may be due to lack of aptitude; in other cases previous negative experiences may be too extreme to overcome. Whatever the reason, you should not think of yourself as a failure if some or even many members of a class leave your instruction with no greater inclination to engage in approach responses than they had when they entered your classroom. Quite often, the best you can hope to do is to hold your own. There are techniques, such as the mastery approach, that you can use to make it more likely that students learn a subject and experience the feeling that they are doing well at it, but even such techniques do not guarantee that a person will become genuinely proficient. Yet proficiency is often a crucial factor. We enjoy doing things we can do well, and we tend to avoid things we do poorly. One of the basic principles of teaching for transfer, therefore, is to try to encourage thorough mastery of a subject.

Implications of research on transfer

Before offering suggestions for teaching for transfer, a review of what has been covered so far in this chapter is in order.

1. Transfer occurs when students apply outside the classroom what they learn inside it.

2. Much of what students learn in any unit or course is forgotten, particularly if teachers fail to think about how they might encourage long-term learning.

3. To focus on long-term goals it is helpful to consider general aims of education, even though they may often seem remote and abstract.

4. One way to make general goals more specific is to follow Gron-lund's suggestions for stating instructional objectives. Another way is to refer to lists of objectives prepared by the National Assessment of Educational Progress.

5. Principles of transfer that have been substantiated by research include: Maximize the similarity between in- and out-of-school situations. Provide plenty of practice. Give a variety of examples when teaching concepts and principles. Make sure that principles are thoroughly understood.

6. Distinguish between specific transfer of skills and general transfer of principles. Whenever appropriate, stress principles, since these are most likely to make learning serve a student in the future.

7. When teaching principles, keep in mind that younger pupils may be unable to grasp or apply abstractions. Also, take into account that before concepts and principles are mastered, verbal association and discrimination learning must take place. Finally, make sure students *understand* principles, since merely reciting them is valueless.

8. Simply because students understand principles, however, they do not automatically use them. It may be necessary to also teach heuristics (techniques of problem solving).

9. Stressing concepts, principles, and problem solving is not appropriate at all grade levels or in all subject areas. Sometimes attitudes may be the most significant learning outcomes to transfer. Students are most likely to develop a positive attitude toward a subject if they

do well at it, feel comfortable in its presence, and associate it with liked or admired individuals.

The following suggestions are based on the points just enumerated.

Suggestions for teaching: Ways to encourage transfer

1. When drawing up lesson plans, think about long-term, general goals, as well as more immediate objectives.

2. Keep in mind that transfer is not automatic.

3. Remember that exclusive emphasis on relevance and practicality may limit rather than enhance transfer.

4. Make the situations discussed and the activities conducted in the classroom as similar as possible to those that the student encounters outside it.

5. Give your students plenty of practice, but make sure they do not begin to rely unthinkingly on a standard way of doing things.

6. Be systematic about helping students master concepts and principles.

7. Encourage and assist your students in applying the principles and ideas they have learned to a wide variety of situations. Give many examples of applications, and urge students to make additional applications of their own.

8. Teach heuristics—techniques of problem solving and methods of inquiry.

9. Try to "send your students away from your instruction anxious to use what they have been taught—and eager to learn more."

    a. Do everything possible to have your students do well at subjects you would like them to continue to study.

    b. Associate subjects with liked and admired individuals.

    c. Try to arrange conditions so that students feel comfortable when in the presence of a subject.

1. When drawing up lesson plans, think about long-term, general goals, as well as more immediate objectives. To avoid perceiving yourself as an assembly-line worker with no feeling of involvement in the creation of a final product, draw up your own list of aims of education. If you take the trouble to record such a list in your Handbook, you may experience the feeling not only that you are contributing to the development of human beings but also that you may be one of the few teachers to attempt to encourage certain traits. Rarely, if ever, do principals say to a teacher, "You have the responsibility this

Handbook heading
Goals of Education

report period for teaching self-discipline, respect for human values, and intellectual curiosity." Even though almost everyone agrees that these are desirable goals, hardly anyone makes a systematic attempt to help students achieve them.

To formulate your list, you might refer to the White House Conference Committee statement, the sets of objectives proposed by National Assessment committees, the taxonomies of educational objectives for the cognitive, affective, and psychomotor domains, and you might also talk things over with classmates. Once you have recorded attributes you feel every public school graduate should ideally possess, try to describe more specific techniques you might use in your classroom to encourage their development.

If you take the trouble to record goals, questions, and suggestions in your Handbook, you are more likely to put them into practice—and do it effectively—if you go a step further and list more specific subobjectives. For ideas about how to do this, refer to Gronlund's observations on instructional objectives (Chapter 8, pp. 395–396). To achieve the National Assessment goal "engage in the process of science," for example, you might teach to help students achieve objectives such as these:

1. Can list five characteristics of the scientific method

2. Can give an example of a scientific study that illustrates all five characteristics

3. Can distinguish between scientific and nonscientific observations

4. Can apply scientific methods in solving a problem presented in class

5. Can apply scientific methods in solving an out-of-class problem.

(Examples of goals, questions, and suggestions are provided in the section at the end of this chapter entitled Becoming a Better Teacher: Questions and Suggestions.)

2. Keep in mind that transfer is not automatic.   Don't rationalize that your students will benefit simply because you make them work hard, memorize large amounts of material, or complete many assignments. Neither should you assume that because you teach a subject that is "logical" or has to do with social problems, your students will automatically acquire related traits or attitudes. Certain subjects can be used to encourage certain kinds of behavior, but the behavior is likely to occur only if you make a carefully planned effort to foster transfer.

3. Remember that exclusive emphasis on relevance and practicality may limit rather than enhance transfer.   In the late 1960s many colleges and universities bowed to student pressure and offered courses and curricula that were *relevant. Relevance* was usually defined as

"having immediate practical value" or "being related to current problems." On some campuses, special programs were developed each quarter or semester in response to demands for courses in areas of current interest. The limitations of such programs and courses are revealed by the fact that virtually all of them have disappeared. As Alvin Toffler has pointed out in *Future Shock,* cultural change takes place so rapidly in technological societies that it is almost impossible to remain abreast of new developments. What is relevant one year is likely to be irrelevant the next. (To prove this to yourself, think about the favorite musical groups, dance steps, and clothing styles that were popular when you were in high school. Then ask current high school students to give you a report on the musical groups, dance steps, and clothing styles they favor.) If you spend too much time discussing immediately relevant topics, therefore, you are building planned obsolescence into your lessons. This does not mean that you should *never* deal with topical issues; it is simply a suggestion that you keep in mind that ideas that have stood the test of time are probably more likely to be relevant five or ten years from today than are current fads.

A related point has to do with practicality. You may be tempted to try to convince your students that everything they learn in your classroom will have practical value. One problem with this approach is that if students fail to make immediate use of what you ask them to learn, they may lose faith in you and interest in what you teach. A more basic difficulty is that no one can predict all that pupils need to know. On the whole, it is probably better to teach general rather than highly specific skills, to ask students to accept on faith that they are likely to be able to use what they are learning at some unspecified time in the future, and to point out that some things are worth learning just for the sake of learning.

One pitfall to avoid is to use such arguments for teaching a topic that you happen to like or to have a great deal of information about. Harold Benjamin satirized that situation in *The Saber-Tooth Curriculum.* This delightful book describes education in Paleolithic times, when the three skills most necessary for survival were scaring saber-tooth tigers with firebrands, catching fish by hand, and clubbing woolly horses (for clothing). These three activities became the basis for the curriculum of the school. Unfortunately, however, a new ice age emerged. The saber-tooth tigers got pneumonia and died, and they were replaced by ferocious bears who weren't the least bit afraid of fire. The streams grew muddy so that fish were no longer visible to be grabbed. And the woolly horses were driven elsewhere and replaced by antelopes, which could run too fast to be killed by simple clubbing. Therefore, in time, necessity led to the development of new techniques to insure survival: Clever hunters invented a pit trap for bears and a snare for antelopes, and clever fishermen invented a net to catch the no longer visible fish.

What is relevant today
may be obsolete
tomorrow

Eventually some "radicals" suggested that since saber-tooth-tiger-scaring, fish-grabbing, and horse-clubbing were obsolete, they should be dropped from the curriculum of the school and replaced by pit-digging, net-making, and snare-setting. But the wise old men who controlled the school only smiled indulgently and said:

"Don't be foolish.... We don't teach fish-grabbing to grab fish; we teach it to develop a generalized agility which can never be developed by mere training [in net-making]. We don't teach horse-clubbing to club horses; we teach it to develop a generalized strength in the learner which he can never get from so prosaic and specialized a thing as antelope-snare setting. We don't teach tiger-scaring to scare tigers; we teach it for the purpose of giving that noble courage ... which can never come from so base an activity as bear-killing." (1939, pp. 42–43)

Benjamin's satire calls attention to the problem of relevance. The emergence of a new ice age took several thousand years, but the emergence of new trends in America in the 1970s may take only a few months. It would have been simple and sensible to change the curriculum to be more in line with current conditions several thousand years ago. Today, it may not be so easy. In the 1960s, after the Russians launched Sputnik, the United States plunged into an all-out effort to produce scientists. The effort succeeded so well that the United States not only forged ahead of the Russians in the space race but produced an oversupply of scientists. In addition, changing conditions, some of which were traceable to the end of United States involvement in Vietnam, led to a de-emphasis on science. The result was that many scientists were unable to find jobs they were trained to perform. Individuals with Ph.D.'s in physics found themselves reading electric meters. When high school and college students found out about the shortage of jobs for trained scientists, they stopped taking science courses. Furthermore, the schools responded to the demands of humanistic educators and students that emphasis be placed less on science and technology and more on personal fulfillment. As a consequence, by 1975 science knowledge had declined to such an alarming extent that former astronaut Wally Schirra joined with several National Assessment officials in pleading with educators and legislators to put such courses back in the required curriculum (NAEP Newsletter, March–April 1975). The ups and downs of science in a fifteen-year period reveal the problems that are encountered today if the schools attempt to teach only subjects that are immediately relevant. In order to be prepared for unpredictable trends, it is often desirable to present a standard curriculum made up of a selection of basic subjects.

Standard curriculum may be best preparation

A final limitation of excessive stress on practicality is that it may lead to a restricted and rather dull view of education—and of life. Some of the most satisfying and exciting activities we engage in are *impractical*. It is possible to make an elaborate case for playing tennis (it builds up several muscle groups), listening to classical music (I might impress a future employer with my knowledge), or learning about great art (I might be able to make a wise investment). But why not simply *enjoy* these activities? And, if you teach them, why not do so primarily on the grounds that they are *interesting*?

4. Make the situations discussed and the activities conducted in the classroom as similar as possible to those that the student encounters outside it. One of the clearest illustrations of this point is the scrimmage in athletics or the dress rehearsal in dramatics or music. Here is an observation made by a high school principal:

I always said we were better because we spent our time playing basketball while the opponents spent their time practicing. That is, our practice periods were periods of play—just more and more basketball. There was little formal instruction and no drill. All of the coaching was applied to actual game situations. It always showed when we played our traditional rivals—they were taught. We were so natural—and having such a good time! *They* were thinking, and it showed all over. When the pattern didn't work, someone was jerked. Our kids just did what came naturally from all those scrimmages. We got so good in basketball that the crowds finally began to drop off.

Not all coaches agree with this explanation of success, but many varsity athletes to. Some coaches become so fascinated with clever, intricate exercises and drills that they devote little practice time to actual game play. The same is often true of music teachers and occasionally of dramatics instructors. The glee club or band may spend most of their rehearsal time singing or playing exercises or concentrating on isolated sections of the pieces they are to perform. The result can be a disaster. If a band has never had a complete dress rehearsal for the big concert, the conductor may find himself or herself frantically singing sections of a piece when the instrumentalists get lost. This is the case with almost all skills and many academic subjects. If you want your pupils to apply outside of school what they have learned in school, do your best to give them "scrimmage" or dress-rehearsal experiences in class.

Handbook heading

Ways to Set Up
"Scrimmage" Activities

EXAMPLES

In business classes, make the classroom as much like an office as possible.

In auto shop, make the class as much like a garage as possible.

Use student body and class elections to teach students how to function as voting citizens.

5. Give your students plenty of practice, but make sure they do not begin to rely unthinkingly on a standard way of doing things. Students are much more likely to transfer skills and ideas if they have

thoroughly learned them to the point that they respond almost reflexively when they encounter a particular type of situation in or out of the classroom. Therefore, you should give them plenty of practice in skills and techniques that are likely to be useful. There is a potential problem in providing such practice, though, because organisms of all types have a tendency to more or less automatically follow a formula when presented with many similar exercises. Harry F. Harlow (1949) was one of the first psychologists to demonstrate this tendency. He found that monkeys were able to learn how to solve a particular kind of problem with 100 percent success after three hundred trials. He concluded that they had learned *how* to learn as they solved the problems and that they had also acquired what he called a *learning set* (or a set way of doing things). This was an advantage when the monkeys were confronted with problems identical to those they had practiced, but it worked as a disadvantage when they tried to solve similar, but different, problems.

This tendency is also referred to as *habitual set.* It was first demonstrated by Luchins (1942), who had students solve some problems that involved measuring a given amount of water with jars of different sizes (see Figure 9-4). The first few problems were all solved in the same way. When slightly different problems were presented—problems that could be solved by a much simpler approach—the habitual set established by the previous experience blocked the students' perception of the easier method. When the subjects in Luchin's study were admonished, "Don't be blind," they were much more likely to look for new solutions.

Set ways of doing things not always advantageous

A related characteristic of thinking that may interfere with problem solving is *functional fixedness,* the tendency to associate certain objects only with certain familiar uses. Duncker (1945) demonstrated this mental attribute by giving subjects a problem to solve that involved using an open pair of pliers as "legs" for a simple flower stand. He discovered that subjects who were required to use the pliers conventionally just before being confronted with the novel-use situation were less likely to solve the problem than were subjects who approached it cold.

Learning sets, habitual set, and functional fixedness all illustrate *negative transfer,* which was mentioned in the discussion of skills in the preceding chapter. Most of the time, transfer is positive because what is learned in one situation helps a person in another situation. Sometimes, however, previous learning interferes.

Perhaps the best way to combat learning sets is to use variations of techniques recommended by Morris L. Bigge for structuring discovery sessions. You may recall from Chapter 6 that he suggests first setting up a discussion session so that students agree on a particular conclusion, then introducing some disturbing data or pulling a subject-matter switch to force them to revise their conclusions. A related

Handbook heading
Ways to Prevent Habitual Set

Figure 9-4

Two problems from Luchins' experiment

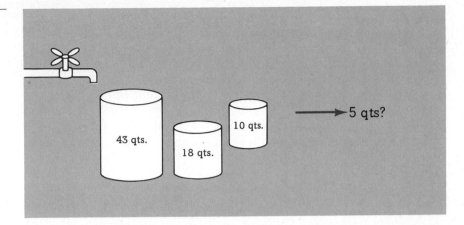

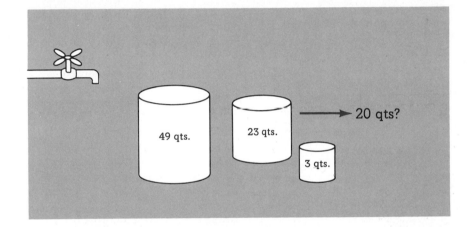

technique was developed by Robert B. Davis (1966), who used a discovery approach to teach math. He frequently resorted to what he called *torpedoing* to prevent students from using formulas in unthinking ways. He presented a series of problems that all could be solved by following the same basic procedure. Then he inserted a problem that looked the same but could not be solved with the tried and true formula. This forced students to seek other approaches.

6. Be systematic about helping students master concepts and principles. In his statement on transfer, Bruner explained why mastery of principles is at the heart of the educational process. Once students thoroughly master a principle, they are able to apply it in many ways. Since concepts and principles are so important, your students will benefit from your following a systematic approach when you teach them. Gagné's description of the conditions of learning offers guidelines. The first point to keep in mind is that concepts and principles

follow S-R learning, chaining, verbal association learning, and discrimination learning in the hierarchy. Therefore, you should first make sure that necessary background information has been acquired. Next, you might follow this five-step procedure to teach concepts and principles. (For Gagné's own discussion of this sequence, see pages 195–203 of *The Conditions of Learning*.)

1. Inform students about the form of performance to be expected when learning is completed.

EXAMPLES

Let's figure out what kinds of things roll.

Let's see if we can discover something about the composition of the earth just beneath the surface.

2. Question students in a way that requires them to discuss the previously learned concepts that make up the principle.

EXAMPLES

What do we mean by *round?* What are some round things in this room?

Remember when we talked about the eruption of that volcano in Hawaii?

3. Use verbal cues to guide the students to put the principle together by linking the several concepts in the proper order.

EXAMPLES

What do round things do if we put them on a slanting surface?

Where did the lava come from when the volcano erupted? What temperature was the lava?

4. By means of questions, lead the students to provide one or more concrete applications of the principle.

EXAMPLES

If we put this basketball on the top of this slanted desk top, what will happen?

Suppose we dug a hole hundreds of feet deep on the island of Hawaii. How would we find it at the bottom—warmer or colder than on top?

5. If it seems desirable, use questions to encourage the students to state the principle in their own words.

At this point you are urged to select a principle you will want the students in your class to learn and then indicate on a page of your

Handbook what you would say to the class to assist them in mastering the principle. If you take the time and trouble to do this, you will benefit from one of the most valuable aspects of principle learning; that is, you will learn to relate the principle to actual situations. To encourage you to do this consistently is one of the primary reasons for asking you to add applications of your own to your Handbook. As you do so, you are, in effect, demonstrating to yourself that you understand the principle under discussion well enough to apply it; and this, in turn, means that you are more likely to remember it and use it in the future.

7. Encourage and assist your students in applying the principles and ideas they have learned to a wide variety of situations. Give many examples of applications and urge students to make additional applications of their own.   When you emphasize applications, point out that any given principle has almost limitless uses. If you apply a principle to only one or two situations, your students may assume it has limited value. Do your best to emphasize the fact that the "sky's the limit" as far as application of general ideas is concerned. (This is the same point stressed in Chapter 6 in the list of suggestions for teaching principles and in the discussion of problem solving. The point is repeated here not only to emphasize it but also to illustrate it.)

8. Teach heuristics—techniques of problem solving and methods of inquiry.   The final stage in Gagné's hierarchy of learning is problem solving. He places it at the end of the line because, "When problem solution is achieved, something is also learned in the sense that the individual's capability is more or less permanently changed" (1970, p. 216). In a sense, all the lower states of learning are important primarily as means to problem solving. S-R psychologists and field theorists agree that teachers should do everything possible to encourage students to function as independent problem-solvers. They disagree, however, as to the best way to do this.

Skinner advises teachers to concentrate primarily on teaching subject matter but also to condition students to pay attention, to study efficiently, and to engage in more varied behavior. If productivity and perseverance can be encouraged by systematically widening the ratios of reinforcement, he maintains, programmed learning is likely to foster problem solving.

Richard Crutchfield has developed some programmed techniques to try to accomplish these goals. He argues:

It is not enough ... that an individual merely be able to generate many new ideas; he must also have a highly aroused general set or propensity to do so, especially when confronted by cognitive tasks which require it. And he must know how best to apply his skills to the task. (1966, p. 64)

Programmed approach
to problem solving:
Repeated successful
experiences

True to the associationist approach, Crutchfield observes, "Sensitization and activation of the child's cognitive skills occur mainly through repeated experiences of their successful use by the child" (p. 64). (Notice the emphasis on repetition and reinforcement.) In Crutchfield's opinion, current educational practice is seriously deficient in providing most pupils with such repeated experiences. For one thing, he points out, very few school experiences require a pupil to engage in genuine problem solving and thinking. Furthermore, many school tasks are too easy and appear meaningless; and cheap success or lack of proper reinforcement fails to shape the desired behavior. To overcome these inadequacies, Crutchfield has developed some pictorial programmed materials for use in promoting problem-solving skills in fifth and sixth grade children. He reports that the program, called the Productive Thinking Program produces "substantial increments" in performance (Olton and Crutchfield, 1969). It appears that he has made good on Skinner's claim that problem solving can be taught through a program, independent of programs for teaching subject matter (see Figure 9–5).

Field theorists share many of Crutchfield's views regarding the desirability of encouraging the development of cognitive skills. They argue, however, that the discovery approach is superior to programmed learning as a means of doing this. As they see it, a single discovery session is capable of providing the same kinds of learning produced by two or more separate programs because pupils in a discovery session are learning subject matter while they are learning problem solving. Field theorists also object to the use of prepared programs on the grounds that such learning tends to make students too dependent on the materials. A student who discovers things independently, it is argued, develops self-confidence and autonomy as a problem-solver. This point of view has been argued by Suchman:

Concepts are ... most meaningful, are retained the longest and are most available for future thinking when the learner actively gathers and processes data from which the concepts emerge. This is true (a) because the experience of data gathering (exploration, manipulation, experimentation, etc.) is intrinsically rewarding; (b) because discovery strengthens the child's faith in the regularity of the universe, which enables him to pursue causal relationships under highly frustrating conditions; (c) because discovery builds self-confidence, which encourages the child to make creative intuitive leaps, and (d) because practice in the use of the logical inductive processes involved in discovery strengthens and extends these cognitive skills. (1961, p. 149)

Suchman suggests that in order to take advantage of these benefits of inquiry, the teacher follow certain procedures:

Discovery approach to
problem solving: Pose
problems, guide
searching

The teacher can help the child by posing problems that are reasonably structured and will lead to exciting new discoveries. The teacher can also coach him in the techniques of data collection and organization that will lend power and control to his searching. (p. 150)

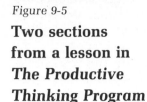

Figure 9-5

**Two sections
from a lesson in
*The Productive
Thinking Program***

From Martin V. Covington et al., Basic Lesson Five, *The Productive Thinking Program* (Columbus, Ohio: Charles E. Merrill Publishing Co., 1972), pp. 22–23.

This description summarizes features of the discovery approach noted in Chapter 6 but places special emphasis on the techniques of inquiry. As noted in Chapter 6, Suchman initiates such inquiry training by showing fourth and fifth grade children short films on such simple physics demonstrations as the following: A bimetallic knife is held over a flame, and it bends down; then it is put in water, and it straightens out; next it is turned over and held over the flame again, and it bends up; finally it is put in water again, and it straightens out. The children are encouraged to find out why by asking questions that can be answered only by yes or no. Tape recordings of all sessions are made and later analyzed so that in subsequent sessions the experimenter can help the children ask more effective questions. She or he does this by pointing out that the most valuable questions are those that identify questions or events, that narrow the focus of inquiry, that "manipulate" the conditions of the experiment and lead to certain outcomes, that test hypotheses of cause and effect, and that check on the validity of conclusions. By the time the students in Suchman's experiments have been exposed to several films and post-mortem sessions, they have become more adept at the techniques of inquiry.

The techniques for teaching problem-solving skills developed by Crutchfield and Suchman are most appropriate for upper elementary and lower secondary school pupils. For older students, you might find the following techniques more useful.

Various attempts have been made to analyze how the great problem-solvers of history have made discoveries, with the hope that their mode of operation might be taught to others. One of the earliest and most frequently cited analyses (Wallas, 1921) describes the process of discovery as consisting of four stages:

Discovery: Preparation, incubation, illumination, verification

Preparation—the acquisition of knowledge, the gaining of an awareness of how different ideas fit together, or the experience of being presented with a problem

Incubation—a period in which the various ideas are sorted out, sometimes in an unconscious way

Illumination—the "Aha!" experience when the solution dawns in thought

Verification—empirical testing of the tentative solution

Perhaps *the* classic example of this process is the way Archimedes solved the problem of specific gravity. He had been asked, you may recall, to figure out whether a crown was solid gold—or just gold plated—without damaging the crown in any way. He had previously thought about the lawfulness of the universe and had a wide background of experience in many things (preparation). At first Archimedes was unable to solve the problem (incubation), but as he lowered himself into his bath one day, he suddenly grasped the solution (illumination) and ran naked down the street shouting "Eureka!" He later checked out his theory and found that it was valid (verification). Such discovery experiences are dramatic examples of insight learning.

Heuristics: Systematic techniques of problem solving

The kind of discovery described by Wallas (and illustrated by Archimedes) was spontaneous and more or less unteachable. Even so, the sequence serves as a basis for devising strategies or devices to be used in problem solving. Such techniques are discussed in a book titled *How to Solve It* by the eminent mathematician Gyorgy Polya.

Here is a brief adapted outline of the basic heuristic methods described in *How to Solve It*. (For the sake of brevity, portions of the passage have been paraphrased; exact quotations are enclosed in quotation marks.)

UNDERSTANDING THE PROBLEM

The first step is to "understand the problem. What is the unknown? What are the data? What is the condition? . . . Draw a figure, introduce suitable notation. Separate the various parts of the condition."

DEVISING A PLAN

The second step is to "find the connection between the data and the unknown. Have you seen it before? . . . Do you know a related problem?"

CARRYING OUT THE PLAN

The third step is to "carry out the plan. Check each step. Can you see that each step is correct? Can you prove that it is correct?"

LOOKING BACK

The final step is to "examine the solution obtained. Can you check the result? Can you check the argument? Can you derive the result differently? Can you see it at a glance? Can you use the result, or the method, for some other problem?" (1957, pp. xvi–xvii)

To illustrate how you might use Polya's suggestions to teach students how to use heuristics, suppose you decide to ask a high school social studies class to figure out how their city might cope with increasing automobile traffic. You might structure the problem by making a statement of this type: "The streets in this city were laid out during horse-and-buggy days. They are no longer adequate for large numbers of modern automobiles and trucks. There is a limited amount of money available for street construction. Which streets should be widened and altered?" Next, divide the class into groups of five or so, and ask them to consider questions under headings you print on the board. Suggest that each group list questions and procedures under each heading, giving an example or two to get them started. Here are possible headings to be listed and some sample questions you might mention:

UNDERSTANDING THE PROBLEM

What kinds of information do we need to find answers to the question? Should we try to get hold of maps, data from traffic counts, diagrams of traffic patterns?

DEVISING A PLAN

How can the needed information be obtained? Do various city agencies have information we can use? Which ones? If some information is not available (e.g., traffic counts), should we try to get it ourselves? Should we interview people who live on different streets and ask them how they would feel about having those streets widened.

CARRYING OUT THE PLAN

How should we organize and present information? Who will obtain information? Who will check on the accuracy of information we acquire?

LOOKING BACK

Once we arrived at a semifinal recommendation, how can we examine it and improve it? Should we offer several alternatives? Should we announce a tentative proposal and then invite citizens to comment on it?

Polya's description of heuristics leads to the following suggestions for helping students become more systematic problem-solvers.

1. Either present problems yourself (keeping in mind the suggestions of the various discovery advocates—Bruner, Bigge, Suchman—on exactly how to do this) or encourage your students to state problems of their own. Some teachers go a step further and require their pupils to state specific hypotheses to be tested. You might consider this approach if it seems appropriate.

2. Encourage and help your students to find information relating to the problem. You can do this by teaching them how to use reference works, how to get the most out of the library, and so on, or by using the question approach advocated by Bruner and Suchman. A limitation of using only the question approach is that students may not gain any experience with other ways of finding information. How many out-of-school problems, for example, can be solved by a question and answer approach?

3. Perhaps allow for an incubation period. A possible disadvantage of programmed learning, as noted earlier, is that reinforcement is usually immediate, which might prevent learners from doing some reflective thinking and coming up with more complete answers on their own. The same limitation, however, *might* apply to group discovery sessions. If pupils are required to verbalize immediate solutions to a problem or ask spur-of-the-moment questions, the value of an incubation period—in which ideas are permitted to sort themselves out and jell—is eliminated. Consequently, you might experiment with a technique of presenting problems that permits pupils to do leisurely and independent ruminating before they attempt to pose an answer.

4. When illumination occurs, urge your students to state the solution in the form of a hypothesis if appropriate; in some situations the solution or observation is so obviously true that it does not need to be verified.

5. Test the hypothesis or alternate hypotheses.

Encourage your students to follow the same procedure outside of class. One way to encourage out-of-class applications is to ask students to report on successful problem solving that takes place outside of school.

A different way of emphasizing many of these same techniques for

If students are taught how to solve problems, they will later be able to deal with a variety of difficulties in a systematic way.

Peter Travers

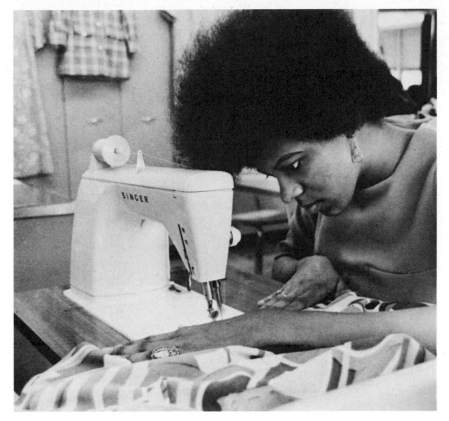

developing problem-solving abilities is derived from the work of Crutchfield and Suchman. Following is a list of suggestions you might want to use as a guide for shaping problem-solving sessions if the list based on Polya's outline of heuristics does not seem immediately useful.

1. Help students recognize and define problems. Assist them in perceiving when a question is the factual type that can be answered by consulting a reference book such as an encyclopedia and when it is the type that requires more intensive reasoning for solution.

2. Help students to ask the right questions and to take a careful look at all available facts.

3. Encourage the generation of many ideas. This could be done in either group or individual brainstorming sessions. It might include the use of heuristics, such as those described by Polya. You might also explain, and even demonstrate, the nature of habitual set and functional fixedness so that your students will understand how and why mental blocks occur and recognize that there are times when a problem should be set aside for a while.

4. Suggest to your students that although a critical attitude is necessary at the verification stage, the generation of ideas should be free and intuitive. Also, point out that persistence in trying to solve problems is desirable but that stubborn persistence may block learning.

5. Try to develop persistence in problem solving by starting out with simple problems amenable to quick solution and gradually working up to thornier ones.

Handbook heading
Teaching Problem-
Solving Skills

If you can think of some specific problems to present to your classes in teaching them the techniques of problem solving, note them in your handbook. You might also take a stab at outlining a plan of attack—listing specific steps to follow—for solving any problems you note. You could use as a guide Wallas's four stages in the problem-solving process or the list of points derived from the work of Crutchfield and Suchman.

9. Try to "send your students away from your instruction anxious to use what they have been taught—and eager to learn more." This is the main point Robert Mager emphasizes in his *Developing Attitude Toward Learning.* He states that one way to convert this goal into a more specific objective is to resolve to try to teach so that students will make at least as many approach responses toward a particular subject after they leave your classroom as they did before they entered it. Approach responses might consist of such things as out-of-class reading, the decision to take additional courses in a subject, or the choice of a hobby related to a particular topic of study. When teaching many subjects, particularly the sciences, it is appropriate to try to induce students to be eager to use what they have learned in quite specific ways. Many suggestions for doing this have just been offered. But with other subjects, it is more appropriate to try to encourage the kinds of attitudes listed in the Taxonomy of Educational Objectives: Affective Domain. Under "Willingness to Respond," for example, you are urged to list the kinds of voluntary habits related to your subject that you would like students to adopt (e.g., voluntarily reading books and magazine articles, participating in free-time activities). Under "Satisfaction in Response," you are urged to list goals such as "finding pleasure in reading," "enjoying literature." These goals stress feelings and enjoyment more than usefulness, and many of the objectives proposed by National Assessment committees also reflect such goals. If you will be teaching nonscientific subjects, therefore, you may wish to concentrate more on attitudes than on practicality.

Handbook heading
Encouraging Positive
Attitudes (Approach
Tendencies)

The survey Mager made of favorite and least favorite subjects provides leads you might follow if you decide to try to arouse such positive feelings.

a. Do everything possible to have your students do well at subjects you would like them to continue to study. Perhaps the single best way to do this is to use the mastery approach that will be discussed at length in Chapter 13.

b. Associate subjects with liked and admired individuals. Probably the most specific way to do this is to try to be an admirable person yourself by being enthusiastic, competent, and fair. In addition, you might call attention to admirable personalities associated with a field of study or type of activity. Just as advertisers use sports heroes and entertainment figures to push their products by taking account of the Freudian principle of identification and the S-R theorists' stress on modeling, you might call attention to admirable individuals who made significant contributions in a particular field.

EXAMPLES

When mentioning a contribution made by an eminent person in some field, give some interesting personal information about that person.

Encourage students to read biographies and autobiographies of outstanding individuals in a field of study.

c. Try to arrange conditions so that students feel comfortable when in the presence of a subject. "Comfortable," as Mager uses the word, is not the same as "relaxed" or "effortless." More accurate synonyms are "unthreatened" or "agreeable." You have probably had at least one teacher who made life in his or her classroom so tension filled and disagreeable that you hated to go through the door. And when you walked out of class for the last time, you most likely made a resolution, consciously or unconsciously, to avoid that subject in the future. Even though you ask students to exert themselves as they learn, you can establish a warm, supportive, pleasant atmosphere for them to do it in. (Many suggestions for doing this were noted in the chapters on the cognitive-discovery view of learning and the humanistic approach.)

A basic reason for striving to send students away from your instruction eager to learn more is that any unit or course can provide only a sample. If students are to really get into a subject or keep up with new developments, they should continue to study or read about it after a course is completed. You might encourage continued learning not only by building positive attitudes but also by telling students how and where to get additional information.

EXAMPLES

If teaching a technical subject, distribute a bibliography of books that might be read for pleasure as well as information. If teaching a subject such as literature, give students a list of your own favorite reading-for-pleasure books.

Keep a personal library of books in your classroom, and invite students to browse and sample.

Make available copies of magazines or journals in a given field, and suggest that students look for related publications in a library.

Encouraging creativity

The nature of creativity

The phrase *problem solving* implies that there is some sort of specific difficulty that needs to be overcome, or some kind of explanation to be sought. Most discussions of problem solving written by scientists reflect the fact that the experiments and studies they carry out have a specific purpose. The first part of most reports of scientific investigations is typically headed "The Problem," and the last part usually summarizes what has been discovered that contributes to a solution of the problem. In some cases, the solution may involve an interpretation of data that might be called "creative" because a new way of looking at things has been proposed. A. Newell, J. C. Shaw, and H. A. Simon (1962) have described four criteria for assessing the degree of creativity in problem solving. They suggest that problem solving is creative when (1) the product of thinking has novelty and value, (2) the original problem was so vague and undefined that the statement of the problem had to be formulated, (3) the achievement of a solution required a high degree of motivation and persistence, and (4) the solution was arrived at only when previously accepted ideas were modified or rejected. These criteria might be summed up by saying that creative problem solving involves novelty, originality, persistence, and value.

Creative problem solving is of special interest to scientists, but it is clearly not the only kind of creativity. Several psychologists who have studied problem solving acknowledge this point by emphasizing that they are discussing *scientific* creativity (e.g., Barron and Taylor, 1963). Scientists write about creative problem solving because that is what they hope to achieve. Furthermore, scientists are eager to apply what they have learned in order to improve some aspect of human affairs; thus, they stress value as a criterion of scientific creativity. Many scientists who have studied problem solving and creativity have been eager to use what they have discovered to help children in school develop skills and attitudes that will help them become creative problem-solvers. Techniques developed by Crutchfield, Bruner,

Suchman, and Polya, and the suggestions offered in the preceding section of this chapter are intended to serve that purpose.

It seems possible that this stress on learning problem-solving skills may be due, in part at least, to the scientist's desire to have everyone think like scientists. Not everyone agrees with this view. A number of observers (e.g., Lewis Mumford, 1967) have argued that asking all people to think and act like scientists may lead to disaster. Humanistic psychologists maintain that preoccupation with science leads to impersonal relationships, compartmentalization and fragmentation of experience, and a tendency to ignore or resist emotions and feelings. Although these charges may be true if individuals are asked to more or less *live* scientifically, they probably do not apply when students are simply asked to take advantage of the methods of science when they are confronted with a problem of some kind. It seems certain that all human beings would benefit if they were taught heuristic skills in school because they are certain to encounter problems the rest of their lives. Even so, psychologists' stress on creative (scientific) problem solving may cause readers of their views to ignore nonscientific creativity.

Human beings appear to possess a universal need to express themselves artistically. Even in the most primitive cultures, individuals have experienced the desire to draw, paint, sing, play musical instruments, and dance. Furthermore, they have felt the urge to decorate and beautify utilitarian objects. Eating utensils have been shaped and embellished to please the eye, for example, and clothing has been created not only to provide warmth but also to be attractive. In more advanced societies, certain individuals have devoted their lives to writing novels, creating dramatic productions, choreographing ballets, and composing music. Artistic creativity is both similar to and different from scientific creativity. Both types involve novelty, persistence, and originality, but they differ in regard to value. The creative scientist typically produces an idea that can be applied to improve the human condition in some tangible way or to further knowledge in a field of study. The awarding of Nobel Prizes for notable achievements emphasizes this point. The artist, by contrast, may engage in activities that have no *practical* value but may bring a sense of fulfillment not only to the creator of a work, but also to those who admire the creation. A painting by Rembrandt, a play by Shakespeare, a symphony by Beethoven, a novel by Dickens—none of these works has practical value, but each may contribute to a special sense of pleasure.

Human beings can survive if they do not engage in artistic or self-fulfilling activities, but their lives are often enriched if they do. Therefore, it seems desirable for children and adolescents to learn not only to solve problems, but also to appreciate the arts and perhaps to be creators as well. Several of the goals and objectives listed earlier stress such activities. You may have chosen a major in college because some form of artistic or self-expressive activity gave you pleasure, and you may be interested in becoming a teacher because you hope to help others share that pleasure. If so, you may find the following observations on encouraging creative self-expression of greater interest than the preceding section on problem solving.

Suggestions for teaching: Encouraging creative self-expression

1. When appropriate, encourage self-expression in spontaneous and planned activities.

2. Respond enthusiastically to forms of self-expression, and arrange for the class to serve as an appreciative and sympathetic audience.

3. Encourage the development of talents and skills in self-expression.

   a. Encourage young children to sample many kinds of self-expressive activities.

   b. Try to neutralize or counteract negative experiences in early attempts at developing a skill.

   c. Provide incentives, and supply reinforcements for practice.

4. Do not hesitate to supply instruction.

5. Acquaint students with the lives and achievements of great artists and performers.

6. Make available and tell students where to find sources of ideas.

7. For students who seem to lack the talent or perseverance to become skilled performers or artists, stress the values of learning to appreciate the achievements of others.

1. When appropriate, encourage self-expression in spontaneous and planned activities. Some critics of the schools (e.g., George Leonard, 1968) maintain that all children enter kindergarten with a natural spontaneity and lack of self-consciousness but that by the fourth grade these qualities have been "crushed by" regimented learning. Leonard and others who make such statements fail to take account of significant differences between five-year-olds and ten-year-olds. Kindergarten children are thrilled by the novelty of school. They are at a stage of cognitive development where they are egocentric and largely unaware of the thoughts of others. They spend much of their school time engaging in free play or loosely structured activities. Fourth graders, by contrast, are old hands at school. They are at a stage of cognitive development where they are just becoming acutely sensitive to the thoughts and feelings of others. Some of them may be experiencing puberty, which leads to drastic physical as well as psychological changes, which, in turn, arouse concern about what others think about how individuals look and behave. Fourth graders are

Younger children, who tend to be egocentric in their thinking and not too aware of the thoughts of others, enjoy such self-expressive activities as dressing up and play-acting.

Ingbert Gruttner

expected to learn fairly complex skills, and even if the teacher uses an open school approach, they are still expected to complete assignments. If fourth graders are more self-conscious and less spontaneous than kindergartners, is this only because they have been "crushed" by their teachers? Or is it primarily because they are growing up, becoming more aware of the thoughts of others, and because they are expected to complete tasks designed to help them learn?

Even if you accept these explanations, it still will be desirable to make an effort to perpetuate the enthusiasm, spontaneity, and lack of self-consciousness of young children. These qualities may tend to diminish for reasons such as those just noted, but that does not mean that they cannot be perpetuated or encouraged. If you do decide to ask children to engage in self-expressive activities, however, you may find it helpful to keep in mind the point made in discussing such types of behavior in the chapter on humanistic learning: older pupils have legitimate reasons for feeling self-conscious, and they should not be forced to be creative in public ways.

2. Respond enthusiastically to forms of self-expression, and arrange for the class to serve as an appreciative and sympathetic audience. Some critics of S-R theory argue that it is antithetical to individuality and self-expression. The fact remains that self-expression is influenced by reinforcement in the same manner as any learned activity. It seems reasonable to assume that a professional artist or performer specializes in self-expression because these activities have been reinforced in a variety of ways. Therefore, if you hope to encourage students to get into the habit of expressing themselves, you should reinforce that kind of behavior. One way to do this is to respond favorably to their efforts at creative expression. Another way is to arrange for the class to serve as a sympathetic audience.

Handbook heading
Ways to Provide a
Sympathetic Audience

EXAMPLES:

If you ask all pupils in a second grade class to make a painting or write a poem, exhibit every child's work on the walls of the room.

In the upper elementary grades, schedule occasional "amateur hours" when any child who wants to can give a brief performance of some kind.

If a student does an especially imaginative and artistic project, show how much you appreciate it. (It is probably better to do this privately, for reasons to be discussed in point 3a.)

In a high school art class, have positive critique sessions during which each student's work is displayed and all members of the class join in explaining what they particularly like about it.

3. Encourage the development of talents and skills in self-expression. Young children may be pleased with almost any kind of self-expression. The falling leaf interpretation of some kindergartners, for example, may resemble an imitation of a sack of potatoes being dropped by a clumsy farmhand, but five-year-olds are not likely to be aware of it. As children mature, however, they are better able to recognize that some works and performances are superior to others. This probably accounts, in part at least, for the tendency of older children to specialize in particular forms of self-expression. If an elementary school girl is dissatisfied with her efforts at drawing and realizes that her drawings are not nearly as attractive as those of talented classmates, she may choose to concentrate on playing the trumpet in the school band.

Choice of an expressive
activity depends on
abilities and
experiences

In order to explain differences in the artistic abilities and achievements of individuals, it seems necessary to assume that the older child's choice of a particular expressive activity depends in part on inherited abilities or talents and in part on positive and negative experiences. If one child seems to have a gift for mimicry, for example, and thrives on the attention and applause of parents, relatives,

*Older pupils,
particularly those who
prefer not to call
attention to themselves,
may enjoy
self-expressive
activities such as
writing or painting.*

Ingbert Gruttner

and peers early in life, dramatics would be appealing. If another child seems to have a knack for handling words and if initial attempts at performing in public are either unsatisfying or embarrassing, writing poems or stories would be a natural choice.

a. Encourage young children to sample many kinds of self-expressive activities.   Taking this into account, it seems desirable to encourage young children to engage in a wide variety of expressive activities so that they will be likely to discover their talents. E. Paul Torrance suggests that teachers can encourage creative work in their pupils by "respecting the ideas that they present for consideration . . . by encouraging opportunities for practice and experimentation without evaluation and grading, and by encouraging and giving credit for self-initiated learning and thinking" (1970, p. 22). To put these suggestions into practice, you might respond positively to initial efforts at any creative activity. (Remember that frequent reinforcement is desirable at the beginning of any learning experience.) You could also schedule frequent "creativity periods" during which free experimentation would be encouraged. If possible, you should avoid grading creative work, since most of your students will probably strive to figure out what you want. For the same reason, you should probably avoid singling out a particular piece of work for lavish public praise. If you make a big fuss over a first grader's drawing of a rabbit, for example, you are likely to find yourself inundated by rabbit drawings. Once children develop a degree of skill, however, some kind of evaluation in the form of constructive criticism may be necessary if they are

Handbook heading
Ways to Respond to
Creative Efforts

to improve. If you always offer praise and never point out faults, pupils may not acquire the ability to criticize their own work, which means they are not likely to improve.

b. Try to neutralize or counteract negative experiences in early attempts at developing a skill.   The development of talent is often a delicate process. Therefore, you might be on the alert for potentially damaging experiences. Suppose a boy seems to have all the qualities needed to become a skilled musician and is initially excited about learning to play the violin. Suppose further that he makes his concert debut during a class amateur hour and that a string breaks, causing some members of the class to howl with laughter. If someone does not persuade the child that the broken string was just an unfortunate accident and say something to the effect that the performance was really excellent and that the next one will be even better, a potential virtuoso might lose interest in further practice.

The last word in the preceding sentence sums up what is probably the most important factor in the development of self-expressive activities that will provide satisfaction and pleasure later in life. If students do not practice—and practice a great deal—they will not become genuinely skillful at any form of self-expression. One of the major tragedies of talent development is that children are not helped to persevere when they are beyond the initial enthusiasm stage but not yet at the mastery stage. Accordingly, you may find that it will sometimes be desirable to use principles of S-R theory to encourage perseverance.

c. Provide incentives, and supply reinforcements for practice.

EXAMPLES

Suggest that students reward themselves with an apple (or the equivalent) or by engaging in a favorite activity after they have practiced a musical instrument at home for thirty minutes.

Tell students in a high school dance class that after they have done the basic exercises, you will show them a film of Rudolph Nureyev.

Inform students in a junior high school art class that when they complete twenty-five drawings of objects around their homes they can borrow a reproduction of a drawing by a famous artist to put up on their bedroom wall.

4. Do not hesitate to supply instruction.   Some teachers do not give formal instruction in artistic or self-expressive techniques on the assumption that doing so might inhibit individuality and stifle creativity. Others believe that periods devoted to such activities should function as therapeutic sessions during which students can let off

Help pupils cope with disappointments, encourage practice

Handbook heading
Ways to Encourage Diligent Practice

steam. Both these arguments may be somewhat shortsighted for reasons related to the preceding point on skill development. Students who are allowed to simply play around with art or other forms of self-expression may get a certain amount of release of tension, but they are not likely to develop any real skill. Accordingly, they are not likely to engage in similar activities after a class is completed. And if a person does not engage in an activity for any length of time, true individuality in expression will never develop. On the other hand, if instruction in techniques is provided, students benefit from discoveries made only after earlier artists had spent years engaging in trial-and-error experimentation. If a teacher insists that all students follow a particular technique and rewards only those who use it, individuality might be inhibited. But if you take pains to show a variety of techniques, explain why certain methods are to be preferred to others, and then urge students to use what they have learned in their own way, it would seem that individuality would be fostered rather than blocked.

5. Acquaint students with the lives and achievements of great artists and performers.   As students become more expert at some form of expressive activity, they are likely to benefit from exposure to the works of the greatest artists and performers in that field. One reason for this is that they may observe techniques to be imitated. Another is that they may be inspired to model their behavior after that of a particular individual. To encourage this, you might urge students to read biographies and autobiographies of the giants in a field of artistic

Contact with outstanding creative artists (such as the conductor of the Boston Symphony Orchestra's concerts for children) may inspire some students to pursue a career in the arts.

Courtesy of Boston Symphony Orchestra

endeavor. An additional advantage of having students become acquainted with the lives of great artists and performers is that they will learn about the amount of perseverance required to become genuinely proficient. A student who is having doubts about continuing to take art classes, for example, may be inspired to stick with it after reading about the early struggles of Mary Cassatt and other Impressionists.

A final advantage of showing the works of great artists is that they offer ideas students might use as starting points. Many great artists borrowed ideas from their predecessors, and there is no reason why students shouldn't do the same. In the early stages of experimentation with any form of self-expression, it is almost essential that students be given some leads to follow.

6. Make available and tell students where to find sources of ideas. Acquainting students with great works of art and great performances may inspire them to improve their artistic abilities. For those who prefer crafts, a similar approach is to introduce them to books and articles that provide samples of work completed by others. The novice weaver or rug maker, for example, might start out by copying a design completed by someone else. After developing skill and confidence, the student might then attempt an original design. The novice woodcarver might start out by making a copy of a piece by a master carver and then progress to original works. The craft worker usually gets more pleasure out of completing something that is entirely original, but a well-made copy can also be a satisfying achievement.

Handbook heading
Helping Students Find
Inspiration

7. For students who seem to lack the talent or perseverance to become skilled performers or artisans, stress the values of learning to appreciate the achievements of others. Even though you do your best to encourage students to develop skills of self-expression, you should not expect that all of them will respond. One explanation, which will be discussed more completely in the next chapter, is provided by Abraham Maslow's hierarchy of needs. Maslow suggests that individuals usually do not experience a desire to engage in forms of self-expression unless they feel physically comfortable, psychologically safe, loved, and esteemed. Children who lack confidence, who are anxious, who feel neglected, or who are not admired may find it difficult to get into the mood to be creative. (On the other hand, some of the greatest artists in history immersed themselves in art partly because the lower needs in Maslow's hierarchy were *not* satisfied.) Even when persons seek to enjoy aesthetic and related activities, however, they may be limited by inhibitions, lack of natural talent, the inability to stick with something until it is mastered, and similar factors. If students give the impression that they are convinced they are

not capable of direct involvement in successful self-expressive activities—even after making a genuine effort—the next best thing may be for them to learn how to appreciate the achievements of others. One of the best ways to help students appreciate the details and subtleties of masterful performances is to have them at least try the skills themselves. A former piano student, for example, will be able to appreciate some aspects of a flawless virtuoso performance more completely than someone who never played the instrument. A pupil who made an abortive effort at stone sculpture may grasp the magnificence of Michelangelo's works in ways that a nonsculptor could not understand. Although experience may be helpful as a prelude to appreciation, it is not essential. You can help students gain vicarious satisfaction as they observe the accomplishments of others by your enthusiasm and knowledge as you point out the details of great works of art or of brilliant performances. To develop critical abilities, expose students to many examples, so that they can begin to distinguish between superior and inferior accomplishments and refine personal tastes.

SUMMARY OF KEY POINTS

Jerome Bruner has emphasized that learning should serve us in the future. Another way to make the same point is to say that you should strive to teach for transfer: Your students should be inclined to continue to use what they have learned after they leave your classroom. While teaching for transfer is extremely important, it is also frequently frustrating because you may be unaware of some of the most valuable changes you have brought about in your pupils, changes that do not become apparent until months or years after they leave your classroom.

Even though you may be unable to trace precisely the impact you have on your students, there are still compelling reasons for thinking about the general aims of the educational enterprise. You may understand some aspects of American education and also comprehend long-term goals if you take into account that the schools are expected to transmit the culture of a society. What is considered to be important in a given culture can often be brought into focus by describing general goals, but such goals are often too abstract to be converted into guidelines for teachers. Objectives such as those proposed by National Assessment committees are likely to be of greater value to teachers than statements of general aims.

Most lists of goals and objectives describe more or less permanent abilities and characteristics. In speculating about how to teach to

Developing creative thinking through school experiences

E. Paul Torrance is perhaps the most active worker in designing programs for encouraging creativity. The title of this supplementary note is the same as that of a concise paper he prepared for A Source Book for Creative Thinking, edited by S. Parnes and G. Harding. (For a more complete description of Torrance's views on fostering creativity, see his Guiding Creative Talent [1962].) In this paper he lists twenty principles for developing creative thinking through school experiences. Some of these ideas have already been discussed in this book—in the sections on the discovery approach in earlier chapters and in the discussions of problem solving and creativity in this chapter. But for emphasis and review, the complete list of twenty suggestions is given here. (For the sake of brevity, portions of the passage have been paraphrased; direct quotations are enclosed in quotes.)

1. "Value creative thinking." Be on the alert for new ideas, and encourage your pupils to develop all their creative talents.

2. "Make children more sensitive to environmental stimuli."

3. "Encourage manipulation of objects and ideas."

4. "Teach how to test systematically each idea." Starting as early as the third grade, show pupils how to define a problem and keep testing each idea. The heuristics described by Polya might be used as a guide.

5. "Develop tolerance of new ideas." This includes tolerance of unorthodox—and perhaps irritating—creative personalities.

6. "Beware of forcing a set pattern."

7. "Develop a creative classroom atmosphere"—a free, relaxed, unharried one.

8. "Teach the child to value his creative thinking." Encourage students to note their ideas in concrete form whenever possible, perhaps in a special notebook set aside for that purpose.

produce such long-lasting learning, it is instructive to examine principles of transfer that have been substantiated by evidence. Such principles include: Maximize the similarity between in-class and out-of-class situations. Provide plenty of practice and examples. Make sure principles are understood.

In some situations instructors should strive to encourage specific transfer and teach skills that will be used in specific circumstances. At other times it is preferable to teach for general transfer, since mastery of principles will equip students with information they can use in a wide variety of ways. One important point to remember about general transfer, however, is that abstract principles can be applied only by formal thinkers. Students who have demonstrated their ability to engage in formal thinking should be prepared to solve problems by

9. *"Teach skills for avoiding peer sanctions."* If a highly creative pupil rubs too many classmates the wrong way, help that pupil become more aware of the feelings of others.

10. *"Give information about the creative process."* You might do this by acquainting students with Wallas's four steps in problem solving and by noting some of the heuristics described by Polya.

11. *"Dispel the sense of awe of masterpieces."* Indicate some of the methods and difficulties experienced by famous creative people to dispel the notion that only a gifted few experience brilliant and perfect insight on the first try.

12. *"Encourage and evaluate self-initiated learning."* Avoid overstructuring the curriculum.

13. *"Create 'thorns in the flesh.' "* Ask controversial questions, and call attention to disturbing data.

14. *"Create necessities for creative thinking."* Confront your students with provocative problems. You might use the suggestions of Bruner and Bigge as guides.

15. *"Provide for active and quiet periods."* Remember the impact of habitual set and functional fixedness.

16. *"Make available resources for working out ideas."*

17. *"Encourage the habit of working out the full implication of ideas."*

18. *"Develop constructive criticism"*—not just criticism.

19. *"Encourage the acquisition of knowledge in a variety of fields."*

20. *"Develop adventurous-spirited teachers."* Try to put these various ideas into practice yourself. (1962, p. 45)

mastering necessary background information underlying principles. If students thoroughly understand principles, they are not likely to forget them, particularly if the principles are actually applied from time to time.

Students not only transfer skills and principles, they also develop attitudes about subjects of study that influence later behavior. It is possible to determine attitudes by observing approach or avoidance responses. Pupils are more likely to make approach responses if they do well at a subject, associate it with liked and admired individuals, and feel comfortable when studying it.

When planning how to teach for transfer, there is a temptation to try to make the curriculum up to date and relevant. Because of rapid and unpredictable cultural change, however, there may be virtues in presenting a standard, all-purpose curriculum. Another inclination when teaching for transfer is to supply students with "formulas" for handling particular kinds of problems. Such an approach may be unfortunate if students fall into habitual patterns and are unable to develop new ways of solving unique problems. Other factors to keep in mind about problem solving are that *preparation* and *incubation* are usually necessary before *illumination* occurs, and that illumination should later be *verified*. A number of ways for teaching problem-solving skills have been developed. Richard Crutchfield uses a programmed approach designed to give pupils repeated successful experiences as problem solvers. J. Richard Suchman favors a discovery approach: he poses problems and guides students as they search for answers. Gyorgy Polya recommends the use of *heuristics,* or the use of systematic techniques of problem solving.

In addition to teaching problem solving you may also wish to encourage the development of talents and skills in creative expression. To grasp why students may differ in their preferences for creative activities, keep in mind that choice of such activities depends on abilities and experiences. Because the development of creative talent is often a delicate process, it may be necessary to help pupils cope with disappointments and to encourage them to persevere and practice diligently.

BECOMING A BETTER TEACHER: QUESTIONS AND SUGGESTIONS

Goals of Education

Would it be beneficial for me to think about the kind of final "product" I am helping to create? Suggestion: Look over the list of White House Conference goals; the taxonomies for the cognitive, affective, and psychomotor domains; and the sets of objectives prepared by National Assessment committees. (Reminder: Either go to the library and look at the detailed lists of National Assessment objectives for grade levels and subjects I will be teaching or send for copies of appropriate lists.) Pick out goals or objectives that seem pertinent; think about how I might try to at least partially achieve them; jot down suggestions to myself. (To illustrate how this might be done, here are a few sample goals, questions, and suggestions you might list for different grade levels and subject areas.)

Primary grades

Goal from the White House Conference list: The fundamental skills of communication. Question: How can I teach reading and writing so that pupils will *enjoy* those skills? Suggestions: Be enthusiastic about reading. Have reading-for-fun periods. Encourage pupils to keep a diary.

Goal from the White House Conference list: Effective work habits and self-discipline. Question: How can I encourage pupils to persevere and stick to a job until it is finished? Suggestions: Check section in Chapter 5 on how to use behavior modification to encourage such behavior. Also, list ways to help pupils use behavior mod on themselves.

Objectives from National Assessment list for reading: Comprehend what is read; have an interest in reading. Question: How can I make sure pupils comprehend what they read and feel positively about reading? Suggestions: Ask pupils to read to me and to each other and then explain what they read. Use Mager's ideas on developing positive attitudes: Help pupils feel they are doing well at reading. Show them that people they admire read a lot. Make them feel comfortable with reading (e.g., don't make them read in front of others).

Category from the Taxonomy: Cognitive Domain: Knowledge. Question: What knowledge will pupils need in order to get off to a good start in reading? Suggestion: Make sure pupils know what objects are before they read about them.

Category from the Taxonomy: Affective Domain: Acquiescence in responding. Question: What kinds of regulations do students need to comply with? Suggestion: Ask the class to help formulate necessary rules and regulations.

Elementary grades

Goal from the White House Conference list: Understanding of the physical world and man's relation to it as represented through basic knowledge of the sciences. Question: How can I set up science units so that pupils will apply what they learn outside of class? Suggestion: Urge pupils to keep notebooks in which they jot down how what they learn in class helps them understand things they notice at home and on trips or see on TV.

Goal from White House Conference list: Ethical behavior. Question: How can I encourage pupils to want to be considerate and honest? Suggestion: Check books on values clarification for strategies that might encourage consideration for others. Read section in Chapter 7 on how to use Kohlberg's moral dilemma technique.

Objective from National Assessment list for writing: Adequate written communication in social and scholastic situations. Question: How can I help pupils write more effectively in and out of school? Suggestions: Give them lots of practice in writing. Give them time in class to write social letters. Look into pen-pal arrangements. Give lots of written assignments and find out how to get some teacher aides to help read papers carefully and make constructive criticisms.

Category from Taxonomy: Cognitive Domain: Knowledge of terminology. Question: What terms will pupils need to know in order to understand each chapter in the social studies text? Suggestion: Go through each chapter before it is assigned; pick out significant terms; give the pupils an ungraded quiz; have them check their answers as volunteers explain what each term means.

Category from Taxonomy: Affective Domain: Controlled or

One of the goals of a dedicated biology teacher is to encourage pupils to continue to engage in the scientific study of nature after class work is completed.

Francis Laping/DPI

selected attention. Question: How can I get pupils to take advantage of what they are learning about nature and see things most people don't see? Suggestion: Arrange a field trip through a park, and invite everyone to make a notebook of special things they recognize about trees, flowers, rock formations, insects, birds, animals, and so on. Then have the class form groups of five and compare their notebooks.

Secondary grades

Goal from the White House Conference list: Physical health. Question: How can I use physical education classes to promote physical fitness now *and* after students graduate? Suggestion: Emphasize exercises, sports, and games that typical adults can engage in by themselves, with spouses, or with small numbers of friends.

Goal from the White House Conference list: Civic rights and responsibilities. Question: How can I teach social studies so that pupils are persuaded they should not only vote but should be *informed* voters? Suggestions: the next time a state or national election is scheduled, have the class go through all the steps they should go through when they become eighteen—that is, register to vote, get information about the candidates and propositions, become familiar with ballots and voting machines. Also, have them discuss reasons why people who argue that there is no point in voting because elections are never decided by one vote may be overlooking several important considerations.

Objective from the National Assessment list for science: Understanding and applying the fundamental aspects of science in a wide range of problem situations. Question: How can I teach science so that students will use scientific methods outside of class? Suggestion: Start out the year with a unit on ways scientific methods correct for weaknesses of unsystematic observation. Then ask students to write brief reports on how they used these methods to check on some out-of-class situation, e.g., a claim made in a TV commercial.

Objective from the National Assessment list for literature: Continuing interest and participation in literature and the literary experience. Question: What can I do to encourage students to read good books after they graduate, instead of choosing only trashy novels to read or spending four hours every night staring at a television screen? Suggestions: Have all kinds of good novels scattered around the room. Urge the pupils to sample these, so they might become intrigued enough to read them all the way through later. Also, remind them when a famous novel is going to be dramatized on television, and suggest that they read the book before or after they watch the TV production. Also, point out differences between a classic novel and current samples of garbage writing.

Category from the Taxonomy: Cognitive Domain: Knowledge of criteria. Question: How can I teach art so that students will be able to evaluate works created by others and themselves? Suggestion: Refer to several criteria in pointing out reasons why some paintings might be considered better than others. Than ask students to apply the same criteria to their own paintings by ranking them in order from best to worst—and listing reasons for the ranking.

Category from the Taxonomy: Affective Domain: Controlled or selected attention. Question: What kinds of construction details in furniture do I want students in woodworking or home economics courses to be able to recognize? Suggestion: After discussing details of furniture design and construction, take a field trip and ask each student to rate bedroom and dining room sets. Then, when we get back to the classroom, have them divide up into groups of five and compare their notes.

Ways to Set Up "Scrimmage" Activities	Are there ways I can give pupils experiences under "game conditions"? Suggestion: When making up lesson plans next week, try to work in at least one exercise where students are asked to perform under conditions that are similar to or identical with those they will encounter when they are on their own.
Ways to Prevent Habitual Set	Am I presenting subject matter in such a way that students are using a formula in unthinking ways? Suggestion: Introduce a problem or situation that looks the same as others but is slightly different—and demands a novel solution. (For leads, refer to Bigge's techniques for structuring discussion sessions mentioned in Chapter 6.)
Ways to Teach Concepts and Principles	Have I thought about ways of teaching concepts and principles? Suggestion: The next time I plan to teach a concept or principle, refer to Gagné's sequence, and write out a step-by-step procedure for presenting the idea to the class.
Teaching Problem-Solving Skills	Should I develop a unit on how to solve problems? Suggestions: Look over the techniques for teaching problem solving advocated by Crutchfield, Suchman, and Polya. Then select or combine techniques they recommend in an exercise or unit designed to teach pupils how to solve problems. Finally, give pupils a series of problems to solve,

and have them form into groups of three or four to explain to each other how they proceeded.

Encouraging Positive Attitudes (Approach Tendencies)

Am I doing an effective job of inculcating positive attitudes toward the subjects I teach? (Do students give the impression that they are eager to avoid me, my classroom, and books on any subjects I teach?) Suggestion: Look over Mager's description of why students like and dislike different subjects. Then list ways to help students do well, associate subjects with liked or admired individuals, and feel comfortable while studying.

Ways to Provide a Sympathetic Audience

The last time one or more students completed a creative work, did I arrange for the rest of the class to function as a sympathetic audience? Suggestion: The next time I want to have students share or display their creative efforts, urge the rest of the class to be constructively appreciative.

Ways to Respond to Creative Efforts

Have I thought about how my reactions to creative efforts may shape student behavior? Suggestion: Draw up a list of guidelines to follow when commenting on creative work (e.g., Don't single out individuals for lavish public praise). Make it a point to comment on every student's work, not just the work of those I think are doing the best job. Occasionally offer constructive criticism.

Ways to Encourage Diligent Practice

Am I helping students persevere during tedious practice sessions that eventually may lead to genuine proficiency in some creative activity? Suggestion: The next time I schedule a practice session intended to help students master skills that may lead to satisfying creative expression or performance, use behavior modification techniques to shape perseverance (e.g., reward students with the opportunity to see or hear an expert performer after they have spent thirty minutes working on fundamental skills in a particular mode of creative expression).

Helping Students Find Inspiration

Am I encouraging students to find inspiration by learning about the achievements of great creators? Suggestion: Schedule a library period, and urge pupils to locate and read works on the lives and works of great artists or books that offer ideas and describe techniques of craftsmanship.

SUGGESTIONS FOR FURTHER STUDY

9-1

National Assessment Goals

The most concise outline of National Assessment goals is provided in *Update on Education* (1975) by Simon S. Johnson. Detailed lists of objectives and subobjectives are described in separate booklets. For information about these publications, request a publications list from National Assessment of Educational Progress, 300 Lincoln Tower, 1860 Lincoln Street, Denver, Colorado 80203.

9-2

Bruner on Transfer

One of the clearest and most concise accounts of the general nature of transfer is presented by Jerome Bruner in the first two chapters of *The Process of Education* (1960).

9-3

The Saber-Tooth Curriculum

As a young instructor of future teachers, Harold Benjamin was struck by what he considered absurdities in American education. He found release from his frustration with the "educational establishment" by writing a satire—*The Saber-Tooth Curriculum*—under the pseudonym J. Abner Peddiwell. In a series of imaginary "lectures," a professor of education describes how education was conducted in Paleolithic times. Even though *The Saber-Tooth Curriculum* was written in 1939, many of the sacred cows ridiculed by Benjamin forty years ago are still with us. If you enjoy satire, this book will both entertain and enlighten you. If you read *The Saber-Tooth Curriculum,* relate Benjamin's criticisms of education to current trends and practices in the schools.

9-4

Research on Transfer

For a concise but complete analysis of transfer, look for *The Transfer of Learning* (1965) by Henry Ellis. Excellent observations on transfer for the elementary school teacher appear in Chapters 9 and 10 of *The Learning Process and School Practice* (1970) by May V. Seagoe.

9-5

Mager on Transfer of Attitudes

In many courses, the most important single type of transfer will be attitudes students take with them when they leave the classroom. If you would like to make a systematic effort to increase the likelihood that your students will make more approach responses to the subject you teach after they leave your classroom than they did before they entered it, examine *Developing Attitude Toward Learning* (1968) by Robert F. Mager.

9-6

The Productive Thinking Program

Richard S. Crutchfield and his associates have developed a series of programmed picture stories designed to "strengthen the elementary school student's ability to think." A discussion of the Productive Thinking Program appears in Chapter 4 ("Developing the Skills of Productive Thinking") of *Trends and Issues in Developmental Psychology* (1969), edited by Paul H. Mussen, Jonas Langer, and Martin Covington, and a curriculum library may have a complete set of the materials used in the program. The sample illustrations shown on page 483 of this chapter may induce you to order your own set of the lessons in the Productive Thinking Program. For information, write to Charles E. Merrill Publishing Company, 1300 Alum Creek Drive, Columbus, Ohio 43216. (A complete package of materials consists of Basic Lessons, a Teacher's Guide, a Chart of Thinking Guide, Reply Booklets, and Problem Sets workbooks.)

You might also consider using similar techniques to develop your own Productive Thinking Program. One possibility would be to base individual or class projects on comic books that present detective stories, perhaps even Sherlock Holmes. For insight into how a master of detective fiction provides the reader with all the clues before the detective solves the case, read an Agatha Christie mystery featuring

Hercule Poirot or Miss Marple. See if you can figure out the answer before the last chapter. All the clues will be at hand. If heuristics attracts you, read and try to solve a Poirot mystery on your own. Then read another, and make full use of heuristics. Poirot does; and by employing "method" and his "little grey cells," he always manages to solve a case. You might even use Agatha Christie novels in a Productive Thinking Program at the junior and senior high school levels.

9-7

Inquiry Training

J. Richard Suchman has sought the same goal as Crutchfield—that is, fostering a student's ability to think or solve problems—but he favors a discovery rather than a programmed approach. To find out more about how Suchman institutes inquiry training (so you can compare his method to that of Crutchfield), look for *The Elementary School Training Program in Scientific Inquiry* (1963); "Inquiry Training: Building Skills for Autonomous Discovery," which appeared in volume 7, number 3 (1961) , of the *Merrill-Palmer Quarterly;* or "Inquiry and Education" in *Teaching Gifted Students: A Book of Readings,* edited by James J. Gallagher (1965). If you read any of these, you might record your reactions and comment on how you might use techniques of inquiry training in your classes.

9-8

Bruner's Approach to Inquiry Training

Jerome Bruner's techniques of inquiry training are similar to Suchman's although somewhat less systematic. You will find a description of how Bruner encourages students to acquire general methods for solving problems in Chapter 3 of *Toward a Theory of Instruction* (1966). If you read this chapter, summarize your reactions to Bruner's approach and, if appropriate, tell how you might apply similar techniques in your classes.

(Note: Bruner uses exercises that are primarily mathematical. Suchman concentrates pretty much on phenomena of physical science. Crutchfield, on the other hand, features a variety of behavioral situations in his lessons. So Crutchfield's approach may be the most helpful to you in a wide range of situations.)

9-9

Polya on heuristics

The teacher of mathematics or physical sciences is likely to find Gyorgy Polya's *How to Solve It* paperback (1954) especially interesting. The concise set of guidelines it offers might be used in encouraging students to learn to solve problems. Even if you will not be teaching math or science, you may find Polya's description of heuristics helpful and thought provoking (and of assistance in solving Agatha Christie mysteries). If you read this book, you might note your reactions and, if possible, indicate what possibilities you see for heuristics in your classes.

9-10

Early Lives of Creative People

In *Cradles of Eminence* (1962), Victor and Mildred Goertzel describe the background of four hundred eminent people who have lived in the twentieth century. Although not all of these famous individuals were creative, many of them were, and an analysis of the forces that molded their personalities sheds light on the kind of environmental experiences that seem to predispose a gifted person to develop his or her potential. The chapter headings summarize the main subjects discussed: Chapter 1, "Homes Which Respected Learning and Achievement"; Chapter 2, "Opinionative Parents"; Chapter 3, "Failure Prone Fathers" (half of the fathers of the four hundred were failure prone); Chapter 4, "Dominating Mothers"; Chapter 5, "Smothering Mothers" (smothering mothers produced dictators or poets—or both); Chapter 6, "Troubled Homes" (percentages from troubled homes: actors, 100 percent; authoritarian politicians, 95 percent; novelists and playwrights, 89 percent; composers and musicians, 86 percent; and military leaders, 86 percent); Chapter 9, "Early Agonies"; Chapter 10, "Dislike of School and Teachers." Some of these chapter headings may lure you to browse through *Cradles of Eminence* and relate points noted in the book to techniques for encouraging creativity in your classes.

9-11

Torrance on Creativity

E. Paul Torrance has probably done more and written more about developing creativity in children than any other psychologist. For ways to stimulate your students to be as creative as possible—or at least to avoid squelching their creativity—look through one or several of Torrance's book or articles. *A Source Book for Creative Thinking* (1962), edited by S. Parnes and G. Harding, contains an article by Torrance (as well as contributions by others). *Guiding Creative Talent* (1962) and *Gifted Children in the Classroom* (1965) are more extensive discussions by Torrance. If you read any of these, you might note your reactions and comment on ideas you think might be worth trying with your students.

9-12

Teaching Poetry

If you will be teaching the elementary grades or secondary school English, literature, or creative writing, you might look at *Wishes, Lies, Dreams: A Way of Teaching Children Poetry* (1970) by Kenneth Koch. This book describes techniques developed by Koch and contains many samples of poetry written by his students. Koch found that an effective way to get pupils started is to have the whole class collectively produce a poem. Then individual work is encouraged by suggesting that pupils write poems in which every line states a wish or includes a comparison, a noise, or a color; by telling pupils not to worry about rhyme; and by urging them to write crazy or silly poems. For more information about how to use these and other techniques, refer to *Wishes, Lies, Dreams*.

9-13

The Nature of Creativity

In *Creativity: The Magic Synthesis* (1976), Silvano Arieti offers a comprehensive analysis of the nature of creativity. Arieti discusses the creative process; theories of creativity; psychological components of creativity; creativity in painting, music, religion, science, and philosophy; the creative person; and many other topics.

In Parts 2, 3, and 4 of this book you were acquainted with theories of development and the characteristics of pupils at different age levels, with speculations about how students learn and with suggestions on how to facilitate the learning, remembering, and transfer of facts, concepts, skills, and attitudes. In this part, you will be asked to consider motivation. One of your major concerns as a teacher will be finding ways to arouse and sustain interest in learning. If most of your pupils are apathetic or unresponsive most of the time, it may not make much difference whether you are aware of their developmental characteristics or well informed about

principles of learning. Accordingly, it is important to speculate about what does and does not arouse the interest of pupils.

The significance of motivating students to learn can be emphasized by reviewing points made in earlier chapters. In Chapter 2 you were asked to think about what you will be expected to do as a public school teacher. One of the points stressed was that you are likely to be held accountable for the amount of learning that takes place in your classroom. Another was that you will need to find ways to involve your students in learning experiences for six hours a day, 180 days a year. An implication of both these conditions is that if your students fail to exhibit a desire to learn, you will need to seek ways to remedy the situation.

In Chapter 3 you were introduced to several conceptions of behavior and development. Erikson pointed out that younger children should be encouraged to develop initiative and industry and adolescents should be assisted in developing a sense of identity. When high school students are unable to focus on positive goals, they may engage in a psychosocial moratorium or develop a negative identity. Havighurst stressed that children must be helped to master a series of developmental tasks if they are to avoid aberrations in development.

A major point stressed in Chapter 8 was that many learning experiences may be thought of as occurring in a hierarchy. Students will not be able to apply principles or solve problems unless they have first mastered simpler kinds of learning, some of which may be unavoidably tedious and effortful. A related point, emphasized at the end of Chapter 9, is that impressive, significant, and satisfying forms of creative expression usually occur only after a person has engaged in lengthy and often arduous preparation.

These various points might be summarized in this way:

1. If your students lack self-motivation to learn, you will be expected to help them become motivated.

2. High school students, in particular, need to focus on specific goals.

3. Students who fail to acquire certain habits, skills, and abilities in lower grades are likely to experience difficulties in upper grades.

4. Once individuals become well-informed in a field of knowledge or proficient in a skill, they usually are eager to make use of what they have learned. In order to reach that point, however, it is often necessary to engage in sometimes unrewarding effort.

5. Before individuals can solve problems or engage in significant creative effort, they must acquire a great deal of information and perfect basic skills.

As this brief review makes clear, there are many reasons for analyzing the nature of motivation. In Chapter 10 you will be acquainted with different views of motivation, with special stress on Abraham H. Maslow's theory of growth motivation. Then some of the educational implications of these theories will be presented in the form of Suggestions for Teaching. In Chapter 11 you will learn about the special motivational needs of students who come from backgrounds that cause them to be at a disadvantage in school compared to classmates.

Part Five

Motivation

Chapter 10   Motivation: Theory and applications

Chapter 11   Teaching the disadvantaged

Key points

Views of motivation

S-R View: Behavior shaped by reinforcement

Cognitive view: Urge to maintain cognitive equilibrium

Humanistic view: Desire to seek adequacy or competence

Maslow's theory of growth motivation

Maslow's basic principle: Higher need emerges as lower needs are gratified

Deficiency needs: Physiological, safety, belongingness and love, esteem

Growth needs: Self-actualization, knowing and understanding, aesthetic

Growth-motivated person seeks pleasurable tension, is self-directed

Teachers in a key position to satisfy deficiency needs

When deficiency needs are not satisfied, person likely to be a bad chooser

Encourage growth choices by enhancing attractions, minimizing dangers

Interrelationships of safety and growth

Level of aspiration: Succeed at highest possible level while avoiding failure

Success leads to realistic goals

Need for achievement encouraged by successful experiences

Implications of the views of motivation

Rewards usually extrinsic; learning for its own sake is intrinsic

Few pupils recognize need to master basic skills and information

Arousing and sustaining interest in learning

Goal card: Detailed series of tasks

Praise may threaten or alienate, cause feelings of inferiority, limit creativity

Blame may induce panic, particularly when no help is offered

Interest aroused by activity, investigation, adventure, social interaction, usefulness

Chapter 10

Motivation: Theory and applications

THREE GENERAL conceptions of motivation have already been discussed in earlier chapters. Chapter 3 acquainted you with the S-R theorists' argument that learning takes place because of the way reinforcement shapes behavior, with Jean Piaget's principle of equilibration, and with Abraham H. Maslow's conviction that children *enjoy* growing and *seek* experiences. These basic conceptions were emphasized again in chapters 5, 6, and 7. The S-R view of learning is based on the assumption that teachers should induce students to learn by rewarding them when they engage in desired forms of behavior. The cognitive view stresses that pupils have a built-in desire to maintain cognitive equilibrium and that the teacher's job is to arrange conditions so that discovery will take place. Humanists also emphasize inherent tendencies, but they believe that these energizing forces impel human beings to seek all kinds of gratification, not just cognitive satisfaction. Before analyzing techniques for motivating students to learn, it will be helpful to examine each of these three basic conceptions in greater detail.

Views of motivation

The S-R view

The stimulus-response position championed by B. F. Skinner stresses the impact of reinforcement. Skinner and his followers argue that we begin life as blank slates and that we are shaped by experiences. Consequently, proponents of this view seek to explain motivation by determining why some experiences seem to arouse responses more than others. Early S-R experiments involved observing the behavior of rats that had been deprived of food and noting the way reinforcement led to associations between stimuli and responses. On the basis of such experiments, a conception of motivation was proposed that stressed the importance of physiological drives and the way these serve as the basis for other motives. It was suggested, for example, that a boy would be motivated to learn in order to earn praise from a teacher because early in life phrases such as "good boy" uttered by his mother as she fed him were associated with his hunger being satisfied.

In time, further experiments revealed that although this explanation might account for some aspects of motivation, it placed too much emphasis on the satisfaction of physiological drives. A number of investigators (e.g., Butler, 1953) demonstrated that young animals with all their physiological drives satisfied would engage in many types of behavior simply to satisfy their curiosity or to manipulate things. This finding led to the recognition that not all behavior is necessarily derived from physiological drives, but the S-R view of motivation still places great emphasis on external behavior and on the ways in which responses are reinforced.

Skinner's experiments with rats and pigeons illustrate this view. The animal is deprived of food before it is placed in the learning situation. When it makes a move toward the desired terminal behavior, it is reinforced with a food pellet. Those who favor an operant conditioning approach follow the same general procedure in the classroom, making allowance for the obvious fact that the physiological drives of most students will be reasonably satisfied. Just as the rat is reinforced with food each time it responds in the desired way, students are reinforced for correct answers by being given praise, prizes, candy (the human equivalent of a food pellet), or sometimes money. If a teacher experiences problems in encouraging students to learn, the S-R theorist is likely to maintain that the problems occur because conditions have been improperly arranged or because reinforcement has not been supplied in an advantageous manner.

S-R view: Behavior shaped by reinforcement

The cognitive view

The cognitive view stresses that human behavior is influenced by the way individuals perceive things. Lewin proposed the concept of the life space to explain why people act as they do. At any given moment, people are subjected to many forces that pull and push them in different directions. The direction that behavior takes is explained by assuming that individuals experience some sort of disequilibrium that they feel impelled to overcome. The techniques recommended by Bruner and Bigge for structuring discovery sessions are intended to cause students to want to find out more about some topic or to revise their perceptions. The question that is posed causes pupils to recognize gaps in their thinking, which they are eager to clarify or fill.

This view is related to Piaget's principles of equilibration, assimilation, and accommodation. Piaget proposes that children are born with a desire to maintain a sense of organization and balance in their conception of the world (equilibration). If children assimilate a new experience that is slightly at variance with previous experiences, they will be motivated to accommodate, or modify, their view of things.

Cognitive view: Urge to maintain cognitive equilibrium

The humanistic view

The humanistic view of motivation is similar to the cognitive view in the sense that it stresses a self-directed desire on the part of individuals to do things. Humanists differ from field theorists, however, in their explanation of why such self-motivation occurs. Instead of proposing that a disequilibrium in one's life space is the energizing force—the explanation offered by Lewin and Bigge—Arthur Combs and Donald Snygg stress the need for adequacy: "a great driving, striving force in each of us by which we are continually seeking to make ourselves ever more adequate in life" (1959, p. 45). A similar explanation has been proposed by Robert W. White (whose primary interest was motivation, not humanistic education), who prefers the

Humanistic view: Desire to seek adequacy or competence

© 1957 United Feature Syndicate, Inc.

words *competence* or *efficacy* to *adequacy*. White offered this explanation (1952) after he had analyzed dozens of theories and hundreds of studies on motivation. He concluded that many types of human behavior are not traceable to physiological drives, since individuals engage in activities when all their physical needs are satisfied. Some of the things people do appear to be motivated by curiosity, an urge to explore, or simply an impulse to try something for the fun of it.

The most complete and thought-provoking analysis of self-directed aspects of motivation has been offered by Abraham H. Maslow. Maslow's analysis merits comprehensive coverage because it helps explain why some children are more motivated to learn than others and also why some individuals are better adjusted than others.

Maslow's theory of growth motivation

A hierarchy of needs

Maslow first described sixteen propositions he felt would have to be incorporated into any sound theory of motivation. (These are discussed in Chapter 3 of *Motivation and Personality*.) Maslow eventually proposed a theory of *growth motivation* (or *need gratification*) that he felt met these propositions. He refers to need gratification as "the most important single principle underlying all development," adding that "the single, holistic principle that binds together the multiplicity of human motives is the tendency for a new and higher need to emerge as the lower need fulfills itself by being sufficiently gratified" (1968, p. 55). He elaborated on this basic principle by proposing a hierarchy of needs, starting with *physiological* needs at the bottom; working up through *safety* needs, *belongingness* and *love* needs, *esteem* needs, the need for *self-actualization*, the desires to *know* and to *understand*; and culminating in *aesthetic* needs (described in Chapter 4 of *Motivation and Personality*). Figure 10–1 presents Maslow's list of needs arranged in a literal hierarchical form.

In Maslow's theory of growth motivation, when individuals have the lower *deficiency* needs (physiological, safety, belongingness and love, esteem) satisfied, they will feel motivated to satisfy the higher *growth* (or *being*) needs (self-actualization, knowing and understanding, aesthetic)—not because of a deficit but because of a *desire* to gratify the higher needs.

Differences between deficiency and growth needs

In Chapter 3 of *Toward a Psychology of Being*, Maslow lists and explains twelve ways that deficiency needs differ from growth needs.

Maslow's basic principle: Higher need emerges as lower needs are gratified

Deficiency needs: Physiological, safety, belongingness and love, esteem

Growth needs: Self-actualization, knowing and understanding, aesthetic

Figure 10-1

Maslow's hierarchy of needs

From "A Theory of Human Motivation," *Psychological Review*, vol. 50 (1943), pp. 370–396. Copyright 1943 by the American Psychological Association. Reprinted by permission.

Differences of greatest significance to teachers can be summarized as follows:

Growth-motivated person seeks pleasurable tension, is self-directed

1. Individuals act to get *rid* of deficiency needs (e.g., hunger); they *seek* the pleasure of growth needs.

2. Deficiency motivation leads to reduction of disagreeable tension and restoration of equilibrium; growth motives maintain a pleasurable form of tension.

3. The satisfying of deficiency needs leads to a sense of relief and satiation; the satisfying of growth needs leads to pleasure and a desire for further fulfillment.

4. The fact that deficiency needs can be satisfied only by other people leads to dependence on the environment and to a tendency to be other-directed (e.g., the person seeks the approval of others); growth needs are satisfied more autonomously and tend to make one self-directed.

5. Deficiency-motivated individuals must depend on others for help when they encounter difficulties; growth-motivated individuals are more able to help themselves.

Implications of Maslow's theory

The implications for teaching Maslow's theory of motivation are provocative. One down-to-earth implication is that a teacher should do everything possible to see that the lower-level needs of students are satisfied so that they are more likely to function at the higher levels. Your students are more likely to be primed to seek satisfaction of the need to understand and know in your classes if they are physically comfortable, feel safe and relaxed, have a sense of belonging, and experience self-esteem. Since the satisfying of deficiency needs involves dependence on others and since teachers have the primary responsibility for what takes place in the classroom, it is worth emphasizing again that you will play an important role in the need gratification of your students. The more effective you are in assisting them to satisfy their deficiency needs, the more likely they are to experience growth motivation.

Teachers in a key
position to satisfy
deficiency needs

Even though you do your best to satisfy the lower level needs in this hierarchy, you are not likely to be successful in establishing a situation in which all your students will always function at the highest levels. A girl who feels that her parents do not love her or that her peers do not accept her may not respond to your efforts to show a favorable reaction. And if her needs for love, belonging, and esteem are not satisfied, she is less likely to be in the mood to learn. Only under close to ideal circumstances do the higher needs emerge; only when the higher needs come into play is a person likely to choose wisely when given the opportunity. Maslow emphasizes this point by making a distinction between *bad choosers* and *good choosers*. When some people are allowed freedom to choose, they seem consistently to make wise choices. Most people, however, frequently make choices that are self-destructive. Maslow explains this by describing growth as it takes place under ideal circumstances and as it, more often, actually occurs:

When deficiency needs
are not satisfied, person
likely to be a bad
chooser

Growth takes place when the next step forward is subjectively more delightful, more joyous, more intrinsically satisfying than the previous gratification with which we have become familiar and even bored; . . . the only way we can ever know what is right for us is that it feels better than any alternative. The new experience validates *itself* rather than by any outside criterion. It is self-justifying, self-validating. . . .

Then arise the inevitable questions, What holds [the child] back? What prevents growth? Wherein lies the conflict: What is the alternative to growth forward? Why is it so hard and painful for some to grow forward? Here we must become more fully aware of the fixative and regressive power of ungratified deficiency needs, of the attractions of safety and security, of the functions of defense and protection against pain, fear, loss, and threat, of the need for courage in order to grow ahead.

Every human being has *both* sets of forces within him. One set clings to safety and defensiveness out of fear, tending to regress backward, hanging on to the past, *afraid* to grow. . . , *afraid* to take chances, *afraid* to jeopardize what he already has, *afraid* of independence, freedom and separateness. The other set of forces impels him forward toward wholeness of Self and uniqueness of Self, toward full functioning of all his capacities, toward confidence in the face of the external world at the same time that he can accept his deepest, real, unconscious Self. (1968, pp. 45–46)

Growth, as Maslow sees it, is the result of a never ending series of situations offering a free choice between the attractions and dangers of safety and those of growth. If a person is functioning at the level of growth needs, the choice will ordinarily be a progressive one. However, Maslow adds:

In this process, the environment (parents, therapists, teachers) is important in various ways, even though the ultimate choice must be made by the child:

a. It can gratify his basic needs for safety, belongingness, love and respect, so that he can feel unthreatened, autonomous, interested and spontaneous and thus dare to choose the unknown.

b. It can help by making the growth choice positively attractive and less dangerous, and by making the regressive choice less attractive and more costly. (1968, pp. 58–59)

The first point emphasizes the suggestion made earlier that you should do everything possible to gratify deficiency needs to encourage growth. The second point can be clarified by a simple diagram Maslow has devised to illustrate a choice situation (1968, p. 47):

Enhance the dangers   Enhance the attractions

Safety ◄——————— person ———————► Growth

Minimize the attractions   Minimize the dangers

Encourage growth choices by enhancing attractions, minimizing dangers

This diagram emphasizes that if you set up learning situations that impress students as dangerous, threatening, or of little value, they will be likely to play it safe, make little effort to respond, or even try to avoid learning. On the other hand, if you make learning appear appealing, minimize pressure, and reduce possibilities for failure or embarrassment, your students are likely to be willing, if not eager, to do an assigned task.

Maslow's theory of motivation is congruent with the views of Combs and Snygg and other advocates of humanistic education. Because it is assumed the child will choose wisely if given the chance, the basic approach to education they endorse involves arranging attractive learning situations so that students can select the activities they feel have personal appeal or value. Instead of the teacher supplying reinforcement, the self-chosen activity of the child becomes its own reward. In order to encourage this kind of education, however, it is necessary to seek an optimum balance between freedom and control. In deciding how you might seek a balance between the motivational aspects of these two factors, you will need to consider the interrelationship of safety and growth.

Interrelationship of safety and growth

Impact of one's level of aspiration

The distinction Maslow makes between safety and growth has been analyzed in different terms by other theorists. One of the first descriptions of the push-pull nature of many decisions was provided by the German psychologist F. Hoppe (1930) who analyzed *level of aspiration*. He observed that people tend to raise their goals after success and to lower them after failure. This process offers protection from continual failure and from too easy achievement, which does not provide a feeling of accomplishment. The level of aspiration is set as a compromise between conflicting tendencies: the desire to avoid disappointment accompanying failure, which forces aspirations down, and the desire to succeed at the highest possible level, which pushes aspirations up. In some cases the protective mechanism is thrown out of balance. Individuals who set goals that are too high will inevitably fail. Individuals who set goals that are too low are robbed of a sense of achievement no matter what they do. The ideal situation is for a student to maintain a realistic level of aspiration.

The nature of aspirations was demonstrated in an experiment by Pauline Sears (1940), who worked with three groups of upper elementary school subjects. A "success" group was composed of children who had had a consistent history of success in all academic subjects. A "failure" group consisted of pupils with the opposite sort of record. A "differential" group was made up of children who had had successful experiences with reading but unsuccessful experiences with arithmetic. The subjects were given a series of twenty speed tests in arithmetic and reading. After the first trial, they were asked to estimate the time it would take them to do the next section. Then half the pupils in each group were exposed to a "success condition." They were lavishly praised for their performance after most (but not all) of the next nineteen trials. The other pupils in each group were exposed to a "failure condition." They were criticized rather severely for poor work after most (but not all) of the next nineteen trials. After each trial, all subjects were asked to estimate their time for the next test.

Pupils who were exposed to the failure condition showed greater discrepancies between their estimated and their actual performance. They were also much more variable in the way they reacted—some tending to 'set consistently lower goals, others setting impossibly higher goals for themselves. The pupils with previous histories of academic success were somewhat better able to cope with the experimental failure condition; their discrepancies and variability were not so extreme. The success condition pupils (even those with a previous history of failure) also set realistic goals for themselves, with a tendency to put them slightly above the actual level of performance.

The need for achievement

J. W. Atkinson (1964) has developed a theory of motivation embodying a more comprehensive interpretation of Hoppe's level of aspiration. His theory is derived also from the conception of *achievement motivation* proposed by David McClelland (1961). McClelland believes that in the course of development human beings acquire a *need* for achievement, and he has conducted research to demonstrate the degree to which the need varies among individuals. Atkinson hypothesizes that differences in the strength of the need for achievement can be explained by postulating a contrasting need to avoid failure. Some people, he suggests, are success oriented; others have a high degree of anxiety about failure. By experiments similar to those conducted by Sears, Atkinson and Litwin (1960) showed that success-oriented individuals are likely to set personal goals of intermediate difficulty (that is, they have a fifty-fifty chance of success), whereas anxiety-ridden persons set goals that are either very high or very low. (If anxiety-ridden individuals fail on the hard task, no one can blame them; and they are almost sure to succeed on the easy task.) Atkinson believes that the tendency to achieve success is influenced by the probability of success and the attractiveness of achieving it. A strong need to avoid failure is likely to be developed if people experience repeated failure and if they set goals beyond what they think they can accomplish.

Need for achievement encouraged by successful experiences

The similarity of Atkinson's conception to Maslow's theory of motivation and to Hoppe's interpretation of level of aspiration is apparent. All three emphasize that the fear of failure must be taken into account in arranging learning experiences. The same point has

Pupils differ in the strength of their need for achievement.

Peter Travers

been stressed by John Holt in *How Children Fail* (1964) and by William Glasser in *Schools Without Failure* (1969) and *The Identity Society* (1972). Glasser argues that in order for people to succeed at life in general, they must first experience success in one important aspect of their lives. For most children, that one important part should be school. But the traditional approach to education, which emphasizes comparative grading, allows only a minority of students to feel successful. Most students feel that they are failures, and their motivation to achieve in other aspects of their lives is depressed. This is the basic argument made by advocates (Bloom, 1968) of mastery learning. It is also related to Erikson's theory of development, which stresses the importance of encouraging initiative and industry (rather than doubt and guilt), and to Carl Roger's contention that individuals must develop positive feelings about themselves.

Implications of the views of motivation

Before offering suggestions for developing motivational techniques to be used in the classroom, an analysis of some of the implications of the various theories that have just been described is offered as background.

Possible limitations of the S-R view

The S-R view of motivation emphasizes that it is necessary for a teacher to supply reinforcement in order to guide learning. Although such an approach is appropriate and effective in some situations, if used to excess, it is likely to lead to a conception of motivation that may become extrinsic, manipulative, materialistic, and repressive.

Rewards usually extrinsic; learning for its own sake is intrinsic

When individuals indulge in an activity primarily because they will earn a reward, the motivation is *extrinsic*. When a person engages in an activity for its own sake, the motivation is *intrinsic*. Some activities may provide their own reinforcement, but the S-R advocates' conviction that it is a mistake to leave anything to accidental contingencies of reinforcement leads them to feel uncomfortable about such activities. Instead, they prefer conditions that are arranged to *produce* specific kinds of behavior. Since these situations are usually arranged rather than natural, a person may not find them self-reinforcing, and reinforcement will have to be supplied. When the supplied reinforcement is not directly related to the activity, it is extrinsic.

If you accept the principle that arranged contingencies are preferable to accidental ones and if you decide to supply reinforcement for almost all responses, you are virtually committed to behavior manipulation. Stimulus situations must be devised, and responses in a desired direction must be reinforced. The necessity to supply different and more satisfying reinforcements is likely to cause problems. Students may cease to respond if any particular technique is used too often (and the reinforcement loses its appeal); and when learning becomes more difficult, they may demand greater rewards for greater effort. Consequently, praise may become ineffective; after the first dozen or so pieces, candy or the equivalent may seem unappetizing; the chance to indulge in a self-selected activity may not be considered worth the trouble. It seems almost inevitable that excessive use of rewards will lead to a materialistic "What will I get out of this?" attitude. And as soon as students realize they are in a situation where no one is around to supply a payoff, they are likely to drop an activity abruptly.

When reinforcement is supplied by others, a depressive effect may occur because of factors such as those outlined by Maslow in his comparison of deficiency and growth needs. The fact that deficit needs can be satisfied only by other people leads deficit-motivated individuals to be sensitive to the approval of others and dependent on them, thereby limiting interpersonal relations and reducing their confidence in solving problems on their own. Ideally, students should be encouraged to be autonomous, to see others as individuals in their own right (not just as suppliers of reinforcement), and to be capable of helping themselves. The S-R view of motivation thus stresses deficit motivation and may limit growth motivation.

Some advocates of behavior modification take pains to point out that the techniques they use are for early training only and that the ultimate goal is to encourage eventual self-directed behavior. However, few books or articles on behavior modification actually give instructions as to how a teacher can bring about the transition. Erikson's theory of development and Rogers's observations on psychotherapy and learner-centered education, which stress the importance of having children feel confident about their ability to control their own behavior, make clear the difficulties of designing reinforcement schedules to wean a child from control.

Possible limitations of too much freedom

In his theory of motivation, Maslow asks you to have trust in the human organism and to allow freedom of choice. At the same time, he urges you to remain aware of the complexity of motivation and to remember that the good chooser is the exception rather than the rule. Neill and Holt and some other champions of free education advocate complete freedom of choice. This view, however, fails to take into account Maslow's observation that individuals usually do not function as good choosers unless their deficiency needs have been well satisfied. Since comparatively few pupils are in the enviable position of functioning consistently at the level of growth motivation, it seems reasonable to assume that most students will frequently make unwise choices if they are given a great deal of freedom to arrange their own educational experiences.

The free education view also overlooks the hierarchical nature of learning, described by Gagné in *The Conditions of Learning*. Problem solving, intuitive thinking, and creativity are the most satisfying and valuable learning experiences—the kinds that occur during episodes of self-actualization. In order to become capable of such learning, a person must first master verbal associations, concepts, and principles. Few children can be expected to have the maturity and foresight to realize this and to persevere through the sometimes minimally rewarding work of mastering basic information. If given complete freedom, they may respond only to aspects of the learning environment that have immediate, superficial appeal and never come to grips with a field of study. If diverted from mastering information that has great potential value and might lead to genuine enjoyment of a subject, they are seduced by the attractions of safety into making bad choices.

In light of all of this, it is once again apparent that some sort of balance between control and freedom seems desirable. In thinking about how to develop such a conception of motivation, consider the following goals to strive for in arranging learning. (Many of them are similar to goals noted earlier.)

Few pupils recognize need to master basic skills and information

Goals to strive for in arranging motivational experiences

1. Take into account Maslow's hierarchy of needs, particularly the distinction between deficiency and growth needs.

2. Remain aware that teachers are in a key position to gratify deficiency needs—which can be satisfied only by others.

3. Keep in mind Maslow's description of a choice situation and the desirability of enhancing the attractions of growth choices while minimizing their dangers.

4. Try to see that learning experiences encourage students to develop a realistic level of aspiration and to become success oriented.

5. Do everything possible to minimize anxiety and failure and to maximize feelings of initiative and industry and the development of a positive self-concept.

6. Maximize intrinsic motivation, self-direction, and the enjoyment of doing something for its own sake.

7. Minimize extrinsic motivation, manipulation, and overtones of materialism.

8. Take into account the need to supply encouragement when students are engaged in mastery of background information that will have a delayed payoff.

The following suggestions are offered as starting points for developing ways to achieve these goals.

Suggestions for teaching: Arousing and sustaining interest in learning

1. Do everything possible to satisfy the deficiency needs—physiological, safety, belongingness, esteem.

   a. Allow for the physical condition of your pupils and the classroom.

   b. Make your room physically and psychologically safe.

   c. Show your students that you take an interest in them and that they "belong" in your classroom.

   d. Arrange learning experiences so that all students can gain at least a degree of esteem.

2. Enhance the attractions and minimize the dangers of growth choices.

3. Direct learning experiences toward feelings of success in an effort to encourage a realistic level of aspiration, an orientation toward achievement, and a positive self-concept.

   a. Make use of goals and objectives that are challenging but attainable.

   b. Provide knowledge of results by emphasizing the positive.

   c. Consider the advantages and disadvantages of symbolic and material rewards.

4. Be alert to the damaging impact of excessive competition.

5. For students who need it, encourage the development of a desire to achieve.

6. Take advantage of natural interests, try to create new ones, and encourage learning for its own sakc.

7. When appropriate, permit and encourage students to direct their own learning

8. Provide encouragement and incentives for learning that is essential but not intrinsically appealing.

1. Do everything possible to satisfy the deficiency needs—physiological, safety, belongingness, esteem.

   a. Allow for the physical condition of your pupils and the classroom.

EXAMPLES

Be aware that your students may occasionally be hungry or thirsty. (This sounds obvious, but it is frequently forgotten.) Permit snacks on an individual basis or have a routine—or occasional nonroutine—snack break.

Have a change of pace or a break when appropriate. With young children, make allowance for flexible nap time.

Make a habit of checking the room temperature. Ask students if the room is too warm or cool.

Handbook heading
Satisfying Physiological Needs

   In your Handbook, you might note other practices you can follow to satisfy physiological needs.

   b. Make your room physically and psychologically safe. The need for safety is likely to be satisfied by the general classroom climate you establish, although physical factors of safety may be

Snack time in the kindergarten takes into account the importance of satisfying physiological needs.
Elizabeth Hamlin/Stock Boston

involved, particularly with young pupils. In one kindergarten, for example, several children were worried about the possibility of fire after seeing TV news coverage of a fire in a school. In most cases, however, you can best ensure safety by establishing a relaxed, secure classroom environment.

EXAMPLES

If you see that a pupil fears something—for example, being bullied by older pupils on the playground, fire, enclosed places—explain that you will offer protection or that adequate precautionary measures have been taken.

Establish a classroom atmosphere in which students know what to expect and can relax about routines. Do everything you can to make your room a place that is psychologically safe. Be alert to things you do that are unnecessarily threatening. Try to see things from your students' point of view in an effort to detect anxiety-producing situations.

As much as possible, establish classroom routines in which students can take the initiative. Don't require recitation; wait for students to volunteer. Don't force students to participate in new activities; let them try when they feel ready.

A humiliating or embarrassing experience may so generalize that a student comes to hate or fear everything connected with a classroom. So go out of your way to make such a student feel comfortable and secure.

Handbook heading
Satisfying the Need for
Safety

In your Handbook, you might note other ways to make your classroom an inviting, secure place.

c. Show your students that you take an interest in them and that they "belong" in your classroom.

EXAMPLES

Learn and use names as fast as you can.

Follow the open school practice of keeping detailed records for individual pupils and refer to accomplishments specifically.

Whenever possible, schedule individual tutorial or interview sessions so that you can interact with all students on a one-to-one basis.

If a student is absent because of an extended illness, send a get-well card signed by the entire class.

To encourage esprit de corps, have class planning sessions or have "sharing," that is, invite students to talk about interesting experiences or make appropriate announcements.

Handbook heading
Ways to Satisfy the
Need for Belonging

In your Handbook, you might note other ways to make students in your classroom feel they "belong."

d. Arrange learning experiences so that all students can gain at least a degree of esteem.

EXAMPLES

Play down comparisons; encourage self-competition.
Make use of mastery learning.

Permit students to work toward individual goals.

Give individual assistance to slow-learning students.

(Further suggestions for satisfying esteem needs will be presented with subsequent points.)

2. Enhance the attractions and minimize the dangers of growth choices. When you first begin to teach, you might keep a copy of Maslow's diagram of a choice situation in your top desk drawer. Refer to it when the need arises and ask yourself, "Am I setting things up to encourage effort, or am I encouraging the student not to try?" If you establish situations that cause pressure, tension, or anxiety, your students will choose safety and do their best to remain uninvolved. But if you minimize risks and make learning seem exciting and worthwhile, even the less secure students may feel impelled to join in.

EXAMPLES

Don't penalize guessing on exams.

Don't impose restrictions or conditions on assignments if they will act as dampers—for example, "You must hand in all papers typed and with no erasures or strikeovers." Some students may not even start a report under such conditions.

Avoid "do or die" situations, such as single exams or projects.

To encourage free participation, make it clear that you will not grade students on class recitation.

Point out and demonstrate the values of learning and the limitations and disadvantages ("dangers") of not learning. For example, point out that knowing how to multiply and divide is necessary for personal bookkeeping and also that errors will lead to difficulties and perhaps the necessity to have someone else do the work for you.

Handbook heading
Ways to Encourage
Growth Choices

In your Handbook, you might note other ways to make safety choices appear unattractive or "dangerous" and make growth choices desirable and unthreatening.

3. Direct learning experiences toward feelings of success in an effort to encourage a realistic level of aspiration, an orientation toward achievement, and a positive self-concept. Hoppe described aspiration level, and Sears illustrated its impact in her study of students who worked under success-oriented and failure-oriented conditions. McClelland's theory of achievement motivation and Atkinson's development of it further emphasize how some people are success oriented, others anxiety ridden. Glasser maintains that in order for individuals to succeed at life in general, they must first experience success in one important part of their lives—particularly in school. Erikson stresses the importance of developing initiative and industry; Rogers, the need for a positive self-concept. All these theorists emphasize the vital importance of success. Students who experience early failure in any learning experience will either lose interest or actively avoid further learning—which could bring more failure. Consequently, it is vital to try to arrange learning experiences so that students will experience success. In order to feel successful, an individual must first establish goals that are neither so low as to be unfulfilling nor so high as to be impossible and then must know the goals have been achieved. There is a two-step process: establishing goals and receiving knowledge of results.

a. Make use of goals and objectives that are challenging but attainable. At the beginning of Chapter 8, instructional objectives were discussed. It was pointed out that the first step of basic technique, derived from Skinner's rat and pigeon experiments, is to state the desired terminal behavior. Those who favor programmed instruction advocate the use of objectives stated in behavioral terms, primarily to make instruction more efficient, but they also suggest that objectives be used to arouse, sustain, and direct student interest. When objectives are used for purposes of motivation, however, it is especially important to take into account the observations by Ojemann and invite students to participate in the selection of goals. If you simply state objectives as what you intend to have your students learn, you are unlikely to get as favorable a reaction as you would get if you helped your students to establish their own goals—or at least to think along with you as you explain why the goals are worthwhile. This will shift the emphasis from extrinsic to intrinsic motivation.

In developing goals to serve a motivating function, you may want to use the techniques recommended by Mager and Gronlund to help shift the emphasis from teacher direction to student choice. Having a specific goal to shoot for is one of the best ways to arouse and sustain interest. You might assist your students in stating objectives in terms of a time limit, a minimum number of correct responses, the proportion of correct responses, or a sample of actions.

Handbook heading
Ways to Establish
Attainable Goals

EXAMPLES

"Why don't you see if you can get that report done in the next thirty minutes?"

"Here is a list of ten scientists whose work is described in the third chapter of the text. Why not try to describe a key experiment for at least seven of them by the end of the period?"

"George, you got six out of ten on this spelling quiz, why not try for at least eight out of ten on the retest?"

"After reading this article on the laws of motion, see if you can state them in your own words and give two everyday examples of each."

The form of these examples implies that you are inviting students to participate in the development of their own objectives. Although this is a desirable policy to follow, sticking to it may not always be possible or appropriate. In many situations you may find it necessary to set goals yourself. In making decisions about presentation of goals, consider the advantages and disadvantages of programmed instruction and the discovery approach.

If you set goals by means of programmed instruction, students may or may not be given a detailed description of the terminal behavior, but they will at least know they are working toward improving their spelling or learning about the relationship between heat and light, or whatever. They will also have what amounts to a long series of specific goals in the form of frames in the program. Each time they supply a correct answer, they have achieved a goal of sorts, and this accomplishment, more than awareness of the general purpose of the program, may motivate them to continue.

There are ways other than programs to apply S-R theory to encourage goal-directed behavior. The use of goal cards provides a semiprogrammed approach. A *goal card* is a detailed series of tasks to be completed by students. It does not lead them to reach these goals as a program would; it merely enumerates things to be accomplished. Figure 10-2 is a math goal card used in the first grade in Winnetka, Illinois. It is a highly specific list of things to be achieved.

The proponents of goal cards (Bauernfeind, 1965) favor them for several reasons. Pupils who use them are highly motivated, especially when they record their own progress. The cards facilitate communication between teachers. A substitute teacher, for example, can discover just how much a given pupil knows. The points on the cards can serve as test items. The cards are invaluable in parent-teacher conferences. Everyone knows exactly what the child knows and where she or he is in the curriculum.

A goal card provides one type of incentive or purpose—a specific set of tasks to be performed. With some variations, it could be used with almost any subject matter. All you need do is draw up a list of

Goal card: Detailed series of tasks

Figure 10-2

Math goal card

Pupil _____ Teacher _____ Year _____

Check

Can count 10 objects .... _____
Can read and write numerals up to 10 .... _____
Recognizes number groups up to 5 .... _____
Recognizes patterns of objects to 10 .... _____
Can read and write numerals to 20 .... _____
Can count objects up to 100 .... _____
Recognizes numbers to 100 .... _____
Can read and write numerals to 50 .... _____
Recognizes addition and subtraction symbols .... _____
*Understands meaning of the inequality signs .... _____
Can count objects:
      by 2's to 20 .... _____
      by 5's to 100 .... _____
      by 10's to 100 .... _____
Recognizes geometric figures:
      triangle .... _____
      circle .... _____
      quadrilateral .... _____
Recognizes coins (1¢, 5¢, 10¢, 25¢) .... _____
Knows addition combinations 10 and under using objects .... _____
Knows subtraction combinations 10 and under using objects ...... _____
Recognizes addition and subtraction vertically and horizontally ... _____
*Can construct simple plane figures with straightedge and compass .... _____
Shows understanding of numbers and number combinations (check one):
     1. using concrete objects .... _____
     2. beginning to visualize and abstract .... _____
     3. makes automatic responses without concrete objects ...... _____
*Can tell time:
     1. hour .... _____
     2. half hour .... _____

*Goals starred are not essential for all students.

Comments:

Source: Reprinted with permission of Superintendent of Schools, Winnetka, Illinois.
Note: Only the first part of the Goal Card has been reproduced here.

things to be accomplished, put them in order, and encourage your students to work their way through the items.

If you will be teaching a subject that lacks clearly specifiable terminal behavior or if you feel uncomfortable about being so precise in shaping the learning of your students, you might prefer a field theory approach to providing goals. Morris L. Bigge (1976), who urges instructors to apply field theory principles, suggests that the teacher select problems for discovery sessions by thinking in terms of the life space. To motivate students through application of field theory principles, Bigge maintains, the teacher should try to induce a sense of dissatisfaction. This feeling will stimulate students to seek a solution in order to regain equilibrium in the life space. Since dissatisfaction will function as tension, a field of forces will be set up favoring goal-directed behavior. The situations Bigge proposes for structuring discovery sessions (noted in Chapter 6) illustrate this concept: switching the subject matter, introducing disturbing data, permitting students to make mistakes.

Goal cards provide incentives that are specific and tangible, but they are open to the usual criticisms of S-R theory: They tend to limit individuality, lend an assembly-line aura to learning, and restrict learning primarily to what the teacher has decided in advance should be learned. If they are used as the basis of examinations, the student may think of learning as a means to an end—getting a grade. This is an extrinsic kind of motivation, and forgetting will probably occur as soon as the exam has been written.

The discovery method problem that arouses tension in the life space avoids these disadvantages, but the subtlety of stimulating dissatisfaction that will lead to learning may make successful discussions difficult to arrange. Furthermore, the lack of clearly defined terminal behavior may prevent some students from achieving a sense of closure, and lack of closure will either lead to continued tension in the life space or cause pupils to divert their attention to something else. As usual, you have to pick and choose and balance alternatives. If you are dealing with material that involves clear terminal behavior, goal cards might be ideal motivating forces. If you are dealing with feelings and attitudes, motivating students by inducing a sense of dissatisfaction might be more appropriate. (This discussion of goals re-emphasizes points made earlier in explaining the lists of Key Points. Key Points, or specific objectives, for each chapter of this text are offered in order to provide a workable compromise between goals that are too specific and goals that are too vague. If you respond favorably to the Key Points technique, you might provide your students with a list of such points for a chapter in a text, a unit, or a lecture.)

Regardless of the approach you take when you set goals for your students, keep in mind the importance of success as a basis for the development of a realistic level of aspiration and an orientation toward achievement. Don't set impossibly high standards, and try to avoid situations in which only a minority of students can succeed. In the traditional approach to grading, success in the form of As and Bs can be achieved by only a few students, and it is frequently necessary for them to "defeat" their classmates in order to succeed. The result is apparent: Many pupils have had all desire to learn suppressed because they realize that when only the top 30 percent get respectable grades, the 70 percent at the bottom simply can't win. If you want most of your students to have the desire to learn, obviously you should set goals that they can achieve and provide extra assistance and encouragement (and not public humiliation or evidence of failure) for those less adept at achieving those goals.

EXAMPLES

Make use of techniques of open education: Let students choose activities on their own. Encourage students to learn from each other. Use tests not to compare students but to diagnose weaknesses and to set the stage for remedial instruction. Provide as much individualized instruction as possible.

Use the mastery approach (to be explained in detail in Chapter 13): State objectives, and arrange learning materials to help students achieve them. Use tests to determine if the goals have been met. Provide remedial instruction for those who need it; let students take tests as many times as they need to in order to achieve the established standard of performance.

b. Provide knowledge of results by emphasizing the positive. In order to experience success, as a basis for establishing a realistic level of aspiration, your students must receive detailed information about their performance. In a programmed approach, feedback will be supplied automatically when students respond to a question in a program or compare their performance to criteria included in a set of instructional objectives. As mentioned earlier, the subtlety of the discovery approach (which stresses reducing tension in the life space) may not always provide a sense of accomplishment. In discovery sessions—and in many other classroom situations—knowledge of performance will be supplied by comments you make. If you make observations on recitation, ask questions in a discussion or on an exam, or provide comments on papers of various kinds, the kind of feedback you provide may make the difference between producing feelings of success or of failure. Consequently, you should do your best to comment favorably on successful performance and avoid calling attention to failure, particularly the kind that is already apparent.

Handbook heading
Ways to Supply
Positive Feedback

Advocates of behavior modification urge teachers to make broad use of praise as a reinforcer—to the point of suggesting that you shape your own behavior to increase your productivity as a praiser. Even if you don't use behavior modification techniques, you will almost automatically praise pupils for perceptive comments in class discussion, excellent written work, and considerate behavior. Richard E. Farson points out that it is important to remain aware of some "hidden" aspects of praise. He offers these hypotheses:

Praise may threaten or
alienate, cause feelings
of inferiority, limit
creativity

Praise is not only of limited and questionable value as a motivator, but may in fact be experienced as threatening.

Rather than functioning as a bridge between people, it may actually serve to establish distance between them.

Instead of reassuring a person as to his worth, praise may be an unconscious means of establishing the superiority of the praiser.

Praise may constrict creativity rather than free it.

Rather than opening the way to further contact, praise may be a means of terminating it. (1968, p. 110)

Farson notes that research on the impact of praise does not clearly substantiate its value. Frequently, reproof is just as effective, which suggests that the safest conclusion is that *some* response motivates people better than no response at all. He goes on to comment on how defensive people are about praise. (He suggests you notice how frequently people react to it by saying things like, "Well, *I* like it" or "It was just luck.") He explains this response as suggesting that praise is an evaluation and that any evaluation is threatening. He also remarks that when people praise us, they are sitting in judgment. If praise is accepted, it puts us under an obligation to behave accordingly. To gain insight into these aspects of praise, he suggests that you ask yourself how you feel when you receive praise, that you note what you say in response to it, that you analyze how you feel when you give praise, and that you speculate about what you are trying to accomplish with praise.

In *Between Parent and Child* (1965), *Between Parent and Teenager* (1969), and in *Teacher and Child* (1971), Haim Ginott distinguishes between desirable and undesirable praise, emphasizing some of the points made by Farson. Undesirable praise focuses attention on a child's character and personality—for example, "Good boy" or "I'm proud of you." Desirable praise emphasizes the child's efforts and accomplishments—for example, "That's a good point" or "You've really improved your spelling." Ginott agrees with Farson that praise may intimidate children if they feel obligated to live up to the evaluation. When you praise the students in your classes, you might keep in mind these observations.

Although you should be aware of some of the complications of praise, you should also be aware of the negative impact of blame. If you are disappointed with a class or with a particular student or if you feel tired and frustrated because things aren't going well, you may find yourself reacting with negative comments. If this occurs, keep in mind the possible consequences. An extremely negative reaction to an error may induce panic, making it impossible for the pupil to think enough to replace the wrong response with the right one. When you praise a pupil for a correct response, realize that you are saying in effect, "That's right; do it again." When you reprimand a pupil for a wrong response, you are saying, "That's wrong; stop it." But if you fail to help pupils find the right response or frighten them so that they are unable to think, they are forced to choose between doing nothing at all or repeating the original response.

If pupils are told when they do the wrong thing but not when they do something right, they never have the chance to experience success. Continual failure leads to fear and depression; it also often leads to

Blame may induce panic, particularly when no help is offered

attempts to escape. It is natural to avoid attempting something if failure is inevitable, as has been pointed out previously. Sometimes students practice avoidance by lowering their level of aspiration. Sometimes physical escape in the form of sickness or truancy is the result. Perhaps the most dangerous kind of escape is withdrawing into the world of fantasy.

Since the student gains nothing from failure, why do so many teachers use sarcasm, ridicule, and punishment? Probably because *they* gain something from the experience; berating pupils and watching them squirm provide a sense of satisfaction and power, especially to weak and insecure people. Teachers have been known to burst into a teacher's room to brag about how they just routed a student or class. Such demonstrations of power are tempting, and you might well watch your initial reactions as you assume control of a class.

c. Consider the advantages and disadvantages of symbolic and material rewards. As noted in the discussion of performance contracting and behavior modification in Chapter 5, many behaviorists advocate the use of material rewards. You were asked at that point to speculate about the advantages and disadvantages of the technique. At this juncture, the question is raised again, this time with reference to the behaviorist view of motivation. Those who favor behavior modification believe that behavior must be shaped by supplying reinforcement. If students do not learn, it is because they have not been presented with a properly designed sequence of stimuli or a satisfactory chain of reinforcements.

This view is illustrated most clearly by techniques used by performance contractors who deal with children who have learning problems. In most cases performance contractors use tangible rewards. Dewey Lipe and Stephen N. Jung comment on this point in a review of studies involving incentives: "Central to the emphasis on incentives is the belief that the newer educational programs of the past decade have not produced impressive results and have especially failed the so-called 'deprived student'" (1971, p. 249). In an effort to assist "deprived" students to succeed, behavior modifiers have used a wide variety of incentives. Lipe and Jung mention many in their review:

Providing fruit, cookies, and sandwiches at snack time only to children who behave as they said they would

Using the school-furnished lunch as a reinforcer, along with candy, goldfish, clothes, and jewelry

Providing candies, trinkets, and toys for a successful performance

Making public records of those who perform successfully by circling numbers on cards, writing names on the blackboard, placing marbles in a holder, writing out tickets

Providing tokens in the form of play money, poker chips, or washers that can be traded in for candy, toys, games, or special privileges

Allowing children to watch the first part of an interesting movie but not letting them see the last part unless they complete an assignment

Using a timer to record the number of minutes all students in the class are engaged in study and rewarding them on the basis of the time recorded

Turning on a light at the desk of each student who makes overt signs of studying and rewarding him or her according to the amount of time the light is on

Dividing a "reinforcement" room into three areas marked off by different colors and having different games and activities in each area (to get into the most desirable area, students have to get 90 percent or better on daily classroom work or increase their scores 10 percent over the previous session)

Handbook heading
Guidelines for
Supplying Rewards

If you ever decide to use such incentives, you now have quite an assortment to choose from. Before you do, you are urged to consider the possible disadvantages of controlled education discussed earlier (particularly at the end of Chapter 5 and the beginning of this chapter).

(A variation of using incentives that fits a student-directed approach is to encourage pupils to reward themselves for goals they have selected. This will be discussed a bit later.)

4. Be alert to the damaging impact of excessive competition. In the traditional public school that uses comparative grading practices, competition is used as a basic motivating force. John Gardner (1961) has commented on the problems of balancing the values of competition (which may lead to great achievements) with their dangers (which cause failure and loss of confidence). There is no denying that competition is a fact of life in a meritocracy and that successful people often do extend themselves when they compete. But if competition becomes excessive in a school situation, students may think of learning only as a means to an end (being better than others); they may be more interested in their relative position in a class than in their actual performance. Only a few students will be able to experience success, and the tendency to make safety rather than growth choices will be increased.

Handbook heading
Ways to Use
Constructive
Competition

To avoid these disadvantages, encourage students to compete against themselves. Try to give each pupil some experience with success by arranging situations in which all students have a fairly equal chance in a variety of activities, and make use of group competitive situations that stress fun rather than winning.

EXAMPLES

Have pupils set their own goals, and keep private progress charts.

Follow the open education technique of keeping a separate folder for each student rather than a grade book that indicates only relative performance.

Give recognition for such virtues as punctuality and dependability.

Give recognition for skill in arts and crafts, music, special interests, and hobbies.

Use games such as "Spelling Baseball." Divide the class into two approximately equal teams. Each time a pupil spells a word correctly, award her or his team a base. Four bases, and the team has a run. Each misspelled word is an out. No team members are eliminated, and the pressure is reduced considerably. If some unfortunate makes too many outs, throw an easy word the next time at bat. In order to avoid overidentification with a particular team, use different players for each game. (If permanent teams are set up or if you overemphasize the competitive nature of the game by offering a prize, the technique may backfire.)

5. For students who need it, encourage the development of a desire to achieve. Despite your efforts to gratify deficiency needs, enhance the attractions of growth choices, arrange learning experiences to produce a realistic level of aspiration and a feeling of success, and play down the negative impact of competition, some of your students will

still lack confidence about their ability to learn. In such cases you may try to help students to acquire a general motive to achieve. McClelland (1965) has demonstrated that it is possible for groups of individuals, in intensive training sessions of one to three weeks, to be instilled with needs to achieve that will be reflected in accomplishments far beyond their previous efforts. Although McClelland's technique would be difficult to use in a school setting, some of the practices he follows might be adapted for small-group or individual sessions with students who appear to lack motivation to succeed. In McClelland's training sessions, he does everything possible to make individuals feel that they can develop a motive to achieve, to show them how the motive will be beneficial, to make acquisition of the motive appear to be an improvement in their self-image, to encourage the achievement of concrete goals, to keep records of progress, and to establish an atmosphere of warm and honest support.

David A. Kolb (1965) based an Achievement Motivation Training Program on the work of McClelland, Atkinson, and others. As with McClelland's program, intensive training sessions were provided (as part of a summer school program). In the opening session, the participants (underachieving high school boys) were given information intended to make training effective, and they were acquainted with characteristics McClelland has found typical of high achievers: personal responsibility for actions, willingness to take moderate risks, the desire for knowledge of results of actions. In subsequent sessions, the boys competed in miniature racing-car contests, took various tests, and played the role of manufacturer. In all these activities, they were urged to analyze their reactions and to think constantly about how they could improve their need for achievement. After the training had been completed, its effectiveness was revealed by higher grades.

Like McClelland's program, Kolb's procedures would be difficult to follow in a regular school setting, but it would be possible to encourage students to emulate the qualities of high achievers by taking personal responsibility for attempting work (perhaps in the form of a contract), being willing to shoot for goals beyond those considered safe, and being eager to receive detailed knowledge of results. A. S. Alschuler (1968) used essentially this approach by organizing learning tasks as self-competitive games in which the student is responsible for setting personal goals and is graded on her or his own terms.

Another technique for assisting students in becoming better achievers was developed by J. S. Sorensen, E. A. Schwenn, and J. Bavry (1970). They devised a checklist for self-ratings by elementary grade students on *prosocial behaviors* (see Figure 10–3). Students rated themselves and then participated in individual and small-group conferences with their teacher in which each category on the list was defined by recalling or identifying instances of the behavior

Handbook heading
Ways to Foster a Need
for Achievement

Figure 10-3

Check list of prosocial behavior

Name _____ Sex _____ Age _____ Date _____

Directions:
Put an X under column 1 if you almost always have to be told to do the job.
Put an X under column 2 if you usually have to be told to do the job.
Put an X under column 3 if you sometimes do the job yourself and sometimes have to be told to do the job.
Put an X under column 4 if you usually do the job yourself.
Put an X under column 5 if you almost always do the job yourself.

	1	2	3	4	5
1. I listen to the teacher.					
2. I begin schoolwork right away.					
3. I correct mistakes.					
4. I work until the job is finished.					
5. I work when the teacher has left the room.					
6. If I make mistakes, I still keep working.					
7. I work on learning activities in free time.					
8. I get to class on time.					
9. I do extra schoolwork.					
10. I do my share in class projects.					
11. I read during free time.					
12. I ask questions about schoolwork.					
13. I have pencil, paper, and books ready when they are needed.					
14. I move quietly to and from my classes.					
15. I listen to the ideas of others.					
16. I help my classmates.					
17. I pick up when the work is finished.					
18. I take care of my clothing, books, and other things.					
19. I take care of the school's books, desks, and other things.					
20. I follow directions.					

described. Then each child was asked to select one or more types of behavior in which to improve and to check his or her present rating and desired rating. At the next conference, children rated themselves to determine if improvement had been achieved. The teacher supplied reinforcement in the form of praise for all improvement, kept a conference record to make note of progress and problems, and asked the pupils to describe reasons why working toward improvement would benefit them. Teacher ratings of student behavior after the program had been completed indicated that most students had made significant improvement in the types of behavior listed.

Sorensen, Schwenn, and Herbert J. Klausmeier (1969) used a similar approach to motivate elementary pupils to indulge in more reading. Many books were made available in the classroom. Forms for reporting titles of books read were provided. Conferences with the teacher were arranged. At the conferences, teachers were urged to keep in mind four motivational procedures:

Modeling: doing such things as telling the child that he (the adult) reads frequently and likes to read; being engaged in reading when the child comes in for the conference and starting to read a book as the child leaves the conference. Modeling also includes such procedures as informing the child of the reading behavior of a possible model and indicating the value of independent reading to other persons who may serve as models for the child.

Reinforcement: smiling, nodding affirmatively, saying "good," "fine," etc., when the student shows that he has independently read a book or pages in a book. The adult also reinforces positive attitude statements about reading either made spontaneously by the child or in response to questions.

Feedback: informing the child of progress by telling him how many books or pages in a book he has completed. Feedback was also given on any improvement in word recognition or comprehension skills.

Goal-setting: helping the child select the next book of an appropriate difficulty level and length. The reading of the book or books then becomes the child's goal for the next conference. (1969, p. 351)

The reading frequency and achievement of almost all students increased as a result of this program, and even control pupils not included in the experiment showed improvement, indicating that the interest in reading became contagious.

If you despair over the lack of confidence, interest, or motivation of your students, you might try to encourage the development of the motivation to achieve by using variations of the techniques just discussed. With modifications, they could be used with all grade levels and with all types of students.

Still other techniques for helping students motivate themselves are described in *Personalizing Education: Values Clarification and Beyond* (1975) by Leland W. Howe and Mary Martha Howe. One strategy is called "My Personal Plan of Action" (pp. 342–347). Its purpose is to encourage students to think about things that prevent people from achieving goals and help them plan how to avoid such pitfalls. A work sheet is provided on which students list a goal they want to achieve, note factors that might keep them from achieving it (e.g., being afraid of failure), and then describe techniques they might use to overcome or circumvent these barriers. In some cases students must sign a self-contract on which they specify the goal, the first step they need to take, and the target date for reaching the goal.

A strategy similar to the self-contract is called "Writing My Own PBO's" (pp. 349–354). (PBO's are *personal behavioral objectives*.) After listing a goal, the student analyzes steps to be taken, difficulties that might be encountered with each step, how these difficulties might be handled, who might provide help, and the date a step is to be completed. If students experience a considerable amount of difficulty achieving PBO's, Howe and Howe suggest that token rewards might be supplied: Give a poker chip worth one hundred points for each step that is achieved and when sufficient points are earned. Have students reward themselves by engaging in an enjoyable activity, giving themselves a ticket to a movie or the equivalent. Still another strategy described by Howe and Howe features three forms students can use in evaluating their own progress. These forms are very similar to the Check List of Prosocial Behavior that was developed by Sorensen, Schwenn, and Bavry.

6. Take advantage of natural interests, try to create new ones, and encourage learning for its own sake. In the preceding section, techniques for aiding the development of motivation were discussed. Some advocates of humanistic education—for example, Neill and Holt—argue that if schooling is arranged properly, such training is unnecessary; if children follow their natural interests, they will learn all they need to know. This policy seems unworkable for most situations. Open education, which stresses freedom of choice and cooperative planning and also teacher guidance, appears to have greater promise. By this approach, the student is given considerable freedom to select activities because of their intrinsic interest. The kinds of activities selected from free-choice situations can be used as guidelines for arranging learning experiences likely to appeal to students. May V. Seagoe surveyed reports on such experiences and concluded that children's interests result from successful experience and familiarity. Among the "points of appeal that emerge from studies of specific interests," she lists the following:

Interest aroused by activity, investigation, adventure, social interaction, usefulness

(a) the opportunity for overt bodily *activity,* for manipulation, for construction, even for observing the movement of animals and vehicles of various sorts; (b) the opportunity for *investigation,* for using mental ingenuity in solving puzzles, for working problems through, for creating designs, and the like; (c) the opportunity for *adventure*, for vicarious experience in make-believe, in books, and in the mass media; (d) the opportunity for *social assimilation*, for contacts with others suitable to the maturity level of the child (ranging from parallel play to discussion and argument), for social events and working together, for human interest and humanitarianism, and for conformity and display; and (e) the opportunity for use of the new in real life, making the new continuous with past experience and projecting it in terms of future action. (1970, p. 25)

In *Push Back the Desks* (1967), Albert Cullum describes a number of techniques for use in elementary school classrooms that incorporate most of the qualities described by Seagoe. Although Cullum's techniques were used with elementary school pupils, many of them could be adapted for use with older pupils.

Arrange a "Parade of Presidents," in which each pupil selects a president of the United States and presents a State of the Union message to the rest of the class, each member of which takes the part of a member of Congress.

Teach geography by presenting "Adventure Hunts," in which the pupils imagine they are detectives trying to keep on the track of a person who travels to various parts of the United States.

Have the class build a replica of "King Tut's Tomb," and then encourage students to play the role of archaeologists. Instead of "digging" for mummies, however, the students use flashlights to find problems, puzzles, graphs, and other items dealing with numbers that are written on cards tacked to the inside walls of the tomb. Each problem has a number and a point score. After a student figures out an answer, he or she deposits it in a box designed as a sarcophagus. After each "dig," answers are discussed; and at the end of the year, fancy certificates are presented to the archaeologists who, by accumulating sufficient points, made a minimum number of successful digs.

To sixth graders, hand out dittoed sheets of twenty questions based on articles in each section of a morning newspaper. Each student is provided with a copy of the paper and competes against herself or himself to discover how many of the questions can be answered in the shortest period of time. (Typical questions: Why is the senator from Mississippi upset? Who got the assists on Bobby Hull's record-breaking goal? What did Miss Peach say to Marcia?)

Create a "Renoir Room" (or the equivalent) in which reproductions of Renoir paintings are displayed on all the walls and the students are encouraged to find out as much as they can about the painter.

Have students read and dramatize Shakespeare and Chaucer.

Have students read the poems of Longfellow and paint murals depicting scenes from the poems.

Here are some other ways you might incorporate activity, investigation, adventure, social assimilation, and usefulness into learning experiences:

EXAMPLES

Ask your students to jot down their interests and hobbies on a card; then use the information to plan individual and group learning activities.

Try to make sure that initial experience with a new topic will be successful (by using the level of aspiration techniques mentioned previously).

Have students go to the board and move around and participate in class discussion—not just sit at their desks.

Use discovery approach techniques to provide opportunities to investigate. Set up learning centers with provocative displays and materials such as these suggested by C. M. Charles:

Appreciation center for observing paintings, poems, sculptures, arrangements, etc.

Art activity center equipped for drawing, painting, modeling, etc.

Communications center equipped for listening to, viewing, and dramatizing music, stories, and guided activities

Display center for showing and observing collections, projects, and hobbies

Games center where students can use instructional games, puzzles, and similar aids

Library and reading center containing both commercial and student-made reading materials

Learning centers in an open classroom reflect the cognitive and humanistic views of motivation: It is assumed that pupils will choose what they need to learn, if they are given the opportunity to direct much of their own learning.

Larry Smith/Black Star

Science center equipped for observation and project work

Social science center stocked with maps, charts, documents, reference books, etc., along with materials and equipment for constructing (1972, p. 105)

Permit and encourage considerable interaction between students, either in groups or in pairs.

Continually point out how new learning relates to previous learning and how it can be applied to other class situations.

     In attempting to arouse new interests, you might employ techniques used by advertisers and by the creators of "Sesame Street" and "The Electric Company." Use intensity, size, contrast, and movement to attract attention. Make use of color, humor, and exaggeration to introduce a topic or make a point. Use audiovisual devices of all kinds—films, tapes, charts, models.

EXAMPLES

Redecorate part of your room the night before presenting a new unit; then have the class help you finish it.

Make full use of the audiovisual aids available from the school, district, or county.

If you are a frustrated actor or actress, ham it up on occasion; make a dramatic production out of a demonstration.

     In considering use of such techniques, it might be worth noting this criticism Michael Maccoby has leveled at "Sesame Street":

Programs such as "Sesame Street" excite the children, but only recently has the question been asked (by the BBC) of what character traits are developed. Exciting learning through TV may further the consumer mentality in children, fostering their need for constant stimulation, for being entertained and "turned on." Other methods of learning the alphabet or numbers might take longer, but they might also emphasize *active* character traits, particularly concentration and the child's development of individual rhythms of work. We must consider the possibility that whatever the content of the programs, TV as a medium for teaching may have negative effects on character development, particularly if not combined with activating classroom discussion. (1971, p. 33)

     Even if Maccoby exaggerates the possible dangers of "Sesame Street," it is worth keeping in mind that it is at times desirable to stress that some learning should be undertaken just for its own sake. The demand for relevance is related to this point. As noted in the preceding chapter, *relevance* is often defined as having "immediate, practical, obvious value." Learning experiences that fit the description are likely to have appeal, but there will be problems if you attempt to make *all* learning relevant. At least on some occasions, it is probably a good policy to try to inculcate a feeling that many satisfying human experiences are neither wildly exciting nor highly relevant.

EXAMPLES

Offer history not only because of its usefulness in interpreting current events but also because of the sheer interest of finding out about how earlier people lived and why certain events occurred.

Point out that many aspects of art, music, and literature are not "practical" but represent an attempt on the part of individuals to express their feelings to others. (Many of Maslow's examples of self-actualization center on artistic creation.)

Encourage students to learn about nature simply to increase their appreciation of it.

Set an example by commenting on things that strike you as interesting, even though they are not "practical." (A very successful French teacher was so enamored of her subject that she occasionally leaned against the blackboard, giving the impression that her ecstasy was so great that she needed support. She would then gaze upward and say with great conviction and fervor, "Isn't French *interesting!*"

7. When appropriate, permit and encourage students to direct their own learning. Many humanistic educators argue that when students are permitted to direct their own learning, teachers do not have problems with motivation. To back up this argument, they usually describe anecdotal reports written by teachers who used learner-centered approaches and were amazed by the enthusiasm of their students. It is true that when an individual or a group selects a topic of great intrinsic interest, and when the pieces in the puzzle fall together nicely, a great deal of enthusiasm is often generated. Unfortunately, such experiences tend to be the exception rather than the rule. When some students are invited to direct their own learning, they become even more bored than when listening to a teacher. Others may select a topic that seems appealing at first glance but turns out to be dull and unappealing after it is examined more closely. The impact of the Hawthorne effect must also be considered. When students are first invited to work on topics of their own choice, the suggestion may be reacted to as a refreshing change. If the technique is used repeatedly, however, students may yearn for a teacher-directed session just for the sake of novelty.

Still another factor is that enthusiasm per se may not be a valid criterion for measuring success. This point is illustrated by student-directed projects described by Herbert Thelen (1960). The first was a unit called "How Do Different People Live?" in the second grade; the second was a television series produced by a high school class on the history of a community. The second grade children, perhaps under the influence of a Walt Disney "True Life Adventure," chose to study prairie dogs, despite the efforts of the teacher to convert them to the Algonquin Indians (about whom she had a great deal of information from previous years). The dismay of the teacher turned to delight as the children not only came through with a smashing dramatic production about prairie dogs but also learned a great deal about how animals and people live. The TV series, on the other hand, generated much enthusiasm but no learning of subject matter. The students gained a lot of experience in taking photographs and lettering signs and solving lighting problems, but the production "incidentals" prevented them from thinking or learning about history. (This brings up an interesting question: If you endorse the argument made by some humanists that how students feel about learning is more important than what they learn, what do you do when you have a bunch of committees working happily away on projects that have nothing to do with the curriculum? Is it better to have a class cheerfully laboring on incidentals or somewhat less enthusiastically engaged with genuine subject matter? Before you supply a final answer to that question, remember that you may be held accountable for what your students learn.)

If you keep these various points in mind, you may find that occasional (and fortuitous) use of learner-centered approaches will lead to self-motivated learning. An excellent source to consult when deciding how to arrange such periods is *Personalized Education: Values Clarification and Beyond* (1975) by Leland W. Howe and Mary Martha Howe. In Part 3, "Personalizing the Curriculum," the Howes describe

Handbook heading

Ways to Encourage Self-Direction and Self-Motivation

how you might encourage students to participate in selecting instructional objectives (by using techniques similar to those proposed by Ojemann) and be efficient self-directed learners. (The steps in this process were described in Chapter 7. They are reviewed here for emphasis.) The Howes recommend that after students have selected a topic (by referring to criteria such as "Is this something that really interests us?" "Will the topic help us to develop a better understanding of the world we live in?") students compile a flow chart, which lists anything related to the main topic that can be studied. Then the participants carry out a question census by listing all the questions they think would be important or useful in studying the topic. The next step is to identify available resources that can be referred to in seeking answers to these questions. The final stage of the process is to have students find answers to the questions and arrange these in the form of a written or oral report. (For details and examples, see pp. 364–395 of *Personalizing Education*.)

8. Provide encouragement and incentives for learning that is essential but not intrinsically appealing. It is a good policy to appeal to

intrinsic interests as much as possible, but sometimes it is necessary to use incentives in order to help students master knowledge or skills that are rarely thought of as fascinating in their own right but necessary if pupils are to function in a complex society. Few students are enthusiastic about learning to spell or to multiply and divide, for example, yet these skills are essential. Because of the hierarchical nature of many learning situations—as exemplified by Gagné's conditions of learning—you may need to stimulate, persuade, inspire, and cajole students to learn some material that is essential for everyday living or subsequent learning. In such situations, you may feel it necessary to resort to progress charts, gold stars, and other kinds of incentives. Howe and Howe (1975) are among the most enthusiastic advocates of student-directed learning, yet they recommend use of the behavior modification technique of giving out tokens to be cashed in for privileges or movie tickets. In making use of such extrinsic motivation, do your best to play down overtones of manipulation and materialism. This might be done by pointing out that the awards are merely a crutch or an aid and by encouraging students to remain aware of that fact. An excellent way to foster that awareness is to have students set their own incentives or supply them in the form of objectives.

Handbook heading
Ways to Supply
Incentives

EXAMPLES

"I know that memorizing spelling words is not the most interesting thing in the world, but it's easier for us to understand each other if we all spell the same way. Try making up a chart to help you keep improving; give yourself an apple or something else each time you hit your goal."

"If you have trouble concentrating on this chapter, write out a short answer to each of these ten questions."

"Learning the names of these trees may seem to be drudgery, but when you know them all, we will really be able to cover some fascinating topics. See if you can learn them all by Friday."

The use of Key Points and marginal notes in this book is intended to give you some specific goals to look for as you read.

SUMMARY OF KEY POINTS

Each of the views of learning discussed in Part 3 includes assumptions about how students should be motivated to learn. The S-R view emphasizes that students learn when their behavior is reinforced.

Cognitive theorists are convinced that human beings do not need to be shaped because they come equipped with a built-in urge to maintain cognitive equilibrium. Humanists also support the proposition that people possess inherent urges to learn, but they emphasize that these motivating forces are not restricted just to cognitive activities; they energize activities that lead to feelings of adequacy or competence.

Abraham Maslow has proposed a theory of growth motivation that is based on the principle that a higher-level need emerges as lower-level needs are gratified. He arranged these into a hierarchy, with deficiency needs (physiological, safety, love and belonging, and esteem) at the bottom, and growth needs (self-actualization, knowing and understanding, aesthetic) at the top. The person who functions at the level of deficiency needs tends to feel driven to get rid of stress and to seek attention from others. The growth-motivated person is likely to seek pleasurable tension and to be self-directed. Because deficit needs can be satisfied only by others, and because pupils must go to school, teachers are in a key position to satisfy deficiency needs. The humanists' argument that pupils should be allowed to guide most of their own learning fails to allow for Maslow's contention that individuals who do not have their deficiency needs well satisfied (which includes many students) are likely to be bad choosers. To minimize the likelihood of bad student choices, teachers should arrange learning situations to minimize dangers and maximize the attractions of growth.

The level of aspiration concept calls attention to the tendency of human beings to try to set goals that permit them to achieve success at the highest possible level while at the same time reducing the possibility of failure. It has been shown that pupils are more likely to set realistic levels of aspiration for themselves if they have had successful experiences. Successful experiences also lead to the development of a need for achievement, since individuals who have had a history of failure are reluctant to take risks.

The S-R view of learning calls attention to the importance of supplying reinforcement, but excessive use of rewards may cause students to feel that they should never engage in an activity unless they will win some sort of extrinsic payoff for their efforts. Humanists emphasize the values of intrinsic motivation but often fail to allow for the fact that few pupils have the maturity or foresight to recognize the need to master basic skills and information.

In your efforts to arouse and sustain the interest of your pupils, you may wish to occasionally use goal cards: detailed lists of specific tasks to be carried out. One of the most basic ways to motivate pupils is to praise them, but keep in mind that excessive or faulty use of praise may threaten pupils, cause them to feel alienated from you, lead to feelings of inferiority, or limit creativity. Judicious praise is to be preferred to blame, because sharply criticizing pupils may induce feelings of panic, particularly if they do not know how to correct faulty behavior. In your efforts to arouse the interest of your pupils, strive to arrange lessons that involve activity, opportunities to investigate, a sense of adventure, chances to interact with others, and usefulness.

BECOMING A BETTER TEACHER: QUESTIONS AND SUGGESTIONS

Satisfying Physiological Needs

Am I taking into account the physiological needs of my students? Suggestions: List specific ways to make sure students' physiological needs are satisfied (e.g., let students go to the bathroom as often as they legitimately need to). At frequent intervals, ask students if the room seems too cold or warm. Consider scheduling snack time, or urge students to have a snack between classes.

Satisfying the Need for Safety

Am I doing anything that causes students to worry about their physical or psychological safety? Suggestion: Make up a list of safety need dos and don'ts (e.g., don't make students attempt any activity if they act apprehensive; do make it a point to be sympathetic and supportive after students have had a bad experience).

Ways to Satisfy the Need for Belonging

Do my students give the impression that they feel welcome, relaxed, and accepted when they enter my classroom? Suggestion: Next month schedule some sort of activity, such as a brief personal planning session, that gives me a chance to interact individually with every pupil in the class.

Ways to Encourage Growth Choices

Am I inadvertently causing students to make safety choices? Suggestion: As I plan activities, make it a point to think about how to minimize feelings of threat or danger and maximize conditions that will make students eager, or at least willing, to try.

Ways to Establish Attainable Goals

Am I arranging classroom experiences so that students know what goals they are working toward and feel convinced they have a chance to achieve them? Suggestion: Whenever appropriate, set up goals in cooperation with students or at least in such a way that they feel they are being consulted about objectives. If I do that, they are likely to know what the goals are and feel that they are attainable.

Ways to Supply Positive Feedback

Am I supplying positive feedback so that it reinforces rather than discourages further effort? Suggestions: When supplying oral or written praise, try not to be condescending or to put the student on the spot. Make it a point to observe how pupils respond to praise. If some of them act embarrassed, annoyed, or apprehensive, try to give them future assignments that are self-reinforcing.

Guidelines for Supplying Rewards

Are there certain class activities where the use of tangible rewards would be appropriate? Suggestion: When planning how to set up sessions where students must make an effort to concentrate, consider supplying a tangible reward of some kind. (But carefully observe how students respond, and don't use this technique too often.)

Ways to Use Constructive Competition

Am I inadvertently setting up learning situations that lead to cutthroat competition? Suggestion: Be alert for signs of competition between pupils. If one or two students start to organize a learning contest of some sort, make it a point to arrange relaxing competitive activities in the following weeks.

Ways to Foster a Need for Achievement

Should I try to encourage the development of a stronger need for achievement in some or all of my pupils? Suggestion: Look over the descriptions of techniques for encouraging achievement in Chapter 10, and experiment with one or more of them next week. Then ask the class for their reactions and suggestions.

Ways to Arouse Interest

Am I doing an effective job of making lessons interesting? Suggestion: Print the words *activity, investigation, adventure, social interaction,* and *usefulness* on a card, and keep it in front of me when I plan lessons. Try to develop activities that include as many of these characteristics as possible. (Use techniques described by Albert Cullum in *Push Back the Desks* as a guide. Also, look over my notes on psychodrama, simulation games, and related techniques discussed in Chapter 7.)

Ways to Encourage Self-Direction and Self-Motivation

Am I giving students enough opportunities to motivate themselves? Suggestion: If I have not done so already, ask the class to help plan activities, use the contract approach, experiment with the ten-step process of structuring a discussion described in *Personalized Education* and summarized in Chapter 7.

Ways to Supply Incentives

Do many members of the class act listless and restless during certain work periods? Suggestion: The next time a tedious but necessary bit of activity must be carried out, consult with students and set up some sort of incentive system. Perhaps invite pupils to prepare individual reward menus, and arrange reinforcement in accordance with the Premack principle.

SUGGESTIONS FOR FURTHER STUDY

10-1

Maslow's Theory of Motivation

The second edition of Abraham H. Maslow's *Toward a Psychology of Being* (1968) is filled with so much insight into so many aspects of human behavior and adjustment that you are urged to buy a copy for repeated reference. The headings of the major sections of the book indicate the general topics discussed: Part 1, "A Larger Jurisdiction for Psychology"; Part 2, "Growth and Motivation"; Part 3, "Growth and Cognition"; Part 4, "Creativeness"; Part 5, "Values"; Part 6, "Future

Tasks." If you have only enough time at the moment to sample the book, read Chapter 1, in which Maslow describes his conception of sickness and health; Chapter 3, in which he differentiates between deficiency and growth needs; Chapter 11, in which he contrasts bad choosers and good choosers; or Chapter 14, in which he lists forty-three basic propositions of a growth and self-actualization psychology. (The propositions in Chapter 14 pretty much summarize all his observations on motivation.)

10-2
Brief Overviews of Motivation

The treatment of motivation in this chapter is limited and oversimplified. For more background, read an appropriate chapter in a general or introductory psychology text. (Almost any introductory psychology text will contain a chapter on motivation.) If you find a concise analysis of motivation, you might summarize it and relate it to points made in the text.

10-3
Analyzing Your Own Motivation

Insight into theories of motivation sometimes results from self-analysis. How energetically do you pursue different goals? Do you have a fairly consistent level of aspiration, or do you exert yourself in only a few areas of behavior? What forces drive you to try to achieve at a high level in certain activities? Can you relate your drives to psychological needs? Do you sometimes feel compelled to regain a sense of equilibrium? Do you engage in some of your activities as a means to "expression"? If those questions do not seem simple to answer, analyze your behavior at different times in terms of Maslow's hierarchy. Do you find evidence that you are more likely to want to learn or to satisfy an aesthetic desire when your lower-level needs have been taken care of? If you note exceptions, how might you explain them? (For example, are thoughts of hunger and discomfort displaced by the sight of the love of your life?) If you gain any insight into your own motives, you might describe and comment on your self-analysis and how this might affect your life.

10-4
Forces That Shaped Famous People

In speculations about what motivates people to strive and achieve, the question of determinism is of key importance. Choose a person you know something about or would like to learn about, and analyze—as best you can—the forces that made her or him great. Or browse through *Cradles of Eminence* (1962) by Goertzel and Goertzel and consider the common factors they found in the backgrounds of famous people. Is there evidence to back up Freud's suggestion that in some cases extreme efforts in the arts or politics are due to sublimation of the sex drive? Or analyze the lives of the eminent people described by Goertzel and Goertzel (or any group of your own choice) with reference to Shakespeare's "theory" of motivation: "Some are born great, some achieve greatness, and some have greatness thrust upon them." You may conclude that psychologists haven't come up with any better way to summarize motivation since those words were written over 350 years ago. If any of these questions or suggestions appeal to you, you might record your reactions.

10-5

Choice Situations

Maslow makes a distinction between bad and good choosers. To become more aware of what he means by this, analyze your own feelings and behavior with regard to choice situations. Maslow describes growth as a never ending series of decisions between safety and growth and suggests that people are more likely to make a good choice if they feel confident and self-accepting. If individuals feel threatened, they may be unable to resist selecting a safe—but perhaps undesirable—form of behavior. Think back to choice situations you have faced recently. When you decided to try something and it proved to be an exhilarating experience, did you feel confident and self-accepting prior to the decision? Can you figure out what made you that way? If you procrastinated about a choice and finally took a safe way out by avoiding the situation or reacting in a manner that provided little if any satisfaction, what was it that made you feel threatened? Could you—or someone else—have reduced the threat somehow? If possible, relate your analysis to how you might function as a teacher. What could you do to establish a classroom environment where your students would feel confident and unthreatened enough to make good choices and have more frequent self-actualizing experiences?

10-6

Level of Aspiration

Maslow's distinction between bad and good choosers is essentially a generalized version of Hoppe's observations on the level of aspiration. Hoppe suggested that a person's level of aspiration in a given situation is a compromise between two conflicting tendencies: (1) the desire to avoid disappointment accompanying failure, which operates to force aspirations down and (2) the desire to succeed at the highest possible level, which pushes aspirations up. If you find it difficult to analyze a choice between safety and growth as just suggested, you might attempt an analysis of your level of aspiration in one or two situations. For example, at the beginning of a course when you determined the grade you hoped to achieve, what factors influenced your decision? If the evaluation in the course seemed to be threatening, did you set your aspirations at the C level? How did you react when you got your grade on the first exam? If you set your aspiration level low for one course and high for another, what factors influenced your decision? If you carry out such a self-analysis, you might draw up some implications to keep in mind when you seek to encourage students to develop realistic levels of aspiration.

10-7

Encouraging a Desire to Achieve

If you are intrigued by the possibility of helping students acquire a need to achieve, you will want to read accounts of how this has been done. David C. McClelland provides a book-length description of his theory in *The Achieving Society* (1960) and a more concise view in "Toward a Theory of Motive Acquisition," *American Psychologist,* 20 (1965): 321–333. In addition, articles by and about McClelland are featured in the January 1971 issue of *Psychology Today.*

J. W. Atkinson explains his conception of the need to achieve—as well as many other theories of motivation—in *An Introduction to Motivation* (1964). David Kolb describes how he put the McClelland-

Atkinson ideals into practice in "Achievement Motivation Training for Underachieving Boys," *Journal of Personality and Social Psychology,* 2 (1965): 783–792. A description of a variety of techniques, including the use of the Check List for Student Self-ratings of Prosocial Behaviors was provided in the section titled "A System of Individually Guided Motivation" (pp. 339–355) of *Learning and Human Abilities: Educational Psychology* (3rd ed., 1971) by Herbert J. Klausmeier and Richard E. Ripple. If you sample one or more of these books or articles, you might draw up your own list of guidelines for helping students acquire a need to achieve.

Key points

Inequality of educational opportunity

Significant relationship between social class and school achievement

Coleman report: Impact of strong educational background

Busing intended to lead to mix of pupils from strong and weak backgrounds

Head Start gains faded rapidly

Destiny control: Feeling of being able to shape own future

Contrasting favored and disadvantaged children

Lower-class mother may not have consistent medical care during pregnancy and delivery

Experiences of lower-class child may be restricted to home and neighborhood

Lower-class child may have neutral or negative attitude toward school

Potential dangers of labeling

Improperly interpreted, labels may lead to fatalistic reaction

Properly interpreted, labels may help teachers plan compensatory education

Factors that may influence disadvantaged students

Lower-class pupils may be ignorant of academic know-how

Lower-class adolescents have low career aspirations

Minority-group pupils may experience role confusion

Arranging educational experiences for disadvantaged pupils

Think of individuals, not groups or types

Interpret test scores with caution

Programmed techniques for the disadvantaged

Programmed approach to teaching reading

Behavior modification approach: Reinforce study skills and learning

Combining behavior modification with self-direction

Discovery and humanistic approaches for the disadvantaged

Montessori method: Discovery, programming, and open education combined

Organic reading: Children ask for words

Taking advantage of spontaneous interests

Reports and observations converted into a do-it-yourself text

Chapter 11

Teaching the disadvantaged

In THE ACCOUNT of public schools in Chapter 2, mention was made of Horace Mann's assertion that education would become the "great equalizer." Early educators hoped that the schools would make it possible for any American child, regardless of background, to acquire knowledge and skills that would contribute to success later in life. By the time President Lyndon Johnson established his Great Society program in the 1960s, it had become clear that Mann and his followers had failed to allow for the fact that home experiences during the school years make learning much easier for some children than for others. Accordingly, the federal government decided to try to discover the nature and extent of inequalities in educational opportunity.

Inequality of educational opportunity

James S. Coleman was asked to direct an investigation to determine the extent to which academic achievement is influenced by home and school factors. When Coleman and his colleagues completed their analysis, they reported that no particular school characteristic—such as the quality of the building, the number of books and audiovisual materials available, the academic preparation of the teachers—seemed to make a crucial difference in academic performance. The one factor that did seem to distinguish between successful and nonsuccessful students was social class. A child who came from an upper-class or middle-class home appeared to have a better chance of doing well in school than one who came from a lower-class home. It appeared that upper- and middle-class children were exposed to experiences and attitudes that gave them an advantage in school. Furthermore, these experiences and attitudes seemed to be contagious. When most of the

Significant relationship between social class and school achievement

children in a classroom were eager to learn and equipped to learn, they seemed to serve as models for less-motivated classmates to imitate. Conversely, when most of the children in a classroom lacked interest in learning or came to school poorly equipped to deal with the curriculum, they seemed to set a tone that had a depressive effect not only on classmates but also on teachers. Coleman and his colleagues presented evidence in their report to substantiate the claim that if a "pupil from a home without much educational strength is put with classmates with strong educational backgrounds, his achievement is likely to increase" (1966, p. 22).

Coleman report: Impact of strong educational background

The Coleman report leads to busing

The conclusion that the achievement of lower-class pupils would increase if they were placed in classrooms with upper-class pupils had much to do with the busing policy that has stirred such controversy. The boundaries that decide which school a child will attend are determined by the surrounding neighborhood. Because of economic

In order to insure that most classrooms contain a mix of students with strong and weak educational backgrounds, the courts and governmental agencies concluded that it is necessary to transport some pupils to schools outside of their neighborhoods.

Bruce Roberts/Photo Researchers

factors and zoning and other restrictions, there is usually considerable homogeneity in income and background within a neighborhood. As a result, children from affluent and poor neighborhoods are segregated from each other, a separation that often results in the segregation of educational strengths and weaknesses. Busing was suggested as a means for establishing a ratio of advantaged and disadvantaged students in all classrooms so that those with less strength would benefit from association with more favored peers. This line of reasoning makes sense in theory, but it has not worked well in practice.

Parents from all socioeconomic levels have objected to busing. Upper- and middle-class parents often fear that their children will be adversely affected by the presence of disadvantaged pupils. Lower-class parents argue for more local control of schools and educational policies. Parents of all class levels resent having their children sent out of familiar neighborhoods to schools in other parts of town. Laws requiring busing have sometimes led to confrontations between parents and police.

Busing to produce a mix of favored and less favored children has not been a success, but other suggestions for accomplishing the same objective have met with even greater resistance. In Forest Hills, New York, for example, it was proposed that instead of busing children back and forth to achieve a balance, low-rent housing should be provided closer to middle-class residential areas so that the desired ratio would be achieved through neighborhood integration. So many people objected that the program has been delayed, and it appears that integrated housing is a less workable solution than busing.

Head Start gains fade

Other attempts to equalize educational opportunities have also been disappointing. Head Start was established after some psychologists (e.g., Hunt, 1961; Deutsch, 1964; Bloom, 1964) reasoned that children from lower-class homes did poorly in school because they failed to receive sufficient stimulation during what were considered to be the critical preschool years. Head Start programs were set up with the expectation that they would equip lower-class children with skills similar to those picked up at home by lower- and middle-class children as they interacted with their parents in a rich environment. It was predicted that gains made before Head Start graduates entered school would lead to continued success throughout the grades. Unfortunately, follow-up studies revealed that measured gains made by Head Starters faded rapidly and by the end of first grade there were often no significant differences in the overall academic performance of children who had attended Head Start programs and those from the same kinds of homes who had not (Westinghouse Survey of Project Head Start, 1969).

Busing intended to lead to mix of pupils from strong and weak backgrounds

Head Start gains faded rapidly

The Head Start program is intended to provide compensatory education.

Matt Herron/Black Star

These results prompted two kinds of reaction. The first was the establishment of Follow-Through programs designed to extend through the third grade the kind of compensatory education provided by Head Start. (Several Follow-Through programs will be described later in this chapter.) Proponents of these programs argued that Head Start did not last long enough. The second reaction was based on the assumption that Head Start did not begin early enough. This is the contention of Burton L. White (White and Watts, 1973), who has observed how effective and ineffective mothers interact with their children during the first two years of life. White believes that he has isolated techniques parents can use to help their one- and two-year-old children acquire overall competence and that this general capability will become more or less permanent. It will not be possible to determine if White's hypothesis is correct until children who have been exposed to the techniques he recommends have completed several years of school, which will not occur until the mid-1980s. It may be imprudent to expect dramatic results from White's methods, however.

It seems probable that the same sort of fade reaction that occurred with three- to five-year-old Head Starters is even more likely to occur with one- and two-year-olds. In an analysis of Head Start follow-ups, Susan W. Gray and Rupert E. Klaus (1970) first summarize research leading to the conclusion that graduates of Head Start programs tended to suffer a fade reaction in the primary grades. They explain this by noting that not even the best possible program could be expected to "inoculate" children and make them "immune" to the impact of continued existence in a poor environment. Even if parents succeed in establishing the equivalent of a Head Start program in the home—which is essentially what White and Watts recommend—it seems unrealistic to assume that the program will "immunize" children and offset the impact of later experiences. The extent to which accumulating experiences begin to take effect was the major point stressed in the Coleman report.

The significance of destiny control

Destiny control: Feeling of being able to shape own future

Coleman explained the results of his study by suggesting that lower-class children lack *destiny control*—the feeling of having the opportunity and capability to shape one's own future. Michael Harrington (1965) has emphasized the same point, suggesting that those who live in depressed areas, particularly in the slums of large cities, are characterized by an attitude of pessimism and despair. Children may become trained to become competent during the first two years of their lives and then participate in Head Start and Follow-Through programs to the point of wanting to do well in school and being capable of achieving this goal. But if such children become aware that in order to do well in school they must engage, more or less on their own, in concerted and protracted efforts to overcome limiting conditions in their home and neighborhood environments, they may become discouraged. If discouraging experiences accumulate, lower-class children may eventually conclude that their chances of reaping the benefits of education are so slim that there is little point in striving to earn high grades.

Is socialism the only way to "equalize" America?

In *Inequality: A Reassessment of the Effect of Family and Schooling in America*, Christopher Jencks interprets the evidence in the Coleman report and related analyses. In his view, the evidence indicates that most attempts to bring about equality through the educational system—including desegregation, busing, providing extra funds for educational programs, and Head Start and other forms of compensatory education—have failed. Jencks observes, "There is no evidence that school reform can substantially reduce the extent of cognitive inequality, as measured by tests of verbal fluency, reading comprehension, or mathematical skill. Neither school resources nor segregation has an appreciable effect on either test scores or educational attainment" (1972a, p. 8). He explains the ineffectiveness of educational reform by suggesting that children are influenced much more by what happens outside of school than by what happens in the classroom. (Some observers maintain that the superior school performance of upper- and middle-class students is due not to better forms of education but to the "hidden curriculum" of the home.) Jencks also believes that the relationship between teacher and pupil is more important than the curriculum or methods of instruction.

Jencks maintains that the schools have been asked to do too much and that inequality of opportunity in our society as a whole will remain until inequalities in income and environmental conditions are reduced. In order to accomplish this reduction, he says, "We will have to establish political control over the economic institutions that shape our society. This is what other countries usually call socialism. Anything less will end in the same disappointment as the reforms of the 1960s" (p. 265).

Even though substantial reduction of inequalities in American life may require political action, it seems highly unlikely that socialism will be established in this country in the foreseeable future. Consequently, it makes sense to look for less comprehensive ways to reduce differences between favored and less favored individuals in our society. Education has not functioned as the great equalizer Horace Mann hoped it would be. Jencks is correct when he argues that the schools have been expected to do too much, but the schools are still more likely than any other institution to provide opportunities for individuals from disadvantaged backgrounds to overcome limiting conditions and achieve success. If that is to happen, though, teachers must seek ways to help students who are at a disadvantage in school. They may not be able to cancel out all limiting conditions and it is unrealistic to expect them to bring about dramatic improvements on a massive scale, but efforts to overcome the learning problems of disadvantaged children should be made. In order to plan how to make such efforts, it is necessary to analyze why some students have an advantage in school. Perhaps the clearest way to call attention to determinative factors is to contrast the backgrounds of typical upper-class and lower-class children.

(To call attention to differences in educational opportunity in the clearest possible way, the following discussion contrasts pupils of two extreme hypothetical types. There are many gradations between poor and rich environments. Furthermore, many poverty-level parents do a more effective job of child rearing than many wealthy parents who have the material resources but not the time, ingenuity, or desire to interact with their offspring in meaningful ways. Accordingly, there are many exceptions to the descriptions that follow. The fact remains, many children who come from poverty-level homes possess different characteristics and are exposed to different experiences than children who come from affluent homes. The descriptions that follow call attention to extreme differences likely to characterize one type of child contrasted with another. The descriptions should not be interpreted as stereotyped portraits of all children who come from a particular type of background. Many of America's most successful citizens came from slum backgrounds; many children from wealthy homes were given every possible advantage, yet they were abject failures. Even so, differences between rich and poor do exist in our society, and many of these differences may have an impact on school performance.)

Contrasting favored and disadvantaged children

Characteristics of favored American children

Children born to upper-class couples in America typically benefit from excellent prenatal care and the latest techniques of childbirth. It is likely that the mother makes frequent visits to a medical practitioner during pregnancy and that she is well aware of the importance of maintaining an excellent diet, avoiding the use of drugs of all kinds, guarding against infectious diseases, and checking for the possibility of Rh-blood-factor incompatibility and similar conditions. It is possible that both husband and wife attend natural childbirth classes, and it is almost certian that the baby will be delivered by a doctor selected by and familiar to the parents.

Before and after the child is born, it is probable that the parents consult pamphlets, articles, and books on infant care and perhaps take one or more courses in child development. If so, they might make a well-planned effort to use techniques of child care that have been found to be especially effective. Even if the parents are not so systematic about child care practices, they—and their relatives—will almost certainly inundate the child with clothing, furniture, toys, books, records, and play equipment. It is also likely that the preschool child will be taken frequently to stores, parks, zoos, and the like and exposed to a wide range of experiences. In addition to supervising such experiences on their own, the parents may also go to considerable trouble to select an excellent nursery school for the child to attend.

By the time she or he enters kindergarten, the upper-class child has probably been imbued with the feeling that school is a fine and exciting place to be and that teachers are admirable individuals who are eager to help. Even in the primary grades, it is likely that the child is made aware of the importance of doing well in school, since the parents undoubtedly show great interest in report cards and are conscientious about attending parent conferences and PTA meetings. If the child experiences difficulty with a particular subject, the parents will probably be eager to provide remedial instruction at home or even hire a tutor. In secondary school, it is even more likely that the child is frequently reminded of the importance of earning high grades, since it is assumed without question that education will continue beyond high school. Any talk about higher education proably centers on *which* college or university will be attended, not *whether* additional education is a good or bad idea. Since education is seen as a serious undertaking, it is possible the adolescent will be given a desk, a typewriter, and a complete encyclopedia set (including research assistance from the publisher) during the secondary school years. It is also possible that high grades may be rewarded directly or indirectly by gifts of money, clothing, sports and audio equipment, or even a car.

In addition to acquiring and maintaining positive attitudes toward school, teachers, and educational achievement, the upper-class child benefits from excellent physical care. Because of the ready availability of junk foods, the diet may not be all that it should be, but the child is sure to be well fed. In addition, excellent health care will be provided by a family doctor, a dentist or orthodontist, and other medical specialists. The favored child will go to school well dressed and well groomed (unless current fads stress the opposite). In addition to physical well-being, the upper-class child may have social characteristics that favor acceptance by peers, leading to a sense of belongingness. A child who has seen that parents are treated with respect and deference is likely to expect that she or he will receive the same treatment from others. Many forms of social behavior practiced at home are also appropriate in the classroom, and there will be a tendency to think of home and school as complementary worlds. Furthermore, most of the texts, workbooks, films, and other instructional materials used in class feature children and adults who possess characteristics similar to the child's own characteristics, which encourages a sense of familiarity and identity. Finally, the ways that learning is measured seem to be derived with the upper-class child in mind—they stress reading and writing the English language, familiarity with everyday objects and experiences, and the standard school curriculum.

Contrast this description of a favored American child with the following portriat of a disadvantaged American child.

Characteristics of disadvantaged American children

The lower-class woman who is expecting a child often receives little or no benefits from health knowledge and services. A lower-class woman who seeks medical advice during pregnancy is likely to receive it from a series of different medical practitioners on the staff of a clinic. If she receives medical aid at the time of delivery, the doctor may be a stranger to her. If she is uneducated, she may not know of the availability of programs and information that might contribute to a

Lower-class mother
may not have consistent
medical care during
pregnancy and delivery

healthy pregnancy and a safe and uneventful delivery. A lower-class mother may not be aware of the importance of a good diet during pregnancy (or even be able to maintain such a diet). She may not protect herself from exposure to infectious diseases. She may take a variety of drugs without realizing that even aspirin or the equivalent may cause abnormalities in fetal development. For all these reasons, a lower-class child may be born with physical defects, some of which may go undetected for several years because regular health care is not available.

The lower-class mother may be ignorant of what has been learned about the physical and psychological care of infants and may not even benefit from "tradition" if she has no contact with older female relatives. Because of poverty, the parents may not be able to provide much in the way of clothing or playthings for the child. Also because of poverty, and possibly because both parents work, the child may only rarely venture beyond the immediate neighborhood. The lower-class child may never ride in a car or a bus or be taken to a large department store and may be ignorant of objects and experiences that are completely familiar to more favored children. Many inner-city children, for example, have no conception of what a farm or a garden is.

Experiences of
lower-class child may
be restricted to home
and neighborhood

When the time comes to enter school, the child may be apprehensive at worst or unenthusiastic at best because of attitudes picked up from parents and older siblings and playmates. If parents, siblings, or older peers were school dropouts, they may harbor negative feelings about teachers and education, and these may be communicated directly or indirectly to the child. If older children have negative experiences in school, they may describe these in exaggerated fashion and make the uninitiated younger child feel anxious about what lies ahead. Even if the parents do not feel negative toward education, they may take little interest in what goes on in school, fail to show up for parent conferences, and be indifferent to report cards. Because of lack of familiarity with many objects and situations depicted in instructional materials, together with an absence of encouragement from parents, a lower-class child may get off to a poor start in the primary grades. Inability to read or write will then lead to ever increasing problems and cause the child to fall further and further behind. By the time the student reaches the secondary grades, she or he may have given up on school and may resolve to just put in time until it is legally permissible to drop out. Awareness that many older children in the neighborhood are unable to find employment contributes to attitudes of fatalistic resignation, anger, or resentment. The possibility of higher education seems so remote that it may never be considered at all. Even if an adolescent does respond to the urging of a teacher and resolve to work for high grades, the attempt may be cut short because there is no place at home to study, no desk or reference works to use, no encouragement from parents.

Lower-class child may
have neutral or negative
attitude toward school

The lower-class child may never see a doctor or dentist and may go to school hungry and dressed in hand-me-down clothes. If a language other than English is spoken in the home or neighborhood, the child may find it difficult to understand the teacher, converse with classmates, or read instructional materials. When asked to complete assignments or take tests, the child may have difficulty following instructions, interpreting questions, or supplying answers. If the lower-class child becomes aware that parents and neighbors are treated in demeaning ways or are accorded little respect from others, feelings of self-doubt and low esteem may be intensified.

There are exceptions to the portraits just presented, of course, but many upper-class children resemble the picture sketched here, and the description of the lower-class child includes most of the elements found in a detailed study reported by Frank Riessman (1964). The fact that there are common characteristics among children from different backgrounds as well as exceptions to the general rule calls attention to a problem that has received increasing attention in recent years. A number of critics have argued that the use of labels of any kind may cause difficulties for those who are placed in categories.

Potential dangers of labeling

So far in this chapter the following words and phrases have been used to refer to children who share certain characteristics: *disadvantaged, lower-class, inner-city.* Similar phrases used in other books and articles about such children include *culturally deprived, children of the ghetto,* and *poverty-level pupils.* Some psychologists and educators object to the use of such terms on the grounds that they create a fatalistic image and may lead to stereotyping and self-fulfilling prophecies. Before going any further, therefore, it will be worth evaluating criticisms of categories such as *disadvantaged* and the equivalent.

Arguments against labels

One of the most frequently cited criticisms of the word *disadvantaged* has been proposed by Urie Bronfenbrenner. He argues that a vicious circle may be set in motion if a child is referred to by that term, and he backs up his point by describing a hypothetical situation (1970, p. 138) where a teacher becomes aware that two boys in her class are doing poor work. When she consults the cumulative folders of the two students, the teacher discovers that one is classified as "disadvantaged." The other has not been categorized in any way, but information about parental occupation and home address (presumably) indicates a middle-class background. Bronfenbrenner suggests that the teacher may

Teaching English as a second language

If you find that some of your pupils need instruction in English as a second language, two books you might consult are Teaching English as a Second Language *(1969) by Mary Finocchiaro and* A Handbook of Bilingual Education *(1973) by Muriel Saville and Rudolph Troike. An extensive bibliography of instructional materials for English as a second language (listed for elementary and secondary grades) is provided on pages 405–413 of the* Standard Education Almanac, *ninth edition (1976–77).*

Improperly interpreted, labels may lead to fatalistic reaction

attribute the poor performance of the disadvantaged child to his background, assume she cannot expect him to perform well, and more or less ignore him. Because no such explanation is available to account for the middle-class child's poor performance, Bronfenbrenner hypothesizes that the teacher will assume it is *her* fault and go out of her way to help him learn. Then, because of the self-fulfilling prophecy, the disadvantaged boy will think and act like a poor learner and the middle-class boy will begin to function as a capable learner.

Bronfenbrenner's argument is based on the assumption that when teachers think of children as "disadvantaged," they assume that all pupils so classified are incapable of learning. Such fatalistic reactions undoubtedly occur, but it is possible that thinking of a child as disadvantaged may prompt a reaction opposite to that predicted by Bronfenbrenner. That, at any rate, is the primary reason for using the word in this chapter. You are urged to think of some children as disadvantaged so that you can plan ways to help them compensate for weaknesses due to environmental factors over which they have little or no control.

Properly interpreted, labels may help teachers plan compensatory education

Some children *are* at a disadvantage

The word *disadvantaged* is used in this chapter to call your attention to the need for some children to receive special kinds of instruction. Some educators prefer the term *culturally different,* but it seems preferable to use the term *disadvantaged* to emphasize that the most significant difference between some pupils is the degree to which they have been exposed to out-of-school experiences that equip, or fail to equip, them to perform academically. Only by acknowledging the nature of the disadvantages attributable to certain types of backgrounds can teachers arrange compensatory school experiences.

If lower-class children are just culturally different, why should Head Start experiences fade so dishearteningly? Coleman offers one explanation when he refers to *destiny control.* A pupil who comes from the kind of background outlined in the preceding description of the lower-class child indisputably has less control over her or his own future than a middle-class child. Another explanation for the failure of disadvantaged children to derive permanent benefit from Head Start and similar experiences is summed up by the phrase "hidden curriculum of the home." The parents of upper-class children in America frequently function as teachers, although *tutors* would be a more appropriate word, since instruction is often given to one child at a time. Every time they talk to their children, answer questions, take them on trips, buy books or educational toys, upper-class parents provide knowledge and experiences that accumulate to make school learning familiar and easy. A child who does not receive such continuous tutoring in the home is clearly at a disadvantage when placed in competitive academic situations.

The Head Start program was developed to provide disadvantaged children with the kinds of preschool experiences that more favored children receive at home and in private nursery schools. Children who attended Head Start schools did acquire skills and information that prepared them for public school, but as soon as the special help was withdrawn, their more favored classmates—who were receiving continuous benefits from the equivalent of a permanent home enrichment program—forged ahead. Project Follow-Through appears to be having a positive effect, but it seems likely that when graduates of that program are left to fend for themselves in regular classes, they too may begin to fall behind. Since this is the case, it seems more logical to say not only that many lower-class children come from a different culture, but also that they are at a disadvantage. To make this clear, here is a review of factors that may influence the behavior of disadvantaged students, factors that were mentioned in the portraits of upper-class and lower-class children presented earlier. Once these factors are listed, it will be possible to derive some general guidelines for teaching such children.

Factors that may influence disadvantaged students

1. Most low-income Americans do not receive satisfactory health care. As a consequence, compared to upper-class children, the incidence of birth defects in lower-class children is greater, and the infant mortality rate is higher (as consistently revealed by National Institute of Health statistics). Since poor children to not receive medical or dental care regularly, it is difficult to compile accurate statistics on general health. It seems reasonable to assume, however, that the infant mortality rate reflects a trend that probably continues in later years. That is to say, lower-class children probably continue to suffer from

untreated illnesses at a rate that may be at least twice that of upper-class children. The most significant impact of poor health care on the functioning of disadvantaged children probably takes the form of fatigue or preoccupation with debilitating discomfort.

2. In the absence of information about child-rearing techniques, many uneducated lower-class parents use unfortunate forms of child care. Robert D. Hess and Virginia Shipman (1964) observed mother-child interactions in lower-class homes and found, typically, that the mothers were inattentive and unresponsive to the child, used impoverished language, tended to lack self-confidence, were disorganized in the way the home was run, and functioned quite often at the preoperational stage of cognitive development. These child-care techniques are essentially the opposite of those that Diana Baumrind (1971) found were used by parents of highly competent children. The U.S. Department of Health, Education and Welfare has financed the research of White and Watts with the intention of eventually attempting to teach lower-class mothers to use child-rearing practices likely to lead to competence in their children. It will be several years before this program has been put into practice long enough to evaluate.

3. Disadvantaged children typically have not been exposed to a wide variety of experiences. This point was just emphasized in discussing the "hidden curriculum of the home."

4. Disadvantaged children may not be strongly motivated to do well in school, and they may not be knowledgeable about techniques of becoming successful in school. Upper-class parents who have benefited in a variety of ways from education serve as effective and enthusiastic advocates of schooling. Because doing well in school paid off for them, they are eager to persuade their children to do well academically in order to achieve similar or greater benefits. They also serve as positive models to be imitated. By contrast, lower-class parents who did not do well may describe school in negative terms and perhaps blame teachers for their failure in classrooms and subsequent failures later in life. If the parents were inept students, they

Lower-class pupils may be ignorant of academic know-how

are unable to tell their children about how to study for exams, meet requirements, select courses, or acquire the general all-around academic know-how that upper-class parents pass on to their offspring.

5. Lower-class adolescents typically have low career aspirations. The impact of social class on career choice was revealed by a comprehensive study (J. K. Little, 1967) of all the graduating seniors in Wisconsin's public and private high schools. At the time of graduation, students were asked to note the occupations they hoped to enter. The choices were later compared to the jobs they actually attained. Stu-

Lower-class adolescents have low career aspirations

dents who were in the lower third of their graduating class in socio-economic status had significantly lower aspirations than those in the middle and upper thirds. In addition, the later actual job attainments of the lower-class students were quite close to their expectations.

The low career expectations of lower-class students might be explained by Hoppe's level of aspiration concept and the theory of achievement motivation proposed by David McClelland and J. W. Atkinson (both of which were described in the preceding chapter), as well as by Coleman's emphasis on destiny control. A lower-class student who has had a history of failure in school is understandably reluctant to risk further failure by working toward a remote, difficult-to-achieve vocational goal. To minimize the possibility of failure, the disadvantaged adolescent is likely to choose a low level of aspiration and be characterized by a low need for achievement. Furthermore, parents may not offer much encouragement. R. L. Simpson (1962) found that high school students, regardless of social class, were likely to seek higher education and higher-level careers if their parents urged them to, but they were unlikely to do so if their parents were neutral or negative about preparation for a career. Lower-class parents who drop out of school and are later unable to find satisfying jobs—or any jobs at all—are less likely to urge their children to go to college than are upper-class parents who have discovered firsthand the employment value of a college degree.

Minority-group pupils
may experience role
confusion

6. In addition to having a low level of aspiration and a low need for achievement, disadvantaged children from minority groups may also feel role confusion, lack a sense of belonging, and have poor self-esteem. Erik Erikson first began to postulate his developmental stage of identity vs. role confusion when he observed American Indians. He concluded that conflicts between their own culture and the prevailing American culture caused a great deal of confusion and prevented Indians from developing a clear sense of identity. Proponents of ethnic studies reason that when minority-group children learn about their cultural heritage, they will acquire a sense of pride and belonging.

Abraham Maslow's hierarchy of needs highlights other problems. Young Americans who become aware that they differ from the majority of their agemates in significant ways may have difficulty satisfying the need for a sense of belonging. Those who observe or sense that they, their parents, and their peers are treated as inferior are not likely to develop feelings of self-esteem. Low self-esteem may also be influenced by lack of school achievement or the inability to find employment. (Maslow's hierarchy also emphasizes the significance of nutrition and health—mentioned in point 1. Physiological needs tend to take precedence over other needs. A child who is hungry or sick and is preoccupied with physical discomfort is not inclined to seek satisfaction of belonging and esteem needs, much less be eager to acquire knowledge and understanding.)

Using this list of points (as well as the preceding discussion of labeling) as a framework, it is possible to draw up a number of general guidelines for teaching disadvantaged children.

Suggestions for teaching: Arranging educational experiences for disadvantaged pupils

1. Be alert to the potential dangers of labeling. Concentrate on individuals while guarding against the impact of stereotyping.

2. When evaluating standardized test scores of any kind, keep in mind the possibility that the norms may not be appropriate for disadvantaged children.

3. Allow for the possibility that disadvantaged children may have inadequate diets and fail to receive adequate medical attention.

4. Take account of research leading to the conclusion that some lower-class parents use unfortunate forms of child care. Check to see if Head Start or Follow-Through experiences have been provided. If so, attempt to continue such programs in classrooms.

5. Remain aware that disadvantaged children may not be familiar with many things you take for granted. Try to supply experiences that such children may have missed.

6. Use every possible means for motivating disadvantaged children to do well in school.

7. Teach study and test-taking skills and academic "tricks of the trade."

8. Use teaching techniques that provide frequent feedback. Make use of programmed instruction whenever appropriate.

9. Encourage students to identify with representatives of their ethnic group who have achieved success.

1. Be alert to the potential dangers of labeling. Concentrate on individuals while guarding against the impact of stereotyping.   Under certain circumstances the potential dangers of labeling mentioned by Bronfenbrenner may lead to unfortunate consequences. The negative impact of labels can be minimized, however, if placing children in categories is done primarily for the purpose of improving instruction or securing services. Instead of thinking that a disadvantaged child is beyond help, for example, you might ask yourself, "What kinds of disadvantages does this pupil need to overcome?" By asking that question, you not only avoid the situation described by Bronfenbrenner, you also concentrate on individuals, which is the surest way to avoid succumbing to the perils of stereotyping. It is reported that Samuel Johnson, the famous English literary figure, was once asked, "Are men more intelligent than women?" He replied, "Which man? Which woman?" If you think in the same way, you can avoid the error

Handbook heading
Drawing Up Individual
Pupil Profiles

Think of individuals,
not groups or types

of assigning to individuals characteristics that are sometimes attributed to a group. Instead of searching for evidence, for example, to determine if blacks, on the average, have more or less of a certain characteristic than whites, on the average, simply concentrate on the unique individual characteristics of a particular black or white student.

2. When evaluating standardized test scores of any kind, keep in mind the possibility that the norms may not be appropriate for disadvantaged children. This point will be analyzed more completely in the next chapter when standardized tests are described, but at this juncture an argument that disadvantaged children have the right to be evaluated with reference to appropriate norms merits mention. The state in which you begin your teaching career may have laws stipulating that standardized tests are not to be used as the sole criterion for identifying students as mentally retarded. Such laws will be ineffective, however, if individual teachers take test scores too literally. If a teacher places too much faith in low scores and treats pupils as if they are stupid, the negative impact may be greater than if some of the pupils were placed in special classes. This is not to say that test scores should be ignored; often they can be used to improve instruction (by following procedures to be described in the next chapter). The point stressed here is that low test scores should always be interpreted tentatively and with caution when there is a possibility that specific students are substantially different from the middle-class children who usually form the bulk of any standardization group.

Interpret test scores with caution

3. Allow for the possibility that disadvantaged children may have inadequate diets and fail to receive adequate medical attention. In searching for explanations of why disadvantaged children may have learning difficulties, some of the first factors to be considered are diet and health. Maslow's hierarchy calls attention to the fact that physiological needs take priority over all others. A child who is malnourished or has a debilitating illness or a physical handicap of some sort (e.g., nearsightedness) cannot be expected to function as an efficient scholar. If you suspect that a child needs medical attention, you might inquire about possible aid from governmental agencies or charitable organizations. (This is a situation where labeling may work to the advantage of a child. Only after an individual has been classified as coming from a poverty-level family or the equivalent are certain kinds of aid made available.)

4. Take account of research leading to the conclusion that lower-class parents use unfortunate forms of child care. Check to see if Head Start or Follow-Through experiences have been provided. If so, attempt to

continue such programs in classrooms. Head Start was established in an effort to provide disadvantaged children with preschool experiences similar to those afforded more favored children being reared under close to ideal circumstances. Studies such as that by Hess and Shipman led to the conclusion that a significant number of lower-class parents failed to provide stimulating experiences for their children, and it was hoped that Head Start would supply training that would compensate for lack of proper care in the home. Although the program did expose children to hundreds of experiences they would not otherwise have received, it did not produce permanent gains. Follow-Through programs were established so that compensatory education would be continued for another three years. A public school teacher can do nothing about child-care practices used by parents, but elementary school teachers in particular could use teaching techniques similar to those practiced in Head Start or Follow-Through programs. If you find yourself teaching in a school attended by Head Start or Follow-Through graduates, you might try to meet with the director and instructors of such programs. The meeting could have two advantages: You might pick up many good instructional techniques. You could use teaching approaches similar to those already experienced by the child, thereby contributing to a sense of familiarity and continuity or at least minimizing confusion caused by clashes in philosophy and methods.

Handbook heading
Techniques Used in
Head Start and
Follow-Through
Programs

5. Remain aware that disadvantaged children may not be familiar with many things you take for granted. Try to supply experiences that such children may have missed. For reasons discussed earlier, many disadvantaged children have led extremely restricted lives. They may have had no experience with everyday objects or situations presented in books or featured in instructional materials. When teaching such children, it is prudent to find out what they know and do not know. If inner-city primary grade children have never seen a chicken, cow, tractor, or barn, they will have difficulty reading a simple story about farm life. In a situation such as this, it would be beneficial to try to arrange a field trip to a farm or at least show pictures and slides of farms to familiarize disadvantaged children with what more favored pupils already know. Regardless of the grade level you teach, you might make it a practice to ask disadvantaged pupils if they have had any personal experience with objects and situations mentioned in books and lessons. If they have not, try to supply familiarity with such experiences in direct or pictorial form.

Handbook heading
Experiences to Provide

6. Use every possible means for motivating disadvantaged children to do well in school. Perhaps the major reason disadvantaged children do not do well in school is not lack of ability but lack of interest in

learning. A number of circumstances conspire to prevent lower-class children from acquiring a desire to do well in school: lack of encouragement from parents, the absence of models in the form of parents and siblings who have benefited from schooling, a level of aspiration set low to avoid possible failure, lack of success leading to a low need for achievement. Accordingly, one of the major tasks of the teacher of disadvantaged children is arousing and sustaining interest in learning. (Specific suggestions for doing this will be offered a bit later in this chapter.)

7. Teach study and test-taking skills and academic "tricks of the trade." Disadvantaged students are not likely to maintain a strong desire to achieve in school unless they receive reinforcement for their efforts in the form of good grades. To get high grades consistently, children must usually develop specialized skills as students. If the parents of a lower-class child are unable to tell their offspring about such skills because they never developed them, teachers must give suggestions about how to study, what to look for on tests, how to budget time during exams, and so on.

8. Use teaching techniques that provide frequent feedback. Make use of programmed instruction whenever appropriate. Skinner's experiments with rats and pigeons reveal the extent to which reinforcement schedules influence output. Just as simple animals will emit a steady stream of responses if they are reinforced at frequent intervals, students are likely to continue to work at learning if they receive steady reinforcement. Asking disadvantaged students to work toward remote goals may be expecting too much. They are more likely to respond to instruction if they receive frequent positive feedback. It has been that many disadvantaged children react very favorably to programmed instruction. The step-by-step procedure is easy to follow, and receiving immediate reinforcement for each response provides an incentive to keep trying. If you are unable to use actual programs, you might set up a series of brief assignments and award points leading to a cumulative total so that students get tangible evidence that they are making progress. The Personalized System of Instruction, particularly when used in a mastery approach, is an ideal way to teach many subjects to disadvantaged pupils. (Detailed instructions for setting up a mastery approach will be presented in Chapter 13.)

9. Encourage students to identify with representatives of their ethnic group who have achieved success. Erik H. Erikson has called attention to the role confusion experienced by some minority-group Americans. He has also concluded that one of the most important factors leading to a sense of identity is occupational choice. Minority-group pupils might be helped to reduce role confusion and develop a

Handbook heading
Ways to Encourage
Ethnic Pride and
Identity

"Motivation programs" in several cities encourage minority group students to identify with representatives of their ethnic group who have achieved success.

Fred Kaplan/Black Star

sense of identity if they are urged to strive to emulate the accomplishments of individuals who share their ethnic background and who have become successful in the professions, business, education, and the like. Such a procedure might lead to the development of identity as successful Americans. Once that identity is achieved, individuals would be free to cherish the language and culture of their native countries without running the risk of experiencing role confusion.

EXAMPLES

Encourage students to identify with successful adults who come from the same background.

Place pictures of successful members of different minority groups on bulletin boards; encourage students to read and write biographies of them and to discuss their work.

Invite such individuals to talk to your class.

Search for books that emphasize the positive achievements of minority group members, for example, the *Negro Heritage Library*. Consult the appendix of *A Handbook for Teaching in the Ghetto School* by

Sidney Trubowitz for a bibliography of books "which portray Negro characters, reveal the cultural heritage of the Negro, or tell of lives of Negroes who have made significant contributions to the total American culture" (1968, p. 147).

Invite retired men of different ethnic backgrounds to visit your class and describe the kinds of jobs they held. If they seem to establish rapport with your students, consider asking them to assist you in small-group or individual instruction.

Consider developing a limited program similar to one used in the Multi-Culture Institute of San Francisco. Encourage pupils from various ethnic and religious backgrounds to get together at designated periods and prepare presentations for the rest of the class illustrating and explaining the art, music, beliefs, and ceremonies of their particular group. On special holidays, have the entire class participate in the celebration, including the preparation of appropriate foods.

An excellent way to become aware of specific teaching techniques that might be used with disadvantaged pupils is to read about programs and methods that have been used at one time or another in educating lower-class children. Becoming aware of techniques used by specialists in compensatory education should assist you in selecting and developing methods of your own. In keeping with a major theme of this book, the following programs are analyzed by contrasting programmed with discovery and humanistic approaches.

Programmed techniques for the disadvantaged

Sullivan's approach to programmed reading

Although programmed reading was not developed specifically for use with the disadvantaged, it has proved especially successful with such students. One of the earliest and most comprehensive programmed reading systems was developed by M. W. Sullivan and several associates. The degree to which this technique proceeds in step-by-step fashion is indicated by the fact that the Teacher's Guide for *The Prereader* is 64 pages long, whereas the guide for the first series of lessons (which covers only part of the entire program) is 451 pages long. The reason for the size of these guides is that instructions for every step of the program are provided in detail. Figure 11–1 lists the instructions the teacher is to follow in presenting the first page of the Prereader, Figure 11–2 is a page from the Prereader on which students are to print the appropriate words.

Figure 11-1

Instructions for presenting the first page of *The Prereader* in the Sullivan program

Teacher's Key	Student Response
Look at the page on the right. (Hold your book up and point to it.)	
On the page you see some lines like this. (Draw eight horizontal lines on the board.) On the left side of the top line you see a letter. (Draw a letter *a* at the left of the top line on the board.)	
Who can tell me the name of this letter?	*a*
You all remember how to make the letter *a*. First I draw a circle, like this. (Draw a circle on the board to the right of the letter *a*.)	
Now *you* draw a circle in your book to the right of the letter *a*. Make the circle just touch the line, the way I did.	(Students draw circle.)
After I've made the circle, I draw a straight line down the side of the circle like this. (Finish the letter *a* on the board.)	
Now you finish the letter *a* in your book by drawing the straight line.	(Students draw straight line.)
Now I'm going to make another letter *a*. First I draw the circle. (Draw it to the right of the second *a*.) Then I draw the line. (Draw it.)	
In your book, write the letter *a* just like this one. (Point to the *a* that you just made.)	(Students write *a*.)
Now I want you to go ahead and fill up all the lines on the page with letter *a*'s. I'll come by and help you while you work.	(Students fill page with *a*'s.)
(Check each student's work, making sure that he draws first the circle and then the line, that he writes his letters on the horizontal lines, etc.)	
Now I want you to turn to the next page of your book like this. (Demonstrate by turning the page.)	

Source: Reprinted from the Teacher's Guide to *The Prereader* by Cynthia D. Buchanan, copyright © 1968 by Sullivan Associates, with permission of Behavioral Research Laboratories, Inc.

Programmed approach to teaching reading

In the Sullivan approach, students first print a page full of the letter *a*, then a page of the letter *i*, then a page in which *a* and *i* alternate, then a page of *n*'s, then *a*, *i*, and *n*, then a page of *p*'s, and finally *i*, *n*, *a*, and *p*. Following that, students print a page of *an*'s, a page of *in*'s, then *in*'s and *an*'s alternating. Eventually, they print *pan* and *pin* under pictures of each and then are given a series of pictures next to which they are to print the appropriate word. This basic technique is used to build a vocabulary of several words, which are then combined into sentences. After each response, students are given either corroboration and praise by the teacher or immediate feedback by seeing the correct answer uncovered.

The similarity of the Sullivan program to Skinner's rat and pigeon

Figure 11-2

Page from *The Prereader* in the Sullivan program

Reprinted from the Teacher's Guide to *The Prereader* by Cynthia D. Buchanan, copyright © 1968 by Sullivan Associates, with permission of Behavioral Research Laboratories, Inc.

experiments is apparent: The behavior of the children is shaped by presenting a series of step-by-step movements toward the terminal behavior and by supplying immediate reinforcement for each step in the desired direction. Generalization is counteracted by contrasting letters and words similar in appearance (such as *pin* and *pan*).

The Engelmann-Becker program

Siegfried Engelmann and Wesley C. Becker (two leading advocates of behavior modification) have developed a basic approach to teaching the disadvantaged that epitomizes the S-R point of view. They operate on the assumption that learning is entirely a product of environmental experiences. As Engelmann puts it: "Even if he is working alone, with no 'teacher' present, [the pupil] is still being taught by the physical environment. . . . There can be no learning (except in trivial, autistic instances) without teaching" (1968, p. 461). On the basis of this assumption, Engelmann and Becker argue that intelligent behavior is learned and that therefore "less intelligent" children—such as the disadvantaged (and mentally retarded)—can be taught to be intelligent.

This can be done, they say, by analyzing the concepts and operations that lead to high performance on intelligence tests and then providing students with programmed units to assist them in mastering the concepts and achieving the operations. They also reason that the disadvantaged should be taught in systematic fashion the academic skills they lack. Series of carefully organized lessons are presented at a fast pace, and reinforcement is provided in a variety of ways. Every effort is made to accelerate learning. An attempt is made to teach generalized response systems that can be applied to solving future problems and to shape traits like attentiveness and perseverance.[1]

Other programmed approaches[2]

The behavior analysis program   Donald Bushell, Jr., has developed a programmed approach that uses systematic reinforcement in the form of recess, snacks, art, and stories to teach study skills (e.g., learning when to talk and when to listen, staying with assigned tasks) as well as subject matter. The teacher and mothers, who act as assistants, are seen as behavior modifiers.

The instructional games program   Lassar Gotkin uses various learning games in a programmed approach. One of these, "Matrix Games," consists of cards with a dozen or so pictures of children engaging in various activities. A child is given one of the cards and directed by the teacher or by a fellow student to "put a red circle around the boy drinking milk." Or the teacher might cover up one of the squares and ask the pupils to figure out what the secret picture is. The games are designed to provide a sequence of learning experiences that proceed in such small steps that almost every response will be correct. Learning is active and can be carried out by assistants or the children themselves. Feedback is immediate and almost always positive. In stressing the values of games that children can handle themselves, Gotkin makes this observation: "If there's anything about ghetto life, it's that the kids have been underlings. Their parents have been underlings, and then the kids have been underlings. I'm interested in Child Power—that the kid should be learning to manage himself" (1970, p. 56).

The primary education project   Lauren Resnick has developed a technique, patterned after a model of teaching proposed by Robert

Behavior modification approach: Reinforce study skills and learning

---

[1] Detailed information about the Engelmann-Becker technique can be found in *Preventing Failure in the Elementary Grades* (1969) by Engelmann, *Distar Instructional System* (1969) by Engelmann et al., and *Teaching: A Course in Applied Psychology* (1971) by Becker, Engelmann, and Thomas.

[2] The three programs in this section are described in *Experiments in Primary Education: Aspects of Project Follow-Through* (1970) by Eleanor E. Maccoby and Miriam Zellner.

Glaser, that is a variation of Individually Prescribed Instruction (described in Chapter 5). Skills needed by disadvantaged students were first analyzed, and then a series of learning units was prepared. The preinstruction behavior of each pupil is determined by tests; then each starts at the appropriate point and works her or his way through the series. Three classes of skills are emphasized: orienting and attending, perceptual-motor, and conceptual-linguistic. As much as possible, the students learn by interacting with the materials and each other. The teacher supplies reinforcement such as praise, gold stars, or tokens and gives assistance where necessary.

Steven Daniels's gerbils, goldfish, and games approach

In *How 2 Gerbils 20 Goldfish 200 Games 2,000 Books and I Taught Them How to Read* (hereafter referred to simply as *How 2 Gerbils*), Steven Daniels describes an approach that combines aspects of behavior modification with discovery techniques. Daniels feels that it is important for the teacher of students from slum areas to function as a leader, and in the opening pages of his book he tells what happened when he failed to do this in his first year of teaching. He then describes specific techniques for establishing control (e.g., state rules and enforce them) but notes that "keeping classroom order is primarily the product of a significant and engaging curriculum" (1971, p. 33). This is true because, "when you got nothin', you got nothin' to lose." So the solution is to give students something to lose—an engaging curriculum. To develop and maintain such an atmosphere, Daniels has devised a variety of techniques, some paralleling those advocated by behavior modifiers (but based more on a philosophy of self-selection than on complete external control) and some similar to open education methods.

Combining behavior modification with self-direction

As reinforcement, he pays children ten cents for erasing the board (so they can earn lunch money); he provides three Games Certificates each year that can be used to "buy" free activity on days when pupils can't seem to get in the mood to study; he makes use of preferred activities as incentives for completing less preferred ones; he posts a Reading Progress Board on which students can chart their progress, and he has developed a series of books arranged in order of difficulty. (All these techniques, it should be noted once again, emphasize a good deal of freedom in self-direction on the part of the students. They are not controlled by the instructor as much as in techniques previously described.)

Daniels uses discovery techniques by surrounding students with books and games and providing for considerable choice (to the point of establishing a Do-Nothing corner), using role playing and psychodrama, exposing students to problem-solving situations (such as giving them bus tokens, then dropping them off at various points in the city and giving a prize to the student who gets to City Hall first), and having Games Day every Friday.

Daniels's book is crammed with practical advice and ingenious ideas for educating the disadvantaged (or any type of student, for that matter), and you are urged to put this at the top of your list of books to buy for your professional library.

Discovery and humanistic approaches for the disadvantaged

Although widespread interest in developing techniques to provide better education for disadvantaged children is a recent development, some methods for teaching such children were put into practice many years ago. Two educators who anticipated the current interest in teaching children from deprived environments by using what today are called discovery or humanistic techniques were Maria Montessori and Sylvia Ashton-Warner.

The Montessori method

In the late 1960s, Montessori schools became popular again after a fifty-year period of relative obscurity. In many cases, such schools enrolled children from affluent homes, perhaps partly because it became voguish to do so. The use of Montessori methods with privileged children is something of a paradox, since the original techniques were developed for use with the disadvantaged. This came about as a result of Montessori's training and early interests.

Maria Montessori began her career as a medical doctor and spent her earliest professional years working with mentally retarded children and in public health. She became involved in education when she was asked by the director-general of the Roman Association for Good Building to create a nursery school that was to be part of a model tenement project. Because of her training, early interests, and the nature of the school she was asked to develop, Montessori stressed cleanliness, order, and housekeeping skills as well as reading, writing, and arithmetic. The techniques she developed to encourage such learning anticipated many aspects of both the discovery approach and programmed learning.

In terms of basic assumptions, Montessori advocated views now associated with Maslow rather than Skinner. She noted, "Environment is undoubtedly a secondary factor in the phenomena of life, it can modify in that it can help or hinder, but it can never *create*" (1912, p. 105; italics in original). She referred to prizes and punishments as "the instrument of slavery for the spirit" (p. 21) and recalled that "all

A classroom in a Montessori school.

Courtesy of the American Montessori Society

human victories, all human progress, stand upon the inner force" (p. 24). In contrast to Engelmann, who maintains that "there can be no learning (except in trivial, autistic instances) without teaching," Montessori observed that "a man is not what he is because of the teachers he has had, but because of what he has done" (p. 172).

Although Montessori advocated the humanistic view, she also urged teachers to observe and experiment, noting that "the more fully the teacher is acquainted with the methods of experimental psychology, the better will she understand how to give the lesson" (p. 107). Montessori combined these two ideas by suggesting that teachers observe the natural, spontaneous behavior of children and then arrange learning experiences to encourage its development. She recommended that lessons be brief, simple, and objective (carried out with objects and independent of teacher control) and that they not be arranged "to make the child feel that he has made a mistake" (p. 109).

Montessori method: Discovery, programming, and open education combined

The techniques and apparatus developed by Montessori are a combination of what today would be called discovery and programmed methods and open education. She stressed activity and self-direction but at the same time provided children with "programmed" materials—for example, form boards arranged in sequence and designed to provide immediate feedback. She used what today are called activity centers, but she also urged the teacher to use repetition

Learning materials developed by Montessori in the early 1900s are similar to programmed learning materials produced in the 1960s and 1970s. Both types of materials provide immediate feedback.

Charles Harbutt/Magnum

in daily associations between stimuli and responses: "The lessons in nomenclature must consist simply in provoking the association of the name with the object" (p. 225). She also stressed that the teacher should determine if what today is called terminal behavior had been achieved: "The teacher must always test whether or not her lesson has attained the end she had in view" (p. 225). She encouraged children to interact and to teach and learn from each other but also presented lessons to build a hierarchical series of skills in much the same manner of Gagné recommends today. For example, in teaching reading and writing, she first encouraged practice in handling a pencil, then presented the alphabet in the form of large letters cut out of sandpaper (to permit the child to use several senses at once), then had the child select the letter, trace it and draw it, and finally had the child combine letters into words. (In the Montessori system, children write before they read. Unfortunately, the fact that English orthography is non-phonetic—that is, a sound cannot be determined simply by the combination of letters used to write it—makes her approach difficult to use with English-speaking American children.) Numerals were also presented in sandpaper form, and addition, subtraction, multiplication, and division were taught with blocks and rods.

Obviously, Montessori was a brilliant innovator. Some of her techniques were based on assumptions that are not appropriate to the

American disadvantaged child in the 1970s, but if you will be teaching younger children, you are urged to read at least one book by or about Montessori. (Suggestions will be offered at the end of the chapter.)

Sylvia Ashton-Warner's organic approach

In 1958, Sylvia Ashton-Warner published her novel *Spinster,* in which she described techniques for teaching disadvantaged Maori children in New Zealand. In *Teacher* (1963) she gives a detailed explanation of her approach, the heart of which is *organic reading,* a pedagogical method that epitomizes the humanistic viewpoint, just as the Sullivan approach epitomizes the S-R position. (As you read this description of Ashton-Warner's approach, you are urged to compare it with Sullivan's programmed technique.)

The meaning of *organic* in Ashton-Warner's approach is summed up in these statements: "First words must have intense meaning for a child. They must be part of his being" (1963, p. 33). When five-year-old Maori children first came into her room, Ashton-Warner invited them to come up to her, one by one, and ask her to print a word on a large card. (The child's name was also printed on the corner of the card.) The child said the word after it had been printed, took it to a mat (serving as a desk), and traced it. After each child had been given a word, all the cards were collected and put in a box. The next day the cards were dumped on the floor, and the children took out their words, after which they chose a partner and exchanged vocabulary. As this was being done, the children came up individually to ask for another word. From time to time, the children were asked to read their cards. If they were unable to read any particular word, the card was destroyed. When a Key Vocabulary of thirty words for each child had been accumulated, the children were encouraged to write their own words and, after being provided with additional general vocabulary, to write sentences. During these writing periods, which were limited to twelve children at a time, Ashton-Warner circulated around the group and gave individual assistance. Each day, new words were printed on the board so that all could see them. When a sufficient vocabulary had been acquired, each child wrote a story, which she or he then read to and exchanged with other children. Thus, the children created their own texts. In addition to reading and writing, the children also were free to select from many activities and took frequent field trips that were used as the bases for stories, singing, and dancing.

Marie Hughes and Ronald Henderson have developed a Follow-Through program (described in Maccoby and Zellner, 1970) to help Mexican-American children to overcome English deficiencies, gain experience in manipulating objects, and develop a sense of the sequence of events. Stories told by the children are recorded and class

[margin note, left of text:] Organic reading: Children ask for words

experiences described in illustrated books—a technique similar to that used by Ashton-Warner. Following is a description of the reading program developed by Hughes and Henderson:

When we are trying to teach reading, we try to make it functional; it must be related to experiences the child and his friends have had, it must be useful to the child to be able to read the labels so he can tell what is available where— so he can get the things he wants. We make a lot of use of the primer typewriter to label everything, and then use the labels in referring to materials, places, etc. The better teachers can use this environment easily. Our assumption is that the children are less motivated if you use a more formal program to unlock the recurring environment. (1970, p. 40)

In addition, efforts are made to inculcate positive attitudes toward school, to build the ability to persist, and the expectation of success.

Minischool approaches stressing free education

The First Street School of George Dennison   In *The Lives of Children,* George Dennison describes the short, turbulent history of the First Street School he established in New York City. Dennison explains how he was influenced by Neill, Ashton-Warner, and others in developing the principle that education is a preparation not for later life but for "the present lives of children" (1969, p. 9). To put his philosophy into practice, he created a minischool consisting of twenty-three students and varying numbers of teachers who lived in the neighborhood. Because of the nature and size of this school and because Dennison was unable to sustain it for more than two years, it does not serve as a model for direct imitation in a public school. However, in Chapter 12 of his book, Dennison offers suggestions for those who see merit in the approach, and the appendix consists of comments on teaching techniques by other educators who endorse the First Street philosophy.

Jonathan Kozol's free school approach   In *Death at an Early Age* (1967), Jonathan Kozol exposed the deplorable conditions of life in a Boston ghetto school. In *Free Schools* (1972), he described the kind of school he has created as an alternative. To understand his approach, it is important to take into account the anguish, rage, and frustration of his first experience with teaching. Although Kozol would like to endorse the free philosophy as advocated by Neill and Dennison, he is obviously imbued with a mission—to help black children work their way out of the ghetto. To do that, he argues, they must be equipped with certain skills (such as reading) and taught how to survive and beat the system. (As Kozol uses the word, *free* refers more to freedom from the stultifying impact of public education than it does to a self-directed approach.) He does everything possible to encourage self-direction but recognizes that formal instruction is necessary if students are to learn the skills they will need. He provides this description of what he considers an ideal free school:

There is, within the school, a lot of emphasis on what the old-time teachers used to call "the basic skills." There is also a visible presence of high energy and fun, pupil irreverence and adult unprotectedness, . . . a warm, reassuring and disarming atmosphere of trust and intimacy and good comradeship between children and adults, a sense of trust that builds at all times on the recognition of the difficult conditions that surround their school and of the dangers which exist for each and every one of them on the outside.

There is also something in this school which is too rare in many of the Free Schools that I know: a real sense of stability and of sustained commitment in regard both to the present lives and to the future aspirations of the children in the school. . . . [The teachers] are not afraid to give their kids direct instructions, straightforward criticism or precise and sometimes bitter admonitions. They like *Summerhill* but they do not think it is the only good book ever written. (1972, pp. 74–75)

Herbert Kohl's "spontaneous interest" approach Herbert Kohl describes his experiences of teaching in a sixth grade class in a Harlem elementary school in *36 Children* (1967); and in *The Open Classroom* (1969), he offers some general suggestions derived from these and later experiences. The Kohl approach is not so much a systematic program of instruction as a general philosophy of taking advantage of spontaneous interests, although a few features (e.g., activity centers) of the British open education technique are recommended. You are urged to read *36 Children* to discover how Kohl converted spontaneous class comments into units on myths, themes on the topic "My Block," autobiographies, fables, an alphabet book, and a class newspaper. His basic approach is summarized in this excerpt from *The Open Classroom*:

Taking advantage of spontaneous interests

I considered my role in [the] class was to bring in things to share with the students and to be available to help them. I brought books and articles and poems to class, and left them there. Sometimes we talked about them though often we didn't. However, my bringing what I cared about to the class made it easier for them to bring things that were important to them.

One has to be patient with freedom and have as rich an environment as possible available for students so there will be things they can choose to do. One cannot ask pupils to be free or make choices in a vacuum. There is no limit to what can be brought to class to enrich the environment. A partial list would include:

—second-hand books

—old magazines

—scraps of wood, metal, and cloth discarded by factories

—old billboard posters

—parts of broken machines—cars, TV's, radios, toasters, etc.

—tape recorders and tape

—old toys

—old clothes to be used to create a classroom costume closet

—a sewing machine and needles and thread

—discarded advertising materials such as signs, posters, booklets, sales tags, handbills

—comfortable old furniture or rugs

—light fixtures, flashlights, wire, bulbs, batteries

—typewriters

—posters and buttons of all sorts (1969, pp. 99–100).

The "open education" approach of Taba and Elkins

Kohl titles one of his books *The Open Classroom,* but his basic technique of teaching is much closer to what is often termed *free* education than to *open* education. Techniques for teaching the disadvantaged that exemplify open education have been developed and practiced by Hilda Taba and Deborah Elkins, who explain their approach in *Teaching Strategies for the Culturally Disadvantaged* (1966). The original description of their work appeared in 1950, thus anticipating the open education movement of today, but their methods are essentially the same as those now being advocated by proponents of the open approach.

The basic guidelines for instructional strategies recommended by Taba and Elkins include continual diagnosis to discover gaps in knowledge and areas in need of attention, and the simultaneous pursuit of objectives in six areas: (1) knowledge, thinking, attitudes, and skills; (2) providing for heterogeneity; (3) pacing learning by providing "bite-size" chunks arranged in hierarchical fashion; (4) structuring learning to allow for tangibility, concreteness, and overt activity; (5) extensive use of dramatization, play making, and role playing; and (6) providing experiences in observing and interviewing.

The implementation of these guidelines can be illustrated by a unit called "Human Hands." The unit was introduced at a concrete level. Students were asked to trace their hands, and the tracings were used first as a basis for discussing the beauty and similarity of hands and then as a stimulus for writing on the topic "Important Things My Hands Can Do." The descriptions provided were analyzed and tallied on the board under different categories to encourage awareness of concepts. The final list of categories was reproduced and added to the written theme as the beginning of an individual notebook for each pupil. Then the teacher read a story, and students were asked to discuss how hands were used by the characters; afterward, the original categories were revised and expanded. For homework, the students

Reports and
observations converted
into a do-it-yourself
text

were asked to observe an adult for thirty minutes and write down
everything the person did with his or her hands. These reports were
discussed, tallied, categorized, and added to the notebooks, following
which each student summed up general observations on hands in a
short paragraph, which was later reproduced in a booklet and distributed to the members of the class. Next, help-wanted ads in newspapers were analyzed to illustrate how hands are used in many different
occupations. Magazines were distributed, and students were asked to
cut out pictures of hands; newspaper articles on hands were collected.
All of these were used in group discussion and as the basis for written
exercises to be added to the notebooks.

   The same general techniques were used in the additional themes

*One of the Taba and Elkins exercises urges students to observe and record
ways adults use their hands.*
Arthur Tress/Magnum

"Walls in Our Life" and "Aspirations." The purpose of the latter topic was to build understanding of goals and encourage the development of realistic aspirations. It featured interviews with parents and other adults, the dramatization of original plays, and role playing (some students acted as employers; others as job seekers).

As this brief description indicates, Taba and Elkins recommend teaching methods that illustrate many techniques of open education. *Teaching Strategies for the Culturally Disadvantaged* offers detailed suggestions for setting up and carrying out social studies units for secondary school students, although the basic methods described could be adapted for use with almost any grade level or subject. It is one of the most practical how-to-do-it books on open education *and* the education of the disadvantaged, and it is highly recommended.

James Herndon's experiments with "creative arts"

In *The Way It Spozed to Be* (1968), James Herndon describes his initial experiences in grappling with life in a public junior high school; in *How to Survive in Your Native Land* (1971), he describes later experiments with "survival" in American education. During his first year as a teacher, Herndon struggled to find ways to arouse interest in the standard curriculum by using student-led groups, tape recorders, games like Scrabble, trips to the library, a Friday "film-orgy" (complete with candy), and play reading. At the conclusion of *The Way It Spozed to Be,* he expresses the fatalistic view that what he did probably made no difference and that there was little hope for change. However, he decided to give teaching another try, and in *How to Survive in Your Native Land* he describes how he (and his colleagues) induced his students to invent their own language, drop notes in bottles off the Golden Gate bridge, pretend to be Peace Corps workers, invent an island, and engage in a variety of other learning experiences. Eventually, Herndon found a school where he was allowed to unveil "Creative Arts" (C.A.)—a two-hour block of time during which students voluntarily (with parental permission) participated in a no-assignment, no-grade curriculum. When they weren't making abundant use of their permanent hall passes, students in C.A. built monster kites, drew elaborate mural maps, and wrote, produced, directed, and starred in a scintillating film epic, "The Return of the Hawk."

Despite the apparent success of many of his ideas in regular and C.A. classes, Herndon expresses doubts about the value of any kind of schooling. He also speculates that C.A. and other forms of free education work only because they are better than the regular curriculum. He suggests that the burden is shifted from teacher to children and that teachers may set up such classes in the hope that their students will show them how to teach. Perhaps Herndon is so hard on himself because he began his career with high hopes and did not fully realize the magnitude of the job he was tackling. If Coleman is correct—and there is considerable evidence that he is—the primary reason that educating the disadvantaged rarely works to perfection is the crushing impact of the entire environment in which students exist. As Jencks has pointed out, the schools are expected to do too much. Herbert Kohl, expressing his disappointment about the lack of permanent change in his students, says, "One year is not enough." Herndon seems to have been bothered by the same feeling. But it is apparent from reading his books that he did have a substantial positive impact on his pupils, and it seems certain that all of them learned more than they would have if left to their own devices. Herndon feels uncomfortable about using many of the ingenious teaching techniques he developed because at heart he is a believer in freedom. But it would appear that when he did exert leadership, his students learned more than he might like to admit.

As you read about these programs you become acquainted with a variety of techniques for teaching disadvantaged pupils. To put these various ideas into perspective and to relate them to points discussed earlier in this book, here is a list of suggestions for teaching the disadvantaged. Since motivation is often the key factor in helping such students learn, the following points are organized to parallel the suggestions for motivating students to learn that were offered at the end of the preceding chapter.

Suggestions for teaching: Techniques for teaching disadvantaged pupils

1. Do everything possible to satisfy the deficiency needs—physiological, safety, belonging, esteem.

    a. Allow for the physical condition of your pupils.

    b. Make your room physically and psychologically safe.

    c. Show your students that you take an interest in them and that they "belong" in your classroom.

    d. Arrange learning experiences so that all students can gain at least a degree of esteem.

2. Enhance the attractions and minimize the dangers of growth choices.

3. Direct learning experiences toward feelings of success in an effort to encourage a realistic level of aspiration, an orientation toward achievement, and a positive self-concept.

4. Be alert to the damaging impact of excessive competition.

5. For students who need it, encourage the development of a desire to achieve.

6. Take advantage of natural interests, try to create new ones, and encourage learning for its own sake.

7. Teach specific study and test-taking skills, and encourage students to continue their education.

1. Do everything possible to satisfy the deficiency needs—physiological, safety, belonging, esteem.

Handbook heading
Satisfying the
Physiological Needs of
Disadvantaged Students

a. Allow for the physical condition of your pupils. Since many children from disadvantaged homes are in poor health, have an inadequate diet, and must cope with noisy and crowded living conditions, it may be necessary to pay special attention to their physical condition.

EXAMPLES

Find out whether your students have had breakfast. If many have not, inquire about the availability of breakfast programs provided by college or other groups; see if the school cafeteria might provide breakfast as well as lunch; or supply some fruits and cereals on your own.

Follow Daniels's technique of paying children for chores, such as erasing the board, either in lunch money or in apples, cookies, and the like.

Stress the importance of a good diet.

When students seem sleepy, provide frequent breaks and rest periods.

Make maximum use of a school nurse to diagnose and treat health problems and to emphasize the importance of cleanliness and a good diet.

b. Make your room physically and psychologically safe. Many disadvantaged children live in environments in which physical safety cannot be taken for granted. (In *How 2 Gerbils,* Daniels describes the jungle atmosphere that may be created by neighborhood gangs.) Consequently, you have an opportunity to make your room seem a haven. Herndon observes:

I often wondered how they got along outside my classroom. In the world of and around [the school], most of the kids were scared—scared of failure, scared of being black, scared of their new shoes, scared of tearing their clothes, scared of not knowing how to do right, scared of not getting a pencil or a piece of three-hole lined paper upon which they would be too scared to write anything much if they got it. Perhaps the students of 7B fell back, outside the classroom, as individuals, into this scariness and became apathetic or violent or ugly, or called each other watermelonhead. I really don't know. It seemed as if in the classroom they had found something reasonable to respond to, as often an individual kid will find in school some promise which is kept, something sensible or even beautiful, something not available in their homes or families or in their blocks, and so come to live really only at school, even sometimes to love it and find in it the same joy and despair as any lover. (1968, pp. 33–34)

EXAMPLES

Establish routines and firm control, but do it in a positive way so that less secure students realize you will protect them from possible physical harm and so all pupils will feel that your room is a place where they can feel unthreatened.

Be consistent, honest, warm, firm, and fair.

c. Show your students that you take an interest in them and that they "belong" in your classroom.

EXAMPLES

Go out of your way to know students on an individual basis.

Consider using a personal interest technique practiced by Daniels: Send birthday and Christmas cards.

d. Arrange learning experiences so that all students can gain at least a degree of esteem.   Many disadvantaged children, particularly those from minority groups, have a poor estimate of themselves as a result of many factors, including living conditions, actual experiences with discrimination, stereotyped conceptions created by films and television (consider the image of the American Indian presented in most Westerns), and observation of the difficulty their parents experience in improving their lot. This is what Coleman means by *destiny control,* and he considered it "to have a stronger relationship to achievement than . . . all other 'school' factors together" (1966, p. 23). All these factors highlight the degree to which efforts should be made to help the disadvantaged in satisfying their esteem needs. The most promising way to encourage feelings of esteem is to do everything possible to help students to feel that they can be successful, to encourage self-control, and to provide background in skills that will pave the way for success in higher education.

Handbook heading
Ways to Encourage
Feelings of Esteem

EXAMPLES

Use the Montessori approach as a model. Try to set up learning situations that are brief, simple, carried out with objects, independent of teacher control, and so arranged that the child is not made to feel she or he has made mistakes.

Use materials such as the "Matrix Games" developed by Gotkin to encourage "Child Power," whereby students manage their own learning and get away from the feeling they are underlings.

Be especially wary of degrading criticisms. At the same time, avoid hypocritical praise.

Constantly remind yourself of Ginott's distinction between desirable and undesirable praise; praise the act, not the child.

Make use of student-created materials: books, plays, newspapers, stories, decorations. Follow the Taba and Elkins procedure of "publishing" student work in the form of a class "text."

Follow the advice of Daniels: "The best method I've found for creating self-esteem is to let my students, to the fullest possible degree, run the class. Aside from the fact that they will teach and lead one another better than I can, they feel trusted, important, and worthy of respect" (1971, p. 91).

This list of techniques brings up a question about the use of behavior modification with the disadvantaged. Some teachers have felt that it is important to provide a steady diet of reinforcement in the form of praise or tangible rewards and in this way attempt to build the confidence and self-esteem of their students. The assumption is that the environment must be controlled by others, which leads to the question of whether and how outer control can be transferred to inner control. When almost all classroom activities are planned and prepared and controlled by the teacher, students may get the feeling that they are not trusted or worthy of respect. On the other hand, if the teacher goes too far in the direction of freedom, students may be overwhelmed by the magnitude of the task of educating themselves. A workable compromise seems to be to follow the open education approach: Provide direction but still allow individual choice, and at the same time encourage students to develop some of their own materials and to learn from each other.

2. Enchance the attractions and minimize the dangers of growth choices.   Many disadvantaged children see learning as threatening or not worth the effort, and they conceive of not attempting to learn as safe. As Daniels put it, "When you got nothin', you got nothin' to lose." Herndon has pointed out that many disadvantaged students may choose to engage in horseplay or defiance because they would prefer to appear bad than to seem stupid. He also describes some elaborate and ingenious techniques his pupils devised to make it appear that they knew more than they actually did. Maslow's diagram of growth choice thus takes on special significance when dealing with the disadvantaged, so do everything possible to make growth (in the form of learning) attractive and unthreatening.

EXAMPLES

Don't require students to perform in front of their peers unless they choose to do so.

Provide positive feedback in private and personal ways.

Follow Daniels's lead, and make learning so lively and interesting that students will find safety (not joining in) unattractive.

3. Direct learning experiences toward feelings of success in an effort to encourage a realistic level of aspiration, an orientation toward achievement, and a positive self-concept. For reasons discussed in the comments on satisfying esteem needs, unless disadvantaged pupils are given assistance, they are quite likely to be predisposed more toward failure than toward success. This is a primary reason why programmed approaches—which supply steady reinforcement— are particularly effective with disadvantaged children. In addition, you might use a variety of other techniques to help students to experience feelings of success, develop a realistic level of aspiration, and acquire an orientation toward achievement.

Handbook heading

Activities That Will Make Pupils Feel Successful

EXAMPLES

Use Daniels's reading for pleasure technique. Obtain (perhaps by asking for used volumes in a classified ad) hundreds of books and spread them around the room; invite students to pick out a book, read it to themselves or friends, and post titles read on a Reading Progress Board. Or use Daniels's list of books graded in terms of difficulty. (For instructions on how to set up such a program, together with a list of the books arranged by levels, see pages 135–150 of *How 2 Gerbils*.)

When students are self-conscious or have doubts about their ability to do something well, put everyone under a handicap. Herndon had his students paint left-handed and with huge brushes when they expressed fears that their efforts at art would look inept.

Use the open education approach of having students set individual goals in consultation with you and use techniques (noted in the preceding chapter) under the following headings: (1) "Make use of goals and objectives that are challenging but attainable"; (2) "Provide knowledge of results by emphasizing the positive."

Use the Taba and Elkins unit entitled "Aspirations" as a model for assisting students in understanding such concepts as why people strive for goals and also in learning what sorts of jobs are available and what is involved in getting a job.

4. Be alert to the damaging impact of excessive competition. Most people enjoy competition only when they have a reasonable chance to

come out on top. When disadvantaged children are forced to compete in academic work against those who come from richer backgrounds, they may have little chance to win. It is especially important, then, to hold down competition between students from varying backgrounds. When students are grouped either unintentionally or as a consequence of school boundary lines and all have approximately the same background, the use of games and lighthearted competition might help to arouse interest. But in other situations, it is probably wise to avoid competition as much as possible.

Handbook heading
Nonthreatening Forms
of Competition

EXAMPLES

Both Herndon and Daniels made extensive use of games in their classrooms. Herndon used Scrabble and Spin-the-Pointer (described on page 131 of *The Way It Spozed to Be*), and Daniels set aside every Friday as Games Day and also had three special Games Days during the year. In order of preference, the ten best classroom games for these days were: (1) checkers, (2) playing cards, (3) Monopoly, (4) The Game of Life, (5) The Newlywed Game, (6) Go to the Head of the Class, (7) Ker-Plunk, (8) Tip-it, (9) jigsaw puzzles, and (10) Spill and Spell.

Daniels also describes these competitive techniques:

> The Reading Progress Board was one of the external motivational devices that I used to encourage the children's reading. One wall of the room was covered with dark Portuguese cork. Each student had his name affixed along the bottom, with a colored map-flag pinned over it. As his group finished a book and passed the test, his flag advanced two of the twelve total spaces on the board. If he reached the top by the end of the school year, he was appropriately rewarded—a giant Sugar Daddy candy sucker.
>
> Another incentive that was very effective was the "Group of the Week." The best group each week (a subjective decision, as are most decisions) had its picture taken in full color. The photograph was posted on the wall, and each child got a Hershey bar. A well-read classroom marches on its stomach! (1971, pp. 60–61)

5. For students who need it, encourage the development of a desire to achieve. Most disadvantaged students are likely to need such encouragement. Consider some of the factors mentioned at the beginning of this chapter: lack of an educational tradition in the home, discontent with schools, antagonism toward schools and teachers, inadequate motivation to achieve remote educational goals. For reasons such as these, disadvantaged pupils are not likely to see much reason to strive for high grades. Consequently, it may be necessary to attempt to encourage the development of a desire to achieve in almost all disadvantaged pupils. Techniques described in the preceding chapter can be used for this purpose, but additional attention might be paid to providing school know-how and sophistication and in making learning seem worthwhile.

Handbook heading
Ways to Inspire
Achievement

EXAMPLES

Use the achievement training techniques developed by Kolb (based on the work of McClelland and Atkinson): Encourage students to emulate high achievers by taking responsibility for attempting work, being willing to shoot for high goals, and being eager to receive detailed knowledge of results.

Stress the importance of doing well on exams. Give practice in taking exams.

Supply hints on how to allow for different types of questions. For example, if there is no penalty for guessing, answer all the questions.

Use the Check List of Prosocial Behaviors (Figure 10–3) to help students to improve their study skills.

Emphasize that learning often *does* pay off. Invite former students who have gone on to college and secured good jobs to speak to the class and emphasize the importance of doing well in school.

Exude confidence in the ability of your students to learn, and guard against low expectations and the self-fulfilling prophecy.

In 1956 a program was instituted in a New York junior high school with the following purpose: "to identify, stimulate and guide into college channels able students from low socioeconomic homes." The project was given the title Higher Horizons, and it has received a good deal of publicity because the aims were fulfilled in dramatic fashion: 39 percent more students eventually were graduated from high school compared with pre–Higher Horizons years; three and a half times more students went to college than previously. Although these results are impressive, Higher Horizons has been criticized. It has been pointed out that the expanded budget, the lower pupil-teacher and pupil-counselor loads, and the zeal of those involved to "prove" they could do it made the program somewhat unrealistic as a model for all school districts.

Whatever the validity of such criticisms (which may explain why similar programs have not become a fixture in more school systems), the techniques used can be of value to any teacher in a secondary school in which there are disadvantaged students. If your school district lacks an organized program, you may be able to develop a miniature, private version of Higher Horizons. Here are some of the techniques used in New York:

To identify those with potential and to ascertain strengths and weaknesses, a variety of test instruments were used.

Pictures of black and Puerto Rican doctors, physicists, and journalists were displayed in the classroom to instill motivation and develop the self-image of the students.

Special remedial reading classes of five and six pupils each were organized. *All* teachers, regardless of what subjects they taught, devoted the first ten minutes of each class to drills in reading.

Book fairs and circulating libraries of paperbacks were started. Students who read a certain number of books were given recognition (e.g., badges that said, "Readers Are Leaders").

An intensive counseling service was established to provide guidance concerning career and college possibilities.

A cultural program was initiated. Groups of students were taken to movies and concerts—after having been prepared for the experience by discussing what to look or listen for, what it would be like, and so on.

Classrooms were opened after school hours to provide a quiet place to study. Counselors made arrangements with parents in crowded apartments to turn television sets off between certain hours so students could complete their homework. (The counselors also persuaded younger brothers and sisters not to pester scholars at work.)

Parents were involved in school programs through meetings, home visits, and letters. Workshops were organized to give parents the opportunity to discuss career possibilities for their children.

Obviously, many of these techniques are beyond the resources of an individual teacher, but they do suggest the direction you might take if you would like to attempt to develop some type of Higher Horizons project of your own. Reports on Higher Horizons appeared in *Strengthening Democracy* (vol. 9, no. 4, March–April 1957, and vol. 12, no. 4, May 1960), published by the Board of Education of the City of New York.

In *Got No Time to Fool Around,* Rebecca Segal describes the Motivation Program of the Philadelphia public schools, which is similar in many respects to the Higher Horizons program. The credo of the program is described this way: "The 'M' program is composed of four fundamental parts of a coherent program designed to enrich, broaden, and motivate ... selected students. These are curricular enrichment, parent and community involvement, cultural enrichment, and tutoring" (1972, p. 47).

The program is put into effect by selecting students who, according to teachers' impressions, show promise but lack motivation. These students are designated as "M" students, and they participate in an induction ceremony and receive pins that identify them as participants. Teachers—and special counselors in the "Motivation Office"—do everything possible to build up the self-concept of "M" students, arrange for tutorial assistance, organize field trips to colleges, provide tickets for plays and concerts, and give assistance for gaining admission to college and winning scholarships.

As part of the Philadelphia Motivation Program, students visit the home of a prominent collector and examine some of his first editions.
Courtesy of the Philadelphia Motivation Program

In order to stay in the program, the students must take extra classes in English and math, earn at least a B average, and do outside reading. In addition, parents are urged to attend group discussions on ways to help their children do well in school. To demonstrate the values of making an effort to do well in school, the achievements of "M" graduates are reported, and students who are accepted at college and those who receive scholarships are given special recognition.

Like New York's Higher Horizons, the Philadelphia program requires school-wide cooperation for some of its features, but any teacher can put into practice what is considered to be a key to its success—taking a personal interest in students.

If you can think of other ways to encourage the development of a desire to achieve, including ideas derived from the techniques mentioned in the preceding chapter, note them in your Handbook.

6. Take advantage of natural interests, try to create new ones, and encourage learning for its own sake.   Until recently, a major problem of educating disadvantaged pupils was that almost all school materials were developed to appeal to the interests of a hypothetical middle-class child. Fortunately, more attention is now paid to developing instructional materials that are relevant to the experiences of the disadvantaged. Many texts now depict situations that are familiar to disadvantaged children, and "Sesame Street" characters spend much of their time in city settings. You might try to make a similar effort to relate what you teach to experiences that are familiar to pupils who come from other than upper- or middle-class homes.

Handbook heading
Relating Lessons to
Pupils' Lives

EXAMPLES

Use variations of the Ashton-Warner technique by using words and ideas requested by your students as the basis for lessons, the development of student-created materials, and student interaction.

Use the Kohl approach of building units on comments made in class.

Follow the Taba and Elkins procedure of starting off a unit with a concrete, physical activity; have students trace their hands.

Make reading functional, as described by Marie Hughes and Ronald Henderson.

Get into the habit of verbalizing extensively, and try to get your students to respond.

Use psychodrama, role playing, and simulation games. (For a description of how Daniels used the psychodrama technique, see page 75 of *How 2 Gerbils*.)

Use the classroom courtroom described on page 142 of Bel Kaufman's *Up the Down Staircase* as a guide for setting up similar activities.

In language class, have students write autobiographies or themes on the subject "My Block" and the like.

In math class, hand out mail-order catalogues, give each of the students a hypothetical sum of money, and have them fill out an order including shipping and sales tax charges.

Be prepared for more than the usual amount of "What do we have to learn this stuff for, anyway?" and try to make "impractical" subjects such as literature appealing by encouraging students to write and illustrate their own books and experience the values of such activities directly.

If you can think of other ways to take into account the practical, physical, concrete orientation of disadvantaged students, note them in your Handbook.

7. Teach specific study and test-taking skills, and encourage students to continue their education. Jonathan Kozol argues that for the disadvantaged, being a well-educated person means being able to "wage guerrilla warfare with credentials" (1972, p. 38). If this argument is endorsed, the kind of learning most essential to disadvantaged students would seem to be that which would equip them to get satisfactory grades, pass tests, and meet requirements. Although it will obviously be necessary to master subject matter in order to do this, the fundamental skills would be reading, study habits, and test-taking skills—plus a feeling of self-confidence and the conviction that it is possible to achieve.

Handbook heading
Ways to Teach
Academic Know-How

EXAMPLES

Schedule how-to-study sessions in secondary school classes. Techniques described in discussing aspects of memorization in Chapter 8 might be featured in such sessions (e.g., teach students how to use mnemonic devices, organize notes, minimize interference, etc.)

After handing back exams, discuss why answers were not satisfactory, and offer suggestions for improvement.

Give frequent tests so that students will get plenty of practice answering questions.

Have high school graduates who are doing well in college return to their secondary schools and talk to seniors about study techniques that lead to success.

Urge students to attend some sort of college after they graduate from high school.

Invite counselors from nearby community and four-year colleges to describe the kinds of courses and programs they offer.

Call attention to the kinds of financial and study aids that are provided by most colleges (e.g., scholarships, loans, tutorial programs).

The Coleman Report and subsequent studies indicate that current educational programs for the disadvantaged are insufficient to overcome the impact of the hidden curriculum of the environment. In theory, changing the environment is the most logical way to solve this problem. Considering current attitudes toward socialism, busing, and integration, this solution does not appear to be realistic. Consequently, the best hope is to try to provide disadvantaged children with the kind of education most likely to increase their chances of helping themselves.

The kind of learning that is essential for the disadvantaged, therefore, is different in many respects from that for the student who has benefited from an enriched environment. It is unlikely that any kind of public school education will ever bring about complete equality of educational opportunity, but if you concentrate on assisting the disadvantaged in developing skills that will help them cope with the educational system, they will at least have a better chance than if they were left to struggle by themselves.

SUMMARY OF KEY POINTS

At the time of President Lyndon Johnson's Great Society program, James S. Coleman was commissioned to supervise a study of inequalities of educational opportunity. Coleman and his colleagues found a significant relationship between social class and school achievement: upper-class children had a much better chance of doing well in school than lower-class children. The researchers hypothesized that the educational achievement of children from weak educational backgrounds would increase if they were placed in classes with pupils from strong educational backgrounds. This conclusion led to the policy of busing, since it was assumed that transporting pupils was the most effective way to bring children from weak and strong educational backgrounds into contact with each other. A different attempt to equalize educational opportunities took the form of enrolling disadvantaged preschool children in Head Start programs. Although children who attended Head Start schools undoubtedly benefited in many ways, the gains they made seemed to fade rapidly when they were no longer exposed to special instruction after they entered the primary grades. One explanation for the tendency for Head Start gains to fade is that pupils from poor backgrounds begin to sense that they lack destiny control: They feel that they are not in a position to shape their own futures.

Among possible explanations for the relationship between lower-class background and poor school achievement are: Lower-class mothers may not receive consistent medical care during pregnancy and delivery. The experiences of lower-class children may be restricted to their own homes and neighborhoods. Lower-class children may have neutral or negative attitudes toward school.

Some psychologists point out that applying the term *disadvantaged* to certain children may lead to negative consequences if teachers assume that pupils so classified are incapable of learning. If labels are interpreted properly, however, they may help teachers plan educational experiences intended to compensate for limiting background factors. Factors that may influence disadvantaged children include: poor health care, unfortunate forms of child rearing, lack of academic know-how, low career aspirations at the time of adolescence, role confusion (particularly on the part of lower-class minority-group children).

Two general guidelines for teachers of disadvantaged children are: think of individuals, not groups or types, interpret test scores with caution. Programmed techniques for teaching disadvantaged pupils include: programmed reading, using behavior modification to reinforce study skills and learning, and combining behavior modification techniques with self-direction. Discovery techniques for teaching the disadvantaged include: combining discovery, programs, and open education in a modified Montessori approach; using Sylvia Ashton-Warner's organic reading method by inviting pupils to ask for words to learn, basing lessons on spontaneous interests, and inviting secondary students to convert reports and operations into do-it-yourself texts.

BECOMING A BETTER TEACHER:
QUESTIONS AND SUGGESTIONS

Drawing Up Individual Pupil Profiles

Am I making an effort to avoid stereotyping pupils by thinking of them as individuals? Suggestion: Prepare a profile of each student in the class, starting with those who seem to be having the most trouble keeping up with the curriculum. Then try to arrange learning experiences to help individuals compensate for their weaknesses. The profile might include headings such as: health and vitality, attitude of parents (if opportunities arise for observing how parents respond, or fail to respond, to conferences, report cards, PTA meetings); knowledge and skills most in need of improvement; attitude toward school; academic and/or career aspirations.

Techniques Used in Head Start and Follow-Through Programs

If I teach in the primary or elementary grades, have I checked to find out if any of my pupils were in Head Start or Follow-Through programs? Suggestion: If I discover that some pupils are graduates of Head Start or Follow-Through programs, try to arrange to talk to the directors and teachers of such programs. If possible, observe the teaching techniques they use and also ask for suggestions for specific procedures I might follow, particularly with individual pupils.

Experiences to Provide

Do I make it a habit to check on how familiar pupils are with what is discussed in texts and other curricular materials? Suggestion: Before beginning a chapter or unit, list the major points that are to be covered, and ask pupils to explain in oral or written form if they have had any personal experiences with what is to be discussed. If some pupils lack firsthand experience with objects or situations to be featured, try to supply such experiences.

Ways to Encourage Ethnic Pride and Identity

If I have children from a variety of ethnic groups in my classroom, are there ways I can encourage them to identify with successful individuals from the same backgrounds? Suggestion: Schedule a library session, and urge pupils to look for and read books about successful people who share their backgrounds or characteristics.

Satisfying the Physiological Needs of Disadvantaged Students

Am I doing as much as I should to try to satisfy the physiological needs of pupils who come from disadvantaged backgrounds? Suggestion: Ask pupils to describe (individually and privately, in oral or written form) what they usually eat for breakfast. If some children get no breakfast, or consume only "junk" foods, try to find ways to arrange for them to eat something nutritious early in the school day.

Ways to Encourage Feelings of Esteem

Am I doing a conscientious job setting up lessons so that pupils from weak educational backgrounds will experience feelings of esteem? Suggestions: Pick out students who seem to lack confidence in themselves, and make sure that individually or in small groups they get to take part in esteem-building experiences. With younger pupils use the Montessori method as a guide and arrange experiences so that pupils engage in self-directed learning that is self-rewarding. With older pupils try an exercise patterned after the units developed by Taba and Elkins: Have students write their own text.

Activities That Will Make Pupils Feel Successful

Am I arranging lessons so that students from weak educational backgrounds experience frequent feelings of success? Suggestion: Pick out students who are having learning problems, and arrange programmed learning experiences for them that lead to frequent positive reinforcement.

Nonthreatening Forms of Competition

Do some pupils seem to be bothered when learning situations are too competitive? Suggestion: Each time a competitive learning situation occurs, keep track of students who never seem to win. Then, try to set up activities or games that permit such habitual losers to occasionally come out on top in nonthreatening competitive situations.

Ways to Inspire Achievement

Am I doing anything specific to help students from homes lacking an "educational tradition" to want to do well in school? Suggestion: Check the descriptions of achievement training programs, New York's Higher Horizons program, and Philadelphia's Motivation Program for ideas about specific techniques to use in encouraging a need for achievement.

Relating Lessons to Pupils' Lives

Is it possible for all pupils in my class to "relate" to curricular materials? Suggestion: Set up lessons that encourage students to develop curricular materials based on their own experiences; ask them to suggest how what we are going to study might be related to things they are familiar with.

Ways to Teach
Academic Know-How

Would some of my pupils be more successful academically if they were more sophisticated about study skills? Suggestion: Draw up a list of how-to-study techniques, print it on the board, explain how the techniques might be used, and offer specific suggestions to individual pupils who need extra help.

SUGGESTIONS FOR FURTHER STUDY

11-1

Inequality of
Educational
Opportunity

An evaluation of problems of inequalities in education is offered in *Equality of Educational Opportunity* (the Coleman Report). The report itself is extremely detailed and lengthy, but you will find a brief analysis of Coleman's major conclusions, together with a review of criticisms made by others, in an article by Christopher Jencks, "A Reappraisal of the Most Controversial Educational Document of Our Time," which appeared in the *New York Times Magazine* of August 10, 1969, or in an article by Catherine Caldwell titled "Social Science as Ammunition," which appeared in the September 1970 issue of *Psychology Today*. More comprehensive analyses are to be found in *On Equality of Educational Opportunity* (1972), edited by Frederick Mosteller and Daniel P. Moynihan, which consists of fourteen articles by psychologists, sociologists, and statisticians. In addition, Christopher Jencks offers a book-length interpretation of the Coleman Report—plus research of his own—in *Inequality: A Reassessment of the Effect of Family and Schooling in America* (1972). The significance and ramifications of busing are discussed in *Busing: A Moral Issue* (1972) by Howard Ozmon and Sam Craver.

11-2

Ability Grouping

The Coleman Report suggested that placing disadvantaged children in the same class might produce a form of reciprocal fatalism. At present there is considerable controversy over desegregation in American schools. Attempts to integrate students of disadvantaged backgrounds into middle-class schools are often blocked or sidestepped in one way or another. Some educators argue that it is desirable to group students on the basis of ability. Advocates of this position might not be upset by segregation because such a policy leads to a form of ability grouping. Other educators, impressed by the Coleman Report, feel that any educational arrangement that separates students from rich and poor environments is undesirable, since it perpetuates the tendency for the fortunate child to be given extra opportunities and for the unfortunate child to remain at a disadvantage. Those who favor ability grouping point out that merely placing a disadvantaged child in a room with middle-class pupils is not always beneficial; the student from a poor environment may be intimidated or humiliated by the ease and speed of learning demonstrated by his luckier classmates.

How the educational handicaps of the disadvantaged can be overcome is perhaps the most important problem of contemporary American education. You might examine the issues and try to come up with your own solution. Perhaps you could describe an overall policy you would recommend and then list some specific interim measures to be used until a general solution is found.

11–3

Inner-City Schools

The formal reports that are listed in 11–1 cover the educational problems of disadvantaged children in a comprehensive way. Within the last few years, several accounts of the experiences of individual teachers in inner-city schools have been published. Edward R. Braithwaite described what it was like to teach in a London slum in *To Sir, with Love* (1959). Bel Kaufman's *Up the Down Staircase* (1964), a fictional narration of life in a New York City high school, is probably the most widely read exposition of life in a big-city school. At about the time *Up the Down Staircase* was establishing itself on the bestseller lists, three young men were either starting or finishing descriptions of their experiences in ghetto schools. Jonathan Kozol accepted a position as a substitute teacher in a Boston elementary school. He held the position for about six months before he was dismissed, at which time he expanded the notes he had taken into *Death at an Early Age* (1967). Herbert Kohl told what it was like to be a teacher in a Harlem sixth grade in *36 Children* (1967), and James Herndon commented on academic life in an Oakland junior high school in *The Way It Spozed to Be* (1968) and described further experiences with teaching in a different junior high in *How to Survive in Your Native Land* (1971). At the same time Herndon was finishing his second book, Stephen Daniels described his experiences in a Philadelphia junior high school in *How 2 Gerbils, 20 Goldfish, 200 Games, 2,000 Books and I Taught Them How to Read* (1971). Any of these books will give you awareness of what it is like to teach disadvantaged students.

11–4

Teaching Techniques

The books noted in the preceding paragraph might be read not only for a general impression of what it is like to teach the disadvantaged but also to gain ideas for teaching techniques. If you want to read them for this purpose, you might browse until you find a section describing teaching techniques, or you might sample sections beginning at the pages indicated in the following books:

To Sir with Love, pages 65, 85, 98.

Up the Down Staircase, pages 63, 114, 129, 139, 142, 191, 199.

36 Children, pages 27, 34, 44, 61, 64, 114, 129, 137, 176.

The Way It Spozed to Be, pages 130, 139, 144.

How to Survive in Your Native Land, pages 24, 44, 145, 155.

How 2 Gerbils, pages 39, 48, 57, 66, 71, 73, 91, 94, 98, 112, 124, 132, 150.

11–5

Educating the Disadvantaged

In addition to reading the personal accounts noted in the preceding exercise, you might examine books devoted to descriptions of teaching techniques or books of readings made up of collections of articles on various aspects of the education of the disadvantaged. Five books of the first type are: *The Culturally Deprived Child* (1962) by Frank

Riessman, *Teaching Strategies for the Culturally Disadvantaged* (1966) by Hilda Taba and Deborah Elkins, *The Disadvantaged: Challenge to Education* (1968) by Mario D. Fantini and Gerald Weinstein, *A Handbook for Teaching in the Ghetto School* (1968) by Sidney Trubowitz, and *Experiments in Primary Education: Aspects of Project Follow-Through* (1970) by Eleanor E. Maccoby and Miriam Zellner. Among the more carefully edited books of readings are *The Disadvantaged Learner* (1966), edited by Staten W. Webster, and *Reaching the Disadvantaged Learner* (1970), edited by A. Harry Passow.

11-6
The Montessori Method

If you would like to learn more about the Montessori method, you have a wide choice of books to examine. Montessori's own descriptions of her approach can be found in *The Montessori Method* (1912, paperback edition 1964), *Dr. Montessori's Own Handbook* (1914, paperback edition 1965), and *Spontaneous Activity in Education* (1917, paperback edition 1965). If you read any of these books, you may find that you are intrigued as much by the style of writing as by the descriptions of how Montessori developed her approach to preschool education. For descriptions by others, with suggestions for adapting the original techniques for use in contemporary America, consult *The Montessori Revolution* (1962, paperback edition 1966) by E. M. Standing, *Learning How to Learn: An American Approach to Montessori* (1962) by Nancy M. Rambusch, and *Montessori: A Modern Approach* (1972) by Paula Lillard.

11-7
Coles on Poverty and Desegregation

Robert Coles, a psychiatrist, was strongly influenced by Erik H. Erikson. He spent ten years studying the forces that shape the lives of children, particularly those of migrant workers in the rural South. He offers his interpretations in a trilogy—*Children of Crisis: A Study of Courage and Fear* (1967), *Children of Crisis: Migrants, Mountaineers, and Sharecroppers* (1972), and *Children of Crisis: The South Goes North* (1972)—and also in *Still Hungry in America* (1969) and *Uprooted Children: The Early Life of Migrant Farm Workers* (1970). He analyzes the impact of desegregation in *The Desegregation of Southern Schools: A Psychiatric Study* (1963). Coles also offers his observations on socially handicapped children in *Dead End School* (1968) and on children of the middle class in *The Middle American: Proud and Uncertain* (1971), written in collaboration with Jon Erikson.

11-8
Minority-Group Life in America

Listed below are books you might read to become acquainted with perceptions of those who have experienced minority-group existence in America. If you read one of these books, you might note points you feel are of significance to teachers.

Blacks: *Black Boy* (1945) by A. Richard Wright; *Invisible Man* (1947) by Ralph Ellison; *Notes of a Native Son* (1953) by James Baldwin; *Manchild in the Promised Land* (1965) by Claude Brown; *Soul on Ice* (1968) by Eldridge Cleaver; *Black Rage* (1968) by William Grier and Price Cobbs; *Black Self-Concept* (1972) by James A. Banks and Jean D.

Grambs; *Black Psychology* (1972), edited by Reginald Jones; *Roots* (1976) by Alex Haley.

American Indians: *Custer Died for Your Sins* (1969) by Vine Deloia, Jr.; *Bury My Heart at Wounded Knee: An Indian History of the American West* (1971) by Dee Brown.

Mexican-Americans: *Chicano* (1970) by Richard Vasquez, *Barrio Boy* (1971) by Ernesto Galarza, *Chicanos: Our Background and Our Pride* (1972) by Nephtali DeLeen, *I Am Joaquin* (1973) by Rodolfo Gonzalez.

Puerto Ricans: *Growing Up Puerto Rican* (1972) by Paulette Cooper.

11-9

Pros and Cons of
Labeling

For a comprehensive analysis of the pros and cons of labeling, peruse volumes 1 and 2 of *Issues in the Classification of Children* (1975), edited by Nicholas Hobbs. The chapter in these volumes most relevant to the education of the disadvantaged is "Psychological Assessment and the Rights of Children" by Jane R. Mercer, pages 130–158 of volume 1. A concise review of the points made in the detailed two-volume work is provided by Nicholas Hobbs in *The Futures of Children* (1975).

Assume that it is fifty years from today and that space technology has advanced to the point that a huge satellite has been assembled to orbit around the earth. The satellite is to function as a miniature world where 10,000 people will work and live together. Assume further that you have been chosen to serve as director of the satellite. You have been instructed to select 10,000 people to journey with you into outer space with the understanding that all who agree to live on the satellite will do so for the rest of their lives. (The cost of getting people to and from the space station precludes commuting.)

When you advertise the existence of this opportunity, you receive 500,000 applications from people who are eager to become citizens of a "new world." The exuberance you felt when you first were chosen to create, in effect, a society is dampened considerably when you begin to think about how to deal with your first major problem. How can you select 10,000 people from a pool of 500,000 in a fair and efficient way? You realize that if you fail to explain how you intend to select the chosen few, you will receive so many complaints from disgruntled rejects that you might lose your appointment as director before the society literally or figuratively gets off the ground. You also realize that if you fail to make wise choices, your society might encounter many difficulties or even cease to exist. Accordingly, you decide that you had better be systematic as you seek to identify the best applicants.

The logical first step seems to be to list the kinds of occupations needed to ensure the survival of your society. Once you have done that, you can begin to seek ways to choose people to fill the jobs. The first jobs that come to your mind are those that center on survival in space. You will need trained engineers and technicians to maintain the satellite and keep it functioning properly. You also realize that the satellite will be an ideal environment for scientists of various kinds who can not only study the nature of space but also develop ways to improve living conditions in the space capsule. Next on your list you place doctors and nurses, since it will be essential to maintian the health of the citizens. Before you get much further down the list, however, you suddenly realize that you will need to select not only highly skilled professionals but also laborers who will not balk at carrying out menial tasks. Even though your satellite will be highly automated, you will need people to operate machines that collect and dispose of garbage, clean streets and buildings, harvest crops, and the like. Furthermore, you will need people skilled in the trades to take care of things like construction, plumbing, air-circulation equipment, and so forth. You also realize that the members of your space colony, regardless of their occupations, will need to buy food, clothing, and household items and that they will sometimes want to eat out and be entertained, so you add salespeople, stock clerks, cooks, waiters, dishwashers, television technicians, movie projectionists, ticket sellers, and musicians to the list.

As you compile your list of occupations, you realize not only that some jobs are more demanding, interesting, and enjoyable than others, but also that the jobs vary in terms of the amount of pay they should command. You conclude that if you hope to attract outstanding professionals (e.g., surgeons) who have spent dozens of years training for their jobs and must make many pressure-filled decisions involving personal judgment, you must pay them substantially higher salaries than untrained individuals engaging in unskilled labor (e.g., window cleaners). Awareness of this fact causes you to speculate about other distinctions between jobs and individuals. You decide you will want skilled

professionals to be as intelligent and creative as possible, since they will have to be innovative in solving the unpredictable problems that will occur in an isolated and unique satellite world. But should you try to select intelligent and creative people for the menial, tedious tasks that must be carried out in the same way day after day? For jobs that will be dull, repetitive, and low paying, would it be better to deliberately choose individuals who are not terribly bright or who rarely think about what they are doing, since they are less likely to brood about their position, throw a monkeywrench into the machinery, or be envious of more favored citizens? Furthermore, such individuals would probably be more willing simply to carry out the instructions of supervisors. You do not want your space society to be made up of

Part Six

Evaluation

Chapter 12   Evaluating ability and achievement

Chapter 13   Evaluating classroom learning

unthinking robots, but you come to the conclusion that for some jobs at least, tendencies toward conformity and lack of a high degree of intelligence or creativity may be an asset.

You spend several weeks adding occupations to your list; and when it seems complete, you begin to wrestle with the problem of selecting from the huge number of applicants those who seem best qualified or most deserving of different jobs. The first idea that pops into your mind is to have some sort of lottery arrangement, but you quickly reject it, since you realize that you cannot simply rely on the luck of the draw. If your society is to survive, you must develop some logical, systematic, and efficient way to choose the best person for each job. The next possibility that occurs to you is to conduct personal interviews, but you soon come to the conclusion that this is impractical. You do not have the time, funds, or trained personnel to interview half a million people, and you also realize that the kinds of things that impress interviewers in a ten-minute conversation (appearance, confidence in talking to others) often have little or nothing to do with performance in most situations.

Next, you think about getting three letters of recommendation from people who know each applicant. You also dismiss this notion, however, after recollecting the rather vague things you usually put in such letters and pondering how difficult it will be to evaluate such recommendations. How will you be

able to make a choice, for example, if a hundred applicants for a particular job all have approximately equivalent sets of recommendations? Since descriptions of what others think do not seem to be the answer, you ask yourself; "Why not watch each applicant for a particular job actually perform that job and make ratings of proficiency?" Although, initially, this proposal seems more promising and logical than the other proposals you have considered, you realize that to put it into practice will be very difficult. It occurs to you that watching only one person at a time will be much too time consuming. Even for simple tasks such as dishwashing, you would have to observe each applicant for at least a few minutes. In order to make accurate judgments about the relative skills of individuals carrying out complex jobs (e.g., medical practitioners), you would have to keep a detailed record of their behavior for days or weeks at a time.

As you wrestle with these problems, another difficulty comes to mind. It makes sense to attempt to anticipate what the citizens of your space satellite will need to know, but you are quite certain that many problems of existence in a new world will be unpredictable. You also are determined to set up a society that will not only survive, but thrive. For both of these reasons you decide that it would be desirable to select many young people from the huge pool of applicants. You reason that recent high school and college graduates should be more flexible and adaptable and capable of learning yet to be discovered skills than older individuals who have become set in their ways. At the same time, you realize that flexibility and eagerness to learn are not enough. You will need at least some individuals who presently possess knowledge that has been accumulated over the centuries. You conclude that if you select a few outstanding older applicants who are recognized experts and authorities in many fields, they can teach a much larger number of young people what they have learned on earth and what they will discover about space and space satellites. The citizens of your new world will need to learn many new things, and some of them will have to master jobs that have never been performed before. Thus, you decide that it would be wise to select large numbers of younger applicants who have proven that they are willing and able to learn from others.

The more you think about the problem of selection, the more you begin to realize that you need readily available information about how individuals have performed in a variety of ways over a period of time and also detailed and objective evidence of how much they understand about general and specific areas of knowledge. Eventually you conclude that perhaps the best ways to get such information are to examine school records, particularly grades earned over the years, and to give tests of various kinds. You can ask applicants to send transcripts of all school work, and you can require those who are seeking specific jobs to take examinations designed to measure understanding. It occurs to you that if you refer to grade point averages (GPAs) and test scores, you will be able to assign each applicant a numerical score. To select the ten most deserving applicants for a particular job out of a group of five thousand all you will need to do is identify those with the ten highest composite scores.

You also speculate briefly about having all applicants take an intelligence test. You reason that knowing a person's IQ might be of value in selecting individuals for different jobs. If two applicants for a position in space biology have exactly the same composite GPA and test score, perhaps you could select the one with the higher IQ. Or when filling positions that you know will be tedious and dull, you might eliminate all applicants with IQs above a particular point. You also entertain the thought that ignoring school records and choosing younger applicants solely on the basis of IQ scores might be preferable. Even as you consider these possibilities, however, you wonder whether IQ tests are accurate enough to serve as the basis for making significant decisions about a person's future.

At first glance, this hypothetical situation may seem to have little to do with schooling in America. Actually, though, the problems an individual would face planning a new space society are simply exaggerated versions of problems to be found in any contemporary technological society. The work to be done in any modern society ranges from manual labor to professional skills acquired only after years of specialized training. Some jobs are much more appealing than others; some yield salaries that are a hundred times greater than others. In earlier times, people were often assigned to particular jobs primarily because of what their parents did. In eighteenth-century Britain, the son of a Welsh coal miner, for instance, usually accepted the fact that he would become a coal miner; the son of a London lawyer planned on joining his father's firm; the oldest child of a king of England knew he or she would become the reigning monarch. In recent times, and particularly in our society, an attempt has been made to make the selection of an occupation dependent primarily on an individual's ability.

Hereditary privilege has not been eliminated in America, but the opportunities for individuals of lowly origin to achieve success have been maximized. The child of an American surgeon may benefit from hereditary privilege if enrolled in an exclusive private school to prepare for admission to an Ivy League university, which will help assure admission to a prestigious medical school, which will then lead to eventual partnership with the parent. But the child of a common laborer might win a series of scholarships and eventually achieve greater eminence as a surgeon entirely through personal effort. In order to provide opportunities for individuals to succeed on the basis of their own merit, however, it is essential to compare them in some way and select those who show the greatest potential and ability. For that purpose, each type of evaluation listed in the hypothetical space satellite situation sometimes is used. Interviews, recommendations, and ratings of actual performance all are employed by those who must choose from among applicants for jobs. The two most widely used measures are school performance, usually indicated by a student's grade point average, and test scores. Since these two measures are so widely used, they deserve detailed consideration.

Chapter 12 (Evaluating Ability and Achievement) opens with a critique of the "grading game" in American education. Then the critique is analyzed to help you evaluate arguments for and against the various forms of evaluation illustrated by the hypothetical situation you have just read. Next, standardized tests will be described, and you will be acquainted with criteria you might use to evaluate such tests and with information about administering them and interpreting the scores they yield. Tests that purport to measure intelligence are the subject of considerable controversy at the present time, and some of the reasons for this controversy will be related. Chapter 12 concludes with the suggestion that you try to use test scores to individualize instruction.

Chapter 13 (Evaluating Classroom Learning) offers suggestions you might follow when you make up and score your own tests (and other forms of evaluation), convert scores into grades, and make out report cards. The final section of Chapter 13 provides detailed instructions for using a mastery approach in an effort to minimize many of the undesirable characteristics of evaluation.

Key points

A critique of the grading game

Criticisms of grades: Subjective, restrictive, divisive, competitive

Grading goals: Reduce anxiety and competition, increase meaning

Grades can be a self-controlled basis for success

Important for students to discover strengths and weaknesses

Standardized tests

Achievement tests measure how much has been learned about a subject

Aptitude tests provide estimates of potential ability

Content validity: How well test items cover a type of learning

Construct validity: How accurately test measures a particular attribute

Reliability: How consistent scores are if test is taken again

Essential to follow instructions when administering standardized tests

Grade equivalent score: Performance interpreted in terms of grade levels

Percentile ranks: Percentage of scores at or below a given score

Standard deviation: Degree of deviation from the mean of a distribution

Normal curve: Bell-shaped (symmetrical) distribution

z score: How far a raw score is from the mean in standard deviation units

T score: How far a raw score is from the mean in numerical terms

Stanines: Distribution divided into nine half-SD units

The nature and measurement of intelligence

Jensen: Heredity establishes limits of intelligence

Claim that IQ tests discriminate against minority-group children

Definitions of intelligence stress general or specific factors

IQ scores of the same individuals tested over the years rarely stay the same

Low test scores may lead to unfortunate self-fulfilling prophecy reactions

Using test scores to individualize teaching

Students vary in abilities to comprehend, memorize, and evaluate

Some students are convergent, others are divergent thinkers

ATI: Try to match pupil styles and abilities to forms of instruction

Students rarely can be classified into distinct types

National Assessment reports supply information about pupil weaknesses

Chapter 12	**Evaluating ability and achievement**

$\mathbf{T}$HE HYPOTHETICAL space satellite situation described in the introduction to this part calls attention to difficulties that arise when the abilities of large numbers of individuals must be evaluated. Confronted with the need to somehow sort out individuals with greater and lesser abilities, agencies of various kinds quite naturally seek readily available, reliable, and reasonably accurate information. It would be prohibitively expensive for most educational, governmental, and business organizations to carry out extensive independent evaluations of large numbers of applicants. Even if such agencies had the funds to set up elaborate screening programs, they would find it difficult to locate evaluation instruments or devise procedures that would supply information about such important variables as level of performance over a sustained period of time. The grades students earn in school are not only available without cost; they also yield information about key aspects of pupil performance that tests and interviews cannot supply. It is not surprising, therefore, that student grade point averages often play a major role in educational and occupational decisions.

Reasons for the grade point average

The use of a grade point average (GPA) to reflect academic achievement, which in turn may have a significant impact on achievement later in life, is essentially an American development. In Europe and in most other parts of the world, comprehensive examinations at the end of elementary and high school typically are used in lieu of grades in separate courses. Before offering explanations for these differences and calling attention to the advantages and disadvantages of each system, it is worth noting that in all technological societies the schools perform the preliminary sorting out of individuals. Some critics of American public schools (e.g., Goodman, 1956, 1964) maintain that students in this country are graded because educators are tools of a capitalistic society. In their opinion, business interests have coerced the schools into doing what corporations should do—identify the most likely candidates for different jobs. This argument fails to take into account that in the Soviet Union and other communistic societies students are evaluated even more systematically than in America and for the same fundamental reasons: If a modern society is to survive, assigning occupations primarily on the basis of merit is essential.

It is an unfortunate but inevitable feature of human existence that in any society some individuals must carry out arduous, disagreeable, tedious, menial tasks and receive low pay for their efforts. A small number of highly favored individuals the same age in the same society will succeed in obtaining jobs that are challenging, significant, interesting, and highly remunerative. The majority of individuals in any society work at jobs somewhere between these two extremes. Most desirable and high-paying jobs require extensive academic preparation. In a technological society many of the "in-between" occupations also are likely to require education beyond high school. Consequently, it is logical and necessary to begin to identify the most capable students as early in their school careers as possible. All technological societies sort out students in school, but they differ in the way they go about doing it.

The European approach to educational sorting

The European approach to education stresses early selection on the basis of comprehensive exams. In the 1950s, for example, Great Britain required all students to take the Eleven-Plus Exam, so called because it was administered after children had reached the age of eleven. The actual examination varied from time to time and from place to place, but it typically covered several subject areas and required two to four hours to complete. On the basis of that single examination, eleven-year-olds were placed in either a vocational or a college preparatory program, and a child identified as a vocational student would find it difficult if not impossible to qualify later for the academic program. A significant decision about a person's entire career was made on the basis of a two- to four-hour sample of his or her behavior at the age of eleven. During the years that the Eleven-Plus Exam was used, children were often drilled for months in preparation for the test. Many suffered physical and mental breakdown because of the extreme pressure they experienced at such a young age. Eventually, the Eleven-Plus Exam was eliminated, but Great Britain and many other European countries still separate students into distinct vocational and academic tracks before they enter high school and also select the most promising university candidates on the basis of comprehensive matriculation exams that are administered during the senior year in high school. Similar examinations determine if college students are to be admitted to graduate school. A recent newspaper article reported that pressures generated by such exams are so great in Germany that the ulcer and suicide rates for high school and college seniors are alarmingly high.

The American approach to educational sorting

In the United States a pupil's overall academic record in separate courses—reflected by the grade point average—is typically used as an alternative to scores on matriculation exams. If you have ever complained about being assigned a grade in each course you took in high school or college, ask yourself if you would have preferred taking two-hour oral and written examinations in five subjects during the spring of your senior year. At first you might believe you would prefer one comprehensive culminating test in a subject to dozens of quizzes spread out over a period of years, but consider how you would feel if you flunked the matriculation exam. When you take a series of quizzes in a course and earn a series of grades, you receive continuous feedback and you have the opportunity to work to improve if you become aware that your performance is unsatisfactory. That would not be the case if you took only one exam. There is no denying that offering separate courses may tend to fragment a curriculum and that the GPA approach tends to make students think that earning a grade is the primary purpose of any course, but these disadvantages may not seem so extreme when the alternatives are considered.

John Gardner (1961) has pointed out an additional advantage of the GPA. He notes that the European two-track system virtually eliminates the possibility that a student who either chooses or is assigned to a vocational program at the age of twelve or so can later pursue an academic program in a university. In America, by contrast, stress on separate courses (and the availability of community colleges) makes it possible for almost any student, regardless of previous courses taken, to qualify for admission to college. Furthermore, students who did poor work at one stage of their school careers can make up for it by doing acceptable work at a later stage. Gardner refers to this as the *principle of multiple chances*, and he suggests that it is one of the major strengths of the American approach to education.

American students have more flexibility to achieve academic success than their European counterparts, but this flexibility does not eliminate the extent to which school performance determines their eventual occupation. Under ideal circumstances, however, asking dozens of teachers to assign separate grades is probably the fairest way to evaluate school performance. For one thing, grades earned over a period of years provide a much more complete sample of student ability and achievement than performance on oral or written exams that require intensive effort only for a matter of hours. For another, different teachers are likely to stress different kinds of abilities and respond to different learning and personality traits. Therefore, a student who fails to impress one teacher may do work that will be acknowledged favorably by another.

Unfortunately, teachers do not always make independent judgments, and a few grades assigned early in a student's career may cause him or her to be identified as a poor student. Later teachers who lack confidence in their own judgment may lower grades they had intended to assign when they see what other teachers have said about the pupil. Then a self-fulfilling prophecy reaction may cause a competent individual to function in incompetent ways. Even so, assigning separate grades for separate courses is a logical and potentially valuable way to evaluate school performance. Nevertheless at various times in the history of American education, critics have recommended that grades be abolished. The most recent surge of support for this view occurred in the late 1960s and early 1970s.

A critique of the "grading game"

A fictional analysis of grades

To help you clarify your thoughts on the pros and cons of the GPA, here is a description of a critique of grades written by three humanistic educators. In *Wad-ja-get?* (1971), subtitled *The Grading Game in American Education,* Howard Kirschenbaum, Sidney P. Simon, and Rodney W. Napier present the case against traditional grading in the form of a novel. The story revolves around the efforts of an eleventh grade history class to stimulate a reform of the grading system in their school. In different chapters the views of students, teachers, administrators, parents, and educational psychologists are presented.

The story begins with a letter to the school paper written by two students who list four criticisms of grades: First, grades put too much emphasis on the kinds of learning that can be easily measured. Second, they turn students into robots. Third, they are not fair because some students who work hard get low grades. Fourth, they encourage cheating. When the members of the eleventh grade history class discuss the letter, they bring up contrasting points such as these: Students would be much more relaxed if grades were eliminated. Students would relax so much they would not do any school work. It does not make sense to grade on how hard a person works. Grades undoubtedly encourage cheating. Grades tell students if they are good or bad in a subject. There is no logical reason for assigning grades; it is just a meaningless tradition. The last point arouses the interest of the class, and they decide to look into the history of grading.

The committee assigned to prepare the report traces the emergence of grading practices primarily to the need to select students for college. Having made this point, the committee presents evidence that the screening is often based on highly questionable evidence. They refer to scientific studies, revealing that when different teachers are asked to grade the same essay exams, their evaluations vary to an astonishing extent. The committee also discusses the policy of grading on the bell-shaped curve, which first become popular in the 1920s and 1930s. They point out that a major problem with this type of grading is that classes are rarely "normal"; that is, some contain many more excellent (or poor) students than others.

Next, the committee reveals that the eleventh grade history class is not the first group to criticize grades or search for alternatives. Movements for reform have surfaced every few years. In 1952, for example, an educator (Rogers, 1952) listed criticisms of grades, which the committee summarizes in this way:

Criticisms of grades: Subjective, restrictive, divisive, competitive

1. Grades are unscientific, subjective and seldom relative to educational objectives.

2. They are misleading and focus only on one aspect of the child.

3. They promote superficial, spurious and insincere scholarship.

4. They lead to uncreative teaching.

5. They form a barrier between students and teachers.

6. Pupils perform for the grade and, as a result, show less initiative and independence.

7. Grades tend to divide students into recognizable groups, reflecting inferior and superior qualities, thus often becoming the basis for social relationships.

8. They establish a competitive system, with grades as the basis for achievement. (1971, pp. 62–63)

As an alternative to letter grades, earlier critics usually recommended written descriptions of performance and the elimination of competition. The committee goes on to report that, despite calls for reform, in the 1940s 80 percent of the nation's schools assigned letter grades and that the major reasons seemed to be administrative expediency and the demand of colleges and universities that grades be reported in easily computed form. The committee concludes its report by stating that in the 1960s a reform movement appeared to be gaining such momentum that it seemed likely that letter grades would soon be eliminated or at least become one of several options (such as pass/fail or credit/no credit) open to a student. The final conclusion of the committee is that "there are no *good* reasons—no sound educational ones, anyway—why [grades] should continue to exist" (p. 73).

The next chapter of *Wad-ja-get?* takes the form of an assembly presentation by an alumnus of the high school who has just graduated from the University of California at Berkeley with the highest GPA in his class. To the surprise of his audience, who expected to be bored by an inspirational talk about the virtues of hard work, the alumnus makes the point that his efforts were not worth it because "the grade point game checked me from the real goal of education: the development of myself as a person" (p. 78). He also argues that he worked for grades rather than for learning and invites the students in the audience to look around—at their enemies. He also makes the point that "we destroy the love of learning in children by encouraging them and compelling them to work for petty and contemptible rewards . . . for the ignoble satisfaction of feeling that they are better than someone else" (p. 81). When he concludes his speech, the alumnus is given a standing ovation.

Inspired by the assembly speech, the history class draws up this list of qualities a grading system should possess:

Grading goals: Reduce anxiety and competition, increase meaning

Our grading system should:

1. Eliminate the anxiety which usually goes with grading;

2. Create a relaxed learning atmosphere in the class;

3. Decrease competition for grades among students;

4. Be meaningful. That is, a student's grade should mean something to him personally;

5. Respect quality of work as well as quantity;

6. Allow those students who needed [sic] a high grade to get one. (p. 121)

The students discuss how they might build these qualities into the grading system to be used in the history class and finally decide that the best policy is to have the teacher set minimum standards of performance and assign a B to any student who meets them. Students who fail to earn a B on the first attempt are to be allowed to try again, and those who want to earn A's can do an extra assignment. When word gets around the school, other students and teachers decide to search for alternatives, and administrators and parents also express their opinions. At a faculty meeting, a young professor of educational psychology from a nearby university asks the faculty to grade essay exams and proves that evaluations differ to a considerable extent. He also asks the faculty to explain what is meant by *mean, median, reliability, validity,* and the *normal curve.* When most of the teachers are unable to answer these questions, he tells them, "There's something *immoral* about playing with kids' lives when you don't know which side of the bell-shaped curve is up" (p. 163).

Another committee, composed of representatives of the student body, faculty, administration, and parent groups, eventually lists eight alternatives to traditional grading:

1. Written Evaluation

2. Self-Evaluation

3. Give grades; but don't tell the students

4. Contract System

5. The Mastery Approach or Performance Curriculum

6. Pass/Fail Grading

7. Credit/No Credit Grading

8. Blanket Grading (p. 207)

These alternatives are then evaluated in order to select a school-wide grading policy. Written evaluations are rejected on the grounds that they are too subjective. Self-evaluation, not telling students their grades, the contract system, and blanket grading are considered to be of limited use because they cannot be used on a schoolwide basis. The mastery approach is criticized because the teacher sets goals and because it allegedly requires too much expertise to put into operation. The alternatives that are considered most workable are pass/fail and credit/no credit.

Wad-ja-get? concludes with the final solution to the grading problem: Students may choose either credit/no credit grading or traditional letter grades. If students select the credit/no credit option, it is agreed that a portfolio of their best work will be forwarded to college admissions officers or potential employers.

So much for the points made in *Wad-ja-get?* Now it is appropriate to analyze the arguments presented in the book.

A general critique of the fictional analysis

The first point to consider in evaluating the points made in *Wad-ja-get?* is that the book was written in 1971 at a time when there was a great deal of unrest in our society and in higher education. The reasons for the unrest were complex and varied, but most high schools, colleges, and universities engaged in a good deal of soul-searching and also were in a mood to experiment with alternatives to traditional approaches. A related point is that the late 1960s were years of steady economic growth and high employment. Most college graduates were more or less guaranteed a job, and recruiters from various business concerns often came to campuses searching for employees. By the late 1970s, conditions have changed. Evidence has accumulated leading to the inescapable conclusion that students exposed to experimental curricula and grading systems are less well educated than previous generations of students. After experimenting with new approaches, many educators and students have concluded that traditional forms of evaluation *were* adopted for logical reasons. The economic and employment situation at the present time is such that simply earning a college degree is no longer a guarantee of a job. Employers and graduate school admissions committees are in a position where they can *select* the best candidates. With that situation as a background, consider the following evaluation of the arguments presented in *Wad-ja-get?*

First of all, re-examine the criticisms of grading mentioned by various characters in the book:

1. Grades are unscientific, subjective, and seldom relative to educational objectives.

2. Grades are misleading and focus on only one aspect of the child.

3. Grades promote superficial, spurious, and insincere scholarship.

4. Grades lead to uncreative teaching.

5. Grades form a barrier between students and teachers.

6. Grades force pupils to perform for extrinsic goals, which causes them to show less initiative and independence.

7. Grades tend to make some individuals feel superior to others, which may influence social relationships.

8. Grades establish a competitive system.

9. Grades lead to tension, pressure, and anxiety.

10. Grades turn students into robots (or prevent them from expressing themselves in individual and creative ways).

11. Grades are not fair because students who work hard may get low grades.

12. Grades encourage cheating.

13. Grades make students think of classmates as enemies.

14. Grades prevent individuals from developing themselves as persons.

15. Grades cause teachers to act in immoral ways when they are unsystematic about making evaluations that may have a significant impact on their students' lives.

The following criticisms are not explicitly made in *Wad-ja-get?*, but they should be added to the list:

16. Grades may label some students as poor learners, which may cause teachers to think of them as poor learners without giving them a fair trial.
17. Grades may lead to negative self-fulfilling prophecy reactions.

Most of these criticisms are valid under certain circumstances. They do not need to be, however, as an evaluation of each of the points will make clear.

A point-by-point analysis of criticisms of grades

1. *Grades are unscientific, subjective, and seldom relative to educational objectives.* This criticism may apply to some grades, but it certainly does not apply to all of them. You can avoid the limitations implied in this criticism if you join with the thousands of teachers who use scientific techniques of evaluation, reduce subjectivity to a minimum, and make use of instructional objectives to insure that grades reflect specific goals.

2. *Grades are misleading and focus on only one aspect of the child.* Most elementary school report cards supply information about a pupil's performance in from ten to twenty aspects of the curriculum and frequently include comments on nonacademic behavior as well. Most secondary school report cards consist of several separate grades, but when these are combined (as in a grade point average), they add up to a profile of student performance in a wide range of activities. Therefore, it does not seem to be true that grades are misleading or focused on only one aspect of a child's behavior.

3. *Grades promote superficial, spurious, and insincere scholarship.* This criticism may be valid if instructors resort to forms of evaluation that stress rote memorization, which is admittedly a common error. The students in *Wad-ja-get?* are correct when they maintain that too often teachers make up tests by writing questions on material the learning of which is easily measured. When this occurs, pupils must engage in essentially meaningless, ritualistic learning. Such more or less pointless learning can be substantially reduced, however, if teachers test students on material that is meaningful and likely to lead to a payoff and if they invite students to make some of their own decisions about what they will study and how they will be evaluated.

4. *Grades lead to uncreative teaching.* This statement more or less implies that if grades are eliminated, teaching will automatically become more creative. There is no logical reason to expect that this will occur. The creativity of teachers would seem to depend on how innovative and adaptable they are in presenting lessons that help students learn. If this proposition is accepted, it follows that a teacher who finds ways to help students learn is being creative. For a variety of reasons that will be discussed later in this analysis, it might be argued that teachers who use grades to foster learning are more creative than those who shirk their responsibilities as evaluators.

5. *Grades form a barrier between students and teachers.* This statement also carries with it an implication—that anything that prevents

students and teachers from being friends and equals is bad. Many humanistic educators favor a friend-to-friend relationship in the classroom, and they also advocate eliminating grades. But as noted at several places earlier in this book, teachers of this era may be held accountable for the amount of learning they produce, and quite frequently an indispensable part of learning is discovering and correcting errors. If there are no "barriers" whatever between teachers and students, instructors may feel reluctant to tell their pupils that they are wrong or have done unacceptable work. Accordingly, it is usually desirable for teachers to maintain a cordial, but professional, relationship with pupils. If, as is unfortunately sometimes the case, a teacher deliberately assigns low grades to vent hostility, it is legitimate to argue that grades erect barriers. But it does not make sense to maintain that grades should be eliminated in order to foster a teacher-student relationship that may be undesirable.

6. *Grades force pupils to perform for extrinsic goals, which causes them to show less initiative and independence.* If pupils are forced to spend a great deal of time memorizing and repeating only what a teacher says they must learn in order to earn a grade, this complaint is legitimate. When the statement does not take into account is that sometimes the only way to induce students to learn some things is to resort to extrinsic goals. (Most people show a great deal of initiative in finding ways to avoid work, even if the work will lead to a desirable outcome.) Individuals might be equipped to become more independent if they acquired skills they would rather not acquire if given completely free choice. Accordingly, even the best of teachers sometimes must resort to extrinsic goals to motivate students to learn.

7. *Grades tend to make some individuals feel superior to others, which may influence social relationships.* A possible implication of this statement is that if grades were abolished, feelings of superiority and inferiority and social-class distinctions would disappear. This is obviously not the case. Students think of themselves as superior or inferior and make friendships on the basis of many factors: appearance, parents' income, religious affiliation, race, interests, and abilities. In many ways, grades earned in school are more under an individual's control than most of the factors just listed. Instead of being "assigned" to a social group because of inherited characteristics, for instance, each student is given the opportunity to establish a personal level of competence.

Grades can be a self-controlled basis for success.

8. *Grades establish a competitive system.* This point is related to the previous one. Many Americans feel that one of the major strengths of their educational system is that it is competitive in the sense that any child who is capable and willing to work can achieve success. Education is a fairer means of sorting out students in a meritocracy than is

hereditary privilege, race, or nationality. Even so, teachers can do many things to avoid extreme competitive situations and to minimize public identification of superior and inferior students.

9. *Grades lead to tension, pressure, and anxiety.* Because the educational system performs the preliminary sorting out of individuals in American society, it is inevitable that grading practices lead to a certain amount of tension, pressure, and anxiety. As noted earlier in this chapter, though, a number of arguments can be advanced to defend the view that these feelings will be less extreme and more under a person's control when grades in separate courses are assigned than when comprehensive examinations are used (as in Europe). As was true of competition, however, teachers can take steps to reduce tension and anxiety about grades.

10. *Grades turn students into robots (or prevent them from expressing themselves in individual and creative ways).* This criticism may be true if teachers emphasize memorization and regurgitation of only what they consider to be measurable. What this statement does not acknowledge, however, is that what students learn in order to earn grades may make them capable of individual expression they would have been incapable of in the absence of such learning. (This point was stressed in the discussion of creativity in Chapter 9.)

11. *Grades are not fair because students who work hard may get low grades.* In some cases it is possible and logical for a teacher to give credit for effort, but most of the time it is essential to evaluate actual performance. Otherwise, students may be misled into thinking that they know more than they actually know. Some students in any class are going to learn faster and more easily than their peers. That is a fact of life, and trying to disguise or ignore it by telling all students that they are equally capable (as in a blanket grading situation) probably will do more harm than good.

12. *Grades encourage cheating.* In some respects this criticism is essentially the equivalent of saying that money encourages stealing. Both statements are true, but that does not mean that grades—and money—should be eliminated. Some human beings are more favorably endowed than others. Inevitably, some students are going to earn higher grades than others just as some adults are going to earn more money than others. Less capable individuals, or capable ones who feel that they can get what they want more easily through dishonest than honest means, will be tempted to cheat. Sometimes, as in a classroom with a vindictive teacher who gives unfairly demanding and extremely devious examinations, almost everyone will be tempted to

cheat. Teachers should seek ways to minimize cheating, but even under the best of circumstances, such behavior is not likely to be eliminated. Some individuals always will feel inadequate or think of everything in life as a game to be played the easiest way possible. You can do many things to try to make cheating unnecessary in a classroom, but it is unlikely that you will be able to eliminate cheating entirely.

13. *Grades make students think of classmates as enemies.* This tendency is also a function of the distribution of human abilities and the nature of a meritocratic society. But eliminating grades would not make all students friends any more than it would eliminate feelings of inferiority or prevent the formation of social groups. Students may think of classmates as enemies as the result of any situation where some individuals are recognized as more successful or fortunate than others or where individuals compete. Some students will be elected to school offices, some will not; some will be given expensive cars by their parents, some will not; some will be popular, some will not. The feeling that others are "enemies" may be fostered as much by nonacademic as by academic factors. If teachers use grading techniques that stress relative performance, resentment between students might be stimulated. But there are many things you can do to set up evaluation techniques where students may be eager to help each other do their best on examinations.

14. *Grades prevent individuals from developing themselves as persons.* It might be argued that grades help more than hinder an individual's self-development and self-awareness. In many respects, teachers who give tests and assign grades (both of which are frowned upon by humanists) are more likely than those who do not to contribute to a student's selection of a career, since an important prelude to vocational choice is finding out what one does well and what one does poorly. And, as Erik Erikson has stressed, one of the most significant factors leading to a sense of identity (or an awareness of oneself as a person) is vocational choice. An important part of discovering one's identity is finding out what one *cannot* do as well as what one can do, and grades supply such information. A major disadvantage of pass/fail and credit/no credit grading systems is that they supply vague feedback about ability and performance. It might be argued that students who choose to be graded only in such ways are minimizing the possibility that they will discover important, albeit sometimes disagreeable, things about themselves.

Related to this point is the argument offered by several characters in *Wad-ja-get?* that there are absolutely no sound educational reasons for assigning grades. The use of grades to select students for college and perhaps graduate school is dismissed as illogical. Instead, it is

Important for students to discover strengths and weaknesses

maintained that a score on a single exam is a better means for deter-mining who will go to college. As one of the students in the novel puts it, "I'd rather have to deal with that one SAT score, than be hit on the head with grades all my school life and have them ruin my education" (p. 221). For reasons discussed previously in commenting on European matriculation exams and for reasons to be discussed later in an anal-ysis of standardized tests, it is unwise to put too much faith or emphasis on a single test score. Using a single test score rather than grades assigned over a period of years might make some problems more, rather than less, extreme. Stress on a single exam not only increases anxiety (as indicated by the student ulcer and suicide rates in Germany), it also intensifies the feeling that one is competing against "enemies," and those who get low scores are told in extremely blunt terms that they are inferior to others.

The dust jacket of *Wad-ja-get?* depicts five dejected students ask-ing each other the question that serves as the title of the book. If grades were eliminated in favor of comprehensive exams, as the authors recommend, the students would still ask each other the same question. And they might be even more dejected because they would be unable to excuse poor performance by blaming low grades on personality clashes, subjectivity, or teacher prejudice.

15. *Grades cause teachers to act in immoral ways when they are unsystematic about making evaluations that may have a significant impact on their students' lives.* The obvious way to avoid acting in immoral ways, as defined by the fictional educational psychology professor in *Wad-ja-get?,* is to be systematic about making evalua-tions and to remain aware that the grades you assign may have a significant impact on student behavior.

16. *Grades may label some students as poor learners, which may cause teachers to think of them as poor learners without giving them a fair trial.* It is unfortunately sometimes true that teachers place too much faith in low grades assigned by previous teachers and treat some children as mentally retarded or think of them as being incapable of doing adequate work. To guard against this possibil-ity, you are urged to make your own independent judgments of children after you have given them every opportunity to prove them-selves. This does not mean that grades reflecting poor performance should never be assigned. Accurate evaluations often pave the way for appropriate instruction. It is important, though, to avoid making pre-judgments on the basis of grades assigned by others.

17. *Grades may lead to negative self-fulfilling prophecy reac-tions.* This point is related to the preceding one, and the same gen-eral comments apply. A teacher who discovers that students have

been assigned poor grades by other teachers may tend to think of such children as nonlearners, treat them as such, and cause them to act that way. The antidote here is the same as for labeling: Make independent judgments after giving students plenty of opportunities to make the most of their abilities.

This critique of points made in *Wad-ja-get?* is not intended to give the impression that the arguments made in the book are valueless. Many are valid and can be used to improve evaluation procedures. But when proposals for reform are critically examined, it usually turns out that assigning grades in separate courses is a fairer and more effective approach than any alternative yet proposed. Furthermore, given the present climate in American education, it is almost certain that you will be expected to assign grades. It makes sense, therefore, to consider potential advantages of grades.

Potential values of grades

The following six points summarize potential values of assigning grades. Many of them have been mentioned already; they are restated here for emphasis.

1. America is a meritocratic society, and it has been decided that the educational system should perform the preliminary sorting out of individuals. Assigning grades that reflect performance in different subjects over a period of years is potentially the fairest and most accurate way to evaluate students. (A student's grade point average is usually a more trustworthy indication of academic ability than a single test score is.)

2. In order to prepare for many occupations, young people must continue their education beyond high school. Students themselves, as well as those who have the responsibility for selecting applicants to universities and graduate schools, are provided with valuable information when individuals establish a "track record" in the form of a grade point average.

3. Assigning grades leads to what John Gardner refers to as the principle of multiple chances. When students are evaluated in separate courses over a period of years, they obtain continuous feedback and can make adjustments in their behavior to compensate for poor performance.

4. When students are evaluated in separate courses by dozens of teachers, they discover important things about themselves that may lead to a suitable vocational choice and the establishment of a sense of identity.

5. Grades motivate students to learn many important things. The motivation may often be extrinsic, but it is frequently essential. Most individuals are not self-actualizers and need incentives to learn, particularly when they are unable to comprehend or anticipate that what they are studying is necessary to pave the way for later learning or a delayed payoff.

6. Grades provide feedback, which is often indispensable if learning is to take place. If students have not mastered a subject at one point in the curriculum, it is important to acknowledge this fact and provide remedial instruction. Otherwise, the student will fall further and further behind as more complex lessons are presented.

   With the lists of potential disadvantages and advantages of grades as background, it is now possible to consider how grading practices might be made as fair and effective as possible.

Characteristics of an ideal grading system

Here is the list of characteristics of an ideal grading system proposed by the student committee in *Wad-ja-get?*
   A grading system should:

1. Eliminate anxiety

2. Create a relaxed atmosphere

3. Decrease competition

4. Be personally meaningful

5. Respect quality of work as well as quantity

6. Allow students to earn high grades if they wish to

   The following characteristics, many of which are derived from the preceding discussion of disadvantages and advantages of grades, should be added.
   Grades should:

7. Be scientific, objective, and related to instructional objectives

8. Be based on learning that is selected because it is potentially valuable to students, not because it is easy to measure

9. Not prevent students from engaging in self-selected, self-directed learning

10. Not tempt students to feel obliged to cheat

11. Not falsely label students or lead to unfortunate self-fulfilling prophecy reactions

For reasons discussed in evaluation criticisms of grades, some of these goals are essentially impossible to achieve. No matter what you do as a teacher, for example, you will not be able to eliminate anxiety or consistently maintain a relaxed atmosphere in your classroom. Sooner or later students must be asked to reveal what they know, and quite often this testing will lead to anxiety and tension, no matter how hard you try to avoid them. The best you will be able to do is to hold such feelings to a minimum. The same general reasoning applies to competition. You can do many things to avoid situations where students must "defeat" classmates in order to get high grades, but because of the meritocratic nature of our society, some competition is inevitable. Nevertheless, it is possible and desirable for you to do your best to establish a grading system that reflects most of the points on this list.

This evaluation of grades has been offered to encourage you to think about why the GPA is stressed so much in American education. As the hypothetical space satellite situation described at the beginning of the part introduction emphasized, those who are given the responsibility for selecting promising individuals in many lines of endeavor may be interested in school records because they supply readily available information about individual performance. A student's GPA reflects the more or less independent judgments of dozens of teachers who observed and evaluated performance for months at a time. High school or college graduates with high GPAs have demonstrated that they have the intelligence, drive, and perseverance to maintain a sustained level of impressive output for several years. It is therefore a good bet they will continue to function that way. Is it surprising, then, that admissions officers at colleges and universities and personnel directors of large corporations are interested in an applicant's performance in school?

Although the GPA is widely used for screening individuals and making predictions about their future performance, it is rarely acceptable as the exclusive basis for making such decisions. One reason is that despite their potential advantages, grades are not always fair and accurate. Sometimes test taking and related skills that lead to high grades are of little or no significance in out-of-school situations. In addition, individuals may be inaccurately classified as poor students early in their school years, and the fact that they are treated as such causes them to act like poor students or to give up trying. Moreover, individuals who are highly creative or who think in atypical ways may find it difficult to give teachers what they expect on examinations or assignments and may thus receive low grades. Finally, there is no way to determine if grades earned in one school are comparable to those earned in other schools. For all these reasons, it is usually unwise to use a GPA as the sole basis for selecting individuals for any kind of activity, including subsequent academic activity.

When making judgments about the potential of young people, it is often advantageous to obtain measures of pupil achievement other than those made by teachers. To allow for errors and variations in grading and to supply objective and detailed information about knowledge and abilities, it is usually prudent to obtain standard measures of performance. That is why you would be interested in standardized test scores if you were asked to select 10,000 individuals from 500,000 applicants, and that is why standardized tests are administered so frequently in American educational institutions. Such tests are used to supply information about specific abilities in different subject areas and also to give an index of a pupil's general learning ability.

Standardized tests

The nature of standardized tests

Standardized tests are designed to make it possible to compare the performance of a particular pupil to the performance of large numbers of other pupils. In order to do that with any degree of accuracy, it is necessary to follow a rather elaborate procedure. First, specialists with knowledge and experience in various fields of study describe what a well-informed pupil of a particular grade level should know about a particular subject or subjects. Next, questions that will measure such understanding are written. The questions are then tried out on a representative sample of pupils from all kinds of schools in all parts of the country. The questions that seem to measure understanding most effectively are selected, revised, and arranged in the final version of the exam. The exam is administered to a sample of students that is larger and more carefully selected than that used in the early development of the testing instrument. The performance of these students is reported in such a way that the performance of any individual who subsequently takes the exam can be determined by comparing his or her score to their scores.

Types of standardized tests

The term *standardized test* is generally used to refer to any measuring instrument that is developed through the procedures just described. But the uses to which such tests are put vary. Some standardized tests are used to measure knowledge of specific subject areas, such as reading, arithmetic, English, social studies, and physics. These are usually referred to as _achievement tests_, since they measure how much a pupil has learned—or achieved—in a particular field of study. For the most part, such tests are designed to measure the outcomes of

Achievement tests measure how much has been learned about a subject

previous learning experiences. When achievement tests are prepared, therefore, an attempt is made to measure what is covered in a typical curriculum in a particular subject at a certain grade level.

Other standardized tests are designed to measure aptitudes or abilities rather than achievement. It may be valuable for teachers to know, for example, if students seem to possess qualities that make it easy for them to learn verbal or numerical skills. When people possess qualities that are appropriate for a certain kind of performance, we say they have an *aptitude* for the activity, and that is the term applied to standardized tests designed to measure a person's potential in a given field. In some cases, aptitude tests are designed to measure specific abilities, but they may also be developed to measure an individual's general overall learning ability. Such measuring devices may be referred to by a variety of labels including *scholastic aptitude tests, general ability tests,* or *intelligence tests.* Since these examinations are intended to measure abilities not tied to classroom instruction, those who develop them go to elaborate lengths to avoid asking questions that measure what is covered in a specific school curriculum. Thus, a basic difference between achievement and aptitude tests is that the former are developed to measure what is covered in specific subjects or courses and the latter are intended to measure abilities that are acquired as a result of all the educational experiences a person has had—outside as well as inside school.

It is quite likely that you have had personal experience with both types of standardized test. During your elementary school years, you probably took at least one achievement test. If you happened to go to school in a district that had an enthusiastic test officer, you may have taken such tests every year or so. You may also have been required to take a group intelligence or general ability test. During your secondary school career, you may have been asked to take achievement tests in specific subject areas. When you applied for admission to college, you probably were asked to take the College Entrance Examination Board's Scholastic Aptitude Test or the equivalent. If you plan to go to graduate school, perhaps you have recently taken the Graduate Record Exam.

The major reason you have taken so many standardized tests is that they supply information that is a valuable supplement to teacher evaluations. Few teachers are evaluation experts. It is melodramatic to accuse them of "immoral" behavior (as in *Wad-ja-get?*) if they cannot answer questions about statistical concepts, but it is probably fair to say that there is a haphazard quality to much teacher evaluation. This may not be as much of a disadvantage as the authors of *Wad-ja-get?* make it out to be, however. In the first place, by the time you got out of high school you have been evaluated by approximately seventy teachers. Because so many different people passed judgment on you, it seems likely that the errors they made more or less averaged

Aptitude tests provide estimates of potential ability

themselves out. Secondly, the lack of a highly consistent, systematic approach to evaluation may have increased the probability that any unique and idiosyncratic qualities you possess were recognized somewhere along the line. Thus, there are certain advantages to personal, somewhat subjective evaluation procedures, but scores on standardized tests serve as valuable supplements to teacher impressions. It may be helpful for you to know, for instance, how much the students in your class know about a subject compared to students from all over the country. Provided you use the information to facilitate learning, it may also be of value for you to know which individuals in any group know more (or less) about a subject than their classmates. And when a small number of individuals must be selected from a large number of applicants, asking everyone to answer the same questions that can be graded in an objective way is obviously the fairest procedure to follow. Before placing a great deal of emphasis on such measures, however, it is important to make an estimate of how effective any standardized test really is. For that purpose, you might refer to a list of criteria for evaluating evaluation instruments.

Criteria for evaluating standardized tests

The Center for the Study of Evaluation at the University of California at Los Angeles has developed a list of seven criteria for evaluating standardized tests:

1. Validity

2. Examinee appropriateness

3. Normed excellence

4. Teaching feedback

5. Usability

6. Retest potential

7. Ethical propriety

The list of criteria is presented primarily to acquaint you with factors to consider if you are asked to administer standardized tests or to interpret scores yielded by them. It is not likely that you will ever be given sole responsibility for choosing a standardized test. Most school districts have test officers who make such decisions after consulting with administrators, teachers, and sometimes school board members or parents. Even so, you may wish to carry out your personal analysis to decide how much confidence to place in certain test scores and also to determine how you will use test scores. To do that, you might consult the publications of UCLA's Center for the Study of Evaluation in which standardized tests are rated with reference to the seven criteria. The volumes in the series include:

CSE Elementary School Test Evaluations, 1970

CSE-ECRC Preschool/Kindergarten Test Evaluations, 1971

CSE-RBS Test Evaluations: Tests of Higher-order Cognitive, Affective, and Interpersonal Skills, 1972

CSE Secondary Test Evaluations, 1973

In addition to referring to the CSE publications, you might also consult the most recent volume of the *Mental Measurement Yearbooks,* edited by Oscar K. Buros. These yearbooks, which are published about every five years, contain descriptions and critiques of most standardized tests used in this country.

The criteria listed by UCLA's Center for the Study of Evaluation are frequently referred to in CSE publications and in the *Mental Measurement Yearbooks.* Furthermore, you may wish to use at least some of the criteria when forming your own judgments about tests. Accordingly, a brief explanation of each criterion in the CSE list is in order.

Validity   The term *validity* is usually defined as the extent to which a test measures what it is supposed to measure. If you are eager to find out about the reading ability of third graders, you will want to use a test that actually measures reading ability. If you want to measure the scholastic aptitude of high school seniors, you will want to pick a test that indicates overall scholastic proficiency. These two examples illustrate two different kinds of validity. Testing experts distinguish between *content validity,* or how well the test items seem to cover a given type of learning, and *predictive validity,* or how well a test predicts later performance. If you were a third grade teacher, you might be able to estimate the content validity of a test simply by examining the questions. But in order to find out about the predictive validity of the SAT, you would need information about the relationship between scores on that test and grade point averages earned in college. Another way to estimate how well a test measures what it is supposed to measure is to estimate its *construct validity*. Some tests purport to measure psychological *constructs* or attributes. A measure of construct validity indicates how accurately such tests actually measure particular attributes. A test of musical aptitude, for example, should differentiate between students who respond quickly to instruction in music and those who do not. A test of anxiety should differentiate between students high and low in anxiety.

Examinee appropriateness   Because developing a standardized test is a substantial undertaking that requires a considerable investment of money, time, and expertise, most tests of this type are designed for nationwide use. But the curriculum in school districts in different

Content validity: How well test items cover a type of learning

Construct validity: How accurately test measures a particular attribute

types of communities and in different sections of the country varies to a considerable extent. Therefore, it is important to estimate how appropriate a given test is for a particular group of pupils. When you are estimating the content validity of a test, you should pay attention not only to how well the questions measure what they are supposed to measure but also to whether they are appropriate in terms of level of difficulty and in relation to the curriculum covered in a particular classroom.

Normed excellence   Standardized tests supply *norms,* which make it possible to compare one pupil's score in relation to the scores earned by others. In order to put faith in these norms, however, one should expect that a score earned when a student takes the test at one time will be quite similar to scores earned if the test is taken again by the same student. This is referred to as *reliability,* and the word stresses the point that you should be able to count on a test score being consistent, just as you might count on a reliable worker doing a consistent job time after time.

Reliability: How consistent scores are if a test is taken again

Teaching feedback   Most standardized tests are designed to be used all over the country, but the scores are usually used by particular teachers interested in individual pupils. An achievement test in reading will provide meaningful feedback only if the scores tell teachers something about pupils that can be used in improving instruction. In order for that to happen, the scores should ordinarily reveal significant things about pupil performance and be reasonably easy to interpret.

Usability   Most standardized tests are group tests designed to be given by one examiner to a class of students. (Some intelligence tests, and a few performance tests that measure specialized aptitudes, are individual tests given to one individual at a time.) As a result, the instructions and questions are typically printed in a test booklet, and the answers are recorded on a separate sheet that can be electronically processed. Sometimes special pencils must be used, and quite often students are given a specified number of minutes to work on each section. A test is usable if it provides clear instructions to the teacher (or other administrator) that can be put into practice without a great deal of difficulty or confusion and if it does not force students to waste time dealing with the mechanics of recording answers. (Perhaps you can recall taking standardized tests that were so confusing you were not sure you put the correct answer down even when you were sure you knew it.)

Retest potential   Quite often it is desirable to obtain before-and-after information about student performance. In some school districts where accountability is stressed, pre- and post-instruction measurements may become a common feature of schooling. But if students are to be tested when they enter a classroom or begin to study a unit and then tested again after instruction has taken place, an alternate form of the first exam should be available. Simply giving the same test over again would yield misleading information because students might remember specific questions and answers. Therefore, the availability of an equivalent but different form of a standardized test may be an important point to consider.

Ethical propriety In the 1960s, when some school districts embarked on a veritable test-giving binge, attempts were sometimes made to measure not only achievement but various kinds of "adjustment" as well. Some of the questions used to tap personality variables asked students to consider questions viewed as potentially harmful (e.g., "Do you love your mother more than your father?"). As a consequence, many school boards now insist that all tests be examined to determine if they contain questions that might be classified as offensive or likely to arouse feelings of confusion or guilt.

Administering standardized tests

Reading about evaluations of tests may help you decide how much confidence to place in test scores, but your primary job as a teacher will be administering tests and knowing what the scores mean. These two responsibilities will now be discussed.

The most important point to keep in mind about administering standardized tests is the need for a standard procedure. The instructions for giving the test must be followed to the letter. Otherwise, the scores of some pupils may be distorted by factors that were not present when the test was standardized, and the distortion may reduce the value of the normative data. To illustrate, the experience of teachers in two schools in a small school district will be described.

One school had an easygoing, pleasantly addlepated principal; the other had a very efficient, well-organized principal. A notice was sent to each school announcing that achievement tests were to be administered on a given day. The relaxed principal took a quick glance at the memo, put it on top of a pile of papers, and forgot about it. The other principal obtained copies of the test booklet and called a special teachers' meeting to familiarize everyone with the nature of the test and its administration.

When the tests were delivered to the schools on the specified day, the casual principal took them around to the teachers, said, "You're supposed to give these today," and wandered off. The efficient principal had the booklets distributed to the classrooms, where both the students and the teachers were poised and prepared. It happened that the test featured a rather unorthodox answer sheet. Most of the teachers who were forced to give the test on the spur of the moment did not catch this, and those who did discover it were unable to alert their pupils to it very effectively. The teachers in the other school had warned the students ahead of time and quickly demonstrated the way to record answers before the students got to work. Needless to say, the scores earned by students in the two schools varied considerably.

This may be an extreme atypical example, but it does emphasize the need for insuring that your students have the opportunity to respond to achievement tests in the standard manner prescribed by the test publisher. You should read the teacher's manual that accompanies every reputable achievement test and follow the instructions faithfully. Usually included is information on preparing pupils, seating arrangements, pencils and scratch paper, distributing and collecting the test booklets and answer sheets, enforcing time schedules, and answering questions.

Essential to follow instructions when administering standardized tests

Interpreting standardized test scores

In addition to administering standardized tests, you are also likely to be asked to explain scores earned on such tests to students and their parents. The likelihood that parents will want information was increased when in 1975 Congress added a new part to the General Education Provisions Act titled Privacy Rights of Parents and Students. The Privacy Rights amendment stipulates that all educational institutions must provide "parents of students access to all official records directly related to the students and an opportunity for a hearing to challenge such records on the grounds they are inaccurate, misleading, or otherwise inappropriate" (Federal Register, vol. 40, no. 3, Jan. 6, 1975, p. 1208). This law was passed primarily to reduce the possibility that damaging statements about children recorded in cumulative folders might have negative repercussions. But it seems likely that many parents might demand the right to examine the test scores of their children. Accordingly, you should know how to interpret standardized test scores, particularly because they can often be misleading.

As noted earlier, standardized tests supply norms that make it possible to compare any individual pupil's performance to that of the standardization group. One of the biggest problems confronting the developer of a standardized test is how to make allowance for the unique characteristics of different school systems. For example, if a given topic or technique is taught a year earlier in one district than it is in another, this should be taken into account in interpreting the results within a given district. Generally speaking, the most useful comparisons are those made at the local level, since most students in a particular district have been exposed to a reasonably uniform curriculum. If normative data are not available at the local level, you will need to be especially careful in making inferences about the significance of a score.

No matter what sorts of norms are available, however, you will need to know how to interpret different types of score. Most standardized test scores are reported on profiles developed by the test publisher in terms of some or all of the following: grade equivalents, percentile ranks, standard scores, or stanines. At one time or another, you are likely to encounter each of them.

Grade equivalent scores The *grade equivalent score* is established by interpreting performance on tests in terms of grade levels. A student who made a grade equivalent score of 4.7 on an achievement test, for example, performed at the level the average fourth grader in the standardization group achieved by the seventh month of the school year. The grade equivalent score is used most often at the elementary level, but because it may lead to misinterpretations, it is not as popular as it once was. One problem with grade equivalent scores is the tendency to interpret a score above a student's actual grade level as an indication that the student is capable of consistently working at that level, which might lead parents to agitate for an accelerated promotion. Such scores may show that a student did somewhat better on the test than the average student a grade or two above her or him, but they do not take into account the possibility that the student tested lacks knowledge of certain skills covered in the grade that would be skipped if demands for acceleration were granted.

Grade equivalent score: Performance interpreted in terms of grade levels

Percentile ranks Probably the most widely used score for standardized tests is the *percentile rank*. This score indicates the percentage of students who are at or below the score of a given student. It provides specific information about relative position. Students earning a percentile rank of 87 did better than 87 percent of the students in the particular normative group being used. They did not get 87 percent of the questions right—unless by coincidence—and this is the point parents are most likely to miss. Parents may have been brought up on the percentages grading system, in which 90 or above was an A, 80 to 90 a B, and so on down the line. If you report that a son or daughter has a percentile rank of 50, some parents are horror-struck or outraged, not understanding that the child is average, not a failure. In such cases the best approach is probably to emphasize that the percentile rank tells the percentage of cases below the child's score. You might also talk in terms of a hypothetical group of 100; for example, a child with a percentile rank of 78 did better than 78 out of every 100 students who took the test.

Percentile ranks: Percentage of scores at or below a given score

Although the percentile rank gives simple and direct information on relative position, it has a major disadvantage: The difference in achievement between students clustered around the middle of the distribution is often considerably less than the difference between those at the extremes. The reason is that most scores *are* clustered around the middle of most distributions of large groups of students. The difference in raw score between students at percentile ranks 50 and 51 may be one point. But the difference in raw score between the student with a percentile rank of 98 and one ranked 97 may be ten or fifteen points of raw score, because the best (and worst) students scatter toward the extremes. This quality of percentile ranks means that ranks on different tests cannot be averaged. To get around the difficulty, standard scores are often used.

Standard scores   Standard scores are expressed in terms of a common unit—the *standard deviation*. This statistic indicates the student's degree of deviation from the mean. (The *mean* is the arithmetical average of a distribution calculated by adding all scores and dividing the total by the number of scores.) The standard deviation is most valuable when it can be related to the normal probability curve. Figure 12–1 shows a normal probability curve indicating the percentage of cases to be found within three standard deviations[1] above and below the mean.

The *normal curve* is a mathematical concept that depicts a hypothetical bell-shaped distribution of scores. Such a perfectly symmetrical distribution rarely if ever occurs when the attributes of large numbers of individuals are measured. However, since many distributions of human characteristics of performance do resemble the normal distribution, it is often assumed that such distributions are "normal" enough to be treated as normal. Thus, information derived by mathematicians for the hypothetical normal distribution can be applied to the approximately normal distributions that are found when human attributes are measured. As some of the characters in *Wad-ja-get?* pointed out, though, instructors should not assign grades "according to the curve" unless total scores for students in a given class are distributed in bell-shaped form. This rarely occurs, for three reasons. First, almost any group of students will have been selected in some way (e.g., by attendance boundaries determined by neighborhood, by a process of specialization or elimination, as when high school students choose a vocational or academic program or drop out). Second, some students in any class are almost sure to have had more previous experience with a subject than others. Third, the tests used may be too easy or too difficult for a particular group, which will

Standard deviation: Degree of deviation from the mean of a distribution

Normal curve: Bell-shaped (symmetrical) distribution

---

[1] Several abbreviations of standard deviation are regularly used, including SD, σ, and s. Because SD seems most directly related to the actual term, it is used in the discussion in this text, as well as in Table 12–1. In an effort to reduce confusion, SD is used consistently in this chapter, although some statisticians might prefer σ in some places because a theoretical distribution is depicted.

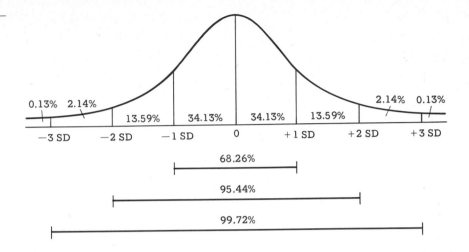

Figure 12-1

The normal probability curve

0.13% 2.14%   13.59%   34.13% 34.13%   13.59%   2.14% 0.13%

−3 SD   −2 SD   −1 SD   0   +1 SD   +2 SD   +3 SD

68.26%

95.44%

99.72%

cause scores to bunch at the top or bottom of the distribution. When very large numbers of pupils are asked to take tests designed by specialists who take pains to cancel out the impact of selective factors, however, it may be appropriate to interpret their scores on such tests with reference to the normal curve.

The derivation of the normal probability curve is quite technical. The computation of a standard deviation for a group of test scores is relatively simple. Tables 12–1 and 12–2 and the steps listed below offer an example and a description of the computation of standard deviation. The first step listed below is illustrated in Table 1; steps 2, 3, 4, and 5 are illustrated in Table 2.

1. Compute the mean: Add up all scores, and then divide by the number of scores. Symbolically: $M = \dfrac{\Sigma X}{N}$, where M = mean, Σ = sum total, X = score, and N = number of scores.

2. Find the difference between each score and the mean. Symbolically: d = X − M, where d = difference, X = score, and M = mean.

3. Square all the differences and add them. Symbolically: Σd^2, where Σ = sum total and d^2 = differences squared.

4. Divide the sum of the squared differences by the number of scores. Symbolically: $\dfrac{\Sigma d^2}{N}$, where Σd^2 = sum total of differences squared and N = number of scores.

5. Compute the positive square root of the figure you obtained in step 4. That square root is the standard deviation.

Before you consider calculating standard deviations and assigning grades by referring to the normal curve, keep in mind the point mentioned in the analysis of *Wad-ja-get?* Unless a distribution of scores

Table 12-1

Calculating the mean from a frequency distribution

Score X	Tally	Frequency f	Product of score and frequency fX
47	/	1	47
46	/ /	2	92
45	/	1	45
44			
43	/	1	43
42	/	1	42
41	/ /	2	82
40	/	1	40
39	/ /	2	78
38	/	1	38
37	/ /	2	74
36	/ /	2	72
35	/ / / /	4	140
34	/ / /	3	102
33	/ /	2	66
32	/ /	2	64
31			
30	/	1	30
29	/	1	29
28	/	1	28
27	/	1	27
26			
25	/	1	25
24	/	1	24
		N = 33	$\Sigma fX = 1188$
		Sum total of scores	

$$\text{Mean (M)} = \frac{\text{Sum total of scores } (\Sigma fX)}{\text{Number of scores (N)}}$$

$$\text{Mean (M)} = \frac{1188}{33}$$

$$\text{Mean (M)} = 36$$

for a class is bell shaped, it is unwise to make inferences about a student's relative position in terms of the normal probability curve. In most cases, only when large numbers of unselected students are tested do distributions of scores tend to take on the characteristic bell shape. Test publishers establish norms with large, representative student populations, so scores based on the normal curve *can* be used in interpreting results of standardized tests. Standard scores have been developed for this purpose.

The first step in deriving standard scores is to calculate a standard deviation. The next step is to determine the position of a given score within the distribution of scores. The standard score provides this information. It tells how far a raw score lies from the mean of a distribution in terms of the standard deviation of the distribution. One type of standard score—the z score—is based on a mean of 0 and an SD

Table 12-2

Calculating the standard deviation (using the frequency distribution from Table 12-1)

Score X	Frequency f	Deviation (X-M) d	Deviation squared (X-M) d²	Product of frequency and deviation squared fd²
47	1	11	121	121
46	2	10	100	200
45	1	9	81	81
44				
43	1	7	49	49
42	1	6	36	36
41	2	5	25	50
40	1	4	16	16
39	2	3	9	18
38	1	2	4	4
37	2	1	1	2
36	2	0	0	0
35	4	−1	1	4
34	3	−2	4	12
33	2	−3	9	18
32	2	−4	16	32
31				
30	1	−6	36	36
29	1	−7	49	49
28	1	−8	64	64
27	1	−9	81	81
26				
25	1	−11	121	121
24	1	−12	144	144
	N = 33		Sum total of fd²	(Σfd²) = 1138

$$\text{Standard deviation (SD)} = \sqrt{\frac{\text{Sum total of fd}^2 \quad (\Sigma fd^2)}{\text{Number of scores} \quad (N)}}$$

$$\text{Standard deviation (SD)} = \sqrt{\frac{1138}{33}}$$

$$\text{Standard deviation (SD)} = \sqrt{34.4848}$$

$$\text{Standard deviation (SD)} = \quad 5.87$$

z score: How far a raw score is from the mean in standard deviation units

of 1. The sign of the z score (+ or −) indicates whether the score is above or below the mean. Suppose you have a distribution of scores that yields a mean of 40 and a standard deviation of 5. Assuming the raw score is 45, the z score is computed thus, with X = raw score and M = mean:

$$z = \frac{X - M}{SD} \qquad z = \frac{45 - 40}{5} = \frac{5}{5} = +1$$

This z score tells you that the pupil who got a raw score of 45 is one standard deviation above the mean.

In order to avoid negative z scores (which are found for all raw scores below the mean) and decimals (which are found for scores not falling exactly at standard deviation division points), T scores have been devised. T scores use an arbitrary number as the mean. With

T score: How far a raw
score is from the mean
in numerical terms

many T scores, 50 is the number chosen; 100 is used with some intelligence tests, and 500 is used on the Graduate Record Exam. To get a T score, multiply the z score by 10 (to get rid of the decimal) and add the product to 50. For a negative z score (which you would get if the raw score was below the mean), you *subtract* the product (10z) from 50. In the example of a raw score of 45, which had a z score equivalent of +1, you get a T score of 60, as follows:

$$T = 50 + 10z$$
$$T = 50 + (10)(1) = 50 + 10$$
$$T = 60$$

If you want T scores but not z scores, you can proceed directly to the calculation of T scores from raw test scores by using the following formula, with X = raw score and M = mean:

$$T = 50 + \frac{10(X - M)}{SD}$$

For the example of a raw score of 45, a mean of 40, and a standard deviation of 5, you would get a T score of 60, as follows:

$$T = 50 + \frac{10(X - M)}{SD}$$

$$T = 50 + \frac{10(45 - 40)}{5} = 50 + 10 = 60$$

To grasp the relationship between z scores, T scores, and percentile ranks, examine Figure 12-2. The diagram shows each scale marked off below a normal curve. It supplies information about the interrelationships of these various scores, *provided* the distribution

Figure 12-2

Relationship between z scores, T scores, and percentile ranks

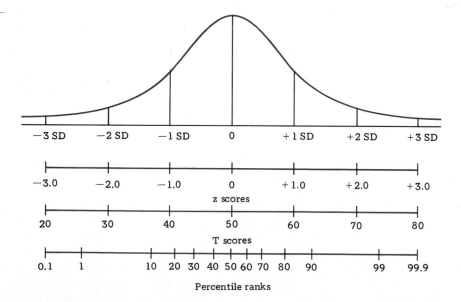

Figure 12-3

Percentage of cases in each stanine, with standard deviation units indicated

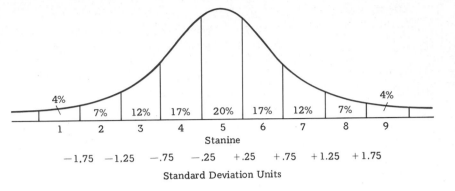

Stanine

−1.75 −1.25 −.75 −.25 +.25 +.75 +1.25 +1.75

Standard Deviation Units

you are working with is essentially normal. In a normal distribution, for example, a z score of +1 is the same as a T score of 60 or a percentile rank of 84; a z score of −2 is the same as a T score of 30 or a percentile rank of about 2. (In addition, notice that the distance between the percentiles clustered around the middle is only a small fraction of the distance between the percentile ranks that are found at the ends of the distribution.)

Stanines During World War II, air force psychologists developed a statistic that is sometimes used by publishers of standardized tests. It is called the *stanine* (an abbreviation of "standard nine-point scale"), reflecting the fact that it is a type of standard score and divides a population into nine groups. Each stanine is one-half of a standard deviation unit, as indicated in Figure 12-3.

Stanines: Distribution divided into nine half-SD units

    Some test publishers cite the success of the air force pilot selection program as evidence that the stanine scale can effectively classify people. However, they fail to point out that the air force used a *battery* of about twenty tests, many of which measured such sensorimotor factors as coordination and reaction time. Most school achievement tests are susceptible to many more errors of measurement than is the air force battery, and any attempts to split a small group into nine subsections, or even three subsections, should be made cautiously. Grouping based on stanine scores (or any scores) should be tentative.

    Figure 12-4 is a profile used in reporting scores on the Stanford Achievement Test. Obviously, you will need to understand percentile ranks, standard scores, and stanines in order to interpret it. Most reputable test publishers provide detailed guides to help you interpret and make the most of the student profiles. But it is usually assumed that you have some familiarity with the general considerations and specific statistics just described.

    Up until recently, scores on standardized tests were often used to group students. In the 1950s and 1960s, many secondary schools divided students into X, Y, and Z classes or the equivalent. Today, this

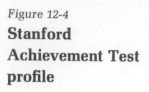

Figure 12-4

Stanford Achievement Test profile

STANFORD Achievement Test
Primary Level II Complete Battery   Form A

Pupil Information Box

Name _____
           last   first   initial

Boy ☐   Girl ☐   Grade _____   Teacher _____

School _____   Date of Testing _____
                                                   Year   Month   Day

City _____   Date of Birth _____
                                                   Year   Month   Day

State _____   Age _____
                                                   Years   Months

	Number Right	Scaled Score	Grade Equiv.	%ile Rank*	STANINE*
TEST 1: Vocabulary					1 2 3 **4 5 6** 7 8 9
TEST 2: Reading Part A					**1 2 3 4 5 6 7 8 9**
Part B					**1 2 3 4 5 6 7 8 9**
Part A + Part B					1 2 3 **4 5 6** 7 8 9
TEST 3: Word Study Skills					1 2 3 **4 5 6** 7 8 9
TEST 4: Math. Concepts					1 2 3 **4 5 6** 7 8 9
TEST 5: Math. Computation					1 2 3 **4 5 6** 7 8 9
TEST 6: Math. Applications					1 2 3 **4 5 6** 7 8 9
TEST 7: Spelling					1 2 3 **4 5 6** 7 8 9
TEST 8: Social Science					1 2 3 **4 5 6** 7 8 9
TEST 9: Science					1 2 3 **4 5 6** 7 8 9
TEST 10: Listening Comp.					1 2 3 **4 5 6** 7 8 9
Total Battery (Test 1 through Test 10)					1 2 3 **4 5 6** 7 8 9
Total Auditory (Test 1 + Test 10)					1 2 3 **4 5 6** 7 8 9
Total Reading (Test 2 + Test 3)					1 2 3 **4 5 6** 7 8 9
Total Mathematics (Test 4 + Test 5 + Test 6)					1 2 3 **4 5 6** 7 8 9

*Percentile Ranks and Stanines based on tables for Beginning ☐ End ☐ of Grade

Reproduced from the Stanford Achievement Test, copyright
© 1973 by Harcourt Brace Jovanovich, Inc. Reproduced by
special permission of the publisher.

is not as likely to be the case because it has been successfully argued
that many standardized achievement and mental ability tests favor
white middle-class students and discriminate against all others. When
such tests are used to group students, it is argued, they perpetuate
inequalities because students with the most educational strength are
separated from those with the least. Furthermore, students who are
identified as slow students early in the grades may be treated as if they
are poor learners and, because of the self-fulfilling prophecy reaction,
come to think and act like poor learners. Such complaints are often

made about achievement tests, but they are made even more energetically about scholastic aptitude or intelligence tests. To understand why this is so, it is necessary to consider the nature and measurement of intelligence.

The nature and measurement of intelligence

If you had been teaching in the 1950s and 1960s, you would have almost certainly found some sort of IQ score (or the equivalent) in the cumulative folder of any student in your class. Today, you may not only fail to find such scores, you may be criticized if you look for them. To understand this abrupt switch in attitudes toward IQ scores, you will need some background information.

Beginnings of the heredity-environment controversy

One reason for the abrupt switch in interest in IQ scores can be traced to differences of opinion about the extent to which intelligence is traceable to inherited tendencies and to what degree it is influenced by experiences. Lack of agreement about the impact of heredity and environment on intelligence has contributed to the decision to place not too much emphasis on IQ scores. A brief history of the controversy may help you understand why this has occurred.

People probably began to argue about the degree to which individuals are born smart or stupid at the time language developed. But current discussions of the nature of intelligence might be traced to a book published in 1869 by the brilliant English scientist Sir Francis Galton. Interest in the theory of evolution proposed by his cousin, Charles Darwin, led Galton to speculate about the intelligence of eminent men of his day. His general conclusion—that intelligence is a hereditary trait—is reflected by the title of his book: *Hereditary Genius*. Galton based his conclusion on the fact that eminent men tended to turn up in succeeding generations of certain families. Galton did not at first consider that England was a society based on hereditary privilege and that the presence of many intelligent people in the same families could be explained just as logically by arguing that they came from a superior environment. Nevertheless, he was interested in gathering information about intelligence and was largely responsible for arousing the interest of many psychologists in seeking ways to measure intelligence.

In the early 1900s the development of industrialism and the rise of meritocratic societies brought people greater freedom to make the most of their intelligence, regardless of their background. At the same time, techniques for measuring intelligence were developed and the debate about the causes of intelligence that continues to this day began in earnest. When people in a society have considerable freedom to achieve success through their own efforts, it is natural enough for parents, educators, and psychologists to begin to speculate about the possibility of finding ways to *make* children intelligent. The view of intelligence propounded by Galton was accepted in Victorian England because it was assumed that heredity determined almost everything about a person. But in America, where the "all men are created equal" philosophy is stressed, it is assumed that individuals acquire many characteristics through their own efforts. Conceptions of intelligence that stress inherited potential have often been less popular in this country than those that emphasize the impact of experiences, and American psychologists have continuously sought to discover ways to teach children to become intelligent.

Attempts to increase intelligence

Enthusiasm for the view that experiences can be arranged to increase measurable intelligence reached its peak when the Head Start programs were instituted in the 1960s. The initial success of programmed learning and behavior modification techniques (as well as the acceptance of Piaget's description of cognitive development) convinced psychologists who supported the S-R view that methods had been perfected for shaping any kind of behavior, including general learning ability. Proponents of S-R theory argued that humans possessed knowledge that would make it possible to systematically create what previously had occurred by accident, and in the 1960s they succeeded in persuading the government to finance Head Start.

As noted in Chapter 11, the results of objective analyses of the Head Start program came as a blow to environmentalists: When evaluated at the end of first grade, children who had been exposed to Head Start programs did no better than children from similar backgrounds who had not attended. The report on the U.S. Commission on Civil Rights offered this conclusion: "None of the compensatory education programs appear to have raised significantly the achievement of participating pupils, as a group, within the period evaluated by the Commission" (1967, p. 138). It was then argued that the lack of success might have resulted from too little training or that the little training there was had come too late. To correct for the first weakness, Follow-Through programs (described in Chapter 11) were instituted. To correct for the second weakness, research was undertaken (by White and Watts, 1973) to try to discover the early experiences that competent children are exposed to. It was assumed that if all children are exposed to the same experiences, all children would become more intelligent.

The Jensen controversy

It is still too early to tell if Follow-Through or the techniques recommended by White and Watts will succeed in increasing the learning ability of disadvantaged children. Although the existence of these programs indicates that the environmentalist view is still strongly endorsed, the lack of success of Head Start has created doubts about this position, doubts that have been intensified in the minds of many by the publication of articles presenting evidence in favor of the genetic view of intelligence. Such articles have appeared regularly over the past fifty years.

A recent report that attracted international attention was "How Much Can We Boost IQ and Scholastic Achievement?" by Arthur R. Jensen, which appeared in the Winter 1969 issue of the *Harvard Educational Review*. Jensen argued that attempts at compensatory education (such as Head Start) failed because they were based on the belief that intelligence is almost exclusively the result of environmental experiences. He presented considerable evidence to substantiate the view that heredity establishes the limits of any individual's intelligence, and he suggested that it would be more fruitful to take into account genetic differences when planning educational programs—as opposed to attempting to "create" intelligence.

The Jensen article aroused a storm of protest, and he was subjected to considerable harassment and even threats of bodily harm. The critiques that quickly appeared included complaints about his interpretation of statistics and his basic premises, and statements that he was a racist and white supremacist. (If you would like to read the original Jensen article plus commentaries by seven critics, see *Environment, Heredity, and Intelligence* (1970), Reprint Series no. 2, of the *Harvard Educational Review*.) Shortly after Jensen's article appeared, other psychologists presented the same basic argument. In the September 1971 issue of the *Atlantic*, Richard Herrnstein of Harvard analyzed the history of intelligence testing and reviewed research on the relative influence of heredity and environment on intelligence. He concluded that 80 to 85 percent of the variability in IQ is due to genetic factors.[2] Then H. J. Eysenck, an eminent English psychologist, published *The IQ Argument* (1971), in which he carried out much the same sort of analysis as Herrnstein and came to essentially the same conclusions.

Jensen: Heredity establishes limits of intelligence

[2] Herrnstein offered an expanded version of his *Atlantic* article, together with an account of the attacks that were made on him because he had written it, in *I.Q. in the Meritocracy* (1973).

Claim that IQ tests discriminate against minority-group children

Environmentalists have responded to these arguments by referring to evidence indicating that minority-group children are victims of deprived early environments (Hunt, 1961; Deutsch, 1964). They claim that there is an "IQ conspiracy" because most intelligence tests have been designed to favor middle-class whites and thus discriminate against lower-class minority group children (Garcia, 1972). They argue that minority-group children do poorly on IQ tests because they have not been equipped with skills to pass tests (Mercer, 1972). They also suggest that minority-group children respond negatively to white testers and are not confident about taking tests and not motivated to do well because they are influenced by a negative self-fulfilling prophecy (Watson, 1972). However, it is possible to cite evidence (e.g., Shuey, 1966; Jensen, 1969; Eysenck, 1971) to refute all these hypotheses.

To help you gain some perspective for evaluating these arguments, definitions and tests of intelligence will now be analyzed.

Definitions of intelligence

Drawing conclusions about research on intelligence is difficult, in part because there is no universally agreed-upon definition of intelligence. Different people mean different things when they talk about this quality. Defining terms is especially important when discussing comparative scores, since an individual's performance may depend on the test used to determine the scores. The conception of intelligence that test authors have in mind determines the kinds of questions they write, which in turn determines the final score. Consequently, it is important to take into account how writers of intelligence tests define the quality they seek to measure.

There is general agreement that the most widely used and *respected* tests of intelligence are the Stanford-Binet and the Wechsler tests. Lewis Terman, the driving force behind the development of the Stanford-Binet tests, designed them to measure a general factor (McNemar, 1942), which might be described as the ability to deal with abstractions. David Wechsler, the chief originator of the Wechsler Intelligence Scale for Children (WISC) (1949), the Wechsler Adult Intelligence Scale (WAIS) (1955), and the Wechsler Intelligence Scale for Children—Revised (1974) has defined intelligence as "the aggregate or global capacity of the individual to act purposefully, to think rationally and to deal effectively with his environment" (1944, p. 3). There are ten subtests on the WISC and WAIS, each specifically intended to measure one aspect of the aggregate of abilities described by Wechsler.

The distinction between general and specific abilities is perhaps the major point of difference in definitions of intelligence. Charles Spearman (1927), one of the earliest authorities on intelligence, spoke of a "g" (for "general") factor, plus several "s" (for "specific") factors.

*Items from the
Stanford-Binet
Intelligence Scale used
to test the intelligence
of young children.
Verbal materials are
also used, but mainly
with older children and
adults.*

A. M. Love, Jr.

Definitions of
intelligence stress
general or specific
factors

L. L. and Thelma G. Thurstone (1941), specialists in the statistical technique of factor analysis, isolated several factors, referred to them as primary mental abilities, and developed a test to measure six of them. The test did not prove very successful, perhaps because later factor analyses (Anatasi, 1968) revealed that despite the Thurstones' efforts to the contrary, the test still seemed to measure a general factor. More recently, J. P. Guilford (1967) proposed a multifactor theory that suggests that intelligence can be divided into 120 components. All this indicates that there are many ways of looking at intelligence and that the way you define it will determine how you try to measure it.

The appraisal of intelligence is further complicated by the fact that intelligence cannot be measured directly. If scientists ever find an organic basis of intelligence, it may then be possible to measure general learning ability through the use of an x ray or an EEG or some future electronic device or chemical analysis.[3] Until that time, however, efforts must be confined to measuring overt manifestations of the

[3] John Ertl, director of the University of Ottawa's Center for Cybernetic Studies, has developed an electronic device called the *neural efficiency analyzer*, which he claims measures the brain's physical ability to learn. The time it takes for flashes of light to register as changes in a subject's brain wave patterns gives an index of the speed of information transmission. According to Ertl, that index serves as a bias-free index of intelligence. The predictive value of neural efficiency scores has yet to be established, but you may encounter reports on studies now underway. For details about Ertl's device, examine the front-page article in the *APA Monitor* for March 1973.

functioning of the brain, and that is why definitions and measurements of intelligence are so elusive. It all depends on what manifestations you choose to observe. Some theorists define intelligence as
what is measured by an intelligence test. This may sound like double
talk, but the intent is not to dodge the issue; it is to emphasize that any
estimate of intelligence depends first and foremost on the questions
asked in the effort to measure it.

Nature of intelligence tests

An intelligence test consists of questions that test-makers believe will
yield an adequate sample of the subject's ability to deal with the types
of problems test-makers consider indicative of intelligence (as they
define it). This is the crucial point in appreciating the values and
limitations of intelligence tests.

Sir Francis Galton emphasized that a test consists of the *"sinking
of shafts at critical points"* (1890, p. 373). When you set out to measure
intelligence, you must decide what the "critical points" are. You must
try to select sample bits of behavior you hope will be "critical" or
indicative of a general ability, yet make your questions fair to all.

The major confounding factor is differences in educational opportunity. Remember, you hope to get an estimate of general learning
ability. This means taking into account that some children benefit
from an especially rich home and school environment. Obviously, the
capacity of children to learn is a function of both their inherited
potential and their experiences. But since those who devise intelligence tests are interested in a general capacity, they want to avoid, as
much as possible, measuring abilities that are largely the result of a
particular set of home or school experiences. If they ask questions too
directly related to a specific kind of home or curriculum, they will
measure only how well children have responded to these experiences.
What about children who have *not* been exposed to that set of home
or curriculum experiences? You can't really say they are dumb,
because you haven't given them the chance to demonstrate that they
are bright. To avoid this sort of handicap, the test questions should be
based on situations common to practically all children. Whether they
have learned from the exposure is what you hope to discover, but you
must try to make sure they have had the opportunity to learn in the
first place.

Another point regarding intelligence tests has to do with the score.
No intelligence test score is an "absolute" measure. Many people—
parents especially—fail to grasp this fact. A common misconception
about the IQ is that it is a once-and-for-all judgment of how bright a
person is. Actually, the score on an intelligence test is merely a qualified guess about how successful a child is—as compared to other children—in handling certain kinds of problems at a particular time. If

children are retested, even with the same questions, they are quite likely to get a different score. If the second test consists of entirely different questions, they are almost certain to get a different score.

Marjorie P. Honzik, Jean W. Macfarlane, and Lucile Allen (1948) analyzed intelligence test scores of a group of children who were tested at frequent intervals from birth through the age of eighteen. The California Preschool Scale was used for the first five years, the Stanford-Binet for ages six to fifteen, the Wechsler-Bellevue at age eighteen. The researchers found that relationships between scores on tests administered a few years apart were high, but the longer the interval between tests, the lower the relationship tended to be. The researchers also reported that between the ages of six to eighteen, the scores of almost 60 percent of the subjects changed fifteen or more points; the scores of almost a third of the group changed twenty or more points; and the scores of 9 percent of the group changed thirty or more points. In only 15 percent of the cases did IQ scores change less than ten points. Some subjects showed upward or downward changes of as much as fifty points. Honzik and her associates reported that children whose test scores showed the most extreme fluctuations were known to have been exposed to unusual variations in their lives.

> IQ scores of the same individuals tested over the years rarely stay the same

Not all teachers have been aware of the changeable nature of IQ scores, and until recently a low intelligence test score in a cumulative record might have branded a child as stupid. (This is a major reason for the Privacy Rights amendment to the General Education Provisions Act.) Teachers who placed too much faith in IQ tests sometimes assumed that children with scores below a certain point were not capable of learning and treated them accordingly. A self-fulfilling prophecy reaction often resulted, causing low-scoring children to share their teacher's estimate of their abilities. In just a year or two, such children not only developed strongly entrenched negative attitudes about themselves and school, they also fell so far behind their classmates that they were unable to catch up if they eventually encountered a teacher who believed in them and urged them to try. To prevent this sort of situation, the National Education Association has called for a moratorium on the use of intelligence tests. Educators in many states endorse the idea, and that is the major reason you may not find intelligence test scores in the cumulative folders of your students. (It seems likely that a major reason for the proposed NEA moratorium on intelligence testing is the realization that it may be difficult to defend such measures if parents argue that the scores are "inaccurate, misleading, or otherwise inappropriate.")

> Low test scores may lead to unfortunate self-fulfilling prophecy reactions

Because of the complexity of measuring IQ and the difficulties of taking into account all variables, it is impossible to come up with any definitive statement about the relative influence of heredity and environment. Authorities may cite the same studies and come up with diametrically opposed conclusions. If you would like to make up your own mind on the question, you are urged to read comprehensive analyses by defenders of each position. For this purpose, you might examine these books: *Intelligence and Experience* (1961) by J. McV. Hunt; *Environment, Heredity, and Intelligence*, Reprint Series no. 2, *Harvard Educational Review* (1970), which includes the Jensen article and several critiques; and *Intelligence: Genetic and Environmental Influences* (1971), edited by Robert Cancro (an exceptionally good collection of articles by seventeen contributors—including Jensen and Hunt—who have specialized in the study of intelligence). Before you engage in such study, however, you might ask yourself if there is any point in trying to come to a definite conclusion on the questions of group differences and the exact proportion of intelligence attributed to heredity and environment.

Is research on intelligence of significance to teachers?

Even if group differences do exist, will they make any difference in your classroom? You could not be sure that a particular student identified as high or low in intelligence actually is high or low until you give her or him a chance to prove it. And even if only 20 percent of the variability of intelligence is due to environmental factors (as some hereditarians claim), that would be enough to make you want to provide the best possible learning environment for each pupil.

Individual and group intelligence tests were developed originally to make *predictions* about relative ability. They were devised at a time when psychologists were intrigued with the possibility of being able to measure abilities accurately enough to foretell how a person would be likely to behave in the future. They were also developed at a time when many theorists were interested in the implications of the normal curve. Furthermore, in the 1950s there was a trend in American education to group students in terms of ability, typically by placing poor, average, and good students into tracks or classes.

Today, comparatively few educators advocate ability grouping. In fact, assigning children to tracks has been declared illegal because it has been successfully argued that disadvantaged children are often mistakenly labeled as poor students early in their school careers and treated that way until they leave school. Today, tests are used not to accentuate differences between pupils, but to find ways to help all pupils to learn at the highest possible level. If this point of view is endorsed, there is no reason to speculate about group differences and the precise degree to which intelligence is determined by nature or nurture. It is more important to use tests to diagnose strengths and weaknesses of individual pupils in order to establish the most effective learning environment. Many critics have concentrated only on certain aspects of Jensen's observations on intelligence, particularly those that have been sensationalized by the press. They have over-looked the fact that this is precisely the procedure he recommends. The final paragraph in his article in the *Harvard Educational Review* sums up his major recommendation:

> If diversity of mental abilities, as of most other human characteristics, is a basic fact of nature, as the evidence indicates, and if the ideal of universal education is to be successfully pursued, it seems a reasonable conclusion that schools and society must provide a range and diversity of educational meth-ods, programs, and goals, and of occupational opportunities, just as wide as the range of human abilities. Accordingly, the ideal of equality of educational opportunity should not be interpreted as uniformity of facilities, instruc-tional techniques, and educational aims for all children. Diversity rather than uniformity of approaches and aims would seem to be the key in making education rewarding for children of different patterns of ability. The reality of individual differences need not mean educational rewards for some chil-dren and frustration and defeat for others. (1969, p. 117)

Using test scores to individualize teaching

The trend toward identifying aptitudes and styles has been develop-ing for a number of years. It is based on the conception of intelligence developed most completely by J. P. Guilford and on what is referred to as *Aptitude-Treatment-Interaction* (often abbreviated ATI).

Guilford's conception of intelligence

Guilford's view of intelligence (which was mentioned briefly in the discussion of cognitive styles in Chapter 3) is a more systematic and complete elaboration of the "s" factors hypothesized by Spearman and the primary mental abilities described by the Thurstones. Guil-ford hypothesizes five intellectual *operations,* four *contents,* and six *products.* The five operations are especially important for speculating about ways to improve instruction:

Students vary in abilities to comprehend, memorize, and evaluate

1. *Cognition:* "Immediate discovery, awareness, rediscovery, or rec-ognition of information in various forms; comprehension"

2. *Memory:* "Retention or storage, with some degree of availability, of information in the same form in which it was committed to storage"

3. *Evaluation:* Ways in which we "reach decisions as to the goodness, correctness, suitability or adequacy of what we know, . . . remember, and . . . produce in productive thinking"

Some students are convergent, others are divergent thinkers

4. *Convergent Production:* Using information in a way that "leads to one right answer or to a recognized best or conventional answer"

5. *Divergent Production:* Productive thinking "in different directions, sometimes searching, sometimes seeking variety" (1959, pp. 470–475)

A few implications of Guilford's description of different operations indicate the significance of his theory: A student low in memory will need a different kind of instruction from a student low in cognition. Any approach to teaching that stresses a single route to a learning goal (such as a linear program) is not likely to appeal to or be understood by all students. Divergent thinkers might be at a disadvantage on multiple-choice tests.

Aptitude-Treatment-Interaction

ATI: Try to match pupil styles and abilities to forms of instruction

Awareness of the kinds of factors just mentioned has led some psychologists to propose that systematic efforts be made to identify the learning strengths and weaknesses of individual pupils and then to provide appropriate forms of instruction. This basic approach is referred to as *Aptitude-Treatment-Interaction* (Cronbach and Snow, 1975) because attempts are made to match student aptitudes with teaching methods (or treatments). Although the ATI idea makes sense from a theoretical point of view, a number of factors may cause difficulties if it is put into practice. F. J. Dowaliby and Harry Schumer (1973), for example, carried out a study that led to the conclusion that low-anxiety students seemed to respond better to learner centered approaches (such as group discussion) and high anxiety students seemed to respond better to teacher-centered methods (such as lectures). In an extreme form of the ATI approach, this information might be used in the following manner. First, a teacher would use tests, rating scales, or questionnaires to estimate the anxiety level of each student in a class. Then low-anxiety students would be given assignments that featured discussion, and high anxiety students would be asked to complete work under the direction of the teacher.

Students rarely can be classified into distinct types

This procedure may sound logical and simple, but several difficulties might be encountered if it were put into practice. The first problem would center on measurements of anxiety. Testing or rating this quality would not only be quite time consuming, but the "anxiety scores" that were established might be of questionable validity. A second problem would occur when an attempt was made to classify students into low- or high-anxiety categories. Almost all human traits that have been measured appear to be distributed more or less according to a bell-shaped curve: A few individuals will rate or score very high or very low; many individuals will have average ratings or scores; others in the group will be spaced out between high, low, and average measures. Consequently, any attempt to divide a group of students into high-anxiety or low-anxiety types will probably lead to artificial and perhaps misleading distinctions. A few pupils in any

*Research on aptitude-
treatment-interaction
has called attention to
the discovery that
high-anxiety students
may not respond to
group discussion
approaches.*

Kenn Goldblatt/DPI

class might properly be classified as high-anxiety or low-anxiety types, but other pupils should probably be designated as fairly high (or low), medium high (or low), slightly high (or low), or average.

Partly because of problems of measurement, partly because there are likely to be several rather than two classifications, and partly because students possess multiple characteristics, it is not likely that all students classified as low or high in anxiety would respond in a predicted manner. Some low-anxiety students, for example, might dislike and do poorly in group discussions because they are reflective rather than impulsive thinkers (cognitive styles explained in Chapter 4). Some high-anxiety students might dislike teacher-centered approaches because they are divergent rather than convergent thinkers. Still another problem might develop if self-fulfilling prophecy reactions occur. A teacher who is convinced that a particular student has a high anxiety level, for instance, might communicate this expectation to the pupil and intensify feelings of anxiety. A related possibility is that exposure to a theoretically inappropriate type of instruction might help, rather than hinder, a student with learning or personality problems. It seems possible that a high-anxiety student who had successful and rewarding experiences engaging in group discussion, to cite just one example, might gain confidence and become less anxious.

For reasons such as those, it does not seem desirable for teachers to make a concerted effort to try to systematically match student characteristics with instructional methods. Nevertheless, there are ways that you might take advantage of ATI research. One is to remain aware that students *do* differ in characteristics and aptitudes, even though the differences may not be measurable in precise terms. Some students will be able to memorize more easily than others; some will tend to be convergent thinkers; some will be more anxious than others; and so on. You might allow for such differences by using a variety of instructional techniques and by permitting students a degree of choice. If you permit students to choose between doing a research paper summarizing the work of experts or working on an original small-group project to be presented to the rest of the class, students may take care of aptitude-treatment-interaction on their own. And if you make balanced use of programmed, cognitive-discovery, and humanistic approaches to teaching, you are almost sure to please some of your students some of the time.

This is an appropriate place to re-emphasize a point made earlier: Just because you clearly prefer one approach to teaching over others, all your students will not necessarily feel the same way. If you enjoyed learner-centered approaches as a student and do poorly on multiple-choice tests, you may tentatively plan to make almost exclusive use of class discussions and to scrupulously avoid objective exams. Before you carry out any teaching plan that features only your favorite approach, however, take account of the fact that not all your students will share your interests, aptitudes, or personality traits.

In the Introduction to Part 3, you were asked to accept the proposition that each view of learning—S-R, cognitive-discovery, humanistic—is of value to teachers. The point was made that *you* may prefer one approach over the others, but this will not be true of all of your students. Mention was made of reviews of research (Stephens, 1967) that lead to the conclusion that comparisons of the effectiveness of different techniques of instruction typically fail to reveal significant differences.

One explanation for the finding that different teaching methods lead to the same overall amount of learning is that some pupils in any class will respond to a particular method better than others. If a comparison is made between test scores earned by groups of students exposed to programmed and discovery approaches, for example, the average scores may be the same. It is almost certain, however, that the scores of some pupils in each class will be higher than others. And it seems reasonable to assume, given evidence from ATI studies, that if the techniques were reversed, different pupils in the same class would be likely to earn higher scores. This would be the case because some children possess aptitudes and characteristics that cause them to respond more positively to one teaching approach than to another. If you desire to give all pupils in your classes the chance to do well at least part of the time, therefore, using a variety of teaching techniques would seem essential.

A second way for you to take advantage of ATI research is to speculate about why some students do less well than others with particular approaches to teaching, assignments, or exams (assuming that you offer variety and opportunities for choice). In the suggestions on how to arrange discovery approach discussion sessions, for example, you were urged to divide the class into small groups (to reduce the anxiety some students might experience if required to recite in front of the whole class). The research mentioned earlier in this section that established a relationship between low anxiety and preference for student-centered learning situations might therefore be used not to match aptitudes and treatments, but to remind you to arrange learning situations to help high-anxiety students enjoy and benefit more from discussion sessions. This approach would not require identification of individuals who were high in anxiety, which would eliminate one of the major problems noted earlier.

For all of these reasons, you might be on the alert for research that relates to Aptitude-Treatment-Interaction. If you encounter reports that describe how students with different characteristics responded to particular methods of teaching, you might ask yourself how you could use that information to arrange learning experiences that might help certain pupils minimize problems.

Using National Assessment data to individualize instruction

Another way you might use test scores to individualize instruction and improve student performance is to take advantage of information provided by National Assessment reports. The National Assessment of Educational Progress was described in the section on instructional objectives in Chapter 8.

As noted earlier, the National Assessment program was instituted in 1964. First, a comprehensive list of educational objectives was drawn up by committees of scholars, public school personnel, and lay citizens. Then questions were written by teams of specialists to determine how well these objectives were being achieved. Next, these questions were formed into tests in ten subject areas: citizenship, science, writing, music, mathematics, literature, social studies, reading, art, and career and occupational development. A sample group was selected consisting of 25,000 nine-year-olds, 28,000 seventeen-year-olds, and 9,000 young adults between the ages of twenty-six and thirty-five. The tests have been administered—and are still administered—to these groups in a continuous cycle, with two subject areas

Figure 12-5

Page from the National Assessment of Educational Progress "Recognizing Literary Works and Characters"

```
                                      Exercise R308

Ages 13, 17, Adult
Objective IA
```

Many people or animals that we read about in books become so well-known that we can name them just from a picture. Above is a picture of a man who appears in a story.

What is the name of the man in the picture?

Write your answer on the line provided.

Sherlock Holmes

	Age 13	Age 17	Adult
Acceptable responses	57.2%	78.5%	75.6%
Unacceptable responses	7.2	4.7	3.2
I don't know.	34.8	15.7	19.9
No response	.8	1.1	1.4

Used with permission of National Assessment of Educational Progress, a project funded by the National Center for Education Statistics and administered by the Education Commission of the States.

being covered each year. The results are reported in terms of geographic region, size of community, type of community, sex, color, and socioeducational background. (No data on specific students, school districts, cities, or states are provided.) The information gives data on general trends (e.g., big cities and small towns are low in science and writing) and specific questions (e.g., only 20 percent of the seventeen-year-olds tested knew that in human females, the egg is released an average of fourteen days after menstruation begins.) Figure 12–5 shows a page from a National Assessment test of ability to recognize literary works and characters.

National Assessment reports supply information about pupil weaknesses

The purpose of the reports is to alert teachers to general areas and specific bits of information that may need special attention if a systematic effort to improve instruction is to be made. You can obtain information about the National Assessment, including a list of all reports and bulletins, by writing to National Assessment of Educational Progress, 1860 Lincoln Street, Suite 300, Denver, Colorado 80203.

Even though no data on specific students or school districts are provided in National Assessment reports, you could easily personalize things by devising your own tests to parallel or supplement the measuring instruments developed by the experts on the National Assessment staff. As a matter of fact, you could probably learn quite a bit about testing if you used National Assessment questions as models to follow.

The hypothetical space satellite situation and the critique of *Wadja-get?* call attention to the fact that the grades students earn in school play a significant role in vocational choice, in the development of identity, and in the determination of a young person's future life. Therefore, you will want to do your best to make the grades you assign as fair and accurate as possible. Techniques for accomplishing these goals are discussed in the next chapter.

SUMMARY OF KEY POINTS

All technological societies use one means or another to identify capable students. In America the grade point average is one of the most widely used measures of student performance. The fact that a pupil's GPA is based on many kinds of performance over a period of years provides opportunities for multiple chances for an individual to correct for weaknesses, and eventually succeed. At the same time, grades may be open to criticism if they are unnecessarily subjective, restrictive, divisive, and competitive. To correct for unfortunate aspects of grading, critics argue that efforts should be made to reduce anxiety and competition and to make grades more meaningful to students.

One advantage of grades is that they may serve as a self-controlled basis for success. Another advantage is that grades provide students, teachers, and employers with accurate information about individual pupil strengths and weaknesses. A potential danger of stress on strict evaluation is that the GPA is not always an accurate indication of a student's true academic ability. For that reason, test scores are usually considered along with grades when students must be classified.

Achievement tests are designed to measure how much has been learned about a subject. Aptitude tests provide estimates of potential ability. Before interpreting standardized test scores, it is important to estimate the validity and reliability of the test. *Content validity* refers to how well the test items cover a particular type of learning. *Construct validity* refers to how accurately a test measures a particular attribute. *Reliability* refers to how consistent scores are if the test is taken again by the same pupils. Standardized test scores are more likely to be valid and reliable if those who give the tests scrupulously follow instructions for administering them.

Scores on standardized tests may be reported in a variety of ways. Grade equivalent scores indicate a pupil's performance with reference to grade levels. Percentile ranks tell the percentage of scores that are at or below a given score. Standard scores are based on the standard deviation interpreted by referring to a normal curve. The z score tells how far a raw score is from the mean of a distribution in terms of standard deviation (SD) units. The T score indicates the position of a particular score in numerical terms based on standard deviation units. Stanine scores indicate a pupil's placement within one of nine half-SD subdivisions of the normal curve.

Some standardized tests are designed to measure a student's scholastic aptitude or intelligence. There has been a great deal of controversy in the United States about the use of these tests—and about the meaning of "intelligence"—because of the impact of the environmental view of determinism. Arthur Jensen has suggested that heredity establishes the limits of a person's intelligence. Other psychologists argue that IQ tests discriminate against minority-group children and cause them to appear less intelligent than they really are.

Discussions of intelligence are often complicated by the fact that there is no universally agreed-upon definition of this quality. Some theorists believe that intelligence consists of a single general ability; others maintain that there are several specific factors that make up what is called intelligence. The measurement of intelligence is complicated by the fact that IQ scores of individuals tested over the years rarely stay the same. Because of the problems of obtaining valid and reliable measures of intelligence, many educators believe that IQ tests should no longer be given in the schools. The main argument in support of this policy is that low test scores (which may not be accurate) could lead to unfortunate self-fulfilling prophecy reactions.

Although test scores sometimes cause pupils to be improperly classified and educated, information about intelligence may be used in positive ways, particularly when an analysis of student strengths and weaknesses make it possible to individualize instruction. J. P. Guilford was one of the first psychologists to propose a detailed description of types of intellectual abilities. He pointed out that students vary in their abilities to comprehend, memorize, and evaluate. He also noted that some pupils are convergent thinkers, others are divergent thinkers. Recognition of differences in student abilities has led to Aptitude-Treatment-Interaction: the attempt to match pupil styles and abilities to forms of instruction. Although ATI makes sense at a theoretical level, it may be difficult to actually put into practice because students can rarely be classified into distinct types. Until ATI research yields more detailed information of use to teachers, it may be preferable for instructors to use National Assessment reports as a guide for identifying pupil strengths and weaknesses.

SUGGESTIONS FOR FURTHER STUDY

12-1

Experiences with Standardized Tests

Do you recall taking a standardized test that seemed exceptionally well or badly administered? (For example, did you ever have a teacher who seemed confused about how to proceed or who made a great show of using a stopwatch or the like?) Do you recall any situation in which the scores you received on a standardized test had undesirable repercussions? (For example, did you ever have a teacher who seemed to evaluate you more in terms of your test profile than on the basis of what you considered your actual performance? Did you find your previously high self-confidence shaken by a low test score and come to doubt your ability to do good work?) After describing any negative or positive experiences you have had with standardized tests, you might draw a "moral" for each experience.

12-2

Taking an Intelligence Test

If you wonder what it is like to take an individual test of intelligence, you might check on the possibility that a teacher of a course in individual testing needs subjects for practice purposes. (In most courses of this type, each student is required to give several tests under practice conditions.) Look in a class schedule for a course in psychology or education designated Individual Testing, Practicum in Testing, or something similar. Contact the instructor and ask whether he or she wants subjects. If you do find yourself acting as guinea pig, jot down your reactions to the test immediately after you take it. Would you feel comfortable about having the score used to determine whether you would be admitted to some program or would qualify for a promotion? Did the test seem to provide an adequate sample of your intelligence? Were the kinds of questions appropriate for your conception of intelligence? You might record your reactions and comments on the implications.

12-3

Evaluating a Standardized Test

In most school systems the selection and use of standardized tests are supervised by a specialist in testing. However, you might wish to make your own evaluation of a test or several alternate tests. To find out the kinds of information available for evaluating standardized tests, examine the seventh *Mental Measurements Yearbook* (1972), edited by O. K. Buros, or one of the publications of UCLA's Center for the Study of Evaluation (listed on page 633). Select two or more tests designed for the same general purpose (by examining the catalogues of test publishers or obtaining sample copies from a test library), and compare them on the basis of the following factors:

Title

Year of publication

Purpose as described by test publisher

Group to which applicable

Cost of test booklets

Cost of answer sheets

Time required

Types of scores

Evidence of validity: size and nature of standardization group, evidence regarding relationship of scores on given test to scores on other tests, and so on

Evidence of reliability: method of estimating consistency of scores, size and nature of sample

Estimate of ease of administration, clarity of instructions, and so on

Kinds of scores and how reported

Comments of reviewers in *Mental Measurements Yearbook* and/or in the publications of UCLA, Center for the Study of Evaluation. (If you do not find a review of a test in the UCLA publications, you might use their list of seven criteria to make your own evaluation.)

After making your comparison, indicate which test you prefer and explain your reasons why.

12-4
Guilford's View of Intelligence

To gain greater insight into J. P. Guilford's factors of intelligence, you might speculate about the significance of his five mental operations—cognition, memory, convergent production, divergent production, and evaluation. Guilford suggests that most forms of evaluations place too much emphasis on only one or two of these operations. As you consider making up tests of your own, give some thought to this point. Were many of the tests you have taken as a student designed to tap only one or two of the operations described by Guilford? Did this have a detrimental effect—and if so, how did it influence you in an undesirable way? How might you avoid or minimize the harmful effects of tests that measure only a limited type of intellectual ability? If you would like to read Guilford's description of his multifactor theory, look for his article "Three Faces of Intellect" in *American Psychologist,* 14 (1959), 469–479, or his book-length analysis in *The Nature of Human Intelligence* (1967).

12-5
Assessing Creative Potential

A number of tests to measure creative potential have been devised, primarily because some studies (e.g., Getzels and Jackson, 1962) indicate that measures of intelligence do not necessarily reflect mental operations associated with creativity. Taking into account different types of intelligence is desirable as a means for broadening the assessment of abilities, but it is possible that a creativity score might *cause* just as many problems as it eliminates. Suppose, for example, that the students in your classes were given a test of creativity and the scores were reported to you. What would you do with them? Would you place children with high scores in special groups or give them special opportunities to demonstrate their ability? Would you evaluate assignments with reference to the scores—that is, look more carefully for signs of creativity in the work of those who earned high scores? Would you distrust your own judgment that the work of a pupil was highly creative if you knew she or he had a low score on the test? Or would you be better off simply encouraging *all* pupils to be as creative as possible and not be concerned about an estimate of creative potential, on the assumption that creativity flourishes when there are abundant opportunities for all individuals to express themselves in their own way? If you are intrigued by the question of the use or abuse of measures of creativity, you might record your observations and perhaps list some guidelines for encouraging free expression that you might apply in your classes.

12–6
Technical Aspects of Testing

If you would like more complete information about group tests of intelligence and achievement, see *Essentials of Psychological Testing* (3rd ed., 1970) by Lee J. Cronbach or *Psychological Testing* (3rd ed., 1968) by Anne Anastasi.

For more complete information on statistics, you might look up one of the following books: *A Primer of Statistics for Non-Statisticians* (1958) by A. N. Frantzblau, *A Simplified Guide to Statistics for Psychology and Education* (1962) by G. M. Smith, *Statistics for the Teacher* (1963) by D. M. McIntosh, *Elementary Statistical Methods in Psychology and Education* (1960) by Blommers and Lindquist, *Statistics for the Classroom Teacher, a Self-Teaching Unit* (1963) by Townsend and Burke, *Evaluating Pupil Growth: Principles of Measurement* (5th ed., 1975) by J. Stanley Ahmann and Marvin Glock, and *Measurement and Evaluation in Teaching* (3rd ed., 1976) by Norman E. Gronlund.

12–7
Aptitude-Treatment-Interaction

For a comprehensive analysis of research on aptitude-treatment-interaction, the best single source is *Aptitudes and Instructional Methods: A Handbook for Research on Interactions* (1975) by Lee J. Cronbach and R. E. Snow.

12–8
National Assessment

For a complete list of National Assessment reports, write to National Assessment of Educational Progress, 1860 Lincoln Street, Suite 300, Denver, Colorado 80203.

Key points

Reducing subjectivity

Halo effect: Tendency for one characteristic to influence all impressions

Cognitive dissonance: Tendency to ignore evidence that is inconsistent

Projection: Tendency to see own undesirable traits in others

Impact of unconscious: May not be aware of reasons for likes and dislikes

Tests: Standard situation, permanent record, fixed criteria

Ways to improve evaluation

Specific goals likely to motivate pupils

Essay exams easy to prepare, hard to score

Reasons for wrong answers may become clear when essay exams are graded

Objective exams difficult to prepare, but can be used many times

Grading of objective exams much less influenced by subjectivity

Almost any pupil will cheat if pressure is extreme

Converting scores into grades

Preparing a frequency distribution

Mean: Arithmetical average, influenced by extreme scores

Median: Middle score, easy to calculate

Comparing pupils is effortful, may discourage low scorers

Learning for mastery

Expectation of a normal distribution leads to low aspirations

Mastery approach: Give pupils multiple opportunities to master goals at own pace

Selecting objectives before writing exams has many advantages

Availability of a study guide opens up many options

Plus-minus grading of answers simplifies evaluation

Chapter 13

Evaluating classroom learning

Aₛ NOTED in Chapter 12, there is not much point in engaging in a debate on the issue "Should grades be retained?" That question was considered in the late 1960s, and many schools went through experiences similar to those described in *Wad-ja-get?* Educational institutions of all types experimented with credit/no credit or pass/fail alternatives to letter grades. By the mid-1970s most of these less stringent forms of evaluation had been dropped in favor of a return to traditional letter grades, for reasons mentioned at a number of places in previous chapters: Scores on standardized tests have revealed that the current generation of students is less well educated than earlier generations. A high rate of unemployment means that individuals must compete for places in graduate school and for jobs. The educational system carries out the preliminary screening of individuals.

As a consequence of these factors, you will almost certainly be expected to assign letter grades or the equivalent when you begin to teach. Since this is the case, the most sensible thing to do is to think about how to minimize the disadvantages of grades and seek ways to make evaluation of student performance as fair and accurate as possible. This chapter offers suggestions you might consult as you strive to make evaluation objective, scientific, related to goals, meaningful, flexible, minimally competitive, and constructive.

Reducing subjectivity

The limitations of personal impressions

To become aware of some of the mechanisms that may cause you to be subjective as you evaluate pupils, imagine for a moment that you decide to base grades not on exams or assignments but solely on personal impressions. If you use only your personal impressions to determine whether a student gets an A or an F, the only way to find out what your pupils are thinking is to listen to their comments in class discussion or notice how they react to your questions. But how many pupils out of a class of thirty are going to be able to recite frequently? And if you ask questions, how will you pick out the pupil to call on?

Suppose you call on students in alphabetical order. The first pupil on your roll sheet gets the first question, and it's an easy one. What's more, it's early in the day, and you are in a good mood. Everyone can answer the question, but you don't know this as you make a mental note that the top-of-the-alphabet student responded correctly. By the time you get to the last student on the list, you are tired and irritable and ask an extremely difficult question. He or she can't answer it. No one else in the class can either, but you aren't aware of that. Or suppose the luckless tail-ender gives a series of brilliant answers during the first part of the grade period but the day before grades are due says something utterly stupid. All those favorable impressions might be wiped out by one unfortunate blooper that sticks in your mind.

Or suppose a boy says something stupid the first day, reminding you that one of the less charitable teachers in your school once labeled him the dumbest student encountered in twenty years. Your first impression is likely to be "This one really *is* a lunkhead." No matter what that boy says during the rest of the year, you may think of him as a lunkhead and interpret his remarks accordingly.

Another student, on the other hand, is a girl who makes a good first impression. Everything she says seems to be a pearl of wisdom because she is attractive, neat, friendly, polite, and attentive; because one of her parents is a surgeon; and because she just won an essay contest.

Compare this pupil to the son of the police officer who just gave you a ticket for going forty-five in a twenty-five-mile zone. Suppose the same boy is given to nose picking, a habit you have always found obnoxious, and looks alarmingly like a rough kid who gave you a bloody nose when you were in the third grade.

These are just a few of the factors that will influence your judgments. Do you think you could still be fair in evaluating the students? Some teachers insist that they *can* allow for all such factors. Many of these influences are so subtle, however, that a person is not aware of them, and you can't allow for something you are unconscious of. Specific mechanisms affect the perceptions of different individuals when they react to each other.

Mechanisms that contribute to subjectivity

Halo effect: Tendency for one characteristic to influence all impressions

Halo effect There is a tendency for prior information, or one impression or characteristic, to influence all other impressions. In the examples just given, a positive halo was induced by a student's appearance and background, which perhaps were associated with stereotypes. A negative halo was attached to a student because of a remark made by another teacher, the student's resemblance to a childhood nemesis, and a disagreeable habit.

Cognitive dissonance: Tendency to ignore evidence that is inconsistent

Cognitive dissonance   We like to think that our attitudes and beliefs form a consistent, logical pattern. If we are exposed to evidence that might lead to incongruities or inconsistencies in our perceptions, we make an effort to reduce this "dissonance," either by perceiving selectively or by supplying an explanation. Once a halo has been established, there will be a tendency to pick out things that fit under it and ignore those that don't. If one of your favorites says something dumb, you can either forget it or excuse it. If a student you have come to think of as dull says something brilliant, you attribute it to luck or to help from someone else.

Projection: Tendency to see own undesirable traits in others

Projection   Sigmund Freud pointed out that we are prone to interpret the behavior of others in terms of traits of our own personality—to project our thoughts and feelings upon others. One of the examples just given mentioned negative feelings about the son of a police officer who gave you a ticket for speeding. If you go forty-five in a twenty-five-mile zone, you are breaking the law and engaging in a form of cheating. A police officer who stops you and gives you a ticket is calling your attention to that fact. Most of us find it difficult to admit that we have done something wrong, so you might strive to protect your ego in such a situation by attributing to others a characteristic you would prefer not to recognize in yourself. Instead of saying to yourself, "I shouldn't have been going that fast and I deserved that ticket," you might look for signs of cheating on the part of others and blame them instead of blaming yourself. The son of the person who reprimanded you would be a perfect target for your feelings of guilt, embarrassment, and anger. You will have twenty-five to thirty potential scapegoats under your control during school hours, and you will constantly be tempted to rationalize your own weaknesses and mistakes by looking for similar types of behavior in your students. If you are honest with yourself, you may sometimes be able to check the tendency to project your inadequacies upon others. Frequently, though, you will not be aware of what you are doing because of the influence of the unconscious.

Unconscious likes and dislikes   One of Freud's major contributions to psychology was his revelation of the importance of the unconscious. As Freud pointed out, only a small fraction of our memories and experiences are within the scope of consciousness—that is, capable of being thought of at will. Many more of our experiences are in the realm of the unconscious. They persist as memories and may influence our behavior, but they cannot be examined or understood because we are not aware of them.

All of us have certain likes and dislikes in regard to physical and personality traits. Some of these we think we understand: "I don't like kids with red hair and freckles because the bully who used to beat me up every other day when I was in the third grade had red hair and freckles." But many other preferences or aversions are based on memories we are not aware of. It is therefore impossible for anyone to be completely fair or unprejudiced in reacting to others. You may be able to handle some of your conscious prejudices, but the far more numerous unconscious influences are beyond your control.

Impact of unconscious:
May not be aware of
reasons for likes and
dislikes

The impact of teacher expectation

The halo effect, cognitive dissonance, projection, and unconscious likes and dislikes all influence the way teachers respond to pupils, and teacher responses may shape pupil behavior, leading to self-fulfilling prophecy reactions. The self-fulfilling prophecy reaction (or Pygmalion effect) has been described previously, but it merits mention again at this point because it illustrates subjectivity on the part of both teacher and pupil.

In a review of articles on teacher expectation, Carl Braun (1976) summarizes and analyzes research on the self-fulfilling prophecy. He explains how the publication of Rosenthal and Jacobson's *Pygmalion in the Classroom* in 1968 triggered dozens of replications. After summarizing these studies, Braun reports that the results are contradictory: Some replications support the hypothesis that what teachers expect influences pupil behavior; other studies do not. Braun agrees with J. D. Finn (1972), who carried out an earlier review of teacher expectation studies, that one way to explain conflicting evidence regarding the Pygmalion effect is to take into account the *interaction* of variables. A teacher may be influenced not just by a single test score, but by a test score, plus appearance, plus grades assigned by other teachers, and so forth.

Braun's review of the studies on each of several factors that might create high or low teacher expectations led to the following findings:

Attractive children are often perceived by teachers to be brighter, more capable, and more social than unattractive children.

Teachers tend to approve of girls' behavior more frequently than they approve of boys' behavior.

Middle-class pupils are expected (by college students in education classes) to receive higher grades than lower-class students.

Teachers are more influenced by negative information about pupils (e.g., low test scores) than they are by neutral or positive information.

Female teachers tend to perceive the behavior of girls as closer to the behavior of "ideal students" than do male teachers.

Teachers appear to spend more time and to interact more frequently with high achievers than with low achievers.

High-achieving pupils receive more praise than low-achieving ones.

After reviewing these findings, Braun developed the diagram reproduced in Figure 13–1 to illustrate several ways pupil characteristics might initially influence teacher perceptions and how teacher reactions (based on those perceptions) might shape pupil behavior.

Because of the influence of the halo effect, cognitive dissonance, projection, and the influence of unconscious likes and dislikes, you will need to make a concerted effort to be fair to your students, not only in evaluating their academic performance preparatory to assigning grades but in all of your interactions with them. Braun's diagram calls attention to many of the variables that might cause you to react positively or negatively to pupils: name, ethnic background, sex, socioeconomic status (SES), physical characteristics, knowledge of siblings, grades recorded on report cards, test scores recorded in cumulative folders. (For elementary grade students, impressions of parents might be added to the "input" cluster at the top of Figure 13–1.)

Factors such as the ones listed at the top of Figure 13–1 may influence you to develop a perception of a particular pupil that will cause you to treat that individual in positive or negative ways. If you had difficulties controlling a boy's older brother, you may expect the younger sibling to be disruptive also, and you may be primed to censure him for the slightest sign of mischief. If another boy is unattractive and has a name and physical characteristics that identify him as a member of a minority group that was ridiculed in condescending ways by friends or relatives throughout your childhood, you may tend to ignore him during class discussions and unwittingly use tougher grading standards to "produce" appropriately low scores on his exams. If you are favorably impressed by an attractive girl's parents and discover that she earned all A's on the previous year's report card, you may smile effusively when calling on her in class (conveying the message that you are expecting an excellent answer) and gloss over inadequacies in her test answers in your haste to assign an A grade.

The diagram Braun developed to illustrate teacher-pupil interactions calls attention to these guidelines for teachers:

1. Try to control the influence of such factors as name, ethnic background, sex, physical characteristics, knowledge of siblings or parents, grades, and test scores. If you think you can be honest with yourself, you might attempt to describe your prejudices so that you will be in a position to try to guard against them. (Do you tend to be

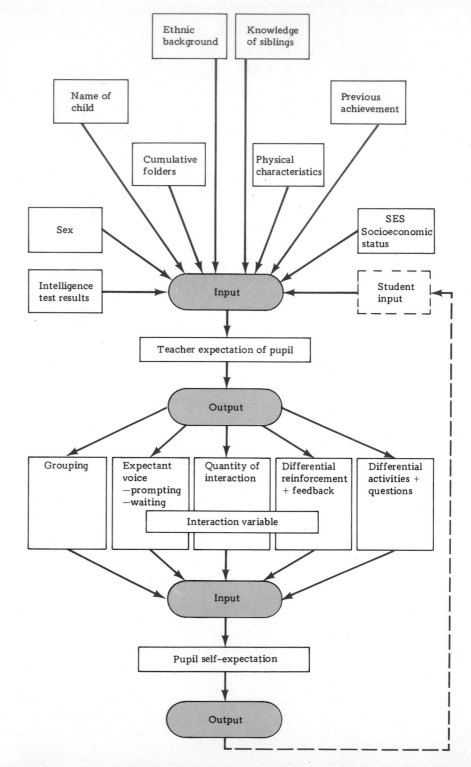

Figure 13-1

The behavioral cycle between teacher input and learner output

Carl Braun, "Teacher Expectation: Sociopsychological Dynamics," *Review of Education Research*, vol. 46, no. 2 (Spring 1976), fig. 1, p. 206. Copyright © 1976, American Educational Research Association, Washington, D.C.

annoyed when you read descriptions of the exploits of members of a particular religious or ethnic group, for example?) Try to think of a pupil independently of her or his siblings and parents.

Handbook heading
Maintaining a Question
and Recitation Record

2. Make a well-planned effort to be fair and consistent in the way you interact with pupils. Keep a Question and Recitation Record to ensure that you call on all pupils in class about the same number of times. Strive to be consistently positive and enthusiastic when asking questions or responding to answers. (Don't hesitate or introduce vocal inflections when calling on less capable pupils. Such public signs of hesitation or lack of confidence may be communicated to the pupil and to classmates.)

Handbook heading
Keeping a Positive
Reinforcement Record

3. Keep a Positive Reinforcement Record in an effort to say favorable things about the work of all pupils. If you discover, after keeping such a record for two weeks, that you have not said a single positive thing to one or more students, make it a point to praise those pupils at least as regularly as others.

4. If you become aware of a pupil's previous low grades or are presented with low test scores, give individuals identified as poor learners the benefit of the doubt. Use the information to try to help low-scoring pupils improve their classroom performance (by using techniques to be discussed later in this chapter), and keep in mind that many factors (e.g., anxiety, misunderstanding instructions) may artificially lower test scores.

5. Strive to reduce the impact of subjectivity and negative expectations by taking advantage of the characteristics of tests.

Testing is such a basic way to control subjectivity that it merits detailed coverage.

Characteristics of tests

Tests: Standard
situation, permanent
record, fixed criteria

Standard situation   On most tests all students are required to answer the same questions. This standardization eliminates the situation in which one student, through the luck of the draw, gets an easy question and a less fortunate student gets a difficult one.

Permanent record of behavior   Written exams mean answers recorded in permanent form. If you rely on intuitive reactions to class recitation, then projection, the halo effect, and cognitive dissonance can run wild. The example of a pupil who says something stupid late in the report period, wiping out previous good impressions, illustrates only one possible error. All impressions based on casual observation and recorded only in memory are susceptible to selective perception. Remember that memory is being exposed to the influence of the unconscious. Having a permanent answer to scrutinize doesn't guarantee avoidance of the influence of the psychological mechanisms just discussed, but it does let you go back over your evaluation several times if necessary, in an effort to eliminate the influence of transitory moods and feelings. You can't do that with a recollection that was distorted and limited by the subjective factors to begin with and is vulnerable to further distortion by subsequent events.

Handbook heading
Taking Advantage of
Test Characteristics

Fixed set of criteria   When you ask all pupils to react to the same questions and you have their answers in permanent form, you can compare each answer to a fixed criterion. In most cases when you prepare exams, you should devise a key to the correct answers, indicating how many points each part of an answer is worth. Then you can compare each test to the key. If you take care not to look at the student's name on the first page of the test, the influence of such factors as name, facial features, habits, and other prejudicial conditions or situations is eliminated. There are still potential contaminating factors—handwriting, grammar, sentence structure—but if you can make an effort to remain aware of them, their influence can often be reduced to such an extent that they have no significant impact on the final score.

The purpose of this survey has been to convince you that formal testing procedures can yield fairer and more accurate evaluations than unsystematic observations. For these advantages of tests to work out in practice, though, evaluation must be carried out under the best possible conditions. The next section discusses techniques you might use to create favorable conditions.

The values of stating objectives

Reconsider for a moment the Taxonomy of Educational Objectives Handbook I: Cognitive Domain, first mentioned in the discussion of instructional objectives in Chapter 8. The six major classes in the taxonomy are:

Knowledge—Can students recall information?

Comprehension—Can students explain ideas?

Application—Can students use ideas?

Analysis—Do students see relationships?

Synthesis—Can students combine ideas?

Evaluation—Can students make judgments?

All six categories reflect evaluations of one kind or another, and the last class is directly concerned with them. This slant is not surprising because the psychologists who developed the taxonomy were members of a committee of college and university examiners interested in improving assessment procedures. The evaluation emphasis of the authors is revealed by an important feature of the book—illustrative test items at the end of each section of the taxonomy (another argument in favor of your buying the book).

Handbook heading
Using Objectives to
Improve Evaluation

In Chapter 8 you were invited to use the taxonomy as a basis for developing specific goals for your classes. At this juncture you are asked to make it a basis for determining whether or not your goals have been reached. In considering these two ideas—goals and evidence that goals have been reached—you will find it instructive to compare again the S-R, cognitive, and humanistic views. The S-R theorist, who favors programmed learning, starts out by describing the desired terminal behavior. The program is written to lead the student to this very specific goal (e.g., knowing how to spell *manufacture,* understanding how a flashlight works). All is simple and straightforward. Things are not nearly so precise for advocates of the discovery approach or of humanistic education. The goals of discovery units are often difficult to pin down (e.g., understanding humanity). The goals of humanistic education are essentially unmeasurable (e.g., meaningful existence). Since the goals are so vague, it may be next to impossible to determine whether they have been achieved.

If you have been favoring discovery and humanistic approaches over programmed learning, take a moment to analyze the values of more structured learning experiences in relation to the potential advantages of grades discussed earlier. Generally speaking, a programmed approach is more likely to make the most of those advantages than a less structured learning situation is.

Goals to strive for in improving evaluation

Certain goals to strive for in improving evaluation emerge from the foregoing examination of the problems of substituting personal impressions for more formal evaluation procedures, the mechanisms that interfere with objectivity, the characteristics of tests, and the values of stating objectives. Other goals can be derived from the analysis of advantages and disadvantages of evaluation described in the preceding chapter. If you are eager to improve evaluation procedures you might:

Do everything possible to arrange evaluation experiences so that they lead to feelings of success.

Minimize public comparisons and competition among students.

Be aware that learning ability is not the same in all pupils, but use this knowledge to give extra assistance to those who need it.

Do everything possible to make evaluations fair and objective. Guard against the halo effect, cognitive dissonance, projection, and the impact of unconscious likes and dislikes.

Make the most of the characteristics of tests; provide a standard situation; obtain records of performance in permanent form; compare student performance to a fixed set of criteria.

Try to use tests so that they emphasize the reinforcement of correct responses and do not punish wrong responses.

Arrange evaluation so that it identifies omissions and weaknesses that need to be corrected before the student moves on to more advanced material.

Try to use evaluation as a motivating device by encouraging students to set and achieve respectable (and realistic) goals.

Stress the importance of establishing and meeting standards. As much as possible, use tests to promote self-competition and improvement.

Set up exams so that they provide feedback for you to use in improving instruction.

When appropriate, state specific instructional objectives, determine if they have been reached, and take steps to supply remedial instruction.

Do everything possible to reduce pressure and tension.

Try to make tests functional in the sense that students recognize or are made aware that the information requested is being learned for good reasons.

Suggestions for teaching: Ways to improve evaluation

The suggestions that follow are intended to help you to control the influence of the mechanisms that lead to subjectivity, to take advantage of the favorable characteristics of tests, and to achieve goals just listed for improving evaluation.

1. As early as possible in a report period, decide when and how often to give tests.

    a. Consider distributing a course outline on the first day of class. (Remember the value of goals.)

    b. Announce tests and other assignments well in advance. Give a detailed description of what will be covered, how it will be evaluated, and how much it will count toward a final grade.

    c. Be considerate in scheduling.

2. Prepare a content outline of the materials to be covered on each exam, and take care to test on each part. (Doing this will enable you to get a good sample.)

    a. Take into account the kinds of terminal behavior you hope to achieve.

    b. Select the type or types of questions most likely to measure the desired terminal behavior accurately and efficiently.

3. Make up the questions, aiming for clarity, objectivity, and ease of grading.

    a. Be certain the instructions and questions are clearly understood. (Doing this will help provide a standard situation.)

    b. Do your best to write questions that reduce subjectivity to a minimum and are relatively easy to score.

4. Make up and use a detailed key.

    a. Evaluate each answer by comparing it to the key.

    b. Be willing and able to defend the evaluations you make.

5. When grading is completed, analyze, if possible, each question, in an effort to improve future exams.

1. As early as possible in a report period, decide when and how often to give tests.

    a. Consider distributing a course outline on the first day of class. (Remember the value of goals.)   The response from your students will be more positive if, on the first day of class, you take the trouble to describe the organization of a given unit or course and provide information on all tests and assignments. (The reasons for doing this were discussed in the analysis of instructional objectives in Chapter 8.) Students will feel more comfortable if they have such an outline and will be more motivated to get to work. In addition, *you* will benefit from having a clear idea of what you hope to accomplish. You not only will be better organized but perhaps also will avoid the agony and inefficiency of making up exams on the spur of the moment.

Handbook heading
Outlining Units of
Study

    b. Announce tests and other assignments well in advance. Give a detailed description of what will be covered, how it will be evaluated, and how much it will count toward a final grade.   If the test is to be used as a learning device as well as a means of evaluation, provide specific goals. If you are coy or absentminded, you may discourage careful study. Consider these two announcements and imagine how you might react to each: "We'll have an exam in a week or so; it, uh, will cover, uh, everything we've discussed so far." "We'll have an exam next Wednesday; it will be on the material covered in class starting with the topic of _____, and on pages 216 through 275. There will be five short-answer, essay questions and a fifteen-item matching question on that mimeographed outline I handed out." Which set of goals would look more attainable to you? Which would be more likely to motivate you to actually prepare for the exam? Suppose the first teacher then gave you a fifty-item true-false test on a twenty-five page section of the text (out of 400 pages covered so far), whereas the second gave you exactly the kind of test described. How would you feel about each class the next time an exam was scheduled? What would be your attitude toward doing a conscientious job of studying for each class?

Specific goals likely to motivate pupils

For the most part, it seems preferable to announce tests well in advance. Pop quizzes tend to increase anxiety and tension and to force students to cram on isolated sections of a book on a day-by-day and catch-as-catch-can basis. Simple homework assignments or the equivalent will encourage more careful and consistent study than pop quizzes. When tests are announced, it is comforting to students to know exactly what material they will be held responsible for, what kinds of questions will be asked, and how much a given test or assignment will count toward the final grade.

Handbook heading
Announcing Tests and Assignments in Advance

If you assign term papers or other written work, list your criteria for grading the papers (e.g., how much emphasis will be placed on style, spelling and punctuation, research, individuality of expression?). In lab courses most students prefer a list of experiments or projects and some description of how they will be evaluated (e.g., ten experiments in chemistry, fifteen drawings in drafting, five paintings in art, judged according to posted criteria).

Handbook heading
Being Considerate in Scheduling

c. Be considerate in scheduling. You may reduce antagonism toward tests if you are thoughtful about scheduling them—or about scheduling deadlines for other assignments. For one thing, it is a bit unfair to have exams on Monday. Students ought to be able to enjoy the weekend without having the threat of an exam to nag them. Another unreasonable tactic is to set the deadline for a term paper or project the day after a vacation.[1] It's human nature to put off some things until the last minute, and the guilt and uneasiness aroused by procrastination can spoil an entire holiday. In the upper grades you might also consider such occasions as a big game, a dance, or elections. If possible, allow students to choose between two or three dates you have selected for exams or deadlines so that the majority can pick a day when they will not be loaded down with other assignments.

---

[1] In end-of-course evaluations at the college level, a significant number of students have reported that they appreciate prevacation deadlines—even though they may at first be irritated at the thought of getting to work early in a quarter or semester.

2. Prepare a content outline of the materials to be covered on each exam, and take care to test on each part. (Doing this will enable you to get a good sample.)

a. Take into account the kinds of terminal behavior you hope to achieve.   If you have drawn up lesson plans or otherwise described the terminal behavior you are aiming for, you already have such an outline. If you have not done this by the time the first test is due, it is almost essential to make amends at that point. The more precisely and completely goals are described at the beginning of a unit, the easier and more efficient evaluation (and teaching) will be. Using a clear outline will help assure an adequate sample of the most significant kinds of behavior.

When the time comes to assess the abilities of your pupils, you can't possibly observe and evaluate all relevant behavior. You can't listen to more than a few pages of reading by each first grader or ask history students to discuss on an exam more than a few pages of the hundred or so assigned. Because of the limitations imposed by large numbers of students and small amounts of time, your evaluation will have to be based on a *sample* of behavior—a three- or four-minute reading performance, questions covering perhaps one-tenth of the material assigned for an exam. It is therefore important to obtain a representative, accurate sample.

Handbook heading

Obtaining an Accurate Sample of Pupil Behavior

EXAMPLES

At the elementary level, perhaps the report card (if your school uses a detailed list of skills and abilities) can serve as the basis for determining what you will evaluate.

If a test is on material presented in class, outline what you have covered, and make up questions from each section.

If the test is on text material, ask questions from every part of the assigned reading, including at least one question from every major section of the book.

b. Select the type or types of questions most likely to measure the desired terminal behavior accurately and efficiently.   The cognitive and affective taxonomies of educational objectives will help you decide what kinds of questions to use. For example, mastery of knowledge can be measured most efficiently by objective tests. Application of skills and ideas can be measured best by performance tests. Objectives centering around analysis, synthesis, or evaluation are appropriate topics for essay exams. If you are systematic about listing goals, with or without the use of the taxonomies, you will probably discover that no single kind of question is appropriate for all types of learning. This is often an advantage, since it provides a wider base for evaluation and is likely to reduce feelings of pressure somewhat.

EXAMPLES

On many elementary school report cards, a pupil is not given an overall mark in reading but is graded on oral reading, reading speed, comprehension, and so on.

In English the grade might be based both on ability to write themes and on understanding of grammar and punctuation as measured by a formal test.

In a physical education class, you might grade on knowledge of the rules of the game as well as performance.

In a biology class, pupils might be graded on their ability to handle a microscope or do a dissection as well as on knowledge of the text.

When the time comes to decide what kinds of questions to use and how many of each type, you may be tempted to settle for those that are easiest to write or that you personally preferred as a student. A better procedure is to look over the following points contrasting essay and objective tests. Most test items are variations of these two basic types of questions, and the listing below indicates the advantages and disadvantages of each type. The seven points are from *Essentials of Educational Measurement* by Robert L. Ebel. (For more detailed information you are urged to read the book, which is an exceptionally clear analysis of evaluation.) Ebel seems to be writing here primarily about the comprehensive essay exam.

An essay test question requires the student to plan his own answer and to express it in his own words. An objective test item requires him to choose among several designated alternatives. (1972, p. 123)

An essay test consists of relatively few, more general questions which call for rather extended answers. An objective test ordinarily consists of many rather specific questions requiring only brief answers. (p. 126)

Students spend most of their time in thinking and writing when taking an essay test. They spent most of their time reading and thinking when taking an objective test. (p. 130)

Essay exams easy to prepare, hard to score

An essay examination is relatively easy to prepare but relatively tedious and difficult to score accurately. A good objective examination is relatively tedious and difficult to prepare but relatively easy to score accurately. (p. 131)

An essay examination affords much freedom for the student to express his individuality in the answer he gives, and much freedom for the scorer to be guided by his individual preferences in scoring the answer. An objective examination affords much freedom for the test constructor to express his knowledge and values but gives the student only the freedom to show, by the proportion of correct answers he gives, how much or how little he knows or can do. (p. 131)

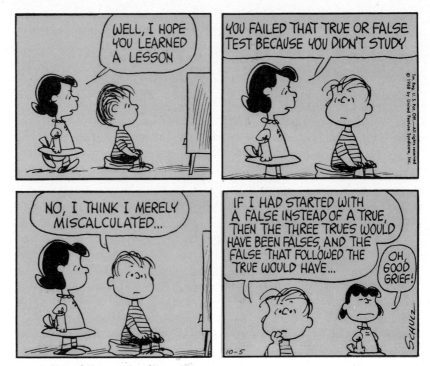

An essay test permits, and occasionally encourages, bluffing. An objective test permits, and occasionally encourages, guessing. (p. 136)

The distribution of numerical scores obtained from an essay test can be controlled to a considerable degree by the grader; that from an objective test is determined almost entirely by the test. (p. 137)

If the term *essay exam* is expanded to include short-answer essay as well as comprehensive essay, the following seven points of comparison might be added to those noted by Ebel:[2]

Reasons for wrong answers may become clear when essay exams are graded

[1] In scoring an essay exam, the teacher gains insight into how and why a student gave a wrong answer. This provides specific and valuable information that can be used in a variety of ways. Scoring an objective test usually indicates only that a student selected a wrong answer; it does not reveal the line of thought that led to its choice (though a separate analysis may be made later).

[2] An essay test is likely to be analyzed in some detail, particularly since it is rather easy to go over the test with the entire class in a short period of time. On a multiple-choice test, frequently only the

---

[2] Many of these points are derived from observations made by Banesh Hoffmann in *The Tyranny of Testing*, a searching analysis of the possible dangers of too much concern for "objectivity" in evaluation.

score is reported to students because reviewing all the questions in class or individually would be prohibitively time consuming. To do the job properly, you would need to explain—for each question—why the right alternative was correct and why the three or four wrong alternatives were incorrect.

[3] The secretarial aspects of preparing essay tests are fairly undemanding, especially if the questions can be written on the board. The secretarial task of preparing objective tests, particularly multiple-choice tests, is often burdensome. If no secretarial help is available, it may take hours to type up stencils and run off, collate, and number the exams (numbering is necessary to check for missing copies).

[4] Essay questions are usually easy to remember. This fact increases the possibility that students in one class will pass on the entire contents of a test to students in other classes. Consequently, it may be unfair to use the same assortment of essay questions more than once, a circumstance that limits the chance of improving a test for future use and also makes comparisons between classes less precise. Objective (especially multiple-choice) questions are harder to memorize and pass on to other students, so an objective test can be used, improved, and used again, and the same test can be given to more than one class.

Objective exams difficult to prepare, but can be used many times

[5] Teachers who use essay tests spend the bulk of their exam time reading student answers. This is an undeniably tedious job but does provide insight into faulty generalizations, misinterpretations, and omissions that can lead to better instruction and student performance. Teachers who use objective tests spend the bulk of their exam time writing questions—and perhaps doing secretarial chores. With multiple-choice tests the greatest amount of time is devoted to devising *wrong* answers. This activity is not likely to help instruction, although it may improve testing.

[6] Since an essay exam is open to a certain amount of adjustment in the way answers are scored, the result may be higher student morale; but it should be recognized that re-evaluations are highly vulnerable to the halo effect, cognitive dissonance, and projection—even though teachers do their best to control for them. Answers to objective questions are usually nonnegotiable. This inflexibility may cause a certain amount of resentment, but it does eliminate subjectivity.

Grading of objective exams much less influenced by subjectivity

[7] On essay tests, it is possible to give a student credit for a "lukewarm" answer. Such adaptability tends to reduce anxiety and pressure and also permits the grader to give partial credit for reasoning. On objective tests, some right answers may be chosen for completely illogical reasons; some wrong answers for logical, defensible, and ingenious reasons. These responses may occur with only a few

questions, and the errors may not alter the total score significantly, but awareness of this aspect of objective testing will bother some students to the point of bitterness, especially if they are not given an opportunity to explain their answers.

(A technique for permitting students to explain why they selected certain answers will be described later.)

Short-answer items can often serve as a compromise between multiple-choice and essay questions. They can be especially effective in assisting you in achieving many of the goals mentioned earlier. You provide students with a standard situation, obtain answers in permanent form, and can make up a detailed key to use in evaluating answers, but you also permit a degree of freedom for individual interpretation. In addition, short-answer questions require students to recall information and express it in their own words, which is a more demanding and realistic form of behavior than choosing among alternatives provided by someone else. Furthermore, you will get insight into the thinking that led to misinterpretations and will thus have information you can use to provide specific remedial instruction. This information will not only help the student; it will also help you improve your teaching and your testing.

Quite often you may need to consider practical as well as pedagogical and theoretical factors when deciding which types of test questions to use. You may feel at the moment, for example, that essay questions are preferable to multiple choice in terms of measuring understanding and allowing opportunities for individual expression of ideas. But if you must give several exams each report period to five different sections of thirty secondary school students each, you may find that you do not have the time or patience to grade thousands of essay exams.

When the time comes to actually prepare exams, you might first look for questions supplied by publishers of the texts you are required to use. If such questions are available, you can develop exams simply by selecting an appropriate number of items. You might also use questions supplied by publishers, as well as those included in standardized tests or in National Assessment examinations or booklets, as models to follow when you write your own test items. The niceties of test-item writing are intricate and complex, and you are urged to examine one of the books mentioned in sections 13–6 and 13–7 of the Suggestions for Further Study at the end of this chapter. They contain guidelines to follow when preparing questions. An excellent way to prepare yourself for test writing would be to consult one or more of these books and try your hand at writing some questions, as proposed in Suggestion 13–5. Then you could draw up your own set of guidelines for question writing to be inserted in your Handbook.

Writing good test questions is a fine art, and you are likely to find

Handbook heading
Guidelines for Writing
Test Questions

that your first efforts will cause considerable confusion. Even veterans of twenty or thirty years of test writing still find it difficult to anticipate aspects of a question that will be vague or misleading. Consequently, you will want to make it a habit to evaluate your tests. Many test specialists believe that the best way to do this is to carry out an *item analysis* and select questions that discriminate most effectively between high and low scores. Although the process of selecting items that discriminate and rejecting those that do not makes sense if the aim is to highlight differences in the test-taking abilities of students, it has limitations when it is examined from a pedagogical point of view—or from an operant conditioning position. The aim of a teacher should be to help as many students as possible to learn as much as possible. In this sense, exams function not only as evaluation devices but also as programs. And programs should be written to maximize the proportion of correct answers. If there are too few questions that most students (particularly the less able ones) can answer, the students most in need of encouragement are reinforced the least. When exams are thought of as programs, items (frames) that help almost all students to realize they understand the point should be retained, not eliminated.

In analyzing the effectiveness of the questions you write, you might use *clarity* as the primary criterion. If a question makes it possible for students to explain to you (and to themselves) that they understand an objective, retain it. If it causes confusion, either reject it or examine the errors and misinterpretations and rewrite it. This is not intended as a suggestion that you make questions artificially easy, just that you do everything possible to make them clear.

3. Make up the questions, aiming for clarity, objectivity, and ease of grading.

a. Be certain the instructions and questions are clearly understood. (Doing this will help provide a standard situation.)   The first of the test characteristics mentioned previously was that all students are in the same (standard) situation. With essay tests this is the case only if all pupils interpret the questions in essentially the same way. To help guarantee such response, try to refine out all traces of ambiguity when you make up questions.

At first, in constructing tests you may tend to make questions rather vague, rationalizing that the brighter students will know what you want and that interpreting the question properly is a measure of their ability. This is not necessarily a valid argument. Some students may misinterpret a question and write an excellent "wrong" answer. Then you face a dilemma: Should you give credit for such an answer or give a zero because what you expected was not forthcoming? After a certain amount of pondering, punctuated by loud squeals of protest from outraged victims, you may become convinced that you are responsible for helping every student understand exactly what is called for. Otherwise, the test becomes a guessing game. It reveals how shrewd pupils are at figuring out what is wanted, not always how much they really know about the subject matter. To avoid this pitfall, try to be complete and specific in writing questions. Even when you have done your best and congratulate yourself that you have removed every trace of ambiguity, probably some pupils *still* won't get what you are driving at. Therefore, you are urged to clarify exam questions at any time—even after the exam has started.

Some teachers categorically refuse to answer questions about a test that is in progress. There are arguments in favor of this policy if multiple-choice tests are being used, although even then many students appreciate occasional clarification. But with essay tests such a policy may reduce the likelihood of a standard situation and also increase tension. To ease things, urge students to come up and ask for clarification during the test or circulate so that they can ask questions. You might even suggest that they write out a paragraph or two to show you their line of thought so that you can tell them whether they are on the right track.

Students who are a bit tense during an exam tend to act like a drowning person grasping at a straw. If there is a familiar word or phrase in a question, they react to a minor point and madly start writing an answer without reading the rest of the instructions. By going out of your way to clarify questions, you minimize indiscriminate responses. Such reactions indicate nervousness rather than ignorance, and you will come closer to finding out what a student knows if you prevent it.

Handbook heading
Trying to Insure that
Questions are
Understood

b. Do your best to write questions that reduce subjectivity to a minimum and are relatively easy to score.   Multiple-choice and other questions have a clear advantage over essay exams in objectivity and ease of scoring. But even essay exams can be made objective and relatively easy to score by use of a detailed key—also by concealing the name on the paper as you are reading it.

Handbook heading
Preparing a Detailed
Key

4. Make up and use a detailed key.   One of the most valuable aspects of a test is that it permits comparison of the permanently recorded answers of all pupils according to a fixed set of criteria. Use of a complete key can do more to reduce subjective influences than anything else. Such a key can save you time and trouble, not only in grading papers but also in defending your evaluation of questions.

You will often detect misleading words or statements in a question when working out *your* answer to it. What's more, you may be able to clarify what you want and provide a standard format at the same time by the way you arrange a question on the page. Suppose you want students to consider the point under present discussion. If you simply say, "Discuss the importance of using a key," each pupil may take a slightly different approach in what he or she writes. You will have to read each answer very carefully and credit points as each major idea is discussed. This will take a great deal of time. In effect, it will be necessary to analyze the organization of the answer in order to grade the content. A standard organization and format will make grading quicker: You can ask first of all for a discussion of the use of a certain point as it relates to the general characteristics of tests, leave a blank space for the answer (indicating it will be worth five points, say), and do the same for the other subpoints.

a. Evaluate each answer by comparing it to the key.   This suggestion points up the desirability of devising questions and arranging a format in such a way that grading will be easy. Whenever possible, indicate the exact number of points you have awarded to each answer. The more precise your designations, the more satisfied your students will be and the more complete your knowledge of results.

Handbook heading
Defending Evaluations
b. Be willing and able to defend the evaluations you make.   You will probably get few complaints if you have a detailed key and explain to the class how each answer was graded when exams are returned. To a direct challenge about a specific answer to an essay question, your defense might be to show complainers an answer that received full credit and invite them to compare it with their own. If they respond, "I *still* don't see why I didn't get full credit," about all you can say is, "Well, I didn't think you did a complete or clear job in your answer. Take a look at this answer and see if you think yours is as good." You will probably get a reluctant acceptance of the decision, but even if you don't, the attempt may reduce the likelihood of a permanent grudge that might lead to poor work the rest of the report period or year.

A major disadvantage of multiple-choice tests is that they provide so little detailed knowledge of results—and precise, specific knowledge of results is extremely important to efficient learning. It is next to impossible to go over a multiple-choice test in class. At least one student will have picked out each of the wrong alternatives and will want to explain why, while the other members of the class doze or fume as they wait to give *their* explanations—or make out a list of right answers to pass on to someone in another section. Going over a fifty-item test may take hours. It may even take hours with just one student, particularly if he or she is a divergent thinker or argumentative.

A partial solution to this problem is to let students pick out two or three questions they thought they answered correctly and write out an explanation of why they selected an answer different from the one you selected. If their reasoning seems valid, you might give whole or partial credit for the answer. This policy may reduce the resentment and pressure that students associate with multiple-choice tests and also give you the chance to receive feedback. Such knowledge of results can help you improve not only your test questions but also your teaching and the learning efficiency of your students.

5. When grading is completed, analyze, if possible, each question, in an effort to improve future exams. Properly graded exams not only provide students with valuable knowledge of results, they also can give you valuable insight into your skill as a test-maker (and teacher). A basic criterion for judging a test is to check on whether it actually measures what it is intended to measure. To obtain information about the validity of your exams, conduct a post-mortem after each test. Even as you are grading essay exams, you may obtain information about content validity if you recognize that some questions are vague and misleading. It is prudent to record ideas on how to improve questions on your key as you grade papers so that they will be available when you need them later. More information will come from students who register complaints—if you permit them to complain.

Handbook heading
Checking on the
Validity of Exams

With multiple-choice and other objective tests, you are not likely to become aware of which questions are effective and which can be improved unless you carry out a systematic item analysis. Many test specialists do this by grouping students in the top and bottom 27 percent of the class and comparing the way they answered each question. (For books on why one chooses 27 percent and how to go about the analysis, see suggestion 13–7 at the end of the chapter.) Such an analysis will disclose the difficulty of each item and show which questions discriminated best between good and poor students. The obvious drawback to this procedure is the amount of time it takes.

Some testing specialists have suggested that a less onerous way to get the same information is to hand back exams and have students indicate by a show of hands whether they got each question right or wrong. Although this does save the teacher a lot of work, it is potentially embarrassing to students and also maximizes the likelihood that the answers to all the questions will circulate through the school.

An alternative is the invitation that students explain their answers. If students are permitted to explain why they selected certain answers, you will gain insight into ways they interpreted the questions, which will assist you in improving test items and perhaps also in doing a better job of teaching. The straight item-analysis approach does not provide the latter information. In order to use either test-analysis technique, however, you will need to go over the right answers. Although this is most desirable pedagogically, it may be unfortunate from a testing point of view, since students in other classes may get tips on the test, which will tend to reduce its validity. About the only solution is to build up a file of questions and use a slightly different assortment each year.

Should you ever change a grade?

Some teachers categorically refuse to change a grade once a paper has been evaluated and returned. It is argued that teachers will be exposed to too much pressure if they agree to listen to complaints and that the "operators" will talk their way into a higher score through persistence or cajolery while the shy, silent types take their lumps. All this is true, and you can save yourself a lot of trouble if you issue an "all decisions are final" ultimatum, but there are counterarguments.

For one thing, you will almost always have to read papers rapidly. It is possible to skip a key word or phrase in an essay exam or term paper and give an unfairly low score. In addition, you may be tired and irritable toward the end of a grading session and unconsciously toughen your standards. Or, if you grade papers in several separate sessions, you may not maintain a consistent mood or interpretation of the key. Then there is the factor of relativity. Any paper you grade after an exceptionally good (or bad) paper may suffer (or benefit) by comparison.

For all these reasons, consider the use of limited gripe sessions after handing back papers. If you feel a student has a legitimate complaint, you might change the score. If you feel the complainer is a borderline case who is only trying to talk his or her way from a C+ to a B−, you might stay firm. One technique for dealing with an aggressive complainer is to say that you will look over the paper that evening and report back if the score is changed. This eases the pressure you may experience if the student is peering over your shoulder and pushing you hard. If you permit one student to "interpret" what he or she "really meant," you should do the same for all other students—which would be impossible in most cases, unless you permit a five-minute conference for everyone who wants it.

One final point has to do with the defense of different kinds of grades. If you favor an open-ended approach to teaching, perhaps you think you might like to use a single, comprehensive term paper as the basis for the final grade in a course. Suppose you give a young man a B on such a paper, and it turns out that if he had received an A, he might have been admitted to his first-choice college. He asks you to look over the paper again. You do this very carefully but become even more convinced that it deserves a B. You can't pin down all your reasons, but you have a general, intuitive feeling that the paper is definitely not in a class with the papers to which you assigned A's. Consider the way he will feel (and how you will feel) when you try to explain this to him. Then imagine how both of you would feel if you had used quizzes, exams, and several short papers and were able to point to a set of ten numerical scores in your gradebook. If it were possible to show him that his total was thirty points below that of the student who got the lowest A, do you think he would feel less resentful about his grade than he would under the single-paper circumstances?

In evaluating your tests, you must be cognizant of their general level of difficulty. Analyze them to be sure they are not unreasonably difficult. Keep in mind points made in previous chapters in regard to providing goals, the disadvantages of intense competition, and the fact that success is necessary for the development of realistic goals. Making one or two test questions "challenging" is one thing. Going all out to flunk as many students as possible is another. You may discover that you have overestimated the ability of your pupils when you first make up exams, particularly at the high school level. (You may assume that the pupils have as much specialized knowledge of a subject as you have.)

To decide whether your exams are on an appropriate level of difficulty, check for consistency. If some students do an excellent job but most do a poor job, low scores may be due to lack of study. If *all* pupils get low scores, it is probably the teacher who is at fault—because of ineffective presentation, questions that are too hard, overly rigorous scoring, or a combination of these factors. Perhaps the worst consequence of unrealistically difficult exams is that they encourage cheating. Several articles recently published report that the high school student of this era does not feel guilty about cheating. According to some interviewers, cheating is accepted as a matter of course because "everybody does it." The look-out-for-yourself philosophy of American life has been blamed, but probably more fault lies with the emphasis on grades as the basis for entrance to college. Experimental studies of honesty (Hartshorne and May, 1930) reveal that almost anyone will cheat if the pressure is extreme enough. Some people will cheat most of the time, and a few will hardly ever, but practically everyone has a "breaking point." It seems sensible, therefore, to do everything possible to make exams just and reasonable. If you go out of your way to confound the test-takers or if you resort to trickery, you are literally inviting pupils to fight back by cheating.

Few students are so callous that they can ignore feelings of guilt, even if they regard the use of crib sheets or the equivalent as somewhat justified. The probable consequence will be an intensification of negative attitudes toward you and your subject, which will block present and future learning. The best way to avoid this is to be fair and objective about tests and grades. More specifically, give your students questions that will keep them busy. Trying to pick up stray bits of information from a neighbor's paper or from a crib sheet is a time-consuming business. Ask questions that require everyone to write for the entire period.

One more point about cheating: Effective teachers do their best to put temptation behind the pupil. Perhaps you can remember teachers who seemed almost to *encourage* cheating. A more constructive policy is to make a quiet "announcement" if you think you detect skullduggery: "A couple of people seem to be curious about papers other

Almost any pupil will cheat if pressure is extreme

Handbook heading
Ways to Minimize and Handle Cheating

than their own. Let's have independent effort." This warns the back-slider, but in such a way that the situation can usually be handled with a minimum of ill feeling.

Perhaps the most common reason pupils feel obliged to cheat is that they feel they cannot compete successfully against fellow students. Unfortunately, in traditional forms of evaluation, grades are based on comparative standing. Arranging students in order from best to worst not only makes almost all students speculate about ways to increase their scores artificially and illegally but also leads to several other unfortunate by-products. The disadvantages of comparative grading become clear when traditional ways of assigning grades are analyzed.

Converting scores into grades: Traditional approach

Preparing a frequency distribution

The approach to assigning grades that has been most widely used in American education is based on analyses of how measures of pupil performance are distributed. There are several ways to depict a distribution of scores. Perhaps the simplest is to take a sheet of lined paper and list the scores consecutively from lowest to the highest. Then place a tally for each pupil beside the appropriate score (see Figure 13–2). If you are reasonably careful to put the tallies about the same distance from the margin, you will end up with a frequency distribution indicating how the scores are arranged. Just looking at the distribution will provide a good deal of information, but your interpretation of the relative values of the scores will be clarified if you calculate the average score (the *mean*) or the middle score (the *median*). Since the mean and median supply information about the central part of a distribution, they are called *measures of central tendency*.

Calculating a measure of central tendency

The mean   The calculation of the mean was illustrated in Table 12–1, p. 640 (to set the stage for the explanation and illustration of the calculation of the standard deviation presented in Table 12–2). To review, the mean is the arithmetical average compiled by adding up all the test scores and dividing the total by the number of scores. If you have thirty to five-times-thirty pupils listed and an exam (or series of exams) with quite a few points, you are in for a sizable amount of figuring. It's difficult to do a sum like that in your head, and even if you own or have access to a small electronic calculator, the chore may take quite a bit of time. To simplify the job, you might follow the

Figure 13-2

Frequency distribution of scores and computation of the mean

Score	Tally	Number of tallies (f)	Number of tallies times score (fX)
47	I	1	47
46	II	2	92
45	I	1	45
44			
43	I	1	43
42	I	1	42
41	II	2	82
40	I	1	40
39	II	2	78
38	I	1	38
37	II	2	74
36	II	2	72
35	IIII	4	140
34	III	3	102
33	II	2	66
32	II	2	64
31			
30	I	1	30
29	I	1	29
28	I	1	28
27	I	1	27
26			
25	I	1	25
24	I	1	24
		N = 33	Total = 1188

$$\frac{1188}{33} = 36$$

Formula: Mean (M) = $\dfrac{\text{Sum total of scores } (\Sigma fX)}{\text{Number of scores (N)}}$

procedures originally illustrated in Table 13-1 and shown again in Figure 13-2. Multiply each score by the frequency of that score, add those products, and divide by the number of scores.

The mean is often computed by psychologists and test specialists because it is the first step to be followed when calculating a standard deviation (which was explained in Chapter 12). Although a researcher or person developing a standardized test may be interested in interpreting scores with reference to a normal curve (which can be done once standard scores are calculated), most classroom teachers do not share that interest because they hardly ever deal with groups of pupils who are distributed normally. In most classes, there are likely to be "abnormal" numbers of high or low students. Such abnormalities tend to distort the mean as a measure of central tendency because it is influenced by extreme scores. Therefore, you may find that it is preferable to calculate the median rather than the mean. The median not only has the advantage of being immune to the influence of extreme scores, it is much easier to find than the mean.

Mean: Arithmetical average, influenced by extreme scores

Median: Middle score, easy to calculate

The median   The median is the middle score of a distribution, and it can be figured simply by counting tallies. To find the median of the distribution depicted in Figure 13–2, first take the number of scores (33), add 1, and divide by 2. (The reason you add 1 is to find the middle score.) Thirty-four divided by 2 is 17, which means that the seventeenth tally from either the top or the bottom is the middle score in the distribution. If you count the tallies from either end of Figure 13–2, you will hit the score of 35, which is the median for the distribution.

With an odd number of scores, as on the distribution in Figure 13–2, you will always land on the same score when you count from top or bottom. With an even number of scores, you will end up halfway between two tallies that may be opposite different scores, for adding 1 to an even number of scores and dividing by 2 will always yield a 0.5 value. A simple way to allow for this is to circle both tallies that straddle the actual median. (To illustrate, add one more tally to the distribution in Figure 13–2 opposite 44 and then calculate the median. You should arrive at a median of 35.5.)

Converting scores into letter grades

What you eventually do with your distribution of scores and your measure of central tendency depends on several factors. If you favor the goals for improving evaluation mentioned earlier, you will want to avoid—as much as possible—assigning letter grades in a way that exaggerates differences between pupils. In many cases, you will be unable to completely avoid comparisons. In a large school in which several teachers handle multiple sections of a course, a degree of standardization between teacher and classes is often considered necessary. For the assignment of final letter grades to be reasonably fair, the conversion of scores will probably have to be done according to school or department guidelines.

To grasp some of the problems you will face when the time comes to assign grades, imagine that you are either a fourth grade teacher or a tenth grade instructor of five sections of social studies.

If you expect to teach in the elementary grades, assume that you will be asked to assign grades of A, B, C, D, or F for *achievement* and O (Outstanding), S (Satisfactory), or N (Needs improvement) for *effort* in the following subject areas: reading, English, spelling, mathematics, social studies, science, health, music, art, and physical education. Assume that standard texts are used for reading, English, mathematics, social studies, science, and health, and that the publisher of each book has supplied examination materials, most of which take the form of multiple-choice questions. Assume further that you will make up your own short-answer exams and also assign projects of various kinds. Finally, assume that the first of four progress reports is to be presented to the parents in a personal conference; the other three reports are to be recorded on cards to be sent to parents.

You undoubtedly realize at this point that if you hope to assign grades fairly, objectively, and in a manner you can explain and defend to students and parents, you will need to be well organized. You should record some indication of pupil performance in each subject fairly regularly. Otherwise, the day and night (and perhaps early morning) before report cards are due, you will find yourself desperately trying to pull grades out of thin air. Therefore, before the school year starts, it would be wise to take a stab at drawing up a tentative master plan for evaluating each subject on the report card you will be expected to use. It also would be wise to prepare some grade sheets for different subjects.

Chances are that the principal of your school or an experienced colleague will explain that many evaluation standards at the elementary school level are already available. Quite often curriculum materials are arranged in a series of progressively difficult lessons grouped according to grade levels. Test questions and standards to be used in determining if a student has mastered a particular level are often supplied by the publisher of the materials. In some school districts, committees of teachers draw up lists of objectives and specify criteria of successful performance at different grade levels. It is not likely, therefore, that you will have to start from scratch when you begin to formulate plans for coping with elementary school report cards. To evaluate reading achievement, for example, you may be able to use test materials that accompany a series of readers. To evaluate understanding of an orderly and sequential subject such as mathematics, you may be able to use a goal card similar to that illustrated in Figure 10–2, p. 531. To measure performance in spelling, you might find (or be given) a standard list of words with various levels of performance already established (e.g., to earn an A, fourth graders should correctly spell eighteen out of twenty words randomly selected from a standard list). It is likely, however, that you will need to take the primary responsibility for deciding how to evaluate at least some areas of academic performance. And you probably will need to develop some of your own methods for recording evaluations and making distinctions between letter-grade levels.

To help you get some firsthand experience assigning grades by traditional procedures, Figure 13–3 represents a hypothetical page from a fourth grade teacher's grade book (the same teacher who must record grades on the card described earlier). Assume that the information provided is to be used in assigning the first report period grade in social studies. In the first two columns are scores earned by pupils on twenty-item multiple-choice tests supplied by the publisher of the text. (Each item was worth one point.) The third column indicates the score on a ten-item short-answer test you prepared covering material shown in films and analyzed in class. (Each item was graded on a 3-point scale for a total of 30 points.) In the fourth column is the score assigned for an individual project (15 points possible). The "total points" and "grade" columns are left blank in Figure 13–3 so that you can gain some experience computing totals and measures of central tendency, and so that you can assign grades.

Total the scores earned by the students listed in Figure 13–3, make a frequency distribution of the total points, compute the mean and median of the distribution, and assign a grade to each pupil. (In the absence of information about personal characteristics and learning habits of the pupils listed, you cannot grade "effort," but you might at least think about how you would attempt to measure this quality.) After you have computed your totals and measures of central tendency and have assigned grades, compare them to those arrived at by classmates. If you detect discrepancies between totals, means, medians, or grades, explain the procedures you followed to fellow students and invite them to do the same.

If you will be teaching one of the secondary grades, examine Figure 13–4. It represents a page from the grade book of the tenth grade social studies teacher mentioned earlier. Assume that the students whose names and grades are recorded make up a section that has not been grouped in any way: that is, pupils were assigned in a random manner. The first two columns contain scores earned on thirty-item multiple-choice exams. (Each question was worth one point.) The third column indicates the score on an end-of-report-period exam made up of a variety of questions adding up to a total of 60 points. In the fourth column is the numerical score assigned to a term paper or individual study project.

Handbook heading
Using a Numerical
Scale to Grade Papers

Evaluating projects or term papers on a numerical scale is not difficult if you follow this procedure. First, decide how many points

Figure 13-3

Page from a fourth grade teacher's grade book: Scores to be used to determine grade in social studies

	1st Exam (20 pts.)	2nd Exam (20 pts.)	3rd Exam (30 pts.)	Project (15 pts.)	Total Points	Grade
Adams, Ann	15	16	20	10		
Baker, Charles	16	14	23	12		
Cook, Donald	18	18	26	14		
Davis, Rebecca	18	19	28	15		
Evans, Deborah	13	15	14	11		
Ford, Harold	9	10	14	5		
Grayson, Lee	16	14	21	11		
Hood, Barbara	14	14	21	10		
Ingalls, Robert	19	18	27	14		
Jones, Thomas	11	11	19	8		
Kent, Judith	18	17	26	13		
Landis, Karen	15	15	18	9		
Moore, James	14	16	21	10		
Norton, Carl	16	14	22	13		
Orton, John	17	16	23	12		
Peck, Nancy	15	15	22	9		
Quist, Ann	14	14	21	10		
Richards, Mary	15	15	22	11		
Smith, Jerry	16	17	24	12		
Thomas, Eric	12	13	18	9		
Watts, Albert	17	17	25	12		
Vernon, Joan	13	14	20	9		
Zacharias, Saul	15	16	22	13		

the project or paper is to count toward the final grade. (The hypothetical teacher whose grade book is depicted in Figure 13-4 decided to set the term project value as a maximum of 30 points, the same as the first and second exams.) Next, draw up a chart to convert letter grades to numerical values. If you decide that a report should be worth 30 points, figure the cutoff point for an A as 90 percent of 30, the cutoff point for a B as 80 percent, and so forth; then prepare a table like this:

LETTER GRADE	POINTS
A+	29 or 30
A	28
A−	27
B+	26
B	25
B−	24
C+	23
C	22
C−	21
D+	20
D	19
D−	15–18
F	Substantially lower in quality than poorest papers

As you examine projects or read papers, sort them into four piles ranging from poor to excellent. Next, divide each of the four piles into up to three subpiles, depending on the degree of variability of projects or papers. (If one or more papers are substantially poorer in quality than those in the D category, an F is probably justified.) Finally, assign numerical scores by referring to your chart.

The total point and grade columns in Figure 13–4 are left blank, so that you can gain some direct experience computing totals and measures of central tendency and determining grades. If you expect to teach at the secondary grade level, you are urged to total the scores for the students listed in Figure 13–4, make a frequency distribution of the totals, compute the mean and median of the distribution, and assign a grade to each pupil. Then compare your totals, your measures of central tendency, and your grades with those of classmates. If there are discrepancies, explain the procedures you followed, and invite classmates to do the same.

If you take the trouble to compute totals and measures of central tendency and assign grades to the pupils listed in either Figure 13–3 or 13–4, you are likely to discover several things:

1. Figuring grades by comparing total scores can be a rather tedious and time-consuming job. (Keep in mind that elementary grade teachers may be expected to assign grades in six to ten or more subject areas; secondary school teachers may have to fill out report cards for five sections on the same day.)

2. Mistakes in addition and division are common. (It will be surprising if your sum of total scores, mean, and median are the same as those of all other classmates who calculated them.)

Figure 13-4

Page from a secondary school teacher's grade book

	1st Exam (30 pts.)	2nd Exam (30 pts.)	3rd Exam (60 pts.)	Term Project (30 pts.)	Total Points	Grade
Adams, Ann	28	26	56	26		
Baker, Charles	24	23	46	23		
Cook, Donald	22	20	42	22		
Davis, Rebecca	22	23	47	22		
Evans, Deborah	27	28	58	28		
Ford, Harold	14	13	30	20		
Grayson, Lee	21	22	44	22		
Hood, Barbara	25	24	51	26		
Ingalls, Robert	17	16	35	21		
Jones, Thomas	18	18	36	22		
Kent, Judith	29	30	58	29		
Landis, Karen	25	26	56	27		
Moore, James	20	21	40	21		
Norton, Carl	22	24	50	23		
Orton, John	19	18	37	21		
Peck, Nancy	25	24	49	24		
Quist, Ann	25	26	53	27		
Richards, Mary	21	23	44	25		
Smith, Jerry	16	16	32	20		
Thomas, Eric	22	24	48	23		
Watts, Albert	24	25	51	26		
Vernon, James	19	17	39	21		
Zacharias, Saul	20	22	44	22		

3. Even if individuals prepare identical distributions and accurately compute measures of central tendency, they are not likely to assign letter grades exactly the same way. (It is almost a certainty that you assigned grades to some pupils in Figure 13-3 or 13-4 that are higher or lower than those assigned by classmates.)

4. Only a few students will earn high grades and experience the feel-

Comparing pupils is
effortful, may
discourage low scorers

ing that they have been successful. The majority of students in any class will feel inferior and unsuccessful.

5. Students who do poor work on a first exam may conclude that it will be almost impossible to pull up their grade, and they may make a decision to study thereafter just enough to earn a passing grade.

If you take account of factors such as these, you can see that assigning grades by comparing levels of performance has a number of disadvantages. In some situations, as when students are competing for a limited number of places in graduate school, comparative grading may be essential and desirable. In most school situations, however, it would seem to make more sense to encourage all students to strive for a superior level of performance by announcing that there is room at the top for everyone who can prove her or his ability. One way to minimize comparisons and motivate all pupils to do their best is to grade according to levels of performance rather than relative standing. The learning for mastery technique permits you to do this.

Learning for mastery

An approach to evaluation that will permit you to assign grades in terms of the traditional A to F pattern but still meet the goals for evaluation described earlier is the technique of learning for mastery. As with many "new" educational developments, the general idea of mastery learning was introduced and experimented with years ago. In the 1920s, Carleton Washburne (1922) devised the Winnetka Plan, and Henry C. Morrison (1926) developed a similar scheme at the University of Chicago Laboratory School. Both defined mastery in terms of objectives, provided students with well-organized learning units, used tests to determine if students had achieved the objectives at the completion of a unit, and provided remedial instruction for students who needed it. Although the technique was popular in the 1930s, it was largely forgotten in the 1940s and 1950s, probably because attacks on the "softness" of the schools and the drive to surpass Soviet achievements in space put emphasis on identifying and selecting the most promising students. Then in the 1960s, critics began to describe some of the unfortunate by-products of highly competitive education, and at the same time, programmed techniques—particularly those stressing instructional objectives and units of study—were being perfected. Thus, the stage was set for the re-emergence of the concept of learning for mastery.

John B. Carroll (1963) in his article "A Model of School Learning" proposes that the focus of instruction should be the *time* required for different students to learn a given amount of material. He suggests that teachers should allow more time and provide more and better instruction for students who learn less easily and rapidly than their peers.

Benjamin Bloom used the Carroll model as the basis for mastery learning. The traditional approach, he argues, promotes the concept that if a normal distribution of students (with respect to aptitude for a subject) is exposed to a standard curriculum, achievement after instruction will be normally distributed. This approach, Bloom maintains, fosters the expectation of both teachers and students that only a third of all students will adequately learn what is being taught, and that expectation leads to a disastrous self-fulfilling prophecy.

Expectation of a normal distribution leads to low aspirations

This set of expectations, which fixes the academic goals of teachers and students, is the most wasteful and destructive aspect of the present educational system. It reduces the aspirations of both teachers and students; it reduces motivation for learning in students; and it systematically destroys the ego and self-concept of a sizable group of students who are legally required to attend school for 10 to 12 years under conditions which are frustrating and humiliating year after year. (1968, p. 1)

Here is the alternative Bloom suggests:

Most students (perhaps over 90 percent) can master what we have to teach them, and it is the task of instruction to find the means which will enable our students to master the subject under consideration. Our basic task is to determine what we mean by mastery of the subject and to search for the methods and materials which will enable the largest proportion of our students to attain such mastery. (p. 1)

Although Bloom's approach is basically similar to the technique used in the 1920s by Washburne and Morrison, the widespread and effective use of mastery learning did not occur until the formulation of desirable ways to devise instructional objectives (as in books by Mager and Gronlund), sophisticated descriptions of the hierarchical nature of learning (such as Bloom's Taxonomy of Educational Objectives and Gagné's conditions of learning), and complete instructional systems (such as Individually Prescribed Instruction and Computer Assisted Instruction). Another factor that has contributed to the improvement of mastery learning is the distinction between *formative* and *summative* evaluation, first pointed out by Michael Scriven (1967). In most cases, evaluation is used to indicate a level of performance at the conclusion of a unit of instruction; that is, it sums up how much learning has taken place. Scriven suggests that more attention should be paid to evaluation that forms part of the teaching-learning process and provides continuous feedback to improve learning and instruction. Tests would thus be used to "form" learning by helping to diagnose weaknesses, thus making remedial instruction easier.

Ingredients for a successful mastery approach

Carroll observes that "teaching ought to be a simple matter if it is viewed as a process concerned with the management of learning" (1971, p. 29). He suggests that the function of the teacher is to follow this procedure:

Specify what is to be learned.

Motivate pupils to learn it.

Provide instructional materials [to foster learning].

[Present] materials at a rate appropriate for different pupils.

Monitor students' progress.

Diagnose difficulties and provide remediation.

Give praise and encouragement for good performance.

Give review and practice.

Maintain a high rate of learning over a period of time. (pp. 29–30)

The open education approach makes use of many of these procedures. Although the teacher allows for considerable student initiative rather than specifying what is to be learned, open education makes allowance for different rates, stresses diagnosis of learning difficulties, provides remedial instruction, supplies recognition for good performance, makes allowance for review and practice, and encourages a high rate of learning over a period of time. If you will be teaching at the elementary level, in particular, you may wish to follow procedures of open education. However, you may wish also to experiment with the sequence exactly as outlined by Carroll. The following suggestions, which can be adapted for use at any grade level and in any subject area, are based on Carroll's outline.

Mastery approach: Give pupils multiple opportunities to master goals at own pace

Suggestions for teaching: Using a mastery learning approach

1. Go through a unit of study, a chapter of a text, or an outline of a lecture, and pick out what you consider to be the most important points—that is, those you wish to stress because they are most likely to have later value or are basic to later learning.

2. List these points in the form of a goal card, instructional objectives (as described by Mager or Gronlund), or key points or the equivalent. If appropriate, arrange the objectives in some sort of organized framework, perhaps with reference to the Taxonomy of Educational Objectives or Gagné's conditions of learning.

3. Distribute a list of the objectives at the beginning of a unit, and tell your students that they should concentrate on learning them and that they will be tested on them.

The open education approach makes allowance for different rates of learning, stresses diagnosis of learning difficulties, and provides remedial instruction.

Bohdan Hrynewych

4. Consider the possibility of making up some sort of study guide in which you provide specific questions relating to the objectives and a format for students to use to organize their notes.

5. Make up exam questions on the objectives (based on the study guide questions, if you provide them).

6. Arrange these questions into at least two (preferably three) alternate exams for each unit of study.

7. Make up tentative criteria for grade levels for each exam and for the entire unit or report period (for example: A—not more than one question missed on any exam; B—not more than two questions missed on any exam; C—not more than four questions missed on any exam).

8. Test students either when they come to you and indicate they are ready or when you feel there has been ample opportunity for all ꞏ idents to have learned the material. Announce all exam dates in advance, and remind students that the questions will be based only on the objectives you have mentioned. Indicate the criteria for different grade levels, and emphasize that any student who fails to meet a desired criterion on her or his first try will be given a chance to take an alternate form of the exam.

Handbook heading
Making the Most of
Mastery Learning

9. Grade and return the exams as promptly as possible; go over questions briefly in class (particularly those that more than a few students had difficulty with); and offer to go over exams on an individual basis.

Make allowance for individual interpretations, and give credit for answers you judge to be logical and plausible, even though they differ from the answer you expected.

10. Schedule make-up exam times, and make yourself available for consultation and tutoring the day before. (At the same time that make-up exams are given, you can give the original exam to students who were absent.)

11. If students improve their score on the second exam but still fall below the desired criterion, consider a safety-valve option: Invite them to provide you with a filled-in study guide (or the equivalent) when they take an exam the second time, or give them an open-book exam on the objectives they missed, to see whether they can explain them in other than written examination terms. If you feel a student does this satisfactorily, give credit for one extra answer on the second exam.

12. To supplement exams, assign book reports, oral reports, papers, or some other kind of individual work that will provide maximum opportunity for student choice. Establish and explain the criteria you will use to evaluate these assignments, but stress that you want to encourage maximum freedom of choice and expression. (Some students will thrive on free choice, but others are likely to feel threatened by open-ended assignments. To allow for such differences, provide specific directions for those who need them, general hints or a simple request that "original" projects be cleared in advance for the more independent thinkers.) Grade all reports Pass or Do Over, and supply constructive criticisms on those you consider unsatisfactory. Announce that all Do Over papers can be reworked and resubmitted within a certain period of time. Have these reports count toward the final grade; for example, three reports for an A, two for a B, one for a C. (The student should also pass each exam at the designated level.) You might also invite pupils to prepare extra papers to earn bonus points to be added to exam totals.

This basic technique will permit you to meet the goals listed earlier and to work within a traditional A to F framework, but in such a way that you increase the proportion of students who do superior work without lowering standards. It also permits you to make the most of the procedures suggested by Carroll.

The advantages and also some further explanations of the steps in the suggested procedure will now be discussed.

Miscellaneous comments on mastery learning

The values of stating objectives　　Teachers who do not make use of objectives, typically, make up exams by haphazardly scanning a text

Is the mastery approach unworkable?

The authors of Wad-ja-get? dismiss the mastery approach as unworkable. In the fictionalized account of grading by Kirschenbaum, Simon, and Napier, mastery learning is rejected for two reasons: First, a student points out to the teachers on the committee charged with developing an improved grading system, "You are still setting our goals for us. When do we learn to set our own goals? What do you think we kids are rebelling against anyway? With your scientific grading, I'd feel even more like a rat in a maze than I do now" (p. 211). Second, a teacher on the committee argues that setting up a mastery approach is so complicated it can be handled only by curriculum specialists, and the school district does not have sufficient funds to hire such experts. Before an evaluation of these arguments is presented, you are reminded that the final recommendation made by the committee in Wad-ja-get? was to give students a choice between traditional grading and a credit/no credit system.

The argument that mastery learning is unsatisfactory because teachers set goals is weak, inconsistent, and illogical. Goals are also set by teachers in traditional grading and in credit/no credit grading, yet these approaches are not rejected for that reason. The student, speaking for the authors, complains about scientific grading, yet in other parts of the book teachers are accused of being "immoral" because they are not scientific. Finally, it is entirely possible for teachers to invite students to participate in drawing up objectives and in determining levels of performance when a mastery approach is used—if appropriate. In some courses, though, particularly those involving material that is technical or unfamiliar, it would be absurd to ask students to list objectives, since they are ignorant of what they need to know. (The faculty of a medical school, to note an extreme example, does not ask first-year students to describe what they will need to know in order to become competent physicians.)

The argument that mastery learning is so complex that it can be set up only by curriculum experts suggests that the authors of Wad-ja-get? did not bother to find out very much about the mastery approach. If they had read any of the books and articles on mastery learning published before they wrote their novel, they might have discovered that any teacher can set up a mastery approach. If they had actually experimented with mastery learning, they might have discovered that this approach makes it possible for an instructor to meet more of the criteria listed earlier for an ideal grading system than any of the alternatives mentioned in Wad-ja-get?

or other form of instructional material for information that seems appropriate for exam purposes. Exams are usually written under pressure, so it often turns out that the material selected is whatever happens to fit into a question format most easily. Unfortunately, such information is rarely of primary importance (names, dates, and statistics are examples of information that is easy to work into questions). However, because students read primarily to prepare for exams, they will feel obliged to concentrate on such information when they study. Skinner emphasizes this point when he observes, "What is taught often tends to be simply what can be measured by tests and examinations" (1968, p. 235), and he adds, "A predilection for scorable right answers distorts our definition of knowledge" (p. 245). If you have ever studied for an exam by deliberately seeking sections of the text you thought the instructor might use in test questions, you know what Skinner means.

In light of research on remembering and transfer, such an approach to testing appears irrational. A traditional test is something of a guessing game. If students are simply told that they will be tested on a hundred pages of text, for example, they may devote much of their study time to trying to anticipate what will be asked and the rest of the time memorizing to the point of being barely able to recall the information until the test is written. If they have been diligent, shrewd, and lucky, students will be able to answer most of the questions on the exam. If they have not fathomed the mind of the instructor, they will be unable to answer many questions, even though they have studied hard, and they are likely to leave the examination room brooding about all the valueless "junk" they learned. (When passing tests is the primary goal in the class, any information that cannot be used in answering questions is likely to be considered worthless.) Students are also likely to make a resolution not to "waste" so much time studying for the next exam.

Because of factors such as these, the traditional approach to grading favors forgetting and works against remembering because it increases the likelihood of interference and reorganization, because no attempt to seek structure or interrelationships is made, and because preparing for and taking tests is likely to be seen as a disagreeable experience that the student will tend to repress. To avoid this kind of situation, you are urged to pick out objectives before you organize a unit and make up exams, choose only information you feel is likely to have high payoff value, stress the relationships between points you select, and do everything possible to help and persuade your students to thoroughly learn a relatively small number of objectives. You are also urged to give them the opportunity to make up for a bad start by trying a second time. This approach is much more likely to lead to genuine understanding and to encourage transfer than the one-shot technique that is so common in American classrooms.

When you provide a list of objectives for a test, you are saying to the student (either directly or indirectly): "These are the points I think are important, and I am asking you to learn them because they are most likely to equip you with ideas you will be able to use later. The

Selecting objectives before writing exams has many advantages

other information in the book is for you to interpret and use in your own way." If you are successful in using objectives in your teaching, your students are likely to react to this approach by scanning the text as they prepare for your exams. In the process, they may well discover sections that they will read on their own or that they will later examine more completely when they are under less academic pressure. Even if it doesn't always work out this way, they probably will have a more useful repertoire of thoroughly learned and organized ideas than if they were required to attempt to cover everything.

The values of a study guide   If you have time to devise some sort of study guide, you will not only assist your students in mastering the objectives but will also open up possibilities for alternatives to final exams. Such a guide might consist simply of a page of specific questions with blank spaces under each one. Or it could take the form of a program or of a few general questions. Regardless of its form, the existence of a guide provides students with suggestions and incentives for study. It also means you can use safety-valve options with formal exams or replace formal exams with take-home or open-book exercises or with oral interviews. You might handle these yourself, or you could have students test each other by following the procedure suggested by Keller (see p. 243). A variation of the Keller Plan has been developed by Gerald Dykstra (described in Carroll, 1970, p. 37). He has created a technique in which primary grade pupils are asked not only to pass a test on a unit themselves but also to teach it to another pupil before going on to the next unit. Flash cards are used for the testing. (This technique could be used with students at all grade levels, and completion or short-answer tests might be used instead of flash cards.)

The choice regarding open- or closed-book exams will depend on grade level and subject area, as well as your feelings about exam pressure. When you provide students with lists of objectives in advance and announce that they will have more than one opportunity to take an exam and that you will do everything possible to help them improve their performance, you remove some of the most anxiety-producing aspects of testing, particularly since you substantially reduce competition between students. Even so, some students will still feel pressure; many will complain about being required to memorize material, arguing that if they need to know something they can look it up.

In making a decision about open- or closed-book exams, take into account that memorization will lead to overlearning and that thoroughly learned material is more likely to transfer. In many situations, we have to act on the spur of the moment or be prepared to see new relationships, so it is not always possible to look things up. In addition, it is necessary to become *equipped* to look things up by learning information well enough in the first place to know that it

Availability of a study guide opens up many options

exists and where it is available. Finally, remember that *preparation* precedes *inspiration* in the process of discovery and that individuals can "leap about intuitively" (as Bruner puts it) only after they have mastered the structure of a field of knowledge.

If you do decide on closed-book exams, you might point out to students who complain of test anxiety that the best antidote is thorough preparation. since students will know in advance what will be stressed, all that is needed for a relaxing test experience is thorough knowledge. Answering questions with skill and confidence can lead to feelings of self-esteem, satisfaction, and even enjoyment. Some students have never experienced these sensations because they have been convinced that they could never do well or have always attempted to get by with the least amount of effort. The mastery approach makes it possible to change these attitudes. (Of course, some students panic just as much over an open-book exam or an interview as they do over a traditional closed-book exam.)

Various uses of formative and summative evaluation   Scriven and Bloom suggest that formative tests be ungraded and used to prepare students for summative evaluation at the completion of a unit. Although this may be the best policy for some types of material, you may wish to follow the suggestions outlined here and have a series of short exams that function as both formative and summative tests. If a final summative exam is used as the basis for the final grade, students may feel considerably more pressured than if they are asked to take a series of exams. Scriven and Bloom recommend that units be arranged in heirarchical fashion. If you do this, ungraded exams that determine a student's readiness to go on to the next unit are appropriate. But if you develop units that are not based on a hierarchical structure, which may be the rule rather than the exception, you may find that basing the final grade on a series of tests will be the best plan.

Should you decide to follow this procedure, consult Figure 13-5 for a possible format for your grade book. If your grade book does not lend itself to such a recording technique, you might purchase a columnar pad designed for accountants. Using a series of exams and the suggested format will let you provide immediate feedback about progress, make-up exams, the need for remedial work, and overall performance. It eliminates the need to compare students and to laboriously total up scores and make frequency distributions before assigning final grades.

Determining criteria for different letter grades   One of the most crucial decisions in a mastery approach centers on the criteria you establish for different grade levels. If you hope to defend the grades you give to parents, fellow teachers, and administrators, you should do everything possible to make sure that an A in your class is equivalent to an A given by your colleagues. This is especially important because James H. Block (1971) has reported that the proportion of A grades in mastery classes is typically higher than in traditional classes, not because of low standards, but because more students are motivated to do A and B work. Therefore, you should be prepared to defend your grades by retaining copies of exams and the keys used to evaluate them and by explaining the criteria for different grade levels.

In establishing criteria, refer to the discussion on instructional objectives in Chapter 8, particularly the observations of Mager (p. 393) and Gronlund (p. 391). You might set up standards for an exam in terms of the percentage of correct answers, a minimum number of correct answers, the number of correct answers provided within a given time limit, or a sample of applications. An approach that has worked well in practice is to make up ten-question exams, grade each answer plus or minus, and use these standards: zero or one wrong—A, two wrong—B, three wrong—C, four wrong—D.

Plus or minus grading has definite advantages. It not only provides a definite number of correct and incorrect answers but also simplifies and speeds up grading. If you make up exams with an equivalent number of questions but evaluate each on a 5-point scale, you will be forced to read each answer with great care and then make a studied judgment of its relative value. If you use a plus-minus approach, you simplify both the judging and the totaling of the final score. In many cases, you will find that the answer is obviously right or wrong and that you can evaluate it in a matter of seconds. You can read answers that are marginal more carefully, and if you eventually do mark them minus, you can be comforted by the fact that the student will have another chance. And it is obviously much simpler to count the number of wrong answers than it is to add up ten scores ranging in value from 1 to 5. With practice, you may find grading exams so quick that you will be able to provide feedback the next day.

Plus-minus grading of answers simplifies evaluation

Providing remedial instruction   For students who do not meet the criterion on a first try at any exam, remedial instruction might be provided by following the techniques described by Bloom and James H. Block (1971): (1) small-group study sessions in which two or three students having difficulty get together to go over their errors and help each other find and correct omissions; (2) individual tutoring; (3) suggestions that the student reread the material; (4) provision of alternate learning materials (in the fashion of a branching program), such as workbooks, programmed units, audio-visual materials, or academic games and puzzles; and (5) reteaching.

The way you schedule make-up exams will depend on how you provide remedial instruction. In the Keller Plan, students are allowed a retest as soon as they feel they are ready. You might use this technique if you can set aside a particular part of the school day for the purpose. You may find it simpler, however, to set aside specific preannounced times when retests (and also make-up tests for absentees) can be taken. Students who have already met the criterion for that exam can work on supplementary reports (if you decide to require them) or read for pleasure while the testing goes on.

Experience has shown that students will procrastinate if given too much freedom to select retest dates. To help them make the most of what they remember from their preparation for the first exam and from remedial study and instruction, you are urged to schedule retest dates no later than two weeks after the first exam. If you use the technique of having a series of short tests serve both formative and summative functions, you will not need to give a comprehensive final exam. Consequently, you can schedule the last make-up exam in place of the final. When your students realize that those who meet the criterion for each test will not have to take an exam during the final exam period, they will have a potent incentive for doing well the first time.

If you do use a series of tests, you are urged to have students meet a criterion for each test rather than averaging their scores. The reason for this is that students who do well on the first exam may taper off toward the end of a report period and go to elaborate lengths to estimate the least amount of effort required to end up with a high final grade. To maintain high output and also to guarantee that students who did poorly on a particular set of objectives will make a second effort to improve their performance, it seems preferable to establish the requirement of meeting the criterion on each test.

Providing encouragement, support, and safety-valve options   If you decide to use a mastery approach and provide remedial instruction and retests, you are almost certain to discover that some students still will not meet the criterion for an A or a B on individual tests. Many will not have studied diligently enough. If you teach in the upper grades (in particular) and expose students to mastery learning for the first time, some who have been identified as C or D students since the first grade will probably have developed a habit of not studying very hard. They are likely to have figured out that there is little point in exerting themselves if they get only a second-rate reward for their efforts. It may take considerable encouragement from you to help such students overcome the habits of a school lifetime and strive to do their best.

When test anxiety seems to be the cause of poor performance, you might go out of your way to make students feel relaxed. One technique is to invite anyone who isn't sure he or she is on the right track to come up during exams and ask you for an indication of "warm" or "cold" for any particular answers. If an answer isn't what you are looking for, supply a subtle hint.

In still other cases, poor performance may be due to a deficiency in the intellectual skills and aptitudes involving memory and interpretation of test questions. For such students, you might use the technique suggested earlier: Tell them to do an especially conscientious job of writing out study notes and to bring the notes to class and hand them in along with the exam when they take the retest. If some students still fail to meet the criterion, look over their notes; if they reflect careful and diligent study, give credit for one more question. (Experience has shown that it may be necessary in a few cases to make sure students are handing in their own notes. A simple way to check on this is to compare the handwriting on the exam and on the notes.)

Does a mastery approach lower the value of high grades?   At this point a question may come to mind: Does a student who takes an exam a second time and still fails to meet the criterion deserve yet another opportunity to earn an A or B by completing additional work (such as doing an especially conscientious job of filling in a study guide)? Does another chance debase the grade or render it meaningless? In analyzing these questions, consider traditional grading practices, which stress the sorting-out function. In many courses, tests and grades are designed specifically to distinguish between high-scoring and low-scoring students. (This is especially true when item-analyses are carried out for the purpose of selecting questions that discriminate between high and low scorers.) Students who earn a high grade in a traditional course, however, may do so primarily because they possess a particular set of characteristics and abilities that come into play only in the contrived and artificial test situation. Those who do not possess these traits find it difficult if not impossible to meet standards for an A or B. Unless they are given encouragement and assistance in improving (which is the exception rather than the rule), they may become convinced that they cannot learn. It seems much more sensible to do everything possible to encourage all students to do superior work by searching for ways to help those with weaknesses to compensate for their dificiencies.

If it seems illogical to go to what may seem elaborate lengths to help a student earn an A in a mastery scheme by providing an option that does not stress memorization or test-taking skills, consider the logic of a relative standing policy, which makes it necessary for a teacher to sort into four or five gross categories students distributed over a range of total scores. Typically, the difference between the lowest A and the highest B (for example) will be a few points out of several hundred. If students are very close to a higher grade, why not extend an invitation to improve instead of "punishing" them for not answering quite enough questions correctly?

One of the most destructive, illogical, and inconsistent aspects of the traditional grading approach is that it tends to make an instructor feel guilty if too many students earn A's. An abundance of A students

Supplying feedback for multiple-choice questions

If you are required to give frequent exams to large numbers of pupils, you may be obliged to use multiple-choice exams. Such exams have a number of advantages, but they also have a major pedagogical limitation—a limitation that may be magnified if a mastery approach is used. For reasons discussed earlier, in the comparison of objective and essay exams, it is extremely difficult to provide detailed feedback to students when multiple-choice exams are used because of the time required to go over each option for each question. When faced with this problem, many teachers conclude that the best policy is to simply post or announce scores and not even attempt to go over questions. This policy is unfortunate in any kind of learning situation, but it is a crucial weakness if a mastery learning approach is used. One of the major strengths of a mastery approach is that students are informed of their mistakes and encouraged and helped to correct them before taking an examination over. It is essential, therefore, to go over each question on all exams used in a mastery approach.

If you are eager to try mastery learning but discover that you must use multiple-choice exams, prepare a "feedback booklet" as you prepare the examination booklet. Just after you make up a question, write a brief explanation of why you considered one option to be a better answer than the others. (You may discover that you can improve the question if you test your ability to justify your answer.) Assemble the explanations into a booklet similar to the test booklet, and invite any student who would like to find out why certain answers were marked wrong to examine your

is likely to be interpreted as a betrayal of academic standards, and instructors who have a reputation for assigning only a tiny proportion of A's may be thought of as the "best" teachers in a school. If the overall amount of learning that takes place in the classes of instructors in the latter group is taken into account, they probably deserve the opposite reputation, for reasons outlined by Mager in *Developing Attitude Toward Learning.* One of the most positive contributions of mastery learning may be that it will encourage you to make extraordinary efforts to help all your students to do A work—which is, after all, what you should try to do. Furthermore, you may find that your students will develop a class esprit de corps. Instead of creating a dog-eat-dog atmosphere in which students study by themselves, keep their notes secret, and pray that classmates will do poorly (to hold the average down), they are likely to be eager to study with each other and willing to share insights and perhaps go out of their way to help less gifted classmates meet the criterion for an A or a B.

Being realistic about mastery learning   Although this discussion of mastery learning has been intended to make you enthusiastic about

defense of the answers you selected. At the same time you announce the availability of the feedback booklet, you might also tell students that they will have the option of explaining their answers for up to three questions. Tell them that if, after reading your explanation, they feel they selected a different answer for logical and justifiable reasons, they may write a defense of their reasoning. If you agree the reasoning is sound, give credit for the answer. (This is one way you can allow for divergent thinking when using multiple-choice exams.)

If you decide to try this technique, assemble feedback booklets when you assemble exams. On exam days invite pupils to come up to your desk as soon as they complete their exams and score the answer sheets immediately. Set aside one part of the room as a "feedback corner," and invite students to peruse feedback booklets as soon as their answer sheets have been marked. Remind them of the option of writing out explanations for up to three of their answers on the back of the answer sheet, and tell them you will look over their explanations that afternoon and indicate the next day if you gave any credit for their explanations. (You should supply such information promptly in a mastery approach so that students will know whether or not to study for a retest.) An added advantage of student explanations is that you receive information you can use to improve your questions. If you find that several pupils criticize a question for the same reasons, eliminate that question, or rewrite it to overcome the limitations noted by your students.

the approach, you should be aware that it is not a panacea. For one thing, some students will disappoint if not infuriate you by the lengths they will go to in trying to beat the system—even after you have done everything in your power to make the system fair, just, and sensible.

Under a mastery approach, you are most likely to be able to improve the learning, attitudes, and self-concept of the typical C student. Those who have previously felt incapable of competing for high grades will usually give it a try in a mastery scheme, and many who try are likely to put out more effort, learn more, and earn higher grades than they ever have under comparative educational practices. Students who find it difficult to learn, however, may feel even more inadequate under a mastery approach than a traditional approach. When every opportunity to learn is provided and slow students are still unable to respond and do as well as their classmates, they must face the fact that they can no longer blame the system.

Mastery learning reduces competition and comparisons, but it does not eliminate them. Students who learn easily will meet the criterion for an A with little effort; they are likely to go through the required sequence so rapidly that they have considerable time for independent study. Those who learn slowly will engage in a constant battle to keep up with the required work. Because fortunate students learn faster and can engage in more self-selected study, they will probably get further and further ahead of their less capable class-mates. Despite suggestions that prestige colleges ought to practice open admissions, it is most unlikely that they will do so. Furthermore, the number of jobs at the top of a scale based on interest, pay, and influence will always be limited. A mastery approach cannot by itself alter the fact that students who learn easily and rapidly are still likely to be rewarded by admission to the best colleges and to get the best jobs. Even so, you may discover that a mastery approach is well worth the extra time, effort, and trouble it requires. A greater proportion of your students will probably learn more, enjoy school more, develop better attitudes toward learning, and feel more confident and proud of themselves than they would under comparative grading techniques. Just don't expect miracles, and be prepared for the fact that some of your students—no matter how hard they try or how much assistance you give them—will still be unable to do as well as most of their classmates in the time available.

Converting scores into grades: Mastery approach

To grasp some of the differences between traditional grading and the mastery approach, assume once again that you are either a fourth grade teacher or an instructor of five sections of tenth grade social studies. This time, however, assume that you have decided to use a mastery approach. Figure 13-5 depicts one way a teacher at *any* grade level might record grades when mastery learning is used.

The first difference you will notice between the grade book page depicted in Figure 13-5 and the pages shown in Figures 13-3 and 13-4 is that there are two columns under each exam heading. Room is allowed for two scores because in a mastery approach pupils are urged to find out about the errors they made on the first try on an exam, ask for clarification, engage in further study (with or without teacher assistance), and take an alternate form of the exam in an effort to improve their score. The obvious advantage of this policy is that students who do less well than they had hoped on a first exam will be motivated to try harder—instead of giving up, which is a common response in a traditional approach.

Another difference between the grade records shown in Figures 13-3 and 13-4 and the grades recorded in Figure 13-5 is that space is allowed in the mastery plan record sheet for grades on three projects, not one. The reason for assigning more projects is to switch emphasis from *quality* (a factor that may be under the control of only quite capable students) to quantity (which is within the capability of all students). Only an exceptional student may have the intelligence,

Figure 13-5

Page from a teacher's grade book: Mastery approach featuring point grading

	1st Exam		2nd Exam		3rd Exam		Exam Total Points	Projects			Grade
	1st Try	2nd Try	1st Try	2nd Try	1st Try	2nd Try		1	2	3	
Adams, Ann	16	18	17	18	18			P	P	P	
Baker, Charles	13	14	14		18	14		P			
Cook, Donald	14	16	15	16	17			P	P		
Davis, Rebecca	19		19		20			P	P	P	
Evans, Deborah	16	18	17	18	16	18		P	P	P	
Ford, Harold	18	16	17		15			P	P		
Grayson, Lee	10	13	12	14	12	15		P			
Hood, Barbara	16		17		15			P	P		
Ingalls, Robert	16	18	16		15			P	P		
Jones, Thomas	11	14	12	16	15			P			
Kent, Judith	18		19		19			P	P	P	
Landis, Karen	14	16	18		16			P	P		
Moore, James	17		17		17			P	P		
Norton, Carl	17	18	19		16	17		P	P	P	
Orton, John	10	10	11		9						
Peck, Nancy	14		15		14			P			
Quist, Ann	16	18	17	18	18			P	P	P	
Richards, Mary	16		17		15			P	P		
Smith, Jerry	13		15		14			P			
Thomas, Eric	18	16	18	17	15			P	P		
Watts, Albert	14		15		16			P			
Vernon, Joan	11	14	13	14	12	14		P			
Zacharias, Saul	16	18	17		16	19		P	P	P	

organizational ability, and perseverance to produce an excellent comprehensive project, but almost any student should be able to produce a series of brief projects at a satisfactory level.

You can figure grades using data presented in Figure 13-5 by assuming that the following information was distributed to students the first day of the report period.

INSTRUCTIONS FOR DETERMINING YOUR GRADE IN SOCIAL STUDIES

Your grade in social studies this report period will be based on scores on three exams (worth 20 points each) and satisfactory completion of up to three projects. Here are the standards for different grades:

A—Average of 18 or more on three exams, plus three projects at Pass level

B—Average of 16 or 17 on three exams, plus two projects at Pass level

C—Average of 14 or 15 on three exams, plus one project at Pass level

D—Average of 10 to 13 on three exams

F—Average of 9 or less on three exams

Another way to figure your grade is to add together points as you take exams. This may be the best procedure to follow as we get close to the end of the report period. Use this description of standards as a guide:

A—At least 54 points, plus three projects at the Pass level

B—48 to 53 points, plus two projects at Pass level

C—42 to 47 points, plus one project at Pass level

D—30 to 41 points

F—29 points or less

If you are not satisfied with the score you earn on any exam, you may take a different exam on the same material in an effort to improve your score. (Some of the questions on the alternate exam will be the same as those on the original exam; some will be different.) Projects will be graded P (Pass) or DO (Do Over). If you receive a DO on a project, you may work to improve it and hand it in again. You may also submit an *extra* project, which may earn up to 3 points of bonus credit (in case your exam scores fall just below a cut-off point). As you take each exam and receive a Pass for each project, record your progress on this chart.

First Exam		Second Exam		Third Exam		Project 1	Project 2	Project 3	Grade
1st Try	2nd Try	1st Try	2nd Try	1st Try	2nd Try				

You are urged to follow these insructions and figure the grade for each pupil listed in Figure 13-5. When you have finished, compare the time and effort expended figuring mastery grades to the time and effort you spent calculating traditional grades. In addition, compare your mastery grades with those assigned by classmates to determine if there are any discrepancies. Finally, speculate about how students would respond to a mastery approach as compared to traditional grading techniques.

A different way of setting up a mastery approach is illustrated in Figure 13-6. The grade sheet and the information supplied in that figure can be interpreted by taking into account the following instructions from a course outline given to students the first day of a report period.

INSTRUCTIONS FOR DETERMINING YOUR GRADE IN SOCIAL STUDIES

Your grade in social studies this report period will be based on scores on three exams and successful completion of up to three projects. The exams

Figure 13-6

Page from a teacher's grade book: Mastery approach featuring + or − grading

	1st Exam		2nd Exam		3rd Exam		Projects			Grade
	1st Try	2nd Try	1st Try	2nd Try	1st Try	2nd Try	1	2	3	
Adams, Ann	~~2~~	1	1		1		P	P	P	
Baker, Charles	~~4~~	3	~~4~~	3	~~5~~	3	P			
Cook, Donald	3		3		~~4~~	3	P			
Davis, Rebecca	2		2		2		P	P		
Evans, Deborah	3		~~4~~	3	3		P			
Ford, Harold	~~6~~	3	~~4~~	3	~~4~~	3	P			
Grayson, Lee	~~2~~	1	~~2~~	1	1		P	P	P	
Hood, Barbara	1		0		1		P	P	P	
Ingalls, Robert	~~8~~	2	2		~~8~~	2	P	P		
Jones, Thomas	~~8~~	4	4		4					
Kent, Judith	0		1		0		P	P	P	
Landis, Karen	~~4~~	3	3		3		P			
Moore, James	~~8~~	2	2		2		P	P		
Norton, Carl	~~8~~	2	~~8~~	2	~~8~~	2	P	P		
Orton, John	~~8~~	2	2		2		P	P		
Peck, Nancy	~~2~~	1	~~2~~	1	1		P	P		
Quist, Ann	~~8~~	2	~~4~~	2	2		P	P		
Richards, Mary	~~2~~	1	~~2~~	1	1		P	P	P	
Smith, Jerry	~~4~~	2	~~8~~	2	~~8~~	2	P	P		
Thomas, Eric	~~2~~	1	1		1		P	P	P	
Watts, Albert	~~4~~	3	3		3		P			
Vernon, Joan	~~8~~	3	~~4~~	3	~~4~~	3	P			
Zacharias, Saul	~~8~~	1	~~2~~	1	~~8~~	1	P	P	P	

will consist of ten questions each, and your answers will be graded plus or minus. The projects will be graded P (Pass) or DO (Do Over). Here are the standards for different grades:

A—Miss not more than one question on any exam, three projects at Pass level

B—Miss not more than two questions on any exam, two projects at Pass level

C—Miss not more than three questions on any exam, one project at Pass level

D—Miss four questions on any exam

F—Miss five or more questions on all three exams

If you are not satisfied with the grade you earn on any exam, you may take a different form of the exam to try to improve your score. (Some of the questions on the alternate form of the exam will be the same as those on the original exam; some will be different.) You may hand in an extra project, which may earn up to two bonus points (in case you fall just below the cutoff point on one or two exams).

If you eventually take a crack at putting a mastery approach into practice using techniques similar to those just described, keep in mind these points (most of which were mentioned earlier):

Try to set aside a specified period one day each week for exams. When deciding how many exams to give, be sure to allow at least two days for each exam. If possible, also schedule at least one make-up exam day.

Grade and return papers as soon as possible after exams so that students will know whether or not to study for a second try. If you use a point-per-exam approach, it is preferable to make up multiple-choice exams that can be graded as quickly as students finish them. If you prefer short-answer questions, try using plus or minus grading. It is considerably simpler and faster than point grading.

On second-exam days allow students who were satisfied with grades earned on a first try to work on projects or engage in individualized study.

Start out using grade standards that reflect the traditional pattern of 90 percent and above for an A, 80 to 89 percent for a B, and so forth. If it turns out that less than 10 percent of your pupils are earning A's after the first exam, however, feel free to lower the standards. Chances are that your exams are a bit on the tough side.

You have been asked to consider the virtues and techniques of mastery learning because you will almost certainly be expected to assign grades. This chapter concludes with a brief list of suggestions you might follow when you prepare to record grades on report cards.

Report cards

Because American schools must deal with millions of pupils, you will, almost inevitably, be asked to fill out report cards. They may possess many disadvantages, but they appear to be unavoidable.

Types of report cards

As noted in Chapter 2, most schools schedule four report periods each year. Over 70 percent of elementary schools use report cards with a classified scale of letters. Almost 60 percent of such schools use parent conferences, sometimes as the exclusive means of evaluating a student's progress, sometimes in conjunction with report cards. About 25 percent of all elementary schools use a written description instead of letter grades. Report cards for the elementary level are usually like the one describe earlier in this chapter in the discussion of converting scores into grades. Typically they consist of two major sections: one for academic achievement and the other for "work habits," "attitudes," or "citizenship." The teacher is ordinarily required to grade all pupils on their ability in subjects such as reading, mathematics, English, spelling, social studies, health, science, music, art, and physical education. Often subcategories are found under reading, writing, and arithmetic. For example, you may have to rate pupils on ability in oral reading, reading comprehension, and library participation. In many cases grading is on the five-step A to F scale. At the primary level and occasionally in upper elementary classes, a three-step system may be used: O (Outstanding), S (Satisfactory), N (Needs improvement). Many elementary school cards also distinguish between actual achievement and estimates of ability, effort, or aptitude. These categories and other subheadings such as work habits, attitudes, and citizenship are frequently graded O, S, or N. (Typical work habits include "listens attentively," "follows directions," "accepts responsibility," "does work neatly," "makes good use of time," "respects rights of others.")

In secondary school the great majority of report cards are austere affairs that call for a stark A, B, C, D, or F for each subject. Sometimes a catchall "citizenship" column is added; almost invariably it is reserved for negative reactions—either a check mark or an N for "Needs improvement."

Suggestions for teaching: Making out report cards

Some report cards are bound to vary from the "typical" ones just described. Even so, the common elements they are all likely to share justify offering the following suggestions:

1. Before classes begin, examine a copy of the card used in your school, and make sure you are aware of the local ground rules for grading.

2. Pick out the important and reportable areas.

3. Test and observe specifically for the gradable skills.

4. Whenever possible, compute subtotals " as you go."

5. If you must grade "citizenship," take special care to guard against the halo effect, cognitive dissonance, and projection.

6. Do your best to make separate and independent evaluations of achievement and citizenship.

1. Before classes begin, examine a copy of the card used in your

school, and make sure you are aware of local ground rules for grading. Some decisions about grades must be made on a school- or district-wide basis. In order to provide a degree of consistency so that all teachers of a given class or subject apply roughly similar standards, guidelines regarding grades and distribution are sometimes necessary. Consequently, it is important to be clearly aware of local ground rules before you begin to develop lesson plans or to plot tests and assignments.

Handbook heading
Checking on Ground Rules for Grading

2. Pick out the important and reportable areas. As you study the card, select the most important *and* gradable categories, and decide how to work within the local regulations. The more elaborate cards at the primary and elementary levels may have thirty categories to be evaluated four times a year. It is impossible to make systematic observations of more than a few skills and abilities, so if you are confronted with an extremely detailed card, you may be forced to pick out those skills you and other teachers and consultants consider most important. The primary teacher is most likely to face this problem. As the children progress through school, the report cards gradually approach that ultimate, one-letter judgment.

3. Test and observe specifically for the gradable skills. This suggestion is intended for the primary teacher because of the complexity of many report cards at this level. If each pupil must be judged on such specific qualities as oral reading, reading comprehension, and library participation, making out thirty report cards can be onerous. Preparing for this chore ahead of time simplifies it. For example, every day you might have an oral reading period during which five or ten pupils read. If each pupil reads five times during a report period and you grade performance on a ten-point scale, the points can be totaled and a distribution prepared before the deadline. A simple glance at your distribution then permits you to assign grades quickly and easily. Without such a system, you may find yourself at 2:00 a.m. the day grades are due desperately dredging your memory for recollections of how well each pupil can read. Resorting to this haphazard alternative brings into play the halo effect, cognitive dissonance, projection, and the influence of the unconscious.

Handbook heading
Measuring Gradable Skills

4. Whenever possible, compute subtotals "as you go." If you plan ahead and space tests and exercises over the grading period, you can also get a jump on the usual last-minute rush of calculating and assigning grades. (In the example mentioned above, each pupil's set of five scores might have been totaled after she or he had completed the fifth oral reading.) This means determining just a few sets of totals each day for several days as opposed to undergoing a hectic all-night

Some observations on parent-teacher conferences

Teachers at the elementary level usually must report student progress in whole or in part through parent conferences. In some schools this means "interpreting" a standard report card to the parents, and in others it simply means giving an oral analysis of strengths and weaknesses. Parents often dislike the latter kind of report unless the teacher shows them something specific to back up her or his remarks. One parent, for example, said that she and her husband got the same answer to all their queries about their son's progress: "He's doing just fine." He was doing "fine" even in reading, although he was two grade levels below the level he should have been. The parents suspected that the teacher didn't know their son's status.

If your school features parent conferences, keep in mind that unless you have kept systematic records of student performance, your only recourse will be to keep smiling (and perspiring) and repeating, "He's doing just fine." Picture an interview with aggressive parents who have ambitions for their son far exceeding your estimate of his abilities. Whether an actual report card is used or not, life will be much simpler if you can support your judgments with evidence. Such evidence will also permit you to do a better job of teaching.

session. In the upper levels, you might sum up the points for homework, papers, quizzes, and exams a few weeks before the final. Marking finals is almost always a pressure-filled task, and if on top of that you must add up five or ten numbers for each of thirty to five-times-thirty pupils, you may be reduced to a state of exhaustion coupled with panic. It's much easier to add just one number to the subtotal and proceed from there to final distribution and grades. This policy will also put you in a position to provide the pupils with their relative positions before they take the final exam. As a teacher, you may have some misgivings about the desirability of doing this, but since most students clamor for such a semifinal report, you may feel obligated to supply it. (You can avoid many of the problems just described if you use a mastery approach.)

5. If you must grade "citizenship," take special care to guard against the halo effect, cognitive dissonance, and projection. Given the choice, you may prefer to avoid grading pupils on their "work habits" or "citizenship." How to define *citizenship* is the first problem. Even with a workable definition, the difficulties involved in observing for it with accuracy are so great that you would have little time left for teaching or evaluating scholastic performance. When you are forced to evaluate such factors as "shows self-control" or "considers the rights of others," consider the *anecdotal report* as a device for making

your reactions more systematic and less subjective. The anecdotal report takes several forms, but a common technique is to take a pad of paper or an inexpensive notebook and put the name of each pupil at the top of a page. Five minutes or so at the end of each day is all that is necessary to conduct a post-mortem of the day's events. This could become almost automatic. Try to remember and record things that turned out well and things that didn't, and in the latter case analyze what went wrong so that you can prevent a similar disaster in the future.

As you recollect what happened, make an effort to recall specific incidents involving individual pupils. For example, two boys got in a fight as they were lining up for recess; a not so bright pupil gave an outrageously wrong answer that provoked gales of derisive laughter from the class; class elections were held. As you jot down each event on your page for the appropriate pupil, you are making a record that may later prove valuable. If a particularly belligerent boy has a fight a day, you have evidence to back up a "Needs improvement" grade under the "shows self-control" column. If you become aware later in the year that the maladroit boy who made the dumb remark seems to have changed from an extrovert to an introvert, the reminder of his embarrassing experience could be the tipoff that this was the original cause of the shift in his behavior; building up his confidence by feeding him easy questions you know he can answer may counteract the low esteem of his classmates. Or the simple notation that a certain girl was elected class secretary for October could come in handy during a parent conference or in a conversation at Back-to-School Night or a PTA meeting.

This sort of record is most appropriate for the elementary teacher, but it can also be of use to a secondary teacher. Such notes can help correct for inaccuracies resulting from distortions of memory. On the other hand, you have to guard against the influence of cognitive dissonance. The more you describe a certain kind of behavior in your notes about a pupil, the more likely you are to look for—and find—more incidents of the same kind and to ignore evidence that is dissonant. The antidote to this trap is to be aware of it and make an effort to be open-minded in noticing similar behavior in other pupils.

6. Do your best to make separate and independent evaluations of achievement and citizenship.   With a report card that has separate sections for scholarship and citizenship, keep these two factors separate in your mind and in your grade book. If you are asked to distill your judgment into only one letter grade, it will be even harder to be fair.

Perhaps as a student you considered one of your teacher's hypocritical and deceitful. A common form of "deceit" is to grade pupils below their actual achievement and explain, if challenged, that they showed "lack of effort," "a poor attitude," or "unsatisfactory recitation." Such statements may be nothing more than thinly disguised excuses for venting personal animosities. The teacher is thinking, "I don't like you and this is my way of getting back at you." In many cases the reason the teacher doesn't like certain pupils is that the pupils have made it abundantly clear that they don't think much of the teacher. For a teacher to exact revenge in the form of a deliberately lowered final grade is indefensible. But it's oh-so-tempting, and you may have to take particular care to avoid falling into the trap. The best safeguard is to draw the lines on your final grade distributions *before* you know which name is attached to which tally and then stick to your decision. If the tallies are so close you have to compare papers, then make a determined effort to control your emotions.

Handbook heading
Evaluating
Achievement
Independently of
Personality

If you feel justified in giving a pupil an N (Needs improvement) in one or more categories listed under "work habits" or "citizenship," you might try to help the pupil *make* improvements by using an approach similar to that illustrated by the Checklist of Prosocial Behavior presented in Figure 10–3, p. 539. If you give a pupil N in "listens attentively," "follow directions," and "makes good use of time," for example, you might ask her or him to first carry out a self-rating regarding those types of behavior. Then ask the pupil to describe specific things that might be done to improve that rating, and mention that you will schedule a conference in a week or so to hear about steps that have been taken to bring about a change for the better. Your sympathetic support, plus the student's thinking about how to improve, will often lead to an S or even an O under those sections of the "work habits" section for the next report period. Thus reinforced, the pupil is also more likely to continue to behave in the desired way.

SUMMARY OF KEY POINTS

If grades are to be fair and accurate, teachers must make efforts to reduce the impact of subjectivity. They should guard against the halo effect by not permitting one characteristic of a pupil to influence all impressions of that pupil. They should try to be aware of cognitive dissonance and be willing to recognize bits of student behavior that seem inconsistent. In some situations, teachers may be tempted to protect themselves by projecting (or attributing) to others traits they would rather not admit are characteristic of their own behavior. Finally, teachers should allow for the possibility that they will be unaware of some of the reasons why they like or dislike pupils. The impact of such mechanisms that interfere with objectivity can be reduced if tests are properly used. When pupils take tests, they are able to respond to a standard set of questions, their answers are recorded in permanent form, and the teacher can compare answers to a fixed set of criteria.

When making up tests and related measures of pupil performance, teachers should keep in mind that stating specific goals makes evaluation simpler and more effective. Goals not only improve grading efficiency; they also serve as incentives for pupils. When deciding which types of exams to use, teachers might take into account that essay exams are easy to prepare but hard to score. Essay exams also have the advantage of permitting teachers to examine the reasoning that led to wrong answers. Objective exams, on the other hand, are often preferable to essay exams when it is desirable or necessary to use the same exam over and over again (as with multiple sections of the same subject). Another advantage of objective exams is that the grading of answers is much less influenced by subjectivity. If any type of exam is made too difficult or is perceived as unfair by students, many of them may feel driven to cheat.

Once an exam has been given and corrected, it is necessary to convert scores into grades. The first step is to prepare a frequency distribution. In order to interpret such distributions, it is usually necessary to calculate at least one measure of central tendency. The mean, or arithmetical average, is calculated by adding all scores and dividing by the number of scores. If an examination consists of large numbers of points, the calculation of the mean requires considerable effort, which may be somewhat negated by the fact that the mean is influenced by extreme scores. The median, or middle score, can be calculated simply by counting tallies and is often a more accurate indicator of central tendency than the mean because many distributions include extreme scores. Even though the median can be calculated easily, the preparation of a frequency distribution does require a certain amount of effort, and any method of evaluation that emphasizes the relative performance of different pupils tends to cause low scorers to feel discouraged.

Another unfortunate by-product of basing grades on distributions is that teachers as well as pupils may begin to assume that only a minority of students in any class can do excellent work. Learning for mastery makes it possible for almost all students to be motivated to strive to meet high standards. When mastery learning is used, students are given multiple opportunities to achieve goals at their own pace. The key to mastery learning is to state goals in specific terms at the beginning of a unit. All students who achieve the goals for a unit, regardless of how long it takes them to do it, earn high grades for that unit. Stating goals not only increases the numbers of students who aspire to do excellent work; it also improves the preparation of examinations. If teachers who use the mastery approach prepare some form of study guide, they may be able to use various kinds of examinations and also introduce safety-valve options. For the mastery approach to work most effectively, answers must be graded quickly. One excellent way to speed up the evaluation process is to grade answers plus or minus.

BECOMING A BETTER TEACHER: QUESTIONS AND SUGGESTIONS

Maintaining a Question and Recitation Record

Do I ask pupils to recite in a fair and consistent manner? Suggestion: Maintain a Question and Recitation Record. List the names of all pupils in a class on a sheet of lined paper, and put a tally next to the appropriate names each time I ask a question of or call on a pupil. (Make the tallies in an unobtrusive way, and not while the student is reciting—which might give the impression I am grading recitation or making notes for some "subversive" reason.) Check the tallies at periodic intervals and take steps to insure that there will be an approximately equal number of tallies next to each name by the end of the report period.

Keeping a Positive Reinforcement Record

How confident am I that I spread around reinforcement in an equitable manner? Suggestion: On the same sheet of paper I use for the Question and Recitation Record, add a column labeled "Positive Reinforcement." Record a tally in that column each time I praise or respond positively to each pupil. Take steps to make sure that there will be an approximately equal number of tallies opposite each name in the positive reinforcement column by the end of the report period.

Taking Advantage of Test Characteristics

Am I using evaluation procedures that take advantage of the characteristics of tests? Suggestion: Evaluate my testing techniques by asking myself these questions: (1) Are all pupils being exposed to a standard situation? (2) Am I obtaining permanent records of pupil behavior, records that can be referred to at a later date? (3) Am I evaluating pupil responses with reference to fixed criteria?

Using Objectives to Improve Evaluation

Can I improve my evaluation procedures by being more conscientious about focusing on objectives? Suggestion: Each time I plan a unit, think about how I will measure achievement in terms of mastery of specific objectives. Then write objectives and prepare tests and other forms of evaluation that measure achievement of these objectives.

Outlining Units of Study

The last time I introduced a unit, did I explain what would be covered and tell students what they would be expected to do? Suggestion: The next time I plan a unit, make out a syllabus to be distributed the first day. Outline what will be covered and explain how the grade will be determined.

Announcing Tests and Assignments in Advance

Do I always give pupils ample warning about tests and due dates? Suggestion: Make it a practice to announce at the beginning of a unit of study all tests and dates on which papers and projects are due. Then, at frequent intervals, remind the class of these deadlines.

Being Considerate in Scheduling	Have I ever asked pupils for their reactions when I announce when exams will be scheduled or papers will be due? Suggestion: Each time I announce an exam or a project deadline, ask the class if there are any reasons I have overlooked that may make it difficult for them to meet those deadlines.
Obtaining an Accurate Sample of Pupil Behavior	When I look over grades I've recorded, do I feel confident that they are based on an adequate sample of pupil behavior? Suggestion: The next time I prepare an exam or get ready to evaluate pupil contributions or performance, think about ways to help insure that I will base my judgments on an adequate sample of behavior, not just haphazard bits and pieces.
Guidelines for Writing Test Questions	Have I read any books on techniques of writing good test questions? Suggestion: Read the appropriate section of at least one of the books mentioned in suggestions 13-6 and 13-7 (or sections of books I find in the library), and draw up a list of guidelines for writing test questions.
Trying to Insure That Questions Are Understood	Am I sure that students know what I want when I ask test questions? Suggestion: Make it a point to convince students that they are free to ask for clarification of questions.
Preparing a Detailed Key	The last time I corrected an exam, did I use a complete key? Suggestion: The next time I write exam questions, write a key that I can use in evaluating those questions. Then put myself in the position of a pupil and check to see if the question clearly asks for the information listed in the key.
Defending Evaluations	Do students feel free to question my evaluations? How did I handle the last student who complained about a grade? Suggestion: Each time I hand back an exam or a graded assignment, invite pupils to discuss their grades with me. Make sure I write test questions and prepare a key of answers that will permit me to defend myself if I am challenged by an irate student or parent.
Checking on the Validity of Exams	Do I ask myself about how valid my tests are as I grade papers and record marks? Suggestion: As I evaluate student answers and total up points, check on the content validity of my exams: Do the questions really seem to cover what I wanted them to cover?
Ways to Minimize and Handle Cheating	Have I taken specific steps to try to limit cheating? Suggestion: After the first exam in any report period, look over scores and ask students if they thought it was a fair test and of reasonable difficulty. If it appears that I expected too much, announce that I will revise the grades. How did I handle the last incident of cheating I detected? Suggestion: Each time I have to deal with a cheating incident, carry out a post-mortem and think about ways to handle similar incidents more effectively in the future.

Using a Numerical
Scale to Grade Papers

Should I be using numbers instead of letters to record grades? Suggestion: If I have been using letter grades when evaluating papers and projects, try out the numerical system described in Chapter 13 next time I must grade such assignments.

Making the Most of
Mastery Learning

Have I tried the mastery approach? Suggestion: The next time I plan a unit, set it up in the form of a mastery approach by following suggestions supplied in Chapter 13.

Checking on Ground
Rules for Grading

If the principal of my school has not explained grading procedures, have I inquired about local ground rules? Suggestion: Ask a veteran teacher for a run-down on grading guidelines, rules, and regulations.

Measuring Gradable
Skills

Am I obtaining data to use when grades are to be assigned? Suggestion: Examine the report card I will have to fill out and take steps to record scores or ratings that will permit me to assign grades quickly and objectively.

Recording Anecdotal
Reports

Should I be keeping anecdotal reports to refer to when citizenship grades are to be assigned? Suggestion: Take a stab at compiling an anecdotal report log for a few days, just to see if it seems to supply helpful information.

Evaluating
Achievement
Independently of
Personality

Am I being as objective and honest as possible when I assign grades? Suggestion: The next time I assign grades, constantly think about whether I am permitting feelings to influence my evaluations. If I harbor a grudge against a pupil for any reason, be especially careful not to get "revenge" by assigning a grade lower than that actually earned.

SUGGESTIONS FOR FURTHER STUDY

13-1
Speculating About
Cheating

Whether or not you approve, the fact remains that the schools *do* perform the preliminary sorting out of able and less able individuals in our society. You may question the kind of ability that current school practices "reward," but the GPA (or equivalent) is unlikely to diminish in importance within the next few years. Because considerable pressure to get high grades is exerted on students in American schools, a significant number of pupils feel driven to cheat. Analyze your own experiences and feelings regarding cheating as a first step to speculating about how pressure for grades could be reduced in your classes. Knowing that you will almost surely be required to assign grades—probably with reference to some sort of distribution—what might you do to lessen your students' tendency to cheat? (As you record your thoughts, concentrate on specific techniques that might be applied within the present system.)

13-2

Analyzing Experiences
with Subjectivity

To gain greater insight into the impact of mechanisms that interfere
with objectivity, examine your own experiences with reference to the
concepts noted in this chapter. Have you ever realized at a later time
that your initial feelings about a certain individual were dominated by
one good or bad characteristic that caused a halo effect? Did you ever
find it difficult to believe an action or a report that was contrary to
what you expected of an acquaintance? Could your irritation at a
habit in someone else perhaps be due to your dislike of acknowledging that you have the same habit yourself? Have you ever reacted very
favorably or unfavorably to an individual you met for the first time
without understanding exactly why? You might record one or more
incidents of the type just described and draw implications from them
as you approach the point of interacting with large numbers of
students.

13-3

Analyzing Tests

You might be able to increase the likelihood that your students will
react favorably to your first exams if you take the time to analyze
exams *you* have especially liked and disliked. Write a description of
the one you liked best and least. Then refer to the characteristics of
tests noted in this chapter. Did you favor a test that involved a permanent record of behavior you and the teacher could re-examine as often
as desired? Were your answers evaluated according to a reasonable,
clear set of scoring standards? If the test you liked best did not have
these characteristics, what *were* the qualities that made you respond
favorably? If the test you disliked had some of these characteristics
but still seemed unsatisfactory, why were you bothered? Record your
reactions, and, if possible, come up with a set of dos and don'ts to
follow in making up exams.

13-4

Objective vs. Essay
Tests

This chapter includes a comparison of objective tests and essay
exams. If you will be teaching at the secondary level, it might be of
interest to carry out a similar analysis of your own. For example, you
might compare observations made by Banesh Hoffmann in his book
The Tyranny of Testing (1962) with those offered by Henry Chauncey
and John E. Dobbin in *Testing: Its Place in Education Today* (1963).
Hoffmann is a distinguished mathematician who felt that psychologists and educators were too involved in testing to recognize certain
weaknesses and inconsistencies of objective tests. Chauncey is president of Educational Testing Service, and Dobbin is an influential
member of the same company (the leading publisher of standardized
tests). In Chapter 3 of *The Tyranny of Testing,* Hoffmann describes
some problems of grading essay exams. In Chapter 4, "Objectivity and
Ambiguity," he points out that *objective* is a misnomer, since the term
refers only to the process of grading. The person who decides which
multiple-choice answer is correct is making just as subjective a judgment as the person evaluating an essay answer. In Chapter 5, he criticizes the emphasis on the "best" answer and suggests that the person
taking the test is required to attempt to fathom how the mind of the
test-writer functions. In Chapter 6, he argues that multiple-choice tests
discriminate against the brightest, most creative students. Chauncey

and Dobbin present counterarguments in a section beginning on page 77 of *Testing: Its Place in Education Today* and in the appendix, "Multiple-Choice Questions: A Close Look." If you are undecided about the relative merits, strengths, and weaknesses of multiple-choice and essay tests, compare the views of Hoffmann with those of Chauncey and Dobbin, or make an analysis of your own. At the conclusion of your analysis, you might list some general guidelines to follow when you write exam questions.

13-5
Making Up Sample Test Items

A good way to become aware of the difficulties and complexities of evaluation (as well as to understand different types of tests) is to devise some test questions. Compose several kinds of questions based on a chapter or two from this text or from a text in a subject you hope to teach. You might try to write three to five multiple-choice, three to five completion, five true-false, a matching question (if the material seems appropriate), three short essay questions, and one or two long essay questions. (If you encounter difficulties or simply want some advice, consult one of the books mentioned in the next two suggestions.) Be sure to make up your key as you write the questions. Then ask one or two classmates to take your test. Request that they not only record their answers but also add any critical remarks about the strengths and weaknesses of specific items. Summarize the answers and criticisms, and draw up a list of guidelines to follow when you construct classroom examinations.

13-6
Writing "Thought" Questions

In *Classroom Questions: What Kinds?* (1966), Norris M. Sanders describes how to write and pose questions that require students to *use* ideas rather than simply remember them. Sanders bases his approach on the Taxonomy of Educational Objectives. The hierarchical nature of learning stressed in the taxonomy is too often ignored, he feels, when questions are asked. Teachers are partial to memory-level questions and thus restrict students to the bottom of the hierarchy of learning. The memorization of facts should not be an end in itself, but a means to permit students to interpret ideas, make applications, analyze, and synthesize. Proper use of questions helps students perform these higher-level operations *as* they answer. In *Classroom Questions: What Kinds?* Sanders devotes a chapter to questions that might be used in testing each of the categories in the taxonomy: memory, translation, interpretation, application, analysis, synthesis, and evaluation. Many examples are offered, and each chapter concludes with questions designed to test the reader's understanding of the discussion. For more on the possibility of using the Taxonomy of Educational Objectives not only to plan lessons but also to make up questions, secure a copy of *Classroom Questions: What Kinds?* (it is an inexpensive paperback).

13-7
Techniques of Evaluation

An excellent collection of somewhat technical discussions on ways to improve evaluation is *The Evaluation of Instruction* (1970), edited by M. C. Wittrock and David E. Wiley. For general discussions of testing, consult *Evaluating Pupil Growth: Principles of Tests and Measurements* (5th ed., 1975) by J. Stanley Ahman and Marvin D. Glock, *Test Construction: A Programmed Guide* (1970) by Lowell A. Schoer, *Measurement and Evaluation in Psychology and Education* (3rd ed., 1969) by Robert L. Thorndike and Elizabeth Hagen, or *Improving Marking and Reporting in Classroom Instruction* (1974) by Norman E. Gronlund. Especially recommended is *Essentials of Educational Measurement* (1972) by Robert L. Ebel. In Chapter 5, Ebel describes "How to Plan a Classroom Test." In Chapters 6, 7, and 8, he gives specific suggestions for writing essay, true-false, and multiple-choice items. Ebel also comments on how to judge the quality of the exams you write (Chapter 13) and tells how to analyze marks and marking systems (Chapter 12). An excellent reference on how to write different types of test questions is "Writing the Test Item" by A. G. Wesman in *Educational Measurement* (2nd. ed., 1971), edited by R. L. Thorndike.

13-8

Schools Without Failure

William Glasser, a psychiatrist, has analyzed traditional approaches to education and concludes that American schools cause too many students to fail. How we might reverse this trend is the subject of *Schools Without Failure* (1969). Glasser feels that the first years in school are of crucial importance and that overemphasis on memorization and grades leads numerous children to be labeled or to think of themselves as failures early in their academic careers. His prescription for reform advises "involvement, relevance and thinking." He recommends group discussion as the basic pedagogical method, argues for greater emphasis on having students relate what they learn in school to their lives outside it, and suggests that a grading system in which a student gets either a Pass or a Superior (but never an F) be substituted for the usual system. Perhaps because of his medical background, Glasser proposes a simple, definite diagnosis and prescribes simple, definite treatment. For an overview of *one* way schools might attempt to minimize failure, you might read *Schools Without Failure*. Chapter 1 is devoted to a general analysis of the problem, Chapter 6 is a critique of tests and grades, and Chapter 10 consists of Glasser's description of how teachers should use group discussion as *the* main approach to teaching. (Glasser gives other suggestions in his more recent book, *The Identity Society* [1972].) If you would prefer different analyses of some of the same points Glasser covers, you might read John Holt's observations on failure in *How Children Fail* (1964), Banesh Hoffman's critique of grades in *The Tyranny of Testing* (1962), the discussions of the discovery approach provided by Jerome Bruner in *Toward a Theory of Instruction* (1966). You might also consult *Learning Theories for Teachers* (3rd ed., 1976), by Morris L. Bigge or *Education and the Human Quest* (1960) by Herbert A. Thelen. If you read Glasser's book or one of the others, you might summarize the arguments presented and add your own reactions.

13-9

Learning for Mastery

If you are impressed by the arguments of Glasser and Holt regarding the negative impact of failure, you may wish to use an alternative to traditional comparative grading. Holt advocates an intellectual smorgasbord with emphasis on free choice and self-direction; Glasser recommends group discussion. Both believe that grades should be eliminated. Such methods are appropriate and effective in certain situations, and you may wish to use them from time to time. It is not likely that you will be able to rely on either technique exclusively, however, because of the organization and administration of public schools in this country. You may find that learning for mastery is a more satisfactory way to reduce the impact of failure while still working within a system of letter grades. If you would like to learn more about this technique for the purpose of drawing up a detailed set of guidelines, consult *Mastery Learning: Theory and Practice* (1971), edited by James H. Block (a concise paperback), or *A Handbook of Formative and Summative Evaluation of Student Learning* (1971), edited by Benjamin S. Bloom, Thomas Hastings, and George F. Madaus (a volume that provides encyclopedic coverage).

In both chapters of Part 6 on evaluation your attention was called to frequency distributions. In Chapter 12 the normal curve was diagrammed and its uses in conjunction with the standard deviation were described. The analysis of standardized tests in the same chapter emphasized that when large numbers of pupils are asked to respond to identical sets of questions, scores reflecting their performance typically are distributed in bell-shaped fashion. In Chapter 13 suggestions were offered for plotting frequency distributions depicting pupil performance on classroom exams, particularly when you are faced with the necessity of assigning grades.

The normal curve, standard scores, and frequency distributions all call attention to a significant fact of academic life: Students vary in ability and performance. Many students cluster around the center of a distribution of measures of general or specific academic abilities, but some inevitably rate very high or very low; others are between the middle and the extremes. The learning characteristics of some atypical pupils can be traced to differences in general academic ability. Other people are exceptional because of glandular, physical, or neurological abnormalities. Still others may be atypical because of lack of satisfaction of needs, leading to behavior disorders.

For these reasons, and many others as well, there are tremendous individual differences between pupils. This part examines some of these differences and offers suggestions you might try in dealing with them. Chapter 14 describes characteristics of and teaching techniques for pupils who are exceptional because of intellectual, neurological, glandular, or physical attributes and/or learning traits. Chapter 15 is devoted to the subject of classroom control. Some pupils respond more favorably to instruction and to school routine than others. In some cases pupils may be difficult to control because of types of exceptionality described in Chapter 14. In other cases the causes of pupil misbehavior may be a function of unsatisfied deficiency needs. Regardless of the cause, disruptive classroom behavior interferes with instruction and learning. Accordingly, you will be eager to maintain control of classroom activities. Chapter 15 opens with an analysis of the impact of different types of leadership. Next, causes of misbehavior are discussed. The bulk of the chapter is devoted to descriptions of dozens of specific techniques you might use to establish and maintain control in your classroom.

Part Seven

Individual differences

Chapter 14   Teaching exceptional students

Chapter 15   Maintaining classroom control

Key points

The education for all handicapped children act

Handicapped children to have individualized educational programs

Tests should not discriminate against minority-group children

Mainstreaming: Exceptional children should be taught in regular classes

Teaching slow learners

Slow learners may have low tolerance for frustration

Slow learners lack confidence and are low in self-esteem

Slow learners have short memory and attention spans

Slow learners oversimplify, concentrate on one quality, cannot generalize

Teaching rapid learners

Rapid learners skilled at absorbing, organizing, and applying abstract concepts

Some rapid learners convergent, others divergent thinkers

Pupils with learning disabilities

Learning disabilities: Disorders in basic processes involved in understanding and using language

Learning disabled have memory problems, short attention span, emotional and social difficulties

Teaching hyperactive pupils

Teachers should call parents' attention to hyperactive pupil behavior, not recommend treatment

Using behavior modification techniques with hyperactive pupils

Identifying and teaching handicapped students

Visual problems indicated by atypical reading habits, eye sensitivity, inconsistent school performance

Hearing problems indicated by inattention, odd mistakes, irrelevant answers, voice peculiarities

Helping students deal with behavior disorders

Maslow: Behavior disorders traceable to lack of satisfaction of needs

Lewin: Behavior disorders represent unsatisfactory attempts to reduce tension

Reactions to frustration: Aggression, defense mechanisms, withdrawal

Teachers may be more concerned about disruptive behavior than withdrawal

Serious symptoms: Depression, unsociability, fearfulness, suspiciousness

Extreme, inappropriate reactions suggest underlying difficulties

Unwise for teachers to attempt to function as therapists

Sympathetic listening by teachers may help pupils cope

Chapter 14

Teaching exceptional students

IN 1972 Elliot L. Richardson, who was then U.S. Secretary of Health, Education, and Welfare, authorized what came to be called the Project on Classification of Exceptional Children. In announcing the project, Richardson emphasized that it was intended to call attention to and correct for unfortunate consequences of labeling children as retarded, emotionally disturbed, hyperactive, or delinquent. He requested that those in charge of the project review classification procedures, assess the impact of present labeling procedures on the lives of children, and make recommendations for improving practices. Nicolas Hobbs of Vanderbilt University was asked to supervise the efforts of close to one hundred experts in various fields who participated in the project, and he also edited the project reports. Two volumes of detailed analyses of thirty-one aspects of classification are presented in *Issues in the Classification of Children* (1975). A summary and synthesis of material covered in the comprehensive reports are offered in *The Futures of Children* (1975).

Disadvantages and advantages of labeling

Hobbs begins *The Futures of Children* by pointing out that there are 7,083,000 children from newborn to nineteen identified as handicapped by the Bureau of Education for the Handicapped, U.S. Office of Education. He then summarizes disadvantages and advantages of referring to these children as handicapped, or exceptional, and of classifying them under more specific labels, such as mentally retarded or emotionally disturbed. Following is a paraphrased digest of some of the points made by Hobbs (1975c, pp. 3–4) in discussing labeling.

Children who are labeled as handicapped or exceptional may be permanently stigmatized, rejected, and denied opportunities for full development. Yet if they are not labeled, they may fail to benefit from special programs intended to help them.

Children who are labeled as mentally retarded or the equivalent may be assigned to inferior educational programs in schools or be placed in institutions without giving them the benefit of legal protection extended to "normal" individuals. Yet, we possess knowledge needed to evaluate children with reasonable accuracy and have developed educational techniques that are quite effective in helping children with low intelligence make the most of their abilities.

Large numbers of minority-group children are inaccurately classified as mentally retarded on the basis of scores earned on inappropriate tests. Yet such children often *do* need instruction that differs from that given to majority-group children in typical classrooms.

After mentioning these points, Hobbs lists several assumptions that served as guidelines for the project and the reports. Assumptions that are of significance to teachers include:

Classification of exceptional children is essential to get services for them, to plan and organize helping programs, and to determine the outcomes of intervention efforts (p. 5).

Public and private policies and practices must manifest respect for the individuality of children and appreciation of the positive values of their individual talents and diverse cultural backgrounds. Classification procedures must not be used to violate this fundamental social value. (p. 6)

Special programs for handicapped children should be designed to encourage fullest possible participation in the usual experiences of childhood, in regular schooling and recreational activities, and in family and community life. When a child must be removed from normal activities, he should be removed the least possible distance, in time, in geographical space, and in the psychological texture of the experience provided. (p. 9)

Categories and labels are powerful instruments for social regulation and control, and they are often employed for obscure, covert, or hurtful purposes: to degrade people, to deny them access to opportunity, to exclude "undesirables" whose presence in some way offends, disturbs familiar custom, or demands extraordinary effort. (p. 11)

Categories and labels may open up opportunities for exceptional children, facilitate the passage of legislation in their interest, supply rallying points for volunteer organizations, and provide a rational structure for the administration of governmental programs. (p. 13)

After listing these assumptions, Hobbs comments on the social functions of categories and labels. He notes that quite often identifying and treating individuals who are atypical as atypical are done as much for the protection and convenience of the public at large as for the welfare of the individuals concerned. Placing mentally retarded children in institutions, for example, is often the simplest way to provide care. This tendency may be encouraged because "normal" individuals who have not had contact with "abnormal" ones may feel threatened or repelled by those who are atypical. If an abnormal person is given a label, normal individuals may feel that a protective barrier has been erected between "us"' and "them." This tendency leads to unfortunate consequences: It encourages the false compartmentalization of individuals. It sanctions placing some groups apart from others. It may serve as a rationalization for neglectful or "inhuman" treatment. Those who are not handicapped by atypical characteristics or forms of behavior may desire to avoid contact with exceptional individuals because habitual patterns of interaction with others may be inappropriate when dealing with those who differ from the norm in significant ways. Some handicapped individuals are disfigured or unattractive; many of them are dependent, at least in part, on others; and both these qualities may lead to avoidance tendencies. Such tendencies may emerge and be sustained to a considerable extent simply because of lack of contact and familiarity. Most people do not have (or seek) the opportunity to interact with handicapped or culturally different individuals in a sustained way under favorable circumstances. As a consequence, when they find themselves confronted by individuals who are different, they may experience anxiety, discomfort, or even revulsion. Such reactions are often intensified if the atypical person is labeled.

E. Goffman (1963) has pointed out that the term *stigma* was originally used to refer to bodily signs (often cut or burnt into a person's body) calling attention to something unusual or bad about an individual. This barbaric procedure is no longer practiced, but attaching a label to a person may produce the same effect. A child who is assigned to a class for the mentally retarded, for example, may be ostracized by neighbors and peers. Furthermore, the label may lead to stereotyped and erroneous perceptions, negative expectations, and self-fulfilling prophecy reactions. Semanticists (e.g., W. Johnson, 1946) point out that when we attach labels to people, each of us tends to conjure up an image based on our own perceptions of selected representatives of that group. If different people are asked to explain what they think of when they see the phrase *mentally retarded,* for example, their reactions will probably vary to a considerable extent. Someone who lives near a family with a Down's syndrome child will think of that individual. Someone who once saw a film on severely retarded individuals being cared for in an institution may recall scenes depicted in the movie. Someone who supervised a summer recreation program for children classified as mildly retarded will think of them. A person who associates an individual or certain types of behavior with a label may come to expect that the behavior of all people who have been assigned that label will be essentially the same. Because of cognitive

dissonance, behavior that seems inconsistent may not be acknowledged or even perceived. And when children who are labeled in certain ways are consistently treated as if they have particular
characteristics, the impact of expectation will cause them to fulfill the
prophecies made by others—and themselves.

The Education for All Handicapped Children Act

Growing awareness of trends such as these stimulated the Bureau of
Education for the Handicapped and the National Advisory Committee
for the Handicapped (as well as other groups and individuals) to persuade Congress to pass (in November 1975) Public Law 94-142, the
Education for All Handicapped Children Act. Public Law 94-142
established the following policies:

A free public education will be made available to all handicapped children
between the ages of 3 and 18 by no later than September of 1978 and all those
between 3 and 21 by September of 1980. . . .

> Handicapped children
> to have individualized
> educational programs

For each handicapped child there will be an "individualized educational
program"—a written statement jointly developed by a qualified school official, by the child's teacher and parents or guardian, and if possible by the
child himself. . . .

Handicapped and nonhandicapped children will be educated together to
the maximum extent appropriate. . . .

> Tests should not
> discriminate against
> minority-group children

Tests and other evaluation material used in placing handicapped children
will be prepared and administered in such a way as not to be racially or
culturally discriminatory, and they will be presented in the child's native
tongue.

There will be an intensive and continuing effort to locate and identify
youngsters who have handicaps. . . .

The States and localities will undertake comprehensive personnel development programs, including inservice training for regular as well as special
education teachers and support personnel, and procedures will be launched
for acquiring and disseminating information about promising educational
practices and materials coming out of research and development efforts.
(Goodman, 1976, pp. 6-7)

> Mainstreaming:
> Exceptional children
> should be taught in
> regular classes

The most significant point about these policies, as far as teachers
are concerned, is that many exceptional children who previously
were placed in special classes are now to be instructed by regular
classroom teachers. The placement of exceptional children in regular
classes is referred to as *mainstreaming*, and this chapter is intended to
make you aware of "promising educational practices and materials"
you might use if you are given the responsibility for educating different types of exceptional children.

Before suggestions you might consult for teaching exceptional

The Education for All Handicapped Children Act has led to mainstreaming—the placement of handicapped pupils in regular classes.

Courtesy of Kennedy Memorial Hospital

children are presented, a few general guidelines based on points already made in this chapter should be listed.

Guidelines for teaching exceptional children

First of all, even though there are reasons for not placing children in categories, each of the following sections of this chapter refers to a particular type of exceptional child. This organization reflects a point made by Hobbs: It is impossible to discuss how to arrange learning experiences for certain types of children unless one first describes the characteristics of such children. It does not seem necessary or desirable for teachers to act as if exceptionality simply does not exist. But when thinking about how to plan educational experiences for any of the types of exceptional children described in this chapter, you are urged to make an effort to avoid the pitfalls of stigmatizing or stereotyping. One way to guard against these pitfalls is to concentrate on individual characteristics. (Hobbs suggests the use of a profile of assets and liabilities for each exceptional child in particular settings.) Another approach is to examine your own reactions to exceptional children by thinking about the possible impact of cognitive dissonance and of the self-fulfilling prophecy.

Secondly, if you have had little or no contact with handicapped

Handbook heading
Preparing Individual Profiles of Strengths and Weaknesses

individuals, you might try to observe special classes or programs in your local school system. If you have had at least some contact with mentally retarded children in a special class or with blind, deaf, or orthopedically handicapped children, you should feel more confident and comfortable if such pupils are later assigned to your classes.

Edwin W. Martin, Jr., Associate Commissioner of the Bureau of Education for the Handicapped, comments on the effect of widespread unfamiliarity with exceptional individuals:

Most teachers share with most Americans the experience of having known or worked with few handicapped persons. Our social mechanisms for excluding handicapped children from schools, from transportation, from public parks, playgrounds, and buildings, from jobs, and from social contacts have worked all too well. This lack of familiarity and confidence in human relations with handicapped persons means that many teachers will need special assistance if they are to interact successfully to help handicapped children learn. (1972, p. 520)

In addition to seeking "special assistance" (by using suggestions and references supplied in this chapter), you might attempt to find ways to have at least some contact with handicapped individuals before you begin your teaching career.

The points just made apply to teaching all exceptional children. The following sections offer descriptions of characteristics and suggestions for teaching the following types of exceptional pupils: slow learners, rapid learners, those with learning disabilities, hyperactive children, students with physical and neurological handicaps of various types, and children experiencing difficulties coping with behavior disorders.

Teaching slow learners

The distribution of measured intelligence

As soon as psychologists developed ways to measure attributes and plotted their findings graphically, they discovered that most characteristics of human beings seem to be distributed in the form of a bell-shaped curve. Such curves reflect the fact that most people are average, and the frequency of average individuals is indicated by the shape of the top of the bell in the center. (Simply imagine that all people who have exactly the same amount of a characteristic are standing on top of each other.) Smaller numbers of people are above or below average, and when they are represented graphically, they trail out toward the rim of the bell on either side. (At the extreme ends, perhaps only one person out of a large sample will be found.)

When intelligence tests were first developed and administered to large numbers of children, it was discovered that IQ scores typically formed a bell-shaped distribution when plotted graphically. Since this was the case, those who developed later intelligence tests, such as the Stanford-Binet, used statistical procedures derived from the normal curve to select questions during the standardization process that would produce a bell-shaped distribution of scores. Subsequent use of the Stanford-Binet with large numbers of children has revealed that scores on this test do turn out to be distributed more or less normally. It seems likely that this distribution is due, in part at least, to the way the test was standardized. But it also seems likely that intelligence *is* distributed in a way that is reflected by the normal probability curve. Support for that assumption derives from the fact that the Stanford-Binet (and any other intelligence test) is made up of individual items, each of which is somewhat independent by others. Any individual's score, therefore, will be based on a somewhat unique pattern of correct and incorrect answers. The test developers could not be sure that children who later took the test would respond to the questions in precisely the same way as the original standardization group. Consequently, it seems reasonable to assume that the bell-shaped distribution of intelligence test scores is not an artifact. The shape of the curve may appeal to test-makers and statisticians, but it represents a host of problems for teachers because it means that the intelligence of pupils in any class is certain to vary to a greater or lesser extent.

Most tests of intelligence have been designed to produce mean scores of 100 and a standard deviation of 15. The mean and standard deviation were described in Chapter 12. If you recall the explanations of the statistics provided earlier, you know that it is possible to use that information, together with knowledge of the normal curve, to predict how intelligence test scores will be distributed. Figure 14-1 depicts information previously reported in Figure 12-1. It shows the proportion of individuals with various IQ scores that one would expect to find within different standard deviation units above and

Figure 14-1

Theoretical distribution of intelligence test scores

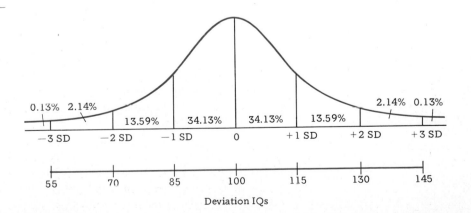

below the mean. Since we are presently concerned with exceptional children, focus on the percentage of individuals who are two standard deviations or more below the mean.

The classification of low-IQ children

An individual who has an IQ at a point on the distribution that is two standard deviations below the mean has an IQ of 70. If the population of the United States is taken as 208 million people, one would expect, on the basis of the theoretical normal curve distribution, that 4,732,000 persons would have IQs of less than 70. On the basis of actual sampling surveys of measured intelligence, H. C. Haywood (1974) estimates that 6,791,800 persons in a population of 208 million have IQs below 70. The discrepancies in estimates based on the normal curve and on actual test scores are explained by Haywood in this way:

The theoretical distribution rests partially on the assumption that the level of general intelligence attained by any individual is genetically determined. There is a growing body of evidence that this is not wholly true; that is, experiences encountered by any individual after birth, and indeed up to adulthood, appear to play a large part in determining his ultimate intellectual growth, especially when one considers intelligence to be represented by a single global score. Variables which appear to influence intellectual growth and the expression of intelligence include ethnicity, social class, chronological age, race, relative cultural advantage-disadvantage, nutrition, education, general health, and specific child-rearing practices. One obvious fact that renders the empirical distribution asymmetrical is that there are many accidents that result in brain damage, hence lower intellectual functioning, but none that are known to result in higher intellectual functioning. (Quoted in Hobbs, 1975a, p. 197)

The theoretical distribution of intelligence is also based on the assumption that intelligence tests are equally fair and appropriate for all children. It does not appear that this is a valid assumption. Jane R. Mercer (1975) called attention to the possibility that IQ tests discriminate against certain children when she investigated the backgrounds of 812 Riverside, California, residents classified as retarded. She found that in this group there were 300 percent more Mexican-Americans and also 50 percent more blacks than their proportion in the general population, but only 60 percent as many Anglo-Americans. Furthermore, persons in the lowest socioeconomic categories were greatly overrepresented and those at the upper levels underrepresented.

Mercer concluded that the public school system was the primary labeler in the community and argued that in order to prevent poverty-level and minority-group children from being improperly branded as mentally retarded early in their school careers, improvements in diagnosis must be made. Specifically, she recommended that both IQ and adaptive behavior should be considered whenever decisions were made regarding special class placement, that sociocultural factors should be taken into account in interpreting test scores, and that all assessment procedures should take into account the civil rights of those being classified. Mercer also proposed that children from poverty-level and minority-group homes be given supplemental help (e.g., tutorial assistance, training in English, speech therapy, remedial reading) so that they could remain in regular classes, that they be free of stigmatizing labels, and that they be encouraged to maintain their ethnic identity and self-respect.

As a result of reports prepared by Mercer and by other psychologists who have studied the problem (and of lawsuits based on the evidence reported), some states have passed laws prohibiting schools from using intelligence test scores as the sole basis for classifying children as retarded. Even so, IQ scores are almost indispensable when decisions must be made regarding the placement in special classes of children low in intelligence. Evidence and arguments presented by Mercer and others have not eliminated the use of IQ tests or the classification of some children as mentally retarded. Instead, arguments that tests discriminate against some children have led to increasing use of estimates of *adaptive behavior* when measures of intellectual functioning must be made. The use of IQ scores *and* adaptive behavior to categorize children low in intelligence is illustrated by the American Association on Mental Deficiency (AAMD) classification of mentally retarded and slow-learning children.

For reasons discussed in commenting on the disadvantages and advantages of labeling, there has been a trend toward reducing or eliminating the use of classification schemes. At the same time, as Nicholas Hobbs points out, it is sometimes essential to classify children who differ in significant ways from the norm in order to plan and finance special educational programs for them. The need for classifying children who are low in intelligence has been recognized by the AAMD, which has proposed this definition: "Mental retardation refers to significantly subaverage intellectual functioning existing concurrently with defects in adaptive behavior and manifested during the developmental period" (Grossman, 1973, p. 5). The AAMD applies the term *mental retardation* to children having IQs of 67 and below and classifies those with IQs within that range into the following categories:

Mild retardation	IQ between 67 and 52
Moderate retardation	IQ between 51 and 36
Severe retardation	IQ between 35 and 20
Profound retardation	IQ of 19 and below

It is not likely that you will encounter children classified as mentally retarded in regular classes because their retardation is so extreme they need specialized forms of care and instruction.

Children who have IQs above 67, but learn at a reduced rate compared to peers, are referred to as *slow learners,* or as *borderline* children. The upper limit of the slow learner category is established by an IQ score of 85 (one standard deviation below the mean). As a consequence of the Education for All Handicapped Children Act, children classified as slow learners are more likely to be placed in regular classes today than they were a few years ago. Children who have scores toward the upper end of the 68 to 85 range will often have learning characteristics that are indistinguishable from pupils who have IQs slightly above 85. Furthermore, children who have IQs in the 90s will probably learn at a slower rate than classmates who have average and above-average IQs. Accordingly, you are likely to have pupils in your classes who function as slow learners, even though they might not be formally categorized as such under the classification scheme proposed by the AAMD. In recognition of this fact, the term *slow learner* is used in this chapter to refer to all pupils who learn at a significantly slower rate than classmates. (If you read books or articles about subaverage IQ individuals that mention the AAMD classification, *slow learner* or *borderline* will probably refer to children with IQs between 85 and 68.)

Characteristics of slow learners[1]

Children who are below average in intelligence follow the same developmental pattern as their peers with higher IQs, but they differ in the rate and degree of development. Accordingly, low-IQ children may possess characteristics typical of average-IQ children who are younger than they are. One general characteristic of such children, therefore, is that they may often appear immature compared to their agemates. You may be able to understand some of the behavior of slow learners if you think of them as being the equivalent of younger children placed in a class with older, more sophisticated children. Immature children are likely to have many experiences of frustration when they find they are unable to do things their classmates can do, and many slow learners tend to have a low tolerance for frustration. Such behavior might be understood by taking into account the likelihood that a slow learner will need to expend more effort coping with situations more favored peers take in stride. Related to frustration proneness is a tendency toward self-devaluation. When slow learners become aware that they experience difficulty doing what classmates

Slow learners may have low tolerance for frustration

Slow learners lack confidence and are low in self-esteem

[1] Many of the points in this section are based on a discussion of characteristics of mentally retarded children in *A Curriculum Guide for Teachers of the Educable Mentally Handicapped* (undated) by Herbert Goldstein and Dorothy M. Seigle.

do with ease, they are likely to develop doubts about their abilities and suffer from lack of confidence and low self-esteem.

Slow learners have short memory and attention spans

The intellectual characteristics of slow learners include tendencies to oversimplify concepts, the inability to generalize, short memory and attention span, the inclination to concentrate on only one aspect of a learning situation and to ignore incidentals, and retarded language development. Several of these characteristics can be understood more completely if they are related to Piaget's description of cognitive development. The slow learner in the elementary school may think in preoperational terms until quite late in the grades. Slow learners in secondary schools may never move beyond the level of concrete operations. Younger slow learners will tend to classify things in terms of a single feature. Older slow learners may be able to deal with concrete situations but find it difficult to grasp abstractions, generalize from one situation to another, or state and test hypotheses.

Slow learners oversimplify, concentrate on one quality, cannot generalize

Now that you have familiarity with characteristics of slow learners, it is time to turn to a discussion of techniques of teaching. The following suggestions take into account the characteristics just described, as well as points made by Samuel Kirk (1972, pp. 214–216) and O. P. Kolstoe (1970, pp. 22–23).

Suggestions for teaching: Instructing slow learners

1. As much as possible, try to avoid placing slow learners in situations that are likely to lead to frustration. When, despite your efforts, such students give indications that they are close to their limit of frustration tolerance, encourage them to engage in relaxing change-of-pace pursuits or in physical activities.

2. Do everything possible to encourage a sense of self-esteem.

3. Present learning tasks that are simple and contain the smallest possible number of elements, at least some of which are familiar to the pupil.

4. Give a series of brief lessons that can be completed in short periods of time, instead of comprehensive assignments that require sustained concentration and effort.

5. Build overlearning into lessons. Keep going back over material previously learned, but make drill as interesting and enjoyable as possible.

6. Try to arrange what is to be learned into a series of small steps, each of which leads to immediate feedback. In other words, use techniques of programmed instruction.

7. Devise and use record-keeping techniques that make it clear that assignments have been completed successfully and that progress is taking place.

1. As much as possible, try to avoid placing slow learners in situations that are likely to lead to frustration. When, despite your efforts, such students give indications that they are close to their limit of frustration tolerance, encourage them to engage in relaxing change-of-pace pursuits or in physical activities.   Since slow learners are more likely to experience frustration than their more capable peers, it is desirable to try to minimize the frequency of such experiences in the classroom. Probably the most effective way to do this is to give slow learners individual assignments so that they are not placed in situations where their work is compared to that of others. No matter how hard you try, though, you will not be able to eliminate frustrating experiences, partly because you will have to schedule some all-class activities, partly because even individual assignments may be difficult for a slow learner to handle. If you happen to notice that such a pupil appears to be getting more and more bothered by inability to complete a task, you might try to divert attention to a less demanding form of activity or have the pupil engage in physical exercise of some kind.

Handbook heading
Helping Slow Learners
Deal with Frustrations

EXAMPLES

Have a primary grade pupil who is having trouble with arithmetic problems do some artwork or run to the end of the playground.

Have a secondary grade pupil who is frustrated by inability to complete an assignment take a note to the office.

2. Do everything possible to encourage a sense of self-esteem.   Slow learners are prone to devalue themselves because they are aware they are less capable than classmates at doing many things. One way to combat this tendency toward self-devaluation is to make a point of showing that you have positive feelings about less capable students. If you indicate that you have positive feelings about an individual, that person is likely to acquire similar feelings about himself or herself. The best overall strategy to use in building self-esteem, however, is to help slow learners successfully complete learning tasks, and suggestions 3 through 7 in this list offer ideas you might use.

3. Present learning tasks that are simple and contain the smallest possible number of elements, at least some of which are familiar to the pupil.   Since slow learners tend to oversimplify concepts, try to give them lessons that are simple to begin with. If possible, select learning tasks that contain only a few elements, at least some of which have been previously learned.

Handbook heading
Giving Slow Learners
Simple Assignments

EXAMPLES

Give primary grade slow learners books that tell a simple story and that contain words the child has recently learned.

Ask secondary school social studies students to prepare a report on the work of a single police officer, as opposed to preparing an analysis of law enforcement agencies (which might be an appropriate topic for the best student in the class).

4. Give a series of brief lessons that can be completed in short periods of time, instead of comprehensive assignments that require sustained concentration and effort. Slow learners tend to have a short attention span. If they are asked to concentrate on demanding tasks that lead to a delayed payoff, they are likely to become distracted or discouraged. Therefore, it is better to give a series of short assignments that produce immediate feedback than to use any sort of contract approach or the equivalent where the student is expected to engage in self-directed effort leading to a remote goal.

EXAMPLES

Ask primary graders to read one page at a time instead of a chapter at a time.

Ask secondary school English students to read a series of short short stories instead of a novel.

5. Build overlearning into lessons. Keep going back over material previously learned, but make drill as interesting and enjoyable as possible. Slow learners have a short memory span and find it difficult to place what is learned in their long-term storage system. Explanations for this include their tendency to oversimplify concepts and their limited ability to generalize. A person with high intelligence is able to grasp the structure of a field of study and comprehend relationships, and both of these abilities make memorizing simpler and forgetting less likely. The slow learner, by contrast, tends to learn one isolated thing at a time. This is essentially what is meant by rote memorization, and it is unfortunate that many individuals with low intelligence can learn only by repeatedly going over specific items again and again. When teaching slow learners, it is necessary, therefore, to engage in what amounts to drill, but you might do your best to avoid making this drill seem pointless or tedious. (Several suggestions for making drill interesting were offered in the section on memorizing in Chapter 8.)

Handbook heading
Using Overlearning
with Slow Learners

EXAMPLES

Have primary grade slow learners form a group and practice the same ten spelling words every day for a week. Then include the same words in lists presented during following weeks. To give such sessions a bit of variety, use different games, such as spelling baseball or having children pick out cards containing a word to be spelled.

In a secondary school home economics class, have students bake a series of cakes by following recipes that are essentially the same but produce a variety of desserts.

6. Try to arrange what is to be learned into a series of small steps, each of which leads to immediate feedback. In other words, use techniques of programmed instruction.   In the discussion of programmed learning in Chapter 5, the point was made that the technique often leads to negative reactions on the part of bright students because of the lowest common denominator effect and impatience with the need to supply a series of brief answers. The same characteristics of programmed instruction are advantageous for slow learners. Students who lack confidence, tend to think of one thing at a time, are unable to generalize, and have a short memory and attention span usually respond quite positively to programmed instruction. The systematic step-by-step procedure, the emphasis on only one specific idea per frame, and the provision of immediate feedback all fit very well with characteristics of slow learners. Therefore, you might look for published programs in the subject or subjects you teach or develop your own

Handbook heading
Using Programmed
Instruction with Slow
Learners

programmed materials, perhaps in the form of a workbook of some kind.

EXAMPLES

In the primary grades, use programmed readers, and look for programs in spelling and arithmetic.

At the secondary level, distribute a list of questions on a chapter, and urge slow learners to be especially conscientious in completing brief answers to one question at a time.

7. Devise and use record-keeping techniques that make it clear that assignments have been completed successfully and that progress is taking place. When a student experiences difficulties in learning it is especially important to provide tangible proof that progress is being made. When students correctly fill in blanks in a programmed workbook and discover that their answers are correct, they are encouraged to go on to the next frame. You might use the same basic approach in more general ways by having slow learners keep records of progress. (This technique might be used with *all* students in a class, not just slow learners.)

Handbook heading
Giving Slow Learners
Proof of Progress

EXAMPLES

Make individual charts for primary grade pupils. As they successfully complete assignments, have them color in marked-off sections; or paste on gold stars or the equivalent; or trace the movement of animal figures, rockets, or whatever, toward a destination.

At the secondary level, make up a chart of which scores on a series of tasks are to be recorded. Then encourage students to record each score as the work is completed.

At any grade level, use a mastery approach: Establish criteria. Present lessons. Measure achievement. Provide remedial instruction if necessary. Measure achievement again. Record successful completion of each unit and total points as they are accumulated.

Teaching rapid learners

Pupils who learn at a slower rate than most of their classmates are likely to respond more favorably to instruction if they are taught in accordance with the suggestions just made. Pupils who learn at a significantly *faster* rate than their peers also may need to be taught in special ways if they are to make the most of their abilities.

Characteristics of rapid learners

The AAMD classification of mental retardation refers to specific IQ scores in establishing the upper and lower limits of various categories. It is not possible to be that specific about the test scores of atypically bright pupils. In the 1920s, Lewis Terman and Melita Oden (1925) proposed an IQ of 140 as the cutoff point for classifying children as *gifted*. The 140 IQ dividing line was widely endorsed until the 1960s when a number of psychologists (e.g., Getzels and Jackson, 1962) called attention to the fact that many children who deserved to be classified as gifted did not earn IQ scores of 140 or above, primarily because the tests used to measure IQ seemed to discriminate against divergent thinkers. Because of controversies over interpretation of the term *gifted* and over ways to identify individuals who deserve to be labeled as such, the term *rapid learner* is used in this book to refer to children who are exceptionally capable students. Such pupils may or may not earn IQs in excess of 140.

After surveying a number of definitions and lists of characteristics and proposals for identifying exceptionally capable learners, James J. Gallagher concluded that what such individuals have in common "is the ability to absorb abstract concepts, to organize them more effectively, and to apply them more appropriately than does the average youngster" (1975, p. 19). That is probably as concise and accurate a description of rapid learners as can be found. Perhaps the only points that need to be added to Gallagher's description are that some rapid learners are ideal students and impress their teachers that way and that other rapid learners may be thought of as pests or perhaps classified by some teachers as below averge in ability. A few differences between these two types merit mention.

Some pupils with high IQs respond to instruction easily, give answers that are precisely what teachers want, and are models of good conduct. In terms of Guilford's description of intellectual operations, such students might be classified as extremely competent *convergent thinkers*. When teachers are asked to nominate the most capable pupils in their classes, they tend to choose children of this type. Although such individuals tend to do exceptionally well in school and in later life, they are typically not very innovative (Terman and Oden, 1959). They become successful doctors, lawyers, professors, and businesspeople, but they are not likely to make original contributions in their fields. Other rapid learners do *not* respond to instruction in expected ways. They may act bored, often respond to questions in unorthodox or unsettling ways, and perhaps give the impression that they are uncooperative or disruptive. Many pupils of this type might be classified as brilliant *divergent* thinkers. Allowing for the possibility of unconventional types of mental superiority helps explain why

Rapid learners skilled at absorbing, organizing, and applying abstract concepts

Some rapid learners convergent, others divergent thinkers

Einstein and Edison (to note only two of the most frequently mentioned examples) were considered to be extremely poor learners by their teachers. The later achievements of Einstein and Edison suggest that gifted divergent learners may become highly productive and creative—provided their spark of genius is not completely squelched in school.

The following suggestions for teaching rapid learners may be more useful if you allow for the possibility that not all bright students will use their gifts in the same ways.

Suggestions for teaching: Instructing rapid learners

1. Consider discussing the possibility of acceleration with extremely capable students, their parents, and school consultants and administrators.

2. Provide horizontal or vertical enrichment.

3. Consult with rapid learners regarding individual study projects, perhaps set up in the form of a learning contract.

4. Encourage supplementary reading and writing.

5. Foster the development of creative hobbies and interests.

6. Check into the possibility of correspondence courses or tutoring.

1. Consider discussing the possibility of acceleration with extremely capable students, their parents, and school consultants and administrators. It is doubtful that you will ever be asked to take the sole responsibility for deciding whether a child should be accelerated, but if you are teaching at the primary level, you may well initiate consideration of such a move. When some pupils learn everything in a small fraction of the time their classmates require and you simply don't have time to give them the individualized instruction they need, you might consult with the pupil, parents, and your principal about the possibility of some form of acceleration. In the elementary years, this usually takes the form of skipping a grade.

Perhaps the biggest drawback to skipping a grade is that the teacher who inherits the accelerated pupil may have to scramble to fill in the work missed. Many school districts meet the problem by providing either individualized or group instruction for a month or so in the summer. If such a program exists in your area, there should be little reason to hesitate to recommend a pupil for skipping.

It should be mentioned, though, that not all pupils who skip a grade look upon their new status as an unmixed blessing. Some children are better off unaccelerated. Children who seem perfectly happy with agemates and are somewhat immature in nonintellectual characteristics might respond to schooling more favorably if they do *not* skip a grade, even though their school performance is quite exceptional.

Acceleration is usually confined to the elementary grades, but an administrative arrangement for permitting skipping at the secondary level is to have the brightest pupils go through junior high in two years with a summer session sandwiched in between. The curriculum is set up so that the rapid learner can be just that. Another procedure allows high school seniors to take college-level courses for credit. Sometimes pupils—if they are permitted to take enough units—can enter college as sophomores.

2. Provide horizontal or vertical enrichment.   Most discussions of enrichment techniques distinguish between *horizontal* and *vertical* enrichment. Horizontal enrichment consists in giving a rapid learner who has finished an assignment ahead of everyone else more material at the same general level of difficulty. The vertical approach involves giving more advanced work of the same general type. Take a math period as an example. Assume that you have started the class on a workbook assignment in math. About the time you get your pencil sharpened and turn around to start giving individual help, you bump into a girl with an IQ of 146 who has come up to announce that she has finished and ask what you would like her to do next. One reaction is to say, "Go back to your seat and do the next five pages of problems." If these problems are at the same level of difficulty, that's horizontal enrichment. If the forest of waving hands signaling the need for special help induces panic, a vertical enrichment assignment may be forthcoming: "Why don't you read the next chapter and see how well you can handle the problems we are going to take up next month."

These examples emphasize the pitfalls of literal horizontal or vertical enrichment. If you assign the fast workers more of the same, it won't take them long to figure out that there is little point in making much of an effort. This can ruin motivation, destroy the ability to concentrate, and squelch interest. On the other hand, if you urge rapid learners to take off on their own, what will happen when you reach next month's problems? The more often you resort to vertical enrichment assignments that simply anticipate what is to come, the bigger the problem becomes. Before long you are rummaging around the storeroom for next year's text. And that can *really* lead to a mess when the clear, innocent voice pipes up to announce to the teacher of the next higher grade that she's already finished the standard text. Mr. or Ms. So-and-so gave it to her.

To avoid such unpleasantness, use some discretion in applying horizontal and vertical enrichment. Don't let an assignment of more of the same seem like punishment. If the skill in question is not likely to

How should you handle an obnoxious "genius"?

Imagine that you are teaching in a third grade. It is the end of the first month of school. A new boy is assigned to your room. During his first week in class he manages to antagonize just about everyone. He gets perfect scores on all his work and makes sure the entire school is well aware of this. He shouts out answers to questions when you call on other children. (He gives the impression that he can't help doing this—he is just bursting with information.) He makes remarks about the stupidity of children who can't answer as rapidly or as accurately as he does. When he recites, he somehow works in all kinds of slightly relevant information he has memorized. He even corrects you on particular points (you spoke of "crocodiles" when you should have said "alligators"); and upon looking the matter up, you discover that he is right. How could you encourage him to be humbler without squelching his undeniable gifts?

Handbook heading
Providing Horizontal and Vertical Enrichment

be improved substantially by more repetition (e.g., problems in addition), find some related exercises of equivalent difficulty (e.g., a book of math "puzzlers"). In reading classes, permit superior pupils to read several other books at the same level of difficulty, instead of stultifying them with an additional dose of primer material. In high school classes, have optional extra assignments for the fast workers.

If you choose to give an assignment at a more advanced level, take care not to anticipate what is to be covered in ensuing semesters and years. Try to obtain curriculum materials that will supplement, not duplicate, the standard curriculum. A series of books from a different publisher is the most logical source of such materials, and most school districts have consultants who can help you obtain what you need. In any event, it pays to do some planning. Trying to take care of enrichment problems by tossing spur-of-the-moment instructions over your shoulder as you dash off to provide remedial help for the slow learners is ineffective at best and potentially disastrous.

Handbook heading
Individualized Study for Rapid Learners

3. Consult with rapid learners regarding individual study projects, perhaps set up in the form of a learning contract.   One of the most effective ways to provide enrichment when straight horizontal or vertical techniques fail to fill the gap is through the assignment of individual study projects. These assignments should probably be related to some part of the curriculum. If you are studying Mexico, for example, a rapid learner could be permitted to devote free time to a special report on some aspect of Mexican life that intrigues her or him.

To provide another variation of the individual study project, you could ask the rapid learner to act as a research specialist and report on questions that puzzle the class. An incident in a third grade classroom illustrates this technique. A child asked about sponges and triggered a whole series of related questions that the teacher couldn't answer. There happened to be a boy with an IQ of 150 in this class, and he agreed to spend his reading period with the encyclopedia and give a report on sponges the next day.

Still another individual study project is the creation of an open-ended, personal yearbook. Any time a rapid learner finishes the assigned work, he or she might be allowed to write stories or do drawings for such a journal. When possible, though, unobtrusive projects are preferable. Perhaps you can recall a teacher who rewarded the fast workers by letting them work on a mural (or the equivalent) covering the side board. If you were an average student, you can probably testify that the sight of the class "brains" having the time of their lives splashing paint around the wall was not conducive to diligent effort on the part of the have-nots sweating away at their workbooks. Reward assignments should probably be restricted to individual work on unostentatious projects.

Another way to set up independent study projects is to use the contract approach described in several of the earlier chapters of this book. Consult with pupils on an individual basis and come to mutual agreement about a personal assignment that is to be completed by a certain date. One point to keep in mind about a contract approach is that this technique may be one of the best ways to take into account the characteristics of rapid learners summarized by Gallagher: Such pupils have the "ability to absorb abstract concepts, to organize them more effectively, and to apply them more appropriately than does the average youngster." If highly capable students are uged to really come to grips with a topic, seek out relationships, organize ideas, and apply them, they should gain maximum benefit from their learning efforts. Another point to remember, though, is that even very bright pupils may not be able to absorb, organize, and apply abstract concepts until they become formal thinkers. Up until the sixth grade or so, it may be preferable to ask bright pupils to carry out a series of brief assignments (as described on activity cards) rather than attempt a comprehensive independent project.

4. Encourage supplementary reading and writing.   A common complaint about modern American education is that pupils don't do enough reading and writing. At any grade level an excellent enrichment goal is to try to remedy relative illiteracy. Encourage the capable students who have time on their hands to spend it reading and writing. A logical method of combining both skills is the preparation of book reports. It is perhaps less threatening to call them book *reviews* and emphasize that you are interested in personal reaction, not in a précis

or abstract. Some specialists in the education of the gifted have suggested that such students be urged to read biographies and autobiographies. The line of reasoning is that potential leaders might be inspired to emulate the exploits of a famous person. Even if such inspiration does not result, you could recommend life stories simply because they are usually interesting.

5. **Foster the development of creative hobbies and interests.** At the elementary level, a rapid learner might devote spare class time to the intensive development of a hobby. If the pupil has an interest in poetry or rocks or butterflies, encouragement from you may lead to future specialization.

At the secondary level, pupils who are gifted in your particular subject might be urged to spend class time on a paper for an essay contest, a science fair project, or a dress or desk to be entered in the county fair. A related point is that you should help high school seniors who are talented in your field to apply for scholarships. Some schools—and teachers—place winners each year, basically because they take the trouble to assist logical candidates.

The suggestions for encouraging creativity offered at the end of Chapter 9 are appropriate for rapid learners, regardless of grade level.

6. **Check into the possibility of correspondence courses or tutoring.** In small school districts one or two brilliant children are occasionally found to have IQs several dozen points higher than those of other above-average pupils. One way to provide for them is tutorial instruction. In some cases this is given by a principal or teacher with released time. Because of the expense, the solution is more likely to be a correspondence course. Combining these two techniques has met with a good deal of success. Called the **Sponsor-Correspondent Plan,** its purpose is to establish a liaison between the brilliant pupil and someone with training and experience in the area of the pupil's greatest interest. Often the person who serves as a sponsor is a retired expert in the field.

Suppose a brilliant boy in a small high school is fascinated by inorganic chemistry. Because of his intellect and his single-minded drive, he learns more about the subject than his teacher—who also teaches three other subjects—knows. The teacher asks a nearby college or professional organization if it knows of a retired inorganic chemist who might enjoy assisting a young enthusiast. If such a person is found, the sponsor and the pupil correspond with each other and, as often as circumstances permit, have personal conferences. Highly successful experiences with this technique have been reported, and if you find yourself teaching in a small school and bedeviled by an embryonic Einstein, it could be your salvation.

Pupils with learning disabilities

Students who are classifed as mentally retarded or as slow learners experience difficulties in school that seem to be traceable primarily to low general intelligence. Other students, however, may experience difficulties because of specific disabilities of various kinds. In the late 1960s this point was recognized when Congress passed the Learning Disabilities Act of 1969. In this act, the following definition, originally proposed by the National Advisory Committee on Handicapped of the U.S. Office of Education (1968), was offered:

Learning disabilities: Disorders in basic processes involved in understanding and using language

Children with special (specific) learning disabilities exhibit a disorder in one or more of the basic psychological processes involved in understanding or in using spoken or written language. These may be manifested in disorders of listening, thinking, talking, reading, writing, spelling, or arithmetic. They include conditions which have been referred to as perceptual handicaps, brain injury, minimal brain dysfunction, dyslexia,[2] developmental aphasia,[3] etc. They do not include learning problems which are due primarily to visual, hearing, or motor handicaps, to mental retardation, emotional disturbance, or to environmental disadvantage. (p. 14)

Characteristics of pupils with learning disabilities

A more specific list of characteristics of pupils with learning disabilities (discussed more completely in Kirk, Kliebhan, and Lerner,, 1978) includes the following:

Learning disabled have memory problems, short attention span, emotional and social difficulties

Difficulty in sensory-motor or perceptual-motor learning

Difficulties with visual or auditory perception

Language disorders

Problems in forming concepts

Memory problems, particularly poor ability to recall things that look or sound alike

Short attention span

Maturational lag (slow rate of maturation of processes that may affect the ability to learn to read)

Emotional problems centering on lack of self-confidence and low self-esteem

Difficulties in learning social skills due to lack of sensitivity to people and poor perception of social situations

Samuel Kirk (1972, p. 45) estimates that from 3 to 7 percent of the

[2] Dyslexia is an impairment of the ability to read.
[3] Aphasia is a loss or impairment of the ability to use oral language.

school population have learning disabilities severe enough to require remedial instruction. The nature of learning disabilities is revealed by the characteristics of the test that is most often used to detect them, the Illinois Test of Psycholinguistic Abilities (ITPA) developed by Samuel A. Kirk, J. J. McCarthy, and Winifred D. Kirk (1968). The test was designed for use with three- to ten-year-olds, and it measures the following abilities:

a. the ability to receive and understand what is seen and heard;

b. the ability to make associations and understand interrelationships of what is seen and heard;

c. the ability to express oneself by verbal and motor responses;

d. the ability to grasp automatically the whole of a visual pattern or verbal expression when only part of it is presented; and

e. the ability to remember and repeat visual and auditory sequences of material. (Kirk, 1972, p. 55)

A profile of ITPA scores of a child with disabilities in several visual areas is reproduced in Figure 14-2.

The definition of learning disabilities included in the congressional act and the nature of the ITPA reveal that such disabilities are most significant during the primary grades, although they may continue to lead to difficulties throughout a student's school career and even beyond. If you will be teaching in the primary grades, therefore, you should be on the alert for pupils who experience difficulties in reading, writing, or oral expression. Most school systems have psychometrists who administer the ITPA and similar tests, and they often have specially trained teachers who supply remedial instruction. But a child will not be tested or given help unless a classroom teacher is alert enough to detect problems and conscientious enough to make a referral.

Techniques for teaching pupils with learning disabilities

Handbook heading
Teaching Pupils with
Learning Disabilities

If you happen to teach in a school that does not have a specialist trained to work with pupils with learning disabilities, the best single source to consult for suggestions is *Psycholinguistic Learning Disabilities: Diagnosis and Remediation* (1971) by Samuel A. Kirk and Winifred D. Kirk. To give you an idea of some of the remedial techniques recommended in this book, here are brief descriptions of two approaches: the kinesthetic method and phonic methods.

The kinesthetic method was developed by Grace Fernald (1943). She discovered that physical movement and tactile sensation served as helpful supplements to visual perception for children who were experiencing difficulties learning language skills. The technique proceeds in four stages: First, the child traces the form of a familiar word

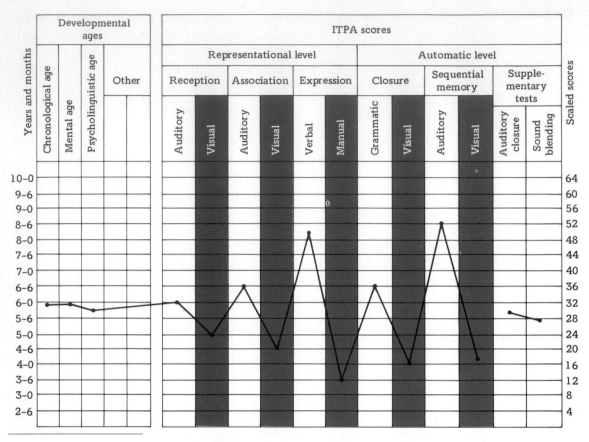

Figure 14-2

Profile of psycholinguistic ages for a child with a visual channel disability

Samuel Kirk, *Educating Exceptional Children,* 2nd ed. Copyright © 1972 by Houghton Mifflin Company. Reprinted by permission.

while saying it and then writes it from memory, comparing each trial to the printed word. Second, the child looks at the word while saying it and then writes it from memory. Third, the child writes the word without vocalizing. Fourth, the child is asked to generalize and read new words from the basis of previously learned words. In evaluating the kinesthetic method, Kirk notes (1972, p. 60) that even though it stresses tracing in the first stage, it might be more accurately called *the training of visual sequential memory,* since the goal is to have the child write words from memory.

Phonic methods, as the name implies, stress the blending of sounds. The child is presented with two- or three-letter words, asked to produce sounds separately and then blend them. After learning to pronounce a word, the child is asked to write it as it is spoken. Finally, several words that have been successfully used are combined into stories. Most phonic methods use principles of programmed instruction by providing a series of steps arranged in sequence, considerable repetition, and immediate feedback for correct responses.

A classroom teacher could use techniques such as these with a child suspected of having a learning disability. Kirk (1972, p. 67), however, ventures the opinion that attempting to help such children in a self-contained classroom is usually less satisfactory than resorting to other alternatives, such as an itinerant diagnostic remedial specialist, a resource room, or a clinic. If these alternatives are not available and if you find that you must take care of the problem by yourself, you might at least seek advice from a specialist, since the kind of remedial measures vary with the type of disability.

It is often difficult to determine the cause of a specific learning disability. Many explanations center on what was once referred to as *minimal brain damage* but is now usually called *minimal cerebral dysfunction* (because it is assumed that cells in the cerebral cortex are not functioning properly). Cerebral dysfunctions are often difficult to trace with any degree of certainty, but it is frequently found that abnormal conditions were associated with the prenatal development and birth of the child. There may have been Rh-factor incompatiblities, for example, or oxygen deprivation (anoxia) at the time of birth. Other possible causes are genetic abnormalities and malnutrition. In many cases, the source of a learning disability may be of no significance because the type of remedial instruction will be the same regardless of the source. With a different type of learning problem, however, it may be desirable to speculate about causes. That type of behavior is hyperactivity, and it has become a source of controversy during the last few years.

Teaching hyperactive pupils

Hyperactivity means excessive mobility. Hyperactive children are extremely restless, often engage in apparently random activity, and are sometimes erratic in their behavior. It is not always possible to trace the causes of hyperactivity (Weithorn, 1973), but it seems likely that in some cases abnormalities in the central nervous system are responsible for the condition or the primary cause may be biochemical.

Drugs and the hyperactive child

Parents and teachers have experienced problems dealing with hyperactive children for years, but the condition has received a great deal of publicity in the last decade, primarily because of a controversy over the use of drugs. Before the 1960s, hyperactive children were frequently placed in special classes of various kinds or taught in situations where stimuli could be held to a minimum (since a common symptom of hyperactive children, along with high activity levels, is distractibility). Then, in the 1960s, when many Americans began to experiment with drugs, it was discovered that amphetamines, which have a stimulating effect on adults, have a calming effect on children. Hyperactive children who had been given amphetamines not only seemed better able to control their tendencies toward physical activity, but also were better able to concentrate, apparently because the drug reduced the number of reactions to stimuli. This discovery, plus the ready availability of amphetamines, led to a dramatic increase in the use of drugs to control hyperactivity.

Parents or teachers who found it difficult to deal with hyperactive children persuaded doctors to prescribe amphetamines on an unprecedented scale. In time, complaints from diverse sources began to be voiced. Some critics argued that large numbers of American children were being drugged into docility for the purpose of converting them into robotlike adults. Others maintained that educators were deliberately producing drug addicts and speculated about what might happen when children who had been given amphetamines to control hyperactivity during the elementary school years reached maturity. After experiencing the physiological changes associated with puberty, it was predicted, young people addicted to "speed" would be stimulated rather than calmed when they took such drugs. Still others maintained that hyperactivity was due not to minimal cerebral dysfunction but to faulty nutrition, and they recommended dietary control and megavitamin therapy instead of drugs.

If you become aware that some of your pupils are taking drugs to control hyperkinetic behavior, you may wish to take into account some observations made by a panel appointed by the Office of Child Development of the U.S. Department of Health, Education, and Welfare. (A description of the report appears on page 6 of the *APA Monitor* for April 1971 [vol. 2, no 4].) The report contained the following information: Minimal brain dysfunction and hyperkinesis are to be found in approximately 3 percent of all school-age children, "Stimulant medications are beneficial in only about one-half to one-third of cases in which trials of the drug are warranted." When successful, the drugs improve the child's "attention, learning and social abilities," and "there is no evidence to show that the proper use of amphetamines in treating [children] leads to subsequent addiction in later life."

The panel made the following recommendations for the proper use of drugs for hyperkinetic behavior: diagnosis by a doctor (with account taken of the child's environment and family relationships as well as physical and psychological factors), close supervision of treatment, and parental understanding and cooperation. It was stressed that "while it is entirely proper for school personnel to draw parents' attention to an individual child's behavior problems in school, teachers and school administrators should scrupulously avoid any attempt to force parents to accept any particular treatment. With parental permission, they should collaborate with the physician in the total program for the child." A final point was that children should not be given sole responsibility for taking their own medication.

Because of complaints about drugs and the availability of alternative methods of treatment, it seems likely that fewer hyperactive children will be given amphetamines by the time you begin to teach. Therefore, you may find that it will be necessary to find other ways to help children control hyperactivity. The following suggestions, which reflect a programmed approach similar to that recommended for slow learners, are based on behavior modification techniques developed by Frank M. Hewett (1968).

Teachers should call parents' attention to hyperactive pupil behavior, not recommend treatment

Suggestions for teaching: Instructing hyperactive children

1. At the start of a day or class period, give pupils who have difficulty concentrating on or completing tasks a record card.

2. When first introducing behavior modification, explain that you will put a check on the card each time an assigned task is accomplished. Then point out that when a specified number of checks have been earned, the card can be traded in for a reward of some kind.

3. At first, award checks for undemanding activities; then require progressively more work before supplying a payoff.

4. If possible, give (or withhold) check marks according to a fixed-interval schedule, that is, every fifteen minutes.

5. If a pupil seems unable to respond to an initial assignment, try a different one.

6. If a student is unable to concentrate on *any* assignment or disrupts the behavior of others, consider placing the individual in an enclosed study area.

Handbook heading
Using Record Cards with Hyperactive Pupils

1. At the start of a day or class period, give pupils who have difficulty concentrating on or completing tasks a record card. Prepare some cards (3 by 5 inches or so) with space at the top for name and date and a series of grids underneath. (See Figure 14-3.) Instruct students to keep the card with them for the entire period or day and present it to you whenever you request it or when an assignment is completed.

2. When first introducing behavior modification, explain that you will put a check on the card each time an assigned task is accomplished.

Figure 14-3

Record card

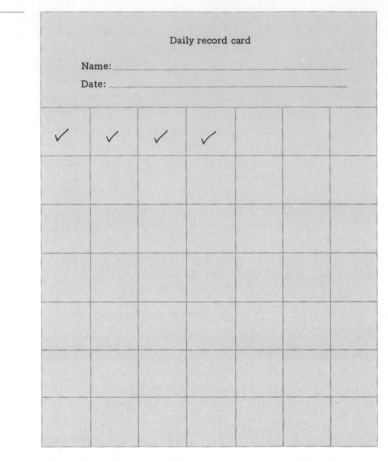

Daily record card

Name: _____

Date: _____

Adapted from Work Record Cards described by Frank M. Hewett in
The Emotionally Disturbed Child in the Classroom (1968).

Then point out that when a specified number of checks have been earned, the card can be traded in for a reward of some kind. Rewards mentioned in discussing behavior modification procedures in Chapter 5 might be used (e.g., an apple or the equivalent, a chance to engage in an activity of the student's own choice, a certain number of points toward a grade).

Using behavior
modification with
hyperactive pupils

3. At first, award checks for undemanding activities, then require progressively more work before supplying a payoff. When this technique is first used, you might award a check for something as simple as getting out a book or writing a name on a paper. Then when the pupil begins to form undesirable work habits, provide a check only when a learning task has been completed (e.g., five addition problems).

4. If possible, give (or withhold) check marks according to a fixed-interval schedule, that is, every fifteen minutes. Hewett recommends

this procedure, partly because fixed-interval schedules seem to produce steady rates of output, partly to decrease competition. It may be difficult for you to put this procedure into practice in a regular classroom if only a few students are on the record card system, but you might at least try to check progress every fifteen minutes during specified work periods and give a check mark if agreed-upon assignments have been completed. It may take a certain amount of trial-and-error experimentation to discover what you can expect from a particular child during a fifteen-minute period. If you require too little work, a pupil may waste time until the last minute or so. If you require too much, the pupil may become discouraged. In seeking the optimum rate for a particular child, it is probably better to err in the direction of assigning too much rather than too little. If you give a student more than he or she can handle in a fifteen-minute block of time, you can always give credit for a good try even if the work is not completed. Failure to give a pupil enough to do, on the other hand, may only increase tendencies toward distractibility.

5. If a pupil seems unable to respond to an initial assignment, try a different one. When a student just can't seem to get started on an assignment, give a different kind of task, or ask the pupil what she or he would like to work on. However, since the goal is to help the pupil eventually to become capable of concentrating on tasks and completing assignments, sooner or later you will probably have to award check marks only when a specified bit of work has been completed in a specified amount of time.

6. If a student is unable to concentrate on *any* assignment or disrupts the behavior of others, consider placing the individual in an enclosed study area. Since hyperactive students tend to be distractible, some theorists (e.g., A. A. Strauss and N. Kephart, 1955) reason that they may be able to learn more easily if they are placed in environments where potentially distracting stimuli are reduced. This might be done in a regular classroom by placing a screen or a curtain in one corner of the room and permitting students to go to this study corner if they feel unable to concentrate in the classroom proper. Such a technique might work for some hyperactive children, but it may not be effective for all of them. W. Cruikshank and several colleagues (1961) carried out a controlled study in which hyperactive children were taught under four sets of conditions: (1) in a room where stimulation was kept to a minimum, (2) in small individual booths, (3) in a regular classroom but with a structured, simplified program where pupils had few choices to make, (4) in situations where the stimulus value of lessons was maximized. The experimenters failed to find evidence that the nonstimulating environments were significantly superior to the other alternatives in terms of average performance. Even so, some children

might respond favorably to placement in a study corner; and if it is feasible, you might set up such an arrangement in your classroom.

Identifying and teaching handicapped students

Individual differences in intelligence and general learning ability are found in almost any class, and occasional students may have specific learning disabilities or be hyperactive, but you may also encounter other kinds of exceptionality from time to time. In the event you take the lead in identifying a child who is handicapped in some way, you may find that you are expected to make special educational provisions for the student. This section focuses on the identification of certain types of exceptionality and provides a brief list of suggestions for teaching the blind and partially sighted, the deaf and hard of hearing, and students with impaired speech.

The blind and partially sighted

Identifying children who need special education because of visual handicaps may very well be instituted by a teacher. Although the handicap of a blind child is usually apparent to almost everyone, a less severe but still damaging visual handicap is often not recognized until an eye specialist conducts a thorough examination. Perhaps the logical person to recommend such an examination is the teacher. You will be in a position to observe the child in situations that demand normal vision. Here are some symptoms of visual problems that you may notice (derived from a discussion in Dunn, 1963, pages 421–422):

Visual problems indicated by odd reading habits, eye sensitivity, inconsistent visual performance

Holding a book abnormally near or far from the eyes

Walking overcautiously; faltering, stumbling, or running into objects not directly in the line of vision

Rubbing the eyes frequently (Some children look as if they are attempting to "brush away" the blur)

Frowning and distorting the face when using the eyes, tilting the head at odd angles when looking at objects

Indicating undue sensitivity to normal light levels by squinting or other facial signs of irritation

Performing inconsistently when reading print at different distances, for example, on the board and in a book

Handbook heading

Checking on the Possibility of Visual Problems

Any suspicion that a child has a visual problem for the above or related reasons should prompt you to alert the school nurse or the parents or both. The child with a severe problem will be eligible for special schools or classes. If the problem is less incapacitating, you will want to consider special teaching techniques in your classroom.

Most states have special schools for blind children, not to mention such nationally famous institutions as the Perkins School in Watertown, Massachusetts. Many workers with the blind favor educating blind children in the specialized environment of a school created expressly for that purpose. In some cases, however, particularly at the secondary level, the parents or local school authorities prefer to have the child remain in a regular classroom. The numerous organizations that offer aid to the blind usually acquaint blind children and their parents with the resources available. For your own information, and in case you encounter a family that is unaware of these resources, here is an abbreviated list:

The Seeing Eye Dog Guide program is located in Morristown, New Jersey.

The Library of Congress Division for the Blind provides free reading materials in the form of Braille, talking books, and tape recordings. (They even pay the postage.) These materials are distributed through thirty regional libraries. Look for the address of the one in your area, or contact the American Foundation for the Blind.

The American Foundation for the Blind at 15 West 16th Street, New York, New York, provides consultative services and scholarship funds and publishes the *Braille and Talking Book Review,* as well as monographs on educational techniques.

Blind children typically attend special schools or classes until they learn to read Braille and acquire techniques for coping with their visual impairment. Because of current emphasis on mainstreaming, they may attend regular classes in public schools during their high school years.

Richard Frear/Photo Researchers

The American Printing House, a private Kentucky corporation located at 1839 Frankfort Avenue, Louisville, publishes catalogues of Braille and talking books, tape recordings, and so on.

The Hadley Correspondence School of Winnetka, Illinois, provides a wide range of home correspondence courses.

The Perkins School in Watertown, Massachusetts, sells Braille typewriters and a stylus and slate for "handwriting."

A local chapter of Lions International, the Variety Club, or the Delta Gamma Foundation will sometimes supply funds for the purchase of a small portable tape recorder and other materials and devices.

If you are wondering what it is like to teach a blind pupil in a regular class, here is a description of a blind college student. This young man came to class with a tape recorder. He recorded the lecture and class discussion and, back in the dorm after class, transcribed the recording on his Braille typewriter. Before the semester started, the text had been recorded for him on tape by an inmate at a state penitentiary. He took exams by typing out his essay answers on a conventional typewriter and by having a fellow student record answers to multiple-choice questions.

Many cities and counties provide special classes for the partially sighted, but if you are asked to teach such a child in the regular class, materials are likely to be available from the special education section of your school district. If materials are not readily available or if you must take the initiative for planning an educational program on your own, here is a list of sources to contact:

The American Foundation for the Blind, 15 West 16th Street, New York, New York, provides a variety of literature about the education of the partially sighted.

The National Society for the Prevention of Blindness, 79 Madison Avenue, New York, supplies information about the prevention of blindness. (It no longer offers other types of information on blindness.)

Stanwix Publishing House, 3020 Chartiers Avenue, Pittsburgh, Pennsylvania, publishes many materials in large type.

In addition, several publishers print large-type versions of standard texts and workbooks, and the American Optical Company sells a Projection Magnifier that optically enlarges the print of texts that have standard type size.

For complete information and suggestions regarding teaching techniques for the partially sighted, you are urged to take advantage of the resources listed above. One general rule of thumb should be mentioned in closing this section on children with visual handicaps: Be alert to the aggravating effect of glare. Many children with poor vision are rendered even less capable of seeing when they are forced to look

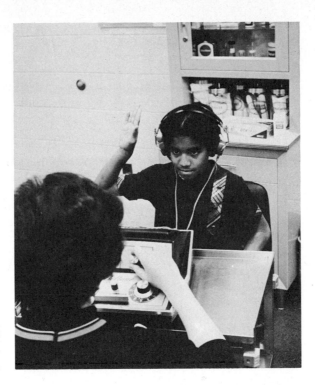

A pupil taking an audiometer (hearing) test.

De Wys, Inc.

at glaring surfaces. Permit them to experiment until they find a location in the room that is free of reflected light. Do not use dead white or coated paper if you can avoid it. Encourage partially sighted children to tilt the top of their desk or use a lapboard so that light does not reflect directly back into their eyes.

The deaf and hard of hearing

In many states, schoolchildren have to take a hearing test every two or three years. Such tests are set up so that the preliminary screening is done in groups. Occasionally a child at the borderline slips by because of the difficulties of testing large numbers of children. Or a hard-of-hearing child transfers into the school district just after the test date. Or a hearing problem begins to develop shortly after a test. (Medical authorities have expressed concern about the literally deafening impact of much popular music. Teen-agers who listen to rock music may suffer a noticeable hearing loss.) For these and similar reasons, keep in mind the following *symptoms of poor hearing,* which could tip you off that an audiometer test is called for:

Peculiar listening posture, habitual turning of the head to position one ear toward the speaker

Inattention and slow response, lack of interest in general conversation

Hearing problems indicated by inattention, odd mistakes, irrelevant answers, voice peculiarities

Mistakes in carrying out instructions or frequent requests to have instructions repeated

Irrelevant answers

Spotty educational record with poor work in subjects that require hearing the spoken voice (work depending on written directions may be done well)

Voice peculiarities—monotone, high pitch, too soft, or too loud

Faulty enunciation and mispronunciation of words

Repeated colds, earaches, ear discharge

Tendency to look at other people's lips, rather than their eyes, in face-to-face situations

Handbook heading

Checking on the Possibility of Hearing Problems

If you find it hard to understand the behavior of a student, consider the possibility of a hearing problem. It is most important to detect a hearing loss as early as possible. Most hearing difficulties detected before the age of eight can be counteracted, and a major educational handicap may result if children with limited hearing manage to conceal their disability—or remain unaware of it. In fact, the hearing difficulty may prevent them from grasping the rudiments of basic skills. Bright children sometimes compensate for defective hearing by resorting to brilliant improvisations to adjust to their condition. In the process they may exhaust themselves mentally and physically and miss out on the fundamental skills that their less capable but normal-hearing classmates are grasping with ease.

Like blindness, total deafness is likely to be detected early in life. Deaf adults who have received special education may be able to react so skillfully to a world built around sound that they are indistinguishable from their more fortunate fellow citizens. Deaf children simply cannot develop the necessary skills by themselves. The main reason is that they will not be able to learn how to talk unless they are given a highly specialized kind of schooling.

Even when they do learn to talk, children who are deaf from birth never learn to pronounce words faultlessly because of lack of feedback, and in some cases incorrect pronunciation may be the only indication you will receive that the person you are conversing with is deaf. Because of the problems of teaching a deaf child, special schools are found in most states. It is next to impossible for a regular classroom teacher with thirty other pupils even to begin to teach a deaf child. Individual attention and much special training are required, and progress is facilitated by elaborate and expensive equipment.

The hard-of-hearing child may be eligible for a special class if one is available. But you are likely to have some hard-of-hearing pupils in your own classes, either because they are not eligible for a special class or because such classes do not exist in the local school system or the school district. In such cases you might consider two remedial measures. First, you could inquire about the possibility of receiving specialized assistance from the school speech therapist, a speech clinic attached to a college, or a summer school or camp sponsored by the Crippled Children's Society (or the equivalent). Children with a hearing loss need the help of specialists to determine whether a hearing aid is advisable and to learn speech (or lip) reading. Usually speech training is desirable to enable them to increase the vocabulary of words they can pronounce properly. Second, there are certain things you can do on your own:

Handbook heading
Techniques for Dealing with Hearing Problems

1. *Use preferential seating.* By trial and error, find the spot in the room where the child can hear best. This is likely to be in front of the room; but because of peculiar acoustics in different settings, it may be elsewhere. Ideally, the child should sit where she or he can hear you as well as classmates. If the pupil has better hearing in one ear, a seat placed at an angle in the appropriate front corner of the room might make it simpler to tune in on most of what you say as well as recitation by classmates.

2. *Take special care to speak clearly.* This seems almost too obvious to mention, but unless you are a speech major or minor, attention has probably never been called to your elocution. A deliberate effort to improve the clarity of your speech will benefit the hard-of-hearing child—and everyone else.

3. *Try to remember to face the class whenever you speak.* This may also seem obvious, but many teachers address half their remarks to the board. Guard against this as much as you can. Face the class not only to gain maximum effectiveness from voice projection but also to permit the hard-of-hearing child to benefit from watching your lips. Make an effort to recognize and to check any nervous habits that might obscure your lips, like scratching your nose or pushing back your glasses.

4. *If the hard-of-hearing child does not understand something, rephrase it instead of repeating it verbatim.* The specialist who offered this suggestion gave two reasons for it. First, repeating the same phrase tends to focus attention on the child's handicap and is likely to make the child self-conscious. But, in addition, probably some of the sounds you used were especially difficult for the child to hear. A different set of sounds gives the pupil another assortment to choose from, so to speak, and at the same time provides additional clues to use in figuring out what you are saying.

These suggestions should help you cope with many hearing problems. However, if it is solely up to you to take the initiative in planning for the education of a deaf or hard-of-hearing child, the following sources of information will be helpful:

Educating the Deaf: Psychology, Principles, and Practices (1978) by Donald F. Moore is an excellent text and reference.

The National Association of Hearing and Speech Agencies, 919 18th Street NW, Washington, D.C., publishes a variety of pamphlets and acts as a clearinghouse on problems of the hard of hearing and the speech impaired.

Deafness Speech and Hearing Publications, Inc., publishes abstracts of articles on deafness and speech. Editorial offices are located at Gallaudet College. You may obtain information about publications on deafness and speech impairment by writing the Office of Public Information, Gallaudet College, Kendall Green, Washington, D.C.

Local chapters of the Crippled Children's Society, often in conjunction with the Shriners, offer financial aid for physical examinations and the purchase of hearing aids, as well as for treatment in clinics and attendance at camps.

Students with impaired speech

A handicap that is often related to poor hearing is impaired speech. Nonhandicapped individuals learn how to talk properly by receiving feedback in the form of their own voices. Since deaf persons cannot hear the sounds they are making, other kinds of feedback are substituted. Sometimes, for example, deaf children are asked to feel their throats. Sometimes they speak into a microphone, and the sound waves are converted into visual images on a screen resembling a TV tube. Children with a hearing loss almost invariably have a speech problem, but because they do not hear how strange their voices sound to others, they may not be bothered about this as much as the speech-impaired child who *does* get feedback. Supplementary measurements or the opinion of a specialist may be necessary to detect certain sight or hearing handicaps. Children with a speech problem proclaim it to the world every time they try to communicate with sounds. Only when we stop to consider how much we depend on oral communication do we begin to comprehend why the entire life of a speech-impaired child seems to revolve around the voice.

A child who is ashamed to speak is not only prevented from participating in many academic activities but is also cut off from others socially. Almost all social situations are predicated on the verbal interchange of ideas and reactions. The child who is unwilling or reluctant to talk is isolated. As a dedicated member of a speech and drama department frequently puts it, "Speech is the star performer in the drama of interpersonal relationships." Less obvious but perhaps more important is the key role language plays in maintaining mental health. When we use words to express our feelings, we release tension and often gain some understanding of ourselves.

The relationship between speech and mental health is circular. Good speech can contribute to good adjustment; poor speech frequently contributes to poor adjustment. At the same time, poor adjustment quite often causes poor speech. Some speech therapists maintain that *every* speech problem is a manifestation of psychological conflict. Even if this is not always the case, a very common consequence of impaired speech is the development of problems of adjustment.

As soon as you become aware of a speech defect in a child, inquire about obtaining assistance from the speech therapist on the staff of your school district. You may not be able to treat the problem yourself, but you *are* in a position to ease the reactions of a child and classmates to the condition, particularly in the case of stuttering. This impairment is especially likely to cause tension not only in the child but in the rest of the class as well. Here are some suggestions for coping with stuttering. (Many of them were supplied by a young man

A student with impaired speech engaging in a speech therapy session.

Katrina Thomas/Photo Researchers

who had struggled with stuttering for twenty-two years. Thanks to some teachers who put these ideas into practice, he overcame his handicap, became a teacher himself, and is now a superintendent.)

Handbook heading
_____
Techniques for Dealing with Speech Problems

1. *Try not to show you are upset.* The pupils in the room will take a cue from you. If you seem repulsed or bothered when a child starts to stutter, the class will probably react in the same way. Even if you *are* upset, do your best to conceal it.

2. *Go out of your way to respond positively to the child.* Most children who stutter have been subjected to numerous experiences of rejection—by parents, peers, and teachers. They need positive reinforcement to compensate for this backlog of negative reactions.

3. *Don't force the child to recite; encourage her or him to volunteer.* If you follow a policy of compulsory recitation, you might make an exception for pupils who stutter. Inform them privately that they are invited to speak up when they want to but that you will never call on them. (You will probably get a more relaxed response from the entire class if you apply this rule to *all* pupils.)

4. *If the child asks to recite and then starts to stutter, control the temptation to finish the sentence yourself.* Children who encounter problems completing a statement know what they want to say. Finishing a word or sentence for them does not assist them in any way. In effect, you are calling attention to their inability to speak normally. Children often stutter because parents and other adults have expressed concern about nonfluency. What such children desperately need is someone who *doesn't* get upset when they begin to stutter.

5. *Don't praise children when they say something in a relatively fluent manner.* This is a natural impulse, but it is a rather backhanded compliment. You may be relieved and pleased that a speech-impaired child has spoken so well, but praise tends to make what is a normal performance seem abnormal. Instead of being complimentary, your remark may become unintentionally sarcastic.

6. *Try to build up confidence through nonverbal activities.* Many stutterers lack self-confidence. Anything you can do to demonstrate to such children and their peers that they are capable in matters other than speech may help them develop sufficient poise to minimize the effects of the stuttering. You might point out accomplishments in subtle ways and perhaps arrange situations so that the child is sure to do well.

If these suggestions are not sufficient to help you handle pupils with speech problems, the best agency to get in touch with is the National Association of Hearing and Speech Agencies, 919 18th Street NW, Washington, D.C.

Helping students deal with behavior disorders

The kinds of exceptionality discussed so far in this chapter have involved differences traceable primarily to intellectual, physical, perceptual, or neurological abnormalities. Some students may experience difficulties in school, though, because of behavior disorders. In some cases problems of psychological adjustment may be due to mental or physical disabilities. More often they are caused by experiences and relationships with others. This section is devoted to an analysis of behavior disorders and suggestions you might follow in trying to help students cope with them.

Extent of behavior disorders

As mentioned previously in Chapter 4, an extensive survey (Rosen, Bahn, and Kramer, 1964) of referrals to psychiatric clinics in all parts of the United States revealed that the highest referral rates occur during the nine-to-fifteen age span, with peaks at nine and ten, and fourteen and fifteen. The referral rates and peaks varied for males and females. Boys were twice as likely as girls to receive psychiatric treatment. Peak referral years for boys were nine and fourteen; peak years for girls were ten and fifteen. The records of psychiatric clinics provide detailed data regarding behavior disorders, but such figures should be interpreted with caution because of the impossibility of making allowance for selective factors of various kinds. The data on referral peaks are supported, however, by teacher evaluations made for an extensive mental health survey of Los Angeles County (1960). Ten- and eleven-year-olds were rated as emotionally disturbed more frequently than those at other age levels.

Estimates of the prevalence of behavior disorders are difficult to make because of the problem of determining a precise point at which a particular form of behavior becomes "abnormal" or "severe," but a number of surveys have been made. Stennett (1946), for example, accumulated data on a sample of fifteen hundred children between the ages of nine and eleven (a peak period of clinic referrals) and estimated that between 5 and 10 percent had "adjustive difficulties" severe enough to warrant professional attention and that 22 percent might be classified as emotionally handicapped.

Types of behavior disorders

Several classifications of behavior disorders have been proposed. (A number of these are summarized by Anthony, 1970, pp. 668–680). The following list is based on chapters in *Child Psychiatry* (4th ed., 1972) by Leo Kanner. Kanner's classification has been selected because his book is regarded as a classic and because, by using the chapter headings in *Child Psychiatry,* you will be able to find quickly additional information on any disorder. Kanner lists the kinds of child behavior that might lead to referral to a physician or clinician under these headings (chapter and page numbers are supplied in parentheses; types of behavior, explanations, or definitions follow):

PSYCHOSOMATIC PROBLEMS

Central nervous system (Chap. 28, p. 357): headache, migraine

Circulatory system (Chap. 29, p. 366): hypertension, fainting spells

Respiratory system (Chap. 30, p. 372): breath-holding spells, asthma

Digestive system (Chap. 31, p. 383): nausea and vomiting, constipation

Muscular system (Chap. 32, p. 402): tics (involuntary, localized motor reactions of short duration), nodding spasms

Urinary system (Chap. 33, p. 417): enuresis (bed wetting)

Special senses (Chap. 34, p. 431): hallucinations (sensory impressions without external stimulation, such as hearing voices when no sound stimuli are present)

PROBLEMS OF BEHAVIOR

Problems of eating behavior (Chap. 36, p. 446): refusal of food, anorexia nervosa (self-starvation), overeating

Problems of sleeping behavior (Chap. 37, p. 473): insufficient and restless sleep

Problems of speech and language (Chap. 38, p. 487): disorders of articulation, stuttering, sensory or receptive aphasia (inability to comprehend other people's language), motor or expressive aphasia (inability to express self through speech or writing)

Habitual manipulations of the body (Chap. 39, p. 518): thumb sucking, nail biting, hair-pulling (habitual manipulations of the body differ from tics in duration, level of awareness, purposefulness, and complexity of movements involved)

Problems of scholastic performance (Chap. 40, p. 534): physical handicaps (poor vision or hearing, prolonged illness), emotional interference, intellectual inadequacy, reading or arithmetical disability

Problems of sexual behavior (Chap. 41, p. 552): masturbation, sex preoccupation, fetishism

Anger (Chap. 42, p. 569): frequent and extreme temper tantrums

Jealousy (Chap. 43, p. 575): sleep disturbances, food capriciousness, enuresis, destructiveness, and restlessness caused by extreme jealousy

Fear (Chap. 44, p. 580): specific fears that incapacitate the child, a general "fear attitude"

Anxiety attacks (Chap. 45, p. 589): recurrent "emotional explosions" involving cardiac, respiratory, and digestive disturbances, shaking and trembling

Separation anxiety (school phobia) (Chap. 46, p. 595): anxiety associated with leaving mother

Hypochondriasis (Chap. 47, p. 598): centering of attention on one or several organs of healthy body, exaggeration of minor ailment, perpetual complaints about aches and pains

Obsessions and compulsions (Chap. 48, p. 608): ideas or fears that keep recurring, are unrelated to present behavior, and seem beyond the person's control (obsessions), irresistible impulses to carry out purposeless actions (compulsions)

Hysteria (Chap. 49, p. 618): disorders not traceable to organic causes involving paralysis, anesthesia, and malfunctioning of bodily organs and systems; amnesia; multiple personality

Delinquency (Chap. 50, p. 642): disobedience, lying, stealing, destructiveness, and cruelty

Schizophrenia (and early infantile autism (Chap. 52, p. 688): seclusiveness, irritability when seclusiveness is disturbed, daydreaming, bizarre behavior, diminution in personal interests, regressive nature of personal interests, sensitivity to comment and criticism, physical inactivity.

Even an exceptionally fortunate and well-adjusted child (or adult) is almost sure, at some time or another, to have headaches, possess little desire for food, experience a nightmare, stumble over words, engage in nervous habits, suffer pangs of jealousy, feel anxious, become preoccupied about health, or experience almost any of the other types of behavior just noted. In many situations such responses are appropriate, and a person who did not develop some of the symptoms listed by Kanner would be abnormal. But when the kinds of behavior just listed become so extreme that they interfere with a child's ability to do school work or to engage in enjoyable social relationships, adults may have to intervene and offer help. The kinds of help that teachers can provide include establishing a classroom atmosphere to limit the incidence of maladjustment, identifying

problem behavior, referring a troubled child to those trained to provide psychotherapy, and being a sympathetic listener.

Helping students satisfy their needs

A basic explanation for the development of problem behavior is that
basic needs are not being satisfied. This point of veiw is emphasized
by the writings of Abraham H. Maslow. His theory of need gratification was mentioned in discussing development in Chapter 3 and in
analyzing motivation in Chapter 10. It merits mention again in this
chapter because it calls attention to things teachers might do to try to
prevent the development of behavior disorders.

A brief review of the aspects of Maslow's theory that have previously been noted will structure the discussion that follows. Maslow
maintains that each individual has an essential inner nature that is
shaped by environmental experiences. The impact of experience is
determined by how people react to situations involving a choice
between safety and growth. If individuals make growth choices, they
will achieve need gratification. If they make unwise safety choices,
their inner nature will be frustrated or denied and sickness will result.

Individuals are more likely to make growth choices if the deficiency
needs (physiological, safety, love and belonging, esteem) have been
satisfied. Since these needs can be satisfied only by others, the way
children are reacted to by parents and teachers is of great significance.
Even though the ultimate choice between safety and growth in any
situation must be made by the child, parents and teachers can supply
support and assistance by gratifying deficiency needs and by making
growth choices attractive and unthreatening.

This summary emphasizes that the most promising techniques you
might use to encourage your students to experience need gratification
have already been discussed—in the chapters on learning, motivation,
and evaluation. If you can make your students feel safe and accepted
in your room and assist them in learning they are likely to experience
feelings of belonging and esteem and be encouraged to make growth
choices that can lead to self-actualization. If you avoid or minimize
situations in which students feel threatened, rejected, or inferior, they
are more likely to make growth choices.

The dynamics of adjustment

To gain additional insight into how to make positive alternatives
attractive, examine Figure 14-4, a diagram of a choice situation
derived mainly from the work of Kurt Lewin. Representing the basic
dynamics of adjustment, it shows one of the simplest and clearest
ways deficit needs determine behavior.

*Maslow: Behavior
disorders traceable to
lack of satisfaction of
deficiency needs*

Figure 14-4
Adjustment diagram

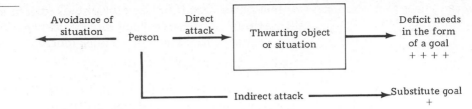

Derived from the work of Kurt Lewin and from a conception suggested by Dashiell (1949), which was further developed by Shaffer and Shoben (1956).

Lewin: Behavior disorders represent unsatisfactory attempts to reduce tension

The adjustment process is instigated by a deficit need, which produces disagreeable tension. To reduce the tension, the person must react in some way, and the action usually is an attempt to overcome a thwarting object or circumstance. If a boy is hungry, for example, he needs to either prepare or obtain food. If a girl feels left out, she needs to gain the feeling she belongs by experiencing acceptance by parents, teachers, or peers. After various exploratory attempts to reduce the tension, sooner or later the person is driven to make a choice. In an ideal situation, the chosen reaction satisfies the need. In a less than ideal situation, the chosen reaction is inadequate and the sense of relief is incomplete. The degree of satisfaction gained depends on whether the person achieves the original goal, accepts a less satisfying but reasonably adequate substitute goal, or fails to reach any goal.

Individuals can meet most deficit needs only by overcoming a frustrating circumstance. Thus, awareness of common reactions to frustration may bring better understanding of the behavior of your pupils and also provide leads on how you might be able to make desirable choices attractive.

Types of reaction to frustration

A very common reaction to frustration is aggression. Most of the time when people are thwarted, they get mad, but the anger can be expressed in positive, neutral, or negative ways. Occasionally, the aggession provoked by frustrating circumstances is channeled into creative effort. In many cases, though, the natural impulse when frustrated is to fight back at the thwarting object or person. This sort of behavior is very apparent in young children. If you try to restrain a child who is engaged in a tug of war over a tricycle, you may receive a kick or a punch. Most adults learn enough self-control to suppress such direct attacks, but they resort to insidious indirect forms of aggression as substitutes. The switching of aggressive feelings from the original source to some other person or object is called *displacement.* The directing of the displaced anger at a particular person or group of persons is called *scapegoating,* a widely prevalent source of prejudice.

Reactions to frustration: Aggression, defense mechanisms, withdrawal

Individuals confronted with a blocked-goal situation may weigh the various alternatives—including those involving aggression—and then choose (consciously or unconsciously) a somewhat less appealing substitute goal that appears easier to achieve. If a substitute goal must be chosen, the person is likely to attempt to protect feelings of self-esteem by resorting to one of the defense mechanisms (e.g., rationalization) described by Sigmund Freud.

Another natural reaction to a frustrating situation is to simply "leave the field," to use a term of Lewin's. The poor student who plays hooky, the shy boy who goes off by himself, the hippie who drops out—all react by withdrawing from the scene. The unfortunate aspect of such reactions is that they are not really solutions, so the person rarely experiences satisfaction. The tension remains and may build up and lead to undesirable behavior.

Even if individuals do not withdraw physically, they may escape through fantasy. An occasional daydream can serve as a safety valve or make a grim situation bearable. It can also pave the way for success. But too much dreaming may render the personal world of fantasy so satisfying that one is unwilling or unable to relinquish it in favor of reality, and mental illness may develop.

Some frustrated pupils may develop a pattern of overt defiance and disruption. Such behavior may be unacceptable to others and may lead to restrictions, punishment, or treatment, but obstreperous students have chosen a reaction to frustration that has merit from a mental health point of view. They gain release for pent-up emotion, even though they do it in a destructive way. For this reason pupils who "act out" their difficulties may be less likely to develop serious forms of mental illness, even though they attract more attention than pupils on the verge of a neurosis or psychosis.

This paradoxical situation was first brought to notice when E. K. Wickman (1928) asked teachers and psychotherapists to name the kinds of behavior they regarded as most "serious." The teachers rated such overt acts as stealing, cheating, and disobedience most damaging. The psychotherapists, on the other hand, considered sensitiveness, unsociability, suspiciousness, and fearfulness more serious than behavior problems. This difference of opinion was thought to stem from teachers' concern over behavior that threatened them or disrupted the class. The psychotherapists, taking into account that aggressive actions release tension, focused on those forms of behavior that were likely to escape notice but predisposed the pupil to serious maladjustment later in life. Alexander Tolor, William L. Scarpetti, and Paul A. Lane (1967) repeated the Wickman study. They found that experienced teachers of their era were more aware of the potential dangers of withdrawal; inexperienced teachers tended to regard aggressive and regressive behavior as abnormal, whereas psychotherapists perceived them to be normal.

Teachers may be more concerned about disruptive behavior than withdrawal

Recognition of various reactions to frustration should guide your endeavors to help students make wise choices in how to react. Keep in mind that the goals set by the student are often the key. A student with an impossible goal is virtually doomed to choose one of the less satisfying reactions. consequently, one way to encourage good choices is to encourage goals that you are reasonably sure students can achieve. But also try to steer your students toward seeking direct rather than indirect forms of satisfaction so that they will not be forced to make extensive use of defense mechanisms. Finally, you should do everything possible to divert students from reactions of withdrawal; these are the least satisfying choices and often lead to serious adjustment problems.

Symptoms of adjustment problems

Although a teacher can do quite a bit to help pupils satisfy their needs, it is inevitable that at least a few students in your classes will exhibit symptoms of poor adjustment. Sometimes basic needs are frustrated by parents. Sometimes predisposing factors in the personality of the child prevent adequate adjustment. Keep in mind that not even the best teacher in the world is able, alone, to rehabilitate some children who are caught in the trap of poor adjustment.

When children get started in the wrong direction in satisfying needs, it is of utmost importance to detect this as early as possible. The longer they resort to a certain defense mechanism or neurotic reaction, the more rigid they become and the more they may resist making a change. One of the biggest difficulties a psychotherapist faces is convincing neurotic clients to let go of the behavior pattern that is dominating their lives.

Neurotic individuals have found something to cling to, and even though it is not completely successful, it does provide a modicum of security. Before they can free themselves to embark on a more gratifying course, they have to build up enough confidence to abandon their own solution. In a sense, the aim of the psychotherapist is to persuade and help the person who has selected an unsatisfactory and unacceptable reaction to frustration to replace it with a more satisfying and constructive form of behavior. The earlier the attempt is made, the easier it is. As an observer with no direct personal or emotional ties to your pupils, you are in an ideal position to detect signs of poor adjustment. If you report them to the proper authorities, psychotherapy can be undertaken before a neurosis or psychosis develops.

To give you something specific to look for, a list of symptoms indicative of difficulties in adjustment is offered. You should guard against the temptation to use it as the basis for "analyzing" all your pupils, your friends, or even yourself. It is important to remain aware of symptoms of poor adjustment, but overdiagnosis should be scrupulously avoided.

Serious symptoms:
Depression,
unsociability,
fearfulness,
suspiciousness

Depression, unsociability, fearfulness, and suspiciousness   These are the first four symptoms, ranking in order of seriousness, noted by psychotherapists in a repeat of the Wickman study done by C. E. Thompson (1940). They are not likely to be obvious and are most frequently found in the pupil who withdraws—literally and figuratively. Perhaps the only additional comment necessary is that "unsociability" should not be equated with "individuality." The key to the difference is the attitude of the loner. If pupils who remain aloof seem satisfied with their lot and do not exhibit the other symptoms, you should probably honor their decision to avoid the crowd. If, on the other hand, isolates seem depressed and furtive, they may be revealing that they are experiencing little need gratification.

Persistent patterns of undesirable behavior   One hallmark of neurosis is persistent behavior. If a particular pupil reacts to almost all frustrations with the same type of defensive behavior, this may be a tip-off that adjustment problems exist. The mentally healthy person is confident and flexible. The mentally ill person is insecure and afraid to experiment. A pupil who suffers from chronic fatigue, seems "nervous" about everything, and worries excessively about insignificant problems may be caught in a neurotic pattern of rigidity.

Extreme, inappropriate
reactions suggest
underlying difficulties

Extreme, inappropriate reactions   Even a well-adjusted person may get angry if pushed far enough or attempt to withdraw temporarily if embarrassed. But when individuals explode over a minor irritation or dissolve into tears at a mild rebuff, they may be signaling that the immediate experience was only the last straw. The *real* reason for the inappropriately extreme reaction is probably the existence of more complicated and permanent difficulties.

Lack of contact with reality   One thing that sets the psychotic apart from the normal is lack of contact with the real world. If pupils think in terms of impossible goals for themselves or seem hard to reach or daydream excessively, they may be indicating that the real world is too much for them to handle and that they are trying to create a private world of their own.

Compulsive behavior giving the appearance that the person can't help herself or himself   Sometimes pupils may give the impression that they are compelled to behave as they do. A troublemaking boy may seem bewildered by his actions; a fearful girl may appear to be perplexed or even dazed by her response. In a sense such pupils *are* driven by forces beyond their control. When this point is reached, it is time for professional assistance.

Difficulties of providing psychotherapy

The reasons for seeking professional assistance become apparent when account is taken of the nature of psychotherapy and the difficulties of providing it.

Unwise for teachers to attempt to function as therapists

Need for specialized knowledge and training The person who is properly authorized to perform psychotherapy is a trained professional. In many states psychologists must pass professional qualification examinations similar to those required for medical doctors. A clinical psychologist is expected to earn a Ph.D. degree and to have undergone an intensive internship. An individual on the counseling

"Miss Peach" by Mell Lazarus. Courtesy of Mell Lazarus and Field Newspaper Syndicate.

staff of a school district is usually required to have an M.A. plus some internship experience. Understanding what lies behind the behavior of any individual requires a kind of training and experience that a regular classroom teacher is virtually prevented from obtaining.

Conflicting roles of a teacher-therapist   A psychotherapist endeavors to establish a climate of permissiveness. a relationship in which there are few rules or limits. A teacher, on the other hand, usually must establish a relationship with a class in which rules and limits *are* recognized. If a teacher tries to be both an authority figure and a psychotherapist, the two roles will conflict. The almost inevitable result will be feelings of confusion and distrust, which will probably not be restricted to the teacher and a particular pupil but may envelop the entire class.

Emotional involvement   Several sections of this book have urged objective, unemotional evaluation of pupil performance. The pervasive influence of subjectivity has been discussed at length. If you tried to act as a part-time "psychotherapist" with a certain pupil, it would be virtually impossible to remain objective in reacting to the school work of that pupil. This does not mean that you should avoid empathizing with any of your pupils; you should, however, be aware that any relationship that puts you in the role of psychotherapist will lead to conflicts. You should take an interest in your students so that you can offer a certain amount of individualized instruction, but the interest should be that between teacher and pupil, not that between therapist and client.

Discontinued support   As a rule, psychotherapy is a long drawn-out process. Adjustment problems are almost always the result of years of causal experiences, and improvement is usually not possible through short, simple treatment. Many schools appoint a counselor to progress through the grades with a certain group of pupils, thus guaranteeing continuity of treatment. The counselor can provide this, but the teacher can't, and that is why the wise teacher arranges for a pupil who seeks frequent counsel to meet with a trained professional.

Suggestions for acting as a sympathetic listener

For the reasons just discussed, it is not prudent for a teacher to attempt to act as a psychotherapist. Nevertheless, there are times when a teacher is the person best qualified to serve as a sympathetic listener. Some pupils confide in a teacher they respect and like but in no one else. Many students, especially at the high school level, have a negative attitude toward the counseling office. In one survey (Arnold, 1965), high school teachers estimated that their students would be twice as inclined to seek help from a teacher as from the counselor. They felt that students with adjustment problems are more likely to turn to someone they are familiar with and that many counselors seemed to be so busy with testing and scheduling that they had little time for therapy.

A voluntary trip to see a counselor, moreover, is a bald admission that a problem is too big for a student to handle alone. Being able to acknowledge that outside assistance is needed is often the biggest and most important step in the process of psychotherapy. When a pupil seeks you out as the first stage in admitting the existence of trouble, you should be sympathetic enough to let him or her talk about it. If you interrupt with, "I'm sorry, but you'd better go see someone in the counseling office," your crude rejection may prevent the very behavior you intended to encourage.

Sympathetic listening by teachers may help pupils cope

The arguments of the preceding section were aimed at discouraging you from setting yourself up as a psychotherapist; they were not intended to recommend *complete* aloofness. By exercising care and ingenuity, you may be able to act as a sympathetic listener without running too much risk of encountering the problems just noted.

If a troubled pupil screws up her or his courage, contrives to find you alone, and begins to talk about personal problems, you are urged to act as a sympathetic sounding board. The very act of expressing troublesome feelings will release tension. Often, merely talking about a problem is all a person needs. With a problem of greater magnitude, however, the relief may be only temporary. In that case, someone in a position to do a great deal of listening over a long period of time is called for. But a troubled pupil may not confer with someone in the counseling office if an initial request for assistance is snubbed.

SUMMARY OF KEY POINTS

There are a number of potential dangers to classifying children as exceptional, but there are also advantages. If labels are used in unthinking ways, they may stigmatize abnormal individuals. At the same time, pupils who need special kinds of instruction may not be identified or given the kind of teaching they need if they are not classified on the basis of particular characteristics. The Education for All Handicapped Children Act was passed to maximize the positive impact of labeling. The act stipulates that all exceptional children are to be given individualized educational programs and that tests used in the classification of children should not discriminate against members of minority groups. The act, as well as related developments in education, have led to emphasis on *mainstreaming*: the policy that exceptional children should be taught—to the maximum extent possible—in regular classes.

Children who fit the AAMD definition of mental retardation are not likely to attend regular classes, but almost any regular-class teacher will need to instruct some pupils who learn at a significantly slower rate than their classmates. Slow learners typically show a low tolerance for frustration, lack confidence and are low in self-esteem, have short memory and attention spans, are prone to oversimplify, think about only one quality at a time, and may be incapable of generalizing.

Rapid learners are skilled at absorbing, organizing, and applying abstract concepts. Some high-IQ pupils who respond well to instruction and supply predictable answers might be characterized as *convergent* rapid learners. Other pupils may be brighter than their test scores indicate but may respond in unpredictable and unorthodox ways. Such students might be thought of as *divergent* rapid learners. Teachers are likely to do a more effective job of instructing rapid learners if they allow for the possibility that both types might be found in the same classroom.

Some pupils have learning disabilities characterized by disorders in basic processes involved in understanding and using language. Learning disabilities often include language disorders, memory problems, short attention span, and emotional and social difficulties. Still other students may by hyperactive. Current thinking about the use of drugs to control hyperactivity stresses that although teachers should inform parents if their children are excessively active in school, teachers should not make recommendations about how the condition might be treated.

Pupils with visual disorders may indicate their need for corrective measures or special instruction by their reading habits, eye sensitivity, and inconsistent performance in activities requiring sight. Hearing problems may be detected if teachers notice that pupils appear inattentive, make odd mistakes, supply irrelevant answers, or have voice peculiarities. Unsuccessful efforts to cope with pressures and frustrations may cause some pupils to develop behavior disorders. Abraham Maslow suggests that behavior disorders may be traced to lack of satisfaction of deficiency needs. A diagram based on the theorizing of Kurt Lewin calls attention to the possibility that behavior disorders represent attempts to reduce tension that were not completely satisfactory. Pupils who are frustrated may respond by reacting aggressively, resorting to defense mechanisms, or by withdrawing physically or psychologically. Studies have shown that teachers may be more concerned about aggressive pupil reactions that disrupt classroom routine than about withdrawal reactions, even though the latter are often of greater significance as indicators of abnormality. Psychotherapists consider depression, unsociability, fearfulness, and suspiciousness as the most serious symptoms of abnormal behavior. Other indicators of underlying difficulties are extreme or inappropriate reactions. Teachers who become aware of such symptoms should call them to the attention of guidance counselors. Although teachers may sometimes help pupils cope with a problem by listening they should not attempt to function as psychotherapists.

BECOMING A BETTER TEACHER: QUESTIONS AND SUGGESTIONS

Preparing Individual Profiles of Strengths and Weaknesses

Am I combating tendencies to stereotype exceptional pupils? Suggestion: Prepare a profile of each pupil in the class, starting with those who are most atypical. List their individual weaknesses and strengths and then try to find ways to help them compensate for and partially overcome limitations by making the most of strengths.

Arranging to Observe or Work with Exceptional Children

Have I had any extensive contact with exceptional individuals? Suggestion: Consider taking a course in the psychology of the exceptional child, and ask the instructor for help in arranging to observe or work with exceptional pupils.

Helping Slow Learners Deal with Frustrations

Do I pay enough attention to the kinds of frustrations faced by slow learners? Suggestion: Make it a point to observe how the slowest learners in the class react when instructional activities tend to call attention to differences in learning ability. If the poorest learners in the group seem disappointed or upset, try to figure out ways to help them cope with inability to do school work as easily as others.

Giving Slow Learners Simple Assignments

When I assign class work, do I take into account that slow learners cannot cope with complex tasks? Suggestion: Prepare some cards that outline simple tasks that can be completed quickly, and ask slow learners to work on such assignments when more capable students are involved with more complex tasks.

Using Overlearning with Slow Learners

Am I remaining aware of the fact that slow learners must go over material again and again in order to master it? Suggestion: Set up individual or small-group study sessions designed to expose slow learners repeatedly to basic material. Try to introduce some variety into such drill sessions, but remember that pupils should be aware that they are learning the same material, even if it is presented in different ways.

Using Programmed Instruction with Slow Learners

Should I be making more use of programmed learning techniques when instructing slow learners? Suggestion: Look in a curriculum library for materials that present information in step-by-step fashion and that have built in reinforcement. Either use these materials with slow learners or develop similar materials of my own.

Giving Slow Learners Proof of Progress

Have I set up lessons so that slow learners will know that they have made at least some progress? Suggestion: Develop a chart or personal learning diary so that slow learners can record tangible indications of progress as they complete assignments.

Providing Horizontal and Vertical Enrichment

Have I been doing an effective job of supplying horizontal and vertical enrichment? Suggestion: In drawing up lesson plans, write down some horizontal and vertical enrichment ideas to use with pupils who finish assignments faster than others.

Individualized Study for Rapid Learners

Am I doing a conscientious job of planning individualized study projects for rapid learners? Suggestion: The next time I ask students to work on a project, explain the contract approach, and invite rapid learners (in particular) to discuss independent learning contracts with me individually.

Urging Rapid Learners to Develop Creative Hobbies and Interests

Am I doing anything to encourage rapid learners who have extra study time on their hands to develop hobbies or interests in creative ways? Suggestions: Pick out pupils who always seem to finish assignments ahead of time or who have exceptional abilities in some area of interest. Urge them to convert a hobby or interest into a specialized field of investigation. At the elementary level, urge pupils to really get involved with a hobby. At the secondary level, encourage pupils to prepare projects for competitions of various kinds.

Teaching Pupils with Learning Disabilities

Are there pupils in my classes who appear to have learning disabilities and who are not receiving special instruction? Suggestion: Check into the possibility of getting teaching suggestions from special consultants or teachers of special classes. If no advice is available, obtain books on the learning disabled, and experiment with kinesthetic and phonic methods.

Using Record Cards with Hyperactive Pupils

Are any of my students so hyperactive it interferes with their ability to learn? Suggestion: Make up some record cards, and use behavior modification techniques with pupils who cannot seem to settle down.

Checking on the Possibility of Visual Problems

Have I made a systematic attempt to discover if any of my pupils have undetected visual problems? Suggestion: List on a card the symptoms of visual problems described in Chapter 14. Observe students during work periods to determine if any of them display one or more of the symptoms. If they do, recommend an eye examination.

Checking on the Possibility of Hearing Problems

Have I made a systematic attempt to discover if any of my students have undetected hearing problems? Suggestion: List on a card the symptoms of hearing problems described in Chapter 14. Refer to it from time to time in evaluating how pupils respond to spoken communications and in assessing the nature and quality of their speech.

Techniques for Dealing with Hearing Problems

If I have one or more hard-of-hearing pupils in my class, am I doing anything to help them respond to instruction more effectively? Suggestion: Make a resolution to follow the suggestions for teaching hard-of-hearing pupils listed in Chapter 14.

Techniques for Dealing
with Speech Problems

If I have one or more pupils with speech problems in my classes, have I thought about how I should react when they cannot speak properly? Suggestion: The next time a student experiences some sort of speech problem in class, evaluate how I handled it by referring to the list of points presented in Chapter 14.

SUGGESTIONS FOR FURTHER STUDY

14-1
Pros and Cons of
Labeling

The pros and cons of classifying children as "exceptional" or "handicapped" are analyzed at length in volumes 1 and 2 of *Issues in the Classification of Children* (1975), edited by Nicholas Hobbs. A briefer treatment of the major points covered in the comprehensive two-volume work is in *The Futures of Children* (1975) by Nicholas Hobbs.

14-2
Mental Retardation

If you are interested in mental retardation, you might wish to do some further reading to supplement the brief analysis in the text. You will find a concise discussion of mental retardation with emphasis on teaching in *The Mentally Retarded Child in the Classroom* (1965) by Marion J. Erickson. For a comprehensive account of the causes of mental retardation and a penetrating analysis of ramifications of retardation, look for *The Mentally Retarded Child* (2nd ed., 1974) by Halbert B. Robinson and Nancy M. Robinson. A briefer account, emphasizing educational planning and techniques, is *Mental Retardation: An Educational Viewpoint* (1972) by Oliver P. Kolstoe. Samuel A. Kirk provides considerable information in concise form in Chapters 4, 5, and 6 of his *Educating Exceptional children* (2nd ed., 1972). A book with emphasis on characteristics is *Understanding the Mentally Retarded Child* (1975) by Richard Koch and Jean Holt Koch.

14-3
Rapid Learners

If you would like to read about the characteristics of *convergent* rapid learners at different stages of their lives, peruse *Genetic Studies of Genius: The Gifted Group at Mid-Life. Thirty-five Years Follow-up of the Superior Child* (1959) by Lewis Terman and Melita Oden. As the title indicates, this book describes the characteristics—up to the time of midlife—of a group of individuals with IQs over 140. (The initial nominations for pupils to be tested were made by teachers, most of whom appear to have selected children described in this book as *convergent* rapid learners.)

For information on teaching rapid learners, look for *Gifted Children in the Classroom* (1964) by E. Paul Torrance or *Teaching the Gifted Child* (2nd ed., 1975) by James J. Gallagher. Gallagher includes chapters on teaching rapid learners mathematics, science, social studies, language arts, problem solving and creativity, and ways of dealing with gifted underachievers and culturally different rapid learners.

14-4
Handicapped Children

If you are interested in teaching children with specific types of handicaps, you might wish to do further reading. For a brief account of visual, hearing, speech, and other problems, look up a text on the exceptional child. *Educating Exceptional Children* (2nd ed., 1972) by Samuel A. Kirk is particularly recommended, but you will probably find several similar books in a college library. For more detail on a specific handicap, consult a teacher of a special class or look in a library card catalogue.

14-5

Types of Maladjustment

For more complete information about causes and symptoms of behavior problems, neuroses, and psychoses, refer to *Child Psychiatry* (4th ed., 1972) by Leo Kanner. The first edition of this classic text was published in 1935, and Kanner might be thought of as the dean of American psychiatrists. He outlines the history of child psychiatry (Part 1), discusses how physical, environmental, and interpersonal factors influence behavior (Part 2), describes clinical methods (Part 3), and provides detailed descriptions of personality problems arising from physical illness, psychosomatic disorders, and disorders of behavior (Part 4). Essentially the same topics are covered in *Behavior Disorders in Children* (4th ed., 1972) by Harry and Ruth Morris Bakwin. Another excellent reference is *Manual of Child Psychopathology* (1972) edited by Benjamin B. Wolman. The part headings of this 1300-page volume are: "Etiologic Factors" (genetic, organic, sociocultural), "Organic Disorders" (brain damage, epilepsy, mental retardation), "Sociogenic Disorders" (neuroses, psychoses, delinquency), "Other Disorders" (speech and hearing problems, learning disturbances), "Diagnostic Methods," "Overview of Treatment Methods," "Specific Treatment Methods," "Research in Childhood Psychopathology," and "The Clinical Professions." Briefer discussions of many of the same topics covered in the Kanner, Bakwin, and Wolman books are provided in "Behavior Disorders" by E. James Anthony and "Childhood Psychosis" by William Goldfarb, Chapters 28 and 29 in *Carmichael's Manual of Child Psychology* (3rd ed., vol. 2, 1970) edited by Paul H. Mussen.

14-6

Maslow on Adjustment

If you did not do additional reading about Maslow's theory of need gratification earlier (in connection with motivation), you may wish to sample *Toward a Psychology of Being* (2nd ed., 1968) after thinking about the dynamics of adjustment. In Part 1 Maslow describes the basic rationale of his theory. In Part 2 he explains the differences between deficiency motivation and growth motivation. Part 6 is entitled "Some Basic Propositions of a Growth and Self-Actualization Psychology." For a fairly definite set of guidelines for helping your students become self-actualizers, read at least these parts of Maslow's book.

14-7

Diagramming Your Behavior

You will gain greater understanding of the diagram of adjustment in this chapter if you try to make a pictorial representation of some of your own behavior. First, draw a diagram of a choice situation you have encountered recently. Analyze your feelings about the situation, and classify your final choice as one of safety or growth. Then ask yourself whether you made your decision because of the balance between dangers and attractions as depicted in the diagram on page 773. Next, speculate about situations revolving round a specific goal (e.g., earning an A in some course, making the varsity in a certain sport, attracting the attention of a member of the opposite sex, being elected to an office). Did you sometimes achieve the exact goal you sought? What were your feelings when this occurred? Did you sometimes find it necessary to divert your attention to a substitute goal? How did you feel about that? Finally, can you recall being so completely thwarted by your inability to achieve the goal that you avoided the situation completely? What was your inner response on that occasion? Could someone else (e.g., a teacher) have helped you deal with the frustrating situations? Note your reactions to the situations described, and comment on the implications of your reactions.

14-8
Mental Hygiene

Mental Hygiene in Teaching (2nd ed., 1959) by Fritz Redl and William Wattenberg covers almost every aspect of adjustment likely to be of concern to teachers. (There are extended sections on classroom applications and special problems, as well as general background information.)

14-9
Case Histories

A great deal of insight into the dynamics of adjustment and the nature of psychotherapy can be gained by reading a detailed case history. Two highly regarded studies are *One Little Boy* (1952) by Dorothy W. Baruch and *Dibs: In Search of Self* (1964) by Virginia Axline. These books will acquaint you with the factors that caused a child to develop serious adjustment problems and reveal how a psychotherapist helped him overcome these problems. Another book that provides insight into the nature of psychotherapy is *The Child's Discovery of Himself* (1966), edited by Mark Moustakas, in which ten therapists describe—in more concise fashion than Baruch and Axline—how children with emotional problems succeeded in overcoming their difficulties.

14-10
Mental Illness

Mental illness has been discussed in textbooks, portrayed in films and on television, and explored in novels. A highly regarded fictional treatment of the subject is *I Never Promised You a Rose Garden* (1964) by Hannah Green (a pseudonym used by Joanne Greenberg), the story of the experiences and treatment of a sixteen-year-old girl who retreats from reality into an imaginary kingdom. If you would like to gain insight into the nature of psychosis and its treatment, you might read this novel.

Key points

Impact of different types of leadership

Submissive or aggressive response to authoritarian leaders

Long-run productivity and friendliness under democratic leaders

Reactions to leadership styles depend on previous experience

Authoritative leaders promote competence, high level of performance

Classroom control

Children need to learn that certain restrictions are necessary

Even "free" children may misbehave if their needs are not satisfied

Causes of misbehavior

Keeping students busy may reduce misbehavior due to boredom

Helping pupils release tension may reduce discipline problems

Providing positive attention may reduce need for negative attention

Analyzing your techniques of classroom management

Ripple effect: Group response to reprimand directed at an individual

Teachers who show they are with it head off discipline problems

Being able to handle overlapping activities helps classroom control

Teachers who continually interrupt activities have discipline problems

Keeping entire class involved and alert minimizes misbehavior

Identify troublemakers; firmly specify constructive behavior

Maintaining classroom control

Establishing rules simplifies clasroom control

After ignoring misbehavior, stress rewards; use punishment as a last resort

Avoid using behavior modification to induce docility

Influence techniques

Establish routines, particularly at the start of activities

Try to give criticisms privately; then offer encouragement

I-messages and the no-lose method

I-messages: Tell how you feel about an unacceptable situation

No-lose method: Come to mutual agreement about a solution to a problem

Chapter 15 | Maintaining classroom control

Chapter 14 presented some observations on need gratification and the nature of adjustment. A feature of need gratification that complicates every individual's pursuit of self-actualization is that, as Maslow puts it, "the [person] needs not only gratification; he needs also to learn the limitations that the physical world puts upon his gratifications, and he has to learn that other human beings seek for gratification, too" (1968, pp. 163–164).

Although it seems desirable to allow students as much freedom of choice as possible (providing they are good choosers), certain natural tendencies must be controlled. Primary grade children are normally inclined to be active. Yet they must learn to control their activity—at least to some extent—in the classroom. Some subjects may have no intrinsic interest for older students. Yet because learning is hierarchical, they may be required to study certain things that they would ignore if left to their own inclinations. Since deficiency needs can be satisfied only by others, students compete with one another for gratification provided by teachers. Thus, your pupils will have to acquire some self-control. They may have to be induced to learn things they would prefer not to learn, and they will surely have to adapt to the fact that their classmates are seeking gratification, too.

Even the best teacher in the world is likely to have at least some trouble keeping a class under sufficient restraint so that learning can take place. This chapter's aim is to prepare you to establish a favorable classroom environment. Research on the impact of different kinds of class atmosphere will be presented and followed by a discussion of specific techniques for influencing and regulating behavior.

Impact of different types of leadership

In a classic study in psychology, Kurt Lewin and two associates (R. Lippitt and R. K. White, 1958) analyzed the impact of different kinds of leadership on group behavior. Lewin, you will remember, was a field theorist. (He was also a German Jew who was driven out of his native land by the Nazis. It is important to consider the effect a democratic society would have upon the victim of a vicious autocracy.)

Lewin and his associates asked eleven-year-old boys to participate in some after-school clubs. The groups were exposed to different kinds of leadership: authoritarian, democratic, and laissez-faire. Here are the instructions given to the leaders, as reported in an article written by Lippitt and White:

Authoritarian. Practically all policies as regards club activities and procedures should be determined by the leader. The techniques and activity steps should be communicated by the authority, one unit at a time, so that future steps are in the dark to a large degree. The adult should take considerable responsibility for assigning the activity tasks and companions of each group member. The dominator should keep his standards of praise and criticism to himself in evaluating individual and group activities. He should also remain fairly aloof from active group participation except in demonstrating.

Democratic. Wherever possible, policies should be a matter of group decision and discussion with active encouragement and assistance by the adult leader. The leader should attempt to see that activity perspective emerges during the discussion period with the general steps to the group goal becoming clarified. Wherever technical advice is needed, the leader should try to suggest two or more alternative procedures from which choice can be made by the group members. Everyone should be free to work with whomever he chooses, and the divisions of responsibility should be left up to the group. The leader should attempt to communicate in an objective, fact-minded way the bases for his praise and criticism of individual and group activities.

Laissez-faire. In this situation, the adult should play a rather passive role in social participation and leave complete freedom for group or individual decisions in relation to activity and group procedure. The leader should make clear the various materials which are available and be sure it is understood that he will supply information and help when asked. He should do a minimum of taking the initiative in making suggestions. He should make no attempt to evaluate negatively or positively the behavior or productions of the individuals or the group as a group, although he should be friendly rather than "stand-offish" at all times. (1958, p. 498)

Each group of boys was exposed to all three types of leadership but in different sequences. Trained observers recorded everything that was said and done during the group meetings. They noticed that the leaders carried out their instructions with considerable fidelity but

AS THE TWIG IS BENT THE TREE INCLINES

LAYING DOWN THE LAW.

Students may respond submissively or aggressively to an authoritarian teacher, depending on their experiences with previous teachers.

The Bettman Archive

Submissive or aggressive response to authoritarian leaders

Long-run productivity and friendliness under democratic leaders

concentrated on observing the behavior of the boys. Under the authoritarian leader, two types of reactions occurred. Some groups responded in a submissive and apathetic way; others responded aggressively. All groups worked actively while the authoritarian leader was present, but the rate of work dropped off sharply when he left the room. All were very dependent on him and demanded much of his attention.

Under democratic leaders, the boys did not produce quite as much as they did in authoritarian-led groups, but since they continued to work after the leader left the room, they produced more in the long run. They were also more friendly toward one another and, as might be expected, more group-minded. Under the laissez-faire regime, the boys were unproductive in the presence of the leader. While he was in the room, they spent most of the time asking him for information rather than doing any actual work. But the teacher-*absent* activity was highest for the laissez-faire group (perhaps because their need for stimulation and activity had been frustrated).

Lippitt and White suggest that the different groups responded to the authoritarian leader in such different ways because of previous group history:

It was clear that previous group history (i.e., preceding social climates) had an important effect in determining the social perception of leader behavior and reaction to it by club members. A club which had passively accepted an authoritarian leader in the beginning of its club history, for example, was much more frustrated and restive to a second authoritarian leader after it had experienced a democratic leader than a club without such a history. There seem to be some suggestive implications here for educational practice. (p. 511)

A number of investigators have reported that students respond negatively to authoritarian teachers. Teachers who act as benevolent authorities, however, often arouse positive responses, if not respect, from pupils.

Laima Druskis/Editorial Photocolor Archives

Reactions to leadership
styles depend on
previous experience

Here are two implications: First, that you might take into account the kind of teacher (or teachers) your students had before they entered your class. Second, you are likely to experience difficulties if you start out with a laissez-faire or democratic approach and then attempt to move toward authoritarianism.

As you read the instructions to the three types of leaders in the Lippitt and White study, you may have found yourself thinking that the authoritarian atmosphere was similar to a structured (e.g., programmed) approach, that the democratic atmosphere is essentially that of open education, and that the laissez-faire atmosphere is basically the same as a humanistic approach (as exemplified by Summerhill). Within limits, these similarities may be said to exist, and some of the boys' reactions might be expected to occur in classroom situations that resemble the club atmospheres. For example, if a teacher controls virtually all aspects of the learning situation and shapes behavior by dispensing rewards, students are likely to be productive when the teacher is present but stop work as soon as her or his influence is withdrawn. In addition, advocates of open education admit that learning is not completely efficient in such an approach, but they maintain that there is a high level of activity regardless of what the teacher does and that group-mindedness and student interaction are high. Finally, descriptions of Summerhill indicate that students were eager to secure attention from Neill and that their overall productivity was low.

But it seems unwise to generalize too directly from this study. Because of his background, Lewin was eager to prove that democracy was incontestably better than autocracy, and the authoritarian leaders seem to have understood this. In their relationships with the boys, they tended to be cold and domineering. A *benevolent* authoritarian leader might have encouraged the boys to be highly productive and at the same time might have succeeded in estalishing high morale and a wholesome group spirit.

The Lippitt and White study triggered a great deal of research on group climates. Richard C. Anderson (1959) reviewed a number studies on the impact of classroom atmosphere and came to this conclusion:

The evidence available fails to demonstrate that either authoritarian or democratic leadership is consistently associated with higher productivity. In most situations, however, democratic leadership is associated with higher morale. But even this conclusion must be regarded cautiously, because the authoritarian leader has been unreasonably harsh and austere in a number of investigations reporting superior morale in democratic groups. (1959, p. 213)

Perhaps one reason that Anderson did not find consistent support for the Lippitt and White conclusion that the democratic approach was clearly superior to authoritarian leadership is a function of differences between clubs and classrooms. The boys in the Lippitt and White study were engaging in voluntary activities and were working toward self-selected goals (very much like a Boy Scout troop working on a project of some kind). In almost all classrooms, however, students are required to participate in activities that have been selected, at least in part, by others. There are usually opportunities for some individuality in learning, but all first graders are expected to learn to read, all fifth graders to learn mathematics, all eleventh graders to learn something about the government of the United States. Furthermore, teachers, as contrasted with the club leaders in the Lippitt and White study, are expected to instruct in such a way that students acquire specific, measurable knowledge and skills. Therefore, the morale of *students* (not club members) might be higher under a teacher who is authoritative (not authoritarian) and who fosters learning than under one who fails to provide instruction because of well-intended but misguided efforts to have the classroom function as a participatory democracy.

Use of the word *authoritative* calls to mind the research of Diana Baumrind (1971) that was mentioned in Chapter 4. Even though Baumrind sought relationships between the behavior of nursery school children and the child-rearing practices used by their parents, her results can be generalized to classroom situations. To refresh your memory, Baumrind found that when parents were *authoritative* (made efforts to influence a child's goal-directed behavior, were interested in having their children internalize adult standards, exerted pressure for performance at the level of the child's capabilities, sometimes asked for the child's opinion, gave reasons for asking for compliance, were warm and supportive, provided sincere praise for accomplishments), their children were rated as competent, mature, independent, self-reliant, self-controlled, explorative, affiliative, and self-assertive. When parents were *authoritarian* (were coercive, asserted power, were not too affectionate or involved), their children were likely to be discontented, insecure, and hostile under stress. When parents were *permissive* (disorganized, ineffective, insecure, babied their children, and used love in efforts to manipulate), their children were likely to be dependent, immature, and lacking in self-reliance and self-control.

Authoritative leaders promote competence, high level of performance

These results might be taken as an indication that teachers who want children to become competent, to engage in goal-directed behavior, to internalize adult standards, and to perform at the level of their capabilities, should be authoritative. That is, teachers should take charge of their classrooms and *arrange* learning experiences but exude warmth and support, ask for student opinions when appropriate, and explain reasons for restrictions.

Classroom control

Some educators advocate almost completely student-determined discipline in the schools. They argue that students should have experience in determining their own behavior. This is a desirable goal, but it overlooks the fact that few rules and laws in society are developed through *direct* democratic discussion by all citizens. Students should therefore learn to live with restrictions imposed by others. As Paul Woodring puts it:

Children need to learn that certain restrictions are necessary

> If by discipline we mean letting the child learn that there are certain restrictions and controls which society places upon the individual and that children are not exempt from these controls, there seems to be no sound psychological reason for avoiding discipline. Indeed, such discipline would seem to be an essential part of education. (1953, p. 137)

Here is Woodring's description of the *kind* of discipline that is essential to education:

> A properly disciplined classroom is one in which the rules are reasonable and

in which they are so well accepted by the children that violations are comparatively rare. It is not one in which violations frequently occur and are severely punished. . . .

The rules appropriate to a classroom are the rules of normal civilized behavior of individuals in a social setting. They involve courtesy and a consideration for others. (p. 136)

Advocates of the permissive approach to teaching sometimes appear to have built a straw man labeled *discipline,* which embodies all the brutal attributes of every sadistic pedagogue who ever lived. They almost suggest that you must choose between being a helpful, friendly guide or a vicious, inhuman autocrat. Although you may sympathize with their desire to eliminate unnecessarily harsh discipline in the classroom, it is a mistake to ignore the possibility that a teacher can be both firm *and* friendly.

Some humanistic educators argue that teachers must resort to techniques of classroom control because they are forcing students to engage in unnatural behavior. It is hypothesized that in a completely unstructured atmosphere, in which children engage only in self-selected activities, all "discipline" problems will disappear. Although there is undoubtedly some truth to the charge that asking students to engage in contrived learning is likely to make close supervision necessary, it is not true that all need for control disappears in a free school. (Read *Summerhill* if you find this hard to believe.) Free education does not automatically lead to satisfaction of the deficiency needs of love, belonging, and esteem; and the possibility of friction between students increases as a consequence of greater opportunities for interaction with peers. The same holds true for open schools. Some

Even "free" children may misbehave if their needs are not satisfied

children may engage in disruptive behavior regardless of the degree of freedom they are allowed because they come from homes where they feel unloved or inadequate. Others may cause difficulties simply to attract attention. And if two belligerent boys happen to want to use the same book or material in an activity center of an open classroom at the same time, an uproar may ensue that could touch off a mild riot.

There is no denying that unnecessarily strict teachers make trouble for themselves. But it does not follow that complete "freedom" will eliminate trouble. The intent of this chapter is to acquaint you with techniques you might use to establish and maintain a classroom environment in which students have the opportunity to learn without being unduly disturbed by others and without being intimidated or coerced by the teacher. The chapter is not intended to convince you that the only possible course of action is to make a full-time effort to trick, bribe, or threaten students into docile obedience. An overcontrolled classroom is likely to cause problems, but a reasonably controlled environment is usually more constructive and conducive to learning than anarchy.

Causes of misbehavior

One way to come to grips with classroom control is to think in terms of determinism. The scientist searches for causes, and it is logical to apply this approach to misbehavior. What are the *reasons* students misbehave? In many cases the reasons are unique, personal, complex, and perhaps beyond your comprehension and control. But some misbehavior comes from common, general causes that can be anticipated, and there are techniques you can use to reduce such behavior.

Boredom

Keeping students busy may reduce misbehavior due to boredom

Many students get into mischief simply because they are bored with classwork and can't think of anything else to do. Obvious solutions: Keep them busy. Make sure they know what they are supposed to be doing (remember the importance of providing goals). Make classwork meaningful and interesting. Try to arrange for students to have something to do at the appropriate level of difficulty, and try to have several activities to choose from.

Handbook heading
Keeping Pupils Busy

Release of frustration and tension

For the following reasons—and many more—students must put up with considerable frustration: A teacher requires them to behave in a manner that is "unnatural." Intellectual endeavor requires mental discipline. Learning is effortful, and practically all pupils resist it to

An excellent way to limit pupil misbehavior due to boredom or tension is to provide occasional relaxing interludes.

Van Bucher/Photo Researchers

some degree, since the natural inclination is to avoid work. The course of study is imposed by outside authority, which generates added resistance. Resentment of compulsory subjects increases with age and is so strong in high school that almost any secondary school teacher of a required course has a built-in source of difficulty. Finally, group activity compels each individual to make concessions and compromises in adapting personal desires to the common will of the group.

When students are frustrated, tension builds up until they are forced to react. You can't prevent this, but there are constructive ways for students to release tension under your control.

Provide frequent breaks and changes of pace. Be on the alert for the point of diminishing returns. Alternate intensive, laborious activities with relaxing ones. If the class is on edge because of the weather, an impending vacation, an important sports event, or whatever, have more breaks and allow more activity and discussion.

Helping students release tension may reduce discipline problems

Desire for attention, recognition, status

Some students misbehave because they want attention, and negative attention is better than none at all. A pupil who is unsuccessful in schoolwork, a poor athlete, and unpersonable may seek recognition and status by being the class pest.

You can minimize this sort of behavior by offering "legal" opportunities for gaining attention and satisfaction. Try to dignify all achievements by stressing improvement. Give positive attention in the form of favorable comments and encouragement. Give recognition for many different kinds of ability.

Providing positive attention may reduce need for negative attention

Analyzing your techniques of classroom management

Remaining aware of the causes of misbehavior may be one way to reduce problem behavior in your classroom, but you might also find it helpful to analyze the classroom management techniques you use. It is easy to slip into poor habits without realizing you have done so, and sometimes such habits may more or less encourage student misbehavior that will force you to resort to punishment. Jacob S. Kounin offers an insightful analysis of aspects of classroom management in *Discipline and Group Management in Classrooms* (1970).[1] He points out that he first became interested in this topic when he reprimanded

---

[1] Some of Kounin's observations were mentioned in Chapter 6 in the discussion of suggestions for handling classroom recitation.

Ripple effect: Group response to reprimand directed at an individual

a college student for blatantly reading a newspaper in class. Kounin was struck by the extent to which the entire class responded to a reprimand directed at only one person, and he subsequently dubbed this the *ripple effect*. Chances are you can recall a situation where you were diligently working away in a classroom when the teacher suddenly became quite angry and bawled out a classmate who was disruptive. If, despite the fact that your behavior was blameless, you felt a bit tense after the incident and endeavored to give the impression that you were a paragon of student virtue, you have had personal experience with the ripple effect.

Once his interest in classroom behavior was aroused, Kounin supervised a series of observational and experimental studies of student reactions to techniques of teacher control. In analyzing the results of these various studies, he came to the conclusion that the following classroom management techniques appear to be most effective.

Teachers who show they are with it head off discipline problems

1. *Show your students you are "with it."*   Kounin coined the term *withitness* to emphasize that teachers who prove to their students that they know what is going on in a classroom usually have fewer disciplinary problems than teachers who appear to be unaware of incipient disruptions. An expert at classroom management will nip trouble in the bud by commenting on potentially disruptive behavior before it gains momentum. An ineffective teacher may not notice such behavior until it begins to spread and then perhaps hopes that it will simply go away. At first glance, Kounin's suggestions that you show that you are with it might seem to be in conflict with the S-R principle that behavior that is not reinforced will extinguish itself. If the teacher's reaction is the only source of reinforcement in a classroom, ignoring behavior may cause it to disappear. In many cases, however, a misbehaving pupil gets reinforced by the reactions of classmates. Therefore, ignoring behavior is much less likely to lead to extinction of a response in a classroom than in controlled experimental situations.

2. *Learn to cope with overlapping situations.*   When he analyzed videotapes of actual classroom interactions, Kounin found that some teachers seem to have one-track minds. They are inclined to deal with only one thing at a time, and this way of proceeding causes frequent interruptions in classroom routine. One primary grade teacher observed by Kounin, for example, was working with a reading group when she noticed two boys on the other side of the room poking each other. She abruptly got up, walked over to the boys, berated them at length, and then returned to the reading group. By the time she returned, however, the children in the reading group had become bored, listless, and were tempted to engage in mischief of their own.

Kounin concluded that withitness and skill in handling overlap-

Being able to handle overlapping activities helps classroom control

Handbook heading
Learning to Deal with Overlapping Situations

ping activities seemed to be related. An expert classroom manager who is talking to children in a reading group, for example, might notice two boys at the far side of the room who are beginning to scuffle with each other. Such a teacher might in midsentence tell the boys to stop and make the point so adroitly that the attention of the children in the reading group does not waver. You might carry out a self-analysis of how you handle overlapping situations when you first begin to teach. If you find that you tend to focus on only one thing at a time, you might make an effort to develop skills in coping with two or more situations simultaneously.

3. *Strive to maintain smoothness and momentum in class activities.* This point is related to the previous one. Kounin found that some teachers cause problems for themselves because they constantly interrupt activities without thinking about what they are doing. Some teachers whose activities were recorded on videotape failed to maintain the thrust of a lesson because they seemed unaware of the rhythm of student behavior (e.g., they did not take into account the degree of student inattention and restlessness; instead they moved ahead in an almost mechanical way). Others flip-flopped from one activity to another. Others would interrupt one activity (e.g., a reading lesson) to comment on an unrelated aspect of classroom functioning (e.g., someone left a lunch bag on the floor). Still others would waste time dwelling on a trivial incident (e.g., making a big fuss because a boy lost his pencil). And a few teachers delivered individual instead of group instructions (e.g., "All right, Dick, you go to the board. Fine, now, Mary, you go to the board"). All these types of teacher behavior tend to interfere with the flow of learning activities. Each time pupils are interrupted they may be distracted and find it difficult to pick up the thread of a lesson. They may also be tempted to engage in mischievous activities. Kounin found that pupil work involvement was greater and deviant behavior less when teachers maintained momentum and smoothness instead of interrupting activities in the ways just described.

Teachers who continually interrupt activities have discipline problems

Handbook heading
Learning How to Maintain Momentum

You might carry out a movement analysis of your teaching from time to time. Think about how you handle a class for a period or a day, and see if you can recall incidents of this sort: Your request for a change in activity seemed too abrupt. You needlessly flip-flopped back and forth between activities. You interrupted a lesson to comment on an unrelated situation that happened to come to your attention. You made a mountain out of a molehill. You gave instructions to individual pupils when it would have been simpler to address several at once. To counteract such tendencies, you might make a concerted effort to maintain a smooth flow of activities the following class periods and days. If you succeed in doing this, it may become habitual.

4. *Try to keep the whole class involved, even when you are dealing with individual pupils.* Kounin found that some well-meaning teachers had fallen into a pattern of calling on students in a predictable order and in such a way that the rest of the class served as a passive audience. Unless you stop to think about what you are doing during group recitation periods, you might easily fall into the same trap. If you do, the "audience" is almost certain to become bored and may be tempted to engage in troublemaking activities just to keep occupied. Some teachers, for example, call on pupils to recite by going around a circle, or going up and down rows, or by following alphabetical order. Others call on a child first and then ask a question. Still others ask one child to recite at length (e.g., read an entire page). All these techniques tend to spotlight one child in predictable order and cause the rest of the class to tune out until their turn comes. You are more likely to maintain interest and limit mischief due to boredom if you use techniques such as the following:

a. Ask a question, and then quickly pick out someone to answer it. With subsequent questions, call on students in an unpredictable order so that no one knows when she or he will be asked to recite. Proceed at a rapid pace so that wrong answers can be more or less glossed over. (If you feel that some students in a class are very apprehensive about being called on, even under relaxing circumstances, you can either ask them extremely easy questions or avoid calling on them at all.)

b. If you single out one child to go to the board to do a problem, ask all other students to do the same problem at their desks and then choose one or two at random to compare their work with the answers on the board.

Keeping entire class involved and alert minimizes misbehavior

Handbook heading
Ways to Keep the Whole Class Involved

Teachers are more likely to maintain control if they keep the whole class involved or busy, even when dealing with individual pupils.
Bohdan Hrynewych

c. When dealing with lengthy or complex material, call on several students in quick succession (and in unpredictable order), and ask each to handle one section. In a primary grade reading group, for example, have one child read a sentence, then pick someone at the other side of the group to read the next sentence, and so on.

d. Use "props" in the form of flash cards, mimeographed sheets, or workbook pages to induce all students to respond to questions simultaneously. Then ask students to compare answers. (One ingenious elementary school teacher observed by Kounin had each pupil print the ten digits on cards that could be inserted in a slotted piece of cardboard. She would ask a question such as "How much is 8 and 4?" pause a moment while the students arranged their answers in the slots, and then say, "All show!")

All these techniques are likely to be effective because they encourage participation by all students, introduce an element of suspense, and hold all students accountable for what is going on.

5. *Introduce variety, and be enthusiastic, particularly with younger pupils.* As Kounin and his associates viewed videotapes of different teachers, they concluded that some instructors seem to get much more in a rut than others. At one end of the scale are teachers who follow the same procedure day after day, respond with the same almost reflexive comments (e.g., "That's fine"), labor a point or continue a lesson so that it becomes almost unbearably tedious—perhaps out of lethargy or reluctance to think of something else for the class to do. At the other end of the scale are teachers who constantly seek to introduce variety, go out of their way to respond with enthusiasm and interest, and move quickly to new activities when they sense that students either have mastered or are satiated by a particular lesson. Apparently because of methodological complexities, Kounin failed to find statistical evidence that students responded differently to teachers at either end of such a scale. It seems logical to assume, however, that students would be more inclined to sleep, daydream, or get into mischief if they are exposed to dull, routine activities. Kounin points out, though, that variety may not be most appropriate in elementary school classrooms because older students may be interested in thoroughly analyzing complex ideas and may be bothered if they are interrupted too frequently.

6. *Be aware of the ripple effect. When criticizing student behavior, be clear, firm, focus on behavior rather than personalities, and try to avoid anger outbursts.* If you take into account the suggestions just made you may be able to reduce the amount of student misbehavior in your classes. Even so, some behavior problems are certain to occur. When you deal with these, you can benefit from Kounin's research on the ripple effect. On the basis of observations, questionnaires, and

Handbook heading
Ways to Set in Motion
"Positive Ripples"

Identify troublemakers;
firmly specify
constructive behavior

experimental evidence, he concluded that "innocent" pupils in a class are more likely to be positively impressed by the way the teacher handles a misbehaver if these conditions exist:

a. The teacher identifies the miscreant and states what the unacceptable behavior is (e.g., "George! You are not to push in line").

b. A suggestion is made specifying more constructive behavior (e.g., "Go to the end of the line and stand three feet in back of Jane").

c. A reason is given explaining why the deviant behavior should cease (e.g., "You almost knocked Mary into the fish bowl when you shoved just now. She might have broken the glass and cut herself").

d. The teacher is firm and authoritative and conveys a no-nonsense attitude.

e. The teacher does not resort to anger, humiliation, or extreme punishment. Kounin concluded that extreme reactions did not seem to make children behave better. Instead, anger and severe reprimands upset them and made them feel tense and nervous.

f. The teacher focuses on behavior, not on personality. This is the same point Haim Ginott stresses in *Teacher and Child* (previously discussed in the analysis of humanistic education in Chapter 7). Ginott urges you to address the situation, not the child's character and personality. Kounin expresses the same point in different words: He concluded that students responded more favorably to teachers who mentioned "task attributes rather than personal attributes" (p. 52). In a situation where one pupil pushes another, for example, it is better to say, "Don't push because you may hurt someone," than to say "You are being thoughtless and rude and making all of us dislike you."

Even if you do everything possible to prevent the development of problems by taking into account causes and by analyzing your classroom management techniques, there will still be incidents of misbehavior. The following pages suggest several ways in which to deal with them.

Suggestions for teaching: Maintaining classroom control

1. Consider establishing some class rules.

2. Be friendly but firm. Act confident, especially on the first day.

3. Have a variety of influence techniques planned in advance.

4. Whenever you have to deal harshly with a student, make an effort to re-establish rapport.

5. Try to avoid threats.

6. Be prompt, consistent, reasonable.

7. Consider using behavior modification techniques.

8. When you have control, ease up—some.

1. Consider establishing some class rules.   As a neophyte teacher you will have a lot on your mind. During the first few weeks you may think that teaching is just one long series of crises. The more of these you can anticipate and prepare for, the less harried and desperate you will be. Anything you can do to avoid coping with problems, especially disciplinary problems, in a completely extemporaneous manner will make life easier. You can prevent a good deal of trouble by explaining on the first day that certain ground rules will apply in your room. Some teachers list these rules in a prominent position on a bulletin board. Others simply state them informally in the first class. Either technique saves time and trouble later because all you have to do is refer to the rule when a transgression occurs. The alternative is to interrupt the lesson and disturb the whole class while you make a hurried, unplanned effort to deal with a surprise attack. Unless you are experienced and skilled, your improvised technique will probably be clumsy and ineffective.

Establishing rules simplifies classroom control

If you introduce rules on the first day, it is important to take a positive, nonthreatening approach. If you spit rules out as if they were a series of ultimatums, the students may feel you have a chip on your shoulder, which the unwritten code of the classroom obligates them to try to knock off. An excellent way to demonstrate your good faith is to invite the class to suggest necessary regulations and why they should be established. (Some teachers use this technique effectively; others think it's a waste of time.) Whatever your approach, encourage understanding of the *reasons* for the rules. You can make restrictions meaningful if you discuss why they are needed. Reasonable rules are much more likely to be remembered and honored than pronouncements that seem to be the whims of a tyrant.

Handbook heading
Inviting the Class to
Help Establish Rules

EXAMPLES

"During class discussion, please don't speak out unless you raise your hand and are recognized. I want to be able to hear what each person has to say, and I won't be able to do that if more than one person is talking."

"During work periods, I don't mind if you talk to your neighbors. But if you do it too much and disturb others, I'll have to ask you to stop."

"I don't mind if you chew gum—provided you don't get too juicy or noisy. If it disrupts the class, I'll have to ask you to stop."

2. Be friendly but firm. Act confident, especially on the first day.   The first few minutes with any class are often the most crucial of all as far as discipline is concerned. Your pupils are sizing you up, especially if they know you are a new teacher. If you act scared and unsure of yourself, you will probably be in for trouble. In self-defense, you

might use this scheme to turn the tables until you have a bit more confidence: Ask the students to fill out cards about themselves at the beginning of the first day of class. (For primary graders who can't write, substitute oral introductions.) This will give you a chance to make a leisurely scrutiny of them as individuals. If you start lecturing right from the sound of the bell, you will be much too busy to do this, and you may misinterpret essentially innocuous reactions as threats. If you follow the card writing by having each student introduce himself or herself, the fact that these are ordinary human beings becomes even more apparent. What is being discussed here is a form of stage fright. Perhaps you have read about singers who pick out a single, sympathetic member of the audience and sing directly to her or him. The sea of faces as a whole is frightening. The face of the individual is not. Even if you don't need to use the cards as a crutch for your confidence, introductions have other values, such as helping you learn names and making you aware of your students as individuals.

Whatever you do the first few minutes, it is important to give the impression that you know exactly what you are doing. The best way to pull this off is to be *thoroughly* prepared.

Handbook heading
Being Completely
Prepared the First Day

3. Have a variety of influence techniques planned in advance.   You may save yourself a great deal of trouble, embarrassment, and strain if you plan ahead. When first-year teachers are asked which aspects of teaching bother them most, classroom control is almost invariably near the top of the list. Perhaps a major reason is that problems of control frequently erupt unexpectedly, and they often demand equally sudden solutions. If you lack experience in dealing with such problems, your shoot-from-the-hip reactions may be ineffective. Initial attempts at control that *are* ineffective tend to reinforce misbehavior, and you will find yourself trapped in a vicious circle. This sort of trap can be avoided if specific techniques are devised ahead of time. Having in mind several methods of dealing with trouble will prepare you for the inevitable difficulties that arise.

However, if you find yourself being forced to use prepared techniques too often, some self-analysis is called for. How can you prevent so many problems from developing? Frequent trouble is an indication that you need to work harder at motivating your class. You might refer to the list of causes of misbehavior in the preceding section for some specific troubleshooting suggestions. Also, check on your feelings when you mete out punishment. Teachers who really like students and want them to learn consider control techniques a necessary evil and use them only when they will provide a better atmosphere for learning. If you find yourself looking for trouble or perhaps deliberately luring pupils into misbehaving, or if you discover yourself gloating privately or publicly about an act of punishment, stop and

Handbook heading
Analyzing My Feelings
After I Deal with
Troublemakers

think. Are you perverting your power to build up your ego or giving vent to sadistic impulses?

You will find an extensive list of *influence techniques* in the section following this discussion of general suggestions for maintaining classroom control.

4. Whenever you have to deal harshly with a student, make an effort to re-establish rapport. If you find yourself forced to use a drastic form of retribution, make a point of having a private "peace conference" with your antagonist as soon as possible. Otherwise, she or he is likely to remain just that—an antagonist—for the rest of the year. It's too much to expect chastized students to come to you of their own volition and apologize. You should institute the peace conference, then explain that the punishment has cleared the air as far as you are concerned and that they can start the next day with a clean slate. You shouldn't be surprised if a recalcitrant pupil doesn't respond overtly with signs or words of gratitude. Perhaps some of the causes of misbehavior lie outside of school and something you did or said may have been merely the last straw. Even if you get a sullen reaction, it is desirable at least to indicate your willingness to meet punished students more than halfway.

At the elementary level, you can frequently make amends simply by giving the child some privilege, for example, passing out paper or being ball monitor at recess. One excellent teacher made it a point to praise a child for some positive action shortly after a severe reprimand.

5. Try to avoid threats. If at all possible, avoid a showdown in front of the class. In a confrontation before the whole group, you are likely to get desperate. You may start out with a "yes, you will"—"No, I won't" sort of duel and end up making a threat on the spur of the moment. Frequently, you will not be able to make good on the threat, and you will lose face. It's far safer and better for everyone to settle extreme differences in private. When two people are upset and angry with each other, they inevitably appear silly at best and completely ridiculous at worst. You lose a great deal more than a student does by having this performance take place in front of the class. In fact, a student may actually gain prestige by provoking you successfully.

Perhaps the worst temptation of all is to try to get back at the entire class by making a blanket threat of a loss of privilege or detention. It hardly ever works and tends to lead to a united counterattack by the class. One elementary school teacher had the reputation of telling her class at least once a year that they would not be allowed to participate in the Spring Play-Day if they didn't behave. By the time pupils reached this grade, they had been tipped off by previous students that she always made the threat but never carried it out. They behaved accordingly. Suppose, in a fit of pique, you tell your class that they must "all stay in forty-five minutes after school." What will you do when they start chattering in a chorus about bus schedules, car pools, music lessons, dentist appointments, and paper routes? You can usually avoid such nightmares by putting a stop to the problem before it begins to snowball.

Handbook heading
Being Prompt,
Consistent, and
Reasonable in
Controlling the Class

6. Be prompt, consistent, reasonable.   No attempt to control behavior will be effective if it is remote from the act that provokes it. For a troublemaker to comprehend the relationship between behavior and counterreaction, one must quickly follow the other. Don't postpone dealing with misbehaving pupils or make vague threats to be put into effect sometime in the future (such as taking away the privilege of participating in Play-Day). By the time the act of retribution comes due, most pupils will have forgotten what they did wrong. They then feel resentful and persecuted and may conclude that you are acting out of sheer malice. A frequent reaction is more misbehavior in an urge to "get even." (In such situations, guilty pupils are not likely to remember that *you* are the one doing the evening up.) On the other hand, retribution that is *too* immediate, that is, applied when a student is still extremely upset, may also be ineffective. At such times, it is often better to wait a bit before requiring restitution.

Being consistent about classroom control can save a lot of time, energy, and misery. Strictness one day and leniency the next, or roughness on one pupil and gentleness with another, invites all students to test you every day—just to see whether this is one of your good days or one of your bad ones or whether they can get away with something more frequently than others do. Having a set of rules is an excellent way to encourage yourself to be consistent.

Harshness in meting out retribution encourages rather than discourages more extreme forms of misbehavior. If pupils are going to get into a lot of trouble for even a minor offense, they will probably figure they should get their money's worth. In the early days of Merrie England all offenses—from picking pockets to murder—were punishable by death. The petty thief quickly became a murderer; it was a lot easier (and less risky) to pick the pocket of a dead man and, since the punishment was the same, eminently more sensible. The laws were eventually changed to make punishment appropriate to the degree of the offense. Keep this in mind when you dispense justice.

7. Consider using behavior modification techniques.   Many of the techniques that have been noted—particularly stating rules, using techniques planned in advance, and being prompt and consistent—are used in a highly systematic fashion in the behavior modification approach to classroom control. In Chapter 5 you were acquainted

with the techniques of behavior modification, including the suggestion that you follow this procedure when confronted by disruptive behavior, as when two boys in a chemistry class engage in a scuffle. (Assume that the scuffling behavior becomes more violent after each phase.)

First, ignore the behavior.

Second, remind the class that those who finish the experiment early will earn five bonus points and be allowed to see a film.

After ignoring misbehavior, stress rewards; use punishment as a last resort

Third, approach the boys and tell them (privately and nicely) that they are disturbing others and making life difficult for themselves because if they do not complete the experiment in the allotted time, they will have to make it up some other time.

Fourth, resort to punishment by informing the boys (in a firm but not nasty way) that they must leave the classroom immediately and report to the vice principal to be assigned to a study hall for the rest of the class period. Tell them they will have to complete the experiment when the rest of the class has free experiment time.

Finish by pointing out that once the work is made up, they will be all caught up and in a good position to do above average work for the rest of the report period.

This sequence is based on studies (e.g., Hall and others, 1971) leading to the conclusion that punishment is most effective when it occurs immediately after a response, cannot be avoided, is as intense as seems necessary, and provides the individual with an alternative and desirable response.

Handbook heading
Experimenting with Behavior Modification

The techniques just described are appropriate for secondary school students. The following behavior modification procedure for maintaining classroom control in the primary grades is recommended by Wesley C. Becker, Siegfried Engelmann, and Don P. Thomas:

1. Specify in a positive way the rules that are the basis for your reinforcement. Emphasize the behavior you desire by praising children who are following the rules. Rules are made important by providing reinforcement for following them. Rules may be different for different kinds of work, study, or play periods.

Limit the rules to five or less.

As the children learn to follow the rules, repeat them less frequently, but continue to praise good classroom behavior.

2. Relate the children's performance to the rules. Praise behavior, not the child. Be specific about behavior that exemplifies paying attention or working hard: "That's *right,* you're a hard worker," "You watched the board all the time I was presenting the example. That's paying attention." "That's a good answer. You listened very closely to my question." "Jimmy is really working hard. He'll get the answer. You'll see."

Relax the rules between work periods. Do not be afraid to have fun with your children when the work period is over.

3. Catch the children being good. Reinforce behavior incompatible with that which you wish to eliminate. Reinforce behavior that will be most beneficial to the child's development. In the process of eliminating disruptive behavior, focus on reinforcing tasks important for social and cognitive skills.

4. Ignore disruptive behavior unless someone is getting hurt. Focus your attention on the children who are working well in order to prompt the correct behavior from the children who are misbehaving.

5. When you see a persistent problem behavior, look for the reinforcer. It may be your own behavior. (1971, p. 171)

The behavior modification approach calls attention to the ways your students will respond to your behavior, to the need for consistency, and to possible ways you might inadvertently reinforce the very behavior you would like to prevent. However, the same possible weaknesses noted in evaluating applications of principles of operant conditioning to learning and motivation also apply to classroom control: Techniques described by Becker, Engelmann, and Thomas may be effective only with young children. Your role in the class may be that of manipulator and dispenser of rewards. Extensive use of reinforcement may lead to satiation. Control will be extrinsic. In addition, some of the disadvantages of an autocratic and dominative classroom atmosphere may result if you are too concerned about shaping behavior.

You may recall that mention was made in Chapter 5 of an article by R. A. Winett and R. C. Winkler (1972) titled "Current Behavior Modification in the Classroom. Be Still, Be Quiet, Be Docile." This title summarizes the conclusion reached by Winett and Winkler after they analyzed dozens of reports of behavior modification procedures used to maintain classroom control: The majority of the behavior modifiers appeared to be primarily interested in shaping robotlike conformity. Injudicious use of the techniques recommended by Becker, Engelmann, and Thomas might easily cause students to conclude that the only way to get a favorable response from a teacher is to be still, quiet, and docile.

A question that comes to mind most directly in regard to behavior modification techniques, but also applies to this entire discussion of classroom control, is: How much control is really necessary? If you insist that your students line up with precision to go out to recess, are you doing so to avoid a jam at the door, or are you perhaps enjoying the power of knowing that you can get pupils to obey your commands? If you shape conscientious work at desks by praising only students who do their work quietly and with apparent industry, are you doing so to instill desirable study habits or perhaps to make classroom life easier for you?

If you find that you are devoting considerable time to shaping classroom behavior, you might analyze your motives: Is the behavior

Avoid using behavior modification to induce docility

Signals such as staring at a misbehaving pupil are examples of influence techniques Redl and Wattenberg classify as "supporting self-control."
Peter Travers

you are trying to produce really necessary and beneficial, or are you controlling for the sake of control? Children should learn to control their impulses and to respect the rights of others, but they should also learn to be self-sufficient and to be capable of making independent decisions. If students are conditioned (and that is exactly what occurs in behavior modification) to respond without thinking when a person in authority gives a command, their capability for independent thought and action may be diminished. In *Brave New World* (1932), Aldous Huxley described a society in which techniques of classical conditioning were used to make citizens easier to control. The application of principles of operant conditioning is not as extreme, and the consequences are more susceptible to analysis by those who are manipulated, but the end result of using too much behavior modification could lead to the sort of behavior that Huxley described in his novel.

8. When you have control, ease up—some.   It is extremely difficult, if not impossible, to establish a controlled atmosphere after allowing anarchy. Don't make the mistake of thinking you will be able to start

out without any control and suddenly take charge. It may work, but in most cases you will have an armed truce or a cold war on your hands. It is far better to start out on the strict side and then ease up a bit after you have established control. (Remember the results of the Lippitt and White study: Groups that started out under democracy resented authority.) Being strict doesn't mean being unpleasant or dictatorial; it simply means that everyone in the room is aware that they are expected to respect the rights of others.

Influence techniques

In *Mental Hygiene in Teaching* (1959), Fritz Redl and William W. Wattenberg present a list of *influence techniques,* which has been adopted as an organizational frame of reference for the following discussion. The sections headed "Supporting Self-Control," "Situational Assistance," and "Reality and Value Appraisal" are based directly on the list. All the subheadings in these sections are exactly as set forth on pages 348–363 of *Mental Hygiene in Teaching.*

Under each section specific examples are offered. Some are based on ideas noted by Redl and Wattenberg; some are the results of reports by students and teachers; some are based on personal experience. You might use the headings in your Handbook. Pick out techniques that seem most appropriate for your grade level or that you feel comfortable about, and add other ideas of your own.

Supporting self-control

Students should be encouraged to develop self-control. This first group of suggestions is designed to foster it.

Handbook heading

Signals to Use to Nip
Trouble in the Bud

Signals   In some cases a subtle signal can put an end to budding misbehavior. The signal, if successful, will stimulate the student to control himself. (This technique should not be used too often, and it is effective only in the early stages of misbehavior.)

EXAMPLES

Clear your throat.

Stare at the culprit.

Stop what you are saying in midsentence and stare.

Shake your head (to indicate no).

Say, "Someone is making it hard for the rest of us to concentrate" (or the equivalent).

Proximity control   Place yourself close to the troublemaker. This makes a signal a bit more apparent.

EXAMPLES

Walk over and stand near the student.

With an elementary grade pupil, it sometimes helps if you place a gentle hand on a shoulder or arm.

Interest boosting   Convey interest in the incipient misbehaver. This relates the signal to school work.

EXAMPLES

Ask the student a question, preferably related to what is being discussed. (Questions such as "Herman, are you paying attention?" or "Don't you agree, Herman?" invite wisecracks. *Genuine* questions are to be preferred.)

Go over and examine some work the student is doing. It often helps if you point out something good about it and urge continued effort.

Humor   Humor is an excellent, all-around influence technique, especially in tense situations. However, remember that it should be *good-humored* humor—gentle and benign rather than incisive. Irony and sarcasm should be avoided.

EXAMPLES

"Herman, for goodness' sake, let that poor pencil sharpener alone—I heard it groan when you used it just now."

(Perhaps you have heard someone say, "We're not laughing *at* you; we're laughing *with* you." Before you say this to one of your pupils, you might take note that one second grader who was treated to that comment unhinged the teacher by replying, "I'm not laughing.")

Situational assistance

Helping over hurdles   Some misbehavior undoubtedly occurs because students do not understand what they are to do or lack the ability to carry out an assignment. Techniques for minimizing problems of this sort were discussed in the section on causes of misbehavior under the subheading Boredom. They are noted again here.

Handbook heading
Ways to Supply
Situational Assistance

EXAMPLES

Try to make sure your students know what they are supposed to do.

Try to arrange for students to have something to do at appropriate levels of difficulty.

Have a variety of activities available.

Establish routines,
particularly at the start
of activities

Support from routines   Trouble sometimes develops simply because students do not know what is expected of them. To avoid this in-limbo situation, it helps to establish a certain amount of routine, perhaps as part of the class rules (if you resort to such rules).

EXAMPLES

Establish a set pattern for getting started at the beginning of the day or period.

Make a specific routine out of lining up for recess, lunch, and other activities.

At the beginning of gym classes (or the equivalent), where wild horseplay is at a maximum, establish a fixed procedure for taking roll (perhaps by having students stand on numbers painted on the floor), for determining activities to be participated in, and so on.

Nonpunitive exile   Sometimes a student will get carried away by anger, frustration, or uncontrollable giggling. If you feel that this is nonmalicious behavior and due simply to lack of self-control, ask the student to leave the room.

EXAMPLES

"Herman, maybe you'd better go out and get a drink of water or do pushups in the hall or something. We'll see you back here in five minutes."

Some high schools have "quiet rooms"—supervised study halls that take extra students any time during a period, no questions asked.

Use of restraint   Students who lose control of themselves to the point of endangering other members of the class may have to be physically restrained. However, such restraint should be protective, not punitive; that is, don't shake or hit. This technique is most effective with younger children; if the pupils are bigger or stronger than the teacher, it may be imprudent. (Even if the high school teacher *is* bigger, such control is usually not appropriate at the secondary level.)

EXAMPLES

If a boy completely loses his temper and starts to hit another child, lead him gently but firmly away from the other pupils or sit him in a chair and keep a restraining hand on his shoulder.

Removing seductive objects   If certain objects or fellow students are too tempting for pupils, the wise thing to do is put temptation behind them.

EXAMPLES

If an elementary grade pupil gets carried away using a projector or stapler or paper cutter or whatever, put it away for a while.

If high school students in a shop or laboratory course seem unable to resist the temptation to fool around with expensive equipment, lock it up or erect a barrier (even a cloth cover will do) of some kind.

Anticipatory planning   Some classroom situations are particularly conducive to misbehavior. If a certain activity seems loaded with opportunities for mischief, try to prepare the class ahead of time and emphasize the need for control.

EXAMPLE

When an elementary school class is going to visit the local newspaper plant or the equivalent, stress the importance of not touching anything, keeping away from the machines, and paying strict attention to the guide.

Reality and value appraisal

Handbook heading
Ways to Use Reality
and Value Appraisal

Most of the techniques in the two preceding sections fall under the category of prevention. The following techniques involve prevention but also function to encourage more constructive behavior. As Redl and Wattenberg put it, "One of the goals of education is to enable people to increase the areas in which they can be guided by intelligence and conscience rather than by blind impulse, fear or prejudice" (1959, p. 358). The approaches to be presented now "appeal to children's sense of fairness and strengthen their ability to see the consequence of their actions" (p. 358).

Direct appeals   When appropriate, point out the connection between conduct and its consequences. This is most effective if it is done concisely and if the technique is not used too often.

EXAMPLES

"We have a rule that there is to be no running in the halls. Herman forgot the rule, and now he's down in the nurse's office having his bloody nose taken care of. It's too bad Mr. Harris opened his door just as Herman went by. If Herman had been walking, he would have been able to stop in time."

"If everyone would stop shouting, we'd be able to get this finished and get out to recess."

Try to give criticisms privately; then offer encouragement

Criticism and encouragement Sometimes it is necessary to criticize a particular student. It is preferable to do so in private, but often public criticism is the only possibility. (And it has the advantage of setting an example for other pupils.) In such cases you should do your best to avoid ridiculing or humiliating the student. Public humiliation may make a child hate you and school, arouse a counterattack, or cause withdrawal. Because of the ripple effect, it may also have a negative impact on innocent students. One way to minimize the negative aftereffects of criticism is to tack on some encouragement in the form of a hint as to how the backsliding can be replaced by more positive behavior.

EXAMPLES

If a student doesn't take subtle hints (such as stares), you might say, "*Herman,* you're disturbing the class. We all need to concentrate on this." It sometimes adds punch if you make this remark when your back is turned while you are writing on the board or helping some other student. (This is one way to show that you are with it.)

Act completely flabbergasted, as though the misbehavior seems so inappropriate that you can't comprehend it. A kindergarten teacher used this technique to perfection. She would say, "Herman! Is that *you?*" (Herman has been belting Lucy with a shovel.) "I can't believe my eyes. I wonder if you would help me over here." Obviously, this gambit can't be used too often, and the language and degree of exaggeration have to be altered a bit for older pupils. But indicating that you *expect* good behavior and providing an immediate opportunity for the backslider to substitute good deeds can be very effective.

Defining limits In learning about rules and regulations, children go through a process of testing the limits. Two-year-olds particularly, when they have learned how to walk and talk and manipulate things, feel the urge to assert their independence. In addition, they need to find out exactly what the house rules are. (Does Mommy *really* mean it when she says, "Don't take the pots out of the cupboard?" Does Daddy *really* mean it when he says, "Don't play with that hammer"?) Older children do the same thing, especially with new teachers and in new situations. The technique of defining limits includes not only establishing rules (as noted earlier) but also enforcing them.

EXAMPLES

Either establish general class rules or develop specific ones as the occasion demands. (Suggestions on how to do this were given earlier.)

When someone tests the rules, show that they are genuine and that there *are* limits.

Postsituational follow-up   Classroom discipline occasionally has to be applied in a tense, emotion-packed atmosphere. When this happens, it often helps to have a post-mortem discussion—in private, if an individual is involved; with the whole class, if it was a group-wide situation.

EXAMPLES

In a private conference: "Herman, I'm sorry I had to ask you to leave the room, but you were getting kind of carried away."

"Well, everybody, things got a bit wild during those group work sessions. I want you to enjoy yourselves, but we practically had a riot going, didn't we? And that's why I had to ask you to stop. Let's try to hold it down to a dull roar tomorrow."

Marginal use of interpretation   Analysis of behavior can sometimes be made while it is occurring, rather than afterward. The purpose here is to help students become aware of potential trouble and make efforts to control it.

EXAMPLE

To a restless and cranky prelunch class you might say, "I know you're getting hungry and that you're restless and tired, but let's give it all we've got for ten minutes more. I'll give you the last five minutes for some free visiting time."

The value of these techniques is that they appeal to self-control and imply trust and confidence on the part of the teacher. However, they may become ineffective if used too often, and that is why so many different techniques have been noted. The larger your repertoire, the less frequently you will have to repeat your various gambits and ploys.

Retribution

When efforts at prevention and subtle control fail, you may occasionally have to resort to forms of retribution. If the misbehavior is a fait accompli, you have no choice but to require the guilty party to pay his or her debt to society. Such payment is a part of education, too. In one sense, retribution is desirable in that it presumably teaches students that they cannot break rules of conduct with impunity. But there are many negative aspects to any form of punishment. The learning theory concept of generalization focuses attention on the major disadvantage: A punished child may come to associate hate and fear with all aspects of school and education. This suggests that you should make retribution as gentle as possible while still demonstrating that the misbehavior should not occur again. Here are some techniques to consider when you have no choice but retribution:

Making the punishment fit the crime   This is one of the most commonly noted rules of retribution, but it is often difficult to put into practice. If you can think of compensating behavior that is directly related to the transgression, all the better.

EXAMPLES

If a boy has been playing around during class, it is appropriate to have him stay in during recess and do the work that had been assigned. (If he tells you smugly that by state law he has to have recess, just tell him he has already *had* his recess.)

If a girl knocks over a vase of flowers during some horseplay, have her clean it up.

Withholding a privilege   This is related to the point just mentioned.

EXAMPLE

If repeated requests to hold down the chatter go unheeded, enforce silence for a day or two. Emphasize that the privilege will be reinstated when everyone has demonstrated control.

Detention   This time-honored technique is not easy to apply in a day of individualized scheduling but may be effective. It is usually unwise to require work on school subjects while the culprit is putting in time, however. A student forced to do math or reading in a situation loaded with guilt, anger, and unpleasantness may come to associate these feelings with academic matters.

EXAMPLES

If the second row from the window is fooling around instead of getting ready for recess, detain them three minutes after the rest of the class goes howling out the door.

An incorrigible talker might be asked to write a theme on the topic "Why Talking in the Class Disturbs Others." (Perhaps the talker really hadn't *thought* about it.) Having students write out sentences such as "I shall not talk in class" is ineffective in most cases. The writing is often carried out automatically, and the writer, while mechanically inscribing a whole row of *I*'s, may be thinking of what a louse you are instead of the significance of the statement. For younger children, this can be a form of torture, especially if an unrealistic number of repetitions is required. One mother, for example, stayed up until midnight giving moral support to her second grader as the boy laboriously wrote out *five hundred* "I will not talk in class" statements. The poor child had bleary eyes and writer's cramp and was in a state of nervous exhaustion by the time he finished. (The mother felt she had to go through with it once the task had been imposed by the teacher, lest the boy decide that his parents would intercede on his behalf whenever he got in trouble. At the end of the year she did tell the teacher what she thought of her.)

Punitive exile   One of the techniques noted by Redl and Wattenberg was "nonpunitive exile." It may also be necessary to use what amounts to *punitive* exile. Pupils who deliberately misbehave and continue to disrupt the class—despite your efforts to get them under control—may have to be exiled in retribution. Recalcitrant pupils may be sent to a "quiet room" or to the principal's office or to any appropriate "solitary confinement" area. As with nonpunitive exile, it is usually desirable to set a time limit so students are invited to return once they have paid their debt to classroom society.

If you routinely send misbehavers out in the hall or to a quiet room and require them to stay there until the end of the period, you may actually encourage mischief. A pupil who is bored and wants a change of scenery may cause enough trouble to merit banishment—or escape. In other words, exile works as retribution only when what you are doing in class is reasonably interesting. (You may be able to minimize the use of exile by putting into practice the suggestions for preventing mischief due to boredom that were noted a few pages back.)

Private Conferences   If none of the milder techniques are effective or if milder techniques are tried and only arouse more hostility, it may be well to schedule a private conference. This is preferable to a confrontation before the entire class—not only for the sake of the pupil but also for your own protection. When you find yourself face to face with misbehavers, it is probably a good policy to let them have their say. Perhaps a student just lost control, regrets the action, and wants to make amends. For your part, you might simply explain why you had to insist that the behavior stop. It is helpful to finish such interviews on as positive a note as possible. Try to get across the point that you intend to let bygones be bygones and that you confidently expect better behavior in the future. (Some of the techniques noted under Situational Assistance apply here as well.)

Appeal to an outside authority   When defiance is open and the behavior is not cut short by the suggestion of a personal conference, it's probably time to obtain an arbiter in the form of the principal or vice principal. For example, a student that you ask to go to a quiet room refuses. The student either implies or says indirectly, "I won't

When confronted by a student, it is usually better to arrange for a private conference or appeal to an outside authority than to engage in a showdown in front of the class.

Peter Travers

go, and what are you going to do about it?'' If you are a petite female without a black belt in judo, you won't have much of a problem deciding what to do. On the other hand, if you are a former middle linebacker and eager to show the class that you are still in shape, you might be tempted to do something dramatic. The wise course of action—regardless of your sex, size, and wrestling ability—is calmly to ask some member of the class to get the principal (or other authority designated for disciplinary control). Then go back to the lesson.

Try to avoid appealing to an outside authority unless all other measures have failed; in a sense, doing so is an admission that you can't handle the problem yourself. Yet you should face the fact that sometimes you will encounter such cases. There may be an impossible-to-avoid personality clashes. Some pupils may be the victims of such disturbing experiences that they can't help themselves, or circumstances may simply conspire to get them out on a limb. It is then far better to get the troublemakers out of the room. A running battle kept up all period or all day makes everyone suffer and severely curtails learning. It is a good idea to find out who the responsible authority is as soon as you report for your first job; you will be more than a bit embarrassed if you send a pugnacious pupil to the principal only to have the culprit sent back two minutes later.

I-messages and the no-lose method

In Chapter 7 ("The Humanistic View of Learning"), mention was made of Carl Rogers's suggestion that teachers should be authentic, genuine, and real. The point was made that one way teachers might show they are real and genuine is to apply Haim Ginott's cardinal principle of communication: "Talk to the situation, not to the personality and character" (1972, p. 84). Instead of shouting, "You slobs are not fit to live in a pigsty!" at two boys who have just thrown bread at each other, Ginott suggests that a teacher deliver an "I-message" and say, "I get angry when I see bread thrown around. This room needs cleaning." According to Ginott, guilty pupils who are told why a teacher is angry will realize the teacher is a real person, and this realization will cause them to strive to mend their ways. Ginott offers several examples of the cardinal principle of communication in Chapter 4 of *Teacher and Child* (1972). In Chapter 6 he offers some observations on discipline: Seek alternatives to punishment. Try not to diminish a misbehaving pupil's self-esteem. Try to provide face-saving exits.

A more extensive analysis of many of the same points Ginott stresses is presented by Thomas Gordon in *T.E.T.—Teacher Effectiveness Training* (1974). T.E.T. grew out of techniques originally described by Gordon in *P.E.T.—Parent Effectiveness Training* (1970). Gordon joins with Ginott in applying principles originally propounded by Carl Rogers. In *T.E.T.*, teachers are urged to be real and genuine, to use I-messages, and to resort to authority and punishment only when absolutely necessary. Gordon also agrees with Ginott that communication is the key, but more specific guidelines for becoming an effective communicator are presented in *T.E.T.* than in *Teacher and Child*.

One procedure recommended by Gordon is for teachers to try to determine who *owns* a problem before they decide how to handle that problem. If a student misbehaves by doing something destructive (e.g., carving a desk top), the teacher owns the problem and must respond by doing something to stop the destructive behavior. But if a student expresses anger or disappointment about some classroom incident (e.g., getting a low grade on an exam), that student owns the problem. Gordon suggests that failure to identify problem ownership may cause teachers to intensify difficulties unwittingly, even as they make well-intended efforts to diminish them. If a pupil is finding it difficult to concentrate on school work because of lack of satisfaction of needs, the situation will not be ameliorated if the teacher orders, moralizes, or criticizes. According to Gordon, such responses act as roadblocks to finding solutions to student-owned problems because they tend to make the pupil feel resentful and misunderstood. The preferred way to deal with a pupil who owns a problem is to use what Gordon calls

Handbook heading
Using I-Messages

I-messages: Tell how you feel about an unacceptable situation

Handbook heading
Speculating about Problem Ownership

active listening: a simplified version of Rogers's nondirective therapy. A nondirective therapist accepts, reflects, and clarifies what a patient says; an active-listening teacher encourages students to talk about what is bothering them. The listener is *active* in the sense that interest is shown and the talker is encouraged to continue to express feelings; the listener does *not* actively participate by interpreting, explaining, or directing.

For teacher-owned problems—those that involve misbehavior that is destructive or in violation of school regulations—Gordon agrees with Ginott that I-messages are appropriate. Instead of ordering, threatening, moralizing, using logic, offering solutions, or commenting on personal characteristics, Gordon urges teachers to explain why they are upset. Proof of the effectiveness of I-messages takes the form of anecdotes reported in *T.E.T.* provided by teachers who used them successfully. A principal of a continuation school for dropouts, for example, reported that a group of tough boys responded very favorably when he told them how upset he became when he saw them break some bottles against the school wall. Almost invariably the anecdotes reported in *T.E.T.* refer to the success of a teacher's first try at delivering an I-message. It seems likely that at least part of the success of the technique could be attributed to surprise or novelty—a kind of Hawthorne effect. As noted in Chapter 7 in comments on Ginott's recommendation that I-messages be used, it is possible that extensive use of the technique might stir up rather than calm down troublemakers. Instead of saying, "Gee! We never realized you felt that way!" they might say, "We're getting awfully tired of hearing about your troubles!"

Gordon urges teachers to try to resolve conflicts in the classroom by using the *no-lose method.* If either person in a conflict loses, there is bound to be resentment. If you tell a girl who is fooling around during a work period that she must settle down or stay after school, *she* loses. If you make a halfhearted and unsuccessful effort to control her and then try to cover up your failure by ignoring her and working with others, *you* lose. Gordon recommends that the preferred procedure is to talk over the problem and come up with a mutually agreeable compromise solution. He offers this six-step procedure for coming up with no-lose solutions, a procedure that you may recognize is similar to techniques recommended by Howe and Howe (1975) for choosing class discussion topics (noted in Chapter 7), and by Polya (1954) for using heuristics (Chapter 9):

1. Define the problem

2. Generate possible solutions

3. Evaluate the solutions

4. Decide which solution is best

5. Determine how to implement the solution

6. Assess how well the solution solved the problem (1974, p. 228)

To put this procedure into practice with an individual, you might approach a boy who is disrupting things during a work period and engage in a dialogue something like this:

You: You're making such a ruckus over here I can't hear the group I'm working with. It looks as if you are having trouble settling down. Any ideas about how we can both do what we need to do?

Pupil: I think this workbook junk is stupid. I already know how to do these problems. I'd rather work on my science project.

You: Well, suppose you do one page of problems. If you get them all correct, we'll both know you can do them and you should be free to work on your science project. If you make some mistakes, though, that means you need more practice. Suppose you do a page and then ask me to check it. Then we can take it from there.

To put the no-lose method into effect when the entire class is upset about something, it would probably be preferable to follow all six steps recommended by Gordon.

In certain situations you are likely to find that the observations of Ginott and Gordon can be quite helpful. You might try to analyze what you say to pupils when you are upset to discover if you tend to violate the cardinal principle of communication by mentioning character and personality instead of concentrating on the situation. If you find that you do criticize personal characteristics, make a concerted effort to comment on the situation. You might also make an effort to determine who "owns" a problem before you decide how to deal with it. If a pupil is not behaving in the desired manner and appears to be unhappy or confused about it, you might try by serving as an active listener. Encourage the student to talk about what is bothering him or her by serving as a sympathetic sounding board. In cases of defiant, disruptive, or destructive behavior, make occasional use of I-messages so that pupils learn that you have feelings that ought to be respected. And if you find yourself confronted by a hostile student or class, you might use the no-lose method to find a mutually agreeable solution to the problem that is the cause of the trouble.

SUMMARY OF KEY POINTS

Several psychologists have studied the impact on pupils of different styles of leadership. Lewin, Lippitt, and White found that groups of boys responded to authoritarian leaders in either submissive or aggressive ways, depending on their previous experiences. Under democratic leaders, the boys engaged in constructive behavior even when working on their own, and were friendly toward each other. Some critics have pointed out, however, that the authoritarian leaders in the Lewin study were unnecessarily harsh. Generalizing from Baumrind's research with preschool children, it might be expected that *authoritative* leaders would encourage pupils to become competent and to strive for high levels of performance. Authoritative leadership may also be considered desirable because children must learn that certain restrictions are necessary if large numbers of individuals are to coexist. Those who advocate that children be taught in situations free from all restrictions fail to allow for the fact that even "free" children may misbehave if their needs are not satisfied.

Some students misbehave because they are bored; others may engage in disruptive acts to gain release of tension. Keeping students busy and giving them positive ways to release tension may reduce behavior problems traceable to these causes. When teachers deal with individual misbehavers, the rest of the class may respond almost as intensively because of the *ripple effect.* Teachers who show they are with it seem to head off many discipline problems before pupils get out of hand. Other effective techniques for maintaining classroom control include developing the ability to handle overlapping activities, maintaining momentum by avoiding unnecessary interruptions, and keeping the entire class involved and alert during recitation periods. Effective ways to handle problems once they erupt include identifying individual troublemakers and firmly informing them about constructive forms of substitute behavior.

Establishing class rules may simplify classroom control because teachers will not have to deal with all problems on the spur of the moment. Behavior modification techniques, such as ignoring misbehavior and rewarding desired forms of behavior, can be used effectively in establishing control, but teachers should guard against the temptation to shape docility. Perhaps the best way to maintain classroom control is to develop a repertoire of influence techniques, such as establishing routines and planning how to deal with disruptive pupils who must be criticized. In dealing with problems, you might make occasional use of I-messages (tell how you feel about an unacceptable situation) or the no-lose method (come to mutual agreement about a solution).

BECOMING A BETTER TEACHER:
QUESTIONS AND SUGGESTIONS

Keeping Pupils Busy

Do the students in my classes frequently act bored, restless, or unsure of what they are to do? Suggestions: Make it a point to check on boredom, restlessness, and random activity, particularly during work periods. If such forms of behavior are common, plan ways to keep pupils constructively busy.

Learning to Deal with Overlapping Situations

Am I with it in terms of knowing what is going on in my classroom, or do I have a one-track mind? Suggestions: Carry out a self-analysis of how I deal with simultaneous activities. Make it a point to continually look around the room as I carry out one activity and be alert for signs of incipient problems. Practice ways to handle more than one thing at a time. List some techniques to prove I'm with it: If I see two boys starting to shove each other just before I turn to write something on the board, tell them to stop as I write with my back turned. Start a sentence, insert a comment directed at a troublemaker, and go right on with the rest of the sentence.

Learning How to Maintain Momentum

Do I flip-flop from one activity to another or unnecessarily interrupt the flow of an activity? Suggestion: The next time I am tempted to interrupt what we are doing to comment on some unrelated incident or activity, fight down the impulse and keep things flowing. Also, make an effort to build momentum into class activities as I draw up plans for the day or period.

Ways to Keep the Whole Class Involved

Am I using techniques that tend to cause some members of the class to tune out? Suggestions: Make up a list of ways to keep everybody involved. Call on pupils in unpredictable order. Ask questions first, and then call on pupils. Ask several pupils to respond in quick succession. Have all pupils in the class respond to questions one way or another.

Ways to Set in Motion "Positive Ripples"

Do I deal with disruptive students in ways that needlessly upset the rest of the class? Suggestion: Memorize a list of steps to follow the next time I have to deal with a misbehaving pupil: Call her or him by name. Specify constructive behavior. Explain why the misbehavior is unacceptable. Be firm and authoritative.

Inviting the Class to Help Establish Rules

Should I ask the class to help establish rules? Suggestion: The next time I meet a new group of pupils, spend a few minutes the first day inviting them to suggest classroom regulations, or at least explain why certain classroom procedures are necessary.

Being Completely Prepared the First Day

Have I thought over exactly what I intend to do the first day or class period with a new group of pupils? Suggestion: Draw up a detailed plan of what I will do the first day, starting off with how I will introduce myself, how I will begin to learn pupil names, whether I will assign desks, and so on.

Analyzing My Feelings After I Deal with Troublemakers

How do I feel after I have to really "put down" a student? Suggestion: The next time I deal harshly with a pupil, make it a point to examine the emotional aftereffects I experience. If I am pleased and smug, should I be? If I am upset, what might I do to avoid experiencing similar emotional tension in the future?

Trying to Re-establish Rapport	The last time I sharply criticized a pupil, did I later make a move to effect a reconciliation? Suggestion: The next time I have to deal harshly with a pupil, make it a point to tell or show that individual that as far as I am concerned, bygones are bygones and I do not hold a grudge. Then try to give that pupil a chance to do something constructive.
Being Prompt, Consistent, and Reasonable in Controlling the Class	Am I being prompt, consistent, and reasonable in my efforts to maintain control of the class? Suggestions: Carry out a personal survey of how prompt and consistent I am as a disciplinarian. Perhaps ask the class to tell me in anonymous statements if they think punishments are reasonable.
Experimenting with Behavior Modification	Have I tried using a behavior modification approach to handle discipline problems? Suggestion: Write down and put into practice a series of steps to follow when dealing with classroom misbehavior: State rules or a description of what needs to be done in order to gain reinforcement. Perhaps invite pupils to prepare individual reward menus. Praise those who are doing what they should be doing. Initially ignore those who are not doing what they should be doing. If negative behavior does not extinguish when it is ignored, point out unfortunate consequences that might occur if that behavior continues. At the same time, stress the desirability of completing the task and gaining reinforcement.
Signals to Use to Nip Trouble in the Bud	What signals might I use to communicate to incipient troublemakers that I am with it? Suggestions: Clear my throat. Pause a few seconds in midsentence and stare at the misbehaving pupils. Move and stand near troublemakers. Direct a question at a pupil who is beginning to engage in disruptive behavior. Make a lighthearted remark about what is going on.
Ways to Supply Situational Assistance	What techniques can I use to help potential troublemakers control themselves? Suggestions: Remind them of what they are supposed to be doing. Set up routines designed to minimize temptation. Send a pupil who seems on the verge of getting into trouble on an errand. Prepare the class and stress the need for control when a potentially "explosive" activity is imminent.
Ways to Use Reality and Value Appraisal	How can I help pupils become aware of how their misbehavior regularly affects themselves and others? Suggestions: Take advantage of object lessons to illustrate why certain rules are necessary and logical. If a student must be criticized, follow it up with encouragement conveying the idea that improved behavior is expected. Ask the class to help establish rules or at least talk about why rules are necessary. After a tense and disagreeable experience, allow a cooling-off period, and then analyze what happened and why it should not happen again. Help pupils gain understanding of their own behavior when they show signs of losing control.

Using Retribution as Positively as Possible	What are some things I can do to make punishment effective without causing negative repercussions? Suggestions: Try to make the punishment fit the crime. Withhold a privilege. Make cautious use of detention. Tell a disruptive student "I want to have a conference at the end of the period (or day)." Find out what the school policy is for handling pupils who are so disruptive they must be sent out of the classroom.
Using I-Messages	Am I applying Ginott's fundamental principle of communication, and am I using I-messages? Suggestion: Just after I reprimand pupils, jot down what I said. Then check to see if I criticized personality or character rather than the situation. If I *did* tell students they were lazy or sloppy or something similar, make a resolution to deliver an I-message the next time I face a similar situation: Tell the student or the class how I feel about what is going on.
Speculating About Problem Ownership	Have I ever tried to figure out who "owns" a problem before dealing with it? Suggestion: Starting tomorrow try to classify the ownership of problems as soon as I become aware of them. If students are doing something disruptive or destructive, use an appropriate influence technique to handle it in an authoritative way. If the problem seems to be due to feelings of confusion, inadequacy, or incompetence, try active listening.
Trying the No-Lose Method	Am I trying to seek compromises when conflicts develop, or am I being too dictatorial? Suggestion: The next time I run into a conflict with an individual pupil or the class, try the no-lose method: Define the problem. Ask for and propose solutions. Come to mutual agreement about one of the solutions.

SUGGESTIONS FOR FURTHER STUDY

15-1 Analyzing Class Atmospheres You Have Experienced	The Lippitt and White study and the observations of Anderson will seem more significant if you think about the different class atmospheres you have experienced. Look again at the descriptions of democratic, autocratic, and laissez-faire leaders (pages 788–789), and recall a teacher who most closely exemplified each type. Then record your recollection of how you and your classmates reacted to the classroom atmosphere. Or compare the classroom atmosphere you found most agreeable as a student with the one you found most disagreeable. Try to highlight the characteristics of the desirable and undesirable class "climates" and record the implications.
15-2 Developing a Personal List of Dos and Don'ts for Classroom Control	The influence techniques described in this chapter may be more meaningful if you analyze your own experiences with classroom control. Think back to techniques you felt were excessively harsh or cruel. Were there incidents in which a teacher embarrassed or humiliated a child or caused considerable mental anguish? If so, describe

the situation and then use it as a basis for drawing up a list of techniques to be avoided at all costs. You might also develop a set of procedures you definitely want to try and insert both lists in your Handbook.

In *Summerhill* (1960), A. S. Neill comments on the advantages of self-discipline. The sequence of topics in this book is a bit disorganized, but if you read "Self-Government" (p. 45), "The Unfree Child" (p. 95), "The Free Child" (p. 104), "Obedience and Discipline" (p. 155), and "Rewards and Punishments" (p. 162), you will have a fairly complete picture of Neill's views on how children should learn self-control.

Haim Ginott has written two best sellers on the subject of communication between parents and their offspring. *Between Parent and Child* (1965) will be of interest to you if you will be teaching at the elementary level. *Between Parent and Teenager* (1969) is more appropriate if you will be teaching at the secondary level. The basic ideas stressed in these books are applied more directly to education in *Teacher and Child* (1971). All three books describe how parents and teachers can make use of techniques similar to those of Roger's nondirective therapy. There is considerable emphasis on assisting children in understanding their feelings. Suggestions are offered on how to praise and criticize and how to achieve a balance between permissiveness and limits to help children develop responsibility, self-control, and independence. Not all the methods described can be used by teachers at all levels, and you may disagree with some of Ginott's recommendations, but as a general guide for establishing and maintaining classroom control his ideas can be quite helpful. If you read any of these books, list the points you think might be useful later.

For a more comprehensive analysis of common causes of behavior problems and suggestions on how to handle them, *Mental Hygiene in Teaching* (2nd ed., 1959) by Redl and Wattenberg is especially recommended. The following chapters may be of particular help: Chapter 10, "Group Life in the Classroom"; Chapter 11, "The Psychological Roles of Teachers"; Chapter 13, "Influence Techniques"; and Chapter 14, "Some Common Dilemmas Teachers Face." Another book on classroom control is *Toward Positive Classroom Discipline* (1971) by H. F. Clarizio. If you will be teaching at the secondary level and you want a down-to-earth list of dos and don'ts, you might browse through *The Teacher's Survival Guide* (1967) by Jenny Gray, subtitled *How to Teach Teen-agers and Live to Tell About It!* Blunt and breezy in style, the book is both entertaining and informative. If you sample one of these books or a similar volume, you might note ideas that strike you as potentially valuable.

Two special New York City schools are described in *The Angel Inside Went Sour* (1971) by Esther Rothman and *Nine Rotten Lousy Kids* (1972) by Herbert Grossman. Rothman describes her experiences as principal of a school for girls considered impossible to handle in regular classrooms. For information about teaching such students, you might sample Chapter 5, "Requiem for a Curriculum," Chapter 6, "The Myth of Discipline," and Chapter 10, "Developing Self-Esteem: A Therapeutic Approach." *Nine Rotten Lousy Kids* is a day-by-day log kept by the teachers in a school for teen-age boys who were to be sent to residential treatment centers, state training schools, or mental hospitals. To sample this book, read one or two sections about incidents that occurred and how they were handled. If you read parts of either of these books, you might note techniques you could use with difficult-to-handle students in your classes.

Key points

Teaching and need satisfaction

Teaching yields intangible rewards

Professional organizations help teachers improve working conditions

Suggestions for dealing with frustrations

Distinguish between things you must accept, things you might change

Seek help when confronted with specific problems

Talk over problems with colleagues or pupils

Avoid taking out frustrations on pupils

Increasing the possibility of self-actualization

Self-knowledge a major path to self-improvement

Be aware of conflicting tendencies toward safety and toward growth

Improving your skills as a teacher

Some ratings may be of value only when compared to others' ratings

Forced-choice ratings solve leniency problem

Verbal interactions between teacher and pupils can be analyzed

Epilogue
Teaching for your own self-actualization

In the two preceding chapters you were asked to consider how you might teach so as to establish in your classroom an atmosphere conducive to the need gratification of your students. In this chapter you are asked to consider your own self-actualization.

Self-actualization is obviously an important issue for personal reasons, but it is important for other reasons as well. As a teacher, you will be involved in relationships with students who have little or no choice in the matter. If you are frustrated by conditions in your personal or professional life, you not only will suffer the consequences yourself but also will inflict them on your students. If you are angry about something, you may take it out on your pupils or infuse them with your hostility. If you are almost totally dissatisfied with teaching, you will communicate this feeling to your pupils in an unmistakable way. The points made in this chapter, therefore, are offered for your students' benefit as well as yours.

In Chapter 2 you were encouraged to think about the advantages and disadvantages of teaching and also to speculate about aspects of teaching you must accept as well as those you might try to change. Now that you have read about what students are like at different grade levels, how they learn, why they are—or are not—motivated to learn, and what you might do to evaluate their performance, you may find it instructive to re-evaluate your original analysis of advantages and disadvantages. One way to do this is to speculate about how well teaching permits satisfaction of the needs in Abraham Maslow's hierarchy.

Teaching and need satisfaction

For a teacher, safety is pretty much equated with security. In the economic sense, teaching provides considerable security—assuming that you have few and simple pleasures. With tenure, steady employment is assured. But in terms of emotional security, the teacher is not guaranteed equivalent satisfaction. In *When Teachers Face Themselves* (1955), Arthur Jersild notes that some teachers are anxious and lonely. Jersild emphasizes "search for self," his basic thesis being that individuals must understand themselves before they can understand others. In his book he discusses the theoretical implications of what teachers report when they are asked to try to understand themselves.

In addition to the personal, search-for-self aspect, Jersild's book reveals that some teachers feel insecure about their jobs. Although the causes are not examined, certain factors stand out. When some students fail to learn, a sensitive teacher can't help wondering, "Is it *my* fault?" Encountering a particular apathetic group of pupils may cause you to brood about whether there *is* any reason for studying your pet subject. Fortunately, there are usually enough signs of flickering interest to sustain you, but you may have days when you wonder whether you belong in a classroom or in business with your in-laws.

The needs for love and belongingness are met very directly in the lower grades. Primary grade students often give overt indications that they like their teacher. Undisguised looks of adoration, Valentine's Day cards, presents at the end of the year—these are unmistakable signs to primary grade teachers that they are liked. At the secondary level, affection is not so obvious. The teacher-authority figure may be disliked by young people who are yearning for independence. Even adolescents who do admire a teacher may take pains to conceal it. If you think you have a strong need for evidences of affection, before you make a final decision about the grade level you prefer, consider the possibility that a secondary school teacher may serve as a target for teen-age hostility. It should be noted, however, that many high school teachers earn respect and subtle signs of high regard from their pupils.

While teaching is a secure occupation, which helps satisfy the need for safety, it is also low paying, which may complicate satisfying the need for esteem. Few tangible marks of "prestige" are within the means of the person who must exist solely on a teacher's salary. In our status-oriented society, this can cause a teacher to feel unsuccessful, at least in terms of material possessions. For the most part, teachers earn *intangible*, though often much more meaningful, rewards than people do in other lines of endeavor. Awareness of doing something important and helping young people to learn and develop their potentialities may be the major source of self-satisfaction and self-esteem for a teacher, as compared with a showplace residence in an exclusive suburb, a Cadillac, and a cabin cruiser.

From this brief review, it is apparent that given the proper teacher qualities and school conditions, teaching can permit a person to achieve satisfaction of the psychological needs. However, it is equally

Teaching yields
intangible rewards

Secondary school teachers are not admired as openly or as universally as elementary school teachers, but positive reactions from just a few secondary school students can do much to satisfy the need for esteem.

Christopher Morrow/Stock Boston

apparent that many barriers prevent the easy or direct reaching of these goals. You will not know whether the satisfactions outweigh the frustrations until you have taught at least a year or two. But it will help to think ahead to how you can make your reactions constructive ones when the inevitable frustrations occur. You will remember from the discussion of reactions to frustration in Chapter 14 that individuals can make a direct attack and strive to overcome a frustrating situation; they can compromise—accepting a lesser goal and resorting to a defense mechanism to ease things; or they can withdraw from the situation, either physically or psychologically.

In many situations the most constructive thing to do is to try to overcome the frustrations. But not all frustrations can be overcome. Suppose, for example, the school board or a state curriculum committee or a local superintendent insists that you teach (or not teach) something in a certain way. To attack the injunction directly would be pointless, since you would have no chance to succeed and would probably suffer considerable mental and professional anguish in making the attempt. (And your involvement might hinder rather than aid your students.) The more sensible thing to do would be to find legal ways to teach within the limits established but in such a fashion that you would still be able to assert your individuality.

It also makes sense to try to bring about change by making suggestions through established channels. These channels are becoming more open every year, especially with the increasing acceptance of collective bargaining as a legitimate way for teachers to express themselves. Nevertheless, even if you are successful in some of your onslaughts on the barriers—and do bring about certain improvements and do find legal ways to get around restrictions—you will still encounter frustrating conditions that are not amenable to much change. This is a fact of life all teachers (and most other people) must simply face. Then you just do what you can and make the best of it. But in making the best of it, you will be more able to maintain a satisfactory personal adjustment if you keep in mind some of the better ways of handling frustrations.

Professional organizations help teachers improve working conditions

Suggestions for dealing with frustrations

Here is a list of suggestions on how to cope with frustrations. With the exception of points 10, 11, and 13, the statements in italics are exact quotations from *Mental Hygiene in Teaching* by Redl and Wattenberg, pages 494–497.

1. *Develop self-awareness.*   This is Arthur Jersild's general theme in *When Teachers Face Themselves* (1955) and *In Search of Self* (1952). The basic idea is that the better people understand themselves, the less likely they are to be overwhelmed by events they cannot control. Furthermore, those who understand and accept themselves are better able to accept and understand others. If you feel that you might benefit from developing greater self-awareness, you might consider joining an encounter group (or the equivalent) under the direction of a competent, well-trained leader.

Handbook heading
Looking for New Possibilities

2. *Recognize new possibilities in teaching.*   If a "standard" technique for dealing with a problem is blocked by a directive or set of conditions, find a new and different way to do it.

3. *Evaluate dissatisfactions.*   If you find yourself dissatisfied with certain aspects of teaching, try to select those portions of the problem

Distinguish between things you must accept, things you might change

that *can* be dealt with and become a relaxed fatalist about the rest. (Confucius put it in the form of the familiar prayer: Give me the strength to change what can be changed, the courage to accept what cannot be changed, and the wisdom to tell one from the other.)

Handbook heading
Listing Priorities

4. *Re-evaluate total load.* If you are inundated by work and pressure mounts, try to eliminate or reduce certain tensions. For example, if you are driven to the brink by having to grade term papers for five classes of thirty pupils each, don't assign term papers unless your teaching load is adjusted.

Seek help when confronted with specific problems

5. *Look for help on specific questions.* If you are hung up on a particular frustration, ask for ideas from your principal or an older teacher or a consultant. In some cases, all it takes is a little more experience or a different perspective to reveal a simple solution. Remember the impact of functional fixedness.

6. *Deliberately expose yourself to new experiences.* Anyone who is conscientious about teaching needs periods of rest and relaxation. Functioning as an inspirational instructor takes a lot out of a person. For this reason it may be wise to cultivate a noneducational hobby, take a nonteaching summer job, or make the most of that three-month vacation.

7. *Seek satisfactions elsewhere.* If conditions in school block the achievement of psychological needs, make a deliberate effort to find satisfaction outside the classroom. For example, a high school teacher who felt unhappy about the lack of overt acceptance and admiration of his students (not because he was a poor teacher but because high school students often make it a point not to show admiration openly) became the scoutmaster of a Boy Scout troop. Another way to satisfy partly frustrated needs is to develop a creative hobby.

Talk over problems with colleagues or pupils

8. *Talk it over with friends.* One purpose of psychotherapy is to provide catharsis—the release of tension. You can get much the same result by talking over your problems with others. There is obviously a limit to how much you can impose on any one person, but an occasional legitimate gripe will rarely strain relationships with a spouse, friend, or colleague, especially if you spread the gripes around and act as a reciprocal "therapist." If you are upset about something (the furnace at home went on the blink at 3:00 a.m.), talk about it, and warn the class that they had better look out for you that day.

9. *Stimulate group discussion.* A variation of the preceding point is "group therapy" sessions. Gripe sessions in a cafeteria or teachers' room are often an effective way to keep body and soul together, especially if there is an element of humor in them. (Looking for the

humorous side of things is a fine, all-purpose method of dealing with frustrations in or outside the classroom.)

Handbook heading
Seeking Physical
Release of Tension

10. *Get physical release of tension.*   When frustrations build up, you might indulge in recreational activities or in physical work to gain release. Raking leaves or mowing the lawn not only helps provide catharsis but may also provide an additional reward—satisfaction of completing a job that has to be done. (One teacher who was known for his patience and sympathy in dealing with students was a viciously competitive tennis player on the local courts. Another even-tempered instructor would garden whenever she felt the need to unwind. Her back yard looked like a horticultural exhibit.)

Avoid taking out
frustrations on pupils

11. *Avoid taking out your frustrations on the class.*   A primary reason for seeking release of tension through gripes or creative hobbies or physical activities is to avoid punishing your students. When you find yourself frustrated, it is natural to want to take out your anger on those thirty scapegoats trapped in your room, especially if they have done more than their share in contributing to your frustration. In a sense, your students are so many sitting ducks. The temptation to shoot them down is sometimes well-nigh irresistible. A certain amount of righteous indignation is probably a good thing for genuinely guilty pupils to be exposed to at the proper time, but too often an angry teacher is more at fault than the alleged provokers. If you are upset because of your own weaknesses or inabilities and compensate by bawling out the class or giving a spot quiz, the students will realize it. A frequent consequence is that they will retaliate, and then you really *will* have some frustrations to cope with.

12. *Get professional help.*   In some cases, personal problems are of such a nature and intensity that they are beyond the help that friends can give or are too extensive to be solved by any of the suggestions noted here. If you feel that you have reached this point, the sensible thing is to seek professional assistance. Since some frustrations may drive an individual to neurosis or psychosis, you should not regard the need for such help as an admission that you are a total failure. Individuals who recognize their need for help are often in better mental health than those who refuse to acknowledge the possibility.

13. *In extreme cases, execute a strategic withdrawal.*   It sometimes happens that a teacher is caught in a bind. If you find yourself teaching in a school where you seem to be penned up in a life space consisting of nothing but negative factors, it may be best to leave the field of forces. Chains of unfortunate circumstances or personality conflicts may lead to an intolerable situation, in which case moving to a different school or a different district may be the sensible rather than

the cowardly thing to do.[1] If you discover, however, that your dissatisfactions are not with local conditions or people but that you simply do not enjoy teaching and that none of the preceding suggestions help very much, it would be logical to look for a different kind of job. At stake is not only your own personal adjustment but also the well-being of your students.

Increasing the possibility of self-actualization

The preceding discussion on satisfying the needs of safety, belongingness, and esteem—and on ways of dealing with the frustration of these needs—has emphasized deficiency motivation. In terms of Maslow's hierarchy, satisfying the deficiency needs sets the stage for growth motivation, satisfaction of the "being" needs, and self-actualization. Many psychologists believe that in order for children to develop more of their potential (and function in a self-actualizing way), they should have contact with adults who are functioning as especially healthy and productive individuals. Since teachers have considerable influence over students, it is only natural to speculate on how you can become a self-actualizing individual—for your students' benefit as well as your own.

The first step toward self-actualization has already been discussed: Do everything possible to satisfy the deficiency needs of safety, belongingness, and esteem. Once these are taken care of, the possibility of self-actualization is enhanced. Maslow described what self-actualizing people are like (see pp. 74–96, 103–114, and 157 of *Toward a Psychology of Being*) but concluded, "We know they are that way, but not how they get that way" (1968, p. 163). Even so, Maslow's observations may help you achieve a greater degree of self-actualization on your own. They will also enable you to understand why self-actualization is such an elusive experience and why you may find yourself dominated by deficiency motivation. Maslow emphasized need gratification and awareness of regressive forces, and he provided some general suggestions on how to encourage growth motivation:

Self-knowledge a major path to self-improvement

1. Self-knowledge seems to be the major path of self-improvement, though not the only one.

[1] If you find that your dissatisfaction with teaching is caused primarily by the structure and bureaucracy of traditional education, you might contact the Teacher Drop-out Center, Box 521, Amherst, Mass. 01002. It has been established to help teachers to find positions in innovative, free, and open schools. Or consult the "Directory of Organizations and Periodicals on Alternative Education," which begins on page 469 of the *Humanistic Education Sourcebook* (1975), edited by Donald A. Read and Sidney B. Simon.

2. Self-knowledge and self-improvement are very difficult for most people. They usually need great courage and long struggle.

3. Though the help of a skilled professional therapist makes this process much easier, it is by no means the only way. Much that has been learned from therapy can be applied to education, to family life, and to the guidance of one's own life.

4. Only by such study of psychopathology and therapy can one learn a proper respect for and appreciation of the forces of fear, of regression, of defense, of safety. Respecting and understanding these forces makes it much more possible to help oneself and others to grow toward health. False optimism sooner or later means disillusionment, anger and hopelessness.

5. To sum up, we can never really understand human weakness without also understanding its healthy trends. Otherwise we make the mistake of pathologizing everything. But also we can never fully understand or help human strength without also understanding its weaknesses. Otherwise we fall into the errors of overoptimistic reliance on rationality alone.

Be aware of conflicting tendencies toward safety and toward growth

If we wish to help humans to become more fully human, we must realize not only that they try to realize themselves but that they are also reluctant or afraid or unable to do so. Only by fully appreciating this dialectic between sickness and health can we help to tip the balance in favor of health. (pp. 165–166)

For a more complete discussion of these ideas, you are referred to *Toward a Psychology of Being*; the final chapter consists of forty-three basic propositions summarizing all aspects of Maslow's observations on human behavior. If you would like to expand your knowledge of yourself as a step toward self-actualization, you are urged to read and ponder those points.

Improving your skills as a teacher

Perhaps the single most effective way to become a self-actualizer as a teacher is to do such an effective job of instruction that you know you are competent and worthy of esteem. In order to do that, you must constantly evaluate what you do in the classroom and seek ways to correct for inadequacies and perfect skills. There are a number of ways you can strive to become a more effective teacher. You might ask for students' suggestions or evaluations, use observation schedules, take in-service courses of various kinds, or constantly use and revise your personal Handbook. Each of these will be discussed separately.

Student evaluations and suggestions

In many respects, students are in a better position to evaluate teachers than anyone else. They may not always be able to analyze *why* what a

Questionnaires and observational schedules provide detailed and systematic information about teacher effectiveness, but some of the most revealing feedback about teaching takes the form of minute-by-minute reactions of pupils.

Ron Benvenisti/Magnum

teacher does is effective or ineffective (which might be true of an experienced expert observer), but they know, better than anyone else, whether they are responding and learning. Furthermore, students form their impressions after interacting with a teacher for hundreds or thousands of hours. Most principals or other adult observers may watch a teacher in action for only a few minutes at a time. Accordingly, it makes sense to pay attention to and actively solicit opinions from students. As a matter of fact, it will be impossible for you to ignore pupil reactions. Every minute that school is in session you will receive student feedback in the form of attentiveness (or lack of it), facial expressions, restlessness, yawns, sleeping, disruptive behavior, and the like. If you become aware that a particular lesson arouses either a neutral or negative reaction, you may feel obliged, in self-defense, to seek a better way to teach the same material in the future. If you find that you seem to be spending much of your time disciplining pupils, you may be almost driven to find other ways to teach.

But in addition to analyzing the minute-by-minute reactions of your pupils, you may also find it helpful to request more formal feedback. One way to do this is to install a suggestion box in your room and invite students to deposit anonymous comments in it whenever they wish. Another approach is to ask a class to express their feelings in a group discussion. After completing a unit you might ask, "I'd like you to tell me what you liked and disliked about the way this unit was arranged and give me suggestions for improving it if I teach it again next year."

A more comprehensive and systematic approach is to distribute a questionnaire or evaluation form and ask students to record their reactions anonymously. You might use a published form or devise your own. In either case, a frequently used format involves listing a series of statements and asking students to rate you on a five-point scale. Some of the published forms use special answer sheets that make it possible to tally the results electronically. One disadvantage of many rating-scale evaluation forms is that some of the responses may not be very informative unless you can compare your ratings to those of colleagues. If you get an overall rating of 3.5 on "makes the subject matter interesting," for example, you may have no way of determining if this means that you need to strive to improve in that aspect of teaching until you discover that the average rating of other teachers of the same grade or subject was 4.2. Published evaluation forms may not be very helpful, unless all other teachers use the same rating scale. This may be a possibility if a school district uses a standard scale to obtain evidence for use in making decisions about retention, tenure, and promotion.

Another disadvantage of many rating scales is indicated by the phrase *leniency problem,* which refers to the tendency for pupils to give most teachers somewhat above-average ratings on most traits. Although leniency may soothe a teacher's ego, wishy-washy responses do not provide information that can be used to improve pedagogical effectiveness. To get around the leniency problem and to induce pupils to give more informative reactions, *forced-choice* ratings are often used. In Figure E-1 you will find a forced-choice rating form, the Descriptive Ranking Form for Teachers, developed by Don J. Cosgrove (1959). This form is designed to give teachers information about how pupils perceive their skill in four areas of performance: (1) knowledge and organization of subject matter, (2) adequacy of relations with students in class, (3) adequacy of plans and procedures in class, (4) enthusiasm in working with students. If you decide to use this form, when preparing copies to be distributed to students you should omit the numbers in parentheses that follow each statement. On your own copy of the form, you should add the parenthetical numbers and use them to prepare your score in each of the four categories listed above.

To calculate your index of effectiveness in each category of the Descriptive Ranking Form for Teachers, assign a score of 4 to the phrase in each group that is ranked 1, a score of 3 to the phrase marked 2, and so on. Then add together the scores for all phrases identified by the parenthetical number 1, and do the same for the other sets of phrases. The cluster of phrases that yields the highest score is perceived by your students to be your strongest area of teaching; the

Handbook heading
Soliciting Feedback
from Students

Some ratings may be of value only when compared to others' ratings

Forced-choice ratings solve leniency problem

Figure E-1

The descriptive ranking form for teachers

This form consists of 10 sets of phrases which are descriptive of instructor performance. Each set is composed of four phrases.

Please consider the instructor you have for this course. In each set of phrases, rank the phrases from 1 to 4 as they apply to your instructor. Give a rank of 1 to the phrase which most applies, and 4 to the phrase which least applies, using Ranks 2 and 3 for intermediate ranks. Every phrase must be ranked. There can be no equal ranks.

Set a
_____ Always on time for class [3]
_____ Pleasant in class [2]
_____ Very sincere when talking with students [4]
_____ Well-read [1]

Set b
_____ Contagious enthusiasm for subject [4]
_____ Did not fill up time with trivial material [3]
_____ Gave everyone an equal chance [2]
_____ Made clear what was expected of students [1]

Set c
_____ Classes always orderly [3]
_____ Enjoyed teaching class [4]
_____ Friendliness did not seem forced [2]
_____ Logical in thinking [1]

Set d
_____ Encouraged creativeness [4]
_____ Kept course material up to the minute [1]
_____ Never deliberately forced own decisions on class [2]
_____ Procedures well thought out [3]

Set e
_____ Authority on own subject [1]
_____ Friendly attitude toward students [4]
_____ Marked tests very fairly [3]
_____ Never criticized in a destructive way [2]

Set f
_____ Good sense of humor [4]
_____ Spaced assignments evenly [3]
_____ Students never afraid to ask questions in class [2]
_____ Well organized course [1]

Set g
_____ Accepted students' viewpoints with open mind [2]
_____ Increased students' vocabulary by own excellent usage [1]
_____ Students always knew what was coming up next day [3]
_____ Students willingly worked for teacher [4]

Set h
_____ Always knew what he was doing [3]
_____ Appreciated accomplishment [4]
_____ Did not ridicule wrong answers [2]
_____ Well informed in all related fields [1]

Set i
_____ Always had class material ready [3]
_____ Covered subject well [1]
_____ Encouraged students to think out answers [4]
_____ Rules and regulations fair [2]

Set j
_____ Always managed to get things done on time [3]
_____ Course had continuity [1]
_____ Made material significant [4]
_____ Understood problems of students [2]

Source: Don J. Cosgrove, "Diagnostic Rating of Teacher Performance," *Journal of Educational Psychology*, 1959, 50, p. 202.

cluster that yields the lowest score is considered to be your weakest. If you get a total of 30 points for all phrases indicated by the parenthetical number 1, for example, that means you ranked high in category 1 (knowledge and organization of subject matter) noted above. If you get only 12 points for phrases identified by the parenthetical number 4, you will need to work harder at being enthusiastic when working with students.

Quite often a homemade form that covers specific points regarding your personal approach to teaching will provide useful information. You might ask a series of questions about specific points (e.g., Were there enough exams? Did you think too much homework was assigned?). Another approach is to ask pupils to list the three things they liked best, the three things they like least, and what they would suggest you do to improve the way a particular unit is taught. When you ask students to respond to questions like these, you usually not only get feedback about liked and disliked teaching techniques, you also get ideas you might use to improve your teaching skill. (On a rating scale you may be rated below average on an item such as "Examinations are too difficult," but you may not know *why* you were rated low or what you might do to change things for the better.)

Observation schedules

While your students can supply quite a bit of information that you may be able to use to improve your teaching, they cannot always tell you about technical flaws in your instructional technique. This is especially true with younger pupils, but even sophisticated graduate students in college may not recognize why certain teaching techniques are ineffective. Consequently, you may wish to submit to a detailed analysis of your approach to teaching. Several observation schedules have been developed for this purpose. *The Flanders Interaction Analysis Categories* (Flanders, 1970) is the most widely used teacher behavior schedule, but over one hundred others are described in the multivolume *Mirrors of Behavior* (1970), edited by Anita Simon and E. G. Boyer. As the title of the Flanders schedule indicates, it stresses verbal interactions between teacher and pupils. The following ten categories are listed on a record blank: accepts feelings, praises or encourages, uses student ideas, asks questions, lectures, gives directions, criticizes, pupil talk-response, pupil talk-initiation, silence or confusion. A trained observer puts a check mark opposite one of these categories every three seconds during a period when teacher and pupils are interacting verbally. Once the observation is completed, it is a simple matter to tally checks and determine the percentage of time devoted to each activity. Then, if a teacher discovers that a substantial amount of time was classified in the "silence and confusion" category and that only a tiny fraction of interactions involved

Verbal interactions
between teacher and
pupils can be analyzed

praise or encouragement, a deliberate effort can be made to alter things for the better.

Perhaps the biggest problem with such observational approaches to teacher evaluation is the need for a trained observer. But it would be possible to team up with another teacher and act as reciprocal observers if you feel that a detailed analysis of your teaching style would be helpful.

If you have access to a videotape recorder, you might analyze your own teaching behavior. One problem with this approach, though, is that it might make you, and your pupils, self-conscious to the point of producing unnatural behavior. There are also problems caused by lighting, recording, and limited camera viewing range. But videotapes have proven to be successful when used in conjunction with what are often called minicourses.

In-service training

W. R. Borg, M. L. Kelley, Philip Langer, and Meredith Gall (1970) and colleagues at the Far West Laboratory for Educational Research and Development have developed a series of minicourses, each of which concentrates on a particular aspect of teaching (e.g., effective questioning). These courses were originally developed for use in teacher training institutions, but they could be used for self-directed in-service training as well. To take one of these courses on your own, you might ask your principal to help you obtain the necessary materials, which consist of films, instruction books, and record sheets.[2]

The minicourse usually begins with a film depicting an excellent teacher demonstrating preferred techniques in some aspect of instruction. As you watch the film, you are asked to follow instructions in a pamphlet, which tells you how to identify components of a skill. Next, you are asked to prepare a short lesson providing practice in the skill. Then, you present the lesson and either persuade a colleague to record your behavior (as well as that of your students), or you videotape your sample lesson. After analyzing the observational record or the videotape, you prepare another lesson designed to correct for errors and bring your teaching closer to that of the ideal.

Borg and his colleagues have developed the following minicourses: Individualizing Instruction in Mathematics; Organizing Independent Learning—Primary Level and Intermediate Level; Teaching Reading as Decoding; Developing Children's Oral Language; Effective Questioning—Elementary Level and Secondary Level; and Higher Cognitive Questioning. They are available from Macmillan Educational Services, 866 Third Avenue, New York, New York 10022.

---

[2] The rental fee for a typical minicourse is $175. Coordinator's and teacher's handbooks cost approximately $5 each. In order to justify these costs, it would probably be necessary to persuade several colleagues to join you in taking a minicourse.

Related teacher-training exercises are described in Program on Teaching Effectiveness, published by the Stanford Center for Research and Development, Stanford, California.

Using your handbook to improve your teaching

Perhaps the most practical way to improve your teaching is to continually refer to and revise your personal Handbook. If you are conscientious in preparing a Handbook of suggestions, you can—in conjunction with the sections in this book entitled Becoming a Better Teacher: Questions and Suggestions—engage in do-it-yourself mini-courses. For example, if you are dissatisfied with a lesson, disappointed about lack of student response, or confused or bothered by the behavior of one or more pupils, you might consult your Handbook for troubleshooting ideas. If you get the impression that you are inefficient, you might refer to the list of suggestions for using programmed techniques in the classroom. If you seem unable to generate interest in class discussions, you might consult your notes on Chapter 6. If some students seem much less interested in learning than others, you might refer to the chapters on motivation and on the disadvantaged.

Developing and using your own Handbook may be the best single way to improve your skills as a teacher because you will be able to use it on a day-to-day basis. A point made in Chapter 2, in the discussion of the advantages and disadvantages of teaching, calls attention to the value of constant appraisal of teaching technique. The same point also serves as an appropriate final statement in a book intended to help you apply psychology to teaching: The fundamental reason children respond to instruction is that well-trained, sensitive, thoughtful professionals seek dozens of ways—every day—to interpret the behavior of individuals and groups of pupils and arrange experiences to help them learn.

SUMMARY OF KEY POINTS

Teaching is a form of endeavor that can lead to satisfaction of many important psychological needs. For the most part, however, the deepest satisfactions are intangible and cannot be translated into material signs of success. Up until recently many teachers simply had to learn to live with frustrating conditions. Today, because of collective bargaining, professional organizations often help teachers improve working conditions. Despite such gains, it is almost inevitable that some problems will be encountered by every teacher. Teachers might deal with frustrations by distinguishing between things that might be accepted and those that might be changed, seeking help when confronted with specific problems, and talking over problems with colleagues or pupils. One extremely important rule for teachers to keep in mind in the classroom is to avoid taking out personal frustrations on pupils.

Abraham Maslow suggested that self-knowledge is a major path to self-improvement. It is important in seeking self-knowledge to remain aware of conflicting tendencies toward safety and toward growth. A person may be eager to try to improve but be reluctant to run the risks of dropping old habits and replacing them with untried techniques. Teachers who are willing to seek ways to improve themselves might use rating scales to discover their strengths and weaknesses. Some ratings, however, may be of value only when compared to the ratings of other teachers. Other ratings may be susceptible to the *leniency problem*: respondents may give uniformly favorable responses. One way to solve the leniency problem is to use a forced-choice rating scale. Other techniques for improving teaching skills involve reports made by trained observers. Many approaches of this type concentrate on verbal interactions between teacher and pupils.

BECOMING A BETTER TEACHER: QUESTIONS AND SUGGESTIONS

Looking for New Possibilities

Have I gotten into a rut, or do I feel backed into a corner by regulations? Suggestions: Try brainstorming new ways to teach. Look through back issues of teachers' journals for ideas. Ask students for suggestions.

Listing Priorities

Do I feel as if I'm on a treadmill or that I can never seem to get caught up? Suggestion: For one week, list all the school-related things I do—during and after school hours. Then arrange these in order from most to least important. Eliminate some of the activities at the bottom of the list.

Seeking Physical Release of Tension

Would I be less uptight in school and at home if I engaged in some kind of physical or creative activity? Suggestion: Figure out ways to unwind at the end of the day by walking, jogging, engaging in sports, trying creative hobbies, gardening, and the like.

Soliciting Feedback from Students

Do I give my students opportunities to tell me what they like and dislike about my teaching style? Suggestion: Within the next two weeks, get some sort of feedback from students. Use a suggestion box, a rating form, a list of questions on the board—but find out what my students think of me as a teacher.

Arranging for an
Observation of My
Teaching

Would it be feasible or desirable for me to have someone observe my teaching? Suggestion: Ask colleagues if they would be interested in a reciprocal observation setup, perhaps featuring the Flanders Interaction Analysis Categories or the equivalent.

SUGGESTIONS FOR FURTHER STUDY

E-1
Satisfying Your Needs
as a Teacher

If you would like to speculate about the satisfaction of your own needs and ways you might become more of a self-actualizer, sample sections of one of these books by Abraham H. Maslow: *Toward a Psychology of Being* (2nd ed., 1968), *Motivation and Personality* (2nd ed., 1970), or *The Farther Reaches of Human Nature* (1971). For more detailed and specific suggestions for dealing with common problems teachers face, read Chapters 14 and 18 of *Mental Hygiene in Teaching* (2nd ed., 1959) by Fritz Redl and William W. Wattenberg.

E-2
Obtaining Information
about Teaching
Effectiveness

If you would like to make a systematic analysis of your teaching effectiveness, either by asking for pupil feedback or by requesting that colleagues observe you in action, an excellent source to consult is Chapter 7, "Rating Methods in Research on Teaching" by H. H. Remmers, in *Handbook of Research on Teaching* (1963), edited by N. L. Gage, pages 329–378. For a detailed explanation of how to obtain and analyze data about your verbal interactions with pupils, examine *Analyzing Teaching Behavior* (1970) by Ned A. Flanders.

E-3
Instructional Theory

Jerome Bruner has stressed the importance of *structure* in almost all his writings. He urges teachers to seek order, organization, and relationships, and to help students do the same. Bruner offers observations on this theme in *Toward a Theory of Instruction* (1966). In an essay (Chapter 3) that has the same title as the book, he proposes that teachers try to develop a theory of instruction. Unfortunately, Bruner's analysis of how a teacher might actually formulate an instructional theory is rather vague and incomplete. Philip L. Hosford recognized that educators would have a difficult time following Bruner's suggestion, and he provides more tangible leads for instructional theory builders in *An Instructional Theory: A Beginning* (1973). After you have taught a year or two and have had time to begin to etablish a personal style of teaching, you are urged to examine Hosford's book, particularly Chapters 5, 6, and 7. If you read these chapters carefully, you may find that you will be able to discover relationships, gain understanding, and become more consistent and effective as a teacher.

Bibliography

Adelson, Joseph, 1971. "The Political Imagination of the Young Adolescent." *Daedalus,* Fall, 1013–1015.

Adelson, Joseph, 1972. "The Political Imagination of the Young Adolescent." In Jerome Kagan and Robert Coles, eds., *Twelve to Sixteen: Early Adolescence,* pp. 106–143. New York: Norton.

Ahman, J. Stanley, and Marvin Glock, 1975. *Evaluating Pupil Growth: Principles of Measurement,* 5th ed. Boston: Allyn and Bacon.

Ainsworth, Mary D., and B. A. Wittig, 1972. "Attachment and Exploratory Behavior of One-Year-Olds in a Strange Situation." In B. M. Foss, ed., *Determinants of Infant Behavior,* vol. 4. New York: Wiley.

Allen, Dwight W., and Eli Seifman, eds., 1971. *The Teacher's Handbook.* Glenview, Ill.: Scott-Foresman.

Almy, Millie C., E. Chittenden, and P. Miller, 1966. *Young Children's Thinking.* New York: Teachers College, Columbia University.

Alschuler, A. S., 1968. "How to Increase Motivation Through Climate and Structure." Achievement Motivation Development Project Working Paper No. 8. Cambridge: Harvard University, Graduate School of Education.

Alschuler, A. S., 1972. *Motivating Achievement in High School Students: Education for Human Growth.* Englewood Cliffs, N.J.: Educational Technology Publications.

Alschuler, Alfred S., 1975. "Psychological Education." In Donald A. Read and Sidney B. Simon, eds., *Humanistic Education Sourcebook,* 23–32. Englewood Cliffs, N.J.: Prentice-Hall.

Anastasi, Anne, 1968. *Psychological Testing,* 3rd ed. New York: Macmillan.

Anderson, Richard C., 1959. "Learning in Discussions: A Resume of the Authoritarian-Democratic Studies." *Harvard Educational Review* 29, 201–215.

Anthony, E. James, 1970. "Behavior Disorders." In Paul H. Mussen, ed., *Carmichael's Manual of Child Psychology,* 3rd ed., vol. 2, 667–764. New York: Wiley.

Arieti, Silvano, 1976. *Creativity: The Magic Synthesis.* New York: Basic Books.

Aristotle, 1941. *The Basic Works of Aristotle.* Edited by Richard McKeon. New York: Random House.

Arnold, Stanley, ed., 1965. *Let Us Teach.* Sacramento, Calif.: Report published by the Senate of the State of California.

Asch, S. E., 1956. "Studies of Independence and Conformity: A Minority of One Against a Unanimous Majority." *Psychological Monographs* 70(9) (Whole No. 416).

Ashton-Warner, Sylvia, 1958. *Spinster.* New York: Bantam Books.

Ashton-Warner, Sylvia, 1963. *Teacher.* New York: Simon and Schuster.

Atkinson, J. W., 1964. *An Introduction to Motivation.* Princeton, N.J.: Van Nostrand.

Atkinson, J. W., and N. T. Feather, eds., 1966. *A Theory of Achievement Motivation.* New York: Wiley.

Atkinson, J. W., and G. H. Litwin, 1960. "Achievement Motive and Test Anxiety Conceived as Motive to Approach Success and Motive to Avoid Failure." *Journal of Abnormal and Social Psychology* 60, 52–63.

Atkinson, Richard C., 1957. "A Stochastic Model for Rote Learning." *Psychometrika* 22, 87–94.

Atkinson, R. C., and H. A. Wilson, eds., 1969. *Computer Assisted Instruction: A Book of Readings.* New York: Academic Press.

Ausubel, David P., 1960. "Use of Advance Organizers in the Learning and Retention of Meaningful Material." *Journal of Educational Psychology* 51, 267–272.

Ausubel, David P., 1963. *The Psychology of Meaningful Verbal Learning.* New York: Grune and Stratton.

Ausubel, David P., 1968. *Educational Psychology: A Cognitive View.* New York: Holt, Rinehart and Winston.

Axline, Virginia, 1964. *Dibs: In Search of Self.* New York: Ballantine Books.

Ayollon, Teodoro, and Nathan H. Azrin, 1965. "The Measurement and Reinforcement of Adaptive Behavior of Psychotics." *Journal of Experimental Analysis of Behavior* 8, 357–383.

Back, Kurt W., 1972. *Beyond Words: The Story of Sensitivity Training and the Encounter Movement.* New York: Russell Sage Foundation.

Baker, Robert L., and Richard E. Schutz, eds., 1971. *Instructional Product Development.* New York: Van Nostrand Reinhold.

Bakwin, Harry, and Ruth Morris Bakwin, 1972. *Behavior Disorders in Children,* 4th ed. Philadelphia: Saunders.

Baldwin, Alfred L., 1967. *Theories of Child Development.* New York: Wiley.

Baldwin, James, 1953. *Notes of a Native Son.* New York: Dial.

Bandura, Albert, 1973. *Aggression: A Social Learning Analysis.* Englewood Cliffs, N.J.: Prentice-Hall.

Bandura, Albert, 1974. "Behavior Theory and the Models of Man." *American Psychologist* 29(12), 859–869.

Bandura, Albert, D. Ross, and S. A. Ross, 1963. "Imitation of Film Mediated Aggressive Models." *Journal of Abnormal and Social Psychology* 66, 3–11.

Bandura, Albert, and Richard H. Walters, 1963. *Social Learning and Personality Development.* New York: Holt, Rinehart and Winston.

Banks, James A., and Jean D. Grambs, 1972. *Black Self-Concept.* New York: McGraw-Hill.

Barber, Theodore X., et al., 1969. "Five Attempts to Replicate the Experimenter Bias Effect." *Journal of Consulting and Clinical Psychology* 33(1), 1–14.

Bardwick, Judith M., 1971. *Psychology of Women: A Study of Bio-Cultural Conflicts.* New York: Harper and Row.

Barker, Roger G., Tamara Dembo, and Kurt Lewin, 1941. "Studies in Topological and Vector Psychology." University of Iowa Studies in Child Welfare 18, No. 1.

Barnes, Buckley R., and Elmer V. Clawson, 1975. "Do Advance Organizers Facilitate Learning? Recommendations for Further Research Based on an Analysis of 32 Studies." *Review of Educational Research* 45(4), 637–659.

Barron, Frank, and C. W. Taylor, eds., 1963. *Scientific Creativity: Its Recognition and Development.* New York: Wiley.

Barth, Roland S., 1972. *Open Education and the American School.* New York: Agathon.

Bartholomew, B. R., 1974. "Teachers' Instructional Problems." *Today's Education* 63(3), 78–80.

Baruch, Dorothy W., 1952. *One Little Boy.* New York: Dell.

Bauernfeind, Robert H., 1965. " 'Goal Cards' and Future Developments in Achievement Testing." *Proceedings of the 1965 Invitational Conferences on Testing Problems.* University of Illinois.

Baumrind, Diana, 1971. "Current Patterns of Parental Authority." *Developmental Psychology Monographs,* No. 1, 1–103.

Becker, Wesley C., ed., 1971. *An Empirical Basis for Change in Eduction.* Chicago: Science Research Associates.

Becker, Wesley C., Siegfried Engelmann, and Don R. Thomas, 1971. *Teaching: A Course in Applied Psychology.* Chicago: Science Research Associates.

Bee, Helen, ed., 1974. *Social Issues in Developmental Psychology.* New York: Harper and Row.

Belch, Jean, ed., 1973. *Contemporary Games.* Detroit: Gale Research.

Berko, Jean, 1958. "The Child's Learning of English Morphology." *Word* 14, 150–177.

Bernstein, Emmanuel, 1968. "What Does a Summerhill Old School Tie Look Like?" *Psychology Today* 2(5), 37–70.

Berscheid, Ellen, Elaine Walster, and George Bohrnstedt, 1973. "The Happy American Body: A Survey Report." *Psychology Today* 7(6), 119–131.

Bessell, Harold, 1968. "The Content is the Medium: The Confidence is the Message." *Psychology Today* 1(8), 32–61.

Biehler, Robert F., 1976. *Child Development: An Introduction.* Boston: Houghton Mifflin.

Bigge, Morris L., 1976. *Learning Theories for*

Teachers, 3rd ed. New York: Harper and Row.

Bilodeau, Edward A., ed., 1966. *Acquisition of Skill.* New York: Academic Press.

Blackie, John, 1971. *Inside the Primary School,* American ed. New York: Schocken Books.

Block, James H., ed., 1971. *Mastery Learning: Theory and Practice.* New York: Holt, Rinehart and Winston.

Bloom, Benjamin S., 1964. *Stability and Change in Human Characteristics.* New York: Wiley.

Bloom, Benjamin S., 1968. "Learning for Mastery." *Evaluation Comment* 1(2). Los Angeles: Center for the Study of Evaluation of Instructional Programs, University of California.

Bloom, Benjamin S., et al., eds., 1956. *Taxonomy of Educational Objectives, Handbook I: Cognitive Domain.* New York: McKay.

Bloom, Benjamin S., J. Thomas Hastings, and George F. Madaus, ed., 1971. *Handbook on Formative and Summative Evaluation of Student Learning.* New York: McGraw-Hill.

Blos, Peter, 1962. *On Adolescence.* New York: Free Press.

Borg, W. R., M. L. Kelley, Philip Langer, and Meredith Gall, 1970. *The Minicourse: A Microteaching Approach to Teacher Education.* New York: Macmillan Educational Services.

Boring, Edwin G., 1950. *A History of Experimental Psychology,* 2nd ed., New York: Appleton-Century-Crofts.

Bradbury, Ray, 1967. *Fahrenheit 451.* New York: Simon and Schuster.

Braithwaite, Edward R., 1959. *To Sir with Love.* Englewood Cliffs, N.J.: Prentice-Hall.

Braun, Carl, 1976. "Teacher Expectations: Sociopsychological Dynamics." *Review of Educational Research* 46(2), 185–213.

Brill, A. A., ed. and trans., 1938. *The Basic Writings of Sigmund Freud.* New York: Random House.

Bronfenbrenner, Urie, 1970. *Two Worlds of Childhood.* New York: Russell Sage Foundation.

Broudy, Harry S., 1972. *The Real World of the Public School.* New York: Harcourt, Brace, Jovanovich.

Brown, Claude, 1965. *Manchild in the Promised Land.* New York: Macmillan.

Brown, Dee, 1971. *Bury My Heart at Wounded Knee: An Indian History of the American West.* New York: Holt, Rinehart and Winston.

Brown, George Isaac, 1971. *Human Teaching for Human Learning: An Introduction to Confluent Education.* New York: Viking.

Brown, Roger, 1973. *A First Language: The Early Stages.* Cambridge: Harvard University Press.

Brueckner, L. J., and H. W. Distad, 1923. "The Effect of the Summer Vacation on the Reading Ability of First-Grade Children." *Elementary School Journal* 24, 698–707.

Bruene, E., 1928. "Effect of the Summer Vacation on the Achievement of Pupils in the Fourth, Fifth, and Sixth Grades." *Journal of Educational Research* 18, 309–314.

Bruner, Jerome S., 1951. "Personality Dynamics and the Process of Perceiving." In R. R. Blake and G. V. Ramsey, eds., *Perception: An Approach to Personality,* 121–147. New York: Ronald.

Bruner, Jerome S., 1960. *The Proces of Education.* New York: Vintage Books.

Bruner, Jerome S., 1961. "The Act of Discovery." *Harvard Educational Review* 31(1), 21–32.

Bruner, Jerome S., 1966. *Toward a Theory of Instruction.* Cambridge: Belknap Press of Harvard University Press.

Bruner, Jerome S., 1971. *The Relevance of Education.* New York: Norton.

Bruner, Jerome S., 1973. *Beyond the Information Given.* Jeremy M. Anglin, ed. New York: Norton.

Bruner, Jerome S., J. J. Goodnow, and G. A. Austin, 1956. *A Study of Thinking.* New York: Wiley.

Bruner, Jerome S., Rose R. Olver, and Patricia Greenfield, 1966. *Studies in Cognitive Growth.* New York: Wiley.

Bruner, Jerome S., and H. Tajfel, 1961. "Cognitive Risk and Environmental Change." *Journal of Abnormal Psychology* 62, 231–241.

Bryan, William L., and Noble Harter, 1897. "Studies in the Physiology and Psychology of the Telegraphic Language." *Psychological Review* 4, 27–53.

Buchanan, Cynthia D., 1968. *Teacher's Guide to the Prereader.* New York: McGraw-Hill.

Buchanan, Edith A., and Deanna Stirling Hanson, 1975. "Free Expression through Movement." In Donald A. Read and Sidney B. Simon, eds., *Humanistic Education Sourcebook,* 345–352. Englewood Cliffs, N.J.: Prentice-Hall.

Burnett, Carol, George Mendoza, and Sheldon Secunda, 1975., *What I Want to Be When I Grow Up.* New York: Simon and Schuster.

Buros, O. K., ed., 1972. *Seventh Mental Measurements Yearbook.* Highland Park, N.J.: Gryphon Press.

Butler, R. A., 1953. "Discrimination Learning by

Rhesus Monkeys to Visual-Exploration Motivation." *Journal of Comparative and Physiological Psychology* 46, 95–98.

Caldwell, Catherine, 1970. "Social Science as Ammunition." *Psychology Today* 4(4), 38–74.

Callahan, Raymond E., 1962. *Education and the Cult of Efficiency.* Chicago: University of Chicago Press.

Cancro, Robert, ed., 1971. *Intelligence: Genetic and Environmental Influences.* New York: Grune and Stratton.

Canfield, John T., and Harold C. Wells, 1975. "Self-Concept: A Critical Dimension in Teaching and Learning." In Donald A. Read and Sidney B. Simon, eds., *Humanistic Education Sourcebook,* 460–469. Englewood Cliffs, N.J.: Prentice-Hall.

Carpenter, Finley, 1974. *The Skinner Primer.* New York: Free Press.

Carroll, John B., 1963. "A Model of School Learning." *Teachers College Record* 64, 723–733.

Carroll, John B., 1971. "Problems of Measurement Related to the Concept of Learning for Mastery." In James H. Block, ed., *Mastery Learning: Theory and Practice,* 24–46. New York: Holt, Rinehart and Winston.

Cazden, Courtney, 1968. "The Acquisition of Noun and Verb Inflections." *Child Development* 39, 433–438.

Center for the Study of Evaluation—Research for Better Schools, 1972. *CSE-RBS Test Evaluations: Tests of Higher-Order Cognitive, Affective, and Interpersonal Skills.* Los Angeles: Dissemination Office, Center for the Study of Evaluation, University of California.

Charles, C. L., and R. Stradsklev, eds., 1973. *Learning with Games: An Analysis of Social Studies Educational Games and Simulations.* Boulder, Colo.: The Social Science Education Consortium.

Charles, C. M., 1972. *Educational Psychology: The Instructional Endeavor.* St. Louis: Mosby.

Chauncy, Henry, and John E. Dobbin, 1963. *Testing: Its Place in Education Today.* New York: Harper and Row.

Chesler, Mark, and Robert Fox, 1966. *Role Playing Methods in the Classroom.* Palo Alto: Science Research Associates.

Claiborn, William L., 1969. "Expectancy Effects in the Classroom: A Failure to Replicate." *Journal of Educational Psychology* 60(5). 377–383.

Clarizio, H. F., 1971. *Toward Positive Classroom Discipline.* New York: Wiley.

Coleman, James S., 1966. *Equality of Educational*

Opportunity. Washington, D.C.: U.S. Department of Health, Education, and Welfare, Office of Education.

Coles, Robert, 1963. *The Desegregation of Southern Schools: A Psychiatric Study.* New York: Anti-Defamation Legue of B'nai B'rith.

Coles, Robert, 1967. *Children of Crisis: A Study of Courage and Fear.* Boston: Little, Brown.

Coles, Robert, 1968. *Dead End School.* Boston: Little, Brown.

Coles, Robert, 1969. *Still Hungry in America.* New York: World.

Coles, Robert, 1970. *Uprooted Children: The Early Life of Migrant Farm Workers.* Pittsburgh: University of Pittsburgh Press.

Coles, Robert, 1972a. *Children of Crisis: Migrants, Mountaineers, and Sharecroppers.* Boston: Little, Brown.

Coles, Robert, 1972b. *Children of Crisis: The South Goes North.* Boston: Little, Brown.

Coles, Robert, 1972c. *Farewell to the South.* Boston: Little Brown.

Coles, Robert, and Jon Erikson, 1971. *The Middle American: Proud and Uncertain.* Boston: Little, Brown.

Colman, John E., 1967. *The Master Teachers and the Art of Teaching.* New York: Pitman.

Combs, Arthur W., 1965. *The Professional Education of Teachers.* Boston: Allyn and Bacon.

Combs, Arthur W., 1975a. "Humanistic Goals of Education." In Donald A. Read and Sidney B. Simon, eds., *Humanistic Education Sourcebook,* 91–100. Englewood Cliffs, N.J.: Prentice-Hall.

Combs, Arthur W., 1975b. "The Personal Approach to Good Teaching." In Donald A. Read and Sidney B. Simon, eds., *Humanistic Education Sourcebook,* 249–261. Englewood Cliffs, N.J.: Prentice-Hall.

Combs, Arthur W., and Donald Snygg, 1959. *Individual Behavior,* rev. ed. New York: Harper.

Comenius, John Amos, 1628. *The Great Didactic.* M. W. Keatinge, ed. and trans., 1896. London: Adam and Charles Black.

Conger, John Janeway, 1977. *Adolescence and Youth: Psychological Development in a Changing World,* 2nd ed. New York: Harper and Row.

Cooley, W. W., and R. Glaser, 1969. "The Computer and Individualized Instruction." *Science* 166, 574–582.

Cooper, Paulette, 1972. *Growing Up Puerto Rican.* New York: Arbor House.

Cosgrove, Don J., 1959. "Diagnostic Rating of

Teacher Performance." *Journal of Educational Psychology* 50, 200–204.

Coulson, William R., 1972. *Groups, Gimmicks and Instant Gurus: An Examination of Encounter Groups and Their Distortions.* New York: Harper and Row.

Covington, Martin V., Richard S. Crutchfield, Lillian Davies, and Robert M. Olton, Jr., 1972. *The Productive Thinking Program.* Columbus, Ohio: Merrill.

Cremin, Lawrence A., 1961. *The Transformation of the School.* New York: Knopf.

Croft, Doreen J., and Robert D. Hess, 1975. *An Activities Handbook for Teachers of Young Children.* Boston: Houghton Mifflin.

Cronbach, Lee J., 1970. *Essentials of Psychological Testing,* 3rd ed. New York: Harper and Row.

Cronbach, Lee J., and R. E. Snow, 1975. *Aptitudes and Instructional Methods: A Handbook for Research on Interactions.* New York: Irvington Publishers/Naiburg Publishing.

Crowder, Norman A., 1963. "On the Differences Between Linear and Intrinsic Programming." *Phi Delta Kappan* 44, 250–254.

Cruickshank, W., F. A. Bentzen, F. H. Ratzeburg, and Miriam Tannhauser, 1961. *A Teaching Method for Brain-Injured and Hyperactive Children.* New York: Syracuse University Press.

Crutchfield, Richard, 1966. "Sensitization and Activation of Cognitive Skills." In Jerome S. Bruner, ed., *Learning about Learning.* Washington, D.C.: U.S. Department of Health, Education, and Welfare, Office of Education.

Cullum, Albert, 1967. *Push Back the Desks.* New York: Citation Press.

Daniels, Steven, 1971. *How 2 Gerbils, 20 Goldfish, 200 Games, 2,000 Books, and I Taught Them How to Read.* Philadelphia: Westminster Press.

Dashiel, J. F., 1949. *Fundamentals of General Psychology,* 3rd ed. Boston: Houghton Mifflin.

Davis, Gary A., Charles J. Helfert, and Gloria B. Shapiro, 1975. "Let's Be an Ice Cream Machine! Creative Dramatics." In Donald A. Read and Sidney B. Simon, eds., *Humanistic Education Sourcebook,* 451–456. Englewood Cliffs, N.J.: Prentice-Hall.

Davis, Robert B., 1966. "Discovery in the Teaching of Mathematics." In Lee S. Shulman and Evan R. Keisler, eds., *Learning by Discovery.* Chicago: Rand McNally.

Deighton, Lee C., 1971. *The Encyclopedia of Education.* New York: Macmillan.

de Beauvoir, Simone, 1952. *The Second Sex.* New York: Knopf.

DeLeon, Nephtali, 1972. *Chicanos: Our Background and Our Pride.* Lubbock, Tex.: Trucha Publications.

Deloria, Vine, Jr., 1969. *Custer Died for Your Sins.* New York: Macmillan.

de Mille, Richard, 1967. *Put Your Mother on the Ceiling.* New York: Walker.

Dennison, George, 1969. *The Lives of Children.* New York: Vintage.

Deutsch, Martin, 1964. "Facilitating Development in the Pre-School Child: Social and Psychological Perspectives." *Merrill-Palmer Quarterly of Behavior and Development* 10(3).

Dowaliby, F. J., and Harry Schumer, 1973. "Teacher-Centered Mode of College Classroom Instruction Is Related to Manifest Anxiety." *Journal of Educational Psychology* 65, 125–132.

Duchastel, Phillipe C., and Paul F. Merrill, 1973. "The Effects of Behavioral Objectives on Learning: A Review of Empirical Studies." *Review of Educational Research* 43(1), 53–69.

Duncker, K., 1945. "On Problem Solving." *Psychological Monographs* 58(270).

Dunlap, Knight, 1949. *Habits: Their Making and Unmaking.* New York: Liveright.

Dunn, Lloyd M., ed., 1963. *Exceptional Children in the Schools.* New York: Holt, Rinehart and Winston.

Ebel, Robert L., 1972. *Essentials of Educational Measurement.* Englewood Cliffs, N.J.: Prentice-Hall.

Ebel, Robert L., ed., 1969. *Encyclopedia of Educational Research,* 4th ed. New York: Macmillan.

Eddy, Elizabeth M., 1969. *Becoming a Teacher.* New York: Teachers College Press.

Elashoff, Janet D., and Richard E. Snow., eds., 1971. *Pygmalion Reconsidered.* Worthington, Ohio: Charles A. Jones.

Elkind, David, 1968a. "Cognitive Development in Adolescence." In J. F. Adams, ed., *Understanding Adolescence,* 128–158. Boston: Allyn and Bacon.

Elkind, David, 1968b. "Giant in the Nursery—Jean Piaget." *New York Times Magazine,* May 26, 25–80. Reprinted in David Elkind, *Children and Adolescents: Interpretive Essays on Jean Piaget.* New York: Oxford University Press.

Elkind, David, 1970. *Children and Adolescents: Interpretive Essays on Jean Piaget,* 2nd ed. New York: Oxford University Press.

Ellis, Henry C., 1965. *The Transfer of Learning.* New York: Macmillan.

Ellison, Ralph, 1947. *Invisible Man.* New York: Random House.

Engelmann, Siegfried, 1969. *Preventing Failure in the Elementary Grades.* Chicago: Science Research Associates.

Engelmann, Siegfried, 1971. "The Effectiveness of Direct Instruction on IQ Performance and Achievement in Reading and Arithmetic." In J. Hellmuth, ed., *Disadvantaged Child,* vol. 3. New York: Brunner/Mazel.

Engelmann, Siegfried, and Theresa Engelmann, 1968. *Give Your Child a Superior Mind.* New York: Simon and Schuster.

Engelmann, Siegfried, and others, 1969. *Distar Instructional System.* Chicago: Science Research Associates.

Environment, Heredity, and Intelligence, 1970. Reprint Series No. 2. Cambridge: *Harvard Educational Review.*

Epstein, Cynthia Fuchs, 1970. *Woman's Place.* Berkeley: University of California Press.

Erickson, Marion J., 1965. *The Mentally Retarded Child in the Classroom.* New York: Macmillan.

Erikson, Erik H., 1963. *Childhood and Society,* 2nd ed. New York: Norton.

Erikson, Erik H., 1968. *Identity: Youth and Crisis.* New York: Norton.

Espenschade, Anna S., 1963. *What Research Says to the Teacher: Physical Education in the Elementary Schools.* Washington, D.C.: National Education Association.

Evans, Gary W., and Gaylon L. Oswalt, 1967. "Acceleration of Academic Progress Through the Manipulation of Peer Influence." *Working Paper* No. 155. Kansas City: Bureau of Child Research Laboratory, University of Kansas Medical Center.

Evans, Richard I., 1967. *Dialogue with Erik Erikson.* New York: Harper and Row.

Evans, Richard I., 1968. *B. F. Skinner: The Man and His Ideas.* New York: Dutton.

Evans, Richard M., 1976. "Effect of Computer Delivered Testing on Achievement in a Mastery Learning Course of Study with Partial Scoring and Variable Pacing." *Morningside College Educational Research Bulletin.* Sioux City, Iowa: Morningside College.

Eysenck, H. J., 1971. *The IQ Argument.* New York: The Library Press.

Fantini, Mario D., and Gerald Weinstein, 1968. *The Disadvantaged: Challenge to Education.* New York: Harper and Row.

Farson, Richard E., 1968. "Praise Reappraised." In Don E. Hamachek, ed., *Human Dynamics in Psychology and Education,* 109–118. Boston: Allyn and Bacon.

Featherstone, Joseph, 1971. *Schools Where Children learn.* New York: Liverwright.

Fernald, Grace, 1943. *Remedial Techniques in Basic School Subjects.* New York: McGraw-Hill.

Ferster, C. B., and M. C. Perrott, 1968. *Behavior Principles.* New York: Appleton-Century-Crofts.

Festinger, Leon, 1957. *A Theory of Cognitive Dissonance.* Evanston, Ill.: Row, Peterson.

Finn, J. D., 1972. "Expectations and the Educational Environment." *Review of Educational Research* 42, 387–410.

Finocchiaro, Mary, 1969. *Teaching English as a Second Language.* New York: Harper and Row.

Flanagan, J. C. 1971. "The PLAN System for Individualizing Education." *Measurement in Education* 2(2), 1–8.

Flanders, Ned A., 1970. *Analyzing Teaching Behavior.* Reading, Mass.: Addison-Wesley.

Fleming, Elyse S., and Ralph G. Anttonen, 1971. "Teacher Expectancy or My Fair Lady." *American Educational Research Journal* 8(2), 241–252.

Frantzblau, A. N., 1958. *A Primer of Statistics for Non-Statisticians.* New York: Harcourt, Brace, and World.

Freud, Sigmund, 1935. *An Autobiographical Study.* James Strachey, trans. New York: Norton.

Freud, Sigmund, 1949. *An Outline of Psycho-Analysis.* New York: Norton.

Friedan, Betty, 1963. *The Feminine Mystique.* New York: Dell.

Friedenberg, Edgar Z., 1959. *The Vanishing Adolescent.* Boston: Beacon Press.

Friedenberg, Edgar Z., 1965. *Coming of Age in America.* New York: Random House.

Fuchs, Estelle, 1969. *Teachers Talk.* New York: Anchor Books.

Furth, Hans, 1970. *Piaget for Teachers.* Englewood Cliffs, N.J.: Prentice-Hall.

Gage, N. L., ed., 1963. *Handbook of Research on Teaching.* Chicago: Rand McNally.

Gagné, Robert M., 1970. *The Conditions of Learning,* 2nd ed. New York: Holt, Rinehart and Winston.

Galarza, Ernesto, 1971. *Barrio Boy.* Notre Dame, Ind.: University of Notre Dame Press.

Gall, M. D., 1970. "The Use of Questions in Teaching." *Review of Educational Research* 40, 707–721.

Gallagher, James J., 1975. *Teaching the Gifted Child,* 2nd ed. Boston: Allyn and Bacon.

Galton, Francis, 1869. *Hereditary Genius.* London: Macmillan.

Galton, Francis, 1890. Statement made in footnote to an article by James McKeen Cattell, "Mental Tests and Measurement." *Mind* 15, 373.

Garcia, John, 1972. "IQ: The Conspiracy." *Psychology Today* 6(4), 40–94.

Gardner, John W., 1961. *Excellence.* New York: Harper and Row.

Gardner, John W., 1965. *Self-Renewal.* New York: Harper and Row.

Gardner, John W., 1968. *No Easy Victories.* New York: Harper and Row.

Gates, A. I., 1917. "Recitation as a Function in Memorizing." *Archives of Psychology* 6(40)

Gesell, Arnold, 1928. *Infancy and Human Growth.* New York: Macmillan.

Getzels, Jacob W., and Philip W. Jackson, 1962. *Creativity and Intelligence.* New York: Wiley.

Gibson, E. J., 1941. "Retroactive Inhibition as a Function of Degree of Generalization Between Tasks." *Journal of Experimental Psychology* 28, 93–115.

Ginott, Haim, 1965. *Between Parent and Child.* New York: Macmillan.

Ginott, Haim, 1969. *Between Parent and Teenager.* New York: Macmillan.

Ginott, Haim, 1971. *Teacher and Child.* New York: Macmillan.

Ginsburg, Herbert, and Sylvia Opper, 1969. *Piaget's Theory of Intellectual Development: An Introduction.* Englewood Cliffs, N.J.: Prentice-Hall.

Glasser, William, 1969. *Schools without Failure.* New York: Harper and Row.

Glasser, William, 1972. *The Identity Society.* New York: Harper and Row.

Goble, Frank, 1970. *Third Force: The Psychology of Abraham Maslow.* New York: Grossman.

Goertzel, Victor, and Mildred Goertzel, 1962. *Cradles of Eminence.* Boston: Little Brown.

Goffman, E., 1963. *Stigma: Notes on the Management of a Spoiled Identity.* Englewood Cliffs, N.J.: Prentice-Hall.

Goldbeck, R. A., and V. N. Campbell, 1962. "The Effects of Response Rate and Response Difficulty on Programmed Learning." *Journal of Educational Psychology* 53, 110–118.

Goldfarb, William, 1970. "Childhood Psychosis." In Paul H. Mussen, ed., *Carmichael's Manual of Child Psychology,* 3rd ed., vol. 2, 765–830. New York: Wiley.

Goldstein, H., J. Moss, and Laura J. Jordan, 1965. *The Efficacy of Special Class Training on the Development of Mentally Retarded Children.* Cooperative Research Project No. 619. Washington, D.C.: U.S. Office of Education.

Goldstein, Herbert, and Dorothy M. Siegle [n.d.] *A Curriculum Guide for Teachers of the Educable Mentally Handicapped.* Danville, Ill.: Interstate Printers and Publishers.

Gonzalez, Rodolfo, 1973. *I Am Joaquin.* New York: Bantam.

Goodman, Leroy V., 1976. "A Bill of Rights for the Handicapped." *American Education* 12, 6–8.

Goodman, Paul, 1956. *Growing Up Absurd.* New York: Vintage Books.

Goodman, Paul, 1964. *Compulsory Miseducation.* New York: Horizon Press.

Goodman, Paul, 1966. *Compulsory Miseducation and the Community of Scholars.* New York: Vintage.

Goodman, Paul, 1967. *Like a Conquered Province.* New York: Random House.

Goodman, Paul, 1969. *New Reformation: Notes of a Neolithic Conservative.* New York: Random House.

Gordon, Thomas, 1970. *P.E.T.: Parent Effectiveness Training.* New York: Peter H. Wyden.

Gordon, Thomas, 1974. *T.E.T.: Teacher Effectiveness Training.* New York: Peter H. Wyden.

Gray, Jenny, 1967. *The Teacher's Survival Guide.* Belmont, Calif.: Fearon.

Gray, Susan W., and Rupert E. Klaus, 1970. "The Early Training Project: A Seven Year Report." *Child Development* 41, 909–924.

Green, Hannah [Joanne Greenberg], 1964. *I Never Promised You a Rose Garden.* New York: Holt, Rinehart and Winston.

Greer, Mary, and Bonnie Rubinstein, 1972. *Will the Real Teacher Please Stand Up?* Pacific Palisades, Calif.: Goodyear.

Grier, William, and Price Cobbs, 1968. *Black Rage.* New York: Basic Books.

Gronlund, Norman E., 1959. *Sociometry in the Classroom.* New York: Harper.

Gronlund, Norman E., 1972. *Stating Behavioral Objectives for Classroom Instruction.* New York: Macmillan.

Gronlund, Norman E., 1974. *Improving Marking and Reporting in Classroom Instruction.* New York: Macmillan.

Grossman, Herbert, 1972. *Nine Rotten Lousy Kids.* New York: Holt, Rinehart and Winston.

Grossman, H. J., 1973. *Manual on Terminology and Classification in Mental Retardation.* Baltimore: Garamond/Pridemark.

Guilford, J. P., 1959. "Three Faces of Intellect." *American Psychologist* 14, 469–479.

Guilford, J. P., 1967. *The Nature of Human Intelligence.* New York: McGraw-Hill.

Halacy, D. S., 1970. *Man and Memory.* New York: Harper and Row.

Haley, Alex, 1976. *Roots.* Garden City, N.Y.: Doubleday.

Hall, R. V., S. Axelrod, M. Foundopoulos, J. Shellman, R. A. Campbell, and S. S. Cranston, 1971. "The Effective Use of Punishment to Modify Behavior in the Classroom." *Educational Technology* 119, 24–26.

Hamachek, Don E., 1975. *Behavior Dynamics in Teaching, Learning, and Growth.* Boston: Allyn and Bacon.

Harlow, Harry F., 1949. "The Formation of Learning Sets." *Psychological Review* 56, 51–65.

Harmin, Merrill, Howard Kirschenbaum, and Sidney B. Simon, 1972. *Clarifying Values Through Subject Matter.* Minneapolis: Winston Press.

Harnischfeger, Annegret, and David E. Wiley, 1976. "Achievement Test Scores Drop. So What?" *Educational Researcher* 5(3), 5–12.

Harrelson, Orvis A., 1975. "Health—The Affective Approach." In Donald A. Read and Sidney B. Simons, eds., *Humanistic Education Sourcebook,* 325–328. Englewood Cliffs, N.J.: Prentice-Hall.

Harrington, Michael, 1965. *The Other America.* Baltimore: Penguin Books.

Hartshorne, Hugh, and Mark A. May, 1929. *Studies in the Nature of Character.* Vol. 2, *Studies in Service and Self-Control.* New York: Macmillan.

Hartshorne, Hugh, and Mark A. May, 1930a. *Studies in the Nature of Character.* Vol. 1, *Studies in Deceit.* New York: Macmillan.

Hartshorne, Hugh, and Mark A. May, 1930b. *Studies in the Organization of Character.* New York: Macmillan.

Havighurst, Robert, 1952. *Developmental Tasks and Education.* New York: Longmans, Green.

Hawkins, Robert P., 1972. "It's Time We Taught the Young How to Be Good Parents (and Don't You Wish We'd Started a Long Time Ago?)," *Psychology Today* 6(6), 28–40.

Haywood, H. C., 1974. "Intelligence, Distribution of" *Encyclopedia Britannica,* 15th ed., vol. 9, 672–677.

Herndon, James, 1968. *The Way It Spozed to Be.* New York: Simon and Schuster.

Herndon, James, 1971. *How to Survive in Your Native Land.* New York: Simon and Schuster.

Herrnstein, Richard, 1971. "I.Q." *Atlantic* 228(3), 43–64.

Herrnstein, Richard, 1973. *I.Q. in the Meritocracy.* Boston: Little, Brown.

Hertzberg, Alvin, and Edward Stone, 1971. *Schools Are for Children: An American Approach to the Open Classroom.* New York: Schocken Books.

Hess, Robert D., and Doreen J. Croft, 1975. *Teachers of Young Children,* 2nd ed. Boston: Houghton Mifflin.

Hess, Robert D., and Virginia Shipman, 1965. "Early Experience and the Socialization of Cognitive Modes in Children." *Child Development* 36, 869–886.

Hewett, Frank M., 1968. *The Emotionally Disturbed Child in the Classroom.* Boston: Allyn and Bacon.

Highet, Gilbert, 1957. *The Art of Teaching.* New York: Vintage Books.

Highet, Gilbert, 1976. *The Immortal Profession.* New York: Weybright and Talley.

Hobbs, Nicholas, 1975a. *The Futures of Children.* San Francisco: Jossey-Bass.

Hobbs, Nicholas, ed., 1975b. *Issues in the Classification of Children,* vol. 1. San Francisco: Jossey-Bass.

Hobbs, Nicholas, ed., 1975c. *Issues in the Classification of Children,* vol. 2. San Francisco: Jossey-Bass.

Hoffman, Lois Wladis, 1972. "Early Childhood Experiences and Women's Achievement Motives." *The Journal of Social Issues* 28(2), 129–156.

Hoffman, Banesh, 1962. *The Tyranny of Testing.* New York: Crowell-Collier.

Holt, John, 1964. *How Children Fail.* New York: Pitman.

Holt, John, 1967. *How Children Learn.* New York: Pitman.

Holt, John, 1969. *The Underachieving School.* New York: Pitman.

Holt, John, 1970. *What Do I Do Monday?* New York: Dutton.

Holt, John, 1972. *Freedom and Beyond.* New York: Dutton.

Holt, John, 1976. *Instead of Education: Ways to Help People Do Things Better.* New York: Dutton.

Homme, Lloyd, and Donald Tosti, 1971. *Behavior Technology: Motivation and Contingency Management.* San Rafael, Calif.: Individual

Learning Systems.

Honzik, Marjorie P., Jean W. Macfarlane, and Lucile Allen, 1948. "The Stability of Mental Test Performance Between Two and Eighteen Years." *Journal of Experimental Education* 18, 309–324.

Hoppe, F., 1930. "Erfolg und Misserfolg." *Psychologische Forschung* 14, 1–62.

Hosford, Philip L., 1973. *An Instructional Theory: A Beginning.* Englewood Cliffs, N.J.: Prentice-Hall.

Howe, Florence, 1971. "Sexual Stereotypes Start Early." *Saturday Review,* Oct. 16, 1971, 76–94.

Howe, Leland W., and Mary Martha Howe, 1975. *Personalizing Education: Values Clarification and Beyond.* New York: Hart.

Howson, Geoffrey, ed., 1969. *Primary Education in Britain Today.* New York: Teachers College Press.

Hunsicker, Paul, 1963. *What Research Says to the Teacher: Physical Fitness.* Washington, D.C.: National Education Association.

Hunt, David E., and Edmund V. Sullivan, 1974. *Between Psychology and Education.* Hinsdale, Ill.: Dryden Press.

Hunt, James McVicker, 1961. *Intelligence and Experience.* New York: Ronald.

Huxley, Aldous, 1932. *Brave New World.* New York: Harper.

Informal Schools in Britain Today, 1971 and 1972. New York: Citation Press.

Jacobs, Paul, Milton Maier, and Laurence Stolurow, 1966. *A Guide to Evaluating Self-Instructional Programs.* New York: Holt, Rinehart and Winston.

James, William, 1958. *Talks to Teachers.* New York: Norton.

Jencks, Christopher, 1969. "A Reappraisal of the Most Controversial Education Document of Our Time." *New York Times Magazine,* August 10, 12–44.

Jencks, Christopher S., 1972. *Inequality: A Reassessment of the Effect of Family and Schooling in America.* New York: Basic Books.

Jenkins, J. G., and Karl. M. Dallenbach, 1924. "Oblivescence during Sleep and Waking." *American Journal of Psychology* 35, 605–612.

Jenkins, J. J., 1963. "Mediated Associations: Paradigms and Situations." In C. N. Cofer and B. S. Musgrave, eds., *Verbal Behavior and Learning.* New York: McGraw-Hill.

Jensen, Arthur R., 1969. "How Much Can We Boost I.Q. and Scholastic Achievement?" *Harvard Educational Review* 39(1), 1–123.

Jersild, Arthur T., 1952. *In Search of Self.* New York: Teachers College, Columbia University.

Jersild, Arthur T., 1955. *When Teachers Face Themselves.* New York: Teachers College, Columbia University.

Johnson, Ronald E., 1975. "Meaning in Complex Learning." *Review of Educational Research* 45(3), 425–454.

Johnson, Sheila K., 1972. "A Woman Anthropologist Offers a Solution to the Woman Problem." *The New York Times Magazine,* August 27, 7–39.

Johnson, Simon S., 1975. *Update on Education.* Denver: The Education Commission of the States.

Johnson, W., 1946. *People in Quandaries.* New York: Harper.

Jones, Ernest, 1953. *The Life and Work of Sigmund Freud.* Vol. 1, *The Formative Years and the Great Discoveries.* New York: Basic Books.

Jones, Harold E., 1954. "The Environment and Mental Development." In L. Carmichael, ed., *Manual of Child Psychology,* 2nd ed., 631–696. New York: Wiley.

Jones, Mary Cover, 1957. "The Later Careers of Boys Who Were Early or Late Maturing." *Child Development* 28, 113–128.

Jones, Mary Cover, and Paul H. Mussen, 1958. "Self Conceptions, Motivations and Interpersonal Attitudes of Early and Late Maturing Girls." *Child Development* 29, 491–501.

Jones, Reginald, ed., 1972. *Black Psychology.* New York: Harper and Row.

Jones, Richard M., 1968. *Fantasy and Feeling in Education.* New York: New York University Press.

José, Jean, and John J. Cody, 1971. "Teacher-Pupil Interaction As It Relates to Attempted Changes in Teacher Expectancy of Academic Ability and Achievement." *American Educational Research Journal* 8(1), 39–49.

Kagan, Jerome, 1964a. *Developmental Studies of Reflection and Analysis.* Cambridge: Harvard University Press.

Kagan, Jerome, 1964b. "Impulsive and Reflective Children." In J. D. Krumbolz, ed., *Learning and the Educational Process.* Chicago: Rand McNally.

Kagan, Jerome, and Robert Coles. eds., 1971. *Twelve to Sixteen: Early Adolescence.* New York: Norton

Kamii, Constance, and L. Dermon, 1972. "The Engelmann Approach to Teaching Logical Thinking: Findings from the Administration of

Some Piagetian Tasks." In D. R. Green, M. P. Ford, and G. Flamer, eds., *Piaget and Measurement.* New York: McGraw-Hill.

Kanner, Leo, 1972. *Child Psychiatry,* 4th ed. Springfield, Ill.: Thomas.

Kaufman, Bel, 1964. *Up the Down Staircase.* New York: Avon Books.

Keller, Fred S., 1968. "Good-Bye Teacher . . ." *Journal of Applied Behavior Analysis* 1, 79–88.

Keniston, Kenneth, 1965. *The Uncommitted.* New York: Harcourt, Brace and World.

Keniston, Kenneth, 1970. "Student Activism, Moral Development, and Morality." *American Journal of Orthopsychiatry* 40, 577–592.

Kerlinger, Fred N., ed., 1973. *Review of Research in Education.* Itasca, Ill.: F. E. Peacock.

Kessen, William, 1965. *The Child.* New York: Wiley.

Kibler, R. J., L. L. Barker, and D. T. Miles, 1970. *Behavioral Objectives and Instruction.* Boston: Allyn and Bacon.

Kilpatrick, F. P., and H. Cantril, 1960. "Self-Anchoring Scaling, A Measure of Individual's Unique Reality Worlds." *Journal of Individual Psychology* 16, 158–173.

Kirk, Samuel A., 1972. *Educating Exceptional Children,* 2nd ed. Boston: Houghton Mifflin.

Kirk, Samuel A., and Winifred D. Kirk, 1971. *Psycholinguistic Learning Disabilities: Diagnosis and Remediation.* Urbana: University of Illinois Press.

Kirk, Samuel A., Janet Learner, and Sister Joanne Marie Kliebhan, 1978. *Teaching Reading to Slow and Disabled Learners.* Boston: Houghton Mifflin.

Kirk, Samuel A., J. J. McCarthy, and Winifred D. Kirk, 1968. *The Illinois Test of Psycholinguistic Abilities,* rev. ed. Urbana: University of Illinois Press.

Kirschenbaum, Howard, 1975. "Sensitivity Modules." In Donald A. Read and Sidney B. Simon, eds., *Humanistic Education Sourcebook,* 315–320. Englewood Cliffs, N.J.: Prentice-Hall.

Kirschenbaum, Howard, and Sidney B. Simon, eds., 1973. *Readings in Values Clarification.* Minneapolis: Winston.

Kirschenbaum, Howard, Sidney P. Simon, and Rodney W. Napier, 1971. *Wad-ja-get? The Grading Game in American Education.* New York: Hart.

Klausmeier, Herbert J., and Richard E. Ripple, 1971. *Learning and Human Abilities: Educational Psychology,* 3rd ed. New York: Harper and Row.

Klausmeier, H. J., J. S. Sorensen, and E. S. Ghatala, 1971. "Individually Guided Motivation: Developing Self-Direction and Prosocial Behaviors." *Elementary School Journal* 71, 339–350.

Koch, Kenneth, 1970. *Wishes, Lies, Dreams: A Way of Teaching Children Poetry.* New York: Random House.

Koch, Richard, and Jean Holt Koch, 1975. *Understanding the Mentally Retarded Child.* New York: Random House.

Koestler, Arthur, 1968. *The Ghost in the Machine.* New York: Macmillan.

Kohl, Herbert, 1967. *36 Children.* New York: New American Library.

Kohl, Herbert, 1969. *The Open Classroom.* New York: Vintage.

Kohlberg, Lawrence, 1966. "Moral Education in the Schools: A Developmental View." *School Review* 74, 1–30.

Köhler, Wolfgang, 1925. *The Mentality of Apes.* New York: Harcourt, Brace and World.

Kolb, David A., 1965. "Achievement Motivation Training for Under-Achieving Boys." *Journal of Personality and Social Psychology* 2, 783–792.

Kolstoe, O. P., 1970. *Teaching Educable Mentally Retarded Children.* New York: Holt, Rinehart and Winston.

Kounin, Jacob S., 1970. *Discipline and Group Management in Classrooms.* New York: Holt, Rinehart and Winston.

Kozol, Jonathon, 1967. *Death at an Early Age.* Boston: Houghton Mifflin.

Kozol, Jonathon, 1972. *Free Schools.* Boston: Houghton Mifflin.

Krathwohl, David R., Benjamin S. Bloom, and Bertram B. Masia, 1964. *Taxonomy of Educational Objectives, Handbook II: Affective Domain.* New York: McKay.

Kumar, V. K., 1971. "The Structure of Human Memory and Some Educational Implications." *Review of Educational Research* 41(5), 379–417.

Kunihara, S., and J. J. Asher, 1965. "The Strategy of the Total Physical Response: An Application to Learning Japanese." *International Review of Applied Linguistics* 3, 277–289.

Lange, P. C., 1972. "What's the Score on Programmed Instruction?" *Today's Education* 61, 59.

Lapouse, R., and M. Monk, 1959. "Fears and Worries in a Representative Sample of Children." *American Journal of Orthopsychiatry* 29, 803–818.

Leacock, Eleanor Burke, 1969. *Teaching and*

Learning in City Schools. New York: Basic Books.

Lefkowitz, William, 1975. "Communication Grows in a 'Magic Circle.' " In Donald A. Read and Sidney B. Simon, eds., *Humanistic Education Sourcebook,* 457–459. Englewood Cliffs, N.J.: Prentice-Hall.

Leonard, George, 1968. *Education and Ecstasy.* New York: Dell.

Lewin, Kurt, 1936. *Principles of Topological Psychology.* New York: McGraw-Hill.

Lewin, Kurt, 1951. *Field Theory in Social Science.* New York: Harper and Row.

Lewin, Kurt, 1954. "Behavior and Development as a Function of the Total Situation." In Leonard Carmichael, ed., *Manual of Child Psychology,* 2nd ed., 918–970. New York: Wiley.

Lieberman, Morton A., Irvin D. Yalom, and Matthew B. Miles, 1973. *Encounter Groups: First Facts.* New York: Basic Books.

Lifton, Walter M., 1975. "Education and Therapy." In Donald A. Read and Sidney B. Simon, eds., *Humanistic Education Sourcebook,* 143–154. Englewood Cliffs, N.J.: Prentice-Hall.

Lillard, Paula, 1972. *Montessori: A Modern Approach.* New York: Schocken Books.

Lindsley, O. R., 1960. "Characterization of the Behavior of Chronic Psychotics as Revealed by Free Operant Conditioning Methods." *Diseases of the Nervous System,* Monograph Supplement 21, 66–78.

Lipe, Dewey, and Steven M. Jung, 1971. "Manipulating Incentives to Enhance School Learning." *Review of Educational Research* 41(4), 249–280.

Lippitt, R., and R. K. White, 1958. "An Experimental Study of Leadership and Group Life." In E. E. Maccoby, T. M. Newcomb, and E. E. Hartley, eds., *Readings in Social Psychology,* 446–511. New York: Holt, Rinehart and Winston.

Little, J. K., 1967. "The Occupations of Non-College Youth." *American Educational Research Journal* 4, 147–153.

Locke, John, 1690. *An Essay Concerning Human Understanding.*

Lopata, Helena Z., 1971. *Occupation: Housewife.* New York: Oxford University Press.

Lorayne, Harry, and Jerry Lucas, 1974. *The Memory Book.* New York: Ballantine Books.

Lowry, Richard, ed., 1971. *Dominance, Self-Esteem, Self-Actualization: Germinal Papers of A. H. Maslow.* Monterey, Calif.: Brooks/Cole.

Lowry, Richard, 1973. *A. H. Maslow: An Intellectual Portrait.* Monterey, Calif.: Brooks/Cole.

Luchins, A. S., 1942. "Mechanization in Problem Solving: The Effect of *Einstellung.*" *Psychological Monographs* 54(248).

Luria, A. R., 1968. *The Mind of a Mnemonist: A Little Book About a Vast Memory.* New York: Basic Books.

Lysaught, Jerome P., and Clarence M. Williams, 1963. *A Guide to Programmed Instruction.* New York: Wiley.

Maccoby, Eleanor E., and Carol N. Jacklin, 1974. *Psychology of Sex Differences.* Stanford: Stanford University Press.

Maccoby, Eleanor E., and Miriam Zellner, 1970. *Experiments in Primary Education: Aspects of Project Follow-Through.* New York: Harcourt Brace.

Maccoby, Michael, 1972. "A Psychoanalytic View of Learning." *Change* 3(8), 32–38.

Macfarlane, Jean Walker, L. Allen, and M. P. Honzik, 1954. *A Developmental Study of the Behavior Problems of Normal Children Between Twenty-One Months and Fourteen Years.* Berkeley: University of California Press.

MacMillan, Donald L., 1973. *Behavior Modification in Education.* New York: Macmillan.

Mager, Robert F., 1968. *Developing Attitude Toward Learning.* Belmont, Calif.: Fearon.

Mager, Robert F., 1972. *Goal Analysis.* Belmont, Calif.: Fearon.

Mager, Robert F., 1975. *Preparing Instructional Objectives,* 2nd ed. Belmont, Calif.: Fearon.

Mager, Robert F., and Kenneth M. Beach, Jr., 1967. *Developing Vocational Instruction.* Belmont, Calif.: Fearon.

Mahan, Harry C., 1967. "The Use of Socratic Type Programmed Instruction in College Courses in Psychology." Paper read at Western Psychological Association Convention, San Francisco, May.

Maresh, M. M., 1964. "Variations in Patterns of Linear Growth and Skeletal Maturation." *Journal of American Physical Therapy Association* 44, 881–890.

Markle, Susan Meyer, 1969. *Good Frames and Bad: A Grammar of Frame Writing,* 2nd ed. New York: Wiley.

Marrow, Alfred J., 1969. *The Practical Theorist: The Life and Work of Kurt Lewin.* New York: Basic Books.

Martin, Edwin W., Jr., 1972. "Individualism and Behaviorism as Future Trends in Educating Handicapped Children." *Exceptional Children* 38, 517–525.

Maslow, Abraham H., 1954. *Motivation and Personality.* New York: Harper and Row.

Maslow, Abraham H., 1968. *Toward a Psychology of Being,* 2nd ed. Princeton, N.J.: Van Nostrand.

Maslow, Abraham H., 1970a. *Motivation and Personality,* 2nd ed. New York: Harper and Row.

Maslow, Abraham H., 1970b. *New Knowledge in Human Values.* New York: Harper and Row.

Maslow, Abraham H., 1970c. *Religions, Values, and Peak Experiences.* New York: Viking.

Maslow, Abraham H., 1971. *The Farther Reaches of Human Nature.* New York: Viking.

McClelland, David C., 1961. *The Achieving Society.* Princeton, N.J.: Van Nostrand.

McClelland, David C., 1965. "Toward a Theory of Motive Acquisition." *American Psychologist* 20, 321–333.

McIntosh, D. M., 1963. *Statistics for the Teacher.* New York: Pergamon Press.

McKeachie, W. J., 1974. "The Decline and Fall of the Laws of Learning." *Educational Researcher* 3(3), 7–11.

McNemar, Quinn, 1942. *The Revision of the Stanford-Binet Scale.* Boston: Houghton Mifflin.

Meacham, Merle E., and Allen E. Wiesen, 1969. *Changing Classroom Behavior: A Manual for Precision Teaching.* New York: International Textbook Co.

Meichenbaum, D. H., K. S. Bowers, and R. R. Ross, 1969. "A Behavioral Analysis of Teacher Expectancy Effect," *Journal of Personality and Social Psychology* 13, 306–316.

Mercer, Jane R., 1972. "IQ: The Lethal Label." *Psychology Today* 6(4), 44–97.

Mercer, Jane R., 1975. "Psychological Assessment and the Rights of Children." In Nicholas Hobbs, ed., *Issues in the Classification of Children,* vol. 1, 130–158. San Francisco: Jossey-Bass.

Messick, Samuel, and Associates, 1976. *Individuality in Learning.* San Francisco: Jossey-Bass.

Mischel, Walter, 1970. "Sex-Typing and Socialization." In Paul H. Mussen, ed., *Carmichael's Manual of Child Psychology,* 3rd ed., vol. 2, 3–72. New York: Wiley.

Montessori, Maria, 1912. *The Montessori Method.* New York: Stokes.

Montessori, Maria, 1949. *The Absorbent Mind.* New York: Dell.

Montesorri, Maria, 1965. *Dr. Montessori's Own Handbook.* New York: Shocken Books.

Montessori, Maria, 1966. *Spontaneous Activity in Education.* New York: Shocken Books.

Moore, Donald F., 1978. *Educating the Deaf: Psychology, Principles, and Practices.* Boston: Houghton Mifflin.

Moreno, Jacob L., 1946. *Psychodrama.* New York: Beacon House.

Morrison, H.C., 1926. *The Practice of Teaching in the Secondary School.* Chicago: University of Chicago Press.

Moss, Howard A., 1967. "Sex, Age, and State as Determinants of Mother-Infant Interaction." *Merrill-Palmer Quarterly* 13, 19–36.

Mosston, Muska, 1966. *Teaching Physical Education.* Columbus, Ohio: Merrill.

Mosteller, Frederick, and Daniel P. Moynihan, eds., 1972. *On Equality of Educational Opportunity.* New York: Vintage.

Moustakas, Clark E., ed., 1966. *The Child's Discovery of Himself.* New York: Ballantine.

Mumford, Lewis, 1967, 1970. *The Myth of the Machine.* Vol. 1, *Technics and Human Development.* Vol. 2, *The Pentagon of Power.* New York: Harcourt Brace Jovanovich.

Murrow, Casey, and Liza Murrow, 1971. *Children Come First.* New York: McGraw-Hill.

Mussen, Paul H., and M. C. Jones, 1957. "Self-Conceptions, Motivation, and Interpersonal Attitudes of Late and Early Maturing Boys." *Child Development* 28, 243–256.

Mussen, Paul H., John J. Conger, and Jerome Kagan, 1974. *Child Development and Personality,* 4th ed. New York: Harper and Row.

Muuss, Rolf E., 1964. *Theories of Adolescence,* 2nd ed. New York: Knopf.

Myers, C. Roger, 1970. "Journal Citations and Scientific Eminence in Contemporary Psychology." *American Psychologist* 25(11), 1041–1048.

National Advisory Committee on Handicapped Children, 1968. *First Annual Report, Subcommittee on Education of the Committee on Labor and Public Welfare, U.S. Senate.* Washington, D.C.: U.S. Government Printing Office.

N.E.A. Research Bulletin, 1969. "Reporting Student Progress." Washington, D.C.: National Education Association.

Neill, A. S., 1960. *Summerhill.* New York: Hart.

Neill, A. S., 1966. *Freedom—Not License!* New York: Hart.

Neill, A. S., 1972. *Neill! Neill! Orange Peel!* New York: Hart.

Newell, A., J. C. Shaw, and H. A. Simon, 1962. "The Processes of Creative Thinking." In H. E. Gruber, G. Terrell, and M. Wertheimer, eds., *Contemporary Approaches to Creative Thinking,* 65–66. New York: Atherton Press.

Norman, D. A., ed., 1970. *Models of Human Memory.* New York: Academic Press.

Northway, J. L., 1940. "A Method for Depicting Social Relationships Obtained by Sociometric Testing." *Sociometry* 3, 144–150.

Nyquist, Ewald B., and Gene R. Hawes, eds., 1972. *Open Education: A Sourcebook for Parents and Teachers.* New York: Bantam.

Offer, Daniel, 1969. *The Psychological World of the Teen-Ager: A Study of Normal Adolescent Boys.* New York: Basic Books.

Office of Economic Opportunity, 1972. *An Experiment in Performance Contracting: Summary of Preliminary Results.* OEO Pamphlet 3400-5. Washington, D.C. U.S. Government Printing Office.

Ojemann, Ralph H., 1968. "Should Educational Objectives Be Stated in Behaviorial Terms?" *Elementary School Journal* 68(5), 223–231.

Ojemann, Ralph H., and Karen Pritchett, 1963. "Piaget and the Role of Guided Experience in Human Development." *Perceptual and Motor Skills* 17, 927–940.

Olton, Robert M., and Richard S. Crutchfield, 1969. "Developing the Skills of Productive Thinking." In Paul H. Mussen, Jonas Langer, and Martin Covington, eds., *Trends and Issues in Developmental Psychology.* New York; Holt, Rinehart and Winston.

Orwell, George, 1946. *Animal Farm.* New York: Harcourt, Brace and World.

Orwell, George, 1949. *1984.* New York: Harcourt, Brace and World.

Owen, Kent, 1975. "Letting Go: Emotion in the Classroom." In Donald A. Read and Sidney B. Simon, eds., *Humanistic Education Sourcebook,* 329–332. Englewood Cliffs, N.J.: Prentice-Hall.

Ozmon, Howard, and Sam Craver, 1972. *Busing: A Moral Issue.* Bloomington, Ind.: Phi Delta Kappa Educational Foundation.

Parnes, Sidney J., 1967. *Creative Behavior Guidebook.* New York: Scribners.

Parnes, S., and G. Harding, eds., 1962. *A Source Book for Creative Thinking.* New York: Scribners.

Parten, Mildred B., 1932. "Social Participation Among Preschool Children." *Journal of Abnormal and Social Psychology* 27, 243–269.

Passow, A. Harry, ed., 1967. *Reaching the Disadvantaged Learner.* New York: Teachers College Press.

Peddiwell, J. Abner [Harold Benjamin], 1939, *The Saber-Tooth Curriculum.* New York: McGraw-Hill.

Perrone, Vito, 1972. *Open Education: Promise and Problems.* Bloomington, Ind.: Phi Delta Kappa.

Peters, William, 1971. *A Class Divided.* Garden City, N.Y.: Doubleday.

Piaget, Jean, 1952a. *The Language and Thought of the Child.* London: Routledge and Kegan Paul.

Piaget, Jean, 1952b. *The Origins of Intelligence in Children.* Translated by M. Cook. New York: International Universities Press.

Piaget, Jean, 1953. "How Children Form Mathematical Concepts." *Scientific American* 189, 74–79.

Piaget, Jean, 1970. *Science of Education and the Psychology of the Child.* New York: Grossman.

Piaget, Jean, and Barbel Inhelder, 1969. *The Psychology of the Child.* New York: Basic Books.

Pipe, Peter, 1966. *Practical Programming.* New York: Holt, Rinehart and Winston.

Plowden, Lady B., et al., 1967. *Children and Their Primary Schools: A Report of the Central Advisory Council for Education.* London: Her Majesty's Stationery Office.

Polya, G., 1954. *How to Solve It.* Princeton: Princeton University Press.

Postlethwait, S. N., and J. D. Novak, 1967. "The Use of 8-mm Loop Films in Individualized Instruction." *Annals of the New York Academy of Science* 142, 464–470.

Postman, Neil, 1972. "Once upon a Time: A Fable of Student Power." In Kevin Ryan and James M. Cooper, eds., *Kaleidoscope: Readings in Education,* 155–159. Boston: Houghton Mifflin.

Postman, Neil, and Charles Weingartner, 1969. *Teaching as a Subversive Activity.* New York: Delacorte Press.

Postman, Neil, and Charles Weingartner, 1971. *The Soft Revolution.* New York: Delacorte Press.

Premack, David, 1959. "Toward Empirical Behavior Laws: 1. Positive Reinforcement." *Psychological Review* 66, 219.

Privacy Rights of Parents and Students, 1975. *Federal Register* 40(3), 1208–1216. Washington, D.C.: U.S. Government Printing Office.

Pulaski, Mary A., 1971. *Understanding Piaget: An Introduction to Children's Cognitive Development.* New York: Harper and Row.

Rambusch, Nancy M., 1962. *Learning How to Learn: An American Approach to Montessori.* Baltimore: Helicon Press.

Raths, Louis, Merrill Harmin, and Sidney L. Simon, 1966. *Values and Teaching.* Columbus, Ohio: Merrill.

Raths, Louis E., Merrill Harmin, and Sidney B. Simon, 1975. "Values and Valuing." In Donald A. Read and Sidney B. Simon, eds., *Humanistic*

Education Sourcebook, 72–81. Englewood Cliffs, N.J.: Prentice-Hall.

Read, Donald A., and Sidney B. Simon, eds., 1975. *Humanistic Education Sourcebook.* Englewood Cliffs, N.J.: Prentice-Hall.

Redl, Fritz, and William W. Wattenberg, 1959. *Mental Hygiene in Teaching,* 2nd ed. New York: Harcourt, Brace and World.

Reich, Charles A., 1970. *The Greening of America.* New York: Random House.

Remmers, H. H., 1963. "Rating Methods in Research on Teaching." In H. L. Gage, ed., *Handbook of Research on Teaching,* 329–378. Chicago: Rand McNally.

Render, Gary F., Charles E. Moon, and Donald J. Treffinger, 1975. "Directory of Organizations and Periodicals on Alternative Education." In Donald A. Read and Sidney B. Simon, eds., *Humanistic Education Sourcebook,* 469–482. Englewood Cliffs, N.J.: Prentice-Hall.

Rennie, Susan, and Kirsten Grimstad, 1975. *The New Woman's Survival Sourcebook.* New York: Knopf.

Reynolds, N.C., ed., 1976. *Mainstreaming: Origins and Implications.* Reston, Va.: The Council for Exceptional Children.

Riessman, Frank, 1962. *The Culturally Deprived Child.* New York: Harper and Row.

Roazen, Paul, 1974. *Freud and His Followers.* New York: Knopf.

Robinson, Francis P., 1961. *Effective Study.* New York: Harper and Row.

Robinson, Halbert B., and Nancy M. Robinson, 1974. *The Mentally Retarded Child,* 2nd ed. New York: McGraw-Hill.

Roethlisberger, F. J., and W. J. Dickson, 1939. *Management and the Worker.* Cambridge, Harvard University Press.

Rogers, Carl R., 1963. "Learning to be Free." In S. Farber and R. H. L. Wilson, eds., *Conflict and Creativity: Control of the Mind.* New York: McGraw-Hill. Also reprinted in *Person to Person: The Problem of Being Human,* Carl R. Rogers and Barry Stevens eds., 1967. Lafayette, Calif.: Real People Press.

Rogers, Carl R., 1969. *Freedom to Learn.* Columbus, Ohio: Merrill.

Rogers, Carl R., 1972. *Carl Rogers on Encounter Groups.* New York: Harper and Row.

Rogers, Carl R., 1975. "The Interpersonal Relationship in the Facilitation of Learning." In Donald A. Read and Sidney B. Simon, eds., *Humanistic Education Sourcebook,* 3–22. Englewood Cliffs, N.J.: Prentice-Hall.

Rogers, Carl R., and B. F. Skinner, 1956. "Some Issues Concerning the Control of Human Behavior." *Science* 124, 1057–1066.

Rogers, Frederick R., 1952. "Education Versus the Marking System." *Education* 52.

Rosen, B. M., A. K. Bahn, and M. Kramer, 1964. "Demographic and Diagnostic Characteristics of Psychiatric Clinic Outpatients in the U.S.A., 1961." *American Journal of Orthopsychiatry* 24, 455–467.

Rosenthal, Robert, 1966. *Experimenter Bias Effects in Behavioral Research.* New York: Appleton-Century-Crofts.

Rosenthal, Robert, 1969. "On Not So Replicated Experiments and Not So Null Results." *Journal of Consulting and Clinical Psychology* 33, 7–10.

Rosenthal, Robert, and Lenore Jacobson, 1968. *Pygmalion in the Classroom.* New York: Holt, Rinehart and Winston.

Rothman, Esther, 1971. *The Angel Inside Went Sour.* New York: McKay.

Rowe, Mary Budd, 1974. "Wait-Time and Rewards as Instructional Variables, Their Influence on Language, Logic, and Fate Control: Part One—Wait-Time." *Journal of Research in Science Teaching* 11, 81–94.

Ryan B., 1974. *Keller's Personalized System of Instruction: An Appraisal.* Washington, D.C.: American Psychological Association.

Ryan, Kevin, ed., 1970. *Don't Smile Until Christmas.* Chicago: University of Chicago Press.

Sanders, Norris M., 1966. *Classroom Questions: What Kinds?* New York: Harper and Row.

Sarason, Irwin G., et al., eds., 1971. *Reinforcing Productive Classroom Behavior: A Teacher's Guide to Behavior Modification.* New York: Behavioral Publications.

Sassenrath, Julius M., 1975. "Theory and Results on Feedback and Retention." *Journal of Educational Psychology* 76(6), 894–899.

Saville, Muriel, and Rudolph Troike, 1973. *A Handbook of Bilingual Education.* Washington, D.C.: Teachers of English to Speakers of Other Languages.

Schaar, Karen, 1975a. "MACOS Assailed, Congress Debates Curriculum." *APA Monitor* 6(6), 1–10.

Schaar, Karen, 1975b. "MACOS: The Controversy Continues." *APA Monitor* 6(7), 1–5.

Schmidt, Gilbert W., and Roger E. Ulrich, 1969. "Effects of Group Contingent Events upon Classroom Noise." *Journal of Applied Behavior Analysis* 2, 171–179.

Schoer, Lowell A., 1970. *Test Construction: A Programmed Guide.* Boston: Allyn and Bacon.

Scriven, Michael, 1967. "The Methodology of

Evaluation." In Ralph W. Tyler and others, eds., *Perspectives of Curriculum Evaluation,* 39–83. Chicago: Rand McNally.

Seagoe, May V., 1970. *The Learning Process and School Practice.* Scranton, Pa.: Chandler.

Sears, Pauline S., 1940. "Levels of Aspiration in Academically Successful and Unsuccessful Children." *Journal of Abnormal and Social Psychology* 35, 498–536.

Sears, Robert R., E. E. Maccoby, and H. Levin, 1957. *Patterns of Child Rearing.* Evanston, Ill.: Row, Peterson.

Sears, Robert R., L. Rau, and R. Alpert, 1965. *Identification and Child Rearing.* Stanford: Stanford University Press.

Segal, Rebecca, 1972. *Got No Time to Fool Around.* Philadelphia: Westminster Press.

Sellar, W. C., and R. J. Yeatman, 1931. *1066 and All That.* New York: Dutton.

Shaffer, Laurence, and Edward Shoben, 1956. *The Psychology of Adjustment,* 2nd ed. Boston: Houghton Mifflin.

Shaw, Alfred L., 1969. "Confirmation of Expectancy and Change in Teacher's Evaluations of Student Behavior." *Dissertation Abstracts International* 30(5-A), 1878–1879.

Shuey, Audrey M., 1966. *The Testing of Negro Intelligence,* 2nd ed. New York: Social Science Press.

Silberman, Charles E., 1970. *Crisis in the Classroom.* New York: Random House.

Simon, Anita, and E. G. Boyer, eds., 1970. *Mirrors for Behavior: An Anthology of Classroom Observation Instruments Continued.* Philadelphia: Research for Better Schools, Inc.

Simon, Sidney B., Leland W. Howe, and Howard Kirschenbaum, 1972. *Values Clarification: A Handbook of Practical Strategies for Teachers and Students.* New York: Hart.

Simpson, R. L., 1962. "Parental Influence, Anticipatory Socialization, and Social Mobility." *American Sociological Review* 27, 517–522.

Skinner, B. F., 1948. *Walden Two.* New York: Macmillan.

Skinner, B. F., 1951. "How to Teach Animals." *Scientific American* 185(6), 26–29.

Skinner, B. F., 1953. *Science and Human Behavior.* New York: Macmillan.

Skinner, B. F., 1958. "Teaching Machines." *Science* 128, 969–977.

Skinner, B. F., 1961. *Cumulative Record,* enlarged ed. New York: Appleton-Century-Crofts.

Skinner, B. F., 1968. *The Technology of Teaching.* New York: Appleton-Century-Crofts.

Skinner, B. F., 1971. *Beyond Freedom and Dignity.*

New York: Knopf.

Skinner, B. F., 1972. *Cumulative Record,* 3rd ed. New York: Appleton-Century-Crofts.

Skinner, B. F., 1974. *About Behaviorism.* New York: Knopf.

Skinner, B. F., 1976. *Particulars of My Life.* New York: Knopf.

Skinner, B. F., and Sue Ann Krakower, 1968. *Handwriting with Write and See.* Chicago: Lyons and Carnahan.

Smith, G. M., 1962. *A Simplified Guide to Statistics for Psychology and Education.* New York: Holt, Rinehart and Winston.

Smith, H. Allen, 1956. *Write Me a Poem, Baby.* Boston: Little, Brown.

Smith, H. Allen, 1959. *Don't Get Perconel with a Chicken.* Boston: Little, Brown.

Snitzer, Herb, 1968. *Living at Summerhill.* New York: Collier Books.

Snow, Richard E., 1969. "Unfinished Pygmalion." *Contemporary Psychology* 14, 197–199.

Sorensen, J. S., E. A. Schwenn, and Herbert J. Klausmeier, 1969. "The Individual Conference: A Motivational Device for Increasing Independent Reading in the Elementary Grades." Practical Paper No. 8, Madison: Wisconsin Research and Development Center for Cognitive Learning.

Sorensen, J. S., E. A. Schwenn, and J. Barry, 1970. "The Use of Individual and Group Goal-Setting Conferences as a Motivational Device to Improve Student Conduct and Increase Student Self-Direction: A Preliminary Study." Technical Report No. 123. Madison: Wisconsin Research and Development Center for Cognitive Learning.

Spearman, Charles, 1927. *The Abilities of Man: Their Nature and Measurement.* New York: Macmillan.

Standing, E. M., 1962. *The Montessori Revolution.* New York: Schocken Books.

Stennet, R. B., 1966. "Emotional Handicap in the Elementary Years: Phase or Disease." *American Journal of Orthopsychiatry* 36(3), 444–449.

Stephens, J. M., 1956. *Educational Psychology,* 2nd ed. New York: Holt.

Stephens, J. M., 1967. *The Process of Schooling.* New York: Holt, Rinehart and Winston.

Stolz, Herbert R., and Lois Meek Stolz, 1944. "Adolescent Problems Related to Somatic Variations." In National Society for the Study of Education, *Forty-third Yearbook: Adolescence,* 85–86. Chicago: University of Chicago Press.

Stone, L. Joseph, and Joseph Church, 1973. *Child-*

hood and Personality, 3rd ed. New York: Random House.

Strauss, A. A., and N. Kephart, 1955. *Psychopathology and Education of the Brain-Injured Child,* vol. 2. New York: Grune and Stratton.

Sturges, Persis T., 1972. "Effect of Instructions and Form of Informative Feedback on Retention of Meaningful Material." *Journal of Educational Psychology* 63(2), 99–102.

Suchman, J. Richard, 1961. "Inquiry Training: Building Skills for Autonomous Discovery." *Merrill-Palmer Quarterly* 7(3), 147–171.

Suchman, J. Richard, 1965. "Inquiry and Education." In James J. Gallagher, ed., *Teaching Gifted Students: A Book of Readings.* Boston: Allyn and Bacon.

Taba, Hilda, and Deborah Elkins, 1966. *Teaching Strategies for the Culturally Disadvantaged.* Chicago: Rand McNally.

Tanner, J. M., 1962. *Growth at Adolescence,* 2nd ed. Philadelphia: Davis.

Tanner, J. M., 1970. "Physical Growth." In Paul H. Mussen, ed., *Carmichael's Manual of Child Psychology,* 77–155. New York: Wiley.

Tanner, J. M., 1972. "Sequence, Tempo, and Individual Variation in Growth and Development of Boys and Girls Aged Twelve to Sixteen." In Jerome Kagan and Robert Coles, eds., *Twelve to Sixteen: Early Adolescence,* 1–24. New York: Norton.

Terman, Lewis, and Melita Oden, 1925. *Genetic Studies of Genius: Mental and Physical Traits of a Thousand Gifted Children.* Stanford: Stanford University Press.

Terman, Lewis, and Melita Oden, 1959. *Genetic Studies of Genius: The Gifted Group at Mid-Life. Thirty-five Years' Follow-up of the Superior Child.* Stanford: Stanford University Press.

Thelen, Herbert A., 1960. *Education and the Human Quest.* New York: Wiley.

Thelen, Herbert A., 1967. *Classroom Grouping for Teachability.* New York: Wiley.

Thomas, Don R., Wesley C. Becker, and Marianne Armstrong, 1968. "Production and Elimination of Disruptive Classroom Behavior by Systematically Varying Teacher's Behavior." *Journal of Applied Behavior Analysis* 1, 35–45.

Thomas, Marlo, 1974. *Free to Be You and Me.* New York: McGraw-Hill.

Thompson, C. E., 1940. "The Attitudes of Various Groups Toward Behavior Problems of Children." *Journal of Abnormal and Social Psychology* 35, 120–125, 188–189.

Thorndike, Robert L., 1968. "Review of *Pygmalion in the Classroom." Educational Research*

Journal 5, 709–711.

Thorndike, Robert L., and Elizabeth Hagen, 1969. *Measurement and Evaluation in Psychology and Education,* 3rd ed. New York: Wiley.

Thurstone, L. L., and Thelma G. Thurstone, 1941. *Factorial Studies of Intelligence.* Chicago: University of Chicago Press.

Toffler, Alvin, 1970. *Future Shock.* New York: Random House.

Tolor, Alexander, William L. Scarpetti, and Paul A. Lane, 1967. "Teachers' Attitudes Toward Children's Behavior Revisited." *Journal of Educational Psychology* 58, 175–180.

Torrance, Ellis Paul, 1962a. "Developing Creative Thinking Through School Experiences." In S. Parnes and G. Harding, eds., *A Source Book for Creative Thinking.* New York: Scribner.

Torrance, Ellis Paul, 1962b. *Guiding Creative Talent.* Englewood Cliffs, N.J.: Prentice-Hall.

Torrance, Ellis Paul, 1965. *Gifted Children in the Classroom.* New York: Macmillan.

Torrance, Ellis Paul, 1970. *Encouraging Creativity in the Classroom.* Dubuque, Iowa: Wm. C. Brown.

Townsend, E. A., and P. J. Burke, 1963. *Statistics for the Classroom Teacher: A Self-Teaching Unit.* New York: Macmillan.

Travers, R. M. W., ed., 1973. *Second Handbook of Research on Teaching.* Chicago: Rand McNally.

Trubowitz, Sidney, 1968. *A Handbook for Teaching in the Ghetto School.* Chicago: Quadrangle Books.

Tyler, Ralph W., 1934. "Some Findings from Studies in the Field of College Biology." *Science* 18, 133–142.

Tyler, Ralph W., 1964. "Some Persistent Questions on the Defining of Objectives." In C. M. Lindvall, ed., *Defining Educational Objectives.* Pittsburgh: University of Pittsburgh Press.

Tyler, Ralph W., 1966. "The Objectives and Plans for National Assessment of Educational Progress." *Journal of Educational Measurement* 3, 1–4.

Ulich, Robert S., 1954. *Three Thousand Years of Educational Wisdom.* Cambridge: Harvard University Press.

U.S. Committee for the White House Conference on Education, 1956. *A Report to the President.* Washington, D.C.: U.S. Government Printing Office.

Vasquez, Richard, 1970. *Chicano.* New York: Doubleday.

Wallas, G., 1921. *The Art of Thought.* New York: Harcourt, Brace and World.

Warfield, G. J., ed., 1974. *Mainstreaming Currents.* Reston, Va.: The Council for Exceptional Children.

Washburne, Carleton W., 1922. "Educational Measurements as a Key to Individualizing Instruction and Promotions." *Journal of Educational Research* 5, 195–206.

Watson, John B., 1913. "Psychology As the Behaviorist Views It." *Psychological Review* 20, 158–177.

Watson, John B., 1919. *Psychology from the Standpoint of a Behaviorist.* Philadelphia: Lippincott.

Watson, John B., 1925. *Behaviorism.* Chicago: University of Chicago Press.

Watson, John B., 1926. *Psychological Care of Infant and Child.* New York: Norton.

Watson, John B., 1928. *The Ways of Behaviorism.* New York: Harper.

Watson, John B., and Rosalie Rayner, 1920. "Conditioned Emotional Reactions." *Journal of Experimental Psychology* 3, 1–14.

Weber, Lillian, 1971. *The English Infant School and Informal Education.* Englewood Cliffs, N.J.: Prentice-Hall.

Webster, Staten W., ed., 1966. *The Disadvantaged Learner.* San Francisco: Chandler.

Wechsler, David, 1944. *The Measurement of Adult Intelligence.* New York: Psychological Corporation.

Weithorn, C. J., 1973. "Hyperactivity and the CNS: An Etiological and Diagnostic Dilemma." *Journal of Learning Disabilities* 6, 41–45.

Wesman, A. G., 1971. "Writing the Test Question." In R. L. Thorndike, ed., *Educational Measurement,* 2nd ed. Washington, D.C.: American Council on Education.

Westinghouse Learning Corporation, 1969. *The Impact of Head Start: An Evaluation of the Head Start Experience on Children's Cognitive and Affective Development.* Westinghouse Learning Corp., Ohio University.

White, Burton L., and Jean Carew Watts, 1973. *Experience and Environment: Major Influences on the Development of the Young Child,* vol. 1. Englewood Cliffs, N.J.: Prentice-Hall.

White, Robert W., 1959. "Motivation Reconsidered: The Concept of Competence." *Psychological Review* 66, 297–333.

White, Sheldon H., 1970. "The Learning Theory Tradition and Child Psychology." In Paul H. Mussen, ed., *Carmichael's Manual of Child Psychology,* vol. 1, 657–702. New York: Wiley.

Whyte, William H., Jr., 1956. *The Organization Man.* Garden City, N.Y.: Doubleday.

Wickman, E. K., 1928. *Children's Behavior and Teacher's Attitudes.* New York: Commonwealth Fund, Division of Publications.

Wilson, Colin, 1972. *New Pathways in Psychology: Maslow and the Post-Freudian Revolution.* London: Gollancz.

Wilson, S. R., and D. T. Tosti, 1972. *Learning Is Getting Easier.* San Rafael, Calif.: Individual Learning Systems.

Winett, R. A., and R. C. Winkler, 1972. "Current Behavior Modification in the Classroom. Be Still, Be Quiet, Be Docile." *Journal of Applied Behavioral Analysis,* 5, 499–504.

Witkin, Herman, R. D. Dyk, H. F. Faterson, D. R. Goodenough, and S. A. Karp, 1962. *Psychological Differentiation.* New York: Wiley.

Wittrock, M. C., and David E. Wiley, eds., 1970. *The Evaluation of Instruction.* New York: Holt, Rinehart and Winston.

Wolf, M., H. Mees, and T. Risley, 1964. "Application of Operant Conditioning Procedures to the Behavior Problems of an Autistic Child." *Behaviour Research and Therapy* 1, 305–312.

Wolman, Benjamin B., ed., 1972. *Manual of Child Psychopathology.* New York: McGraw-Hill.

Woodring, Paul, 1953. *Let's Talk Sense about Our Schools.* New York: McGraw-Hill.

Woodring, Paul, 1957a. *A Fourth of a Nation.* New York: McGraw-Hill.

Woodring, Paul, 1957b. *New Directions in Teacher Education.* New York: Fund for the Advancement of Education.

Woodring, Paul, 1965. *Introduction to American Education.* New York: Harcourt, Brace and World.

Woodring, Paul, 1968. *The Higher Learning in America: A Reassessment.* New York: McGraw-Hill.

Wright, A. Richard, 1945. *Black Boy.* New York: Harper.

Wright, Herbert F., 1960. "Observational Child Study." In Paul H. Mussen, ed., *Handbook of Research Methods in Child Development,* 71–139. New York: Wiley.

Yablonsky, Lewis, 1976. *Psychodrama.* New York: Basic Books.

Young, Michael, 1959. *The Rise of the Meritocracy.* New York: Random House.

Zeigarnik, B., 1927. "Uber das Behalten von erledigten und unerledigten Handlungen." *Psychologische Forschung* 9, 1–85.

Zuckerman, David W., and Robert E. Horns, eds., 1973. *The Guide to Simulation/Games for Education and Training.* Lexington, Mass.: Information Resources, Inc.

Index

Index to suggestions for teaching

Index to suggestions for becoming a better teacher